# Handbook of the Humanities and Aging

**Thomas R. Cole, Ph.D.,** is Associate Professor and Graduate Program Director at the Institute for the Medical Humanities, University of Texas Medical Branch, Galveston. He is a past Chair of the Humanities and Arts Committee of the Gerontological Society and serves on various editorial boards. Senior editor of *What Does It Mean to Grow Old? Reflections from the Humanities* (1986) and author of *The Journey of Life: A Cultural History of Aging in America* (Cambridge, 1992), he is now completing *No Color Is My Kind: The Life Story of Eldrewey Stearnes, Texas Integration Leader* (University of Texas Press), and *The Oxford Book of Aging,* to be published in 1994. With co-editors W. Andrew Achenbaum, Patricia Jakobi, and Robert Kastenbaum, he is editing *Voices and Visions in Aging: Toward a Critical Gerontology,* which Springer will publish in 1992 as a companion volume to the *Handbook of The Humanities and Aging.*

**David D. Van Tassel, Ph.D.,** is Elbert J. Benton Professor and Chairman of the History Department at Case Western Reserve University. He is a fellow of the Gerontological Society of America. He has written and edited many books including: *Aging and the Elderly, Humanistic Perspectives in Gerontology,* with Stuart F. Spicker and Kathleen M. Woodward (1978); *Aging, Death and the Completion of Being* (1979); *The Elderly in a Bureaucratic Society: the Elderly, the Experts and the State in American History,* with Peter Stearns (1986); and in press, *Aging Policy Interest Groups,* with Jimmy E. W. Meyer (1991).

**Robert Kastenbaum, Ph.D.,** entered University of Southern California on a fellowship in philosophy. He emerged as a clinical psychologist, and later served as director of a geriatric hospital before taking up his current responsibilities as professor of communication at Arizona State University. Along the way he founded *International Journal of Aging & Human Development,* and *Omega, Journal of Death and Dying.* He is a past president of American Association of Suicidology and past chair of the Section on Behavioral and Social Sciences of the Gerontological Society of America. Kastenbaum scripted the National Public Radio series: "Essays for the Ear: Youth's the Tune, Age the Song," a project that he draws on in his chapter for this *Handbook.* Dr. Kastenbaum is the author of *Psychology of Death, Second Edition* to be published by Springer in 1992.

# Handbook of the Humanities and Aging

Thomas R. Cole
David D. Van Tassel
Robert Kastenbaum
Editors

SPRINGER PUBLISHING COMPANY
New York

Springer Publishing Company, Inc.
536 Broadway
New York, NY 10012

92 93 94 95 96 / 5 4 3 2 1

---

**Library of Congress Cataloging-in-Publication Data**

Handbook of the humanities and aging / Thomas R. Cole, David Van Tassel, Robert Kastenbaum, editors.
p. cm.
Includes bibliographical references and index.
ISBN 0-8261-6240-1
1. Gerontology and the humanities. 2. Aging. I. Cole, Thomas R., 1949– . II. Van Tassel, David D. (David Dirck). 1928– .
HQ1061.H3355 1992
305.26—dc20 91-21954
CIP

---

Printed in the United States of America

# Contents

# Foreword

It is indeed a privilege to be invited to make prefatory remarks for this impressive, comprehensive, imaginative *Handbook of the Humanities and Aging*. Here are my reflections on the purposes and themes of this book.

"The Humanities and Aging"—I find it hard to think of these terms, these arenas of life, as one *and* the other. Aging is an integral part of life, of the human condition, throughout the lifespan and certainly, as is usually meant, the latter part of each person's existence. The humanities, as approaches to understanding and enlightening us about the full potentials of human beings, in turn by definition include the full range of the "variety, uniqueness, complexity, originality, and unpredictability" of older as well as younger human beings, as the humanities are described by Thomas Cole in his Introduction.

Thus I suggest that this handbook really addresses aging as an integral part of the substance of the humanities—the arts, philosophy, literature, religion, history—, this is, aging *in* the humanities; and vice versa, the contributions of the humanities as an essential part of understanding aging, that is, humanities *in* aging. It seems to me that this integration of the two is really what this handbook aims to and does achieve, from the perspectives of the wide range of accomplished contributors.

My second perspective is that, as a biomedical scientist and as a physician immersed in gerontology and geriatrics, I find the contents of these chapters entirely and totally relevant to my missions. From the point of view of biomedical (and also behavioral and social) research in aging, it becomes clearer all the time that the frontiers of this research are addressing and must address the marvelous, varied, characteristics and capabilities of the full potentials of aging human beings, as revealed in the humanities. We are approaching the time when we will understand the molecular bases of creative thought, memory, wisdom, as well as the intricate steps and interactions that link these phenomena. There will be no place for thinking of "the natural (and behavioral and social) sciences *and* the humanities," but rather the commonalities and interrelations of all knowledge.

Similarly from the point of view of clinicians, those of all professions who provide care to older persons: even with the remarkable advances in understanding health and disease and the technical capabilities for diagnosis and treatment, the core principle continues to be to understand and care for the whole patient, the whole person. In the words of one of my medical heroes, Dr. Francis Peabody, "One of the essential qualities of the clinician is interest in humanity, for the secret of the care of the patient is in caring for the patient" (p. 882). One cannot meaningfully care *for* just a part of a person. And certainly the person, each individual, includes the varied manifestations that are best approached from the perspectives of the humanities.

Finally, it is clear that those working in the humanities share the same challenge as those in gerontology and geriatrics, of being concerned with the implications of their work for individuals at least as much as for societies. In particular in our history of developing knowledge about aging, it has been too easy to focus on overall phenomena, too common to ignore the immensely variable and critical differences in physical, mental, emotional and social characteristics, the uniqueness of each person. The approaches of the humanities, as presented in this volume, can help us all to understand these and the creative features of each person, in relation to the humanistic characteristics of the society in which the person lives.

Thus I see this handbook as a major contribution to the comprehensive understanding of aging, and as well to the comprehensive understanding of the humanities. The editors and authors deserve thanks and the attention of anyone interested in a full understanding of these intimately interrelated fields.

T. FRANKLIN WILLIAMS, MD

## REFERENCE

Peabody, F. W. (1927). The care of the patient. *Journal of the American Medical Association*, 88, 882.

# The Humanities and Aging: An Overview

*Thomas R. Cole*

Over the past 20 years, many people have sensed that something important is missing in a purely scientific and professional gerontology. Mainstream gerontology—with its highly technical and instrumental, avowedly objective, value-neutral and specialized discourses—lacks an appropriate language for addressing basic moral and spiritual issues in our aging society. Researchers, teachers, students, professionals, patients, clients, administrators, and policymakers do not possess a ready way to speak to one another about fundamental questions of human existence.

The predicament of gerontology mirrors a larger historical tendency. Since the late nineteenth century, the growth of experimental science and technology, the culture of professionalism, and the emergence of the modern university have all contributed to the erosion of a common (if contested) language for discussing questions of meaning and value, justice, virtue, wisdom, or the common good. In the contemporary world of postmodern culture, where exploding communications technology both saturates personal experience and undermines traditional assumptions of the self's unity, it becomes increasingly important to identify and talk about moral and spiritual concerns.

In the 1970s, professional humanists—along with humanistically oriented social scientists and clinicians—awakened to these issues in the study of aging. Around 1975 a steady stream of writing began to emerge, and over the next decade, the implications of the humanities for gerontological research, education, public policy, and clinical practice became clearer. By the mid-1980s, when the Humanities and Arts Committee of the Gerontological Society of America commissioned *Where Do We Come From? What Are We? Where Are We Going?: An Annotated Bibliography of Aging and the Humanities*, roughly 1,100 annotated books and articles demonstrated that a whole new field of interdisciplinary knowledge—humanistic gerontology—had been created since 1975.[1]

Despite the recent flood of academic and professional writing in humanistic gerontology, the field has lacked a basic reference work to introduce readers to the state of the art, establish intellectual standards, and help guide future research. It was Robert Kastenbaum who saw a need for this book as a vehicle for the continued growth and maturation of humanistic gerontology. On a yellow napkin at Wendy's in New Orleans between Gerontological Society sessions, Bob initiated the effort to map this new area of knowledge. There ensued a long collaboration between Bob, David Van Tassel, and myself to chart the boundaries and contours of the field, to commission chapters and have them peer reviewed, and to shape the material into a coherent volume.

A "handbook" in the humanities and aging certainly has its ironic side. Handbooks nowadays are too big and heavy to hold in one's hand. And who ever heard of a handbook of philosophy, literature, or history? The word "handbook" implies a kind of manual that distills bits of useful knowledge for solving problems. Knowledge in humanistic gerontology *is* sometimes directly useful for solving problems, for example, in applied ethics or public policy history. But more often, such knowledge is useful because it deepens understanding and enhances opportunities for human flourishing. This, then, must be a handbook with a difference—less scientific and instrumental, more historical, more concerned with the limits and conditions of its own knowledge, and more focussed on questions of representation, meaning, and value than traditional handbooks in gerontology.

The three major U.S. handbooks of aging, covering the fields of biology, psychology, and the social sciences, appeared in their third edition in 1990. These handbooks lie squarely within the Enlightenment vision of progress achieved through science and cumulative knowledge. They are informed by a quest for scientifically valid explanations of aging as a phenomenon dependent, as supervisory editor James E. Birren puts it, "on the influences of genetics, physical and social environments, and individual behavior."

This *Handbook of the Humanities and Aging*, in contrast, approaches aging with a different epistemological stance—one that strives for contextual understanding and interpretation along with explanation and that considers scientific method to be one way of knowing among others. Again, the humanities have become important in late twentieth-century gerontology precisely because conventional scientific and professional gerontology has retreated into a formal, technical rationality that lacks a shared discourse for addressing moral, aesthetic, and spiritual issues or for appreciating their historical and cultural contexts.

What are the humanities? And how can they respond to the conditions of fragmentation, isolation, and value conflict that inhere in contemporary forms of gerontological research, education, policy, and practice? The humanities can be defined in terms of disciplines, subject matter, or methods; but no final definition is possible or perhaps even desirable. Defined by disciplines, the humanities range from languages and literature, history, and philosophy to religious studies, jurisprudence, and those aspects of the social sciences that emphasize interpreting, valuing, and self-knowing.

Defined by its subject matter, the humanities reflect on the fundamental question "What does it mean to be human?" As the Rockefeller Commission on the Humanities put it in 1980: "[the humanities] reveal how people have tried to make moral, spiritual, and intellectual sense of a world in which irrationality, despair, loneliness, and death are as conspicuous as birth, friendship, hope and reason. We learn how individuals or societies define the moral life and try to attain it, attempt to reconcile freedom and the responsibilities of citizenship, and express themselves artistically."[2]

From the perspective of methods, the humanities have been defined by R. S. Crane as the proper cultivation of four essential "arts": language, analysis of ideas, literary and artistic criticism, and historiography.[3] Rather than mathematical proof or reproducible results, humanities research and teaching are dedicated to understanding human experience through the disciplined development of insight, perspective, critical understanding, discernment, and creativity.

But disciplines, subject matter, and methods—whether taken separately or together—cannot adequately characterize the humanities, which ultimately emphasize description, interpretation, explanation, and appreciation of the variety, uniqueness, complexity, originality, and unpredictability of human beings striving to live and know themselves. Charles Frankel has expressed the aspirations of the humanities this way:

> At their most vivid [the humanities] are like the arts as well as the sciences. The humanities are that form of knowledge in which the knower is revealed. All knowledge becomes humanistic when this effect takes place, when we are asked to contemplate not only a proposition but the proposer, when we hear the human voice behind what is said.[4]

In the last twenty years, the subject matter, disciplines, and methods associated with the humanities have barely begun to shape the gerontological imagination: to provide philosophical grounding and historical context for theories, policies, and practices; to clarify values and question assumptions; to cultivate tolerance for intractable ambiguities, appreciation for experience that eludes quantification, and a disposition toward self-examination. This *Handbook* is a vehicle for gathering and presenting contemporary humanistic knowledge about aging. It should become a standard reference for academic and clinical gerontologists, as well as a stimulus for future work in the humanities and aging.

The next phase in the development of the humanities in gerontology will require institutional commitments of teaching positions, fellowships, and research funding. New funds must be committed to integrate the humanities into gerontological curricula, to stimulate new research, and to train humanists in the ways of gerontology. Out of such commitments can emerge better-educated gerontologists and a new generation of humanists who have some knowledge of biological and social gerontology, are familiar with the worlds of clinical practice, social service, or policy, and whose collaborative efforts will help shape the future of gerontology and geriatrics.

Having pointed to some problems in mainstream gerontology, we must also emphasize that the humanities are beset with equally serious difficulties of their own. In American academic life, the humanities disciplines suffer from the problems of specialization and positivism no less than the natural and social sciences. Professional humanists, like other academics, have also become excessively technical and analytic, contributing to a new obscurantism. To advance in the academy, scholars are encouraged to leave aside "big" questions of meaning and purpose, focus on more manageable problems, and detach their thinking from living human needs and problems. The old idea of the "liberally educated" individual has virtually disappeared in the rush toward careerism, the scramble for credentials, and disarray within the traditional humanities disciplines themselves.

Ironically, just as humanists in the last 20 years began making significant contributions to gerontology and the professions in general, the tradition of Western humanism—especially in its Enlightenment form—came under severe attack from within the academy. A wide range of thinkers from overlapping positions—including feminists, postMarxists, various schools of deconstruction, cultural theorists, poststructuralists, and Lacanian psychoanalysts—challenged conventional ideas about science, truth, progress, man, history, and the self. Much that had been taken for granted became contested terrain.

One practical outcome of these debates about the content and production of knowledge has been a widely publicized argument over the core curricula for undergraduate education. Cultural leftists argue that great books and artistic treasures owe their existence not only to great minds but also to the great toil of anonymous contemporaries—an insight at the root of many valuable alternative readings of traditional texts. Some critics have rejected the idea of "great books" altogether, arguing that most ideas, images, and concepts from the humanist tradition are little more than tools used to justify the domination of white male Europeans (and Americans) over women and people of color.

Conservatives have responded to these positions with a range of their own. Some have reacted by essentially circling the wagons, claiming that the attack on the canon reflects the worst aspects of contemporary culture—its rejection of tradition, its rootlessness, and its tendencies toward nihilism, relativism, decadence. Others agree with liberals who are attempting to reconstruct the canon, thereby helping educators transmit a usable cultural heritage that both acknowledges the social costs of all great work and reflects contemporary demands for diversity and pluralism.

Conceiving the *Handbook of the Humanities and Aging* amidst this "crisis in the humanities," we have sought a middle ground. The humanist tradition in the West *is* largely the product of "dead white men," most of whom enjoyed considerable privilege. This fact, however, requires that we contextualize humanistic knowledge, that we enlarge and open it up to previously neglected subjects and invisible sources—not that we reduce the search for truth to politically correct formulas. Sensitivity to issues of race, class, and gender *has* become essential for responsible inquiry. These categories are now necessary dimensions of (but no substitute for) rigorous analysis and interpretation of particular intellectual or social problems.

We are living through a period of great historical change and uncertainty. Profound shifts in contemporary social life have seriously disrupted the self-understanding and confidence of intellectuals. Previously reliable ways of knowing, interpreting, and acting in the world have come under suspicion, undercutting claims for the unity or universality of humanistic knowledge. In our view, there is no reason for alarm or despair in extreme claims that the humanist tradition is irrelevant, or privileged, or dying. It is more accurate to say that the humanist tradition has always been selectively constructed, historically situated, and internally divided. In the humanities as well as the sciences, the modernist dream—of decontextualizing and purifying human reason to achieve unified, formal, and unquestioned knowledge—is over.[5]

This situation recalls us to the practical modesty that informed Renaissance humanists, who accepted the uncertainty, ambiguity, and plurality in all human knowledge but who nevertheless sought wisdom, virtue, goodness, and human completion through the critical exploration of their cultural heritage. That heritage contains a basic style of inquiry that is absolutely central for finding our bearings without excluding or privileging any particular point of view—the "method" of dialogue or conversation as a mutual exploration of possibilities in the search for truth.

There are, of course, varieties of dialogue, exemplified powerfully by such diverse thinkers as Buber,[6] Bakhtin,[7] Hutchins,[8] Bellah,[9] and Tracy.[10] In a classic defense of liberal education, Robert Hutchins described the tradition of the West as a "great conversation." While Hutchins's description of that tradition is certainly problematic by today's standards, his general definition of an ideal conversation is appropriately democratic and intellectually demanding: "Nothing is to remain undiscussed. *Everybody* is to speak his [or her] mind. No proposition is to be left unexamined. The exchange of *ideas* is held to be the path to the realization of the potentialities of [humanity]" (Hutchins, 1954, p. 51).[11]

The "conversation" of humanistic gerontology revolves around a basic question: what does it mean to grow old? This question, of course, has no single or universal answer—at least not one that finite, historical beings can provide. Indeed, the question itself is abstracted from other innumerable questions that arise in historically and culturally specific forms—for example, What is a "good" old age? Is there anything important to be done after children are raised and careers completed? Is old age the fulfillment of life or a second childishness? What are the possibilities of flourishing in old age? What kind of elders do we want to be? What are the paths to wisdom? What are the vices and virtues of the elderly? What kinds of support and care does society "owe" its old? What are the obligations of the old? What are the "gifts reserved for age?"

The *Handbook* presents a range of historical, religious, philosophical, literary, and social science scholarship that engages such questions. We have divided the volume into four major sections: (1) Aging, Old Age and Elders in History; (2) Aging, Spirituality, and World Religions; (3) Artistic Expression, Creativity, and Representations of Aging; and (4) Humanistic Gerontology: The State of the Art. Obviously, we do not claim to have explored humanistic gerontology from all possible angles, perspectives, or in all geographic regions. We have included Far Eastern cultures in the historical section; Jewish, Islamic, Hindu, and Buddist perspectives in the section on religion and spirituality; and world history in the state-of-the-art section. In important areas like Africa and Latin America, there is little or no existing scholarship—a gap we hope will be remedied in the future.

Part I, "Aging, Old Age, and Elders in History," consists of four chapters synthesizing historical scholarship on aging. The first three chapters are devoted respectively to the ancient, medieval, and early modern, and modern and postmodern eras in Western culture. A fourth chapter, "Aging in Eastern Cultures," presents an historical overview of aging in China, Japan, and Korea.

In Chapter One, "A View from Antiquity: Greece, Rome, and Elders," Thomas M. Falkner and Judith de Luce find that while older people in ancient Greece and Rome were not at the center of political, legal, and military power, aging and old age carried a high profile in literature. Humanist texts from antiquity show considerable interest in later life, an interest revealed by old age as an important theme in various genres, the appearance of elderly characters, and in reflections on the nature and value of old age.

Falkner and de Luce are quick to point out that literary interest in old age was not necessarily sympathetic, nor was it always meant to be taken literally. The symbolism and rhetoric of the ages (or stages) of life, for example, were often used to convey ideas about tradition and innovation, morality and corruption, foolishness and wisdom, or activity and contemplation. In addition, the goals and imaginative purposes of literary materials produced by elite men are often at odds with the goals of historical reconstruction, which focus on popular practices and perceptions in the context of social organization.

In Chapter Two, "The Older Person in the Western World," David Troyansky surveys the predominant images of aging and the life course, along with the central socioeconomic and demographic trends impinging on the experience of growing old from the fifth to the nineteenth centuries. Troyansky's overview of retirement practices, age relations, and ideas about aging takes the reader deftly through the later Middle Ages, the Renaissance and Reformation, the Scientific Revolution, the Eighteenth-century Enlightenment, and the Industrial Revolution. He points out that historians have abandoned the search for a single turning point (usually associated with some version of modernization theory) and suggests that there are no simple lessons in the history of aging and old age. Rather, an array of explanatory models, reflecting the empirical diversity of social practices, attitudes towards aging, and images of old age can serve as elements of a humane and historical context for making sense of our lives in an aging society.

In Chapter Three, "Old Age in the Modern and Postmodern Western World," Christoph Conrad presents an overview of the social and cultural changes affecting older people in the last two centuries. He describes the emergence of old age as a structurally distinct stage of life built on retirement and supported by the welfare state. Against this structural background, Conrad traces changing concepts of time, finitude, the role of older people, and intergenerational conflict. In the future, he suggests, Western society's rapidly growing need for long-term care and humane conditions of dying will require serious cultural and institutional change.

Chapter Four, Christie Kiefer's "Aging in Eastern Cultures," presents an historical overview of the images, statuses, roles, and material circumstances of the aged in China, Korea, and Japan. Classical Chinese society was not the changeless, homogeneous gerontocracy that Westerners often imagine. It is true that during much of Chinese history, the old were venerated according to Chinese ideals of family and kinship. But veneration depended on a range of economic conditions, customs, and institutions that varied widely according to locale, family fortune, and historical era.

Korean elders, according to Kiefer, traditionally benefited from a pattern of Confucian lineage, law, and ritual quite similar to that in China, though Koreans preferred primogeniture to the Chinese ideal of married brothers living together under one roof. In the last 40 years, industrialization and urbanization have led to considerable displacement and isolation for old people in both urban and rural South Korea, especially for those without family. The strong sense of filial responsibility and a rising standard of living among the young, however, has contributed to improved living conditions for many grandparents.

Like Chinese and Koreans, traditional Japanese delegated authority to senior males and relied heavily on kinship bonds. But the Japanese also emphasized a strong responsibility to the collective welfare. During the transition to modernity, Japanese leaders reinforced Confucian morality and filial responsibility. The traditional Japanese emphasis on corporate welfare allowed the old to defer to the young in technical matters, and the young were able to show respect for their elders while assuming leadership roles in a new industrial order. Japan's phenomenal population aging since World War II has lead to considerable concern about health care costs, dependency ratios, and traditional family patterns. Although the proportion of old people living with their children has recently declined from 90% to about 70%, the national government still expects families of the dependent elderly to carry most of the financial and in-kind burden of care.

Part II, "Aging, Spirituality, and World Religions," consists of four chapters that survey the place of aging and spiritual development in five of the world's major religions and in the surprisingly relevant, subversive world of fairy tales. The study of spirituality and aging by scholars in theology, religious studies, and in divinity schools is only beginning. Part Two, therefore, breaks new ground by surveying aging in both Eastern and Western religions and by linking these traditions to a nondenominational perspective on spirituality in later life found in the world's fairy tales.

In Chapter Five, "Aging and Meaning: The Christian Tradition," Stephen Post emphasizes the historical consistency of Christianity's vision of aging as a journey focused on the imitation of Christ. In contrast to the contemporary secular belief in medical progress and life extension, Post describes Christianity's emphasis on cultivating the virtues of faith, hope, and love. The Christian journey, which takes place in a dialectic of decline and redemption, envisions the end of life not as mere disintegration or meaninglessness but as completion of self, whose proper relation to both neighbor and God leads finally to life after death.

Chapter Six, Sheldon Isenberg's "Aging in Judaism: 'Crown of Glory' and 'Days of Sorrow,'" surveys Jewish literature over nearly four millenia. Isenberg reminds us that until virtually the twentieth century, Jewish literature retains its patriarchal perspective, allowing very few insights into the experiences or ideas of aging women. Combing the Torah, wisdom books, rabbinic commentaries, as well as philosophical and mystical texts since the second century B.C.E.*, Eisenberg finds consistent themes of blessing and suffering in the literature.

Like the Christian attempt to redeem what T. S. Eliot called "the cold friction of expiring flesh," Jewish writers since the Biblical era have struggled with the uncertain blend of pain, suffering, and fulfillment that accompanies long life. In modern Jewish fiction and poetry, Eisenberg suggests, old men and women symbolize the passing of European *yiddishkeit*, largely destroyed by the Holocaust. Twentieth-century Jewish women's struggles for freedom and the contemporary Jewish renewal movement's interest in "spiritual eldering" are among the recent topics of Eisenberg's survey.

In Chapter Seven, "Islamic, Hindu, and Buddhist Conceptions of Aging," Gene Thursby surveys three religious traditions whose followers have recently emigrated to the West in large numbers and who together represent about 40% of the world's population. All three share a basic assumption: human life is a brief but nevertheless great and rare opportunity that can be rightly understood only in relation to what transcends it. Each tradition understands transcendent reality differently and has shaped its vision of right living accordingly. Islam has generally discouraged ascetic and monastic styles of life and has celebrated the family. Buddhism, from the beginning, has made its monastic com-

---

* B.C.E. = Before the Common Era

munity the model for right living. And Hinduism has attempted to balance asceticism with family values.

In the Muslim holy scripture, the Quran, aging is understood as one sign of the overwhelming mercy, justice, and power of Allah. While children are directed to show kindness and respect for aged parents, female subordination and circumstances of life often lead to neglect or abuse in poor Muslim societies. Hinduism, which contains an extraordinary diversity of convictions and practices, defines an ideal life cycle prescribed for those born into the highest three castes in Indian society. The third and fourth stages provide guidelines for an aging couple to assume the position of grandparents and to prepare for a retiring and contemplative life of spiritual realization. Buddhism, more oriented toward celibacy and renunciation of the world, has emphasized the painful prospects of old age to motivate people to cultivate detachment. Calming anxiety and awakening an "ageless" presence are central to these traditions—but just what aging amounts to depends on the teachings and practices of each.

In Chapter Eight, "Fairy Tales and Spiritual Development in Later Life," Allan Chinen uses the story of the shining fish to exemplify his argument that "elder tales" from around the world share cross-cultural plots and themes, exemplifying an ideal of adult development. The drama of late life in these stories, according to Chinen, involves the journey beyond the self, towards generativity and the illumination of society. Surprisingly, these traditional fairy tales, largely neglected in scholarship on the subject, are a rich interpretive source for addressing issues of spirituality and the development of wisdom.

Part III, "Artistic Expression, Creativity, and Representations of Aging," consists of five chapters: three chapters on aging in the genres of poetry, fiction, and art; one chapter on creativity over the lifespan and a final chapter on storytelling and cultural transmission. In Chapter Nine, "Images of Aging in American Poetry, 1925–1985," Carolyn Smith discusses themes of aging in the poetry of Robert Penn Warren, Langston Hughes, Gwendolyn Brooks, and Elizabeth Bishop. Attending to cultural and gender differences in the lives and work of these poets, Smith reveals a fascinating range of expression from despair to physical frailty that nevertheless embodies strong perceptions of life and death.

In Chapter Ten, "Old Age in Contemporary Fiction: A New Paradigm of Hope," Constance Rooke describes a new genre—the *Vollendungsroman*—that is taking shape in contemporary English–language fiction about aging. The *Vollendungsroman*, a story of "winding up" or completing life, presents an old hero or heroine struggling for affirmation in the midst of loss and death. The urgent and varied strategies of characters searching for narrative coherence and meaning sheds light on the entire range of questions that concern gerontologists.

Chapter Eleven, Mary Winkler's "Walking to the Stars," explores aging in Western art through three categories: grotesque or despicable old age; wise old age; and old age transcended in the face of death. Borrowing from Rudolph Arnheim's dictum that "the principal task of the artist is to introduce appropriate meaning," Winkler discusses artists who have depicted aging under the archetypal image of life's journey. The artist's pencil and the pilgrim's staff, Winkler concludes, may both be understood as means of achieving self-knowledge, commitment to others, and love along the hazardous path of life's journey.

Chapter Twelve, Robert Kastenbaum's "The Creative Process: A Life-span Approach," masterfully discusses the growing research on creativity in lifespan development and gerontology. Rather than conceive creativity as an ability (an approach that traditionally involves exclusively quantitative methods), Kastenbaum argues that we should study the functions and meanings of creativity—an approach that requires qualitative and contextual research focused on individuals. Kastenbaum provides examples of this approach and concludes with a stirring apologia for his position: "creativity belongs not at the periphery, but at the center of all studies of human experience—as a psychobiological resource for survival of both individual and species, and as an intimate link between the individual and what gods, spirits, forces, or whims have given rise to mindedness in an entropy-addicted universe."

One dimension of creativity in later life is storytelling, a traditional practice of the old that persists in radically altered form today. In Chapter Thirteen, "Story of the Shoe Box: On the Meaning and Practice of Transmitting Stories," Marc Kaminsky reinterprets a particular story told often by the late anthropologist Barbara Myerhoff. This story of redemption and perdition, told by a survivor, retold by Myerhoff and again by Kaminsky after her death, is emblematic of the preciousness and precariousness of transmitting culture in our century of mass death.

The importance of stories is by no means limited to great literary figures. Ordinary stories—if they are received—both transmit the past and confirm the integrity of the aging individual. They are, as Kaminsky writes, "arms with which to fight death, arms for mortal oarsmen to go back over the wide water of forgetfulness, so that we may continue to make the round trips toward meaning . . ."

Part Four, "Humanistic Gerontology: The State of the Art," brings together six chapters that review disciplinary knowledge about aging in literature, history, bioethics, philosophy, and in education for older people. Chapter Fourteen, Anne Wyatt-Brown's "Literary Gerontology

Comes of Age," masterfully surveys the exciting and difficult field springing up at the intersection of gerontology and literary criticism. Wyatt-Brown groups this scholarship under several headings: (1) analyses of literary attitudes toward aging; (2) humanistic approaches to literature and aging; (3) psychoanalytic explorations of literary works and their authors; (4) applications of gerontological theories about autobiography, life review, and midlife transitions, and (5) psychoanalytically informed studies of the creative process. The continued growth of literary gerontology, Wyatt-Brown argues, will require that mainstream literary criticism awaken to aging both as a variable in textual analysis and as an element in the creative process.

In Chapter Fifteen, "Aging in America: The Perspective of History," Carole Haber and Brian Gratton discuss the historiography of aging in America that has grown up since the later 1970s. They show that this literature challenges many gerontological assumptions about aging in the past, neatly lay out the basic findings of historical research, and suggest the implications of these findings for social gerontology. Finally, Haber and Gratton pose five central issues that will shape historical research on aging in America during the next decade.

Chapter Sixteen, Peter Stearns's "Elders in World History," ventures some thoughts on the place of old age in the fledging study of world history. Stearns suggests that the common periodization of world history (e.g., the advent of agriculture, the rise of various world religions, the emergence of new kinds of cultural and commercial contacts, industrialization) is a useful place to begin. This periodization reveals considerable cultural continuities across several civilizations, as well as innovations associated with industrialization and urbanization. We need, however, much more historical knowledge about aging and old age within various societies (especially in Latin American and Africa) before we can arrive at better comparative analyses.

In Chapter Seventeen, "Bioethics and Aging," Harry Moody examines a field of considerable relevance for gerontological policy and practice. Moody shows how ethical dilemmas in the care of the elderly have been handled by the "dominant model" in bioethics. He elaborates and critiques the basic style of analysis and problem solving inherent in this "dominant model," which emphasizes the legalistic application of rules and principles. Moody points to virtue ethics, phenomenology, and communicative ethics as alternatives to the individualistic, rights-based emphases of the dominant model. He offers an ideal of ethical deliberation that defines and promotes concrete conditions for communication, clarification, and consensus-building.

Interestingly, the vast majority of philosophical writing about aging has come from social scientists or from fields of the humanities other than philosophy. In Chapter Eighteen, "Wisdom and Method: Philosophical Contributions to Gerontology," Ronald Manheimer asks why so few professional philosophers have entered the arena of aging and why nonphilosophers in gerontology have been drawn to issues of epistemology, ontology, ethics, hermeneutics and the philosophy of science. His discussion greatly enriches our understanding of topics that defy disciplinary boundaries: wisdom, social philosophy and theory construction, ethics, philosophy of education, logic and teleology, and the status and construction of meaning.

Chapter Nineteen, David Shuldiner's "The Older Student of Humanities," discusses the growth of late-life humanities study under four rubrics: age and lifelong learning; social/historical contexts; humanities, literacy, and oral tradition; and forms of late-life humanities study. Whatever their class, ethnic, or educational background, students of the humanities at any age can experience the self-validation and empowerment that emerge from critical thinking in the humanistic tradition. As Shuldiner notes, the most challenging and empowering forms of late life humanities study are cooperative ventures, in which the life experiences of older learners are valued and explored along with those of great writers who have explored the experiences of being human.

In his "Afterword," W. Andrew Achenbaum explores past, present, and future ways of integrating the humanities into gerontological research, training, and practice. Using John Dewey and Simone de Beauvoir as two alternate ideal models for linking the humanities and aging, Achenbaum distinguishes between *humanistic gerontology* and *gerontological humanities*. Surveying recent attempts to bridge the sciences and humanities in American (and to a limited extent European) gerontology, Achenbaum analyzes the marginality of the humanities in gerontological circles. He discusses several options for future development and concludes with a call for *critical gerontology*—a style of inquiry rooted in practice rather than science and technology, and aimed at emancipating old age from its constricted meanings in modern culture. A conference on *critical gerontology* was held at the Institute for the Medical Humanities, University of Texas Medical Branch, Galveston, in January 1991. Revised papers are being shaped into the forthcoming *Voices and Visions in Aging: Toward A Critical Gerontology* (Springer Publishing Co., 1992), which may be read as an interdisciplinary companion to the *Handbook*.

We want to thank many people whose work has made this *Handbook* possible. Organization and preparation of the *Handbook* was supported at the Institute for the Medical Humanities by the Jesse Jones Memorial Research Fund in the Medical Humanities, made possible by a Challenge Grant from the National Endowment for the Humanities. At the Institute, Sheila Keating organized the volume's innumerable little tasks into a useful system for keeping the editors informed. She also typed correspondence and kept track of multiple versions of manuscript chapters. Eleanor Porter prepared the final version for the publisher and worked on permissions as well as proofreading. Cheryl Vaiani prepared useful summaries of each chapter. We are also indebted to many people for their input and service as peer reviewers: Andrew Achenbaum, Robert Atchley, Sandra B. Bertman, Bertram Cohler, Robert Binstock, William Deal, Melvin Goldstein, Eva Kahana, Donald Laing, Ruth G. Lyell, Ronald Manheimer, Gerald Manning, Lawrence McCullough, Rick Moody, Kerry Olitzky, Robert Rubinstein, Stephen Sapp, Harold Stahmer, and Kathy Woodward.

## NOTES

[1] *See* D. Polisar, L. Wygant, T. Cole, & C. Perdomo, (1988). *Where do we come from? What are we? Where are we going?: An annotated bibliography of aging and the humanities.* Washington, DC: Gerontological Society of America.

[2] Commission on the Humanities. (1980). *The humanities in American life,* 1. Berkeley: University of California Press.

[3] R. S. Crane. (1967). *The idea of the humanities and other essays.* Two Volumes. Chicago: University of Chicago Press.

[4] Cited in *The humanities in American life,* 2.

[5] *See* S. Toulmin. (1990). *Cosmopolis: The hidden agenda of modernity* esp. pp. 89–147. New York: Free Press.

[6] M. Buber, "Dialogue," (trans. R. G. Smith). (1965). In M. Friedman (Ed.), *Between man and man,* pp. 1–39. New York: Macmillan.

[7] M. Bakhtin, *The dialogical imagination: Four essays.* M. Holquist, (Ed.) (trans. Caryl Emerson) (1981). Austin: University of Texas Press.

[8] R. Hutchins. (1954). *Great books: The foundation of a liberal education.* New York: Simon and Schuster.

[9] For a valuable discussion of culture as conversation, *see* R. Bellah et al. (1985). *Habits of the heart: Individualism and commitment in American life.* Berkeley: University of California Press.

[10] D. Tracy. (1987). *Plurality and ambiguity: Hermeneutics, religion, hope,* pp. 1–27. New York: Harper and Row.

[11] Hutchins. (1954). *Great Books,* p. 51; for a more recent formulation, *see* David Tracy, *Plurality and ambiguity,* p. 19.

# Contributors

**W. Andrew Achenbaum, Ph.D.**
Professor of History and Deputy Director of the Institute of Gerontology, University of Michigan, Ann Arbor, Michigan

**Allan B. Chinen, Ph.D.**
Assistant Clinical Professor of Psychiatry, University of California, San Francisco, California

**Christoph Conrad, Ph.D.**
*Wissenschaftlicher Mitarbeiter*, Department of History, Free University of Berlin, Berlin, Germany

**Judith de Luce, Ph.D.**
Professor, Department of Classics, Miami University, Oxford, Ohio

**Thomas M. Falkner, Ph.D.**
Professor, Department of Classical Studies, The College of Wooster, Wooster, Ohio

**Brian Gratton, Ph.D.**
Associate Professor, Department of History Arizona State University Tempe, Arizona

**Carole Haber, Ph.D.**
Associate Professor of History and Coordinator of American Studies, University of North Carolina, Charlotte, North Carolina

**Sheldon Isenberg, Ph.D.**
Associate Professor, Department of Religion, Center for Jewish Studies, University of Florida, Gainesville, Florida

**Marc Kaminsky, M.A., M.S.W.**
Founding Co-director, Myerhoff Center at the YIVO Institute for Jewish Research, Brooklyn, New York

**Christie W. Kiefer, Ph.D.**
Associate Professor of Anthropology, Human Development and Aging Program, Department of Psychiatry, University of California, San Francisco, California

**Ronald J. Manheimer, Ph.D.**
Executive Director, North Carolina Center for Creative Retirement, and Research Associate Professor of Philosophy, University of North Carolina at Asheville, Asheville, North Carolina

**Harry R. Moody, Ph.D.**
Director,
Institute on the Humanities, Arts, and Aging, Brookdale Center on Aging of Hunter College, New York, New York

**Stephen G. Post, Ph.D.**
Associate Professor,
Center for Biomedical Ethics, School of Medicine, Case Western Reserve University, Cleveland, Ohio

**Constance Rooke, Ph.D.**
Professor and Chair,
Department of English, University of Guelph, Ontario, Canada

**David Shuldiner, Ph.D.**
Humanities Program Coordinator,
State of Connecticut Department on Aging, Hartford, Connecticut

**Carolyn H. Smith, Ph.D.**
Director of Freshman Writing,
University of Florida, Gainesville, Florida

**Peter N. Stearns, Ph.D.**
Heinz Professor and
Head, Department of History, Carnegie Mellon University, Pittsburgh, Pennsylvania

**Gene R. Thursby, Ph.D.**
Associate Professor,
Department of Religion, University of Florida, Gainesville, Florida

**David G. Troyansky, Ph.D.**
Associate Professor,
Department of History, Texas Tech University, Lubbock, Texas

**T. Franklin Williams, M.D.**
Director, National Institute of Aging,
National Institutes of Health, Bethesda, Maryland

**Mary G. Winkler, Ph.D.**
Assistant Professor,
Institute for the Medical Humanities, University of Texas Medical Branch, Galveston, Texas

**Anne M. Wyatt-Brown, Ph.D.**
Assistant Professor,
Department of Linguistics, University of Florida, Gainesville, Florida

# *PART I*
# *Aging, Old Age, and Elders in History*

1

# A View from Antiquity: Greece, Rome, and Elders

*Thomas M. Falkner and Judith de Luce*

> Indeed when I consider old age, I find four reasons why it is regarded as a misfortune: first, because it keeps one from public activities; second, because it makes the body weaker; third, because it deprives one of almost all physical pleasures; fourth, because it is not far removed from death.
>
> —Cicero, *Cato Maior de Senectute* ("On Old Age," 5.15)[1]

It is ironic that the discipline that is heir to the oldest extant study in gerontology should have been so slow to take up the study of old age and the elderly in classical antiquity. Yet although there are still important gaps in our understanding, one is better equipped to learn something about the subject now than was the case even a decade ago. A spate of recent work has made it possible to define boundaries, establish areas of common knowledge and points of controversy,

---

Falkner wishes to express his gratitude to the College of Wooster for a research leave in 1987–88 and to the National Endowment for the Humanities for a Summer Stipend in 1989, which allowed him to complete the research for this work. De Luce thanks Miami University College of Arts and Science and the Department of Classics for a faculty improvement leave in 1989–90 to continue studying aging, and the Scripps Foundation Gerontology Center where much of the work was done. Special thanks go to Mildred Seltzer and Robert Atchley of Scripps, Rebecca Lukens, Cathy Beltz-Williams, and Pam Messer of the College of Arts and Science.

generate bibliographies, and propose research agenda.[2] Although little of this material has been directly influenced by work in gerontology, classicists, like other humanists, are aware of the interdisciplinary nature of the subject and the need to look at materials and methods outside the discipline as it is normally practiced.

Most important, one has at one's disposal the abundant testimony of the ancients themselves, particularly in the literary tradition, so that a view of old age in antiquity can be had in large part in their own words. That this should be the case is itself something of a paradox. The elderly in Greece and Rome were often, as a class if not as individuals, at a distance from the traditional centers of power (political, legal, military). But this is compensated for by the high profile they carry in literature. Here we find a variety of sources and a wealth of references to old age, though for at least two different reasons. One is the humanism of the texts themselves, whose interest in the final stages of life is reflected across genres in the thematic importance of old age, in the many elderly characters, and in reflections, some brief and some extended, on the nature and value of old age—Cicero's essay here is only the best known. It should be added at once that this interest, however genuine, is not therefore necessarily sympathetic. The second reason is that age as a conceptual system is a vital literary resource, useful for exploring issues that may seem to have no essential connection with old age. Concepts of age are regularly employed for their symbolic and metaphorical value, as poetic vehicles in which the polarities of youth and age are assimilated to other conceptual structures—tradition and innovation, morality and corruption, foolishness and wisdom, activity and contemplation, and so forth. To put it crudely, the texts sometimes talk *about* old age; at other times they talk *through* old age to something else, although these two aspects cannot, of course, really be separated.

In this sense, the problems in studying the elderly in Greece and Rome are the same as those that bedevil the study of socially marginal groups like slaves or women. We are necessarily reliant upon literary sources and indeed are fortunate in the sensitivity and depth of insight such first-person testimony at times affords. On the other hand, as the purposes and imaginative nature of these materials are often at odds with the goals of historical reconstruction, we must avoid the temptation of assuming that what may be unique and even idiosyncratic views of old age necessarily reflect popular practice or perceptions. Although Greece and Rome present us with social orders that are in some respects fundamentally different from each other in their concepts, institutions, and values, they are alike in the attention their respective literatures give to old age and in the prominence of certain themes: the relationship between wisdom and old age, the social and political authority of the elderly, the care of the aged. Yet as these themes are circumscribed by their own literary and textual circumstances, the representations of old age need to be interpreted in the fullest cultural context. This is not a matter of pitting artistic "representations" against social "realities"—to be sure, all of our sources are representational, whether they be discourses, institutions, material artifacts, or the practices of everyday life—but of interpreting each in the light of the other and of establishing a practical relationship between alternative representations of old age.

## OLD AGE IN CLASSICAL GREECE

The Greeks recognized old age (*gêras*) as the last of the four life stages it broadly distinguished for both men and women. For the man (*anêr*) they are those of the child (*pais*); the young adult (*neos* or *kouros*) who has achieved *hêbê*, or physical maturity; the mature man at *akmê*, or prime of life (without a distinctive term); and the elderly man (*gerôn* or *presbys*). For the woman, they are again the *pais*, or child; the young woman (*korê*) sexually of age but not married (as virgin, she is *parthenos*); the mature married woman-wife (*gynê*); and the elderly woman (*graia*).[3] Although the male and female life course each has four stages, the models are not commensurate. The stages of a woman's life are defined primarily in sexual and reproductive terms and run parallel with her biological development: the stage as mother-wife is preceded by that of the child, not yet capable of motherhood and the *parthenos*, sexually of age but not yet married, and is followed by that of the no longer capable of motherhood (*graia*).

Thus, for a woman, the passage to old age and the social changes that accompany it commence with menopause, when she ceases to be useful for sexual or reproductive purposes (Bremmer, 1987). For men, on the other hand, the transition to old age is more social and generational than physical. Although the Greeks had no institutionalized concept of retirement, and males who worked typically continued to do so as long as they could or had to (Finley, 1981), the age of 60 serves as a useful marker. In Athens a man's military obligations ended with his 59th birthday, and in Sparta nobles were eligible at 60 for election to the Gerousia, or council of elders. Greek men tended to marry at about age 30 (to women, on the average, half that age), with the father, often then around age 60, handing over control of the household (*oikos*) to him (Lacey, 1968). Thus, the son's coming into maturity, domestic authority, and economic independence would roughly coincide with the time when his father was considered "old."

Greek pessimism about old age is immediately striking at the level of language. In the poetic tradition, old age is regularly qualified by a range of negative epithets. Homer and Hesiod describe *gêras* formulaically as "hateful," "accursed," "difficult," or "sorrowful." The elegiac poet Mimnermus, whose view is typical of much of Greek lyric, speaks of "difficult and ugly old age, . . . both hateful and dishonored." The old chorus in Euripides' *Heracles* sings of "deadly, sorrowful old age," and that in Sophocles' *Oedipus at Colonus* adopts the conventional view when it describes old age with a string of privatives as "strengthless, friendless, loveless" (Falkner, 1987). For sheer negative effect, few passages can surpass that in the *Homeric Hymn to Aphrodite*, in which the goddess takes leave of her mortal lover Anchises: "soon the common fate of old age will cover you over, pitiless old age which comes beside every man, accursed, wearying, hated even by the gods" (244–246).

For the gods, who are defined in the formula "deathless and ageless," old age is a thing of loathing. Although the Olympic pantheon is ordered in a careful balance of opposing types by gender, marital status, function, and occupation, there is no god of old age, and there is no old god. The Greek gods are free from the twin vicissitudes of old age and death, frozen in youth (like Apollo or Artemis) or maturity (like Zeus or Hera), their perfection maintained by a diet of nectar and ambrosia (Clay, 1983). Hesiod personifies Gêras and identifies the abstraction as one of the offspring of Night (*Theogony*, 225). It was occasionally represented, not as a god but a daimon: a vase in the Louvre shows a balding and shriveled old man being clubbed mercilessly by the youthful Heracles.[4]

It is significant that although the Greeks, unlike many other peoples, did not imagine a mythical time when humans did not die, they were reluctant to recognize old age as an irreducible of human life (Kirk, 1970). In the closest the Greeks had to a myth of "the fall," Hesiod's stories of Prometheus and the "five ages [more accurately, races] of man" in the *Works and Days*, old age was not a part of man's original lot but was a punishment like disease, hard work, and women. In the myth of the five races, Hesiod charts the decline from an original idyllic race of Gold to a corrupt and immoral race of Iron, of which he and his contemporaries are members. He portrays that final race as a kind of senescence of humanity: we will know its end is near when children are born "gray at the temples" (*poliokrotaphoi*, used frequently of old men). That Hesiod should use the metaphor of age in a human history may seem routine and uninspired,but that he should find in old age a symbol for the decadence and depravity of his own times says something about his culture's view of old age.[5] In the Prometheus myth it is among the ills released from the jar of Pandora, and the mortals in Hesiod's original Golden Race did not age but died "as if subdued by sleep" (*Works and Days,* 116). Old age is often described as an outside force and is listed with the fates of death, disease, and poverty, before which men stand helpless. At times it is endowed with its own agency. In Homer, old age "wears," "holds," and "oppresses", and in Mimnermus, it "makes a man hateful, dishonored, unrecognizable."

Why is old age so loathsome a reality? In the quotation with which this essay begins, Cicero (who is drawing upon Hellenistic philosophical sources)[6] suggests four reasons. The Greeks would agree to these and distinguish a fifth: the disfiguring and degenerative effects of old age. In the *Odyssey* we are told that when Athena disguised the hero, she "withered the beautiful skin on his supple limbs, and ruined the fair hair on his head, and put about all his limbs the skin of an aged old man" (13.431–432). Old age was understood, in early thought and later discussions of physiology, as a "drying up" of the bodily fluids and the liquid force of life. The dry skin of old age was a symptom of the general desiccation of old age, hence the related notion of old age as a skin to be scraped or sloughed off (Giacomelli, 1980; Onians, 1951). Greek lyric poetry develops the bodily aesthetic that pits the beautiful bloom of youth against the ugliness of age and laments old age as a time when a man loses interest in love or, as often, love loses interest in him (Bertman, 1989)—for Mimnermus, old age makes him "hateful to boys, worthless to women." In tragedy, especially Euripides, the physical burden of old age is described at times in almost clinical terms, with the speeches of the elderly a litany of their wrinkles, aching limbs, gray hair, stooped backs, trembling feet (Falkner, 1985). The Greek obsession with youth and horror at the physical process of aging help account for the relative invisibility of the elderly in classical sculpture, which found its inspiration in gods and heroes of myth and in the generic idealization of the young man and woman, the *kouros* and *korê* (Richardson, 1969/1933). Apart from the occasional seer or priestly figure, the elderly are conspicuous by their absence. It is not until the Hellenistic period that artists become interested in the elderly form and not until the Roman portrait bust that they will lend nobility and even beauty to all those wrinkles.

In many cultures the physical disadvantages of old age are mitigated by the prestige the elderly have for their great wisdom. Indeed, the figure of the wise old counselor, as a venerable source of tradition and guidance, is central to the *Iliad,* embodied in Nestor and Phoenix and the Trojan city-elders (*dêmogerontes*). Nestor himself defines "speech and counsel" as the *geras gerontôn,* the prerogative of the elders, with a bit of formulaic word play on *geras* (privilege) and *gêras* (old age). It has been rightly observed that Nestor's long and digressive speeches in the *Iliad* are not examples of senile garrulity (Austin, 1966). His counsel is often recognized as best of all of the Greeks, and his tactical advice is sound and sensible, if sometimes obvious. His moral advice, which aims to bolster spirits and soothe tempers among the younger heroes, is characterized by its emulation of a superheroic past of which he is the sole surviving exemplar.

On the other hand, Nestor holds no monopoly on speech and counsel, and it is significant that in the council of the princes both young and old are referred to as elders (*gerontes*). Moreover, Nestor's success as a counselor is limited, and his advice is frequently unheeded and at times widely off course (Falkner, 1989a). The Trojan city-elders fare no better when they recommend that Helen be returned to the Greeks. Their speech, like Nestor's, is beautiful but ineffectual, and Nestor's "honey-sweet words" (1.249–250) are paralleled by the "lily-thin voices" of the Trojan city-elders, who chirrup like cicadas deep in the woods (3.150–152). The Trojan counselors have their counterpart, in the second book of the *Odyssey*, in Halitherses and the other old Ithacans who try in vain to talk some sense into the young suitors. That the youthful protagonists of epic should disregard the advice of the elderly is in one sense a precondition of their own tragic greatness. But the overall impression that elderly counsel is also by and large failed counsel is warranted.

Indeed, one seldom finds in Greek thought the assumption that wisdom comes naturally with old age. Kirk (1971) suggests that the introduction of the alphabet into Greece, probably in the late ninth or early eighth century, had important consequences for the status of old age. In preliterate Greece the knowledge of the past, of the authentic traditions and sacred truths, would largely have been the province of the elderly. When literacy lifted the burden of memory, it was the poets and thinkers, not the elders and storytellers, who became the teachers of the culture, dealing a blow to the proverbial wisdom of old age. Indeed, early Greek literature at times seems intent on undermining any connection between wisdom and age. A fragment of Hesiod reassigns the function of counsel from old age to middle age and replaces it with piety: "deeds belong to the young, counsel to those in the middle, and prayers to the old" (321 West). The iambic poet Archilochus (or someone writing in his tradition) recommends that the elderly live a *bios apragmôn*, a life apolitical and socially disengaged: "an idle life is good for old men, especially if they happen to be simple in their ways or prone to be stupid or talk nothing but nonsense, which is typical of old men" (330 West). Neither did Solon, the first architect of Athenian citizenship, associate old age and wisdom. Like Shakespeare and the Bible, he reckoned a man's appointed years as threescore and ten, but his poetic division of the life course (27 West) into ten "hebdomads" is highly unconventional by Greek standards (Falkner, 1990). Like Hesiod, he saw middle age (36 to 56) as the acme of male life: "in the sixth hebdomad a man's mind is disciplined in every respect, and he no longer wishes to do lawless deeds; and in the seventh hebdomad he is far the best in mind and speech, and in the eighth too—fourteen years in all" (11–14). Old age is a period of relative decline: "in the ninth he still has some ability, but his speech and his intellect are feebler in respect to great excellence; but if he should complete the measure of the tenth hebdomad, it would not be untimely for him to meet his appointed end" (15–18). It is interesting in this regard that one of the sources on the life of Socrates contradicts Plato's account of his trial by presenting the philosopher at age 70, faced with the prospect of both mental and physical decline, resigned to and even eager for death.[7]

The wise old counselors of Greek drama are characterized by a similar kind of ambivalence. Seven of the extant dramas employ choruses composed of elders. In the earliest of these, Aeschylus' *Persians* (472 B.C.), they counsel Queen Atossa and mourn the destruction of their army abroad. In the *Agamemnon* (458 B.C.), the prophetic chorus counsels Clytemnestra and vainly attempts to keep her in her proper place. But in the latter play Aeschylus emphasizes the weakness and helplessness of the chorus, which complains as it hobbles into the orchestra: "we, dishonored in our aged flesh, left behind then by the host of allies, remain here, propping up our childlike strength on staffs" (72–75). Here the impotence of age provides a practical solution to a dramaturgical dilemma, which became acute with the development of plots that involved more "action." Specifically in the *Agamemnon,* what are these bystanders to *do* as they hear the grisly execution taking place within the palace or when the murderess and her accomplice declare themselves? The answer, at least by the scenic conventions that separate chorus and actors, is nothing, and Aeschylus attempts to resolve these "paradoxes of inaction" by composing the chorus of ineffectual groups like old men and women. But by naturalizing their behavior these plays contribute to the impression that old age is equally unable to act or to persuade. Ultimately, one is hard-pressed to identify any real difference between young and old, male and female, or Greek and foreigner in the quality of choral wisdom. It is significant that the *Histories* of Herodotus, which are deeply influenced by tragedy and make extensive use of wise counselors (Lattimore, 1939), show no particular predilection for casting the elderly in this role.

Until the later moralizing treatises that inspired Cicero's "On Old Age," the philosophical tradition was often inhospitable to the elderly. The pre-Socratic philosopher Democritus criticizes those who do not accept death as a natural limit: "the senseless long for life, fearing death rather than old age." Neither does Plato regard wisdom as a necessary by-product of age or experience. In the *Republic*, where belief and behavior will be carefully regimented, the "philosopher-kings" are a select group of men and women aged 50 and older, but they rule not by virtue of their age but of their grueling education. In fact, Plato begins the dialogue with a portrait of the complacent old Cephalus, who excuses himself from the deliberations precisely when they become difficult.[8] And there are few more unsympathetic characterizations of old age than that in which Aristotle discusses the three stages of life (*Rhetoric*, 2.12–14). Here middle age is the prime of life (*akmê*) and the golden mean between youth, which is rash and insolent, and old age, which is cynical, suspicious, small-minded, illiberal, cowardly, selfish, shameless, and calculating.

Aristotle's observations may be drawn as much from the stage as from life. Many of the old men in Euripides are selfish, disagreeable, and hypocritical: Pheres in the *Alcestis*, Tyndareus in the *Orestes*, Cadmus and Tiresias in the *Bacchae*. The image of the foolish, irascible, and hopelessly out of date old man was a staple in the New Comedy of Menander (McCary, 1971), and Menander provides the Greek perspective on old dogs and new tricks: "to heal a corpse and to instruct an old man are the same thing." We get an earlier version of this theme in Aristophanes' *Clouds*, in which the foolish Strepsiades enrolls in Socrates' shop of sophistry. The old man hopes that a crash course in the New Rhetoric will help him argue his way out of his debts, but he finds himself bewildered by the newfangled science, philosophy, and argumentation. In a society like Athens the knowledge and beliefs of the old were of little use in negotiating the subtleties of the new knowledge. But such scenes reflect differences in values as well as age. The old men in Aristophanes are often cast as "Marathonomachoi," the Marathon-fighters who had saved Athens from the Persians in 490 B.C. None of this group could actually have been alive by the end of the century, but in Aristophanes they come to stand for a set of traditional values under attack by the sophists, the politicians, and the whole ethical tenor of the Greek enlightenment. To this extent Aristophanes is directing his satire not only at the elderly but at a dimension of the whole community, which he holds responsible in large part for the situation in which the city finds itself (Hubbard, 1989).

Old women fare no better. Aristophanes predictably focuses not on their lack of wisdom but on their deviation from the feminine and domestic virtues, and he sees in old age the exaggeration of qualities he condemns in younger women as well. In plays like the *Ecclesiazusae*, old women are characterized as feisty, argumentative, bibulous, and even sexually aggressive (Henderson, 1987). The elderly heroines in tragedy, on the other hand, in Euripides in particular, reveal enormous depths of hatred and a frightening capacity for vengeance, as with Hecuba's grotesque punishment of Polymestor in the *Hecuba* or with Alcmene's brutal execution of Eurystheus in the *Children of Heracles*. Euripides' type of the "vengeful old woman" has a tradition going back to Homer's portraits of Hecuba and Eurycleia; nor should we forget that the spirits who embody the very principle of vengeance, the Eumenides, were envisioned as ugly old women (Falkner, 1989c).

When we turn to the lives of Greek intellectuals, in many cases the men who produce the images we are examining, we get quite a different picture. Although old age was, of course, not a condition for intellectual and artistic accomplishment, it was clearly no obstacle. It was believed by some that as the *Iliad* was the product of Homer's youth, the *Odyssey* was written in old age (the later poem being more narrative than dramatic and storytelling being characteristic of old age). Solon capped his career as a lawgiver and political reformer with an old age spent in study, travel, and writing and could say of himself "as I grow old, I am always learning." He seems to have done something of a volte-face on the final couplet of his poem on the "ten ages of man." In a verse aimed ostensibly at another poet, who had prayed for death at 60, he says, "Let death's end find me when I am *eighty*."

More striking is the situation toward the latter half of the fifth century, in Athens and elsewhere, where we can speak without exaggeration of a "graying of Greece" among intellectuals and creative artists. Perhaps the most remarkable aspect of the fifth-century enlightenment is that this period of energetic intellectuality was virtually dominated by the elderly, and Finley (1981) wonders if there is not some connection behind this remarkable longevity and creativity. Aeschylus lived to be 69 and produced his masterpiece, the *Oresteia*, only two years before his death in 456. Pindar composed epinician odes up to his death in 438 at the age of 80. The philosopher Anaxagoras lived to be 72, and he was running a school in Lampsacus when he died in 428 B.C. Euripides died in 406 at almost 80, having just completed perhaps his greatest work, the *Bacchae*. The following year Sophocles died at age 90; among his last works was the brilliant *Oedipus at Colonus*. The rhetorician and sophist Gorgias was still lecturing at Athens and would continue doing so for another quarter century until he reached 110 years; his esteemed colleague Protagoras had died in 415 at about age 70. (Among their most gifted students was Isocrates the orator, who would live to be 108.) And of course, Socrates, charged with corrupting the youth of Athens, made his first and only appearance in a court of law at age 70 in 399. His student Plato would be active until his death at age 83 or so in 437.

Yet the vigorous and productive lives that these biographies suggest seem to have left little mark on the literary imagery of old age. That Greece has an abundance of what Kenneth Clark calls "old age art" tells us little about ordinary elderly men and women, whose daily lives would have been quite different. It may well be the case that old age brought Athenian women, particularly widows, greater freedom. Although they continued technically to be under the control (*kurieia*) of a husband or male relative, one wonders if such women were not largely in control of their own lives: there is clear evidence that they, unlike their younger counterparts, could travel about the city as midwives, participants in religious festivals, and perhaps even as professional mourners (Bremmer, 1987; Lacey, 1968). For these women, whose lives had been constituted in their obedience to their husbands and in the nurturing of their children, old age may well have been a kind of liberation.

For old men the transfer of the family business and estate to their sons would have relieved them, too, of much of their authority and responsibilities. There would be some continuity in their social lives. They would continue to appreciate the cultural amenities of Athens, its religious and dramatic festivals, and enjoy the daily hum of politics and commerce in the agora. But there seems to have been no important function that elderly men as a class performed. Although seers and priests, in both literature and art, are sometimes depicted as old (the example of Tiresias is frequently adduced here), neither occupation is in any real sense age-specific (Finley, 1981). And as age did not necessarily imply wisdom, neither did it confer authority, at least in any political or institutional sense. Age is clearly not a prerequisite for ruling in the Homeric world. In the *Odyssey*, Laertes seems to have abdicated rule of both Ithaca and the household of Odysseus even before his son's departure for Troy, and the Greek princes are all in youth or middle age, with Nestor again the exception that proves the rule. Among the Trojans, Priam's authority seems largely titular and ceremonial, the real authority wielded not by the *dêmogerontes* but by the younger heroes.

The governing council in historical Sparta, on the other hand, was in name and reality a Gerousia, with 2 kings and 28 elders from the Spartan elite elected for life: Aristotle was predictably critical. The early poet Tyrtaeus could say of his city that "the beginnings of counsel (*boulê*) belong to the god-honored kings . . . and the revered elders" (4.3–5 West). But in this regard Sparta is exceptional, and in the variety of political constitutions that developed one is hard-pressed to find evidence of gerontocratic institutions or practices. Although the evolution of the polis moved uniformly to reduce the hold of the aristocracy and to diffuse power more evenly, there is no evidence at the institutional level of structures through which the elderly wielded any kind of real political power.

This is not to say that their participation was limited constitutionally. Van Hoof (1983) rightly observes that the elderly were not marginalized in any structural sense. In Athens old men sat in the assembly and were eligible for election to the various magistracies and the council, and Socrates himself served on and presided over the council only six years before his death. Demographics are an issue here: though we know little statistically (Finley, 1981), given the number of aged male citizens it is unlikely that there were ever more than a handful on the council at any one time. But there is also a sense in which the underlying values of the emerging polis were antigerontocratic. One cross-cultural study (Slater, 1964) suggests a correlation between attitudes toward old age and social and political characteristics:

> Societies in which the elderly have high prestige are generally authoritarian, totalitarian, collectivistic, and static. They are typically governed by monarchs, chiefs, or restricted councils of oligarchs. . . . In societies in which the aged have low prestige . . . government is by general assembly or some other democratic system. Individualism is prevalent and highly valued. (pp. 232–233)

Slater's categories could well be applied to Greek political development. In conservative Sparta, where the authority of tradition and age was enshrined in the Gerousia, the elderly are spoken of frequently and deferentially. Tyrtaeus exhorts the younger warriors to defend their older colleagues and says elsewhere that those who fight bravely in youth "are distinguished among the citizens as they grow old." But in the more democratic constitutions at Athens and elsewhere, the principle of the authority of old age runs at odds with the whole tenor of the times: the egalitarian nature of the politics, the relocation of the male's identity from the patriarchal *oikos* to the polis, and the increasing valuation of reason over and against the authority of mere age (Reinhold, 1970). In such cities, where politics served as an arena for individual competition, where the winds of social, intellectual, and political life shifted often and "modernity" was a positive value, and where political success was often based upon one's rhetorical ability and adaptability to changing circumstance, the elderly may have been at a real disadvantage. Not surprisingly, it was in such an environment that the glorification of youth and disparagement of age became social forces and literary commonplaces.

There is some evidence to suggest that in the late fifth century elderly men participated extensively in the jury service available to Athenians.

In Aristophanes' *Wasps*, for instance, the ranks of the elderly dutifully assemble at the law courts in the predawn hours to volunteer to serve. They are "jury-mad," and the playwright has great fun representing the elderly chorus as a swarm of angry, stinging wasps. One critic says of them that "a mass of old men sitting on a jury is the democratic equivalent of an immemorial feature of human society, the elders of the community sitting as judges" (Dover, 1972, p. 128). But jury service implies neither great wisdom nor great power, and there are other reasons these old men should be so litigious. The first is simply that, relieved of their domestic and military responsibilities, they may have had little else to do. Given the time on their hands, the displays of rhetoric and temper in the law courts may well have been the best show in town. This is not to say that they did not take their charge seriously. Where the "younger generation" (those, like Alkibiades, born in 450 B.C. or later) had come to take Athenian democracy largely for granted and could weigh its merits with a theoretical detachment, for the elderly it represented an issue of vital public interest (Forrest, 1975). For them, these constitutional questions still mattered, and the idea of participation in the machinery of the democracy could still excite their passions.

Other passages in the *Wasps* suggest that there are financial reasons for the public-spiritedness of the elderly. In one a boy who is hoping for a sweet treat is reminded by his father, the old chorus leader, of how far he has to stretch the miserable jury pay he hopes to receive.

> CHO: From this pittance I have to get my barley meal, and firewood, and meat and you—oh no—you want *figs*!
>
> BOY: But Dad, listen. If the magistrate says the court won't sit today, how will we buy our supper? Have you thought your way out of *this* pickle?
>
> CHO: Alack, alas, oh woe is us—I don't have a clue where dinner will come from! (300–308)

The Periclean reforms had established three obols as standard compensation for jury duty, avowedly in service to the ideal whereby participation in the democracy was extended even to the poor. The figure was a minimal subsistence level, the Athenian poverty line, attractive only to those who had no other real source of income. If, in fact, the elderly served on juries disproportionate to their numbers, it is evidence that a significant number of old men and likely a greater number of women lived in real or virtual poverty.

As in many traditional cultures, the institutional center for care for the elderly in Greece was not the polis but the family, in the duties of sons toward their aging mothers and fathers. The Greeks liked to stress the reciprocal nature of this arrangement, sons taking care of their parents as their parents had taken care them. What the son was said to "give back" to his parents was called the *threptêria,* literally the cost of one's rearing. In the *Theogony,* Hesiod reminds his listeners that as bad as is the curse of women, there is a greater one: "whoever avoids marriage and the troublesome ways of women, and is unwilling to marry, arrives at accursed old age in need of a *gêrokomos* ('tender-in-old age')" (603–605).

Sons formed the only pension plan available to the elderly, and the institution become one of the cornerstones of Greek social organization: Schaps (1979) rightly observes that the concern Greek law shows for the well-being of the elderly is evidence of just how vulnerable they were once divested of their property and domestic authority. The economic predicament of the elderly is a pervasive theme in Greek literature, and it contributes to a grim prospect of old age as a whole. The *Iliad* makes poignant mention of several heroes whose deaths rob their parents of the *threptêria,* and the theme is in a sense implicit in the situation of every hero who, in the pursuit of glory and booty, risks depriving his parents of their security in old age. In the last book of the *Odyssey* the hero returns to find his father, Laertes, dressed in rags, tending his orchard alone, and sleeping at night with the slaves. Laertes is neither poor nor neglected—he has a grandson and servants to support him—but his appearance suggests the destitution of those bereft of their sons in old age. So too, incidentally, does Odysseus himself, whose disguise as an "old and wretched beggar" provides an image of those untended in old age.

The payment of the *threptêria* carries the strongest moral overtones. In the *Works and Days,* Hesiod prophesies that children's failure to provide for their parents will be a sign of the imminent demise of the Iron race: "men will dishonor their parents who are aging quickly, reviling them and talking in cruel words . . . and will not give back to the old ones the *threptêria*" (185–188). Here, as elsewhere, support for one's parents in old age is the outward sign of the honor and respect they are owed. The elegiac poet Theognis of Megara says pointedly, "there's no room here . . . for those who dishonour their aged parents" (821–822). It is worse than death, disease, or old age itself "when you raise your children and provide everything they need, and store up possessions for them at the cost of great pain, and they hate their father and call curses on his life, and loathe him like some beggar who comes along" (271–278). In Athens the payment of the *threptêria* was enforcible by law, and politicians taking office swore publicly that they were taking proper care of their parents. Though there are few examples of actual failures to do so, the theme occurs with some frequency in the fifth-century literature. In Sophocles' *Oedipus at Colonus*, the old protagonist—blind, exiled, and homeless—becomes an archetype of filial disregard. His situation is doubly ironic in that he is cared for not by his sons, who acquiesced in his expulsion, but by his daughters, Antigone and Ismene. The institution provides the context to a chilling scene in Euripides' play *Alcestis*, in which Pheres comes under attack for having declined an offer to die in his son's stead. The *agôn* of the play here provides for a legalistic debate over the obligations and the expectations in a filial relationship. Says Admetus: "You cannot say that you betrayed me to die for having dishonored you in old age, since I've been especially dutiful to you. And in return for this you—and the one who bore me—do me this kind of a favor! Well, you'd better get going and get some more children, to feed you in old age and dress your body when you die and lay out your corpse. I swear that *I* will never bury you" (658–665). Pheres objects that he has met all his obligations, having begotten and raised him and made him master (*despotês*) of the household. But he knows of no Greek custom that fathers should also die for their sons. Admetus concludes with a shameless blast against mother and father to "go and grow old!" and threatens to publicly "disown" his father.

It is hard to tell what social significance these disagreeable scenes have. Some suggest they reflect generational conflict in Athens (Reinhold, 1970; Thury, 1989). But the theme is heavily moralized, and here as elsewhere it is related to the disrespect and outright abuse the aged are made to suffer. The weakness and vulnerability of old age became an important way to dramatize the hubris of the wicked, and a character's treatment of the elderly often serves as a measure of his morality. It is not by accident that as the *Iliad* opens with Agamemnon's abuse of the elderly priest Chryses, it concludes in a rapprochement of young and old, with Achilles caring for Priam in place of the warrior he has slain. In the *Odyssey*, the arrogant suitors who devour the stores of his household do violence to Laertes as well as Odysseus. The theme is frequent in the drama of Euripides, whose plays show a special sensitivity to questions of social injustice. His stagecraft finds some of its most effective moments in scenes in which the elderly are verbally and physically abused: thrown to the ground or marched off to execution, supplicating on their knees or collapsing in fear for their lives, pitted against their children or grandchildren in an *agôn* full of spite and disrespect (Falkner, 1985).

In the end, one is struck by the frequency with which the elderly become paradigms of tragedy. Greek literature continually treats us to the spectacle of human happiness lost in the final stretch. Priam, on his knees before Achilles in the last book of the *Iliad*, serves as a kind of *pater dolorosus,* a prototype of human suffering and archetype for all the other examples in Homer of fortune lost or nearly lost in old age: Phoenix and Nestor, Hecuba and Chryses, Laertes, and perhaps even Odysseus himself. In the fifth century this theme is played with even more frequency. Sophocles used it in the great *Oedipus at Colonus,* but Euripides is its foremost spokesman. His tragedies are crowded with the aged heroes and heroines of legend, and perhaps the single most frequent scene in Euripides is that of the elderly in mourning over the bodies of their wives, sons, daughters, grandchildren. To some extent these images are based on history itself. In fifth-century Athens there must have been few families untouched by the chain of misfortunes that rocked the city: the casualties of the Peloponnesian War, the great plague, the catastrophic end to the Sicilian expedition. Although these disasters touched the whole city, the grief of the elderly must have been especially keen, who had known the heights of Athens's earlier glory and had grown up in a time of expansion and prosperity. In Pericles' "Funeral Oration," as reported by Thucydides, we get an idea of their suffering. Here Pericles' only consolation to the elderly is to hold onto the memory of earlier and happier years and to remember that it will not be long until death ends their grief (2.4).

But we also want to keep in mind the symbolic value of these scenes and their relation to the Greek vision of life as a whole. The Greeks seem to have been particularly moved by the idea of tragedy in old age and the loss of happiness near the close of life. It is as though life were a kind of footrace; and even though one might take the lead and hold it almost to the end, if one should stumble, the whole race is lost. Greek literature treats us repeatedly to the spectacle of human happiness lost in the final stretch. In the elderly we see compelling images of how fragile and precarious a thing is human happiness and get a sense of catasrophe that is always lurking just beyond the scene. In these images the Greeks found a logic that was aesthetically satisfying and in keeping with their vision of life itself.

## OLD AGE IN CLASSICAL ROME

The difference between what we can say about old age among the Romans and among the Greeks can be attributed as much to intrinsic differences between the two cultures as to the different sources of information available to us. On many scores—linguistic, religious, political, social, historical—Greek and Roman civilizations shared common ground even before Greece became a Roman province in the second century B.C. But the Romans also diverge sharply from Greek tradition, both in the details of their culture and in the sources for our understanding of that culture. An extensive body of written records and law, for example, provides information not encountered in as great detail among the Greeks. Classical Greek sculpture, above all else the sculpture of youth, rarely depicts specific, recognizable individuals, but the Romans favored strikingly realistic portraits of themselves at all ages; so many of these portraits have survived that we know what real Romans looked like throughout their lives. Latin literature is as intensely personal as the sculpture: a variety of different literary sources is available to us, including letters and satire, that provides vivid, if not always uncensored, glimpses of Roman life. We also know, at least by name and in some cases in considerable detail, far more Roman women and men, many of whom are old. This wealth of information allows us to supplement with specific details from the lives of Roman elders the perspective on old age that we derive from literature.

Relying on both representation and reality, we discover an ambiguous picture of old age. The representations of old age that we find in poetry owe much to the pessimism of the Greeks described above, but Roman culture challenges that literary tradition of a bleak, hateful old age. Men and women would have experienced old age differently, as would members of different economic and social classes, but in general elders were as likely to be esteemed for their wisdom and experience as ridiculed for their frailty. Three examples will highlight the ambiguity. Ovid described himself at nearly 60: "Already my temples copy the swan's snowy plumage and white old age dyes my black hair; already the brittle years and sluggish time of life approach, already it is painful for me, in my frailty, to endure" (*Tristia*, 4.8.1–4). Ovid wrote these lines in exile, where the image of diminished physical and mental vigor could serve as a metaphor for the loss and isolation he suffered from as easily as it could describe Ovid as an old man: "The staggering succession of my troubles wears me out and forces me to become an old man before my time" (*Tristia*, 4.8.19–20).

On the other hand, a Roman political institution provided real opportunity for male elders to remain influential in their community. The senate, the oldest deliberative body in Rome, derived its name from *senex*, "old man," and originally had been composed of 100 *patres*, "a few select men physically weak but intellectually vigorous" (Sallust, *Catilina*, 6.6). They were called "fathers" either because of their age or because the duties they performed for the state were like those of a father (Sallust, *Catilina*, 6.6–7). This explanation hardly suggests that the Romans discounted the political wisdom of their elders, but we will need to return to the senate later.

The enigmatic saying *sexagenarios de ponte*, which appears to advocate hurling 60-year-olds off the nearest bridge into the Tiber (Balsdon, 1979), implies political antagonism between generations rather than the practice of geronticide (Baldwin, 1976). Of the three interpretations Ovid (*Fasti*, 5.621–662) mentions for the practice that gave rise to the saying, the second is relevant here, that "young men threw decrepit old men from the 'bridges' [to the ballot boxes during elections] so that only the young could vote." Whatever the actual origin of the saying, Ovid rejects the suggestion that Romans ever killed their old men.

To understand the relationship between representation and reality, we need to focus on a series of questions. What was "old age" in Rome? What roles did elders play in Roman tradition and institutions? Is there a consistent literary representation of old age? What relationship exists between the literary representation and Roman culture? The discussion of these questions, far from being exhaustive, revolves around the themes of elders' wisdom, influence, and care.

The Romans persistently equated age and particular stages in life with behavior. Cato in *De Senectute* speaks in terms of *tempestivitas*, those qualities appropriate or "seasonable" for a particular age. Cicero argues in his defense of Caelius that sowing wild oats is expected in a young man of Caelius's age but presumably not in an older man. In his third satire, Persius has an older man upbraid a younger one for his debauched life-style. The speaker admits that as a child he played all sorts of tricks to avoid reciting Cato's dying speech, for example, because his energy was absorbed in play, but he warns that there is a time to give up the pursuits of childhood and to settle down to more serious things. Ovid, who refers to his earliest poetry as *iuvenalis* (youthful), says that his youthful poetic efforts were spent in writing elegy, a genre appropriate for a young man (*Amores*, 3.1). Sallust even contends that Catiline was able to win over allies to his conspiracy by playing upon their individual passions, passions that varied according to age (*Catilina*, 14.6).

Old people in particular inspire harsh criticism and vicious jokes when they violate the principle of *tempestivitas*. As a young man himself, Ovid insists in *Amores* 1.9 that an old man cannot be a lover. It is bad enough, according to Juvenal, that young women speak Greek when making love, but a woman of 86 cannot arouse anyone if she does the same: "your face gives an account of your age . . . this speech is not decent in an old woman" (6.199). Seneca warns against childish behavior (*puerilitia*) undermining the tranquility of old age (*Ad Lucilium Epistolae*, 4.2, 36.4). If sexually active elders appear to be unnatural, there is a quality appropriate to them: "Although wisdom and virtue may never be out of season, it is only in old age that they can be deemed positively natural" (Burrow, 1986, p. 151).

Different systems of age classification existed, some of which clearly took inspiration from Greek predecessors. In one of the more detailed schemes, the physician Galen based his classification in part on physiological factors: *pueritia*, or childhood (7–14); *adolescentia*, or youth (14–35); *iuvenis*, or maturity (35–48); *senex*, or old age (48 and beyond).[9]

As did the Greeks, the Romans identified the stages of women's and men's lives differently. That is, whereas physical, legal, and political factors define a man's life, a woman is identified almost exclusively in terms of her sexuality and her role in the family. Menarche was supposed to occur at 14, but a girl could marry as early as 12 (Amundsen & Diers, 1970).[10] Traditionally, she was expected to remain under perpetual guardianship (*perpetua tutela* [Livy, 34.2]) throughout her life, regardless of whether or not she had passed puberty or menopause, although at times women circumvented this guardianship. Such a guardian could be a father, husband, or nearest agnate, in most cases someone with a clear interest in the family property who could act on her behalf. After Augustus, a young *matrona* was expected to have had her first child by the time she was 20.[11]

At the age of 14, a Roman boy passed puberty and could marry; he could also become head of his own family if he were *sui iuris* (i.e., if his *pater familias* was not alive). To be sure, Roman law might also provide him with a guardian until he was 25 and old enough to handle his own affairs, but the law recognized that once past puberty he was no longer a "minor." By 15 he usually assumed the *toga virilis*, signifying his entrance into young manhood, and by 25 the young man could have been elected to the quaestorship, the first magistracy in the political career track that would lead to the consulship. He would enter the consulship around the age of 40.

Each of these stages marks a beginning, but we do not find many comparable points at which one would retire. In fact, the modern concept of retirement does not apply to ancient Rome. At 50 a man was normally exempt from military service (Finley, 1981); at 60 he was excused from jury duty (Baldwin, 1976). A senator was excused after 60 or 65 from what was originally a lifelong obligation (McAlindon, 1957). Rome did not establish mandatory ages for retirement from employment; in most cases men and women would have worked until it was no longer possible to do so (Baldwin, 1976; Finley, 1981).

For a Roman woman the most significant "retirement" came with menopause, which ancient authors thought occurred between 40 and 50, with the upper limit at 60 (Amundsen & Diers, 1970). The social consequences of menopause varied: If a woman had been valued primarily as a mother, menopause might leave her vulnerable, unprotected because no longer valuable; on the other hand, menopause might bring her greater personal freedom precisely because she could no longer bear children and because limiting sexual access to her was no longer necessary. One group of women did "retire," however, and they suggest an opportunity for postmenopausal women. Vestal Virgins, traditionally six in number, served Vesta, the goddess of the hearth. These women who guarded the hearth fire of the city and therefore the welfare of Rome were enrolled in the priesthood between the ages of 6 and 10. When they left the service after 30 years, they could marry, although few actually did. As Vestal Virgins these women enjoyed a number of privileges not shared by their sisters, including freedom from *patria potestas*. They were accorded these privileges because as virgins they were independent of the power of men; postmenopausal women were virgins in a similar sense and could enjoy liberties not granted to women of childbearing age. The *Annals* of Tacitus include portraits of a number of old women whose independence and influence are related to their age.

Not a great many men, and considerably fewer women, would have lived to become *senes*. In spite of the unreliability of some of the evidence, Hopkins (1966) estimates that at birth the average expectation of life would have been between 20 and 30, with infant mortality above 200 per 1,000. The median age of death for wives was 34 and was about 46 for husbands; higher mortality rates among young women because of the dangers of childbirth explain some of the difference. Hopkins (1983) also estimates that, on the average, 15 out of 20 quaestors entering the senate at 25 would reach the age of 40. As Baldwin (1976) notes, however, "life did not begin at forty for the Romans; rather, it began to run out" (p. 221).

The *familia* not only informed Roman social and political life, it provided a structure within which both old men and women exerted considerable influence. The *pater familias*, not necessarily one's biological father but the eldest living male when descent is traced agnatically, headed the family and could exercise extraordinary power (*patria potestas*) over its members, including the right of life and death over his children, the right to expose them, to sell or emancipate them, and to consent to their marriages. In spite of this power, the mother was not uninvolved in her children's lives, however. For example, a mother could play a decisive role in arranging or ending her daughters' marriages (Phillips, 1978; Pomeroy, 1976b). When Sejanus proposed to the Emperor Tiberius that he should marry Livilla, the widow of Tiberius's son Drusus, the emperor refused to give his consent, responding that Livilla could decide for herself and that if she needed advice she could always consult her mother and grandmother (Tacitus, *Annals*, 4.40).

Strictly speaking, only a *pater familias* was recognized as a legal person. A wife or daughter was not, by virtue of her gender, able to act in a legal capacity; the same restriction applied to a son. Thus, a 35-year-old Roman male who was not *sui iuris* was in a legal sense a "minor," unable to engage in a variety of legal matters; yet this same Roman might have been elected to an important magistracy and himself be the father of several children. The peculiar position of this son and the power of his *pater familias* could persist until the older man's death, giving rise to the frustration and resentment we find in the sons in Roman comedy (Hallett, 1984). In some cases, fathers emancipated their sons in order to free them from the legal constraints of dependency.

A final word about the family is required here: Roman law and social custom work to preserve the *familia*, especially its property and the *sacra*, those religious rites peculiar to each family. Laws of guardianship, marriage, adoption, and succession are all formulated for the preservation of the family. The tendency of the Romans toward ancestor worship also reflects this concern for continuity.

The *Laudatio Turiae* provides the most intimate glimpse we have of a real Roman marriage, one that lasted 43 years, until "Turia's" death at the end of the first century B.C. The identity of both the wife and her husband, the author of this eulogy, remains in doubt; what is not in doubt is the extraordinary portrait of a courageous woman who side-stepped many of the social and legal constraints imposed upon her by class and sex, as when she saved her husband during the civil wars. Romans assumed it was the woman's fault if a marriage was childless; when Augustus pressed upper-class families to produce children, childless "Turia" offered to divorce her husband so that he could remarry. Her husband preferred to remain in the marriage in spite of the emperor's clear expectations, and "Turia" died an *univira*, a woman married to one man only, a phenomenon much admired by the Romans (Lightman & Zeisel, 1977).

Within the literary tradition, we rarely encounter an elderly couple like Baucis and Philemon (*Metamorphoses*, 8.624–720), who share an enduring affection for one another. They alone had received the disguised Jupiter and Mercury and had gladly shared what food they had with the gods. Because they were virtuous, Baucis and Philemon were spared from the flood that swept away their neighbors and were granted their prayer: to be the priests of the gods and "because we have lived in harmony for so long, to die in the same hour, so that I won't see my wife's tomb nor will she have to bury me." Like "Turia" and her husband, they contrast sharply with the couples we find in the comic-satiric tradition.

In comedy the relationships among old men, old women, and their sons tell us something about the Roman family. They also anticipate some of the later representations of old age. The structure of the family, all of whose members are dependent upon the *pater familias*, was not the only constraint on a son's behavior. Traditional stories that the Romans told reflect their expectation that children be obedient to their parents (Segal, 1976). Livy, for example, tells the story of the first consul, Lucius Junius Brutus (2.5.6), who had his sons executed because they were rebelling against the newly established republic. Plautus and Terence adapted for a Roman audience the New Comedy of Menander. Although plots and some dramatic conventions may have originated in Greek comedy, Latin authors would not have included in their plays jokes or situations that were unfamiliar to their audience. We can assume, therefore, that Romans recognized in the comedies aspects of their own families. Segal sees in the comic sons' treatment of their fathers, in their deceptions, in their prayers for their fathers' death, behaviors that "openly flaunt the Roman dictates of respect for elders" (p. 14), as when Philolaches in Plautus's *Mostellaria* prays: "Would that I could hear that my father's dead now, so that I could disinherit myself and make [my mistress] heir to my entire estate."

"Even on the stage the silliest character is that of the old man who lacks foresight and is easily deceived" (Duckworth, 1952, p. 242). Some old fathers, like the one in Plautus's *Aulularia* are miserly, suspicious, gullible. As a husband, the *senex* can be harsh, often brutally cruel to his wife: Demaenetus (*Asinaria*) says he would rather drink bilge water than kiss his wife, whom he married for her money and wishes were dead. The *senex* can also be a severe father, but that severity is often intended for the son's welfare, as in Terence's *Heauton Timorumenos*. In Plautus's *Casina*, the lecherous Lysidamas is finally tricked, exposed, and disgraced. Demipho in Plautus's *Mercator* is in love with his son Charinus's mistress. Such aging lovers are funny in part because they violate the principle of *tempestivitas*.

The old *matrona* is far less important in comedy than is the *senex*. She can be nasty, greedy, and suspicious; the fact that her husband is often a philanderer may explain some of these traits. She can also be crafty, like Cleustrata in Plautus's *Casina*, who plots against her husband on her son's behalf. If the relationship between *senex* and son reflects the frustration of a real Roman son living under the control of his *pater familias*, to what extent does the *matrona* resemble a real Roman mother? While she is not old, Duckworth (1952) has suggested that of all of the mothers who appear in comedy, Alcumena in the *Amphitryon*, chaste, honest, innocent, comes closest to a real Roman woman.

The characters of the *senex* and *matrona* anticipate the general descriptions of old age that emerge in subsequent Latin literature. When Lucretius's old man (3.952) laments the approach of death, Nature rebukes him, drawing on the metaphor of life as a banquet, which appears elsewhere in the poem: "You enjoyed the rewards of life and now you grow weak. Because you always want what you don't have, and despise what is at hand, your life has slipped away incomplete and unpleasant, and before you could give it any thought, death stands at your head before you are ready to leave satisfied" (3.956–960). Lucretius is writing within the tradition of Epicureanism, which taught that aging was simply the process of losing more atoms, those particles of which everything is composed, than one takes in. Since the gods do not interfere with the affairs of the living or punish the dead, death is a natural process that should not be feared; no amount of praying for a longer life will do any good.

In his tenth satire, Juvenal includes the prayer for long life among those prayers that have unfortunate consequences (10.188–288): "With what great and unending evils is a long old age filled!" (190–191). The problem is not long life but long life without youthfulness. (This dilemma recalls Petronius's *Satyricon* [48], where Trimalchio claims that as a boy he and his friends saw the Cumaean Sibyl shriveled up like a dried grasshopper and hanging in a jar. She had tricked Apollo into granting her long life but had failed to ask for youthfulness to go along with the years. When the boys asked her what she wanted, she replied: "I wish I were dead.") Juvenal pictures the old man, repulsive in appearance, wrinkled like an ape, palsied, bald, with a running nose, deprived of sensual pleasures. He is prone to disease of every kind, but the worst loss of all, worse than the loss of physical health or sensual pleasure, is a failing memory. So forgetful does he become that he does not remember his own children and violates the principle of maintaining the family's continuity: "And so, in a cruel will he refuses to make his own children his heirs, but hands over his entire estate to [a prostitute]" (236–238). Yet even if he avoids physical and mental deterioration, "nevertheless he must bury his sons, he must gaze upon the pyre of his beloved wife and his brothers and the urns full of his sisters' ashes. These are the penalties paid by those who live long lives. . . . he grows old in unending woe and clothed in mourning" (240–242, 245).

Ovid follows the Pythagoreans when he equates human age with the seasons in *Metamorphoses* 15.199–236 (Burrow, 1986). After the spring of childhood comes summer "like a strong young man," then the "mellow" autumn of maturity, and finally "comes aged winter, shivering and with trembling steps, bald or with white hair." As an old man, Milon laments the loss of the strength of his youth, and Helen "weeps when she looks in a mirror at the wrinkles of age, and asks why she was twice kidnapped" (by would-be lovers). At the end of his life Ovid will warn his stepdaughter Perilla that as with Helen, there will come a day when "that lovely face of yours will be scarred by the years, and hateful old age will lay her hand upon your beauty" (*Tristia*, 3.7.33–35).[12] Ovid assures Perilla that her talent as a poet will not stay old age, but it will outlast her beauty. Juvenal, in his sixth satire, however, warns that the ravages of old age mean abandonment for a woman: "'Why is Sertorius afflame with Bibula?'" If you want to know the truth, it is the face not the wife that he loves. Let three wrinkles appear; let her skin become dry and lose its elasticity, her teeth turn black and her eyes dim," then he will send her away with this parting shot, "you are always blowing your nose."

Horace writes within this tradition when he advises authors to assign appropriate behavior to their characters according to age (*Ars Poetica*, 153–178). Whereas his descriptions of childhood, young adulthood, and maturity are fairly balanced, Horace speaks only in negatives when he turns to old age. The old man is "avaricious, interested only in acquiring more wealth, not enjoying what he already has"; he is "timid and full of complaints, criticizing the current generation and harping on the days of his own youth." This picture hardly matches Horace himself, who had enjoyed the onset of what promised to be a comfortable old age and had completed his fourth book of odes shortly before his death at 57. At least one scholar has suggested that this is the portrait of the "common man [*sic*]," for whom an old age like Horace's would not have been likely (Harcum, 1914).

Cicero's *Cato Maior de Senectute* reflects this literary tradition in spite of the fact that Cato appears to be envisioning an entirely different kind of old age from that seen in Juvenal or Horace. The subject held special interest for Cicero, then 62, as he dedicated the essay to his friend Atticus, who was 65: "I want to write you something about old age, for I want to lighten for us the burden of old age which is either already pressing upon us or surely is fast approaching."

This chapter began with the four factors that render old age painful: Cato dismisses each one, in part by distinguishing not only between the effects of ill health and the effects of old age but between the faults of old age and those of a particular old person. Someone may be "exacting," "anxious," "irascible," "greedy": but these are character flaws, not characteristics of old age. At the same time that he contends that old age can be comfortable, Cato says that one must fight old age "like a disease" by practicing good nutrition and attending to the health of the mind as well as the body. Even the forgetfulness associated with age can be avoided if one has opportunities to exercise the mind. Cato admires those who learn late in life; in fact, he claims that he learned Greek as a *senex* (rather like I. F. Stone, who learned Greek at 70). Finally, Cato regards the absence of sensual pleasures in old age as an advantage, not only because they interfere with reflection but because the greatest pleasures are those of the mind.

Because old age is weak, old men are not required to engage in activities that require bodily strength, but the greatest strength of old age is *auctoritas*, influence. So great is this influence in affairs requiring reflection and experience that in the College of Augurs, Cato reports, debate proceeds in order of age, with the eldest speaking even before those magistrates with *imperium* (supreme power); this distinction outstrips mere physical pleasures.

To regard this essay as the premier discussion of old age among the Romans or to accept it as an accurate description of what old age could be like is to overlook the fact that it is an essay on old age among men of the upper class. There is no comparable discussion of a sleek old age for women in Latin literature. It is highly unlikely that any Roman woman, regardless of class, would have experienced such an old age. She would not have had the opportunity to establish through business or politics the kind of resources and associations that enrich the old age of a Cato. It is just as unlikely that a man of any but the middle and upper classes would have enjoyed such an old age. Laelius interrupts Cato to raise an objection: that "perhaps because of your wealth, resources, and position old age seems more tolerable, but that this could not be the case for many people."[13] Cato concedes that Laelius may be right, but he retreats from considering what old age would be like to those who lack such advantages.

In his old age, Plutarch wrote an essay, *An Seni Sit Gerenda Res Publica* (*Whether an Old Man Should Participate in the State*), which could have been a companion piece to *De Senectute*. In this essay he debated whether old men should withdraw from public life and concluded that, rather than withdraw, they should remain active in public affairs because of the unique contributions they could make to the state. Like Cato, Plutarch insists that old men are invaluable by virtue of their experience and wisdom and because they are free of the jealousy and passion that marks younger men and interferes with their performing their civic duty. States look to elders in a crisis when speech, caution, and foresight are needed, not mere physical strength. "Youth ought to obey and old age rule," concludes Plutarch.

How closely do the visions of Cicero and Plutarch approximate the experiences of real Romans? Clearly, the Romans took advantage of the wisdom and experience of elders: "veneration for old age was no less intense than at Sparta" (Segal, 1976, p. 138). The very existence of the senate suggests this veneration, although the etymology of *senatus* may be slightly misleading. Because the body was augmented annually by the addition of 20 quaestors who had won the right to attend the senate by virtue of their election at 25, at any given time the senate included others besides old men.[14] Plescia (1976) argues that family structure, religion, and political institutions "sanction the supremacy of the Elders," thereby turning Rome into a gerontocracy at least until the second century B.C. But he sees a change with what he identifies as the "Roman Revolution" of 134–127 B.C. as a direct result of the conflict between generations. The cultural revolution in Rome following the victory in the Punic Wars brought Roman youth new philosophical and political ideas from Greece that challenged the system under which they lived; an oligarchy controlled the wealth while the rest of the population was in an economic crisis; and the hostility of the young against the tyranny of the elders contributed to the revolution that brought down the Republic.

In spite of the composition of the senate and the evidence of those who were active in Roman politics, Rome was not a gerontocracy, even before 200 B.C. In a study of the Venetian Republic in the 16th and 17th centuries, Finlay (1978) describes a gerontocracy that contrasts with the nongerontocratic practice in the rest of Europe. When the average age of European princes was 33, in 1518, the Doge was 83;[15] military leaders were 20 years older than the opponents they faced; and although age qualifications for political assemblies might be in the 20s or 30s, "deference to age pushed the de facto eligiblity ten years and more beyond the legal limit" (p. 160).

Rome met some of Finlay's criteria for gerontocracy, "the great respect for age, the existence of a patrician caste, founded upon a monopoly of officeholding," but Rome could not boast a true gerontocracy. Elders did not hold a monopoly on officeholding. The age of entry into the highest office, the consulship, was established at 42 by the lex Villia annalis in 180 B.C. Candidates for that office were likely to emerge as soon as they were eligible. Rather than a gerontocracy, the Romans observed a system of seniority. If a *pater familias* died leaving a 15-year-old son as the eldest male in the family, that son became *pater familias* on the basis of seniority.

More important, to date we do not have compelling evidence that elders either acted in concert as a class or thought of Rome as a gerontocracy or themselves as gerontocrats.[16] The letters of Pliny do not suggest such a gerontocracy, neither do the more autobiographical poems of Horace or Ovid. We have already seen that *De Senectute* may promise opportunities for old men to remain influential in the state, but it could have applied to only a few individuals, not to elders as a class.

Still, Roman politics does not show much bias in favor of youth. Lucian apparently never completed his promised Roman companion to the *Octogenarians,* an essay on famous Greek men who lived at least into their 80s, but he did include three kings of Rome among his Greeks: Numa Pompilius, Servius Tullius, and Tarquinius Superbus. Neither in the republic nor the empire does youth appear to be preferred: Cato the Elder died at 85. Cicero himself died at nearly 64, having written five major works in the final two years of his life. He was still embroiled in the political turmoil of the final years of the republic on the day he died. Among the emperors, Augustus ruled until his death at 76; Claudius became emperor at 50; Galba, at 72; Nerva, at 61.

It is not only in political circles that we encounter productive elders. Both Horace and Ovid lived well beyond middle age, and both incorporated into their work representations of old age as well as reflections on their own aging.[17] The life and works of Horace point to the relationship between what Latin authors say about old age and what that old age may have been like. Horace, who delineated his own version of age classification, applied the standard of *tempestivitas* as much to himself as to the persons who appear in his poems. According to the tradition, erotic passion is one of the sensual pleasures to fail in the face of old age. Horace assures the addressee in *Ode* 2.4 that he is no threat, even as he admires the beauty of Xanthias: "don't mistrust someone whose life has rushed to complete the fortieth year." In *Ode* 4.1 he prays to Venus to transfer her efforts to arouse his interest to a younger man. At 50, Horace is not up to it. An old woman must observe *tempestivitas* as well: Horace tells Chloris in 3.15, "You who are closer to the grave, stop playing among the girls . . . working the wool suits you." Whereas an older man loses interest in erotic pleasure, Horace pictures the old woman still very much interested but unable to satisfy her desires (*Ode* 1.25). Soon she will weep because young men "take pleasure in the green ivy and dark myrtle, but they give up the withered leaves."

Horace uses a season metaphor in the Soracte ode (1.9), in which both old age and Mt. Soracte are wintry, lonely, and still, whereas youth (equated with summer at poem's end) is lively and gay. As we observed above, Horace's own old age was a comfortable and productive one; we have no reason to believe that it resembled the old age of 1.9.

Ovid died at 60, having written continuously since his early 20s. Because he wrote throughout his life, Ovid provides a unique opportunity to study creativity across the life span and into old age. The fact that he spent the last years of his life in exile requires us to distinguish between the salience of old age and the salience of exile in his writing;

but in general we see Ovid, in spite of his complaints that he has lost his strength as a writer, writing constantly as he returns to the genre of his youth to review his career, settle some old scores, and reflect upon the traumas of old age and exile (de Luce, 1989).

Letters present a rich source of information about real Romans, but must be read with some recognition of the conventions of letter writing and the expectations of the letter writer. Pliny's letters both confirm and reject poetic representations of old age. Spurinna, at 77 exercising body and mind through a rigorous daily regimen, could have been modeled on Cicero's Cato (3.1). As an old man he had continued to serve the state as consul, and he enjoyed a vigorous and influential old age; and he is not Pliny's only elderly friend. Pliny's close associations with men considerably older than himself, men who acted as his advisers, support the contention of Cato and Plutarch that old men who had been active in public life could continue to participate by assuming the role of teacher and advisor to younger men. One scholar has questioned whether Pliny's experience and consequently his perception of old age may not be atypical. Pliny grew up surrounded by adults who were not family members. What would have been his opinion of old people had he been surrounded by elders in his family? Wouldn't he, for example, have displayed some of the frustration or annoyance of the young man in comedy chafing under the control of his *pater familias* (Kebric, 1983)? But it is also worth remembering that Pliny has no illusions about the less positive side of old age. At one point (3.6) he describes a Corinthian bronze he had purchased; it is the depiction of an old man with wrinkled skin, hollow chest, and a haggard expression.

We find other literary representations of old men valued for their wisdom and advice, men like Entellus, Acestes, Nantes, Evander, and Anchises, all in the *Aeneid* (Pavlovskis, 1976). In the funeral games in the fifth book, old men, competing successfully against much younger men, draw upon courage and experience and emotional resources (Bertman, 1976). In the sixth book, Aeneas risks traveling to the Underworld to talk to Anchises; he needs the advice of an old man as much as he needs to speak with his father. Yet even with these wise elders the traditional, less positive representations of old age recur, as when, at the entrance to the Underworld, Aeneas encounters "gloomy Old Age" accompanied by Disease, Fear, Need, and Hunger. Although the young men of the fifth book may appear rash at times, Beroe reminds us that old age may be excessively cautious and timid (Bertman, 1976). What is most provocative in the *Aeneid* is the inclusion of both: the timidity and weakness of the old exists along with the wisdom. Burrow (1986) thinks that this double vision is important to the epic, that "infractions of the 'common course of age' in Virgil's epic point towards a grand equalization of ages there, a convergence of old and young characters in the direction of an ideal heroic condition which escapes the limitations of both" (p. 117).

Once again, these are the experiences of old men. What about old women? Old women are both silent and silenced in Latin literature—silent because nearly all of our authors are male, and we are thus deprived of the chance to hear a woman speak in her own voice; silenced, in some cases, because scholars, applying their own cultural stereotypes of old women, have tended to ignore the considerable number of old women who appear in literature. Hallett (1984) has distinguished herself among classical scholars by taking old women seriously and arguing that "the Roman equation of seniority with superiority" would have extended to women as well: "older women command more respect, inspire more awe, and have (or may be perceived as having) greater social and political influence than do younger ones" (p. 38). As an example of the esteem accorded a female elder, Hallett recalls the story of Coriolanus (Livy, 2.40), who had been leading an attack against Rome. Only when his widowed mother appealed to him to cease this attack on his own city did he abandon his march.

Because women were identified almost exclusively in terms of the family, we encounter some of the most impressive if not always the most admirable old women within the context of familial relationships. Tacitus[18] claims that Tiberius was so obedient to his mother that it was not until after her death at an advanced age that Sejanus was able to exert his influence over the emperor. While she was alive, Sejanus did not dare confront her (*Annals*, 5.1–3). Pliny commends Ummidia Quadratilla (7.25) not because she lived so exemplary a life but because of the care she took of her grandson, shielding him from the influence of her resident mime troupe and providing handsomely for him in her will. Pliny tells us that until her death at 79 she remained mentally alert. Juvenal had presented an old mother-in-law (6.231–241) who violated the expectations of appropriate matronly behavior by acting as procuress for her own daughter. Sextus Papirius, according to Tacitus, took his own life to escape the incestuous machinations of his mother. She was banished from Rome for 10 years, until her younger son was old enough to withstand her influence, a measure that would not have been necessary if the authoriy of a mother could be easily dismissed (*Annals*, 6.49). When Silvanus (*Annals*, 4.22) was charged with murdering his wife and a panel had already been named to hear the case, his grandmother, Urgulania, sent him a dagger, a gesture interpreted as a sign of the emperor's wishes because Urgulania was not a stranger to the imperial household. Tacitus does not regard it as strange that Urgulania should attempt to interfere with her grandson (4.22). After Claudius had decided to execute his wife, Messalina, her mother, Lepida, who had stood by her in spite of their earlier estrangement, urged her daughter to seek an honorable death before the executioner could get to her (*Annals*, 11.37).

Old women did not confine themselves to their immediate families, however, as we discover from accounts of other old women in letters and histories. Sallust (24.3) reports that some older women joined the Catilinarian conspiracy, apparently motivated by their desire for more secure financial futures. Some of the old women in Tacitus courageously withstand imperial pressure. Junia, niece of Cato, wife of Gaius Cassius, and sister of Marcus Brutus, died an immensely wealthy woman (*Annals*, 3.76). Defying custom, she named in her will any number of Roman nobles but passed over the emperor. We do not know how old Vibidia was, but she was the eldest of the Vestal Virgins when she confronted Claudius about Messalina, arguing that even an adulterous wife should not be condemned without a hearing (*Annals*, 11.34).

The existence of women like these may help explain the exuberant viciousness of invective against old women exemplified by none other than that genial poet, Horace, in *Epodes* 8 and 12. Poems of invective against old women begin with the woman's immense age, describe her as repulsive, especially in terms of her sexuality, represent her as sexually insatiable and as utterly disgusting as a sexual partner (Richlin, 1983). *Epode* 8 includes all of these elements in its attack on a wealthy woman:

> You, foul by your long century, ask
>   what unmans my strength,
> when you've a black tooth, and old age
>   plows your brow with wrinkles,
> and between your dried-out cheeks gapes filthy
>   an asshole like a dyspeptic cow's?
> But your chest and decaying tits arouse me,
>   like mare's udders,
> and your soft belly and your skinny thigh
>   on top of swollen shins.
> Congratulations, and may images of great men
>   precede your funeral train,
> nor may there be a wife who walks
>   laden with rounder pearls.
> And so what if Stoic booklets like to lie
>   between your silk pillows?
> Do unlettered cocks harden less for that?
>   Or does that phallus droop less,

which you have to work on with your mouth
to raise from its proud crotch?
(translation by A. Richlin [1983, p. 110])

In discussing other aspects of poetic attacks against old women, Richlin (1983) suggests that "their power is doubly resented by satirists, a woman both old and moneyed being doubly anomalous" (p. 114). Juvenal says as much in 3.129–130. Richlin is one of the first scholars to see that these attacks reflect a real fear of old women's power: "It seems at least possible that invective against *vetulae* [old women] constituted a sort of apotropaic satire that attempts to belittle and control the power of old women" (p. 113).

Another figure who appears with some frequency is the witch, who in most cultures, including Roman, is both old and female. If *Epode* 8 reflects the reality of a wealthy woman who exercises influence in part because she is someone from whom one can inherit, then a witch such as Horace's Canidia (*Epodes* 5. 17) reflects the same woman in a different way. Instead of undercutting the woman's power by focusing on her sexuality, Horace presents the witch as an old woman who must resort to magic because she is otherwise without powers or influence.

As in Greece, the responsibility for the care of elders fell to the family, with the agnatic relationship determining the lines of responsibility. When Cicero discusses parental and filial affection in *De Finibus* (3.19.63), he commends the stork, among other animals, because it "acts for the sake of others." Indeed, the Romans passed a law compelling children to care for their aged parents and named it *Lex Ciconaria* in recognition of the bird's legendary solicitude (Kaganoff, 1989). Fathers and sons were expected to demonstrate mutual care; mothers and daughters were expected to demonstrate moral care (Plescia, 1976). This latter provision reflects, among other things, the economic status of women more than the relationship between mothers and daughters. Although some women worked outside the home and others accumulated sizable fortunes, a daughter might not be in a position to provide care. If she were still under perpetual guardianship or in the most restrictive form of marriage, she would not necessarily have the opportunity or means to help. Moreover, ancient sources provide examples of mothers supporting their daughters' interests but almost none of adult daughters supporting their mothers' interests (Phillips, 1978).

Roman law provided for various forms of guardianship for elders, several of which were not specifically formulated for them but certainly could apply to them. In addition to the perpetual guardianship of women, there are provisions for the care of the insane and of spendthrifts. An elder found to be a spendthrift would be assigned a guardian and would be prohibited from a variety of activities, including making contracts and participating in the preparation and witnessing of wills. The primary concern of such a guardian, however, was not the care of the spendthrift but the protection of family property that the guardian might stand to inherit.

Old women could find themselves in particularly vulnerable positions without relations or resources to provide for their care. Greek law provides a useful perspective in this instance: the existence of laws explicitly providing for care for old women suggests their powerlessness (Schaps, 1979). If she had sons, a mother could expect to be supported by them in her old age, just as their father was supported. A childless woman, on the other hand, was not entitled by law to maintenance and had to rely on the goodwill of her relatives. Since the Roman dole did not include women and since various programs to feed children were structured to the advantage of males, we certainly would not expect any institutionalized support for female elders even if some system had existed for the support of men.

We do not have an abundance of documentary evidence for the care of elders, but literature consistently shows children caring for their parents. Aeneas leaving burning Troy with his father on his back is not the only dutiful son; neither is Lausus, trying to save his father, Mezentius, from Aeneas's attack in the seventh book of the *Aeneid*. The most poignant example must be that of Euryalus, in the ninth book. Faced with the opportunity to go on a particularly dangerous mission, Nisus at first tries to dissuade his comrade Euryalus, not only because Nisus would prefer his friend to survive but "nor can I be the cause of such great grief for your unhappy mother who alone out of many mothers dared to follow you" (9.216–218). When Nisus and Euryalus are ready to set out on the mission from which neither will return, Euryalus asks Ascanius to look out for his mother: "I pray you, console her when she is in need, support her in her loneliness" (9.290). Ascanius assures Euryalus, "She shall be a mother to me . . . everything I promised you should you return safely belongs forever to your mother and to your family" (9.297, 301–302). In a society where few children survived to adulthood, the loss of an adult child would be especially devastating, in part because that death threatened to eliminate the family just when one thought the child safely grown (de Luce, 1988). In this context, the lament of Euryalus's mother reminds us of the consequences for her of losing the son who would not only have cared for her but who represented the future of the family: "late respite of my old age, cruel son, how could you leave me here alone" (9.481–483)?

Although he does not elaborate. Pliny implies this kind of loss when he writes of the death of Junius Avitus, a young man whose death Pliny mourns, just as he mourns the plight of Avitus's elderly mother and of the family that survived Avitus (8.23). Scipio Aemilianus, on the other hand, as a young man inherited a large fortune in clothes, utensils, slaves, and so on. He settled much of that wealth on his impoverished mother to enable her to participate in public functions (Polybius, 31.23–26.18).[19]

The Romans also knew of peoples who did not care for their elders, indeed quite the opposite. According to Strabo, the Caspians starved to death those who were 70; the Dervishes in the Caucasus killed and ate men of 70 and strangled and buried women of that age. For some, suicide was preferable to an old age of pain, deprivation, or mental infirmity regardless of how good the care. Strabo and Pomponius Mela report on the deaths of those who took their own lives in old age (Balsdon, 1979). Lucretius says that Democritus took his life when he discovered that his mind had begun to wander (3.1039–1041). Pliny's friend Corellius Rufus died "by his own wish" rather than endure any more pain. "He completed his seventy-seventh year, an age which is long enough even for the very healthy," yet Pliny mourns his death "as if he were a young man in good health" (1.12).

Finally, concern for "care" extended to death, as Pliny's ghost story suggests (2.27): an old man in chains haunted a house in Athens because he wanted a proper burial for his bones. Care entailed not only provision for the living but the performance of burial rites upon death. The ghost story reminds us of the fear that both kinds of care might be missing.

In the end, the picture of old age proves less ambiguous than it first appeared. We have seen that although social and political institutions provided opportunities for elders to exert influence and power, traditional representations often, although not exclusively, depicted old age as a time of lost opportunities, of physical and mental deterioration.

We can attribute some of the difference between the representation and the reality to the difference between literature written in the shadow of Greek tradition and that of peculiarly Roman institutions. We can also attribute the difference to the distinction between what individual elders experienced as opposed to elders as a class. In fact, we still know comparatively little about the subjective experience of old age among the class of elders; we know far more about individual old persons. And in that respect, Harcum's (1914) conclusion can be ours: old age for individual Romans is a "time to be dreaded rather than hoped for . . . Even Cicero could make it only endurable, not desirable" (p. 118).

## NOTES

[1] Except where noted, translations are by the authors.

[2] Eyben (1989) provides an annotated bibliography. Useful general studies of old age in ancient Greek and/or Roman culture can be found in Richardson (1933/1969), Haynes (1962, 1963), Kirk (1971), de Beauvoir (1972), Finley (1981). A number of relevant essays can be found in the collections in Bertman (1976) and Falkner and de Luce (1989).

[3] On the stages of life in Greek thought, see especially Nash (1978). Although Garland (1990) was not available at the time this manuscript was prepared, it offers a detailed study of the Greek life course and its terminology.

[4] A picture of the vase can be found on the frontispiece for Richardson (1933/1969). On Heracles as a symbol of youth and life in conflict with old age and death, see Kirk (1974 pp. 188ff.).

[5] On the role of age in the sequence as a whole, see Falkner (1989b).

[6] On the sources of the *De Senectute*, see the useful introduction in Powell (1988 pp. 24ff.).

[7] Xenophon, *Apology of Socrates*, 6–9.

[8] Later, in a number of passages in the *Laws*, Plato advocates a traditional behavior toward and obligations to the elderly, particularly one's parents, although his arguments have more to do with avoiding generational conflict and the resultant political instability than with wisdom per se (cf. Reinhold, 1970).

[9] For further discussions of age classification, see Eyben (1973), Baldwin (1976), Suder (1978), and Burrow (1986).

[10] For technically precise discussions of Roman law and society, see Crook (1976), Watson (1971), and Nicholas (1975).

[11] Hallett (1984) and Pomeroy (1976a) discuss women's lives in general.

[12] For Ovid and old age, see de Luce (1989).

[13] Finley (1981) looks at the issue of class.

[14] Finley (1981) and Hopkins (1983) discuss the senate and its composition.

[15] In the Renaissance, "old age" began at 40 (Finlay, 1978).

[16] According to Sue A. Taylor, Miami University (interview with author, August 1989), in the absence of a universally acceptable definition of gerontocracy, the question of whether elders as a class regard themselves as gerontocrats is particularly important in identifying a gerontocracy, especially from an anthropological point of view.

[17] Broge (1976), Finley (1981), Esler (1989), and de Luce (1989) all discuss the relationship between poetry and old age in these authors.

[18] We rely here on Tacitus's references to old women and his memorable if not always unbiased accounts.

[19] See also Hallett (1984, pp. 44–45).

## REFERENCES

Amundsen, D. W., & Diers, C. J. (1970). The age of menopause in classical Greece and Rome. *Human Biology, 42*, 79–86.

Austin, N. (1966). The function of the digressions in the *Iliad*. *Greek, Roman and Byzantine Studies, 7*, 295–312.

Baldwin, B. (1976). Young and old in imperial Rome. In S. Bertman (Ed.) *The conflict of generations in ancient Greece and Rome* (pp. 221–233). Amsterdam: Gruner.

Balsdon, J. P. V. D. (1969). *Life and leisure in ancient Rome.* New York: McGraw Hill.

Balsdon, J. P. V. D. (1979). *Romans and aliens.* London: Duckworth.

Beauvoir, S. de (1972). *Coming of age* (Patrick O'Brien, Trans.). New York: Putnam.

Bertman, S. (1976). The generation gap in the fifth book of Vergil's *Aeneid.* In S. Bertman (Ed.), *The conflict of generations in ancient Greece and Rome* (pp. 205–210). Amsterdam: Gruner.

Bertman, S. (1989). The ashes and the flame: Passion and aging in classical poetry. In T. Falkner & J. de Luce (Eds.), *Old age in Greek and Latin literature* (pp. 157–171). Albany: State University of New York Press.

Bremmer, J. N. (1987). The old women of ancient Greece. In J. Blok & P. Mason. (Eds.), *Sexual asymmetry: Studies in ancient society* (pp. 191–215). Amsterdam: J. C. Gieben.

Broge, V. (1976). The generation gap in Catullus and the lyric poetry of Horace. In S. Bertman (Ed.), *The conflict of generations in ancient Greece and Rome* (pp. 171–203). Amsterdam: Gruner.

Burrow, J. A. (1986). *The ages of man.* Oxford: Clarendon Press.

Clay, J. S. (1983). *The wrath of Athena.* Princeton, NJ: Princeton University Press.

Crook, J. (1967). *Law and Life of Rome.* Ithaca, NY. Cornell University Press.

de Luce, J. (1988, April). *Tune illa senectae sera meae requires: Mothers and fathers mourning the death of an adult child.* Paper presented at the annual meeting of the Classical Association of the Middle West and South, New Orleans.

de Luce, J. (1989). Ovid as an idiographic study of creativity and old age. In T. Falkner & J. de Luce (Eds.), *Old age in Greek and Latin literature* (pp. 195–216). Albany: State University of New York Press.

Dover, K. J. (1972). *Aristophanic comedy.* Berkeley and Los Angeles: University of California Press.

Duckworth, G. E. (1952). *The nature of Roman comedy.* Princeton, NJ: Princeton University Press.

Esler, C. C. (1989). Horace's old girls: Evolution of a topos. In T. Falkner & J. de Luce (Eds.), *Old age in Greek and Latin literature* (pp. 172–182). Albany: State University of New York Press.

Eyben, E. (1973). Roman notes on the course of life. *Ancient Society, 4,* 213–238.

Eyben, E. (1989). Old age in Greco-Roman antiquity and early Christianity: An annotated select bibliography. In T. Falkner & J. de Luce (Eds.), *Old age in Greek and Latin literature* (pp. 230–251). Albany: State University of New York Press.

Falkner, T. (1985). Euripides and the stagecraft of old age. In K. Hartigan (Ed.), *The many forms of drama* (pp. 41–49). Lanham, MD: University Press of America.

Falkner, T. (1987). Strengthless, friendless, loveless: The chorus and the cultural construction of old age in Sophocles' *Oedipus at Colonus.* In K. Hartigan

(Ed.), *From the bard to Broadway* (pp. 51–59). Lanham, MD: University Press of America.

Falkner, T. (1989a). *Epi gêraos oudôi*: Homeric heroism, old age, and the end of the *Odyssey*. In T. Falkner and J. de Luce (Eds.), *Old age in Greek and Latin literature* (pp. 21–67). Albany: State University of New York Press.

Falkner, T. (1989b). Slouching towards Boeotia: Age and age-grading in the Hesiodic myth of the five races. *Classical Antiquity, 8,* 41–59.

Falkner, T. (1989c). The wrath of Alcmene: Gender, authority and old age in Euripides' *Children of Heracles*. In T. Falkner & J. de Luce (Eds.), *Old age in Greek and Latin literature* (pp. 114–131). Albany: State University of New York Press.

Falkner, T. (1990). The politics and the poetics of time in Solon's "Ten ages." *Classical Journal, 86,* 1–15.

Falkner, T. & de Luce, J. (Eds.). (1989). *Old age in Greek and Latin literature.* Albany.

Finlay, R. (1978). The Venetian Republic as gerontocracy: Age and politics in the Renaissance. *Journal of Medieval and Renaissance Studies, 8,* 157–178.

Finley, M. I. (1981). The elderly in classical antiquity. *Greece & Rome, 28,* 156–171.

Forrest, W. G. (1975). An Athenian generation gap. *Yale Classical Studies, 24,* 37–52.

Garland, R. (1990). *The Greek way of life.* Ithaca, NY: Cornell University Press.

Giacomelli, A. (1980). Aphrodite and after. *Phoenix, 34,* 1–19.

Hallett, J. P. (1984). *Fathers and daughters in Roman society: Women and the elite family.* Princeton, NJ: Princeton University Press.

Harcum, C. G. (1914). The ages of man: A study suggested by Horace, *Ars Poetica*. *Classical World, 7,* 114–118.

Haynes, M. S. (1962). The supposedly golden age for the aged in ancient Greece: A study of literary concepts of old age. *Gerontologist, 2,* 93–98.

Haynes, M. S. (1963). The supposedly golden age for the aged in ancient Rome: A study of literary concepts of old age. *Gerontologist, 3,* 26–35.

Henderson, J. (1987). Older women in Attic old comedy. *Transactions of the American Philological Association, 117,* 105–129.

Hopkins, K. (1966). On the probable structure of the Roman population. *Population Studies, 20,* 245–264.

Hopkins, K. (1983). *Death and renewal.* Cambridge: Cambridge University Press.

Hubbard, T. (1989). Old men in the early plays of Aristophanes. In T. Falkner & J. de Luce (Eds.), *Old age in Greek and Latin Literature* (pp. 90–113). Albany: State University of New York Press.

Kaganoff, B. (1989, August–September). Fowl names. *Jewish Monthly*, p. 14.

Kebric, R. B. (1983). Aging in Pliny's letters: A view from the second century A. D. *Gerontologist, 23,* 538–545.

Kirk, G. S. (1970). *Myth: Its meaning and function in ancient and other cultures.* Berkeley and Cambridge: University of California Press.

Kirk, G. S. (1971). Old age and maturity in ancient Greece. *Eranos-Jahrbucher, 40,* 123–158.

Kirk, G. S. (1974). *The nature of Greek myths*. Baltimore: Penguin.

Lacey, W. K. (1968). *The family in classical Greece*. Ithaca, NY: Cornell University Press.

Lattimore, R. (1939). The wise advisor in Herodotus. *Classical Philology, 34*, 24–35.

Lightman, M., & Zeisel, W. (1977). *Univira*: An example of continuity and change in Roman society. *Church History, 46*, 19–32.

McAlindon, D. (1957). The senator's retiring age: 65 or 60? *Classical Review, 7*, 108.

McCary, T. (1971). Menander's old men. *Transactions of the American Philological Association, 102*, 301–325.

Nash, L. (1978). Concepts of existence: Greek origins of generational thought. *Daedalus, 107*, 1–21.

Nicholas, B. (1975). *An introduction to Roman law*. Oxford: Oxford University Press.

Onians, R. B. (1951). *The origins of European thought about the body, the mind, the soul, the world, time, and fate*. Cambridge: Cambridge University Press.

Pavlovskis, Z. (1976). Aeneid V: The old and the young. *Classical Journal, 71*, 193–205.

Phillips, J. (1978). Roman mothers and the lives of their adult daughters. *Helios, 6*, 69–80.

Plescia, J. (1976). *Patria Potestas* and the Roman revolution. In S. Bertman (Ed.), *The conflict of generations in ancient Greece and Rome* (pp. 143–169). Amsterdam: Gruner.

Pomeroy, S. B. (1976a). *Goddesses, whores, wives, and slaves*. New York: Schocken Books.

Pomeroy, S. B. (1976b). The relationship of the married woman to her blood relatives in Rome. *Ancient Society, 7*, 215–227.

Powell, J. G. F. (1988). *Cato maior de senectute*. Cambridge: Cambridge University Press.

Reinhold, M. (1970). The generation gap in antiquity. *Proceedings of the American Philosophical Society, 114*, 347–365.

Richardson, B. E. (1969/1933). *Old age among the ancient Greeks: The Greek portrayal of old age in literature, art and inscriptions, with a study of the duration of life among the ancient Greeks on the basis of inscriptional evidence*. New York: Greenwood Press.

Richlin, A. (1983). *The garden of Priapus: Sexuality and aggression in Roman humor*. New Haven, CT: Yale University Press.

Richlin, A. (1984). Invective against women in Roman satire. *Arethusa, 17*, 67–80.

Schaps, D. (1979). *Economic rights of women in ancient Greece*. Edinburgh: Edinburgh University Press.

Segal, E. (1976). O tempora, O mos maiorum! In S. Bertman, (Ed.), *The conflict of generations in ancient Greece and Rome*. Amsterdam: Gruner.

Slater, P. E. (1964). Cross-cultural views of the aged. In R. Kastenbaum (Ed.), *New thoughts on old age*. New York: Springer Publishing Co.

Suder, W. (1978). On age classification in Roman imperial literature. *Classical Bulletin, 55,* 5–9.

Thury, E. M. (1989). Euripides *Alcestis* and the Athenian generation gap. *Arethusa, 22,* 197–214.

Van Hooff, A. J. L. (1983). Oud-zijn in het oude Hellas. *Tijdschrift voor Gerontologie en Geriatrie, 14,* 141–148.

Watson, A.(1971). *Roman private law around 200 B.C.* Edinburgh: Edinburgh University Press.

2

# The Older Person in the Western World: From the Middle Ages to the Industrial Revolution

*David G. Troyansky*

Do older persons have a history that is not simply reducible to their biographies? And if so, does the period from the Middle Ages to the Industrial Revolution have any coherence? To the first question, the recent literature on the history of old age responds with a resounding yes. To address the second, we must recognize that we are dealing with more than one history over the course of a thousand years. There is a history of images of age and a history of the experience of aging. Moreover, different images appear in different kinds of sources. Medical texts do not necessarily project the same image that can be found in theater or painting, and every genre may include a variety of competing or complementary images. Furthermore, representations of older persons are mediated by gender, class, religion, and cultural tradition, and they do not simply reflect a coherent social reality. Nevertheless, certain images seem to predominate in particular periods of history, and certain demographic and socioeconomic trends have imposed limits on people's experience of old age.

What follows can be only provisional, and although it seeks to put things together in a new way, it must rely on research already undertaken. Because so much of that work has adhered to fairly traditional periodization, this chapter does the same. Such chronological treatment should serve as a convenience to the reader, who ought, however, keep in mind that periods and categories overlap and that some elements of "medieval and early modern aging" persist.

## MEDIEVAL AGING (5TH TO 15TH CENTURIES)

Medieval texts reveal an interest in the life course, the *cursus aetatis,* and the appropriateness of certain kinds of behavior in every age of life. Authors in the Middle Ages adopted different schemes from antiquity, which referred to three, four, six, or seven ages. "Scientific" texts fit the life course into the natural world: biologists see three ages; physiologists, four; and astrologers, seven (Burrow, 1986). Religious and historical texts fit the life course into history, opting generally for six stages, the model that Saint Augustine presented in *On Genesis against the Manichees* (388–390) and other works. The days of creation were correlated with the ages of man and history. Such scholarly works as the *Etymologies* of Isidore of Seville (d. 636), Bede's *De temporum ratione,* and Hrabanus Maurus's *De naturis rerum* (840s) popularized the six-part scheme (Sears, 1986).

Individual scholars differed on the duration of each age of life, but multiples of seven years were very popular. Older persons could be identified with the last two stages, called alternatively *gravitas* and *senectus, senectus* and *senium,* or *senectus* and *decrepitas.* Thus, qualities of seriousness and wisdom might be separated from those of weakness and mortality. According to Isidore:

> The fifth age is that of riper years, that is to say, of mature judgment, *gravitas,* and is the gradual decline from youth into old age: the individual is no longer young, but he is not yet an old man. . . . This age commences with the fiftieth year and ends with the seventieth. *Senectus* is the sixth stage and is bounded by no definite span of years, but whatever of life remains after those earlier five stages is marked up to old age. *Senium* is the final part of old age, so named because it is the terminus of the sixth age. (Sears, 1986, p. 61)

Monastic authors emphasized the spritual virtues of the old, but later medieval preachers, seeking a wider audience for their exegesis, focused on problems of decline. They maintained the Augustinian categories of the ages of life but favored Psalms and Paul's Epistles in commenting on old age (Sprandel, 1981). They also developed the Augustinian tradition of using age as a metaphor, according to which old age represents the body and sinfulness, and youth represents the soul and salvation (Minois, 1987).

Illuminated manuscripts, stained glass windows, religious sculptures, and secular murals transmitted such moralizing views. They also broke out of the four- or six-part mold. Some commentators opted for seven ages of life, adding death to the traditional six. Others suggested a correlation with the 12 months of the year, providing an opportunity for greater differentiation of characteristics and ages. Whatever the divisions, in the later Middle Ages authors and illustrators emphasized the vanity of earthly existence and the need to prepare for death; they also represented the ages of life in cyclical or serial images: the Wheel of Life, the Tree of Life, and the Steps of Life. It was the last that would prove most enduring, though it has also been seen as reducing the number of alternative models that people had had in the late Middle Ages (Cole & Winkler, 1985; *Die Lebenstreppe*, 1983; Dal, 1980; Sears, 1986). All such models, however, had less to do with the process of aging per se than with the idea that in every age one should think of death.

Secular medieval narratives employed the idea of the ages of life to judge individuals according to their conformity with or transcendence of cultural norms. Transcendence usually involved the *puer* or *puella senex*, who in youth already displayed the virtues or wisdom of the old. It might, however, involve the old person who attains the innocence or power of youth. Epic literature shared the ideal of transcendence, which took on a heroic complexion but permitted an equalization of ages in which youth could be idealized as youth. Conformity with the ideals of nature eventually replaced the ideal of transcendence in the secular literature of the later Middle Ages. Indeed, the youth who displays the attributes of age would be mistrusted by authors such as Chaucer and Petrarch, who followed the Stoic thinker Seneca in this connection (Burrow, 1986).

A new literature on old age, combining moral teaching with scientific observation, appeared in the late Middle Ages. The Arab physician Avicenna (980–1037) had borrowed from Galenic medicine and explained the causes of aging by examining such factors as climate, nutrition, and exercise. Roger Bacon (d. 1290s) and Arnald of Villanova (d. 1311) took up this approach and suggested ways of slowing or preventing the aging process. In the 1280s, Bacon expressed considerable optimism in *The Cure of Old Age and the Preservation of Youth*, in which he recommended a particular regimen but observed that the air had been polluted by an increasing number of people and animals inhabiting the earth. Arnald further developed Bacon's approach and combined it with considerable mysticism in *The Defence of Age and Recovery of Youth* (Grmek, 1958; Gruman, 1966; Minois, 1987; Sears, 1986).

The prescriptive literature on old age displays a tension between the possibility of an inherently good old age and the desire to avoid the maladies typically associated with aging. The representation of old age in romance is painful to behold:

> Old Age was painted next to Sorrow there,
> Shrunken at least a foot from what her height
> Had been in youth. She scarce could feed herself
> For feebleness and years. Her beauty gone,
> Ugly had she become. Her head was white
> As if it had been floured. 'Twere no great loss
> Were she to die, for shriveled were her limbs—
> By time reduced almost to nothingness.
> (Lorris & Meun, 1962, p. 9)

Thus, Guillaume de Lorris in *The Romance of the Rose*, which later, in the section authored by Jean de Meun, entertains Cicero's ideas from *De Senectute*. But even then, "Reason contrasts Youth and Old Age" and declares:

> But badly are Age's services received;
> For no one loves or prizes Age enough,
> That I know of, to want her for himself.
> None to be old and near life's end desires. (p. 99)

Moreover:

> . . . Age has her home
> Where Labor dwells with Grief, and both combine
> To chain and fetter Age and torture her
> And beat her till they bring her near to Death. (p. 100)*

Nor is less elevated literature any less bleak. The *fabliaux*, popular ribald tales, are filled with hideous crones who are both lascivious and avaricious, but it is probably fair to say that different genres reveal different old persons. Initial investigations into the medieval depictions of the aged reveal more variety than nonspecialists may have expected (C.U.E.R.M.A., 1987; Sheehan, 1990).

---

* From The Romance of The Rose by Guillaume de Lorris and Jean de Meun, translated by Harry W. Robbins, translation copyright © 1962 by Florence L. Robbins. Used by permission of the publisher, Dutton, an imprint of New American Library, a division of Penguin Books USA Inc.

Courtly romance may be said to favor youth over age, but Petrarch, who straddles the divide between the Middle Ages and the Renaissance, had some serious and sympathetic observations to make on aging throughout the life course. His letters and love poems indicate that a participant in urban Italian and southern French courtly culture might transcend the obsession with youth (Folts, 1980). After witnessing the 1361 plague in Milan, Petrarch opted for a consideration of old age that was neither an expression of contempt for the world nor a desire for death. He wrote to Boccaccio, "It is most useless to hold on to death; rather we must learn to improve life. . . . Think rather about doing that work which is always good, which is seen as noble and beautiful at any age, but which in old age is necessary" (Cohn, 1988, p. 91).

It is difficult enough to free the representation of old persons from the context of metaphor and the *cursus aetatis*; it is even harder to perceive its connection with the experience of growing old in the Middle Ages. Yet some glimpses are possible. They are not particularly happy. In the violent atmosphere of the early Middle Ages, youthful strength may have been more valued than aged wisdom. Dying in battle was certainly preferable to dying "of" old age. Customary law assessing damages for wrongful death shows us an old person valued as the equal of a child under the age of 10. Germanic codes also indicate a relatively early end to a father's control over his children (Mitterauer & Sieder, 1982). This was a far cry from Roman patriarchy. For non-elites, old age must have implied a significant loss of power. Nevertheless, some evidence suggests a popular association between age and the supernatural, particularly old women whose experience with birth, disease, and death placed them at the margin of the natural and the magical.

Monastic orders provide examples of scholarly elders, but age does not seem to have been an important factor in selecting authorities. In some early cases, elderly monks were even sent back to their families. But the practice by some rich old people of retiring permanently to a monastery began appearing in the sixth century. Such a move represented a complete break with the world, more so than the partial break experienced by the retired Roman patriciate. It represented a preparation for death in contemplative retreat. By the 11th century, it had become a common experience for the aged elite; some elderly men lived in company with younger monks, others in separate housing (Minois, 1987). Widows frequently ended their days in monastery towns and in lay religious communities (Lorcin, 1975). Donations guaranteed maintenance in old age, and by the 13th century elderly women were making such arrangements with hospitals.

Medieval wills show us the origins of the common early modern practice of notarizing contracts for maintenance in the family of elderly peasants and artisans (Clark, 1982; Mitterauer & Sieder, 1982). Physical disability sometimes forced early retirement, which was negotiated with the succeeding generation. But such retirement was still a stopgap measure worked out in a series of formal or informal agreements. The elder's authority might even outlive him, as testaments might dictate particular long-term arrangements from the grave (Cohn, 1988).

Demographic circumstances precluded the coexistence of two adult generations throughout much of the medieval period. By the late 12th century, however, such coexistence and even a generation gap had emerged (Duby, 1988). In feudal territories, the landlord may well have forced the retirement of less productive elders in favor of their adult children or unrelated peasants. That is the common explanation for the emergence of rural retirement arrangements (Mitterauer & Sieder, 1982). Their extent in the Middle Ages is not well known, so we will return to the topic when we consider the 17th and 18th centuries.

In the great commercial cities of the late Middle Ages, retirement became a somewhat more common practice in the business class. Classical texts provided advice, but economic expansion, urban growth, and demographic change provided the context. Wealth and longevity encouraged a more secular retirement, and lifetime annuity arrangements were made with new public institutions. But the demographic horrors of the 14th century changed the context of European culture. Some historians see a new worldliness; others, a revived religiosity. Much depends upon the choice of city and source. High culture may reveal one reaction to demographic crisis; testamentary practices may reveal something else. In testaments from Siena, for example, a new strategy for the afterlife and pious earthly bequests emerges in the late 14th and early 15th centuries, and a certain selfishness becomes evident in the late 15th and the 16th centuries. Eventually, the Counter-Reformation would encourage a new kind of piety, which would decline only in the 18th century (Cohn, 1988).

Horrific as it was, the Black Death did have some respect for the aged. Younger people seem to have been disproportionately represented among the victims, and the result was a significant aging of the population. Ten percent of the Tuscan peasantry was over 65 years of age in 1427 and 11% of the working class and petite bourgeoisie. A significant literature on the family emerged in the wake of the plague. It called for respect for aged parents, but it is difficult to say what the impact was on behavior (Duby, 1988; Herlihy & Klapisch-Zuber, 1985).

## RENAISSANCE AGING (1300–1648)

The Italy of the Black Death is also the Italy of the Renaissance, and the image of old persons was treated in a great variety of ways in that period. The recognition of a distinct stage of life in old age and the spread of retirement must be admitted. But the meaning was ambiguous. Such ambiguity runs through the recent literature. On the one hand, Minois (1987) sees a nastiness toward the aged in Renaissance culture. He views it as a return to the gerontophobia of classical Greece and Rome. On the other hand, the participants in a University of Maryland colloquium on old age in the Renaissance see something somewhat more positive. They don't deny the cruelty of much literary evidence, but they find even that more comforting than the lack of a model in the 20th century. They can point to an artistic tradition that valued the aged physiognomy, a rich variety of elderly literary characters, and a large prescriptive literature (Seeff & Ansello, in press).

Prescriptions for Renaissance aging varied enormously. It is possible to find Rabelaisian hedonism, Erasmian humanism, Baconian "technologism," and Montaigne's powerful stoicism (Moody in Seeff & Ansello, in press). To a certain extent, these provide models for aging as for everything else in life. The revival of Cicero was another important element of Renaissance humanism. The *De Senectute* had something to say to an elite that might experience retirement from public life. The humanist retreat to one's study, as in the choice of the 38-year-old Montaigne, offered a nonreligious model for leisurely occupations. The scientific discourse on aging was further developed in Zerbi, Du Laurent, Francis Bacon, Luigi Cornaro, and others (Grmek, 1958). However, even the "scientific" approach involved the transmission of literary wisdom. Thus, Zerbi, who has been called the author of "the first practical manual on the problems of old age," quoted approximately 100 lines from the 6th-century elegies of Maximianus of Tuscany (Zerbi, 1988). The elegies were written from the point of view of an old man looking back on an amorous career and give considerable attention to impotence in old age.

Not all literary examples are necessarily prescriptive. The marvelous variety of aged characters in Shakespeare's plays makes it foolhardy to assign him one particular view of the elderly. The ages of life make their appearance in Jacques's famous speech, but elsewhere we find a discussion of the importance of money for the aged (also in *As You Like It*), property and love (*King Lear*), the "impact of bad life-choices" (*Macbeth*), and a certain paranoia at the wreckage of life in later years (*The Winter's Tale*) (Mowat in Seeff & Ansello, in press). The fury of the aged Prospero can be compared to the rage and resurgence of strength in the old age portrayed later by John Milton (Kerrigan, 1986). *King Lear* is routinely cited as the most insightful portrayal of old age in world literature (Asp, 1986; Bagnell & Soper, 1989), but it meant different things to different people. Eighteenth-century rewrites would end happily, and in L.-S. Mercier's French version, *Le vieillard et ses trois filles,* Lear is not a king but simply an old man.

Painting can be a useful source for the historian, and the Renaissance would be an obvious period to explore. However, there has not been any systematic study of the depiction of elderly characters in that or any other period. Nevertheless, a few very impressionistic attempts have been made to characterize the artistic representation of older persons. Thus, Dayonnet, a historian of art, and Lasserre, a physician, give a grand sweep from antiquity to the present. They do not go much beyond describing a few works; and even when attempting to analyze the changing depiction, they simply adapt the standard textbookish parade of styles, using categories like naturalism or realism. They have done an important service in pointing out the old saint (1352) of Tommasso da Modena, wearing the first glasses to be seen in painting, and the sculpture of the aged Anne and Joachim (1470) in Amsterdam. But the art historians have not yet done with old characters what they have begun to do with children.

Is it more than a truism to say that the Renaissance had an interest in the nature of man and that Renaissance painting explored all of the ages of life? At this point we might simply recognize a wide range of aged characters among the portraits of saints, mythical heroes, political figures, and humanists. It has been suggested that the characters portrayed by Breughel the Elder are people who carry the full weight of their decrepitude, that Dürer's portrait of his mother betrays a certain despair, that greater calm can be found in Raphael's work, that a great intensity can be seen in Tintoretto, that the affection shown in the gazes of Ghirlandaio's old man and young boy is remarkable, or that Michelangelo's old persons are full of strength (Dayonnet & Lasserre, 1982). A more systematic study of old persons in art might begin with Ripa's 16th-century *Iconologia* or Cochin's 18th-century *Iconologie,* which describe the themes and types in European painting. But we would still be dealing with the allegorical or metaphorical uses of age.

Literary and iconographic evidence from the Renaissance suggests a shift from the cyclical medieval ages of life to the early modern stepladder stages. The cyclical view emphasized preparation for death at any moment, whereas the *Lebenstreppe* or *degrés des âges* turned life into a rising and falling career, peaking at 40 or 50. Although the new model was quite improbable when compared with the typical "career" in early modern Europe, Thomas Cole (1992) sees this as a "bourgeois" construction of life that accomplished a certain cultural work over the course of many centuries. Like one specialist in the English Renaissance (Chew, 1962), Cole links tha stepladder version of the life course with the idea of the pilgrimage or journey. However, Europeans opted for a variety of shapes or "master narratives" that described a life. The ship that sought a safe harbor after the storm of life was at least as important an image as the stepladder stages.

Whatever representation of the life course we choose to examine, the relationship between discourse and reality is, as always, difficult to identify. However, one can argue that many Renaissance cities were gerontocracies, and social conflicts were often understood as representing intergenerational tensions (Trexler, 1980). Calls for respect might then be seen as merely supporting the patriarchal sociopolitical order and the many attacks on old age in the culture as an expression of resentment of that same order, a recurring theme in both high and popular culture. The particular version that emerged in Florence—that city is better known than any other, largely as a result of work on the 1427 census (Herlihy & Klapisch-Zuber, 1985)—was the result of a peculiar family structure in which the husband was much older than his wife. It may well have isolated the patriarch from wife and children, who identified more with each other. And a literature on family life emerged that discussed the marriage of youth and age. Poggio Bracciolini's life and writing provided a view on the old man's marrying a young woman that was still important in the 19th century. Herlihy (1982) has hypothesized that the importance of the mother in child rearing in Renaissance Florence helped develop the aesthetic sense of youthful Florentines. It would be difficult to prove such a contention, but contemporary texts do hint at such a connection.

There have been attempts to define when old age began in the Renaissance, and different scholars have opted for 50 or 40 years of age, depending upon occupation (Gilbert, 1967). Others point not to particular moments in an individual's life but to turning points in the history of the family and household. Thus, the birth or departure of the last child might be a significant time for the maturing mother (Seeff & Ansello, in press). Either might be considered the gateway to old age. Widowhood too would often represent a significant turning point in a woman's life. The widow of any age and the woman in old age were often cruelly attacked in high and popular culture. They often were seen as dangerously sexed and independent (Beauvoir, 1970; Carlton, 1978). A growing historical literature has cut through some of the imagery, and we have learned that elite and bourgeois widows may have acted with some of the authority of their late husbands (Bideau, 1980; Diefendorf, 1982; Dupâquier, 1981). Still, women alone were generally quite vulnerable, and poor widows and aged spinsters suffered great deprivation. Some institutions served as old age homes, but they hardly were the norm for the needy. Nevertheless, one Florentine hospital, the Orbatello, served as a home for widows and their daughters. The women governed themselves in a way that contrasts markedly with the patriarchy that predominated in the world (Trexler, 1982).

## REFORMATION AND COUNTER-REFORMATION (1517–1648)

Historians of the 16th and 17th centuries have tended to emphasize the similarities between the Protestant and Catholic reformations rather than their differences. They have treated both great religious movements as parts of one large shift in Western consciousness. In both, it may be said that religion left the monastery to enter the world, and ordinary people became newly concerned with spiritual issues. Both display characteristics of individual and communal spirituality, and both can be seen as contributing to the disciplining of the European population. They can also be interpreted as having an important impact on the course of life, on the meaning of the family, and on the meaning of death (Davis, 1977). Some historians have stressed the reinforcement of patriarchy, but others point to the emergence of a new companionship between spouses and between parents and children (Ozment, 1983; Stone, 1977). The question of the development of an idea of childhood as a distinct period of life has stimulated an impressive historical literature (Ariès, 1962). The parallel question of the development of a view of old age has only begun to be addressed (INED, 1982–1983).

A popular image of the Protestant Reformation is that of the patriarch reading the Bible to the members of his household. Often he is depicted as much older than his wife. Genre paintings in both Protestant and Catholic cultures include aged figures engaged in everyday activities. However, they should not be taken as objective depictions of the family. Seventeenth-century paintings of Flemish bourgeois and peasant life often illustrated religious proverbs that included wisdom on the ages of life and the evils of avarice in old age (Chartier, 1989). Very common also is the older person depicted in an attitude of prayer. Aged saints and other spiritual characters reinforced the Augustinian tradition of old age as preparation for death. Counter-Reformation preaching was often quite hysterical in warning of the difficulties of true repentance in old age and calling for mortification of the flesh (Minois, 1987; Troyansky, 1989).

> Alas! it is impossible for old people to be able to escape or to deliver themselves from the miseries, pains, troubles, and other incommodities of life. Thus it is not really the time to think of a true conversion when one has neglected it; it is necessary to have provided for it early. Actions follow the temperament of ages; those of youth are ardent and vital; in adulthood they are strong and robust; but the actions of old people are cowardly,

> negligent, slothful, frigid, coarse, defective, trembling, accompanied by sorrow and *ennui*. (Yvan, *La trompette du ciel*, cited in Troyansky, 1989, p. 85)

Some Protestant preachers adopted a similar strategy of warning aged individuals of the vanity of earthly existence and identifying vanity as a particular vice of old age.

If the Reformation was essentially an exploration of questions of salvation, it was also an era of debate about security in all of its guises. Questions about aging and death were central to a cultural preoccupation with fear and insecurity. It is here perhaps that the Reformation is further from us than we may imagine (Bouwsma, 1980; Delumeau, 1989). Nowhere is this more evident than in the witch craze of the 16th and 17th centuries. Witches were not necessarily elderly, but those accused in the early modern period were likely to be older than their medieval counterparts. The association of old women with magic and death contributed to a kind of gerontophobia (Bever, 1982). Even economically and politically secure individuals may have felt great psychological insecurity in aging (Demos, 1986).

Much remains to be done on religious discourse on aging and the aged, but some scholars have found in Protestant piety and institutions a somewhat kinder view. This has allowed Americanists to see a great reverence for the aged in Puritan New England and observers of Dutch painting to see a new appreciation for domestic life at all ages, from the innocent child to the kind old teacher (Fischer, 1978; Schama, 1987). Such depictions express, by this interpretation, considerable certainty in the believer's salvation. If Catholic texts put the emphasis on the deathbed and the difficulties of salvation in old age, some Calvinist sources describe old age itself as a sign of salvation.

Such a clear and consistent confessional difference is probably an exaggeration. Calvinists too could suffer from anxiety, even into the 20th century (Williams, 1990). Moreover, the good works of the Catholic might engender self-confidence. Nonetheless, the organization of Calvinist churches privileged the role of elders, and secular institutions as depicted in Dutch guild and regent paintings suggest association of age and authority. In England, a higher socioeconomic rank meant earlier promotion in the life course, but age did play a role in the construction of authority (Thomas, 1976).

## SEVENTEENTH AND EIGHTEENTH CENTURIES

Religious hysteria and fear of witches had run their courses by the middle of the 17th century. Several explanations have been offered for the change from baroque to classical tendencies (Rabb, 1975). One lies in the Scientific Revolution, which should also be understood as a philosophical revolution. Science still depended greatly on ancient and medieval sources, but some sort of epistemological break is generally recognized. This had an impact on the elderly, as they began to be studied in new ways. Dissection included the invasion of the aged body. The process of aging was addressed by Descartes, the impact of occupational hazards by Ramazzini. Scientific discourse combined traditional Galenic theory with a new concern for empirical observation.

Closely connected to the more scientific approach to the natural world was the development of the early modern state. States concerned themselves with what would become known as political economy, and this involved a consideration of the strength of populations. Dependency ratios can be gleaned from early demographic texts. State institutions also rewarded civil servants with new kinds of pensions. At first they had little to do with age per se, but eventually they became associated with a particular age and a particular career (Bois, 1989; Ehmer, 1990). Mathematicians studied questions of life expectancy and probability and put pensions on a more scientific footing (Dupâquier & Dupâquier, 1985; Daston, 1988).

The most thorough change in the representation of the elderly can be seen in the period of the popularization of the Scientific Revolution, the Enlightenment of the 18th century. One attempt has been made to link the new appreciation of old age to the era's writers' favorable experience of aging and long intellectual productivity (Kafker, 1981). But secularization and increased life expectancy have been identified as the essential motors of change (Gutton, 1988; Troyansky, 1989). And the principal result was the creation of a sentimental image of old age that would eventually be defined by the middle classes as "traditional." The historical literature certainly indicates no earlier golden age for the aged (Stone, 1978). Indeed, if we are to believe the jacket copy for a collection of articles on preindustrial old age, it has revealed quite the opposite, that aging in the past was attended uniformly by extraordinary horrors (Stearns, 1982). But even the articles in that collection attest to a much more complex situation.

Criticism of traditional religious belief was a commonplace in the intellectual elite of the 18th century. But until the 1970s, scholars were ill-equipped to determine how deeply the secularizing tendencies of the Enlightenment ran. The question of secularization, or "dechristianization," has been raised most provocatively by Michel Vovelle (1973) in his research on the history of death. He examined a wide range of sources in studying the decline of "baroque piety" in Provence in the 18th century, but the key source was the testament. In *Piété baroque et déchristianisation*, Vovelle traced changes in testamentary clauses in order to document decline in religious sentiment at different levels of the social hierarchy. His method was borrowed by other scholars, who appreciated the possibility of quantifying changes in attitudes (Chaunu, 1978; Chiffoleau, 1980), and Vovelle went on to make that change a central feature of his book on the long-term history of death (Vovelle, 1983). Philippe Ariès (1981) was not convinced that Vovelle was finding "dechristianization" but argued that the change was one of religious expression. What had previously been broadcast publicly was now a private matter for more intimate families. Nevertheless, people were expressing a new uncertainty concerning a world to come (McManners, 1981).

Some degree of secularization forced people to pay greater attention to this life. For some it meant that old age was associated more with life than with death. For others it may have meant the loss of an institutional form of solace. One historical demographer who has turned to cultural history even suggests that whatever improvements in life expectancy occurred in the period were mitigated by a loss of faith in eternal life. The result was a decline in life expectancy, though not the kind the demographers are used to measuring (Imhof, 1985).

What else changed? First, there developed a new prescriptive literature on growing old. It certainly borrowed from medical, literary, and religious traditions, but it addressed new questions and a new audience. Medical and scientific texts began to specialize in the maladies of particular ages; religious tracts played down the terror of imminent death; and philosophical treatises addressed questions of how to age rather than how to die. Even the publication of classic texts like Cicero's *De Senectute* was now aimed at a broader spectrum of Western society, and new texts claimed to do for older women what Cicero had done for men. Second, the nation state continued to grow and with it the idea of the socioeconomic order as changing and manipulable. Memories of political turmoil in 17th-century England prompted an early awareness of generational change, as revealed in Clarendon's *Dialogue on Old Age* (Hyde, 1984), but in the later 18th century progressive change came to be expected throughout western Europe. Third, older literary stereotypes that had ridiculed the elderly were seen as distasteful, and several authors called for a new approach to the aged. Fourth, the graphic arts began to see elderly characters as worthy of depiction in their own right, not simply as useful allegorical figures. New sentimental depictions appeared in France and Germany in the middle of the 18th century (Borscheid, 1987; Gutton, 1988; Troyansky, 1989). A case can also be made for the precocity of Dutch appreciations of old age; in the 17th and 18th centuries "there were no wrinkles quite like Dutch wrinkes"

(Schama, 1987, p. 430). There is no denying the brilliance of the depiction of old age in Hals and Rembrandt. It contrasts perfectly with the Spanish baroque, for example, where Ribera's old people are reminders of death and sin, not life and earthly dignity.

The 18th century has been seen as a great high point for older persons, and at least one scholar has seen the more positive vision of old age as describing accurately social conditions (Bois, 1989). It may, nevertheless, be possible to interpret the more positive discourse as masking cruel realities (Troyansky, 1989). Some evidence suggests increasing tensions between generations in the 17th and 18th centuries in southern France (Castan, 1974) and in colonial New England (Greven, 1970). If some such tension was always present when two adult generations coexisted, one might hypothesize greater conflict resulting from longer coexistence. Peasant proverbs had long indicated the difficulties of supporting more than one adult generation (Berkner, 1972). A look at changing demographic circumstances might help to describe the social context for dealing with aging.

Aging that occurred in the 18th century was not yet the demographic aging that resulted, in the 19th and 20th centuries, from fertility decline. It depended, rather, on mortality decline in adulthood. It was not as dramatic as later developments, but it may have been just as important in the emergence of a new view of old age in Western culture. What may have been crucial was the combination of some earlier marriage, an earlier date for the last birth, and longer life, resulting in a longer period of overlap of adult generations. This makes for a rather complicated demographic transition (Bardet, 1983; Perrenoud, 1985; Troyansky, 1989; Wrigley & Schofield, 1981).

One of the factors that seems to have permitted earlier marriage, even among the laboring classes, was the development of mercantile capitalism and household industry. This was the industrialization that occurred gradually, before the emergence of factory-based industrial capitalism. As employment was no longer based upon the land, marriage did not depend upon the ability to support an independent farming family (Gutmann, 1988; Tilly, 1978). New household structures permitted a variety of retirement arrangements. Some of the provisions found in the Middle Ages probably became more common, but regional variety was extraordinary (Held, 1982; Mitterauer & Sieder, 1982; Wall, Robin, & Laslett, 1983). In some regions, parents maintained authority as long as possible; elsewhere, they took an early retirement, transmitted the patrimony, and reserved some portion for their upkeep. This was particularly important for the maintenance of widows.

Historians of 18th-century society and culture have emphasized significant changes at midcentury that anticipated the era of revolution at the end of the century. It was almost axiomatic for some historians to assume that such dramatic changes would be to the detriment of the elderly. Thus, Fischer's (1978) America underwent a "deep change" in the period 1780–1820, and the French revolutionaries criticized everything associated with the Old Regime. But when we look at the ways that revolutionaries have legitimated their revolutions, we see that they often sought the sanction of the aged. The revolt of sons against fathers included many white-haired revolutionaries, and the culture of the French Revolution even included a Festival of Old Age (Ozouf, 1970; Troyansky, 1989).

The Festival of Old Age was one of a series of secular holidays that sought to establish a new public culture in which the ages of life replaced other sorts of social distinctions. In the French Revolution's attempt to renegotiate the social contract, the honored elders of the nation would all be equivalent to the Founding Fathers of the American Revolution (Troyansky, 1991). And yet the new secular festivals failed to thrive. Paradoxically, it was in the new nation that would make a cult of youth and innovation that the old revolutionaries became permanently established as Founding Fathers (Hoffer, 1983).

Beneath the level of public symbols, however, the revolutionary era in the Western world saw the emergence of modern ideas of privacy. The remark by George Sand that the Revolution invented grandparents figures prominently in the first attempt to survey the modern history of private life (Perrot, 1990). The expectation of change brought on by political revolution no doubt had its significance in 19th-century middle-class ideas of aging, but the emergence of grandparenthood probably had more to do with both new demographic circumstances and a new culture of intimacy and sentimentality. Older traditions of resentment were based upon a culture created by adult children. Images of grandparents, however, found in memoirs, autobiographies, and letters indicate a freeing of the generations from the older sorts of conflicts (Premo, 1990; Thompson, Itzin, & Abendstern, 1990).

## THE INDUSTRIAL REVOLUTION (1750–1900)

Economic change featured more prominently than political change in the first histories of old age, which tended to look for one turning point associated with the processes of "modernization" (Achenbaum, 1978). Even those who claimed to be critical of "modernization theory" tended to fall back on premodern / modern or traditional / modern dichotomies (Achenbaum & Stearns, 1978; Ehmer, 1990; Haber, 1983; Kohli, 1986; Quadagno, 1982). And yet even in economic history, the idea of one great change has been abandoned. The idea of an industrial revolution cannot stand alone. Too much of the economic literature opts for the idea of protoindustrialization (Gutmann, 1988; Medick, 1976).

Still, great changes have occurred. Mechanization and the growth of large-scale industry were significant. They had an uneven impact on the Western world. Many elements of rural society survived. Cities drew youth, while the countryside aged (Bois, 1989). Young people also tended to go into new industries, while their elders remained in more traditional ones. Ideas of obsolescence emerged in the 19th century (Ehmer, 1990; Haber, 1983). And parents lost their teaching role in the workplace (Accampo, 1989). Occupational inheritance declined, and it may be possible, then, to link these great transformations to the obvious cultural ferment: the emergence of "generational" thought, the normalization of change.

To a large extent, however, that normalization was restricted to the 19th-century bourgeoisie. The emergence of Romantic youth movements throughout Europe and America (Gillis, 1974), the proliferation of age groups, and the spread of age-consciousness (Chudacoff, 1989), as well as the publication of novels about intergenerational conflict—Stendhal's *The Red and the Black,* Balzac's *Père Goriot,* and Turgenev's *Fathers and Sons* come to mind—reveal more about middle-class aging than any "universal" experience. Middle-class reformers worried about the havoc being visited upon laborers, but their ideas about old people were derived from their own peculiar experience of longer life and greater wealth. It is only now that we can begin to understand the long-term institutionalization of old age as retirement in a "work society" (Kohli, 1986). And there is still little agreement on the timing of change and the relative importance of organized labor, political parties, and the state (Gratton, 1986; Hareven, 1976, 1982; Thomson, 1984).

## THE CONTRIBUTION OF THE HUMANITIES

The context for much of the work on old age has been that of the social sciences. It has sometimes involved a European combination of social sciences and humanities: the human sciences. When Simone de Beauvoir (1970) wrote her massive work on old age, there had not yet been much scholarly research in historical gerontology. Students of art and literature have contributed to our knowledge, but they all run the risk of being as ahistorical as Beauvoir (Bagnell & Soper, 1989; Berman & Sobkowska-Ashcroft, 1987; Freeman, 1979; Moss, 1976). Now we have a literature that is more historical, but it does not have simplistic lessons to teach (*Ageing and Society,* 1984; *Annales de démographie historique 1985;*

Conrad and von Kondratowitz, 1983; Imhof, Goubert, Bideau, & Garden 1982). A challenge for the humanities is to create a useful, humane and historical context in which people can make sense of their lives (Spicker, Woodward & Van Tassel, 1978; Van Tassel, 1979). The temptation is great to call for a revival or adaptation of some older model (Philibert, 1968), but empirical research has discovered a plethora of models, some examples of dignified aging, and some examples of extraordinary cruelty.

Traditions from the ancient, medieval, and early modern periods have weighed heavily on modern ideas and experiences of old age. Religious retreat, rural retirement, and bourgeois career-building have all had their impact. Greater life expectancy (the earthly variety), greater wealth, new ideals of family life and privacy, secularization, and the rise of the state are among the forces that have come into play as people have constructed old age in the long period of history treated in this chapter.

## REFERENCES

Accampo, E. (1989). *Industrialization, family life, and class relations: Saint Chamond, 1815–1914.* Berkeley: University of California Press.

Achenbaum, W. A. (1978). *Old age in the new land: The American experience since 1970.* Baltimore: Johns Hopkins University Press.

Achenbaum, W. A., & Stearns, P. N. (1978). Old age and modernization. *Gerontologist, 18,* 3.

*Annales de démographie historique 1985: Vieillir autrefois.* (1986). Paris: Ecole des Hautes Etudes en Sciences Sociales.

Ariès, P. (1962). *Centuries of childhood: A social history of family life.* New York: Knopf.

Ariès, P. (1981). *The hour of our death.* New York: Knopf.

Asp, C. (1986). "The clamor of Eros": Freud, aging, and King Lear. In K. Woodward & M. Schwartz (Eds.), *Memory and desire: Aging—literature—psychoanalysis.* Bloomington, Indiana University Press. (pp. 192–204).

Bagnell, P., & Soper, P. (1989). *Perceptions of aging in literature: A cross-cultural study.* Westport, CT: Greenwood Press.

Bardet, J.-P. (1983). *Rouen aux XVIIe et XVIIIe siècles: Les mutations d'un espace social.* Paris: SEDES.

Beauvoir, S. de (1970). *La Vieillesse.* Paris: Gallimard.

Berkner, L. (1972). The stem family and the developmental cycle of the peasant household: An eighteenth-century Austrian example. *American Historical Review, 77,* 398–418.

Berman, L., & Sobkowska-Ashcroft, I. (1987). *Images and impressions of old age in the great works of Western literature (700 B.C.–1900 A.D.): An analytical compendium.* Lewiston, NY, and St. David's, Ontario: St. David's University Press.

Bever, E. (1982). Old age and witchcraft in early modern Europe. In P. N. Stearns (Ed.), *Old age in preindustrial society* (pp. 150–190). New York: Holmes and Meier.

Bideau, A. (1980). A demographic and social analysis of widowhood and remarriage: The example of the Castellany of Thoissey-en-Dombes, 1670–1840. *Journal of Family History*, 5(1), 28–43.

Bois, J. P. (1989). *Les vieux: de Montaigne aux premières retraites*. Paris: Fayard.

Borscheid, P. (1987). *Geschichte des Alters, 16. bis 18. Jahrhundert*. Münster: F. Coppenrath.

Bouwsma, W. J. (1980). Anxiety and the formation of early modern culture. In B. C. Malament (Ed.), *After the Reformation*. Philadelphia: University of Pennsylvania Press.

Bracciolini, P. (1877). *Un vieillard doit-il se marier*? Paris: Liseux.

Burrow, J. A. (1986). *The ages of man: A study in medieval writing and thought*. Oxford: Oxford University Press.

Carlton, C. (1978). The widow's tale: Male myths and female reality in sixteenth- and seventeenth-century England. *Albion, 10*, 118–129.

Castan, Y. (1974). Pères et fils en Languedoc à l'époque classique. *XVIIe siècle, 102–103*, 31–43.

Chartier, R. (1989). *A history of private life: 3. Passions of the Renaissance*. Cambridge, MA: Harvard University Press.

Chaunu, P. (1978). *La mort à Paris: XVIe, XVIIe, XVIIIe siècles*. Paris: Fayard.

Chew, S. C. (1962). *The pilgrimage of life*. New Haven, CT: Yale University Press.

Chiffoleau, J. (1980) *La comptabilité de l'au-delà: Les hommes, la mort et la religion dans la région d'Avignon à la fin du moyen âge (vers 1320–vers 1480)*. Rome: Ecole française de Rome.

Chudacoff, H. P. (1989). *How old are you? Age consciousness in American culture*. Princeton, NJ: Princeton University Press.

Clark, E. (1982). Some aspects of social security in medieval England. *Journal of Family History, 7*, 307–320.

Cohn, S. K., Jr. (1988). *Death and property in Siena, 1205–1800: Strategies for the afterlife*. Baltimore: Johns Hopkins University Press.

Cole, T. R. (1992). *The journey of life: A cultural history of aging*. Cambridge: Cambridge University Press.

Cole, T. R., & Winkler, M. G. (1985). Aging in Western medicine and iconography. *Medical Heritage*, (Sept.–Oct.), 335–347.

Conrad, C., & von Kondratowitz, H. J. (1983). *Gerontologie und Sozialgeschichte*. Berlin: Deutsches Zentrum fur Altersfragen.

C.U.E.R.M.A. (1987). *Vieillesse et vieillissement au moyen-age*. Aix-en-Provence: Université de Provence.

Dal, E., with Skarup, P. (1980). *The ages of man and the months of the year: Poetry, Prose and Pictures Outlining the douze mois figurés motif mainly found in shepherds' calendars and in livres d'heures (14th to 17th century)*. Det Kongelige Danske Videnskabernes Selskab, Historisk-filosofiske Skrifter, 9:3. Copenhagen.

Daston, L. (1988). *Classical probability in the Enlightenment*. Princeton, NJ: Princeton University Press.

Davis, N. Z. (1977). Ghosts, kin and progeny: Some features of family life in early modern France. *Daedalus, 106*, 2.

Dayonnet, C., & Lasserre, J. (1982). *La vieillesse dans l'art occidental.* Toulouse: Université du Troisième Age.

Delumeau, J. (1989). *Rassurer et protéger: Le sentiment de sécurité dans l'Occident d'autrefois.* Paris: Fayard.

Demos, J. P. (1986). Past, present, and personal: The family and the life course in American history. New York: Oxford University Press.

Diefendorf, B. (1982). Widowhood and remarriage in sixteenth-century Paris. *Journal of Family History, 7*, 379–395.

Duby, G. (1988). *A history of private life: 2. Revelations of the medieval world.* Cambridge, MA: Harvard University Press.

Dupâquier, J. (1981). *Marriage and remarriage in populations of the past.* London and New York: Academic Press.

Dupâquier, J., & Dupâquier, M. (1985). *Histoire de la démographie.* Paris: Perrin.

Ehmer, J. (1990). *Sozialgeschichte des Alters.* Frankfurt: Suhrkamp.

Fischer, D. H. (1978). *Growing old in America.* New York: Oxford University Press.

Flandrin, J. L. (1979). *Families in former times: Kinship, household and sexuality.* Cambridge: Cambridge University Press.

Folts, J. D., Jr. (1980). Senescence and renascence: Petrarch's thoughts on growing old. *Journal of Medieval and Renaissance Studies, 10*(2), 207–237.

Freeman, J. T. (1979). *Aging: Its history and literature.* New York: Human Sciences Press.

Gilbert, C. (1967). When did a man in the Renaissance grow old? *Studies in the Renaissance, 14*, 7–32.

Gillis, J. (1974). *Youth and history: Tradition and change in European age relations, 1770–present.* New York: Academic Press.

Goody, J., Thirsk, J., & Thompson, E. P. (1976). *Family and inheritance: Rural society in Western Europe.* Cambridge: Cambridge University Press.

Gratton, B. (1986). *Urban elders: Family, work, and welfare among Boston's aged, 1890–1950.* Philadelphia: Temple University Press.

Greven, P. (1970). *Four generations: Population, land, and family in colonial Andover, Massachusetts.* Ithaca, NY: Cornell University Press.

Grmek, M. D. (1958). On ageing and old age: Basic problems and historic aspects of gerontology and geriatrics. *Monographiae Biologicae, 5*(2).

Gruman, G. J. (1966). A history of ideas about the prolongation of life: The evolution of prolongevity hypotheses to 1800. *Transactions of the American Philosophical Society* (new series), *56*(9).

Gutmann, M. P. (1988). *Toward the modern economy: Early industry in Europe, 1500–1800.* New York: Knopf.

Gutton, J.-P. (1988). *Naissance du vieillard: Essai sur l'histoire des rapports entre les vieillards et la société en France.* Paris: Aubier.

Haber, C. (1983). *Beyond sixty-five: The dilemma of old age in America's past.* Cambridge: Cambridge University Press.

Hareven, T. (1976). The last stage: Historical adulthood and old age. *Daedalus, 105*(4), 13–27.

Hareven, T. (1982). *Family time and industrial time: The relationship between the family and work in a New England industrial community.* Cambridge: Cambridge University Press.

Held, T. (1982). Rural retirement arrangements in seventeenth to nineteenth-century Austria: A cross-community analysis. *Journal of Family History, 7,* 227–254.

Herlihy, D. (1982). Growing old in the Quattrocento. In P. N. Stearns (Ed.), *Old age in preindustrial society* (pp. 104–118). New York: Holmes & Meier.

Herlihy, D., & Klapisch-Zuber, C. (1985). *Tuscans and their families: A study of the Florentine Catasto of 1427.* New Haven, CT: Yale University Press. (Abridgment and translation of *Les toscans et leurs familles,* Paris: Ecole des Hautes Etudes en Sciences Sociales, 1978).

History and ageing. (1984). [Special issue]. *Ageing and Society,* 4(4).

Hoffer, P. C. (1983). *Revolution and regeneration: Life cycle and the historical vision of the generation of 1776.* Athens: University of Georgia Press.

Hyde, E. (1984). *Two dialogues: Of the want of respect due to age and concerning education* (Reprint of 1751 2nd ed.). Los Angeles: William Andrews Clark Memorial Library, UCLA.

Imhof, A. E. (1985). From the old mortality pattern to the twentieth century. *Bulletin of the History of Medicine, 59,* 1–29.

Imhof, A. E., Goubert, J.-P., Bideau, A., & Garden, M. (1982). *Le vieillissement: Implications et conséquences de l'allongement de la vie humaine depuis le XVIIIe siècle.* Lyon: Presses Universitaires de Lyon.

Institut National d'Etudes Démographiques (INED). (1982–1983). *Les âges de la vie,* 2 volumes. Paris: Presses Universitaires de France.

Kafker, F. (1981). La vieillesse et la productivité intellectuelle chez les encyclopédistes. *Revue d'Histoire Moderne et Contemporaine, 28,* 304–327.

Kerrigan, W. (1986). Life's iamb: The scansion of late creativity in the culture of the Renaissance. In K. Woodward & M. Schwartz (Eds.), *Memory and desire: Aging—literature—psychoanalysis* (pp. 168–191). Bloomington: Indiana University Press.

Kohli, M. (1986). The world we forgot: A historical review of the life course. In V. W. Marshall, (Ed.), *Later life: The social psychology of aging* (pp. 271–303). Beverly Hills, CA: Sage Publications.

Laslett, P. (Ed.). (1977). The history of aging and the aged. In *Family life and illicit love in earlier generations* (pp. 174–213). Cambridge: Cambridge University Press.

*Die Lebenstreppe: Bilder der menschlichen Lebensalter.* (1983). Cologne: Rheinland-Verlag.

Lorcin, M.-T. (1975). Retraite des veuves et filles au couvent: Quelques aspects de la condition féminine à la fin du moyen âge. *Annales de Démographie Historique,* 187–204.

Lorris, G. de, & Meun, J. de (1962). *The romance of the rose.* New York: Dutton.

McManners, J. (1981). *Death and the Enlightenment: Changing attitudes to death among Christians and unbelievers in eighteenth-century France.* Oxford: Oxford University Press.

Medick, H. (1976). The proto-industrial family economy: The structural function of household and family during the transition from peasant society to industrial capitalism. *Social History, 1*, 291–315.

Medick, H., & Sabean, D. W. (1984). *Interest and emotion: Essays on the study of family and kinship*. Cambridge: Cambridge University Press.

Minois, G. (1987). *Histoire de la vieillesse: De l'antiquité à la Renaissance*. Paris: Fayard.

Mitterauer, M., & Sieder, R. (1982). *The European family: Patriarchy to partnership from the Middle Ages to the present*. Chicago: University of Chicago Press.

Moss, W. G. (1976). *Humanistic perspectives on aging: An annotated bibliography and essay*. Ann Arbor, MI: Institute of Gerontology.

Ozment, S. (1983). *When fathers ruled: Family life in Reformation Europe*. Cambridge, MA: Harvard University Press.

Ozouf, M. (1970). Symboles et fonctions des âges dans les fêtes de l'êpoque révolutionnaire. *Annales Historiques de la Révolution Française, 42*(202), 569–593.

*Pénélope: Pour l'histoire des femmes* (1985). *Vieillesses des femmes, 13*.

Perrenoud, A. (1985). Le biologique et l'humain dans le déclin séculaire de la mortalité. *Annales: E.S.C., 40*, 113–135.

Perrot, M. (1990). *A history of private life: 4. From the fires of revolution to the Great War*. Cambridge, MA: Harvard University Press.

Philibert, M. (1968). *Les échelles d'âqe dans la philosophie, la science et la société: De leur renversement et des conditions de leur redressement*. Paris: Seuil.

Premo, T. L. (1990). *Winter friends: Women growing old in the new republic, 1785–1835*. Urbana: University of Illinois Press.

Quadagno, J. (1982). *Aging in early industrial society: Work, family, and social policy in nineteenth-century England*. New York: Academic Press.

Rabb, T. (1975). *The struggle for stability in early modern Europe*. New York: Oxford University Press.

Raphael, M. (1964). *Pensions and public servants: A study of the origins of the British system*. Paris: Mouton.

Roebuck, J. (1979). When does old age begin? The evolution of the English definition. *Journal of Social History, 12*, 416–428.

Schama, S. (1987). *The embarrassment of riches: An interpretation of Dutch culture in the golden age*. New York: Knopf.

Sears, E. (1986). *The ages of man: Medieval interpretations of the life cycle*. Princeton, NJ: Princeton University Press.

Seeff, A., & Ansello, E. (in press). *Aging and the life cycle in the Renaissance: Proceedings from a 1988 symposium at the University of Maryland*. Dover: University of Delaware Press.

Sheehan, M. M. (1990). *Aging and the aged in medieval Europe*. Toronto: Pontifical Institute of Mediaeval Studies.

Smith, D. S. (1978). Old age and the "Great Transformation": A New England case study. In S. Spicker (Ed.), *Aging and the elderly*.

Smith, S. N. (1976). Growing old in early Stuart England. *Albion, 8*(2), 125–141.

Spicker, S. Woodward, K., & Van Tassel, D. (1978). *Aging and the elderly: Humanistic perspectives in gerontology*. Atlantic Highlands, NJ: Humanities Press.

Sprandel, R. (1981). *Altersshicksal und Altersmoral: Die Geschichte der Einstellungen zum Altern nach der Pariser Bibelexegese des 12.–16. Jahrhunderts*. Stuttgart: Anton Hiersemann.

Stearns, P. N. (1976). *Old age in European society: The case of France*. New York: Holmes and Meier.

Stearns, P. N. (1980). Old women: some historical observations. *Journal of Family History* 5(1), 44–57

Stearns, P. N. (Ed.). (1982). *Old age in preindustrial society*. New York: Holmes and Meier.

Stone, L. (1977). *The family, sex, and marriage in England, 1500–1800*. New York: Harper & Row.

Stone, L. (1978). Walking over Grandma. *New York Review of Books, 24*, 8.

Thomas, K. (1976). *Age and authority in early modern England*. London: British Academy.

Thompson, P., Itzin, C., & Abendstern, M. (1990). *I don't feel old: The experience of later life*. Oxford: Oxford University Press.

Thomson, D. (1984). The decline of social welfare: Falling state support for the elderly since early Victorian times. *Ageing and Society*, 4(4), 451–482.

Tilly, C. (1978). *Historical studies of changing fertility* Princeton, NJ: Princeton University Press.

Trexler, R. (1980). *Public life in Renaissance Florence*. New York: Academic Press.

Trexler, R. (1982). A widows' asylum of the Renaissance: The Orbatello of Florence. In P. N. Stearns (Ed.), *Old age in preindustrial society* (pp. 119–149). New York: Holmes & Meier.

Troyansky, D. G. (1989). *Old age in the Old Regime: Image and experience in eighteenth-century France*. Ithaca, NY: Cornell University Press.

Troyansky, D. G. (1991). Generational discourse in the French Revolution. In D. G. Troyansky, A. Cismaru, & N. Andrews, (Eds.), *The French Revolution in culture and society*. Westport, CT: Greenwood Press.

Van Tassel, D. (Ed.). (1979). *Aging, death, and the completion of being*. Philadelphia: University of Pennsylvania Press.

Vovelle, M. (1973). *Piété baroque et déchristianisation: Les attitudes devant la mort en Provence au XVIIIe siècle*. Paris: Plon.

Vovelle, M. (1983). *La mort et l'Occident, de 1300 à nos jours*. Paris: Gallimard.

Wall, R., Robin, J., & Laslett, P. (1983). *Family forms in historic Europe*. Cambridge: Cambridge University Press.

Williams, R. (1990). *A Protestant legacy: Attitudes to death and illness among older Aberdonians*. Oxford: Clarendon Press.

Woodward, K., & Schwartz, M. (eds.). (1986). *Memory and desire: Aging—literature—psychoanalysis*. Bloomington: Indiana University Press.

Wrigley, E. A., & Schofield, R. S. (1981). *The population history of England, 1541–1871: A reconstruction*. Cambridge, MA: Harvard University Press.

Zerbi, G. (1988). *Gerontocomia: On the care of the aged* (and Maximianus, *Elegies on Old Age and Love*). Philadelphia: American Philosophical Society.

3

# Old Age in the Modern and Postmodern Western World*

*Christoph Conrad*

The purpose of this chapter is to point out what it is like to grow old "modern": what framework society has prepared for its aging members and what society as a whole is likely to face when its collective aging process continues. If the chapter has a message at all, it says that much of what we witness today might be new and unseen in history, but most of it is not specific to old age. The social processes of the 19th and 20th centuries, which encompass industrialization, urbanization, the demographic transition, and welfare state development, as well as secularization and individualization, have created a particular "ecological" framework for today's aging. In this milieu, there are chances and discontents, constraints and uncertainties, options and voids. To understand how these divergent aspects came about and how they concern older people may also help to identify more clearly the growing demand for the humanities: why new customers are posing old questions.

This chapter starts with considering the provocation of "postmodern" thinking, which spills over from the arts, social sciences, and humanities, on our way to conceptualizing aging in past and present. The chapter then proceeds by highlighting three areas of socioeconomic

* Special thanks are due to Bernd Dornseifer and Hans-Joachim von Kondratowitz for their critical reading of the first draft. Tom Cole was not only an excellent editor but rather an accoucheur for this chapter.

change and three correlated areas of cultural and attitudinal change in Western societies since the middle of the 19th century. Therein, three broad themes are each examined from two sides: first from the point of view of social structure, then with an emphasis on cultural patterns and collective attitudes. These themes include (1) the distribution and meaning of "lifetime," (2) the sociopolitical construction of "old age," and (3) the implications of cohort change. The chosen areas are meant to open up central perspectives on the social position of older persons without being exclusive or exhaustive. The closing remarks are devoted to the final challenges that aging presents to society as a whole: physical as well as mental decline and dying.

The approaches chosen and the evidence presented in this chapter range from history and sociology over demography and anthropology to philosophy. Thus, the scope of disciplines differs from the "humanities" in the strict sense. Rather, the chapter's orientation follows that of the "human sciences" in the Western European understanding (cf. Jennings & Prewitt, 1985).

## LOCATING OLD AGE IN THE 20TH CENTURY: BETWEEN MODERNIZATION AND POSTMODERNITY

If one has to treat the societal position of older people in the 19th and 20th centuries in 30 pages, one cannot help but be tempted by falling back into good old modernization theory. The dense and neat dichotomies—traditional versus modern, *Gemeinschaft* versus *Gesellschaft*, stem versus nuclear family, village versus metropolis, and so on—come to mind without fail. These concepts are still widely used; in fact, I shall use them myself in the following. They might even be irreplaceable because we often need a kind of shorthand to evoke the undoubtedly profound changes that all Western societies underwent. However, if there is another "world we have lost," to use Peter Laslett's ironic title, it is the conceptual world of modernization theory. In the introductions to studies on the history of old age, fierce debates were and are still fought around the pros and cons of modernization (Foner 1984; see Haber [chap. 15] and Stearns [chap. 16], this volume). The main problems are found when the timing of changes is considered: family structure or demographic aging seem to follow their own rhythms, with major developments either before the 19th century or after World War II (Laslett 1984, 1989). The "new history" of society and culture in the Early Modern period has successfully urged us to consider "modernizations" before industrialization and to drop the image of an homogeneous "traditional" society (Cole & Winkler 1988; Troyansky, this volume). In other subject areas, fatal blows to models of linear social change have come from such diverse directions as the observation of unequal development in the Third World, of women's status, and from the "dialectic of enlightenment" in the tradition of the Frankfurt School.

When, in 1954, the International Association of Gerontology devoted its third congress to "Old Age in the Modern World," the speakers shared a common view on the main historical trends that made old age a "problem." More than 35 years later, the consensus is broken. Although many of the themes then discussed are of a remarkable actuality—population aging, employment of older workers, residential care, and "education for later maturity," to name only a few (*Old Age in the Modern World,* 1955), it would be misleading simply to update the 1950s story by adding a "postmodern" chapter. To be truthful, a consensus on a viable theoretical alternative to modernization theory is not in sight. This new openness has certainly led to more public interest in cross-cultural and historical research results and should facilitate interdisciplinary dialogues. In the year 2020 or 2030, a cultural historian or a sociologist of knowledge might not be surprised when looking back on the explosion of approaches, methods, and themes so characteristic for the social sciences in the last decades. A society that increasingly promotes a diversity of life-styles and worldviews cannot but have pluralist views on its own past and present.

"Postmodern" seems to be a quite faddish but adequate label for these tendencies. It does not define a new period but rather expresses the emancipation of various cultural avant-gardes from the dictatorship of modernism. Postmodernism in architecture, philosophy, or literature seems to be an attempt to reflect society's changed relationships to its own development, its refusal of the unifying "great tales" (Lyotard, 1985). It would therefore be misleading to integrate it as a new stage in a linear process: from traditional over modern to postmodern society (see the discussion of compounds with "post-" in Bell, 1973). A period name for the structural changes since about the 1950s has, of course, been found with the term "postindustrial society" (Bell, 1973). The trends Daniel Bell and others described—namely, the shift from manufacturing to services; the role of the new science-based, particularly information-based, technologies; and the rise of technical elites—are today commonly accepted features of Western societies. Together with the welfare state, these features form the social and economic ground for the present and future "aging society" (cf. Pifer & Bronte, 1986). Although there is no direct causal link between demographic aging and the evolution toward a postindustrial society, it is simply a fact that the nations with the highest life expectancies and with the highest proportion of older people in the population share some of those features; and, moreover, are all very affluent. Peter Laslett (1989), therefore, proposes to consider "third age" as a collective phenomenon that these societies—from France to Japan, from Australia to the United States—have reached. If, for our purpose, we call "postindustrial" the type of most developed societies, particularly since the 1960s, and "postmodern" the mode of self-reflection that these societies have recently unfolded (see, with critical distance to the concept, Giddens, 1990), we intend to emphasize the following characterists of the postmodern condition: the interplay of continuity and discontinuity in social trends, the pluralization of life-styles and preferences, the dissolution of common value orientations.

The situation in respect to old age may be summarized with much the same words as many other social aspects: it is historically new, conceptually open, and characterized by growing inner contrasts. Large minorities inside the older population experience the recent social changes from a very different position from that of their age mates in the 19th century: whereas most elderly in the 19th century were lagging behind the economic and technological revolutions, today's elderly have been among those pioneering new life-styles since the 1950s (Achenbaum, 1983; Silvermann, 1988). They are the first to age with lots of other elderly around them and the first to experience the dynamics of four- and five-generation families as well as the looseness of bonds from divorced or unmarried families. They spend more time in retirement than anyone before, and they are mostly well-off enough to enjoy it. At the border between work and leisure, retired men and women are among those who are confronted massively with the "cultural contradictions of capitalism" (Bell 1976), fostering opposite value sets in economic and private life. But older people are also confronting their heightened self-esteem with the cultural "de-meaning" of old age in our societies (Cole, 1991; Cole & Winkler, 1988). The plurality of responses to these challenges may reach from denial over withdrawal into self-styled subcultures to search for new meaning.

The socioeconomic discrepancies inside this population are no less formidable than in the younger age groups: between the 55-year-old steel worker who is half unemployed and half early retired and the 70-year-old policy consultant on a second career, between "new old" middle-class wives and widows on culture trips and the permanent hotel dwellers, between senior golf champs and the victims of work disability, chronic diseases, and dementia there are immense and probably increasing inequalities. These contrasts make it doubtful whether the term "old age" can still serve as a conceptual roof for all of these situations (Neugarten, 1974; Pifer, 1986; Thompson, Itzin, &

Abendstern, 1990). A postmodern gerontology might want to explode this artificial unity, reaching from about 50–55 to 100 years, on which its self-defined compentence is focused. One may even speculate that the attempt to build one multidiscipline for all aspects of aging could soon appear as a passing and rather short-lived historical phenomenon.

One characteristic, if not surprising, feature of social change in the past two centuries is that it has touched the elderly in a number of ways without being focused on them. The shifts in the great areas of economic life where men and women are employed, the consequences of technological innovation, the growth of the health sector, the changing role of the family—all have left their mark in the social environment of aging. Most of these evolutions, however, are best understood inside the logic of these various societal subsystems and not as deliberate projects to influence the living conditions of one (marginal) client group (Grob, 1986; Rosenberg, 1986). One should be hesitant to interpret the negative effects of, say, retirement, residential isolation, or the growth of long-term care facilities as a concerted effort to get rid of the elderly. This would mean attributing too much intention to basically incremental processes. Instead, we should equally stress the positive sides of those developments that are often understood as achievements even if they were mostly unintended side effects. For example, the reorganization of work lives, seniority rights for advancement and income, and the rules for exit from employment may have, in the beginning, reflected the interests of management and capital, but they also led to the liberation of the later years from work. Or, to take another example, the household structure of the eldery lends itself to isolation as much as the long-treasured maintenance of autonomy (Ehmer, 1990; Grebenik, Höhn & Mackensen, 1989; Thompson, Itzin, & Abendstern, 1990).

I will therefore try to withstand the impulse to rate whatever happened to the elderly as detrimental (or not) to their once high status. Let's face it: compared to what historians describe as the idealization of old age in enlightened France (Gutton, 1988; Troyansky, 1989) and what has also been found in 18th-century New England (Fischer, 1978) and Germany (Borscheid, 1987), the public image of the elderly could only go downhill in the following centuries. Whether the same was true for their day-to-day living conditions, the political care for their problems, and the scientific attention to their specificity remains to be seen. The impression of a linear downgrading of the elders' status has often been fueled by comparisons between the elite of power and education in past societies, on the one hand, and, say, workers in industrial society on the other, between traditional norms and modern practices. The more differentiated picture that has been drawn for the preindustrial centuries as well as the many signs of improved status of the aged in postindustrial societies (Pampel, 1981; Rosenmayr, 1987) help us to take a fresh look at the 19th and 20th centuries.

## THREE AREAS OF SOCIOECONOMIC CHANGE

### Redistribution of Time

The creation of old age as an independent stage of life is a modern phenomenon, linked to the growth of the "empty nest" in family life, retirement in work life, and income transfers in the welfare state. The democratization of this new phase at the end of life is embedded in a broader process of the redistribution of life time in which the relative portions of time spent in education, work, and leisure have shifted dramatically. At present, this reordering is not yet finished, but the preliminary results are obvious: we live longer, and our working lives are shorter; parents spend relatively less time with dependent children and more in the "empty nest" or without a married partner; we go to school longer and stop working earlier. The demographic side of these changes is well known by now, thanks to the work by historians and demographers (Fischer, 1978; Imhof, 1986; Spanier & Glick, 1980). A vast sociological and psychological literature has been devoted to analyzing the different "life events" or transitions between life stages inside this overall pattern (Hagestad & Neugarten, 1985). Focusing on the second half of life, I will try to capture the contrasting trends of life expectancy and retirement age with the metaphor of "opening scissors."

The emergence of old age as a distinct phase of the life course is based on both *demographic* and *socioeconomic* factors that, since the second half of the 18th century, have created the basis for "full-size life careers" (Imhof, 1987). Not the lengthening but the standardization of the life span is the central demographic contribution; the rectangularization of the survival curve has been widely accepted as the most evocative tag for this profound change (Fries, 1980). Demographic change, however, came relatively late and would not have sufficed to create modern old age: the time left after age 60 or 70 did not increase decisively until the mid-20th century. The necessity to work until death had to be alleviated and finally abolished. Without the changing organization of the labor force and the creation of private and public pension systems, the potential of the "added years" could not have been realized. The new life stage "old age as retirement" was "added" to the life course not only by democratizing longevity but also by reconstructing the later years. In the industrializing countries, the two processes ran parallel to but independently of each other. In Germany, for example, the inauguration of a national pension insurance in 1889 came in a period of continued high infant and adult mortality, rapid population growth, and a very youthful age structure. The same trends hold for countries like Britain or New Zealand. France and Sweden, however, had higher life expectancies and older age structures by the time they created social security systems in the 1910s.

Many observers today think that the social construction of life time has reached a new historic phase of change (Gaullier, 1988). Recent discussions of an "age irrelevant society" (Neugarten, 1974; Neugarten & Neugarten, 1986) and the blurring of boundaries between life stages reflect the awareness of a growing flexibility in transitions during the life course. In respect to the border between work and retirement, the growing unpredictability and variety of forms of leaving the labor force and of income maintenance has created as many new chances as new insecurities for the individual (Guillemard, 1989). For the more distanced observer, all of the keywords of the present debate reveal that the familiar architecture of the life course emerged in a specific cultural, economic, and sociopolitical environment during the late 19th and first half of the 20th centuries. Future analysts may view it as a limited episode in the course of modern industrial societies.

As long as public and private income security provisions are capable of buffering the greater variety of individual risks that flow from the increase of flexibility and choice, the emerging postindustrial reconstruction of the life course can be a welcome source of liberty. In Ralf Dahrendorf's (1979) optimistic words:

> There was a social construction of human lives which consisted merely (for those who lived long enough) of a disciplined childhood, the endless "realm of necessity," and old age. Today there is a social construction of human lives which consists of the mild morning mist of childhood, the stage of education or training, the parallel stages of work and leisure, the stage of active retirement, and the dusk of old age. There might be a social construction of human lives which recognizes much more flexible and variable combinations of work, education and leisure between childhood and old age, and which, in addition, makes them all as rich in chances (as free?) as possible. (p. 92)

A pertinent image for the interplay of demographic and sociopolitical factors would be the opening of scissors: a growing interval between life expectancy after employment and average retirement age. Those who reached age 60 in 1900 could expect to life a further 12 to 14 years, much the same as in 1800 or even 1700. In the second half of the 20th century there has been a steady and, especially in the case of women, impressive gain in years after 60 or 65. At the same time the number of those who could retire from work and receive a pension grew rapidly, and (this is the other half of the scissors) their average retirement age stayed low or even decreased (Conrad, 1988). As a result, we can observe in the records of national social security systems a growing period of life spent receiving pensions. Health status played a major role in this: not only did health status improve in the older age groups, but retirement became "normal" for those who were not so ill that they would die shortly after being awarded a disability pension. Since the mid-1970s, the drop in labor force participation of older workers and so-called early retirement has suddenly opened up the scissors further—and has also led to its growing perception as a problem (Guillemard, 1986a, 1989).

The second important trait of this process and the reason it can be called a redistribution of time makes it part of the growth and diffusion of leisure in industrial society. The shortening of the relative proportion of time spent working over the whole life course evolved from a more or less gradual shortening of the work day and the work week, the introduction of holidays and, simultanously, the extension of schooling in youth and retirement in old age (Cross, 1989; Mayer & Müller, 1986). The new lifetime allocation of work and leisure as a whole is, of course, a keystone of the welfare state; like its other benefits, the new temporal regimen was paid for by an increase in productivity. The growth of free time, particularly in the 20th century, was paralleled by the increasingly intensive use of labor during the "productive" years. The diffusion of retirement as an expectable period of life for the majority of workers succeeded only rather lately—in Britain and Germany probably since the interwar years and then with particular speed, for example, in the United States and France since the 1950s (Conrad, 1988).

## Retirement as a Social Institution

Mass retirement distinguishes old age in the 20th century from any previous society in history. I have already pointed to its share in the overall lifetime budget. Now it is the institutional structure supporting the last stage that has to be considered more closely. In the following, modern old age will be seen as only one pillar of the "institutionalization of the life course."

Pension systems and retirement rules developed slowly from the 18th century to the 20th century, including one professional group after another and reaching full-fledged form in the Western welfare states by the 1950s (Bois, 1989; Graebner, 1980; Hannah, 1986; Myles, 1984; Stearns, 1977). In Europe, the military and public authorities started the sequence with provisions for their agents. Special professional groups, like miners, followed with their corporative self-help institutions. In the 19th century, private employers, particularly in large, highly organized firms, took up the idea of pensions. Finally, central states enacted national laws on disability and old age pensions, following either the insurance model (as in Bismarck's Germany) or the model of a non-contributory flat rate provision (as in Denmark, New Zealand, and Britain).

Retirement in its fully developed form is defined by the end of full-time employment, by reaching the minimum or maximum age limits, and by the receipt of a pension, whether as public transfer payment, from a private fund, or both. As a result, modern states have become responsible not only for the income maintenance of the great majority of the elderly but also for the organizing rules of this stage of life (Atchley, 1982; Kohli, 1987; Mayer & Müller, 1986; Mayer & Schoepflin, 1989). Historically, the concern of governments shifted from poverty linked to old age and disability to the generalization of retirement (Ehmer, 1990). This is not to say that the state is the only causal agent. One can see some of the other factors when looking at the problems that the American or European governments will face when they will try to implement the recently legislated increases in the age of retirement. The labor market and the interests of employers, as well as the preferences of the individuals, can be expected to act as counterforces. Despite varying actors, programs, interests, and timing, the nationalization of social responsibility for late life has evolved in all industrialized countries, capitalist or socialist. Although the resulting living conditions of older citizens show marked discrepancies inside those countries and between them, there can be no doubt that the overall social process does not stop at national boundaries and cannot be reversed in one country alone.

In synthesizing research from sociology and history on both sides of the Atlantic, Martin Kohli (1986, 1987) suggests that the emergence of retirement is only one part of the "institutionalization of the life course"—a more flexible concept that has begun to replace the older sociological construct of "age stratification" developed by Matilda Riley (1987) and others. As an institution, the life course fulfills four vital functions in modern society: it helps to secure social control, succession, integration, and rationalization (Kohli, 1986, 1987). Considering the life course as a societal program to process people through life has the advantage of linking more structurally oriented studies both with the longitudinal or retrospective cohort research and with tendencies in qualitative social research that focuses on subjective interpretations. The rich literary, iconographic, scientific images of the "ages of man" that we admire in medieval or early modern times (Cole & Winkler, 1988) remind us, for example, that the modern life course regimen also needs symbols, rituals, and an "imaginary constitution." It appears, however, that contemporary culture lacks the symbolic means for accompanying transitions in later life (e.g., widowhood). This is not so much because "modernization" has led to a loss of earlier rituals—there were no "rites de passage" for retirement in preindustrial Europe (Schenda, 1983)—but rather because our societies have failed to develop a particular "culture" for the third age (Rosenmayr, 1983).

Students of the institutionalization of retirement have turned primarily to two master thinkers of modernity, Karl Marx and Max Weber, to interpret their findings. With Marx, some explain retirement with the capitalist division of labor and the spread of wage labor. The inability of capitalist industry to secure their workers a living wage over an entire life is the key issue from this perspective. Some have gone so far as to see retirement only as disguised unemployment and a major reason for dependence (Phillipson, 1982; more balanced: Quadagno, 1988), underestimating somewhat that, according to Marx, it is "alienated" work from which the workers are set free. On the other hand, a closer look at the professions and branches that first benefited from retirement provisions and that today have the most privileged status in this respect rather supports the Weberian view, that bureaucratization was very directly involved in the construction of this life stage (Haber, 1983). Moreover, the concept of the life course as an institutionalized program for planning individual biographies, as well as for fitting people's lives into the requirements of employment, gains its fullest resonance against the background of the secular trend toward rationalization so dear to Weber (Graebner, 1980; Kohli, 1986; Mayer & Müller, 1986; for a mediating position, cf. Ehmer 1990; Van Tassel & Stearns, 1986).

## Cohort Change

The structural changes of the life course that we have evoked so far are to a large degree external to the aging process of successive cohorts. The temporal sequencing of life stages and the institutions regulating work and leisure form ecological conditions—indeed, a social policy milieu—for the collective experience of aging. But old age is not an institutional shell that can exist without older men and women. Our third dimension in modern and postmodern aging will therefore highlight the growing pace of social change reflected in the experience of successive cohorts of older people. Their evolution in terms of health, longevity, education, family composition, female labor force participation, financial security, and the like is the main moving force behind the new realities of late life, realities that can be observed in detail since the end of World War II and that will probably become even more prominent in the decades to come (cf., for the U.S., Pampel, 1981).

Today's elderly, of course, are not unique in having been shaped by available opportunities in schooling, by family, and by the labor market. Illiterate and unmarried, a considerable percentage of older people in the 19th century, for instance, contrasted sharply with younger people who had already benefited from the spread of public primary schooling and from improved chances of family formation. To express this more abstractly: at a certain point in time, different *age* groups reflect *cohort* differences in life chances that are created by *period*-specific conditions, policies, and economic transformations. Inside the cohorts—or generations, as they are more commonly but less precisely called—the inequalities of class, ethnicity, and gender remain independent of age, but their strength in any particular domain (e.g., education or social security) can itself be modified by the sociopolitical environment through which the cohorts are living (Riley, 1987; Riley & Riley, 1989).

The extension of social security systems, especially after World War II, decisively shaped the fate of older men and women. Recent studies comparing cohorts before and after these systems were enacted have found drastic differences in experiences and expectations. A panel study of workers who retired in 1972 in Paris asked whether the fathers of the new pensioners and their spouses had themselves experienced retirement. Out of this sample (born around 1907–1908), 51% either had lost their father before he reached 60 years of age or had no legitimate father; "22 per cent saw their fathers work right up to their death, many of them working as farmers, shopkeepers, craftsmen; others, working in industry, stopped work only to die" (Cribier, 1981; pp. 51–52). Only 27% of the parent generation had experienced formal retirement, mostly with a modest pension and for only a few years. Historical and national particularities can be called upon to explain this cohort fate: World War I; the delayed development of a national social security system in France; the weight of agriculture, small crafts, and trades in the labor force. The contrast between generations, however, goes beyond national pecularities. The availability of pension systems and the spread of retirement contributed to the contrast between the children's experience and that of their parents, whose lives were less integrated into the welfare state.

What effects did this have on values and expectations? In her research on mill workers from Manchester, New Hampshire, Tamara Hareven (1986) contacted her oral history informants' children and asked them about their biographies, family orientation, and attitudes toward caring for their older parents. She distinguished two "young" cohorts: children born between 1910 and 1919 and between 1920 and 1929. Describing their life courses, members of the parent generation usually referred to family events and economic crises, whereas their children placed much more emphasis on the age norms shared by the society at large; the youngest respondents even used the terms of popular psychology to label their life stages and transitions. The attitudes toward familial care differed even more:

> While the historic cohorts expected their children to assist them in old age, the children's cohorts did not expect to have to rely on their own children for major support in old age. They prepared for old age through pension plans, savings, and real estate, and expected to rely on social security and assistance from the welfare state. Over their life course they had become accustomed to the welfare state and had developed skills in dealing with bureaucratic institutions. (Hareven, 1984, pp. 175–176)

This decrease in feelings of financial obligation between the generations has also been confirmed by more representative data from opinion polls since the 1950s (Callahan, 1987). It is important to note the emphasis on "*financial* obligations" and not to confuse them with more general feelings of mutual belonging and help. The family's discharge from direct income support for the elderly actually has opened up new chances for emotional and caring relationships in the developed welfare states. Besides, when income flows are observed today—and this is another indicator for the mostly comfortable situation of the retired—they often go from the old to the young (Neugarten & Neugarten, 1986).

For those retiring in the 1970s and 1980s, the pace of cohort differentiation seems to have further accelerated. In her research on French pensioners, Françoise Cribier (1989) has recently compared the retirement class of 1972 with a second cohort that retired in 1984. These two groups, though separated by only a little more than a decade, living at the same time in the same city, and both belonging to the so-called third age (Laslett, 1989), have surprisingly little in common. Incomes, housing conditions, and living standards have improved significantly. The attitudes to work and expectations about pensions differ markedly. Whereas the older cohort did not really trust the generosity of the welfare state, the younger cohort is more aware of its comfortable situation and has noticed the mounting competition between old and young workers—something they worry about when thinking about the future of their children and grandchildren (Cribier, 1989).

Again, cross-national comparison would show differences in timing and scope of these new developments, and closer scrutiny of national data would reveal the persistent social and gender inequalities. Still, the trends detected have a broad international basis, and all lead in the same direction: The reduction of poverty in old age and the diffusion of higher entitlements to social security have considerably improved the position of older persons. The increase of married women's labor force participation and the equally growing participation of women in higher education since the 1950s have widened the experiences and aspirations that women bring with them into the later years (Lehr, 1987). Together with the more comfortable living standard, the better health situation of the elderly has played an enormous role in broadening the basis for new life-styles (sports, tourism, adult education, etc.).

Better health, in this context, means the undisputed improvements in fitness that today's 65- or 70-year-olds enjoy, compared to their age mates of around 1900 or 1950. On the other hand, epidemiologists continue to debate whether the risk of chronic disease and mental deterioration has only been postponed in high age groups, which are, however, reached by more and more members of future cohorts (Haan, Rice, Satariano & Selby, 1991). So far, statistical data do not support the optimistic view that morbidity will follow mortality in its decrease (Brody, Brock, & Williams, 1987; Duncan & Smith, 1989). The price for the impressive improvements in the activity potential and longevity of the elderly is to be paid later in life by the individual; its collective cost will be shifted to younger cohorts by society (Gaitz & Samorajski, 1985).

The general amelioration of social conditions in the later years is particularly relevant for women because they form the great majority in these age groups and live more years in that situation. A narrowing of gender inequalities inside the cohorts therefore has an even greater impact on the life chances in old age than in other age groups (cf. Lehr, 1987). Matilda Riley goes so far as to suggest that women who combine family and employment today are already pioneering the more flexible design of life courses in the future: changing in and out of the labor market to fulfill familial or social tasks in other areas might develop from a symptom for less successful careers to a sign of successful aging (Riley & Riley, 1986). There are many more new features which will be transported by the recent and future cohorts of older men and women into the stage that we label "old age" as a whole (cf. Kiesler, Morgan, & Oppenheimer, 1981).

To a certain extent, every era has its "new old." Still, behaviors and group characteristics unseen and unheard of in earlier cohorts increasingly break their way into the expanding time slot between work or family life and death. The famous Ida M. Fuller, the first person in the United States to receive a Social Security check (in 1940) (Achenbaum, 1978), or the first (unknown) gentleman who continued owning and driving his car into late age were such pioneers. Sometimes it meant touching taboos and breaking rules, as in the case of the first Gray Panthers. For people retiring only few years later than these examples, their once path-breaking behavior has become quite normal or at least an accepted option in a wider range of choices. The aging of those cohorts, for example, who disturbed universities and opposed the Vietnam War in the 1960s, or of those young people today who seem to herald postmaterialistic values (Inglehart, 1989) and massively embark upon new ways of partnership and parenthood, will probably rebuild the realities of old age in the next century to a degree that will make most of current gerontological knowledge obsolete.

## THREE AREAS OF CULTURAL AND ATTITUDINAL CHANGE

The following section will discuss cultural and attitudinal changes in three areas: life time, the social construction of old age, cohort change. The cultural themes, however, are not supposed to be subjective reflections of socioeconomic conditions. Rather, the interaction between these two approaches should heighten our sense of diversity and discontinuity regarding the life world of the elderly.

### Life Time and Finitude

An impressive amount of research on the changing perception of time in the aging process, on the social patterning of time in institutions, or on the shared temporal universe of certain communities has been done (Hendricks & Hendricks, 1976; Mizruchi, Glassner, & Pastorello, 1982). An example drawn from this literature may illustrate how complex and unexpected relationships between time conceptions and life worlds can be. In a provocative study based on anthropological fieldwork in a London day care center, Haim Hazan (1980) described the "time universe" of its members as a sort of mentally "closed shop." The past, and with it the former life course, had ceased to be a dynamic experience at all, serving only as anchor point for a never-ending present without change and future. The regular clients moved both socially and temporally in a limbo state. But even this elaborate effort to buffer the community against the outside world was not immune to social change.

When the anthropologist revisited the center 7 years later, he found significant alterations (Hazan, 1984): More interaction with the degrading neighborhood, changes in organization, and the renewal of membership had led to a more differentiated time frame. Whereas the present-orientation of the former "limbo-people" was the correlate of an egalitarian community without much involvement from management or outside, the breaking up of the closed time universe was linked to a considerable rearrangement in the everyday life of the center. Even among the veterans from the first visit, involvement with other groups, new activities, and more contacts with nonmembers indicated an opening to the linear, past- and future-oriented time concept of the society at large. The changes that the new management introduced in the center led to dissatisfaction and estrangement; the loss of the community spirit was felt. Instead, Hazan recognized a renewed importance of the individual life-course, but also found continued refusal of the future where decline and death were concerned.

It would obviously be hazardous to estimate how typical or exotic this example is. On this phenomenological level, we therefore cannot hope to generalize over long periods, for large groups of older people, or across national boundaries. Instead, I would like to discuss basic tendencies on the level of *mentalités* that shaped the cultural framework for conceptualizing individual time. On this level, profound changes in the temporal orientation of individuals took place during the early modern period (Cole & Winkler, 1988), preparing and rehearsing the breakthrough of secularization and belief in progress since the mid-18th century (Koselleck, 1985).

In his research on Central European populations, studies that have moved subsequently from demography to cultural history and even present-day moral criticism, Arthur Imhof (1985, 1987) highlights the paradox that as increased life expectancy on earth was sought and finally attained, the belief in eternal afterlife was sacrificed. To express the loss of the religious dimension of life as a "shortening of the life span," however, does not capture the full scope of its meaning. One can certainly argue about the central place that demography has in this version of the great change. Of more importance for us is that Imhof, in the tradition of the French historian Jean Delumeau (1989), views the Christian belief in eternal life, with its different departments of hell, purgatory, and heaven, as one of the symbolic instruments people in medieval and early modern times used to create security in a largely unstable world. Genealogies and patterns of inheritance, the corporate bodies of monasteries or guilds, and codes of art and architecture helped to provide continuity, meaning, and security when the individual life was demographically too fragile to be trusted (Imhof, 1988). Hence, the basic functional mechanism that these historians see at work is one of compensation: the less individual forces can be relied on, the more communal support and metaphysical relief are valued. The contrast to modernity seems obvious. It is this Janus face that classical sociology has been painting since the 19th century (Giddens, 1990). Even if we agree with cultural historians that the shifts in collective *mentalités* during the 16th to 18th centuries were so profound that, again, the old premodern / modern dichotomy does not work anymore, there can be no doubt that, for the first time in history, secular and individualistic value systems became a mass phenomenon during the 19th and 20th centuries (Chadwick, 1975; McLeod, 1981). But this dominant trend must not be identified with a mere fading away of religious identities because, as Hugh McLeod stated, the 19th century was also a "great age of religious revival": instead of providing "a focus of social unity," religion became "a major basis for the distinctive identity of specific communities, classes, factions in a divided society" (McLeod, 1981, p. v).

Individualism became the central driving force in the reordering of preferences. With the loss of the "eternal" perspective, every year of earthly life seems more precious than ever: the self and the body moved to the center of individual interests. The effort of bourgeois society to secure a more modest, secular immortality (i.e., fame after death) through family, work, and posterity has lost more and more of its persuasive power in the 20th century. Yet not everybody has necessarily become an unbeliever: recent surveys from Europe and North American still show how widely the belief in a life after death is shared. Ireland and the United States lead the scale with approximately 70% of positive answers, whereas in Denmark only one-quarter of the population believes in heaven and hell; Great Britain, France and West Germany cover the middle ground (Himmel & Hölle, 1986). The recent lifting of the iron curtain between the two Germanies showed that socialist education was at least successful in reducing metaphysical convictions to a minority phenomenon: In 1990, 51% of West Germans answered in the affirmative the question "Is there life after death?" whereas only 14% of East Germans did (Roski, 1991, p. 74). Still, modern society as a whole has moved away from a cultural system in which the eternal life of the soul was the dominant, if not the only, framework for interpreting the meaning of life (Chadwick, 1975). Individualization has reached even these matters without simply abolishing the particular contents of the Christian religions altogether. In the words of Niklas Luhmann (1984): "And then men had to know, so to speak, themselves if they were immortal or not" (p. 349).

The long-term costs and benefits of such overarching processes as secularization and individualization that people experience over their life course are hard to determine. It may be that younger members of modern and postindustrial societies benefit more from the softening of social control and the increase of opportunities, whereas older members rather regret the destabilization of traditional values and suffer from the speed of social change. The loss of common social meanings for life and death may be felt more acutely by older people. The demographic revolution of the last century, with its concentration of dying in the later years, has certainly contributed to this specialization of fundamental questions. More important is probably what Harry R. Moody (1986) calls "the dual displacement of meaning." "By dual displacement I mean first, the displacement of leisure / contemplation / meaning from the rest of adulthood into old age and second, the displacement of death / finitude / judgment from the afterlife into the present life" (p. 35). Or, to put it in crude economic terms: shifting the costs of modernism onto the end of life may maximize the total benefits during most of the life time but overburden the last years. This trade-off helps to explain why the "dual displacement" could have been so widely accepted in modern societies.

Can the humanities play a compensatory role here? Let us consider this question together with some of the social trends already reviewed. Several factors have contributed to create a growing need for humanistic reflection in older people themselves as well as in the gerontologic professionals. The increasing time spent in retirement, the liberation from paid work and from many family tasks, the financial security, the better health, and the higher formal education—all of these induced an enormous demand for meaningful and symbolically high-ranking activities that ought to be broadly accessible. Traditionally reserved for a tiny minority of well-off people in their later years, the consumption as well as the production of performing arts, philosophy, literature, and so on, are undergoing a broad process of democratization (Moody, 1988). This is a significant feature of postindustrial aging. However, the role the humanities play in the more sophisticated part of this new leisure market is not a priori capable of repairing the problems of meaning hinted at above. Equally, the input of arguments or specialists from the humanities into policy planning or ethical decisions is not by itself a guarantee that the deep-rooted ambiguities of contemporary culture can be overcome (Callahan, Caplan, & Jennings, 1985).

## Old Age as a Social Problem

Aging has always been likely to become a private trouble, but it has not necessarily been a social problem, to take up a well-known distinction by C. Wright Mills (1978). Like child labor, migration, women's status, or working-class housing, old age began to be considered a social problem or a social question during the 19th century. But only limited aspects of aging, namely, the high risk of poverty and the disability of older workers, were publicly discussed and acted upon. It should, of course, be remembered that the stereotypical connection of "old and poor" was common in medieval and early modern cities and that, at the end of the 18th century, progressive thinkers developed far-reaching plans for preventing and relieving the hardships of the elderly; in France these plans even gained political support but were not realized (Troyansky, 1989). Systematic attention for old age as one of the legitimate objects of public social policies (besides sickness, accidents, unemployment) emerged only in the late 19th and early 20th centuries, however. Interestingly, not before the 1920s could aging as such be conceptualized as a potentially troublesome issue for society: it was in demographic and economic thinking that this abstraction took shape when population aging became a specter in Europe (Bourdelais, 1989; Thane, 1990). Since the end of World War II, a whole range of disciplines and specialized agencies has developed to work on this "problematic" life stage, as it was then generally considered.

The modern conception of old age as a social problem had two fundamental consequences. On the one hand, it furnished the justification for the creation and extension of income maintenance systems, as well as for the growing provision of social and health services. On the other hand, practically all older persons who became clients of public or private welfare institutions were (and are) also treated as dependent and to a certain degree helpless. The often-criticized paternalism hidden in social policies must be understood as a heritage of their historical development.

The specific national and historical conditions for framing the issue of old age determined the outcome in terms of concrete policy programs as well as publicly formulated attitudes. In 19th-century Germany, for example, a shift in focus from the concern with mass pauperism to the "workers' question" brought with it a specialization toward provisions for interrupted or lost earnings among the working class. Accidents and sickness were at the forefront of concern; cyclical unemployment was added only hesitantly at the end of the century, and old age merely figured as a subcase of disability. Although women already formed the majority of the elderly in the 19th century, the expert debate on work and health risks in the life course was a predominantly male affair. Before Bismarck's pension law of 1889, sociopolitical programs had already focused on the insurance principle and on the risk of disability. The issue of providing for the old and helpless, particularly old widows, remained under the responsibility of the poor law. Several studies on older women stressed the neglect they suffered in the sociopolitical discussion. Ofter stereotypes hid the precarious but rather successful coping strategies of aging women (Roebuck & Slaughter, 1979; Stearns,

1980). The general ambivalence in society's attitudes toward aging seems even more pronounced when gender differences are more closely observed (Goeckenjan & Taeger, 1990). At the same time, the medical profession gained greater definitional power over problems of aging. Doctors served as experts in all areas of social policy implementation and acted as advisers to a growing middle-class public. This "medicalization" has been identified as a major source for a more negative valuation of old age (Kondratowitz, 1991; for France, see Stearns, 1977; for the U.S. see Haber, 1984).

In Great Britain, sociologists and historians debated the origins and effects of "dependency" in a quite radical way. Led by the renowned specialist of poverty, Peter Townsend (1981), some younger researchers, like Alan Walker and Chris Phillipson, saw the creation of dependency not as a unintended side effect of the modern welfare state but as a systematic outcome of old age policies (Phillipson, 1982; Walker, 1983). According to this school of "radical" gerontology, exclusion from the work force, modest levels of public pensions, reduced autonomy through professional social services and institutionalization all work together to produce a dependent status. This constructed dependency, in turn, is considered by doctors and social workers as the justification for ever-increased intervention.

The moving force in this process is capitalist industrialization, which, in its latest phase, creates the welfare state as a means of social control. This factor seems vastly overemphasized if one considers recent historical research on social realities before industrialization and draws comparisons with noncapitalist countries. As the recent evidence since the lifting of the iron curtain suggests, the mode of production in the formerly socialist countries has not particularly benefited those who were no longer part of the production, among them the retired. The reservations put forward by the historian Richard Smith (1984) are based on a long-run analysis of English demography and poor law. Though he recognizes the novel features of the 20th-century welfare state and of the aging population in it, Smith points out that dependence had been a persistent feature of old age at least since the Middle Ages. The particular dominance of nuclear families in England and other parts of northern and western Europe always led to hardship in cases of widowhood or disability. In such cases, "it seems that 'risk devolution' and poor relief have been centred on the community rather than on the family" (p. 424).

Still, the strong feature of the "political economy" of old age is that it treats the present client position of the elderly not as natural, but as a social construction. This opens important ways for a fundamental critique of the provision of services, of institutional care, or of early retirement programs (Guillemard 1986b; Phillipson & Walker, 1986). But one should be careful not to imply that there has ever been (or will ever be?) an alternative without some kind of dependence, either in a golden past with family care and work until death or in a socialist society without frailty or scarce ressources. Moreover, the extension of welfare state responsibility for the elderly has also changed the principles of dependence and paternalism. It is no longer only the "truly needy" but the great majority of older citizens who are the clients of social policy programs. Irrespective of the existing differences in welfare states, critical observers like to point out that governments have become as dependent on the expectations and voting decisions of (potential) clients as certain groups, such as pensioners, have become dependent on public transfers. To push the argument to its limits, one might even argue that the share of social expenditures going to people over 60 years of age (more than 50% in Western Europe and North America) is a direct indicator for how highly the "social citizens rights" of this particular group are valued or of how efficiently the elderly's interests have been promoted (Conrad, 1990; Myles, 1984; Pampel & Williamson, 1989).

The attitudinal consequences of the "problem status" of old age are to be seen in a broader context. First of all, one should not be too worried about the fact that since the late 19th century old age has been increasingly thought, labeled, and treated as a social problem (Achenbaum, 1978; Fischer, 1978; Haber, 1983). This seems only a particularly denigrating form of interaction between the "experts"—doctors, social workers, and the like—and the elderly when the focus is on old age alone. As soon as other age groups or differently defined social groups are brought into a comparison, it becomes evident that constructing certain life situations as problems is, from society's point of view, a quite normal way to handle them. It might well be that this definition process had greater cultural and material consequences for the position of older people in society than for that of youth, women, or ethnic minorities. But, again, my aim is to underline that what happened to the aging was (and is) not unique.

The second point is a more contemporary and practical aspect. The negative image of aging in the public mind has often been blamed for disadvantages and prejudices older people had to suffer. From its early years as a discipline and academic advocacy group, gerontology has made great efforts to identify and correct such "false consciousness' in the public, in groups of specialists, or opinion leaders. Following the sociopsychological model that low expectations lead to low performance, the profession voluntarily adopted the advice, proposed most prominently by Margret Mead, that public attitudes can be changed more easily than societal institutions can. Among others, Mead called for "cultural reorientation" in respect to aging (Calhoun, 1978, p. 76). This meliorist effort of modern enlightenment found its most prominent expression in the attack against "ageism." Although the notion of "ageism," as well as the concomitant link between civil rights concepts and anti-age discrimination, has mainly stayed a U.S. phenomenon (Butler, 1975), the reformist attitude of many gerontologists regarding stereotypes is shared in Europe (Lehr, 1987).

Hence, aging and old age have increasingly become the targets of concerted efforts of image building, the attempt to correct prevailing prejudices being only one example. Again, this is obviously not limited to the later years but applies to other areas, such as childhood, the family, and sexuality, as well. Like any attempt at image politics, such efforts take place in a competitive landscape; the way they work is closely related to that of semantic politics, an area of considerable attention from researchers and policy marketers in recent years (Edelman, 1977, 1988). The inherent goals and values of these campaigns merit close attention; there is more at stake than simply an outside, advertising image of aging. As Cole and Gadow (1986) and Callahan (1987) make clear in their critique of Gruman (1978), the acceptance of certain limits of the "perfectibility" of late life has important ethical implications.

Intentional efforts to shape new attitudes toward the elderly or new norms of aging are not a 20th-century invention. The amazing effort of public pedagogy of the enlightened elite in the late 18th century covered many areas of popular life, stylizing the virtuous old man (rarely the old woman) (Göckenjan & Taeger, 1990), in a model figure never seen before—or after (cf. Bois, 1989; Borscheid, 1987; Troyansky, 1989). About a hundred years later, a less conscious but nevertheless consequential trend to treat "problems" of aging in a scientific manner arose among personnel managers, social reformers, and doctors. As already mentioned, some historians identify this movement in professional circles as the major turning point in negative attitudes toward the elderly (Haber, 1983; cf. Cole, 1991; chap. 10). Perhaps more important in Europe than in the United States was the role demographers played in framing a negative view of aging. During the interwar years, the European countries reacted to the heavy losses of young men and to the dramatically fallen birth rates during World War I with a highly emotional discussion of the aging of their national populations. In a climate of sharp social tensions over the consequences of the Great War, inflation, unemployment, and the financing of relief programs, the demographic diagnosis had deep ideological undertones. In Weimar Germany, the terms used for the aging of the population were particularly pejorative: *Überalterung* meant not only aging but literally "overaging"; *Vergreisung* denoted the process of becoming senile.

Since the end of World War II, image building has become a kind of social engineering. Richard B. Calhoun (1978) has analyzed the sometimes involuntary coalition of gerontologists, doctors, journalists, and marketing experts who were the major proponents of the "new old" in the United States. With a sharper critical edge, Chris Phillipson (1982) described the British attempts to keep older workers in the labor force during the 1950s. The first wave of research on retirement, its causes and effects, helped to spread a negative image of this new stage of life. A cyclical relationship between social policy aims and publicly promulgated images of aging has been put forward for France by Anne-Marie Guillemard (1986a, 1986b). She distinguishes three periods in French postwar "politics of old age": a first phase, until about 1960, dominated by the extension of retirement and pensions; a second phase, from 1960 to 1975, in which various programs aimed at changing the way of life of the elderly and at integrating them into society coincided with "activity theories" in gerontology; and a third phase, after 1975, that brings back the concern for retirement, that is, early retirement in this case. At the same time, the ambitious integration projects of the 1960s and 1970s have survived as political efforts to favor home care.

Among the students of aging and the helping professionals there seems to have been a rough sequence in the promotion of concepts of old age (Calhoun, 1978). Traditional attitudes toward the "poor old folks," together with concepts related to bodily deficiency, were still dominant in the 1940s and 1950s. A first move for a positive image of aging put forward the idea of "successful aging" and the activity theory. During the 1960s, the latter became well known through the debate with disengagement theory. Meanwhile, the more positive outlook on old age had made its way into numerous programs for integration in the community, preretirement training, residential care, and the like. The late 1970s and 1980s saw the speedy commercial promotion of the "new old." In recent years, "successful aging" has made a renaissance, interestingly, mostly concerning the individual, not the societal level. Some critics of gerontology's changing involvements in image building have remained unimpressed by the recent upsurge in professional optimism: "The currently fashionable positive mythology of old age shows no more tolerance or respect for the intractable vicissitudes of aging than the old negative mythology" (Cole, 1989, p. 381). For the historian of long-term attitudinal changes, further questions remain unanswered. Our evidence on attitudes toward the aging is largely limited to certain professionals (social workers, doctors, etc.) who are very outspoken and determine the philosophy of the institutions they work in. Broader changes in 20th-century *mentalités* and cultural themes, however, are much harder to pinpoint. At least for Western Europe, there is a great deal of research needed before we can go beyond the usual but probably one-sided references to youth cult, generation conflict, and devaluation of experience. (See Thompson, Itzin, & Abendstern, 1990.)

## Generations in Conflict?

Intergenerational conflict is an age-old theme. Historically, and also in the recent past, it has often served as a catch-all explanation for youth unrest. Some social scientists rightly point to the richness of various strands of theory regarding the location of generations in time, their role as collective actors in social change, and their relationships with each other (Attias-Donfut, 1988). For the study of aging, various concepts of "generation" share with the concept of life course the advantage of seeing the later years together with younger age groups; whether in the family or in society at large, "generations" focus on relationships (Garms-Homolová, Hoerning, & Schaeffer, 1984). While gerontologists acknowledge these and other important features of generational analysis (Bengtson, Furlong, & Laufer, 1974), they react quite allergically to predictions of a future conflict of old and young over how to distribute the national product or how to allocate health resources (Binstock 1983, 1985). To project familiar notions of relations between parents and children onto the societal level may indeed not be a particularly cogent analysis.

Instead, age as a political issue has to be placed in the wider context that we have already mentioned in our discussions of the social construction of old age as a problem and as retirement. Contrary to modernization theory, not all ascribed characteristics of people have lost their importance or have been replaced by achieved ones. As Morris Janowitz (1978) put it:

> With the advent of advanced industrialism, age paradoxically becomes more and more a societal-wide dimension of self-identification and collective attachment.... Likewise... the ascriptive characteristics of race and sex emerge as profound sociopolitical issues, in good measure because they produce inequality in social stratification and economic rewards. (p. 132)

The 1980s witnessed a growing perception of competition between young and old people about the distribution of resources in the welfare state (cf. Cole, 1989). To believe certain American magazines, a "war between the generations" was declared. While the emotional tone and the scope of the attack against the "Greedy Geezers" (*The New Republic,*

March 28, 1988; see Fairlie, 1988) is clearly an American phenomenon, echoes of this debate began to be heard in the late 1980s in countries like New Zealand, Britain, West Germany, and even France (Conrad, 1990). Explaining the timing of these rather dramatic attitudinal changes is not easy. Obviously, the fear of demographic aging or the mere proportion of old people in the population was not sufficient to trigger them. The idea that today's elderly are the "winners" of the post–World War II economic boom and social security extension is a necessary precondition. But a third ingredient was needed: the bleak outlook of the baby boom generation on jobs, family formation, future burdens from public debt, ecological destruction, and so on (see Binstock, 1983).

Let us step back and consider the relationship of cohort change to this outburst of envy and fear of (relative) deprivation so evident in the generational equity debate. To clarify the talk about "ages in conflict" we have to take the so-called generations as what they really are: successive cohorts, sometimes, but not necessarily those of parents and children. Those born in the late 1940s and 1950s are living with the permanent experience of crowding: from the kindergarten to the labor market, there are always too many age mates. Their economic prospects are, relatively speaking, much less rewarding than of those who were born in the 1920s and 1930s. The consequences of this greater stress for the baby boomers are visible, according to Richard Easterlin (1987), in delayed family formation, lower fertility, psychological problems, and deviant behavior. To equal the relative economic success of their parents, married women have to go out working more often, and they have to cut back in family size. When they enter retirement, however—that is, from about 2010 on—the baby boomers will face another difficult period. They will not only again be crowding the institutions, from pension funds to nursing homes, but also they cannot be sure that their children and grandchildren will then finance the welfare state as generously as the baby boomers themselves are now doing for their parents.

The New Zealand historian David Thomson (1989), himself a baby boomer, has analyzed the fate of the older cohorts. His study focuses on the success story of the "welfare generation": those born around 1920–1935 who married after World War II and benefited during their family cycle from an unprecedented development of social services and transfer schemes. But after collecting all of the benefits and going through the long economic boom of the postwar period, this generation failed, particularly since the 1970s, to guarantee the same advantages for the next generation. Instead, in nearly all Western nations, they remodeled once youth-centered public programs into a welfare state centered around old people. While housing subsidies, child allowances, tax reductions, and public funds for higher education were reduced in relative value, pension expenditures continued their amazing postwar career. In Thomson's startling model, demography plays only a minor role; the shifting priorities of the welfare state exceeded the slow aging of the population. Only in the next century will demographics aggravate a drama in which the main parts are acted today. Taken together, the basis of the current talk of growing conflicts between the generations lies in these two highly divergent cohort fates. The potential cleavage between the baby boomers and the next generation, which will become manifest in the first decades after the year 2000, may become even more prominent. But one should not, as family sociologists warn us, mix up these concerns with the quality of relations inside family and kinship (Garms-Homolova, Hoerning, & Schaeffer, 1984).

The philosopher Norman Daniels (1988) has proposed more general arguments against "equity" protagonists. In his view, the distribution of resources between age groups over the whole life span is primordial, and unequal treatment of children and the elderly at the same time or of birth cohorts is secondary. Daniels's model of the "prudential lifespan account" would allow development of guidelines for distribution and redistribution between the life stages under the condition that everybody can expect the same treatment over his or her life course. In the long run, immediate inequalities would not only be compensated, but the "prudent" allocation of resources over the life span would also maximize the general well-being: "We feel we pay through the nose as working adults, but we are free-loaders in youth and old age" (Daniels, 1989, p. 63). This theoretically based optimism has not reassured those empirical analysts who find in today's and tomorrow's inequities between cohorts enough dynamite to make the invisible "generation contract" crumble.

> Even if the historical uniqueness of the fate of successive cohorts after the Second World War is probably not prone to political "compensation," social security reforms must give younger people a good reason for sustaining the common stake that different generations have in the welfare state. (Johnson, Conrad, & Thomson, 1989, pp. 12–13)

Since the exchanges between the age groups in contemporary societies are public as well as private and encompass not only pensions but also transfer flows in education, health, infrastructure, or through inheritance, a key role is played by the state on all levels. In the immediate future, government policies must consciously try to mediate between conflicting cohort and age group interests; indeed, the state cannot but act, as a French economist put it, as an "arbiter of generations" (Kessler, 1990).

## THE LAST THINGS BEFORE THE LAST

Even a highly selective overview such as this cannot end without some words on the dark side of the later years: physical frailty, dementia, the need for long-term care, institutionalized dying. Gerontologists are certainly right in reminding us that, at a given moment, most older people are not the victims of any such situation and that, in contrast, many of the mentally or physically handicapped are younger than 60 or 65 years. Aging is not a disease, and in contemporary society, old age as a stage of life does not equal disability or sickness. As important as such a statement, however, is the acknowledgment that the aging individual faces a high risk of becoming dependent on others and that society faces an absolute increase in the number of those most at risk. What, for the individual, is surrounded by uncertainty presents itself to society as a fact of life that must be collectively coped with one way or the other (Riley, 1983). Even if one disagrees with Daniel Callahan's (1987) agenda setting for medical policy, his book has the merit of pressing the public to consider suffering and death as an essential part of human life as a whole. Other chapters of this volume are devoted to this "huge new area of moral uncertainty" (Pifer & Bronte, 1986, p. 12; cf. Moody, this volume). From the historian's point of view, there may be added some simple factual points that can help us to understand the "newness" of our situation.

The mortality revolution of the late 19th and early 20th centuries led to the concentration of most deaths in the age groups above 60. Today "those in the Third and Fourth Ages," remarks Peter Laslett (1989, p. 18), "do almost all the dying for the whole society." In a parallel movement, again shared by all developed countries, the spectrum of causes of death has shifted from acute, infectious diseases to chronic, degenerative diseases, especially to those not easily "repaired" by modern medicine. Since about 1950, life expectancy, even at high ages, has been increasing more strongly. One consequence is the rapid multiplication of the "old old," those men and women who have successfully survived until 80 or 85. The impact of medicine's involvement in this process is far from clear. For the first part of this deep demographic change (until the 1930s and 1940s), rising living standards and public hygiene had a much higher impact on life expectancy than did personal medical care. In the second half of the 20th century, pharmaceutical products, especially vaccines, and the so-called life-extending technologies have gained considerable importance for public health. Their application has also benefited the elderly to a growing extent. But the growing life expectancy of today's old people has much to do with their former lives under more beneficial circumstances. One should be careful not to attribute too much of modern longevity, and thus of today's health cost problems, to the efficacy of medicine (Avorn, 1986).

But demography is not the whole story and will not be the only force to push the future development. The medical system (including nursing homes as well as hospitals) also changed its involvement with older people. Although this is not yet a well-researched area, medical institutions and insurance and welfare policies, as well as attitudes to family care, seemed to undergo tentative changes during the interwar years and decisive changes since the 1950s. In short, hospitals opened their doors to older patients and expanded the departments particularly catering to their needs. The contrast with the beginning of the century is astonishing. In French and German cities of around 1900 the typical hospital patient was a young, unmarried man, most often a worker. Women and children and also older people were by far underrepresented. Infants and their mothers were soon integrated into public health programs, but it took somewhat longer for older men and women. Since the 1950s, the age profile of hospital patients has turned around: the elderly are now overrepresented among them; nursing homes have developed into a growth industry. The reasons for this turn are manifold; one important factor is the integration of pensioners and their wives in the national health insurance systems. This step was completed by the late 1940s in Western Europe; the United States even instituted a special health insurance system for older people (Medicare, in 1965).

This de facto integration of older people into the medical system of modern welfare states does not, however, correspond to an equally profound change in the conceptual and therapeutic orientations of medical experts. Older people continue to be considered thankless patients. Specialization in their often chronic and multiple morbidities does not rank high in the symbolic hierarchy of the medical profession, and hospitals with a particularly high proportion of very old patients tend to be smaller, less well-equipped, and less-valued institutions (cf. Haber, 1984; Rosenberg, 1986; Cassel, 1986). Health policy specialist Jerome Avorn (1986) diagnoses "the mismatch of conventional medical paradigms with the changing epidemiology of illness" (p. 291). This is an acute example of the "structural lag" between the age composition of our societies and their obsolete institutional setup (Riley, 1987). The future adaptation to an aging society will demand a serious reversal of the traditional preferences that put acute treatment over long-term care, curing over prevention, life extension over a humane process of dying. For more "successful aging" in the future, our societies still seem to lack not only the attitudes but also the institutional arrangements that would allow an "art of dying"—an *ars moriendi,* as early modern Europeans put it—to be an accepted part of the life course (see Imhof, 1991; Kastenbaum, 1979; Riley, 1983).

## REFERENCES


Achenbaum, W. A. (1978). *Old age in the new land: The American experience since 1790.* Baltimore, London: Johns Hopkins University Press.

Achenbaum, W. A. (1983). *Shades of gray: Old age, American values, and federal policies since 1920.* Boston, Toronto: Little, Brown.

Atchley, R. C. (1982). Retirement as a social institution. *Annual Review of Sociology, 8,* 263–287.

Attias-Doufut, C. (1988). *Sociologie des générations: L'empreinte du temps.* Paris: Presses Universitaires de France.

Avorn, J. L. (1986). Medicine: The life and death of Oliver Shay. In A. Pifer & L. Bronte (Eds.), *Our aging society: Paradox and promise* (pp. 283–297). New York, London: Norton.

Bell, D. (1973). *The coming of post-industrial society: A venture in social forecasting.* New York: Basic Books.

Bell, D. (1976). *The cultural contradictions of capitalism.* New York: Basic Books.

Bengtson, V. L., Furlong, M. J., & Laufer, R. S. (1974). Time, aging, and the continuity of social structure: Themes and issues in generational analysis. *Journal of Social Issues, 30*(2), 1–30.

Binstock, R. (1983). The aged as scapegoat. *Gerontologist, 23,* 136–143.

Binstock, R. (1985). The oldest old: A fresh perspective or compassionate ageism revisited? *Milbank Memorial Fund Quarterly, 63*(2), 420–451.

Bois, J.-P. (1989). *Les vieux, de Montaigne aux premières retraites.* Paris: Fayard.

Borscheid, P. (1987). *Geschichte des Alters: 16.–18. Jahrhundert.* Münster: F. Coppenrath.

Bourdelais, P. (1989). Vieillissement de la population ou artefact statistique? *Gérontologie et Société, 49,* 22–32.

Brody, J. A., Brock, D. B., & Williams, T. F. (1987). Trends in the health of the elderly population. *Annual Review of Public Health, 8,* 211–234.

Butler, R. N. (1975). *Why survive? Being old in America.* New York: Harper & Row.

Calhoun, R. B. (1978). *In search of the new old: Redefining old age in America, 1945–1970.* New York: Elsevier.

Callahan, D. (1987). *Setting limits. Medical goals in an ageing society.* New York: Simon & Schuster.

Callahan, D., Caplan, A. L., & Jennings, B. (Eds.). (1985). *Applying the humanities.* New York, London: Plenum Press.

Cassel, C. K. (1986). The meaning of health care in old age. In T. Cole & S. A. Gadow (Eds.), *What does it mean to grow old?* (pp. 179–198). Durham, NC: Duke University Press.

Chadwick, O. (1975). *The secularization of the European mind in the nineteenth century.* Cambridge: Cambridge University Press.

Cole, T. R. (1989). Generational equity in America: A cultural historian's perspective. *Social Science and Medicine, 29,* 377–383.

Cole, T. R. (1991). *The journey of life: A cultural history of aging in America.* New York: Cambridge University Press.

Cole, T., & Gadow, S. A. (Eds.). (1986). *What does it mean to grow old? Reflections from the humanities.* Durham, NC: Duke University Press.

Cole, T. R., & Winkler, M. G. (1988). "Unsere Tage zählen". Ein historischer Überblick über Konzepte des Alterns in der westlichen Kultur. In G. Göckenjan & H. J. von Kondratowitz (Eds.), *Alter und Alltag* (pp. 35–66). Frankfurt: Suhrkamp.

Conrad, C. (1988). Die Entstehung des modernen Ruhestandes: Deutschland im internationalen Vergleich 1850–1960. *Geschichte und Gesellschaft, 14,* 417–447 (French version in *Population* (Paris), *45*(1990), 531–563).

Conrad, C. (1990). Gewinner und Verlierer im Wohlfahrtsstaat: Deutsche und internationale Tendenzen im 20. Jahrhundert. *Archiv für Sozialgeschichte, 30,* 297–326.

Cribier, F. (1981). Changing retirement patterns: The experience of a cohort of Parisian salaried workers. *Ageing and Society, 1,* 51–71.

Cribier, F. (1989). Changes in life course and retirement in recent years: The example of two cohorts of Parisians. In P. Johnson, C. Conrad, & D. Thomson (Eds.), *Workers versus Pensioners: Intergenerational justice in an ageing world* (pp. 181–201). Manchester: Manchester University Press; New York: St. Martin's Press.

Cross, G. (1989). *A quest for time: The reduction of work in Britain and France, 1840–1940.* Berkeley: University of California Press.

Dahrendorf, R. (1979). *Life chances: Approaches to social and political theory.* Chicago: University of Chicago Press.

Daniels, N. (1988). *Am I my parents' keeper? An essay on justice between the young and the old.* New York: Oxford University Press.

Daniels, N. (1989). Justice and transfers between generations. In P. Johnson, C. Conrad, & D. Thomson (Eds.), *Workers versus pensioners: Intergenerational justice in an ageing world* (pp. 57–79). Manchester: Manchester University Press. New York: St. Martin's Press.

Delumeau, J. (1989). *Rassurer et protéger: Le sentiment de sécurité dans l'Occident d'autrefois.* Paris: Fayard.

Duncan, G. J., & Smith, K. R. (1989). The rising affluence of the elderly: How far, how fair, and how frail? *Annual Review of Sociology, 15,* 261–289.

Easterlin, R. A. (1987). *Birth and fortune: The impact of numbers on personal welfare* (2nd ed.). Chicago, London: University of Chicago Press.

Edelman, M. (1977). *Political language: Words that succeed and policies that fail.* New York: Academic Press.

Edelman, M. (1988). *The construction of the political spectacle.* Chicago: University of Chicago Press.

Ehmer, J. (1990). *Sozialgeschichte des Alters.* Frankfurt: Suhrkamp.

Elias, N. (1986). *The loneliness of the dying.* Oxford: Basil Blackwell.

Fairlie, H. (1988). Talkin' 'bout my generation. *The New Republic,* March 28, 19–22.

Fischer, D. H. (1978). *Growing old in America (expanded ed.).* Oxford, New York: Oxford University Press.

Foner, N. (1984). Age and social change. In D. I. Kertzer & J. Keith (Eds.). *Age and anthropological theory* (pp. 195–216). Ithaca, NY: Cornell University Press.

Fries, J. F. (1980). Aging, natural death, and the compression of morbidity. *New England Journal of Medicine, 303,* 130–136.

Gaitz, C. M., & Samorajski, T. (Eds.). (1985). *Aging 2000: Our health care destiny.* New York, Berlin: Springer-Verlag.

Garms-Homolová, V., Hoerning, E. M., & Schaeffer, D. (Eds.). (1984). *Intergenerational relationships.* Lewiston, NY, Toronto: C. J. Hogrefe.

Gaullier, X. (1988). *La deuxième carrière: Âges, emplois, retraites.* Paris: Editions du Seuil.

Giddens, A. (1990). *The consequences of modernity.* Cambridge, Oxford: Polity Press.

Göckenjan, G., & Taeger, A. (1990). Matrone, Alte Jungfer, Tante: Das Bild der alten Frau in der bürgerlichen Welt des 19. Jahrhunderts. *Archiv für Sozialgeschichte, 30,* 43–79.

Graebner, W. (1980). *A history of retirement: The meaning and function of an American institution, 1885–1978.* New Haven; CT: Yale University Press.

Grebenik, E., Höhn, C., & Mackensen, R. (Eds.). (1989). *Later phases of the family cycle: Demographic aspects.* Oxford: Oxford University Press.

Grob, G. N. (1986). Explaining old age history: The need for empiricism. In D. Van Tassel & P. N. Stearns (Eds.), *Old age in a bureaucratic society* (pp. 30–45). New York: Greenwood Press.

Gruman, G. J. (1978). Cultural origins of present-day "age-ism": The modernization of the life cycle. In S. F. Spicker, K. F. Woodward, & D. D. Van Tassel (Eds.), *Aging and the elderly: Humanistic perspectives in gerontology* (pp. 359–387). Atlantic Highlands, NJ: Humanities Press.

Guillemard, A.-M. (1986a). *Le déclin du social: Formation et crise des politiques de la vieillesse.* Paris: Presses Universitaires de France.

Guillemard, A.-M. (1986b). State, society, and old-age policy in France: From 1945 to the current crisis. *Social Science and Medicine, 23,* 1319–1326.

Guillemard, A.-M. (1989). The trend towards early labour force withdrawal and the reorganisation of the life course: A cross-national analysis. In P. Johnson, C. Conrad, & D. Thomson (Eds.), *Workers versus pensioners: Intergenerational justice in an ageing world* (pp. 164–180). Manchester: Manchester University Press; New York: St. Martin's Press.

Gutton, J.-P. (1988). *Naissance du vieillard.* Paris: Aubier.

Haan, M. N., Rice, D. P., Satariano, W. A. & Selby, J. V. (Guest Eds.). (1991). *Living longer and doing worse? Present and future trends in the health of the elderly.* Special Issue, *Journal of Aging and Health* 3(2).

Haber, C. (1983). *Beyond sixty-five: The dilemma of old age in America's past.* Cambridge: Cambridge University Press.

Haber, C. (1984). Geriatrics: A specialty in search of specialists. *Zeitschrift für Gerontologie 17,* 26–31.

Hagestad, G. O., & Neugarten, B. L. (1985). Age and the life course. In R. H. Binstock & E. Shanas (Eds.), *Handbook of aging and the social sciences* (2nd ed., pp. 35–61). New York: Van Nostrand Reinhold.

Hannah, L. (1986) *Inventing retirement: The development of occupational pensions in Britain*. Cambridge: Cambridge University Press.

Hareven, T. K. (1986). Historical changes in the social construction of the life course. *Human Development, 29*(3), 171–177.

Hazan, H. (1980). *The limbo people. A study of the constitution of the time universe among the aged*. London, Boston: Routledge & Kegan Paul.

Hazan, H. (1984). Continuity and transformation among the aged: A study in the anthropology of time. *Current Anthropology, 25*, 567–578.

Hendricks, C. D., & Hendricks, J. (1976). Concepts of time and temporal construction among the aged. In J. F. Gubrium (Ed.), *Time, roles, and self in old age* (pp. 13–49). New York: Human Sciences Press.

Himmel und Hölle (1986). *Die Zeit*, No. 3, January *10*, 57.

Imhof, A. E. (1985). From the old mortality pattern to the new: Implications of a radical change from the sixteenth to the twentieth century. *Bulletin of the History of Medicine, 59*, 1–29.

Imhof, A. E. (1986). Life-course patterns of women and their husbands: 16th to 20th century. In A. B. Sørensen, F. E. Weinert, & L. R. Sherrod (Eds.), *Human development and the life course: Multidisciplinary perspectives* (pp. 247–270). Hillsdale, NJ: Erlbaum.

Imhof, A. E. (1987). Planning full-size life careers: Consequences of the increase in the length and certainty of our life spans over the last three hundred years. *Ethnologia Europaea, 17*, 5–23.

Imhof, A. E. (1988). *Die Lebenszeit: Vom aufgeschobenen Tod und von der Kunst des Lebens*. Munich: C. H. Beck.

Imhof, A. E. (1991). *Ars Moriendi. Dic Kunst des Sterbens einst und heute*. Vienna, Cologne: Böhlau.

Inglehart, R. (1989). *Culture shift in advanced industrial society*. Princeton, NJ: Princeton University Press.

Janowitz, M. (1978). *The last half-century: Societal change and politics in America*. Chicago: Chicago University Press.

Jennings, B., & Prewitt, K. (1985). The humanities and the social sciences. In D. Callahan, A. L. Caplan, & B. Jennings (Eds.), *Applying the humanities* (pp. 125–143). New York, London: Plenum Press.

Johnson, P., Conrad, C., & Thomson, D. (Eds.). (1989). *Workers versus pensioners: Intergenerational justice in an ageing world*. Manchester: Manchester University Press; New York: St. Martin's Press.

Kastenbaum, R. (1979). Exit and existence: Society's unwritten script for old age and death. In D. D. Van Tassel (Ed.), *Aging, death, and the completion of being* (pp. 69–94). Philadelphia: University of Pennsylvania Press.

Kessler, D. (1990). L'arbitre des générations. *Le débat, 60*, 271–277.

Kiesler, S. B., Morgan, J. N., & Oppenheimer, V. K. (Eds.). (1981). *Aging: Social change*. New York: Academic Press.

Kohli, M. (1986). The world we forgot: A historical review of the life course. In V. W. Marshall (Ed.), *Late life: The social psychology of aging* (pp. 271–303). Beverly Hills, CA: Sage.

Kohli, M. (1987). Retirement and the moral economy: An historical interpretation of the German case. *Journal of Aging Studies, 1*, 125–144.

Kondratowitz, H.-J. von. (1991). The medicalization of old age: Continuity and change in Germany from the late eighteenth to the early twentieth century. In M. Pelling & R. M. Smith (Eds.), *Life, death, and the elderly: Historical perspectives.* London, New York: Routledge.

Koselleck, R. (1985). *Futures past: On the semantics of historical time.* Cambridge, MA: M. I. T. Press.

Laslett, P. (1984). The significance of the past in the study of ageing. *Ageing and Society, 4,* 379–389. (Special issue: History and ageing).

Laslett, P. (1989). *A fresh map of life: The emergence of the third age.* London: Weidenfeld & Nicolson.

Lehr, U. (1987). *Zur Situation der älterwerdenden Frau: Bestandsaufnahme und Perspektiven bis zum Jahre 2000.* Munich: Beck.

Luhmann, N. (1984). *Soziale Systeme: Grundriss einer allgemeinen Theorie.* Frankfurt: Suhrkamp.

Lyotard, J.-F. (1985). *The post-modern condition.* Minneapolis: University of Minnesota Press. (Original work published 1979)

Mayer, K. U., & Müller, W. (1986). The state and the structure of the life course. In A. B. Sørensen, F. E. Weinert, & L. R. Sherrod (Eds.), *Human development and the life course: Multidisciplinary perspectives* (pp. 217–245). Hillsdale, NJ: Erlbaum.

Mayer, K. U., & Schoepflin, U. (1989). The state and the life course. *Annual Review of Sociology, 15,* 187–209.

McLeod, H. (1981). *Religion and the people of Western Europe 1789–1970.* Oxford: Oxford University Press.

Mills, C. W. (1978). *The sociological imagination.* Harmondsworth, UK: Penguin. (Original work published 1959)

Mizruchi, E. H., Glassner, B., & Pastorello, T. (Eds.). (1982). *Time and aging: Conceptualization and application in sociological and gerontological research.* Bayside, NY: General Hall.

Moody, H. R. (1986). The meaning of life and the meaning of old age. In T. Cole & S. A. Gadow (Eds.), *What does it mean to grow old?* (pp. 9–40), Durham, NC: Duke University Press.

Moody, H. R. (1988). *Abundance of life: Human development policies for an aging society.* New York: Columbia University Press.

Myles, J. (1984). *Old age in the welfare state: The political economy of public pensions.* Boston, Toronto: Little, Brown.

Neugarten, B. L. (1974). Age groups in American society and the rise of the young-old. *Annals of the American Academy of Political and Social Science, 415,* 187–198.

Neugarten, B. L., & Neugarten, D. A. (1986). Changing meanings of age in the aging society. In A. Pifer & L. Bronte (Eds.), *Our aging society: Paradox and promise* (pp. 33–51). New York, London: Norton.

*Old age in the modern world: Report of the Third Congress of the International Association of Gerontology, London 1954.* (1955). Edinburgh, London: Livingstone.

Pampel, F. C. (1981). *Social change and the aged: Recent trends in the United States.* Lexington, MA, Toronto: Lexington Books.

Pampel, F. C., & Williamson, J. B. (1989). *Age, class, politics, and the welfare state*. Cambridge: Cambridge University Press.

Phillipson, C. (1982). *Capitalism and the construction of old age*. London: Macmillan.

Phillipson, C., & Walker, A. (Eds.). (1986). *Ageing and social policy: A critical assessment*. Aldershot, UK: Gower.

Pifer, A. (1986). The public policy response. In A. Pifer & L. Bronte (Eds.), *Our aging society: Paradox and promise* (pp. 391–413). New York, London: Norton.

Pifer, A., & Bronte, L. (Eds.). (1986). *Our aging society: Paradox and promise*. New York, London: Norton.

Quadagno, J. S. (1988). *The transformation of old age security: Class and politics in the American welfare state*. Chicago: University of Chicago Press.

Riley, J. W., Jr. (1983). Dying and the meanings of death: Sociological inquiries. *Annual Review of Sociology, 9*, 191–216.

Riley, M. W. (1987). On the significance of age in sociology. *American Sociological Review, 52*, 1–14.

Riley, M. W., & Riley, J. W., Jr. (1986). Longevity and social structure: The potential of the added years. In A. Pifer & L. Bronte (Eds.), *Our aging society: Paradox and promise* (pp. 53–77). New York, London: Norton.

Riley, M. W., & Riley J. W., Jr. (1989). The lives of older people and changing social roles. *Annals of the American Academy of Political and Social Science, 503*, 14–28.

Roebuck, J., & Slaughter, J. (1979). Ladies and pensioners: Stereotypes and public policy affecting old women in England, 1880–1940. *Journal of Social History, 13*, 105–114.

Rosenberg, C. E. (1986). The aged in a structured social context: Medicine as a case study. In D. Van Tassel & P. N. Stearns (Eds.), *Old age in a bureaucratic society* (pp. 231–245). New York: Greenwood Press.

Rosenmayr, L. (1983). *Die späte Freiheit: Das Alter—ein Stück bewusst gelebten Lebens*. Berlin: Severin & Siedler.

Rosenmayr, L. (1987). On freedom and aging: An interpretation. *Journal of Aging Studies, 1*, 299–316

Roski, G. (1991). Bleiben sie Heiden? *Das Profil der Deutschen. Spiegel Spezial, 1*, 72–76.

Schenda, R. (1983). Bewertungen und Bewältigungen des Alters aufgrund volkskundlicher Materialien. In C. Conrad & H.-J. von Kondratowitz (Eds.), *Gerontologie und Sozialgeschichte* (pp. 59–71). Berlin: Deutsches Zentrum für Altersfragen.

Silvermann, P. (Ed.). (1988). *The elderly as modern pioneers*. Bloomington: Indiana University Press.

Smith, R. M. (1984). The structured dependence of the elderly as a recent development: Some sceptical historical thoughts. *Ageing and Society, 4*, 409–428.

Spanier, G. B., & Glick, P. C. (1980). The life cycle of American families: An expanded analysis. *Journal of Family History, 5*, 97–111.

Stearns, P. N. (1977). *Old age in European society: The case of France*. London: Croom Helm.

Stearns, P. N. (1980). Old women: Some historical observations. *Journal of Family History, 5,* 44–57.

Thane, P. M. (1990). The debate on the declining birth-rate in Britain: The "menace" of an ageing population, 1920s–1950s. *Continuity and Change, 5,* 283–305.

Thomson, D. (1989). The welfare state and generation conflict: Winners and losers. In P. Johnson, C. Conrad, & D. Thomson (Eds.), *Workers versus pensioners: Intergenerational justice in an ageing world* (pp. 33–56). Manchester: Manchester University Press; New York: St. Martin's Press.

Thompson, P., Itzin, C., & Abendstern, M. (1990). *I don't feel old. The experience of later life*. Oxford, New York: Oxford University Press.

Townsend, P. (1981). The structural dependency of the elderly: A creation of social policy in the twentieth century. *Ageing and Society, 1,* 5–28.

Troyansky, D. G. (1989). *Old age in the Old Regime: Image and experience in eighteenth-century France*. Ithaca, NY: Cornell University Press.

Van Tassel, D. D., & Stearns, P. N. (Eds.). (1986). *Old age in a bureaucratic society: The elderly, the experts, and the state in American history*. New York: Greenwood Press.

Walker, A. (1983). Social policy and elderly people in Great Britain. In A.-M. Guillemard (Ed.), *Old age and the welfare state* (pp. 143–167). Beverly Hills, CA, London: Sage.

4

# Aging in Eastern Cultures: A Historical Overview

*Christie W. Kiefer*

---

Most East Asian societies have given important roles to the elderly, so there is a great deal to say about their place in the rich and ancient written history of the area. In this chapter I will try to simplify and clarify the subject, focusing on a few central points and keeping in mind the concerns of Western gerontologists. I am principally interested in how the major Eastern societies—China, Korea, Japan—contrast with the West and with each other and what the main shifts have been in the social images, statuses and roles, and material circumstances of the aged throughout their histories. I will treat each of the major societies separately, only noting its salient contrasts with the others. Finally, I will try to draw some general conclusions about the effects of social organization, economy, and social change on the status of the elderly.

## CHINA

### Classical Society

Classical Chinese society is generally viewed by Westerners as an almost changeless, culturally homogeneous Leviathan in which old people held positions of respect and power—as a kind of ageless gerontocracy, the antithesis of our volatile and youth-oriented Western societies. Although there is some truth in this view, as there is in most stereotypes, it needs some modification and refinement if we really are to understand Chinese history.

Compared with most modern Western societies, the old were venerated in many parts of China or at least in many families in those parts during much of history. But their veneration depended on economic conditions, customs, and institutions that varied according to locale, family fortune, and historical era. Like many customs, respect for the aged evolved gradually and unevenly, although it often continued out of habit in times and places where it seemed out of place. Old people who were highly respected tended to fulfill a number of key functions in their families and communities, and those who were unable for any reason to perform such functions tended to get far worse treatment. In fact, poverty-stricken childless elderly were numerous enough to attract the attention of several reformers before the turn of the 20th century (Bauer, 1976; Levinson, 1967).

It is simply not possible, then, to talk about the "role of the elderly" in classical China without overgeneralizing. But here we encounter a certain difficulty. Although we know something about scholarly *views* of old age and about actual conditions in some elite families who left detailed records, we can only infer that these details were not universal norms. We actually know little about the treatment of the elderly among the silent majority of history.

With this in mind, let us begin with classical philosophy, which was often encoded into law as well as custom and had a major role in shaping the distribution and evolution of what we now think of as the classical Chinese type of family.

The origins of the Chinese family system are too ancient to be known by us, but Confucian scholarship tells us at least that kinship played a powerful role in the society as early as the sixth century B.C. Confucius considered the Zhou Dynasty (1050–700 B.C.) to have been the golden age, an age in which respect for harmony and order were at their peak; the government, benevolent; and the people, happy. He took as his main philosophic problem the restoration of this ancient order, and he believed that the answer lay in mutual respect among people, fostered through the perfection of individual character. The method of perfection was the performance of rituals, and the most important rituals were those venerating the ancestors. Neither Confucius nor Mencius (372–289 B.C.?) advocated a one-sided veneration of the aged by the young but rather sought to produce social harmony by clarifying and beautifying "natural" social virtues such as the love between parents and children. They proposed an analogy between social and personal evolution—that the achievement of proper character took time and that just as ancient societies (such as China) were usually more righteous than upstart ones, so the elderly were more likely to be wise than the young (Bauer, 1976; Murphy & Murphy, 1968).

The view of human nature held by Confucius and Mencius was obviously an optimistic one. People are naturally social and, if encouraged in their spontaneous sentiments, will produce a good society. The old will teach good habits; the young will listen and learn. But this optimistic view was soon challenged by the contrasting thought of Xun Zi (298?–238 B.C.), the Chinese version of Thomas Hobbes. Xun Zi and his followers distrusted human nature and emphasized the importance of keeping folly under control through the exercise of authority.

This view has played a major part in Chinese thought. Although Confucianists have liked to cite Mencius as their fountainhead, Bauer (1976) calls such protestations insincere. "[I]n the course of time, Confucianism actually inclined increasingly toward the conceptions of Hsun-tzu [Xun Zi]" (p. 49). Such a Confucianism was probably an encouragement to the strict enforcement of filial piety and ancestor worship and to the institutions that gradually evolved in support of these ideas.

In the T'ang Dynasty (618–906), Confucianism was systematically incorporated into laws that granted authority to parents and parent-figures throughout society, and these laws continued for many centuries. About the 13th century, for example, Gernet (1962) says:

> According to the T'ang Code [which was still in force] those who lifted a hand against parents or grandparents deserved to be beheaded. . . . A father who broke the bones of his son in administering an overdose of punishment was subject to a less severe penalty than if he had done the same to a stranger. (p. 145)

C. K. Yang (1959) notes that similar laws continued in force until the end of the Qing Dynasty in 1912.

The legal power of the elderly tended to gain strength as it was incorporated into classical Chinese culture, especially features of kinship groups and kinship-based magico-religious beliefs about fate, death, and the afterlife.

In all human societies, kinship ties—bonds of blood and marriage—link the individual to the larger groups of community and nation. There is still lively debate among China scholars about how best to describe the main features of descent, household and lineage organization, and authority that distinguish kinship, which varies considerably by class, region, and period. Anthropologist Maurice Freedman (1958, 1966) was the chief author of a widely held view we might call "the ideal of patrilineal descent." In this view, variation centers around a near-universal ideal, which affects not only the rules and forms of kinship but many other social institutions as well. This is the ideal that male descendants of a common male ancestor (and their wives and unmarried daughters) constitute a natural economic and religious unit and that joint action in these spheres should be a major principle of social life. According to this model, the usual rules favor an authority structure in which males are dominant and rank is determined by generation first, then age within generation. Because a woman joins her husband's descent group at marriage, the group consists of related males, their wives, and unmarried daughters. Sons share equally in the inheritance of their father's (and childless uncles') property. Household composition varies considerably. Much has been written about the ideal of the patrilineal extended family household—parents, their sons, and their sons' wives and children under one roof—but the most common historical household seems to have been a two-generational one of four to six people (Fried, 1973).

The descent group, or lineage, then, can be seen as a group of related households tracing their origin back to a common ancestor. The size, composition, and functions of this group have varied so greatly that I will not try to describe or explain it in detail. For some purposes, such as ancestor worship ceremonies, one might find hundreds of relatives, tracing their ancestry back five or six generations, working together—a form that developed gradually between about A.D. 1,000 and 1,300 (Ebrey, 1986). For other purposes, such as the arrangement of marriages and conduct of daily business, one might find the co-descendants of a common grandfather in the cooperative group (e.g., Potter, 1968).

In a highly unequal society, large lineages or lineage branches with much property (or good connections) conferred respect and influence on their members, but this might not have been its original purpose. Ebrey (1986) points out that lineage solidarity (a) developed following the Confucianist T'ang Code, which prescribed ancestor worship, and (b) was accompanied by the development of the paraphernalia of Confucian ritual: ancestral halls, lineage-owned fields whose income was set aside for ritual, and well-kept genealogies. The important point is that lineage came to play a vital role in securing a reputation and a livelihood, in the conduct of ritual, and in the sense of one's social identity and worth; and the lineage was ruled by its oldest male members.

These functions of the lineage developed in lockstep with post-T'ang Chinese religion. Personal fortune was thought to be closely tied to lineage fortune, which was in turn influenced by supernatural powers, many of which were subject to manipulation by lineage ritual or by the intervention of ancestral spirits. The extreme seriousness (not to mention expense) of funeral and memorial rites, both occasional and daily, so often noted in traditional China stemmed largely from popular belief in the efficacy of the rites themselves in securing good fortune. Partly, of course, they also stemmed from the more mundane desire to impress one's neighbors. Not only could ancestors confer good luck if well cared for, they could and would inflict harm if neglected. Even in modern times, Martin Yang (1945) could write about a village in Shandong Province: "A great part of the household activities is regulated by the invisible power of the ancestors" (p. 45).

To the extent that a family participated in this pattern, the elderly naturally exercised real authority over younger kin. Custom as well as law dictated that they should occupy the most honored positions in the family (the seats of honor at meals and ceremonies, the most polite speech and deferential gesture), as well as the first choice of limited resources (the best food and furniture, the allocation of extra money and goods). For the young, rebelliousness carried a serious price, just as compliance and concern conferred admiration if not success. Older members of such "Confucian ideal" families, at least, could indeed demand and get respectful behavior and material support in their waning years.

This description fits the rural situation in traditional China better than the urban. At least in the 19th and early 20th centuries, many city dwellers were so-called sojourners, or what we might call migrant workers today, keeping close ties with their families in the countryside, sending money home, and hoping to return as soon as finances permitted (Ikels, 1980; Lang, 1946; Skinner, 1977). For those unlucky enough to grow old in the city, there were surname and district associations, as well as trade guilds, that provided some sociability and security (Crissman, 1967; Ikels, 1980). These associations arranged credit, kept contact with the home district, and provided funerals for members. Although there was no formal retirement system, an employer would often keep a loyal older worker on in a gradually diminishing capacity "until he became perhaps little more than a 'night watchman' sleeping on the floor in the front of the shop in exchange for his meals" (Ikels, 1980, p. 90). Some urbanites without families could depend on same-age co-workers for collective security, and some managed to adopt children; but many grew less secure as their health and vigor faded, until they were destitute and isolated.

## Sentiment and Tradition

All of this tells us that the philosophical, religious, and legal views about the elderly *in families* tended to support their dignity and power, but it does not tell us much about the actual sentiments attending relations between the old and the young, even in respectable families. Human behavior, after all, is the result of customs and decrees that interact with personal feelings. On this question our materials come almost entirely from postclassical times, but we can probably infer certain continuities from the past. Chinese technology has changed slowly until now, especially in the countryside, and wholesale ideological reeducation did not begin until after the Communist revolution. Even in times of war and upheaval, a way of living and thinking that is millennia old is not likely to change too radically, and we shall see that even the strenuous attempts of the monolithic modern state to reshape the family may not have altered sentiments very much.

Of course, sentiments depend on the particulars of relationships as much as on cultural norms—the personalities and private circumstances of those involved. But perhaps we can find some broad social factors that have influenced feelings toward the elderly more or less systematically. I have already mentioned as one such factor the degree of an old person's involvement in family leadership, the only guarantee of the sort of respect for parents prescribed by Confucian tradition. In fact, economic leadership in the family has continued to reinforce Confucian practices in modern times, when they have lost much of the force of tradition. When Marjory Wolf (1968) asked a Taiwanese peasant why people spend a lot of money on funerals, her informant said, "Many people correct their old parents when they are still alive, saying, 'This is old-fashioned,' and 'That is no longer done.' But when their parents die they discover how good the old people were to them and wish they were still alive to advise them" (p. 44).

Certain other features of traditional Chinese culture, features not strictly related to age itself, have helped to reinforce acceptance of gerontocratic leadership. One is a relatively low priority placed on sexuality, erotic beauty, and romance; another is a preference to do business through stable reciprocal role relationships, as opposed to the ad hoc market relationships that are more popular in some Western societies, especially the United States (Davis-Friedmann, 1983).

The Western emphasis on individualism over familialism results in a relatively strong emphasis on physical attractiveness in heterosexual relationships. It is not only *good fortune* to be sexually attractive, in American culture it is also *important*—an emphasis that naturally places the elderly at a disadvantage. Eroticism in China, by contrast, occupies a place alongside epicureanism, desirable only if one can afford the luxury. In such a culture, the old are not seen as lacking anything physical of important social value.

The habit of getting one's needs met through the use of lifelong arrangements of mutual reciprocity also suggests the relative value of the old. The Chinese impulse is not so much to seek a partner who will deliver the most for the least, but to assure that value given will be returned in the long run, via the sense of obligation and indebtedness that develops between longtime allies. An old partner is a good partner, other things being equal.

To return, however, to the place of the old in the family, it is clear that not all families were alike. Influences on filial sentiment seem to have been the family's level of wealth and the value of the labor an old person was able to contribute. The relationship between family wealth and respect for the aged appears in a number of descriptions. Davis-Friedmann (1983) puts it succinctly in writing about pre-Communist China: "Few families were wealthy enough to sacrifice the interests of the economically strongest to those of the weakest" (p. 48). Martin Yang (1945) also notes that the aged in very poor rural families could not count on much filial support or feeling. Children in these families tended to establish separate households when they married; and although they were obligated to support their aged parents, they often showed little inclination to do more than the minimum. In such families, the superannuated old, who could no longer contribute to the hard work of survival, held little respect and were not much missed when they died. Yang also notes that parents who failed to husband the family property and pass it on to their children "were actively resented and quickly forgotten" when they died. The message of this to parents was, of course, quite clear. While young enough to work, they had a heavy obligation to build up family fortunes. In old age, their obligation to preserve the family wealth was no less serious. I will return to this when I discuss ancestor worship.

On the positive side, the conditions of rural life gave the aged ample opportunity to contribute to family well-being, even as their strength and health faded. Under preindustrial conditions, old people can do many of the less strenuous jobs that require patience and experience. The timing of work has to be planned, floodgates and fires watched, cookstoves fed, animals and people doctored and nursed, children minded, tools mended, prayers offered, ceremonies directed. Moreover, farm work tends to follow generational cycles and to reach a peak during the years when there are many children who are too young to produce as much as they eat. This period tends to correspond with the old age of the grandparents.

Many accounts, then, point to the close correspondence of filial sentiment and the elders' thriftiness and their contributions to family labor. Yang (1945) notes that the death of one who has long outlived his strength, far from being grieved, "is a relief to relatives and friends" (p. 12).

## Ancestor Worship

I have referred to traditional beliefs in the power of ancestral spirits to influence the fortunes of the living. These beliefs were part of a complex of ancestor worship that included elaborate funeral rituals and periodic ceremonies honoring the souls of the departed. As with other customs, the details varied according to era, locale, and social background, but on the whole such observances were the most elaborate and expensive events in village life, calling for large processions, accompanied by music, and great quantities of food, fireworks, wine, and ritual offerings.

The relationship between ancestor worship and the treatment of the living elderly was indirect and is difficult to reconstruct, but one arresting feature was the firm belief that the elders did not leave the nexus of the family when they died. On the contrary, even those who had held little authority when living often took on considerable stature and required considerable care and expense in the afterlife. They were honored with lavish funerals at death, received offerings of incense and prayers in daily life, and presided over the gathering of many descendants at annual rites.

The linkage between the degree of respect shown ancestors and the cost to the living may help to explain the strange fact that this complex has continued to inflict staggering costs on a relatively poor society for centuries. Traditional families were very much at the mercy of their oldest members, who had the legal right, at least, to dispose of family fortunes as they saw fit. But the combination of powerful *postmortem* status and costly ritual care put an additional burden on the *living* senior members of traditional families to look after the financial fortunes of their heirs. If they failed to do this, they might leave behind a family too poor to do them proper honor in the next life.

This relationship is implied in Francis Hsu's (1948) ethnographic work near Kunming, in Western China, in the 1930s. Hsu found that the living aged were not particularly venerated here and that they appeared to accept the indifference of the young philosophically. On the other hand, many were intensely interested in their own afterlives, taking great pleasure in the selection and design of their tombs and cultivating spiritual knowledge in preparation for ancestorhood. "[T]here are any number of elderly people," writes Hsu, "men and women, who are interested only in reading scriptures, becoming devotees in temples, ensuring the quality of his or her coffins and graveyards [*sic*], and preparing windsheets" (p. 132). In this village, incidentally, it was common to consult the dead directly by means of seances, and fear of angry ancestral ghosts was a pervasive concern.

We might summarize the gerontology of traditional China, then, by noting that it was not a gerontocracy but a lineage- and family-ocracy, in which both daily life and ritual revolved around the all-pervasive dependence of each individual on his or her network of kin. The virtual identity of age and respect grew from the authority structure of this system, a structure that was based on age and gender but also on performance.

## Posttraditional China

The end of traditional Chinese society was really not an event but a process, one that is still going on, in fact. From the fall of the Manchu government in 1912 until the Communist takeover in 1949 was a period of great upheaval, during which once more war and population movement disrupted lineage and family relations. This itself was not new in Chinese history, but the modern chaos was accompanied by an attack on Confucianism by Chinese intellectuals and social reformers.

It was also the period of the most intensive research to date by Western-trained scholars on everyday Chinese life. Much of what we know about the premodern culture comes from careful, on-site studies of villages and towns done in the 1920s and 1930s (Fei, 1939; Gamble, 1954; Hsu, 1948; Lang, 1946; Yang, 1945).

Blows to the prestige and comfort of the elderly were many in the first half of the present century. In the near-continuous political upheaval of the period—especially the Republican movement of 1911, the May Fourth movement of 1919, and the Second Revolution of the mid-1920s—educated urban youth surged into political leadership in great numbers (Yang, 1959), bringing with them a taste for Western values and ideas and a disdain for Confucian teaching. The war with Japan and the Communist insurgency of the 1930s and 1940s displaced many families from their land and scattered them across the subcontinent and beyond. Traditional village organization was in many cases replaced by youthful cadres during the revolution.

These changes undoubtedly produced extreme hardship for those elderly who lost or were separated from their children and/or their land and possessions. For those lucky enough to have preserved their livelihood and family position, there must have been great insecurity, resulting from both overall social instability and legal changes that undercut their power in the family. But customs and sentiments rarely change much in a mere half-century; and judging by the ethnographies, the general conditions of classic society continued into the 1940s in rural areas that survived the wars.

Estimates of the numbers of elderly during this period vary from source to source, but Gamble (1954) gives the proportion of those over 65 in the general population as 5.5% in 1930, exactly the same as in the United States at that time. Thirty-two percent of the household heads in his village of 5,000 families were over 65, and 4% were over 70, figures that match reasonably well with the rates of three-generation households in rural Korea and Japan at about the same time.

## Aging in the People's Republic

Protection of the status of the old has not been a major priority in Communist China, but neither have the elders been neglected. Confucian values are often identified with the evils of pre-Communist rule, and the old are sometimes patronized in official literature as long-suffering but ignorant reminders of an unjust past. The young are encouraged to show compassion for them, however, and laws require their material support in the family and community. Denunciation of aged parents and teachers met with official acquiescence if not approval during the cultural revolution, although it seems to have been limited to that peculiar movement. In 1983, the government established a National Committee on Aging with local committees in every province. These committees are charged with educating the public on the economic importance of the elderly, with seeking ways to improve the lot of the old, and with seeing that official policies benefiting the old are carried out (Olson, 1990).

Whatever the priorities of the current govenment, the lives of the elderly appear considerably improved in some respects over pre-Communist times. Deborah Davis-Friedmann (1983) records that there is an "easy rapport" between the young and the old throughout China now and that the grandparental generation are proud of their age. One analysis of modern Chinese literature concludes that grandparents were seen in a more positive light in the 1960s than they had been at any time since the 1930s (Chen, 1970).

Life expectancy has been rising quite dramatically. In 1950 it was 53.9 years for men and 50.22 for women (Mathews & Mathews, 1983) and now stands at 66.4 years for men and 69.3 years for women (China State Statistics Bureau, 1966). This, of course, is largely the result of declining infant mortality. In the last census (1982) the over-60 population was 7.67%; the over-65, 4.9%, or 49 million people (China State Statistics Bureau, 1986). The fact that this is a lower rate than Gamble (1954) reported for 1930 is probably a reflection of two things: (a) the boom in population between the mid-1950s, when health care and nutrition began to improve, and the mid-1970s, when vigorous family planning efforts were instituted; and (b) the decimation of the over-65 generation, who were young adults during the Sino-Japanese War and the revolution. All retired urban workers are now covered by national health insurance, which provides free preventive checkups as well as free care (Olson, 1990).

The well-being of the old, in spite of official anti-Confucianism, stems partly from the tenacity of cultural attitudes and partly from improvements in living standards that have materially helped the old. Better material conditions have resulted from better bealth care and nutrition, a more equal distribution of wealth, and a fairly stable economy. In urban areas, guaranteed job security, pensions, and housing allowances have especially helped the older workers. The Chinese wage system emphasizes seniority, so older workers usually make substantially more than the young do. Since 1978, workers with 15 to 18 years of service retire on 70% of their maximum wage, with the result that many retirees have larger incomes than their working children.

In the cities there are even retirement homes for those pitiful figures of former times, the childless elderly. High employment rates and stable wages have also made it possible for more people to get married, thereby avoiding childlessness in late life. Although the rural elderly have not shared equally in these blessings, they have been helped by government restrictions on population movement, which have tended to preserve rural families by keeping the sons at home. We will see the importance of this when we take up the case of the Korean elderly.

Health improvements have had several effects. A higher infant survival rate means more living children and grandchildren in old age. For the time being, this means both fewer childless aged and greater numbers of children, increasing the chance that at least one will shoulder the burden of caring for parents. This situation will pass once the current generation of young parents, with their small families, reaches old age. The present population boom also means more crowding in urban areas, but privacy has never been as important in China as it is in the West. Since the mid-1970s, the boom has created chronic unemployment among youth, but since 1978 even this has worked to the advantage of many older workers. In that year it became possible for retiring workers in state-owned factories (some 16% of the population) to pass their jobs directly to successors in their own families. This is an example of a pro-youth policy, designed to provide jobs by encouraging retirement and supporting the status of the aged. Like passing on property at death in former times, it tends to strengthen the authority of the prospective retiree.

In the countryside, meanwhile, old people once again live much as they did before the collectivization period of 1956–1983, working hard as members of a family economy. Davis-Friedmann (1983) writes: "Leisure among the rural elderly is a privilege reserved for a tiny minority" (p. 19). Children are legally required to care for their parents in the countryside, and poor households, including the childless elderly, also have the "five guarantees" from their community: food, fuel, clothing, education, and burial. Women generally retire from field labor when their first grandchild is born and carry out the traditional grandparental chores at home, thereby freeing daughters-in-law for outside labor. Many old people contribute importantly to the rural family economy by growing cash crops for private sale.

The government's official attack on Confucianism is expressed in a 1950 law that gives children the right to choose their own mates and a 1959 law that forbids parents to betroth their minor children, collect a bride price, or demand a dowry. The custom of extravagant funerals has been criticized repeatedly by officialdom, and during the Great Leap Forward, in 1958, the government even tried to remove graveyards from arable land and outlaw all but the simplest funeral customs. The following year many lineage temples were seized and converted to productive use, a move the Nationalists had tried in the 1930s. These measures were largely forgotten after the failure of the economic policy that prompted them, but the Cultural Revolution of 1966 to 1970 witnessed the return of vigorous criticism of Confucian-style ritual. In recent years the norm of lavish funerals has come back yet again.

The fate of efforts to diminish ancestor worship and eradicate the cult of the lineage illustrates the tenacity of entrenched customs. Even though urbanization and industrialization have eroded some of the conditions that promote family solidarity and personal network formation in Chinese society, the family ideals remain strong when compared with those of the West. The elderly continue to embody family values in situations where they create the family with their labor, nurturing it even in their waning years. There they continue to be symbols of family honor and continuity, perhaps even more than before, as other aspects of the society change. In balance, the anti-Confucian revolution seems to have improved their lives, a fact that reveals something about Confucianism as well: Like culture itself, Confucianism is not the slavish repetition of dead ideas but the articulation of a framework of vital traditions. What matters is not so much what those traditions are called but how they help to accomplish work and give meaning to life.

The Chinese Communist government finds the traditional functions of the family system extremely useful. Families assure the care of the dependent, organize work, and teach obedience to authority. But the survival of familialism has preserved some of its other functions as well.

In the face of official ideology, it contributes vital meaning to the lives of young and old alike, greatly strengthening their sense of purpose, continuity, and belonging. The survival of these functions in turn assures the continued security and prestige of the elderly. It also puts limits on the kinds of policies any government can enforce.

## KOREA: CONFUCIAN MELTDOWN

China and Korea share a long history, and the similarities between the traditional societies are so great that the latter is often treated as a variation of the former. Although there is much regional and class variation in Korea, the pattern of lineage organization and the Confucian basis of law and ritual are indeed very familiar to the Sinologist. If anything, the Confucian emphasis on the duty of sons to fathers has traditionally been stronger in Korea than in many parts of China.

From the viewpoint of gerontology, important differences between the two societies can be found in the area of kinship. The traditional Korean kinship system resembled the Chinese insofar as it was patriarchal and patrilineal, with large lineage organizations playing important economic and political roles. Also like China, rank was determined by sex, generation, and age, giving the oldest male of the oldest generation authority in the household as well as the lineage. The strength of patriarchal authority can be gathered from the notes of a French missionary (Dallet, 1874):

> A son must never play with his father nor smoke before him nor assume too free a posture in his presence, and so in well-to-do families there is a special apartment where he can be at ease with his friends. A son is the father's servant. Oftentimes he brings him meals, serves him at table, and prepares his bed. He must greet him respectfully when he leaves the house and when he comes back. If the father is old or sick, the son hardly leaves him for an instant, and sleeps nearby so as to provide him with all his needs. If the father is in prison, the son comes to live in the vicinity. (p. 128)
>
> No virtue, in Korea, is esteemed and honored as much as filial piety, none is taught with more care, none is more magnificently recompensed by exemptions from taxes, by the erection of monumental columns or even temples, and by honors and public offices. (p. 129)

The chief difference between Korean and Chinese kinship was in the manner of inheritance and the ideal family structure. Whereas Chinese sons expected to share in their father's property, the Koreans preferred primogeniture. The important family property—typically land—went to the oldest son, who in turn bore the burden of caring for the elderly parents. Younger sons were expected to form their own households once they married, so the typical structure was the two- or three-generation household containing a married couple, their unmarried children, and their oldest son's wife and unmarried children, if any. This contrasts with the Chinese ideal (not often achieved in practice, as I have noted), in which married brothers would live together under one roof.

Rules for the succession of fathers and sons differed from place to place within Korea. In the southwest, for example, fathers held family headship until they died, whereas in Cheju Island, they retired when their oldest son married (Lee, 1975). Mothers often retired after the age of 60 or so as well, handing over to their daughters-in-law the key to the family rice granary.

But as with China, the discussion of aging is complicated by the fact that Korea too had a system of endogamous social classes, which differed considerably in custom and life-style. In recent times the important Korean classes have been the landed gentry, or *yangban,* and peasants. In historical accounts of Korean customs it is seldom clear just which class is being observed. Dallet (1874, quoted above), for example, was probably writing about customs among upper-class Koreans rather than those of the average peasant, but he does not say. Ethnographic works since World War II have tended to focus exclusively on the peasant class (Han, 1977; Lee, 1975; Osgood, 1951). Judging by the accounts of my own Korean friends, the problem persists in Korean ethnography today. The modern history of the peninsula has been extremely turbulent and poorly documented at the level of everyday life. There is still little sociological study of class differences and only a perception that such differences are indeed important.

Japan invaded Korea in 1895, and in 1910, after 15 years of bloody fighting, fully occupied the country, ruling until the end of World War II. During that period, the Japanese government was consciously using Confucian principles in the homeland as the moral hasis of a patriarchal regime. This principle was extended to Korea, in an attempt to keep control over a rebellious population through instruction in filial piety. By this strategy, the Japanese also hoped to secure the loyalty of the *yangban,* some of whom saw their own interest in the preservation of the authoritarian tradition.

The invaders were natural targets for the militant nationalism that was sweeping Asia at the time. Many young Koreans learned nationalist politics in America (and also, ironically, in Japan) and began to build opposition to the repressive Japanese rule. Anything the Japanese promoted took on the taint of accommodationism, with the result that many nationalists denounced Confucian practices, more than a few converting to Christianity to avoid taking part in ancestor worship.

As in China during the same period, however, political opposition to ancient practices apparently had only a superficial and temporary effect, at least in the rural areas and among the traditional elite. The authority of the elders in the family remained strong, the three-generation household remained the preferred type, and traditional funeral and memorial customs continued where they were economically and logistically possible. Osgood (1951) found that half of the households in rural Kanghwa Island were of the three- or four-generation type, and the rest were nuclear families, so there were no elderly living alone in his village in 1949. Lee (1975) found that three-generation households were 29% of a rural village in Ch'ung-ch'ong-buk-do Province in 1971, and Han (1977) found them to be 23% of a fishing village off the southern tip of the peninsula at about the same time. Given that the over-60 population ran at about 5% to 7% in these villages and family size at around six members, it is reasonable to assume that most old people lived with children in parts of rural Korea until at least the mid-1970s. The ethnographies also show the continuity of patriarchal authority within the three-generation family in these villages. In discussing the Korean elderly since 1945, of course, I must limit my remarks to South Korea, as I have almost no information on the north.

In the past 40 years, the big challenge to the traditional culture has come from urbanization. The urban portion of the population tripled between 1940 and 1966, from 11.6% to 33.6%, and it continues to rise. In 1988 alone, the net migration to South Korea's eight largest cities was 313,491, a staggering 7.8% of the national population. The population of Seoul reached nearly 10 million in 1986, having doubled in the past 10 years; Pusan and other metropolitan centers are growing at about the same rate (National Bureau of Statistics, 1989).

This translates into a major drain of young people, especially men, from rural areas. Families are being dispersed, there is a mania for modern education, and living conditions in the cities have become so crowded that many children have no room to keep their parents with them. The trend also leads to the replacement of family and village functions by bureaucratic structures, as business and government offer more services. In the long run, Korea has entered the typical industrial cycle of improved health, rising life expectancy, lower birth rates, and the so-called graying of the population. Life expectancy at birth now stands at 69 years for women and 63 for men; but women aged 65 can expect another 14 years of life; men, another 10 years. The proportion of those over 65 in the population rose from 3.1% in 1972 to 4.5% in 1985 (National Bureau of Statistics, 1989).

As usual, the effects of the process on the aged are mixed. The depletion of the rural population means many elderly must choose between a lonely and isolated life in their rural villages and moving to an overcrowded city, where many lack knowledge of both the physical terrain and the habits and skills necessary for independence. Life in an industrial city is still so new to most Koreans that they have not developed the needed basic sensitivity to the needs of strangers. In the anonymous crowded streets, buses, and apartment buildings, old people are rudely shoved aside or narrowly missed, sometimes with an insulting shout in the bargain.

In the traditional society, nearly all social transactions were *particularistic,* meaning that they involved long-term relationships based on mutual personal familiarity and trust, reciprocal obligation, and well-understood ritual and etiquette. Of course, this is impossible in rapidly growing cities, where most transactions are anonymous and where residents come together from different regions with different traditions and habits. The solitary elderly Korean in Seoul or Pusan is likely to get poor service and rude treatment, for the same reason he or she would in New York or Los Angeles: Anyone slow and uncomprehending is simply "in the way."

Idleness and isolation are also serious problems of the Korean elderly today. Farming has declined as the staple of family income, and the skills of the elderly are less needed. Although most old people of all social classes make an effort to be useful, many cannot find even menial jobs. I have noted the shift from multigenerational households, common in the countryside, to nuclear, one-person, and couple-only households in the city. Lee (1975) found that even in the early 1970s the proportion of three-generation households in Seoul was only 14%, half the rate in a small rural village a few hours to the south, suggesting a lonely and isolated life for many elders who move to the city.

However, this interpretation of housing patterns is not always justified. Cultural gerontologists tend to assume that separate housing imposes a hardship on the aged in familistic societies, but my experience in Japan suggests that this is an overly simple view. True, some elderly will be forced against their will, by crowding, high rents, and unfilial children, to live apart from their families as a result of urbanization. For others, however, living separately is the expression of a preference, made possible by a rising standard of living. Remember there is often little for the elderly to do in an urban household, especially if the grandchildren are in school. As telephones and cheap public transportation become more available, separate living need not mean loneliness, and it may be an attractive option for those elderly healthy enough to look after themselves.

Even with regard to financial and emotional support, the modern Korean situation is not completely bleak. Pension systems are not yet well developed, but a remaining strong sense of filial responsibility, together with a rising standard of living among the young, contributes to improved living conditions for many grandparents. The government is trying to combat boredom and social isolation among the urban elderly by promoting senior centers and old people's clubs, with some success. One study found that about two-thirds of the elderly in each of two Seoul neighborhoods regularly took part in the Old People's Association, which provided entertainment, social contact, and a certain amount of health screening and education (Chin, 1990). The goal of the government is to achieve 100% participation in these associations nationwide in the next few years.

By far the greatest assets of most Korean elderly, however, remain the sentiment that holds families together and the tenacity of Confucian attitudes of respect. Young people generally show more deference to their elderly relatives than do Westerners. Among the more prosperous lineages, ancestor worship is not only still performed, it has taken on new importance as a vehicle of conspicuous consumption for the newly affluent (Chin, 1990). Funerals and 60th-birthday celebrations, although changing in form to accommodate social change, are still major events in family life. The new affluence of many young people has even added a dimension to filial feeling: They view their own success as the direct result of their parents' self-sacrifice and suffering. Under the circumstances, Korean elders show the same easy confidence and pride in their seniority that Western visitors to China find remarkable there.

There are both differences and similarities between China and Korea affecting the lives of the elderly, then. The greatest difference is that the booming Western-style economy of Korea has greatly raised the national living standard but at the cost of severe disruption of families and a growing disparity in wealth between the rich and the poor. Chinese policies restricting population movement tend to keep rural families together and to minimize the problems of urban unemployment and overcrowding that afflict the Koreans. Second, the South Korean government has put a priority on economic development and has paid less attention to pensions and other minimum guarantees for the elderly than the Chinese have.

The similarities are striking, given the very different recent histories of the two Confucian-based cultures. In both China and Korea, age-old traditions of family solidarity and the delegation of respect and leadership to the elderly have acted as a brake on the shift of power from old to young that is widely believed to accompany modernization (Cowgill & Holmes, 1972). This brings us to the case of Japan, the East Asian culture that has moved the farthest toward a Western-style market-industrial economy.

## JAPAN

### Traditional Culture

Adapting ideas from other cultures seems to have been a talent of the Japanese from their prehistoric beginnings. Chinese influences appeared before the writing of Japanese history in the sixth century A.D. and thereafter really transformed the culture over the next 300 years. Buddhism was relatively strong in China in the sixth century and was the first major institution to be borrowed by the Japanese, but critical Confucian influences also entered by the early seventh century. The "Seventeen Article Constitution" of Prince Shotoku gave Japan its first formal semblance of a ruling code in 604. The first article pays homage to Buddhism, but the other 16 articles "read like a Confucian tract" (Reischauer & Fairbank, 1958, p. 476), seeking to make Japan's loosely organized feudal estates into a central hierarchical kingdom.

Buddhism, Confucianism, and many other Chinese and Korean ideas were added onto prehistoric Japan's religion, politics, and ethics, forming an alloy that proved to be, like the ancient Japanese sword, both durable and flexible. The result was a culture that resembled classical China's in its hierarchical structure, its strong family basis, its reverence for the aged and the dead, and its taste for formal rules and rituals.

But Japan was different in some ways that have important bearing on the status of her elderly. Even before Chinese writing made historiography possible, the Japanese seem to have had a social organization based on middle-sized territorial units, held together by bonds of kinship and *fictive* kinship, for the purpose of efficient collective work. The ethical and psychological core of these groups was orchestrated effort on behalf of the group as a whole—a quality Befu (1962) calls "corporate emphasis." It was an emphasis on the responsibility of the individual to collectivity that resulted in ascending pyramids of loyalty, uniting individuals in households, households in extended families, and extended families in larger territorial productive and defensive units.

Like Chinese and Koreans, traditional Japanese tended to delegate authority to the senior males of their collectivities and to rely heavily on kinship bonds. They tended to practice patrilineal primogeniture, passing assets and authority on to the oldest son of the senior male. But they always seemed to have their eye on the goal of promoting the collective interest first and respected formal rules mainly as a gesture (albeit an important one) in the interest of public relations. Hence, the well known Japanese habits of separating title from real authority and credit from real accomplishment, of making ad hoc situations and relationships *look* traditional, and of holding the whole group responsible for the actions of the individual.

In a formalistic society with strong Confucian elements, this meant that the aged, especially men, received respect and obedience in public but in private often deferred to more capable subordinates. It also meant that the responsibility of the individual for the well-being of the group did not end with physical decline or retirement but continued until—and beyond—death. The coincidence of formal respect and informal sentiment often depended on the degree to which the old person contributed to the peace and well-being of the collectivity. On the other hand, the care of the aged was an important responsibility of younger relatives, especially daughters-in-law, to the collectivity also.

Japanese social morality also has another quality that seems less developed on the East Asian continent, a brand of nationalism that one finds only in a relatively homogeneous, relatively isolated island nation. For many centuries, Japanese civilization developed inwardly, with intense commerce among its local cultures and only sporadic contact with the outside world. The result is that the average Japanese has a very strong indentity—call it national or cultural—as a Japanese. Words like *kokutai*, the "body national," and *Yamato minzoku seishin*, the "timeless Japanese character," enter easily into their speech.

What has this to do with aging? A great deal, I believe. The corporateness of traditional Japanese life, together with the almost mystical sense of oneness with other Japanese, had a profound effect on people's social conscience. Virtually everyone belonged not only to a family but also to some larger collectivity—village, urban neighborhood, Buddhist monastery, commercial enterprise—and shared in the fate of all of its loyal members. The result was (and still is) a remarkable optimism among all levels of society, from hereditary royalty to the poorest peasant. Although the Japanese worldview had its cynical side, expressed for example in Buddhistic fatalism, the general level of commitment to the whole society was remarkably strong compared with most other civilizations.

The result of this, in turn, was a high value on generalized altruism and empathy as character traits. Overt aggression certainly had its place in war or revenge, but even then it was not to be enjoyed. I believe this is partly what Joseph Campbell (1962) meant when he said of Japan, "as no where else in the world, one has the sense there of a permeation of the social body by a spirit essentially heroic and aristocratic" (p. 462).

Without an understanding of this optimism and capacity for empathy, often naive to the Western eye, one cannot grasp the Japanese feeling for the aged. It is not so much that the aged were revered as that one's character was likely to be measured by one's compassion for them, especially the sick and the frail. To neglect, mistreat, or ignore one's elders was more than a breach of manners; it was a sign of defective character. Of course, the aged themselves would be judged by their compassion for the young.

As in Korea and to some extent in China, the cultural ideal upheld a comfortable and pleasant old age. Late-life birthdays, starting with the 60th and including the 66th, 77th, and 88th, were joyous occasions, when family and friends could show their pleasure at having a loved one reach such a ripe age. After retirement, old men were free to wear red (a color symbolic of childhood) and to indulge in preferred foods, pastimes, and drink. Older women also were allowed increased license when it came to liquor, sexual joking, and a relaxed and open style in their relations with men. It was important for the young not only to attend to the health and sustenance of their feeble elders but to indulge the old person's feelings as well.

Lest the picture of aging in the traditional society seem unreal, of course one must mention a few problems. With poor sanitation and nutrition for most people, there was the sheer unlikelihood of reaching old age. Life expectancy at birth was about 50 years in the 1800s, and the over-65 portion of the population was less than 5%. Family life also had its difficulties. Japanese brides, like Chinese and Korean brides, were required to leave their natal home and live with their husbands. If the husband was an eldest son, this meant that the bride was under the strict control of her mother-in-law, and the relationship was often a miserable one. Many brides spent the first quarter-century of their marriages plotting their revenge, which would, of course, be exacted upon their own sons' wives. The position of mother-in-law itself, then, was generally looked upon with suspicion, the more so because of the Japanese distaste for overt conflict. The ambivalence of the young toward the old is preserved in figures of everyday speech, like *umeboshi baba* (dried-plum crone), and *jiji kusai* (like an old codger).

## The Transition to Modernity

Japan's transition to modernity began in the mid-1800s and progressed quickly. A group of well-educated petty nobility seized power from the bankrupt and ineffectual feudal government and pushed through sweeping reforms in education, law, economics, and government. There were, of course, revolts and intrigues during this transition, but the willingness of the average citizen to wait, perhaps naively, for promised reforms was undoubtedly indispensable to the speedy success of the reformers' efforts. They were also helped by the fact that the West had preceded them not long before, giving them plenty of examples both of success and of failure.

The Japanese leaders decided that Confucian morality and the strength of the Asian-style family would help stabilize their new nation through the modernization process. They made laws strengthening the position of parents in the family and requiring the young to support their aged relatives. They developed universal public education and made sure that Confucian morality loomed large in the curriculum. In all of their propaganda, the nation and the family were portrayed as moral equivalents and as objects of reverence and self-sacrifice.

This strategy apparently worked well in Japan, the result being a people almost fanatically devoted to both national and family goals. Reverence for the old did not seem to be a contradiction, even in a modernizing society in which the knowledge held by the elderly was often obsolete: The corporate emphasis on group life allowed the old to defer to the young in technical matters and the young to show their seniors respect while themselves taking leadership in the emerging culture. In short, new skills could be added to the group repertoire without challenging many of the traditional customs.

As education and living standards rose, the small group continued to be the focus of social life and the basis of productivity and security. Families, businesses, even neighborhoods and villages, pooled resources and absorbed losses during the turbulent growth years. There was remarkably little cynicism, even during the bad years of World War II, and the position of the elderly within the small group remained one of honor and security. There were some family-less old people who had to rely on charity for survival, but they seem to have been scarce. Communities and temples built shelters to house them, but there were only 23 such shelters in Japan in 1913, ranging in size from "several" to 30 beds. By 1941, there were still only 130 homes (Kinoshita & Kiefer, 1991).

Life in the rural areas changed only slowly during this period, and the three-generation household continued to be the ideal form. As late as 1960, 34% of the households in rural Japan contained at least two adult generations—that is, parents and their married children (Koyama, 1962)—comparable to the rural Korean and Chinese rates in recent times. In many of these Japanese households, the aged parents retire and pass the headship on to the children; but both law and custom encourage deference and generosity toward them.

Low-cost public health insurance plans were mandated in 1938, run by local governments and voluntary associations. Pensions for most workers retiring after the age of 55 were required beginning in 1942 (Dore, 1963). Many retirees received sizable retirement bonuses amounting to about a year's salary, but the 1942 law also required companies with more than five employees to pay pensions of approximately one-third of salary. The law was complicated, and it is difficult to know how many older workers actually benefited from it or to what extent.

By 1945, the end of Japan's disastrous attempt at empire-building, the country had learned how to construct and operate a fully modern industrial economy using many of the traditional social tools—especially the Confucian-style family and the small quasi-family corporate group. The economy now lay in shambles, but the Japanese people on the whole seemed to share the hardship of defeat with tolerable equality. The great majority of the elderly continued as respected and reasonably secure members of families, judging by early postwar ethnographies (Dore, 1963; Benedict, 1949).

## Postwar Japan

Since the war, the story of Japan's elderly has been dominated by their phenomenal proliferation in the population. In the early decades of the 20th century, the proportion of those over 65 in the population was typical of the rest of the industrial world—about 5%. It remained at this level until after World War II, then began a dramatic climb to its present rate of 11.9% and rising. In 30 more years, the Japanese expect to have 12% of their population *over 75* and 23% over 65. Since World War II, men's life expectancy at birth has risen from 50 years to almost 75; women's, from 54 years to 80.5; making Japan the most longevous nation in the world. The gains have naturally followed rising incomes and health standards, now among the highest in the world as well.

The Japanese themselves, avid consumers of statistics, are both fascinated and troubled by this aging boom. Popular magazines are full of articles on retirement, geriatric health, and the care of old parents. Bookstores devote long shelves to these subjects, and television and films are full of advice and drama about growing old.

Much of this interest is solicitous of the gray-haired set, but there are also signs of resentment. Faced with the possibility of a mother-in-law who may live another 40 or 50 years, today's brides are reluctant to marry oldest sons without some guarantee of separate quarters. The rate of old age dependency is viewed with alarm by many young parents, whose priority is on the education of their children. When national health care costs began to soar in the 1970s, many were quick to blame the elderly and to call for a curtailment of geriatric services.

The position of the national government is to encourage veneration of the aged and to expect the families of the dependent elderly to carry most of the financial and in-kind burden of caring for them. "Honor the Aged Day" is a national holiday; well-known elderly artists, writers, and craftsmen are named "Living Cultural Treasures." In 1958 the National Health Insurance Law was passed, providing low-cost health benefits to all Japanese who were not already covered, and these benefits soon grew to cover 70% of most medical costs for the aged. The 1963 Law for the Welfare of the Aged improved geriatric health services and pensions nationwide, and in 1973 full health coverage was declared free for the elderly. In that year also, pensions were substantially improved so that they approached Western standards of wage replacement in some industries (Kiefer, 1990).

Still, there is a good deal of controversy in Japan about who should do what for the elderly. Three-fourths of Japan's young adults agree that aged parents should live with their children, at least if they are too frail to live alone (Prime Minister's Office, 1982), but the proportion of old people actually living with their children has gradually declined over the years, from almost 9 out of 10 in 1960 to about 7 out of 10 today. This probably reflects improvements in the financial and physical vigor of the elderly themselves, as well as improved services to support the independent but frail ones. Like old people everywhere, Japanese elders like to see their children fairly often but not be squeezed together into inadequate space.

The strong commitment of the individual to the family and community in Japan does not cease in old age. Although the average septuagenarian now has a reasonably secure income and access to essential services, few are content to give up trying to contribute. One out of every three Japanese over 65 works and on the whole is more willing to take a low-paid, menial second job than are American retirees.

In the light of this sense of responsibility, the new longevity contains a troubling paradox. A life prolonged by modern medicine and sanitation means not only a longer *productive* life; for most people it also means a longer *post*productive life, a lingering frailty and impairment before death. When questioned about what they fear most, the Japanese aged answer much as the aged in every advanced society do: they fear endless helplessness under the laborious care of their offspring. There are even shrines and temples where Japanese elderly go to pray for a speedy death.

The desire of self-reliance is seen in the recent boom in retirement housing in Japan. At least those who have substantial cash (typically from the sale of property) can buy into one of the many new apartment complexes for the aged. A growing number of these so-called Silver Business condos offer health care and homemaker services in addition to organized activities, meals, and, of course, private living space.

The impression this trend gives, to Japanese as well as foreign eyes, is that the Confucian family is gradually being replaced by the checkbook and the professional geriatric caregiver, Western-style. The sarcasm this evokes is not completely justified in my view. Even Confucianists like privacy and autonomy, and although the Japanese have become accustomed to living in much smaller quarters than Westerners do, the quality of the average retirement community is quite good, even by the most modern standards.

In sum, Japan is an example of a society with strong Confucian traditions that has become remarkably like Western societies in its material culture and government. The aged there appear, for the time being, to be relatively respected, integrated, and secure, as they do relative to the young in China and Korea, and certainly they are a lot wealthier. Being affluent in an affluent society, they have many more choices than do their Confucian brethren elsewhere, but there have been some obvious losses as well. The sight of the impaired elderly—the bedridden, the housebound, the helpless—dependent on the generosity and sweat of the young for survival, is increasingly common there. It is a sight that causes the middle-aged and the still-healthy old some sleepless nights.

## THE LESSONS OF ASIA

From about the T'ang Dynasty until the mid-19th century, some 900 years, household, lineage/village, and state formed the three levels of social integration in traditional East Asian cultures. True, there were major changes during this period. Population quintupled in China between the 15th and 19th centuries, a time during which the semi-autonomous village economy gave way to a heavy dependence on commercial farming and cottage industry (Eastman, 1988). However, cultural change was gradual until about the 1850s, after which we can no longer speak of East Asia as "traditional."

In the traditional period, the household, under the headship of the oldest male, directed daily work and worship, wielding the scepter of custom as well as the threats of expulsion and direct punishment in its rule. In some areas, patrilineal, patriarchal lineages and villages existed, and these functioned to maximize the power and wealth of their members and thereby spread a Confucian ideology. These organizations, along with a host of voluntary and governmental institutions, organized collective work and ritual at the intermediate level. Households provided wealth, leadership, and ritual support to the lineage and village in return for protection, prestige, support in time of need, special services (like teaching and medicine) and help with large undertakings. Lineages and other intermediate institutions in turn supplied the state with order and the discipline of their members, with education and talent, with trade and commerce, and with taxes. In return, the state provided an avenue for upward mobility through honors and wealth and, intermittently at least, kept peace between lineages and villages. The result in the more settled rural areas of East Asia was, for long periods, a slow rate of technological change and a relatively homogeneous culture in which cooperation in face-to-face groups was the norm.

These factors seem to support the well-being of the aged. Slow change and homogeneity support the usefulness of old people's knowledge of technique and custom. Close cooperation uses their knowledge of people and assures that they will not be abandoned in need. After the 15th century, high population density also became a factor, tending to hold families close together and to lend unusual authority to family leaders. The three-generation household, though never the majority pattern, has tended to remain fairly strong as an ideal in modern times. It is, as I have discussed, an institution well adapted to agricultural production with simple technology.

Given the strength of this basic cultural framework in large parts of East Asia for nearly a millennium, it is not surprising that the social position of the aged has been relatively strong in all three societies. Perhaps the most important lesson is that the effect of the basic cultural pattern seems to hold fairly constant, even though it was never universal in any of these cultures and even though the three have taken dramatically different paths toward modernization. China maintains an anti-Confucian policy while still supporting the status of the aged in the lineage and village. The slow pace of industrialization there, together with the shortage of housing and jobs, has also lent strength to the traditional role of the aged. Korea has opted for a policy of laissez-faire development, with resulting explosive growth and internal migration. Even there the family retains important functions as caretaker of the dependent aged. Japan consciously used Confucianism as a source of social control and economic stability during a century of industrialization. But because the pattern of leadership there always allowed for the separation of symbolic role and economic function, the aged retained prestige even when their skills were obsolete. With these lessons in mind, perhaps we can look with new eyes at the role of the aged in the modernization of the West. To some extent industrialization has given us the Western family, and to some extent it has been the other way around.

## REFERENCES


Bauer, W. (1976). *China and the search for happiness.* New York: Seabury Press.

Befu, H. (1962). Corporate emphasis and patterns of descent in the Japanese family. In R. Smith & R. Beardsley (Eds.), *Japanese culture: Its development and characteristics* (pp. 34–41), Chicago: Aldine.

Benedict R. (1946). *The chrysanthemum and the sword.* Boston: Houghton Mifflin.

Campbell, J. (1962). *The masks of God: Oriental mythology.* New York: Viking Press.

Chen, A. (1970). Family relations in modern China fiction. In M. Freeman (Ed.), *Family and kinship in Chinese society,* (pp. 94–103) Stanford, CA: Stanford University Press.

Chin, S. (1990). *Late life rituals in Korea and among Koreans in America.* Unpublished doctoral dissertation, University of California, San Francisco.

China State Statistics Bureau. (1986). *Yearbook of China 1986.* Oxford: Oxford University Press.

Cowgill, D., & Holmes, L. (1972). *Aging and modernization.* New York: Appleton-Century-Crofts.

Crissman, L. W. (1967). The segmentary structure of urban overseas Chinese communities. *Man, 2*(2), 185–204.

Dallet, C. (1984). *Histoire de l'Eglise de Coree* Human Relations Area Files (Trans.). Paris: Victor Palme. (Original work published 1874)

Davis-Friedmann, D. (1981). Chinese families and the four modernizations. In R. Oxnam & R. Bush (Eds.), *China briefing 1981* (pp. 67–77). Boulder, CO: Westview Press.

Davis-Friedmann, D. (1983). *Long lives: Chinese elderly and the Communist revolution.* Cambridge, MA: Harvard University Press.

Dore, R. (1963). *City life in Japan.* Berkeley: University of California Press.

Eastman, L. E. (1988). *Family, fields, and ancestors.* New York: Oxford University Press.

Ebrey, P. (1986). The early stages of descent group organization. In P. Ebrey (Ed.), *Kinship organization in late imperial China: 1000–1940* (pp. 16–61). Berkeley: University of California Press.

Fei, H. (1939). *Peasant life in China: A field study of peasant life in the Yangtse Valley.* London: Routledge & Kegan Paul.

Freedman, M. (1958). *Lineage organization in southeastern China.* London: Athlone.

Freedman, M. (1966). *Lineage and society: Fukien and Kwangtung.* London: Athlone.

Fried, M. (1973). China: An anthropological overview. In J. Meskill & J. M. Gentzler (Eds.), *An introduction to Chinese civilization* (pp. 341–378). New York: Columbia University Press.

Fukutake, T. (1967). *Asian rural society: China, India, Japan*. Seattle: University of Washington Press.

Gamble, S. (1954). *Ting Shien: A north China rural community*. Stanford, CA: Stanord University Press.

Gernet, J. (1962). *Daily life in China on the eve of the Mongol invasion, 1250–1276*. Stanford, CA: Stanford University Press.

Han, S. (1977). *Korean fishermen*. Seoul: National University Press.

Hsu, F. L. K. (1948). *Under the ancestor's shadow*. New York: Columbia University Press.

Ikels, C. (1980). Coming of age in Chinese society. In C. Fry (Ed.), *Aging in culture and society* (pp. 80–100). New York: J. F. Bergin.

Kiefer, C. (1990). Aging and the aged in Japan. In R. Rubinstein (Ed.), *Anthropology and aging: Comprehensive reviews* (pp. 153–172). Dortrecht, Netherlands: Kluwer.

Kinoshita, Y., & Kiefer, C. (1991). *Refuge of the honored: Social organization in a Japanese retirement community*. Berkeley: University of Califormia Press.

Koyama, T. (1962). Changing family structure in Japan. In R Smith & R. Beardsley (Eds.), *Japanese culture: Its development and characteristics* (pp. 47–54). Chicago: Aldine.

Lang, O. (1946). *Chinese family and society*. New Haven, CT: Yale University Press.

Lee, K. (1975). *Kinship system in Korea*. New Haven, CT: Human Relations Area Files Press.

Levinson, J. (1967). *Liang Ch'i Ch'ao and the mind of modern China*. Berkeley: University of California Press.

Mathews, J., & Mathews L. (1883). *One billion: A China chronicle*. New York: Random House.

Murphy, G., & Murphy, L. B. (1968). *Asian psychology*. New York: Basic Books.

National Bureau of Statistics. (1989). *Korea statistical yearbook 1989*. Seoul: Economic Planning Board, Republic of Korea.

Olson, P. (1990). The elderly in the People's Republic of China. In J. Sokolovsky (Ed.), *The cultural context of aging* (pp. 143–161). New York: Bergin & Garvey.

Osgood, C. (1951). *The Koreans and their culture*. New York: Ronald Press.

Potter, J. (1968). *Capitalism and the Chinese peasant*. Berkeley: University of California Press.

Prime Minister's Office. (1982). *Rōjin Seikatsu to Iken: Kokusai Chōsa Shō* (The lives and opinions of old people: A cross-national survey). Tokyo: Ministry of Finance Printing Office.

Reischauer, E. O., & Fairbank, J. K. (1958). *East Asia: The great tradition*. Boston: Houghton Mifflin.

Skinner, G. W. (1977). Introduction: Urban social structure in Ch'ing China. In G. W. Skinner (Ed.), *The city in late imperial China* (pp. 521–554). Stanford, CA: Stanford University Press.

Tsai, W. (1989). New trends in marriage and the family in mainland China: Impacts of the Four Modernizations Campaign. In S. Leng (Ed.), *Changes in China: Party, state, and society* (pp. 225–246). New York: Universities Press of America.

Wolf, M. (1968). *The house of Lim*. New York: Appleton Century.

Yang, C. K. (1959). *Chinese Communist Society: The family and the village*. Cambridge, MA: M.I.T. Press.

Yang, C. K. (1973). The role of religion in Chinese society. In J. Meskill & J. M. Gentzler (Eds.), *An introduction to Chinese civilization* (pp. 643–674). New York: Columbia University Press.

Yang, M. C. (1945). *A Chinese village: Taitou, Shandung Province*. New York: Columbia University Press.

# *PART II*
# *Aging, Spirituality, and World Religions*

5

# Aging and Meaning: The Christian Tradition

*Stephen G. Post*

From the wider history of Christian thought the following proposition emerges with general continuity: Old age requires the acceptance of bodily deterioration viewed as an opportunity to grow in virtue, for the loss of health and bodily firmness that eventually forces a withdrawal from past activities can open up new horizons of meaning. Christian thought, though by no means ageist, categorically rejects the imposition of images of fulfillment befitting the young and middle-aged on those for whom the outwardly active and productive life becomes, finally, an impossibility. The current counterpoint to ageism is the myth that the old can or should be like the young; but this myth is itself ageist, for it denies to those who grow old their genuine alternative to despair, namely, the completion of a journey in the pursuit of moral and spiritual maturity.

In Christian thought, the infirmities of old age and the limitations they impose are frankly acknowledged. By emphasizing moral and spiritual values, rather than material and bodily ones, Christian thought transforms the stage of outward decay into one of inward fulfillment. This dialectic between decline and redemption is a mainstay of Christian thought, for even the most tragic circumstances can be redeemed through the power of love for God and neighbor, of faith in a merciful God, of hope in a world unseen. As Thomas R. Cole (1983) has underscored, "hope and triumph were linked dialectically to tragedy and death" in the Puritan tradition, a tradition wih roots as far back as

Augustine and beyond to the redemptive imagery of crucifixion as salvific journey.

This dialectic is in tension with secular modernity, which attempts to abolish the decline of aging through promises of protracted youth, perhaps through biomedical research on the "scavenger cells" that destroy the "free radicals" partly responsible for biological decline. From a Christian perspective, the hope for a technological "fixing" of human frailty and finitude stems from a tragic existential unwillingness to come to terms with the stark realities of the human condition. It is this peculiar unwillingness that underlies much of the depression and confusion that plague those who grow elderly.

How can the problem of meaning and biological aging be faced when myths about progressive biomedical abolition of growing old are so prevalent? Daniel Callahan (1990) rightly points out the way medical advance or the endless promises thereof "reshapes our notion of what it is to live life," dismantling "the cultural attitudes and institutions designed to live within those barriers" (p. 25). Or as Cole (1983) suggests, "Unable to infuse decay, dependency, and death with moral and spiritual significance, our culture dreams of abolishing biological aging" (p. 39). We would be better off to retrieve the wisdom of the writer of Ecclesiastes, who in his old age lamented, "I said to myself, 'Come, I will plunge into pleasures and enjoy myself'; but this too was emptiness" (2:1). The contemporary myths of eternal bodily life and of youthful old age are both tragic and finally painful for the very persons they are intended to inspire.

Cole (1986) notes that "for at least the last sixty years Western observers have sensed an impoverishment of social meaning in old age" (p. 3). The endeavor to mitigate this impoverishment with nothing deeper than an extension of the youth culture and of life itself is testimony to a failure of cultural and spiritual imagination.

In the modern West, old age is viewed as a period of consumption, as a "golden age" of vibrance and energy, as though decline can be avoided. This retirement ideology is neither fair nor sensitive to the elderly. A meaningful and realistic view consistent with the facts of human decay and mortality emerges from the tradition of virtue, of moral and spiritual journey. On this point, Christianity is consistent with other major world religions, for the grief of loss and decline can be healed and transcended only through the discovery that what appeared meaningful to an earlier version of the self may actually have been less meaningful than the self once supposed. In the past the meanings discovered in growing old were embedded in religious and philosophical worldviews that valued resignaion, self-transcendence, and the virtuous life. Modernity, with its Enlightenment myth of scientific-economic perfection (Passmore 1970), alienates the old from these worldviews. Without these worldviews, many older persons, having lost social-professional status and bodily firmness, grow depressed or decide that they no longer wish to go on living (Tolchin, 1989).

The Christian meaning of growing old emerges from the humble cultivation of faith, hope, and love. It is the cultivation of virtue that provides purpose to what would otherwise be a stage of inner dis-intergration and incoherence. One aims at near *completion* of the self in its relation to both neighbor and God, making progress on the journey of life that leads finally to afterlife. Harry R. Moody (1986) states this thesis as follows:

> In this view, the elderly are not held to be morally superior but rather further along on a journey of life, with life seen as a movement of lifelong fulfillment whose consummation is found only in death and afterlife. The sufferings of old age, in the traditional view, are seen against the wider background of the cosmos. The loss of that wider perspective is partly what deprives aging of meaning. (p. 31)

Aging is understood as a valued movement toward a new birth under a sacred canopy, consistent wih religious meanings that inform life in all of its stages.

The eminent historian of American Methodism, E. Brooks Holifield (1986), writes that throughout the early 19th century, "Methodists retained the dual sense of death as both penalty and promise" (p. 90). Methodist devotional writings urged the believer to be always mindful of death because the Christian "lives for death" and should manifest a "joyful, heavenly, and serene" contenance grounded in the knowledge that through Christ "the sting of death was plucked out" (p. 91). Only death without faith is meaningless. Of the Reformed or Calvinist tradition, Kenneth E. Vaux (1984) writes that the Christian should "resist efforts to extend indefinitely the human life span" and "accept aging and death as inevitable events comprehended in life's mystery" (p. 81). Whether Methodist or Reformed, Catholic or Lutheran, the message is the same: In growing old, clutch not at the things of the world or at the youth of the past but rather affirm in the strongest way the values of faith, hope, and love, without which those in decline cannot arise.

This chapter moves from a critique of modernity and a brief introduction of some themes in the wider Christian tradition to a consideration of the theological virtues, the origins of death in sin and finally to the writings of the later Dostoyevsky that beautifully articulate the Christian perspective on growing old.

## THE VIRTUES

According to Christian tradition, the elderly are not highly regarded simply because they have grown old and survived longer than others. Christianity is not "gerontocratic" (Achenbaum, 1987); that is, it does not give special respect to the elderly simply because they are old, as do some other religious and cultural traditions. Rather, Christianity has perennially held the elderly to high standards and has been ready to make serious moral demands of them.

These moral demands are not specific to the elderly, for they pertain to any stage of life. William J. Bouwsma (1976) points out that "Christian adulthood" is "assumed to be a potentiality of any age of life" (p. 85). This adulthood is defined as "total conformity to the manhood of Christ" (p. 85), a Calvinist articulation of the medieval moral ideal of *imitatio Christi*, the imitation of Christ. No one actually achieves such a level of moral perfection in this life, so Christians can only hope to develop toward it. Bouwsma writes thus: "As movement in a direction, it [adulthood] also implies progress that remains incomplete in this life" (p. 87). Meaning in old age comes from maintaining the direction, the voyage to the very end of life, thereby avoiding the cessation of growth. This goal is age-neutral; it "lacks interest in chronological disparity" (p. 91). At any stage in the journey, the worst evil is arrested development.

So the Puritan theologian Cotton Mather (1912) of 17th-century Massachusetts Bay had to address sternly those who slide away from Christian virtue as they grow old: "The scandalous profaneness of those who even to old age, neglect preparing for and approaching the Table of the Lord, is to have yet more pungent rebukes bestowed upon it" (p. 47). The moral pressure Mather wielded was rather severe if we are to judge from his harsh and uncompromising language. Yet this severity is fully consistent with Christian precedent, and it demands no more of the elderly than it does of other believers.

It was Saint Paul who, imprisoned in Rome, spent his last years "proclaiming the kingdom of God" (Acts 28:31). And it was Paul who declared: "When I was a child, my speech, my outlook, and my thoughts were all childish. When I grew up, I had finished with childish things" (I Cor. 13:11). This theme is echoed in Ephesians, authored *circa* A.D. 100 by a member of the later Pauline school after Paul's death:

> We are no longer to be children, tossed by the waves and whirled about by every fresh gust of teaching, dupes of crafty rogues and their deceitful schemes. No, let us speak the truth in love; so shall we fully grow up into Christ. (Eph. 4:13–16)

The proposition that according to Christianity, "the goal of human devlopment is to grow into the 'mature manhood' of Christ" is an accurate one, true to the Pauline heritage (Achenbaum, 1987, p. 133). It is as valid for the very old as it is for the very young, and for his reason, Calvinist culture did not spare children the rod.

The Christian emphasis on moral adulthood and maturity will strike some as utterly arid and dry. But this is a mistaken impression, for "adulthood merges with childhood in its appreciation for play" (Bouwsma, 1976, p. 92). Playfulness is understood as the "natural expression" of faith, of the sense that this world is penultimate only, that "ultimate seriousness" lies with God. So it is that Christian virtue, while stern and demanding, is simulaneously and perhaps surprisingly joyful.

## Christian Virtue

In all theories of virtue, the concern is with habitual behavior and continuities in character. "Character" refers to the sum of virtues and vices that define the self. Deeply ensconced in Western moral thought since Plato and Aristotle are four cardinal virtues: prudence, courage, justice, and temperance. Christianity added to these four classical virtues the three theological ones of faith, hope, and love (Meilaender, 1984). Aging, from a classical Christian perspective, involves primarily a shaping of character consistent wih all of the virtues, both cardinal and theological. Meaning in the fullest sense derives not merely from a "courageous" acceptance of growing old (the existentialist notion of bravely living unto death) nor from maintaining a prudent, just, and temperate character, although these Greco-Roman virtues were accepted in Christian moral thought. In addition to this Greco-Roman ideal, theological virtues were emphasized and given more ultimacy because they had to do with the eternal well-being of the soul.

It is important to underscore the relevance of courage, justice, patience, prudence, and, as William F. May (1986) notes, *hilaritas*, or gaiety. But the specifically Christian virtues remain theological ones, in the absence of which even the courageous fall short. The Christian will find meaning by transcending his or her despair through faith in the continuing reality of a merciful and just God, through hope in everlasting life, through acts of authentic other-regarding love, and through a continued interior search for the peaceful presence of God within the soul.

The Christian perspective on aging as a journey in moral and spiritual (or inward) growth is antithetical to the view of aging as an opportunity for leisure and self-indulgence. Harry R. Moody (1986) characterizes the latter view as follows:

> The modern distaste for contemplation is accompanied by a nostalgia for leisure, a wish to escape from haste, and a sentimental image of retirement as the "Golden Age" of life. Late life becomes the period when, freed from alienated labor, the "real self" can be fulfilled, as in the ideology of retirement. (p. 35)

Christianity rejects this ideology of leisure and moral laxity. Theologian Stephen Sapp (1987) describes this rejection as follows:

> Indeed, many typical retirement activities—golf, bridge, travel, and the like—illustrate that narcissistic values continue to thrive in the later years: All of these "pastimes" are quite *self*-centered, focusing attention upon oneself and doing little for anyone else. (pp. 150–151)

The ideal of a love that is at least as other-regarding as self-regarding remains the Christian moral norm even in the fullness of years.

The command to love God and neighbor in a life of virtue is in a carefully qualified sense even more relevant to the elderly than to the young, for the latter have youth as an excuse for their diversions, and they still have years remaining for moral growth. The culture of narcissism is, of course, morally unacceptable for the Christian of any age, but it is especially tragic among the old because they stand in greatest proximity to their moment of judgment before a sovereign God (see Fingarette, 1977).

## Catholic and Protestant Continuities

The emphasis on virtuous aging is so characteristic of Christian thought that exceptions cannot be found. Surely, every medieval Christian understood aging as a spiritual journey progressing through stages toward the divine, though beatitude, the full vision of God, could never be realized in bodily life. The great Protestants from Luther and John Wesley to Jonathan Edwards exerted themselves all the more as they aged, all for the sake of divine providence. Wesley, the founder of Methodism, is reknowned for evangelical activities while a white-haired old man in his 80s (Holifield, 1986). To those in the Methodist tradition, the devotion of Wesley in his old age provides a model of excellence in their journey toward "holiness."

To be sure, with Protestantism the Catholic's contemplative vision of God was more or less set aside, replaced with *sola scriptura* and *sola fides* (i.e., with the Bible and faith). The fundamentally otherworldly orientation of Catholicism now had its rival, for Protestantism emphasized obedience to divine commandment within the world—sociologist Max Weber's "inner-worldly asceticism." For Protestants, under the providence of God, age was to be accepted gratefully as a divine blessing, after the model of the Hebrew patriarchs, who obeyed God's will to their dying breath (see Feldman, 1986). But tension between otherworldly and inner-worldly asceticism aside, neither Catholic nor Protestant ethics made allowance for elderly believers to retire from the rigorism of the faith, hope, and love, as though the commandment of Jesus to love God and to love neighbor as much as self no longer applied to them on the basis of age. The pervasive moral norm of *imitatio Christi* or "adulthood" was age-neutral, and those who fulfilled it reasonably well were highly respected.

In the early Church, the venerable Saint Augustine provided an influential model of virtuous aging that is second to none, and that inspired both Catholicism and Protestantism. And in modernity, no Christian thinker considered meaning and aging more systematically than did Fyodor Dostoyevsky (1977, 1988) in his later writings. Dostoyevsky was, of course, steeped in Eastern Orthodox Christianity. Other Christian thinkers would prove fertile ground for insight into meaning and aging, though with Augustine and Dostoyevsky this theme is especially well articulated. Before turning to these two thinkers, I will touch on the understanding of aging itself as a punitive phenomenon, the result of original sin, in order to suggest why virtue among the elderly is such a consistent Christian emphasis.

## AGING AS PUNISHMENT FOR SIN

The moral and religious demand placed upon the aging and elderly in the Christian tradition is partially rooted in the presumption that decline and death are the results of original sin. Aging and death were understood by all Christians as unnatural consequences of that sin. In the absence of Adam's sin, human beings would not have died, nor would they have experienced the decline of old age. Theologian Nicholas Berdyaev (1937) thus writes, "Death is the evil result of sin. A sinless life would be immortal and eternal" (p. 252). Stanley Harakas (1986) likewise notes that "Theologically, Eastern Christianity viewed death as an enemy, a consequence of the Adamic sin, and therefore a condition to be struggled against" (p. 157), not through attempts to prolong life but through the effort to live according to the highest standards of generosity and interior mystical quest.

Thomas Aquinas (1952) provided a reliable summary on death and original sin in the *Summa Theologica* (I, question 97, article 1): "Whether in the State of Innocence Man Would Have Been Immortal?" Here Aquinas cited Paul: "By sin death came ino the world" (Rom. 5:12). In the state of "original righteousness," that is, before Adam and Eve sinned, the body was "incorruptible," that is, beyond mortality:

> For man's body was indissoluble not by reason of any intrinsic vigour of immortality, but by reason of a supernatural force given by God to the soul, by which it was enabled to preserve the body from all corruption so long as it remained itself subject to God. (p. 514)

Had Adam and Eve obeyed God, the "corruption" and "punishment" of aging and death would not have been inflicted upon them. Martin Luther and other major Protestants held a view identical to Aquinas's based on a literal reading of "You are dust and to dust you will return" (Gen. 3:17–19), God's condemnation immediately after the trespass. Theologian Reinhold Niebuhr (1941) summed up the tradition succinctly: "The doctrine that death is a consequence of sin is of course variously stated; but it remains a consistent doctrine of Christian orthodoxy" (p. 176).

Paul wrote of death as follows: "For since it was a man who brought death into the world, a man also brought resurrection of the dead" (1 Cor. 15:21). Aging and death result from a divine *order of retribution,* rather than from the natural order. Jesus provides salvation from physical death through an offer of immortality to those who believe. Thus could Paul conclude, "O Death, where is your victory? O Death, where is your sting?" (1 Cor. 15). Paul exhorted others to work ceaselessly toward the end of eternal blessing, and counseled against any weakening of resolve: "Therefore, my beloved brothers, stand firm and immovable, and work for the Lord always, work without limit, since you know that in the Lord your labour cannot be lost" (1 Cor. 15:58). Old age provides no holidays.

In the Pauline framework, aging and decline are understood as divinely ordained retributions that should be responded to with steadfast faith and Godly endeavor. Persons are cast into the debtors' prison of aging and finitude from whence they can be rescued only through repentance and faith in Christ. Accordingly, by a purposeful adherence to God's will, aging as a period of indemnification for sin can be successfully endured, and the reward of eternal life gained. Virtue alone can take the sting out of death so that death no longer need be feared. Unfortunately, the traditional Christian way of defeating death has been secularized and medicalized so that in modernity we quest mistakenly for a technological "fix" that will eliminate growing old.

Were aging and eventual death interpreted as part of the natural order, they would not be so heavily infused with moral meaning; they could be taken in stride. Outside of this interpretation, the elderly could still try to make the best use of their time in the face of mortality, perhaps to leave behind creative works for which to be remembered (Kass, 1985). However, the elderly could just as well be idle without fear of consequences, fulfilling the norms of "retirement ideology." But within the classical Christian framework, growing old is an essential opportunity for the achievement of virtue.

A cogent expression of the unnatural tragedy of mortality is found in Augustine's (1950) writings. Under the rubric "Of the life of mortals, which is rather to be called death than life," he begins: "For no sooner do we begin to live in this dying body, than we begin to move ceaselessly towards death. For in the whole course of this life (if life we must call it) its mutability tends towards death" (p. 419). It is agreed to by all Christians, he contends, that aging and death issue not from the "law of nature, by which God ordained no death for man, but by His righteous infliction on account of sin; for God, taking vengeance on sin, said to the man, in whom we all then were, 'Dust thou art, and unto dust shall thou return'" (p. 423). Such a "righteous infliction" ought not to be endured flippantly or taken lightly. A major test of Christian orthodoxy was, according to Augustine, acceptance of aging and death as proof of original sin and a life of purposeful virtue under the shadow of retribution.

## Theological Revisions

For the last two centuries, Protestant theological liberalism challenges the traditional view of aging and death as "unnatural corruptions." Freidrich Schleiermacher (1986), for instance, writing in 1830, held that neither the Genesis account of Adamic sin nor the New Testament "compel us to hold that man was created immortal" (p. 244). In his 1940 Gifford Lectures, Niebuhr (1941) protested against the traditional Pauline viewpoint because "such an interpretation obscures man's organic relation to nature and could be made meaningful only if it were assumed that sin had introduced death into the whole of nature" (p. 175).

However, fundamentalist Protestantism, which takes the Bible literally, still maintains the premodern perspective. Henry C. Thiessen (1979), whose writings present modern fundamentalism in its most systematic and articulate form, concludes thus:

> When God said that for disobedience man would "surely die" (Gen. 2:17), he included the body. Immediately after the trespass, God said to Adam,

> "You are dust, and to dust you shall return" (Gen. 3:19). The words of Paul, "As in Adam all die" (I Cor. 15:22) have reference primarily to physical death. (p. 183).

According to Thiessen, those who "reject the doctrine of original sin hold that death is a natural evil, flowing from man's constitution" (p. 183). However, "the Scriptures teach that death is part of the penalty of sin" (p. 183).

Whatever the current status of the Pauline doctrine, it has bequeathed to Christianity an emphasis on aging as a penalty to be redeemed in faith and subsequent moral seriousness. Aging is a time neither for selfishness nor for sloth but for a sober and disciplined pursuit of virtue under the justice of a sovereign deity who has imposed a just sentence for sin. So in the medieval period sloth was viewed as particularly unseemly among the elderly, as was their clinging in avarice to material possessions; thus the moral gravity of growing old, as Augustine and Dostoyevsky so profoundly conveyed it.

## THE AUGUSTINIAN STRAIN

The virtues expected of the aged, in essence continuous with Paul, are beautifully expressed in the framework of Augustinianism, and in the life of Augustine himself.

"Religion," as Augustine defined it, borrowing from Cicero, refers to the "re-binding" of a fallen and sinful self to the divine. Oliver O'Donovan (1980) writes of Augustinian neighbor-love,

> When he elaborates the content of neighbor-love, Augustine does not give much prominence to the natural needs of the body or soul which we may suppose the neighbor to have. In practical terms, love of neighbor is evangelism. He is a man, and men find their blessedness in God. The only service of lasting significance that we can render him is to lead him to that blessedness. (p. 112).

The most basic fact of human experience, Augustine contended, is that there is neither happiness nor peace without loving God. Therefore, exhorting the neighbor toward God is the highest form of benevolence.

The poet T. S. Eliot (1936), an insightful Augustinian, wrote as follows:

> How can we love our neighbor? . . .
> You, have you built well, have you forgotten the cornerstone?
> Talking of right relations of men, but not of relations of men to GOD.
> (p. 112)

Eliot's poems are full of moving references to the "light" above, "too bright for mortal vision," and to the "waste and void" of worldly pursuits as human beings struggle "in torment towards God" (p. 118).

Another Augustinian, Kenneth E. Kirk (1932), in his 1928 Bampton Lectures, wrote:

> Further, it must be agreed that, for various reasons, Christianity has often forgotten this primary supernaturalism of its charter, and has allowed itself to be presented as a moral system among other moral systems, with the religious element reduced to little more than an emotional tinting of its ethical scheme. (p. x)

"Supernaturalism" is a word that immediately alienates some, but without language to describe what transcends the natural, Kirk could hardly write of "the vision of God."

Another major 20th-century Augustinian was Max Scheler (1960). In his important 1917 address entitled "Christian Love and the Twentieth Century," Scheler expressed indignation over the "bankruptcy" of Christian ethics. Specifically, Scheler warned against the tendency to dilute Christian neighbor-love to "the milk and water of welfare-morality" (p. 363). Modern "humanitarianism" revolted against love for God "with special force during the Enlightenment" (p. 367), contends Scheler, and the result is that "spiritual goods" are no longer the chief human goals. The human being is understood as a strictly "natural" entity, so the true needs of the soul are hidden and obscured. Scheler writes this:

> What is primarily envisaged by the new "love of man" (of man alone) is no longer his invisible spirit, his soul and his salvation, solidarily included in the salvation of all children of God, with his bodily welfare taking an incidental place as a condition of his perfection and happiness.... It envisages man the external phenomenon, his sensual well-being. And increasingly it envisages this well-being in isolation from the objective hierarchy of real and spiritual goods.... No; love now appears valuable only at second hand, as a means of promoting the welfare and sensual contentment of man or social groups. Of course, even in the Christian view we should on all occasions seek to further the welfare of our society, economically, socially, in respect of public health and so on.... But in the final analysis we should promote welfare for the sake of man's *spiritual* personality. (p. 367)

In other words, Scheler (1960) is concerned that a spiritual image of human fulfillment has been lost sight of. In its place at the top of the hierarchy is a sensual one that was once penultimate and has now become ultimate. The "humanitarian erasure of the *first part of the commandment of love*" meant the loss of the full intent of neighbor-love, and this erasure is motivated by "a kind of suppressed hatred of God, a conscious insurrection against him and his order" (p. 368). The reduction of the content of neighbor-love constitutes, according to Scheler, "the withering of the central, guiding, goal-setting forces in the European mind" (p. 371). Neighbor-love is no longer directed "at man's spiritual core" (Scheler, 1961, p. 108). Scheler (1960) insists that neighbor-love requires more than accepting the other as is; it makes demands of the neighbor, requiring "a movement, an intention, towards potential values still 'higher' than those already given and presented" (p. 154).

## Growing Old, Augustinian Style

Modern men and women struggle with meaning as they age, the Augustinian contends, because there is no meaning to be had that does not begin in love for God and related virtues. Aging has meaning only because it can involve the agent on a path of spiritual-ethical maturation. This, anyway, is the outgrowth of the Augustinian hierarchy of values.

As Augustine (1961) argued, "There is no rest to be found where you seek it. In the land of death you try to find a happy life; it is not there. How can life be happy where there is no life at all?" (p. 82). Meaning in aging derives from a retrospective critique of the pride, sloth, avarice, and sensuality of earlier years: "But I was too proud to call myself a child. I was inflated with self-esteem, which made me think myself a great man" (p. 60). Augustine recalls his youthful experience with a group known as the "Wreckers," who, "swollen with conceit," used innocent persons as "fodder for their spiteful jests" (p. 58). Echoing Paul, he writes: "In my youth I wandered away, too, from your sustaining hand, and created of myself a barren waste" (p. 53). Even traditional education was an opportunity for sinful pride: "Let me tell you, my God, how I squandered the brains you gave me on foolish delusions" (p. 37). Sexual lust too marked the prison of youth: "Foolhardy as I was, I ran wild with lust that was manifold and rank" (p. 43). With age, Augustine could proclaim: "The good of the spirit is to cling to you for even, so that it may not, by turning away from you, lose the light which it gained by turning towards you and relapse into that existence which resembles the dark depths of the sea" (p. 312). Old age is not a time to "relapse," to slide back into vice.

In old age, Augustine spent his last years "exercising myself in the Holy Scriptures" (cited in Brown, 1967, p. 428). He was "not a man living in the past. His eyes were on the present" (p. 430). When he died

(A.D. 430), his last ten days were spent in prayer while no one but his doctors was permitted to enter his room lest he be distracted (p. 432).

The Augustinian standard is rigid and demanding. It implies that a great many persons never achieve true meaning in growing old. They may think that they live meaningfully through accumulating wealth, through worldly recognition and status, and the like. But there can be no genuine meaning in the idolatry that pervades the lives of those who are trapped in worldliness. Meaning, age, and "light" are intertwined: "Let there be light; and the light began" (Augustine, 1961, p. 313).

Through aging, held to issue from the sin of Adam and Eve, the virtuous self *gains* detachment from vain pursuits. This is how aging can be spiritually creative. Dante summed up the medieval ideal:

> ... gently slip cheerfully into the arms of God.... And even as the good sailor, when he draws near to the port, lowers his sails, and gently with mild impulse enters into it, so ought we to lower the sails of our worldly activities... so that we may come to that port with all sweetness and peace." (cited in Barash, 1983, p. 6).

Through aging the self can discover that it is ontologically structured toward God and morally bound to encourage the neighbor upward toward the divine.

Unfortunately, the contemplative spiritual tradition of Augustinianism is lost to modernity. Moody (1986) recognizes that meaningful aging is difficult in a society that places no value on the contemplative vision of God, and he therefore credits efforts to bring spirituality into the discussion of meaning:

> In recent years we have seen a rapprochement between life span development psychology and concern for spiritual growth. An encouraging development has been the appearance of work that draws on the resources of spirituality. The spiritual traditions have never accepted the idea that human fulfillment is the product of social roles or relentless activity in the world. Nor have they accepted the idea that the meaning of old age can be separated from the meaning of life as a whole. (p. 40)

Ours is a culture in which the zestful active life is the accepted norm, but this norm is inappropriate for those whose bodies become weak and even devastated.

This norm is perhaps a vestige of the Calvinist work ethic stripped of its theological groundings, and it is one that makes persons from more inwardly oriented cultures cringe. Whatever its origins, it devalues the perennial inner quest and the theological virtues associated with that quest. The retrieval of the Augustinian strain has been defended best in modernity by Dostoyevsky, so it is to his writings that attention will now turn.

## DOSTOYEVSKY

The most powerful contemporary image of meaning and aging as Christianity interprets it comes from the pen of Dostoyevsky (1970, 1988), who made it his special vocation to capture for posterity the virtues of the Christian who grows old.

Dostoyevsky published his *The Adolescent (or A Raw Youth)* in 1874. The reception was unfriendly, and the book is not one of the author's best known. Yet as a study on a Christian growing old, this book is a classic. Most of the themes from *The Adolescent* are echoed in *The Brothers Karamozov,* published in 1879. In this later work, the reknowned Elder Zossima manifests the Christian ideal of meaningful aging in remarkable fashion.

Of Dostoyevsky, J. I. Packer (1988) has written this: "Dostoyevsky is to me both the greatest novelist, as such, and the greatest Christian storyteller, in particular, of all time" (p. vii). He was, as Malcolm Muggeridge (1988) proclaims,

> a God-possessed man if ever there was one, as is clear in everything he wrote and in every character he created. All his life he was questing for God, and found Him only at the end of his days after passing through what he called "the hell-fire of doubt." (p. 1).

Dostoyevsky lived 60 years, dying in 1881.

### Makar

In *The Adolescent,* Makar Evanovich Dolgoruky is a former serf, now old and gray, and the legal husband of "the adolescent's" mother. The adolescent, Arkady Dolgoruky, narrates his dialogue with Makar, who comments to Arkady:

> So a pious old man must be content at all times and must die in the full light of understanding, blissfully and gracefully, satisfied with the days that have been given him to live, yearning for his last hour, and rejoicing when he is gathered like a stalk of wheat unto the sheaf when he has fulfilled his mysterious destiny. (Dostoyevsky, 1988, p. 219)

Arkady, a well-educated youth, asks Makar what "fulfilling one's mysterious destiny" refers to. Maker responds thus:

> What's mystery? Everything's mystery, my friend, everything is God's mystery. There's mystery in every tree, in every blade of grass. When a little bird sings or all those many, many stars shine in the sky at night—it's all mystery, the same one. But the greatest mystery is what awaits man's soul in the world beyond, and that's the truth, my boy. (p. 220)

The adolescent claims that scientific reason has removed mystery from existence, but Makar holds a more mystical worldview.

Arkady notes of Makar that "there was *gaiety* in his heart and that's why there was *beauty* in him. *Gaiety* was a favorite word of his and he often used it" (Dostoyevsky, 1988, p. 229). One is reminded of May's (1986) mention of *hilaritas*. Makar seems to rejoice in the existence of things around him, whether human or nonhuman, animate or inanimate. His appreciation of the mystery of the world moves him far beyond a merely utilitarian relationship with the people and objects he encounters. He does not seek to turn the world to his advantage, he exhibits no "will to power." Things are valued simply on the basis of their being. Arkady evidently feels this "gaiety" of heart, this mystical love for the world that is so different from mere aesthetics.

Makar is anxious to communicate, animated by a remarkable love for Arkady, who narrates: "Moreover, I'm sure I'm not just imagining things if I say that at certain moments he looked at me with a strange, even uncanny love, as his hand came to rest tenderly on top of mine or as he gently patted my shoulder." (Dostoyevsky, 1988, p. 221) It is love that is Makar's chief virtue. Speaking of death he comments:

> And grass will grow over his grave in the cemetery, the white stone over him will crumble, and everyone will forget him, including his own descendents, because only very few names remain in people's memory. So that's all right—let them forget! yes, go on, forget me, dear ones, but me, I'll go on loving you even from my grave. I can hear, dear children, your cheerful voices and I can hear your steps on the graves of your fathers; live for some time yet in the sunlight and enjoy yourselves while I pray for you and I'll come to you in your dreams. . . . Death doesn't make any difference, for there's love after death too! (p. 226)

Makar goes on to teach the adolescent that finally even the learned professors "remain restless" because fulfillment comes only with God: "They never think to face the only truth, though life without God is nothing but torture" (p. 228). The intellectual worships idols in the form of ideas and curses "the only source that can brighten our lives" (p. 228). And he observes that Makar likes most to talk about religion, about legends of ascetics from the remote past he had heard "from simple, illiterate folk" (p. 229).

This appreciation for "simple" folk indicates that the virtue of love does not depend on discursive and intellectual processes; it is not a cognitive virtue. It is a matter of the heart, of the affections, that issues in a profound kindness that is more easily felt than described. Sometimes Makar's memory does fade, and he will periodically lose track of conversation, as though mildly demented. Yet within him is an active love for God, neighbor, and creation that surpasses what cognition can ever achieve. As Pascal once said, the "heart has its own reasons, that reason does not know." Even in his most cognitively compromised moments, there is more affective personhood and virtue in Makar than meets the rationalist's eye.

Arkady, the would-be young intellectual, remains unconvinced by Makar's simplicity of heart and makes reference to the accomplishments of the professions: "Then I drew for him as complete a picture as I could of all the useful things a learned man, a doctor, or anyone devoting his life to the service of man could accomplish" (Dostoyevsky, 1988, p. 232).

But Makar comments that few, if any, "stick to their duties without going astray." People are tempted by sensuality, vanities, and envy, "so a man may forget the great cause and try to satisfy all these little cravings" (p. 233).

Makar prefers to be unworldly and in proximity to the God who gives the heart meaning and therefore peace. As he concludes,

> What Christ said was, "Go and give all you have to the poor and become the servant of all men," for if you do so you'll become a thousand times richer because your happiness won't be made just of good food, rich clothes, satisfied vanity, and appeased envy; instead, it will be built on love, love multiplied by love without end. And then you will gain not just riches, not just hundreds of thousands or a million, but it will be the whole world that you will gain! (Dostoyevsky, 1988, p. 233)

In Makar one discerns the Russian Christ figure, Dostoyevsky's "idiot" who has nothing to do with the ways of the world. His values and experiences pose a challenge to worldy images of human fulfillment in aging and to all of the cultural norms of secular society.

## Zossima

*The Adolescent*, like many of Dostoyevsky's other works, serves as prelude for *The Brothers Karamozov*, in which the author refines so many earlier themes. In *Karamozov*, "a lady of little faith" comes to the monk Zossima trying to find meaning in her life as she grows older. The virtuous, aged monk tells her: "Try to love your neighbors, love them actively and unceasingly. And as you learn to love them more and more, you will be more and more convinced of the existence of God and of the immortality of your soul" (Dostoyevsky, 1970, p. 64). She walks away challenged by the encounter.

Before his death, Zossima, like Augustine in his *Confessions*, tells of his youthful diversion. He comes finally to a discussion of his imminent death:

> My life is coming to an end—I know it, hear it. But with every day that is left to me I feel that my earthly life is already blending into a new, future life, anticipation of which sets my soul atremble with ecstasy, makes my mind glow and my heart weep with joy. (Dostoyevsky, 1970, p. 352)

Here is a joy like that of Makar, rooted in an exuberant communion with all things.

He warns against the "isolation that you find everywhere, particularly in our age." "Today everyone asserts his own personality and strives to live a full life as an individual. But these efforts lead not to a full life but to suicide, because, instead of realizing his personality, man only slips into total isolation." (Dostoyevsky, 1970, p. 366). This isolation is hell: "Fathers and teachers, what is hell? I think it is the suffering of one who can no longer love" (p. 390).

An absolutely meaningless old age, we can suggest, would be one in which love was frozen, as water in winter, leaving only isolation and suffering. It would be one lived in isolation from God, neighbor, and inner self.

Zossima dies, having to the very last moment served his friends and fellow monks as a teacher in the image of Paul and Augustine. The few passages cited above can hardly begin to provide a sense of the depth in Zossima's death, but they do bring to life the central role of the specifically theological virtues.

## FINAL REMARKS

The Christian image of a meaningful old age brings together joy and seriousness in the context of an integrated journey focused on the imitation of Christ. Virtues are essential for this journey, for they put the elderly on a path toward levels of fulfillment to which human beings are ontologically structured. Fortitude, wisdom, prudence, and the like can give meaning to aging for the secular existentialist, and this is pure gain. But from the Christian perspective, faith in a merciful God, hope in life eternal, and love lived in spiritual availability to others, especially the young, are surely the virtues without which the integrity and completion of life's journey is impossible.

Moreover, this journey takes place in the dialectic of decline and redemption. The Christian accepts decline and death and will not deny these things. This acceptance is not only good for the soul but good for society. As Callahan (1990) rightly maintains, a just person, a person dedicated to the common good, must acknowledge values other than medical progress, for each bit of progress brings with it expenditure of resources that might be better directed to other essential social needs. Medical progress and the extention of the human life span is a two-edged sword, for it benefits as well as harms. The Christian must ask what kind of life he or she wants to leave for society and for future generations. A Christian ethic is, finally, a social ethic critical of idolatrous medical progress that is simultaneously social regress. How many urban ghettos are a virtual wasteland except for the tower of some awesome hospital structure through which the homeless and oppressed will never pass? Meaning in growing old is related to justice, to a love that applies not just to family and friends, but to the good of all. My only difference with Callahan is that this sense of justice, to be worthy of authenticity, must come from within the hearts of those who grow old, rather than through public policy impositions. Christians might find meaning, additionally, in witnessing to the perennial truth that the body is finally impermanent and that a few more days or months or even years of life is not a moral imperative.

What, though, can be said about meaning for those who suffer a radical cognitive decline due to dementing illnesses? Persons suffering from severe Alzheimer's disease, for instance, are perhaps incapable of striving for virtue after the example of Augustine or Dostoyevsky's characters. And yet even amid such cognitive devastation it is important not to overlook the possible presence of an affective level of experience and virtue. It can never be concluded empirically that the severely demented person has "ceased to exist," that he or she is merely a "shell" of a former self. There are moments, after all, when Makar is less than his full self. The "tyranny of normalcy" (Hauerwas, 1986)—that is, our modern emphasis on cognition as determining "personhood"—should not obscure the possibility that currents of virtue move through a river of forgetfulness. Christian thought tries to see beyond devastation to the completion of life as a journey and the soul's return to port. It sees, as well, that to entrap these souls at their journey's end through the imposition of medical technology that goes beyond care consistent with dignity is cruel indeed. The Christian welcomes the transition from life to life everlasting and need not linger in the bizarre new world of betwixt and between that is the most futile legacy of biomedical progress.

Finally, meaning for those who grow old depends in part on the imaginations of those who are still young. It is difficult for the young to see the very old as anything but unproductive and burdensome. We need to teach the young about alternative images of human fulfillment and meaning that center on the Christian journey toward fullness. It is this focus, rather than a distorted emphasis on how young the old can be, that is worthy of serious consideration in the struggle against ageism. The elderly can themselves contribute to this vision of growing old by serving the young and by providing examples of self-transcendence.

## REFERENCES

Achenbaum, W. (1987). Societal perceptions of aging and the aged. In R. H. Binstock & E. Shanas (Eds.), *Handbook of aging and the social sciences* (pp. 129–148). New York: Van Nostrand Reinhold.

Aquinas, T. (1952). *The summa theologica.* In R. M. Hutchins (Ed.), *Great books of the Western world* (Vol. 19). Chicago: Encyclopedia Britannica Press.

Augustine. (1950). *The city of God* (M. Dods, Trans.). New York: Modern Library.

Augustine. (1961). *The confessions.* New York: Penguin.

Barash, D. P. (1983). *Aging: An exploration.* Seattle: University of Washington Press.

Berdyaev, N. (1937). *The destiny of man* (N. Duddington, Trans.). London: Geoffrey Bles.

Bouwsma, W. J. (1976). Christian adulthood. *Daedalus, 105,* 77–92.

Brown, P. (1967). *Augustine of Hippo.* Berkeley: University of California Press.

Burnaby, J. (1939). *Amor dei: A study in the religion of St. Augustine.* London: Hodder & Stoughton.

Callahan, D. (1990). *What kind of life: The limits of medical progress.* New York: Simon & Schuster.

Cole, T. R. (1983). The "enlightened" view of aging. *Hastings Center Report, 13*(3), 34–40.

Cole, T. R. (1986). Introduction. In T. R. Cole & S. Gadow (Eds.), *What does it mean to grow old? Reflections from the humanities,* (pp. 3–7). Durham, NC: Duke University Press.

Dostoyevsky, F. (1970). *The brothers Karamozov* (A. H. MacAndrew, Ed.). New York: Bantam Books.

Dostoyevsky, F. (1988). *The adolescent (or a raw youth).* In Hutterite Brethren (Eds.), *The gospel in Dostoyevsky: Selections from his works.* Ulster, NY: Plough.

Eliot, T. S. (1936). *Selected poems.* New York: Harcourt, Brace, and World.

Feldman, D. N. (1986). *Health and medicine in the Jewish tradition.* New York: Crossroad.

Fingarette, H. (1977). *The self in transformation.* New York: Harper & Row.

Harakas, S. S. (1986). The Eastern Orthodox tradition. In R. L. Numbers & D. W. Amundsen (Eds.), *Caring and curing: Health and medicine in the Western religious traditions* (pp. 146–172). New York: Macmillan.

Hauerwas, S. (1986). *Suffering presence*. Notre Dame, IN: University of Notre Dame Press.

Holifield, E. B. (1986). *Health and medicine in the Methodist tradition: Journey toward wholeness*. New York: Crossroad.

Kass, L. (1985). *Toward a more natural science: Biology and human affairs*. Chicago: University of Chicago Press.

Kirk, K. E. (1932). *The vision of God*. London: Longmans, Green.

Mather, C. (1912). *The diary of Cotton Mather*. Boston: Massachusetts Historical Society.

May. W. F. (1986). The virtues and vices of the elderly. In T. R. Cole & S. Gadow (Eds.), *What does it mean to grow old?* (pp. 41–61). Durham, NC: Duke University Press.

Meilaender, G. C. (1984). *The theory and practice of virtue*. Notre Dame, IN: University of Notre Dame Press.

Moody, H. R. (1986). The meaning of life and meaning of old age. In T. R. Cole & S. Gadow (Eds.), *What does it mean to grow old?* (pp. 11–40). Durham, NC: Duke University Press.

Muggeridge, M. (1988). Preface. In Hutterite Brethren (Eds.), *The gospel in Dostoyevsky*. Ulster, NY: Plough.

Niebuhr, R. (1941). *The nature and destiny of man* (Vol. 1). New York: Charles Scribners Sons.

O'Donovan, O. (1980). *The problem of self-love in St. Augustine*. New Haven, CT: Yale University Press.

Packer, J. I. (1988). Introduction. In Hutterite Brethren (Eds.), *The gospel in Dostoyevsky*. Ulster, NY: Plough.

Passmore, J. (1970). *The perfectibility of man*. New York: Charles Scribner's Sons.

Sapp, S. (1987). *Full of years: Aging and the elderly in the Bible and today*. Nashville, TN: Abingdon Press.

Scheler, M. (1960). *On the Eternal in man* (B. Noble, Trans.). London: SCM Press.

Scheler, M. (1961). *Ressentiment* (W. W. Holdheim, Trans.). Glencoe, IL: Free Press.

Schleiermacher, F. (1986). *The Christian faith*. Edinburgh: T. & T. Clark.

Thiessen, A. C. (1979). *Lectures in systematic theology*. Grand Rapids, MI: Wm. B. Eerdmans.

Tolchin, M. (1989, July 19). When long life is too much: Suicide rises among elderly. *New York Times*, A1, 10.

Vaux, K. L. (1984). *Health and medicine in the Reformed tradition: Promise, providence, and care*. New York: Crossroad.

6

# Aging in Judaism: "Crown of Glory" and "Days of Sorrow"

*Sheldon Isenberg*

How has Jewish civilization in its varied, related manifestations expressed itself on the ending of life's trajectory? Jewish history covers nearly four millennia, and the literature produced during that time, given the modest numbers of people involved, is immense and varied. We shall consider the literature of three overlapping periods. First, the literature of the Bible covers more than a millennium, from the patriarchal period through the 2nd century B.C.E. Second, the literature of traditional, or classical, Judaism includes the legal (*halakhic*) and nonlegal (*aggadic*) rabbinic collections as well as philosophical and mystical texts that cover the long stretch from Pharisaic-Rabbinic Judaism to contemporary orthodoxy, from the 2nd century B.C.E. through today. Third, western European Jews moved into modernity early in the 19th century, with some earlier encounters, whereas the mass of eastern European Jews entered the posttraditional world toward the beginning of the 20th century, most of them as American immigrants. We shall look at both continuities and radical transformations in modern Jewish conceptions of aging.

This study focuses on Jewish voices transmitted in writing, although for centuries much had been preserved in oral forms. Of course, in Jewish literature, as in virtually all literature of all traditions, male voices and perspectives are heard nearly exclusively until the modern period. We are usually told specifically about aging males and beliefs about and attitudes toward their process, so we must continually remind ourselves that we are woefully ignorant of what at least half of the Jews were feeling and saying. Only in the modern period, from the moment that it was possible for women's voices to be heard, can we begin to consider a more complete range of Jewish perspectives, including diverging images of Jewish men and women in the aging process.

Relatively little appears to indicate that problems of aging were singled out until the modern period.[1] In premodern texts the elderly are not listed with the poor, orphans, or widows, those groups requiring public care. Because traditional sources assume that the extended family is the setting for caring for aging parents, it is likely that care for the elderly was not specifically an extrafamilial issue. Perhaps the elders for whom families could not provide were thought of as poor or widowed.

But in the late 17th century care for the aging emerged as a Jewish communal concern. In the mid-18th century the first Jewish home for the aged was built in Amsterdam. By the end of the 19th century most of the major European Jewish communities had established similar institutions. In contrast to traditional sources, contemporary Jewish fiction expresses explicit concerns for problems of aging, reflecting developments in modern society such as extended life spans, the nuclearization and atomization of the modern family, and the proliferation of segregated living arrangements for the aged (Herr; Olitzky, 1989).

## POSITIVE AND NEGATIVE STRANDS

In each of the major strata of traditional Jewish literary reflection we find positive and negative valuations that persist as diachronic strands weaving through the generations of texts. As we shall see, the worldviews through which these strands weave shift over time, with a radical break in the modern period. We should not expect univocity of such a long tradition, especially one that, although very prescriptive of behavior, has encouraged creative speculation and theorizing about living—and dying—Jewishly.

The opening verses of the Bible assert that life per se is good; there is no serious contradiction of that primordial evaluation of God's creation in the thousands of years that follow. The positive strands value long life as a divine blessing, often romanticizing the process by ignoring the suffering associated with aging. The reference in Proverbs (16:31) to gray hair as "a crown of glory" is typical. Even when the negative strand warns of old age as "days of darkness" (Qohelet 11:8), it never calls into question the ultimate value of life.[2]

Long life is valued for different reasons. Aging enables the ripening of what had been seeded, a time of continued growth and harvest, a time for sharing the wisdom of experience (Prov. 22:6). In biblical and classical Judaism, a happy old age is seen specifically as an opportunity and reward for fulfilling current cultural values, a view that tends to play a socially conservative role. In Deuteronomy, for instance, long life is a reward for keeping the covenant requirements specified in that layer of tradition, whereas a short life signifies faithlessness to that covenantal understanding. Because Jewish tradition as a whole often focuses on the mental and spiritual dimensions in which aging presents opportunities for the accumulation and integration of the wisdom of experience, an extended life implies an increase in wisdom and Torah as well as in political authority. Fulfilling the core values associated with attaining a happy extended life and even immortality, is often viewed as protection against a difficult aging.

Such promises address the universal vulnerability to the physical, emotional, and mental disintegration that so often precede dying. The negative strand speaks of aging as the side of death we know about: dissipated power; loss of autonomy, respect, and self-worth; alienation from family and society; and the intimate loss of the capacity to enjoy living. In a late Midrash an old man is described as "apelike . . . and childlike . . . his children and household mocking at him, disregarding him and loathing him."[3]

Negative aspects of aging are also justified in various ways. Suffering in old age is often seen as a punishment for not living in accord with God's will, the correlate of the belief in old age as a reward. A contrasting voice, heard in all ages, and a central theme of skeptical wisdom literature questions the implied belief in a morally responsive universe. This negative wisdom strand scoffs at our presumption to comprehend God's moral calculus or will.

## THE HEBREW BIBLE

Although biblical literature gives us insight into the values and concerns of biblical Jews, just as signifiant is its authority for Jews and Christians throughout the ages. In Jacob Neusner's (1988b) terminology, traditional Judaism is "Torah-centric" (pp. 81–85). Torah is a central term that has several interrelated meanings. In the Bible, *torah* does not refer to a body of literature but means, generally, "teaching" or "way." For Judaism, the Bible or *Tanakh*, after its canonization, is "written Torah."[4] The Bible is the basis of nearly two millennia of rabbinic commentary, whether narrative, nonlegal (*aggadic*), or legal (*halakhic*). Claiming the authority of revelation, the rabbis called the results of their holy hermeneutics "oral Torah." Only in the 20th century, with the decline of traditional education, can we no longer take for granted the authority of and familiarity with the Bible for the average Jew.

The references to old age in the Hebrew Bible, although limited, are spread out through a literature that accumulated in oral and written forms over the course of a millennium or so (Reuben; 1987). The positive and negative voices heard at the beginning of the biblical tradition are continuations of themes found in earlier cultures that formed the historical-cultural matrix of the Israelite tradition.

## Biblical Ages and Origins

Traditions tend to gild their origins in myth and legend. Myths about beginnings are often cast heroically (Eliade, 1963). The early chapters of Genesis tell the story of the universe, stretching from its creation to the beginnings of the Jewish people. Narratives about creation, the flood, and the Tower of Babel are connected by genealogies of fathers and sons—the names of no mothers or daughters are listed—that link Adam, the first father, to Abraham, the first Jewish father. Primordial time is different: a universe is created in a week, and lifetimes cover centuries. Adam's life spanned 930 years, and Methuselah was said to have died at 969 years. In these genealogies quantity of years indicates quality of life.

The first biblical genealogies record not only monumental life spans but also the ages, ranging from 60 to more than 800 years, at which men were still virile and fertile (Genesis 5). Methusaleh, for instance, "begat" Lamech at 187 years and continued to beget for nearly another 800 years. The focus on engendering children corresponds to God's directive to all Creation and specifically to humanity: "Be fruitful and multiply."

The numbers taper as they approach the legendary patriarchal-matriarchal history that occupies the rest of Genesis, marking a transition from the narratives about creation of the world to those about the sacred national history of the Israelites. The theme of infertility adds suspense to the story of the transmission of Abraham's covenant, in which God promises the continuation and proliferation of his progeny. In the story of the conception of Isaac, the "right" inheritor of the covenant, that tension is heightened by the advanced ages of his parents: Sarah is 90; Abraham, 100. Until that moment the fulfillment of the covenant is in question.

The lives of the founding couple are of legendary length, although the numbers are less exaggerated than those found for earlier genealogies. It is significant that in these legends of long-lived women and men, there is only one story that tells of interaction between grandparent and grandchildren (Genesis 48). The first biblical figure described as aged (*zagen*), Abraham died still vigorous at 175; Sarah, at 127.[5] According to the priestly narrator, Abraham was 75 when he entered into the covenant, initiating Israelite history, still without heirs. Even Abraham's servant Eliezer, also called *zaqen*, was spry enough to cross the great desert to find a wife for Isaac.

But the patriarchal history provides sharp contrast in the story of Isaac, who, in his old age, feeble and blind, was manipulated by his wife and children. Even with the propensity to mythologize the founding fathers and mothers, a strain of realism about the infirmities attendant on aging emerges. In a narrative about a later period, an 80-year-old ally of King David, invited to join the royal household, responds grimly: "Your servant is far too old . . . I cannot tell good from bad, I cannot taste what I eat or drink; I cannot hear the voices of men and women singing. Why should I be a burden any longer to your majesty?" (2nd Sam. 19:32f.). David himself, after a long life of unrelenting activity and royal accomplishment, spends his last days sick and surrounded by intrigue, so lonely and cold that a young woman had to be found to help warm his body at night (1 Kings 1:1–4).

## Blessings and Curses

Long life, then, may be a blessing or a curse. In those strata where a happy, vigorous old age is experienced as a reward for fulfilling God's will, each layer of tradition adds its own understanding of God's will to the accumulating tradition.

In all of Jewish history, there is no more significant figure than Moses, the leader of the Exodus who receives God's Torah on Mount Sinai on behalf of the people. The Bible's own narrative framework presents much of Torah as God's speech to Moses, to be transmitted to the people. More than a millennium later, the rabbis began to cloak their own legislation with the authority of Moses' Torah (Urbach, 1987). According to the biblical tradition, when he died at the age of 120, "his eye had not dimmed, nor had his life force [moisture] fled" (Deut. 34:7). Yet he died short of completion of his life's dream, for God did not permit him to lead the people into the promised land. The ending of Moses' life thus connects positive and negative strands: his vigorous old age as leader of the people and transmitter of Torah and commandments is framed by a life divinely shortened as punishment for his disobedience of a divine directive.

Priesthood, monarchy, and prophecy emerge during the First Temple period (10th through 6th centuries B.C.E.). The prophetic understanding of the Israelite covenant relationship with God informs the final book of the Pentateuch, Deuteronomy, and gives shape to a major portion of the historical narrative that follows. The prophets understood the historical fate of the nation to be dependent upon the Children of Israel's fulfillment of their covenant obligations: great empires won and battles lost, all in relation to the Israelite performance of their duties. This prophetic view of history has continued as a major Jewish hermeneutical principle across the ages.

In this view the people's fate and the individual's quality of life are tied to ethical fulfillment of the covenant demands. Thus, long life was valued as a reward for fulfillment of the *mitzvot* of God's Torah, and a short life indicated punishment. At the core of Deuteronomy's covenantal vision is the choice given by God to adhere to Torah or not. Obedience brings blessing, including "length of days"; disobedience brings disaster (Deut. 38:19f.). The covenant not only protects the continuation of the people through time; it also protects against the dangers of daily living that might prematurely end a life.

## Elders and Elders

The Deuteronomic narrator presents the story, distasteful to him, of the disintegration of David and Solomon's kingdom as the result of the refusal of Solomon's son, Rehoboam, to accept the wisdom of the elders; "the elders" (*z'genim*) were described as a political force to be considered in an unsettled monarchy. The same Deuteronomic tradition records the following advice: "Remember the days of old, consider the years of many generations; ask your father and he will show you; your elders, and they will tell you. (Deut. 32:7)

In various Biblical narratives the elders play important governing roles, representing the interests of their extended families or tribes. In the desert, the elders were commanded to stand with Moses at the "Tent of Meeting," where they would also be official recipients of the divinely revealed laws. For that voice, the Torah of Moses is really the Torah of Moses and the elders. The text and readers know that, at the time of reading, Moses is dead—but there are still elders.

Elders play a variety of roles through the First Temple period (ending ca. 586 B.C.E.), including appointing kings and declaring war. They constituted an institution with analogues throughout the ancient Near East.[6] However, there is no specific age requirement for being counted as an official *zagen*. Although chronological age provides no guarantee of mature judgment, the symbolization of the experience and wisdom to serve the community by advanced age is compelling and universal in the ancient Near East. The metaphor remains, as we shall see.

More directly relevant, of course, is the generic use of "elder." In the biblical law codes, the automatic respect due to the aged is part of what makes the Children of Israel a "holy nation," according to the priestly tradition. One of the Ten Commandments (Exod. 20:12) connects the instruction to honor mother and father with the promise of a long life in the land. Respect for the preceding generation that gave life and sustenance is a life-and-death matter. In the priestly Holiness Code we find "Rise before the aged and show deference to the old" (Lev. 19:32), a commandment that reverberates throughout Jewish history. No matter how the biblical tradition evaluates a long life from the perspective of the one living it—positive, negative, or mixed—the attitude that others should hold is clear: respect.

This attitude converges with the notion that long life brings with it a wisdom born of experience. Respect for all elders—particularly parents—is so strong a principle in the Bible that the punishment for disobedience of the covenant, according to Deuteronomy, is that "the Lord will raise against you a nation that does not revere the old or pity the young" (28.49f.)

The prophetic tradition teaches that mistreatment of the elderly by any human community is a sign of being outside God's will, devoid of any morality. A symptom of the deepest evil, it reveals complete alienation from God's demands of humanity. Isaiah declares that a sign of God's punishment is precisely a disorderly and sinful society, characterized by infighting, a society in which "the young shall bully the old and the despised, the honored" (3:5).[7]

## ESCHATOLOGICAL REWARDS OF OLD AGE

The development of eschatological and apocalyptic perspectives, after the destruction of the First Temple, marks a significant shift in the Jewish experience of time. For some biblical voices the prophetic relation of action to immediate reward and punishment seemed too mechanical and failed to match common experience. Eschatological and apocalyptic literature project reward and punishment into an end time when all the struggles of human existence have been completed. A characteristic expectation of the end time is that "the just" will live to ripe old ages, if not forever. Psalm 92, an eschatological song, looks forward to the time when "the righteous . . . shall still bring forth fruit in old age; they shall be full of sap and richness" (92:15). This promise is to be fulfilled after the Lord's enemies have been destroyed. With the end of all that is evil in the world, all of the causes for suffering and untimely deaths will also come to an end.

Zechariah promises that at the end time "old men and old women shall again sit in the streets of Jerusalem, each with staff in hand for very age" (8:4). The presence of the aged is a sign of the transformation of the world into what it should be. When a new heaven and new earth shall have been created, "there shall be no elder who will not complete his days" (Isa. 65:20). This theme extends into an infinite prolongation of life in other eschatological speculations—an end to death (25.8).[8]

## Wisdom and Old Age

Proverbs, Job, and Qohelet (Ecclesiastes) attest to the participation of Israelite thought in and contributions to the widespread wisdom tradition of the ancient Near East. Collections of aphorisms, proverbs, allegories, and scholarly lists may have served as materials for "wisdom schools" to train governing elities and/or may simply reflect non-institutionalized popular wisdom. Here too we find the strands of contrasting attitudes: the positive view in the socially conservative book of Proverbs that old age is a ripening and opposing views in Job's outraged questioning and Qohelet's skeptical fatalism.

Proverbs focuses on that part of the tradition that saw old age as wisdom, beauty, and strength, warning both about the dangers of ignoring the wisdom of the elders and about despising the aged mother (23.22). The whole book is framed as the advice of an experienced parent or teacher to an already adult son or student about to set out in the world (Prov. 1:8). Heeding this wise instruction will result in "length of days, and years in life, and peace" (Prov. 3:2) The correlative warning is clear: "the upright shall live on in the world . . . but the wicked's life on earth will be cut short" (Prov. 2:21–22). The general perspective on aging throughout the book is that old age is a blessing for the righteous, who please God, for true wisdom is rooted in fear of God: "The *savya*, the grey hair, is a crown of glory, it shall be found in the way of righteousness" (Prov. 16:31) A good aging, however, depends on early training in wisdom: "Train the young man according to its way, so that even in his old age it shall not depart from him" (Prov. 22.6).[9]

A very different picture emerges in the less trusting wisdom of Job, who questions the power or honor due to mere quantity of years. Most of the Book of Job is a forceful refutation of the prophetic view of a moral universe, including the equation of long life with wisdom and virtue. Life is not just, says the poet, for the connection between one's fate and actions is mysterious. When his conservative advisors claim the wisdom of age as they argue against Job's questioning of God's justice

(15:7–10), Job dismisses this conventional wisdom, asking sarcastically, "Does wisdom come with age, and understanding in length of days?" (12:12).

Thus, the negative strand as it manifests in the wisdom literature denies the automatic connections between age and wisdom. Indeed, the central message of Job is that what happens to us is beyond our ken. Ironically, when Job accepts the limitations of his wisdom, his suffering ceases, and he is rewarded by God with another 140 years of life: "So Job died, old and sated with days." Many scholars regard this return to the prophetic view of long life as a reward as a later, pious addendum.

The latest of the canonical wisdom books, Qohelet, or Ecclesiastes, begins with a theme to be repeated throughout: "Utter futility! says Qohelet, utter futiliity! Everything is futile!" (1:2).[10] The passage of time has no meaning; no accomplishments will be remembered by coming generations. Wisdom gives no special insights (8:16f.), for death ultimately reclaims all. In this context Qohelet contrasts youth and old age:

> Indeed, let anyone who lives many years rejoice in all of them, but remember the days of darkness, for they will be many; everything that comes is absurd. Rejoice young man, in your youth and let your heart be glad during the days of your prime . . . for youth and black hair are fleeting, And remember your wife in the days of your youth, before the evil days come and the years approach of which you will say, "I have no pleasure in them . . ." Absurdity of absurdities, says the Qohelet, everything is absurd. (11:7–12:8)

Thus ends Qohelet's words. The meaninglessness and vulnerability of old age evoke the cry of futility. Nevertheless, in contrast to comparable texts from Egypt and Mesopotamia, Qohelet does not draw the conclusion that life is not worth living, that one might just as well end life at will. The fundamental biblical impulse toward life persists in the darkest speculations: "Yes, sweet is the light, and it is good for the eyes to behold the sun."

Elsewhere, we find the negative perspective of a wisdom psalm (Ps. 90:10) somewhat less severe: 'The days of our years are threescore and ten, and if by reason of strength, they be fourscore years, yet is their strength labor and sorrow." But in another wisdom psalm, we read an elder's plea: "Do not cast me off in old age; when my strength fails me, do not forsake me . . . and now that I am old and my hairs are gray, forsake me not, O God" (71:9, 18). Here again, the suffering of old age is neither reward nor punishment but cause for fear if one is "cast off," so we can only appeal to God.

## TORAH AS THE SOURCE OF VALUE

Positive voices often value long life, not for itself but for the enlargement of life's container of virtue and meaning: the more life, the more Torah. For instance, the stanza chosen to open the Book of Psalms celebrates the one who takes pleasure in God's *torah*. The desire to fulfill God's will brings the promise of a happy, vigorous old age ("his leaf does not wither" [1:3]). This strand makes not only obedience to but also study of divine instruction the criterion of value, for the wisdom gained from Torah exceeds that gleaned from the experiences of a long life (Ps. 119.99f.).

This theme continues into the Hellenistic Jewish wisdom literature. Ecclesiasticus, the Wisdom of Ben Sira (25:4–6), from Hellenistic Palestine (ca. 180 B.C.E.), has deep appreciation for the generic wisdom that comes from the experience of a full life, reminding us of some passages from Proverbs: "Much experience is the crown of old men, their enhancement is reverence for the Lord" (Olitzky, 1989, p. 340)[11] In contrast, the apocryphal Wisdom of Solomon, written in Egypt perhaps a century later, affirms that "it is not length of life that makes for an honorable old age . . . but rather is it wisdom which constitutes a man's silvery brow, and a spotless life the true ripeness of age" (4:8–9).

Indeed, God may snatch the life of a good person in youth to protect him from the influence of the wicked and godless (4:7ff.), for "swiftly perfected youth [shall condemn] the old age of the unrighteous rich in years" (4:16). The truth that scoundrels too may enjoy old age disintegrates the belief in a tie between length of life and virtue. At the same time, the prophetic notion that length of days is a reward for virtue in this life is transformed by the belief that righteousness leads to immortality—the death of the righteous is only apparent. Nonetheless, sin brings death (2.21–3.9) (Nickelsburg, 1981).

## AGING IN RABBINIC JUDAISM

The rabbinic tradition is collected in the Talmud and Midrash. The literature deals with a period that includes the Maccabean period (second century B.C.E.), the destruction of the Second Temple in 70 C.E., the codification of early rabbinic law and lore collected in the Mishnah and Tosefta in Palestine around 200 C.E., and the formation of the two great commentaries on the Mishnah, the Palestinian and Babylonian Talmuds, which were completed by the end of the 5th century C.E. The other great rabbinic collections are the *midrashim*, legal and nonlegal materials arranged as commentaries on the biblical text. The rabbis rooted their writings in the Bible, usually by creatively interpolating their beliefs and values into their readings of the text. Rabbinic Judaism is not only intrinsically important but also serves as the matrix of many forms of posttraditional Judaism.

References to aging and its problems in the immense rabbinic literature are relatively rare, although still more than we shall be able to consider. Given all of the complaints one might have heard about old age—such as those expressed by Qohelet—the only specific regret in the sayings of the early Palestinian rabbis collected in the Mishnah is the loss of intellectual potency for the study of Torah. There is no mention of physical and emotional disintegration, on the one hand, and no claims for prolongation of life as a result of study, on the other. The rabbinic belief in an afterlife in which rewards and punishments were measured out relieved the pressure to view an extended life as a reward.

Several references to old age are found in the fourth chapter of the tractate *Avot,* which contains collections of wisdom-like sayings of the early rabbis. This totally *aggadic* (nonlegal) tractate has become the most widely read part of the Talmud. Included in the Siddur, the prayer book, these sayings were often studied on the Sabbath afternoon, a custom that continues in some communities. One rabbi says: "He who learns when a child—what is he like? Ink put down on a clean piece of paper. And he who learns when an old man—what is he like? Ink put down on a paper full of erasures." Another says: "He who learns from children—what is he like? One who eats sour grapes and drinks fresh wine. And he who learns from old men—what is he like? He who eats ripe grapes and drinks vintage wine." Judah ha-Nasi, the compiler and editor of the Mishnah, says: "Do not look at the bottle but at what is in it. You can have a new bottle full of old wine, and an old bottle which has not got even new wine" (4:20) (Neusner, 1988a).

For the rabbis, study is the major purpose of the male life; not to study is not to live. But when age diminishes one's capacity to absorb and learn, study is futile. In this first view, then, youth is an advantage in studying. The next view, not wholly incompatible, argues that learning from the young is far inferior to learning from the old, the experienced. Judah ha-Nasi rejects the generalizations of both, noting, in consonance with a negative strand of the wisdom tradition, that age is irrelevant to the wisdom of Torah. Youth can absorb old wisdom and old people can be ignorant fools. Nevertheless, although the age of the container is not important, the age of the contents is![12]

The Tosefta, a collection of materials contemporaneous with and overlapping the Mishnah, records the following saying that identifies wisdom with age (Tos. Avodah Zara 1.19): "If young people advise you to build the Temple, and old men say destroy it, give ear to the latter; for the building of the young is destruction; and the tearing down of the old is construction" (Neusner, 1981). The young are profoundly distrusted when it comes to public religious policy. If old men, whom we might expect to conserve the past, advise to destroy, then listen! The passage, referring to Rehoboam's refusal to consider the advice of the elders, is a continuation of the biblical strand that enjoins deference to elders. The Palestinian rabbis may be recalling the destructive and internally divisive wars against Rome that culminated in the destruction of the Second Temple and enormous suffering.

The use of *zaqen* as metaphor for the highest values of the tradition continues through the Mishnah and into the Talmudic literature. In the Mishnah, *zaqen* is used to designate a *hakam*, a sage or scholar steeped in Torah, and especially members of the Sanhedrin, who were said to have advised the priestly temple hierarchy on ritual matters (Yoma 1:3,5). The use of "elder" to designate a man distinguished in Torah study continues in Talmud and Midrash (Ben-Sasson).

## TALMUD AND MIDRASH

### Torah as Good Medicine

Rabbinic tradition amplifies the virtues and failings of biblical figures in Midrash. A story is told that at the circumcision party for Isaac, Sarah—more than 90 years old—nursed a hundred babies to counter the suspicion that Isaac was not really her child but a foundling (Ginzberg, 1961). In contrast, Barzilai the Gileadite's description of his decrepitude in old age (2nd Sam. 19:32f.) drew a wide range of rabbinic comments preserved in the Babylonian Talmud. Rab called him a liar because he knew someone older than Barzilai's 80 years whose taste buds were still functioning; Raba, however, accepted the accuracy of Barzillai's self-observation but imagined that his problems arose from his dissolute life. In either case, the validity of Rabbi Ishmael's view is sustained: wisdom comes with age—if you are a scholar (Shabbat 152a). This continues the thread in which longevity is taken to be more valuable for someone who is occupied with study of Torah than for an ignoramus. But there is also an implicit threat that a difficult old age awaits the nonscholar (i.e., the nonrabbi).

It is not just that study keeps the mental dimension of aging at bay but also that filling one's mind with Torah is per se an antidote to senility. This motif appears in the Mishnah:

> When someone falls into sickness or old age or troubles and cannot engage in his work, he dies of hunger. But with Torah this is not so; for it guards him from all evil while he is young, and in old age it grants him a future

> and a hope. Of his old age what does it say? "They shall still bring forth fruit in old age." (Ps. 92.14; Kiddushin 4:14).

This corresponds to the *aggadic* identification of Torah study as the "elixir of life" (*Ta`anit* 7a).[13]

Even the mind that has begun to disintegrate with age, if it once held words of holy Torah, is to be valued: "Be careful [to respect] on old man who has forgotten his knowledge through no fault of his own, for it was said: 'Both the whole tables and the fragments of the tables were placed in the Ark'" (*Berachot* 8b).[14] The container of Torah is sanctified by its contents, even when those contents are no longer accessible. In the same vein: "Respect even the old man who has lost his learning" (Kiddushin 32a). No wonder that in this Torah-centric community, the text inscribed by those to whom Torah was life was known as the Tree of Life (*etz hayyim*)! Torah may not always being long life as its reward, but to be occupied with Torah makes any length of life worth living.[15]

## Honoring the Carriers of Torah

In the Babylonian Talmud, tractate *Kiddushin* 32–33, there is an extended discussion that attempts to establish a calculus to relate the biblically mandated honor due an elder to that required by the rabbis for a scholar. To authenticate the principle of honoring the learned, some rabbis read biblical passages that require respect to the aged as referring only to scholars, making the Mishnaic practice into a hermeneutical principle. Surely, says one rabbi, Torah would not mandate honor to an "aged sinner"—or, by implication, to an ignoramus.

But the alternative reading, that "elder" refers to chronological age, is discussed in the same passage. In this characteristic spectrum of views, Rabbi Issi commands respect for any "hoary head." Rabbi Johanan goes further, maintaining that the value of life experience even transcends the boundary between Jew and non-Jew. On the other hand, for Rabbi Nahman, Raba, and Abaye, the respect due to a scholar was greater than that due even an elder nonscholar. Rabbi Issi's view that age per se is worthy of respect reflects the simple reading of the biblical command to rise up before the aged and is echoed in the Midrash: "Concerning he who welcomes an old man, it is as if he has welcomed the Shekhinah (*Genesis Rabbah*, Toledot 43.6).[16] Respect for the aged is equivalent to respect for God.

## The Negative Strand

The negative strand, reminding us of the organic sufferings of old age, continues to spin through Talmud and Midrash. There are some passages that give specific warnings: "[One must pray in the later years that] his eyes may see, his mouth eat, his legs walk, for in old age all powers fail" (Herr, p. 345). In other passages we find references to stages of life. One vehicle was the midrashic adaptation of a Greek counting of seven stages of life.

A comparison of the treatment of the final stage of life in two texts, one found in the Midrash Tanhuma and the other in the Midrash Rabbah to Qohelet, is illuminating. The account of the stages is the same, but each version adds a different comment about the final stage, that is, the apelike countenance of the old (a literary image apparently originating with the Greek savant Solon). Midrash Tanhuma gives a graphic description of the seventh and final stage as impotent senility, when elders are at the mercy of their hostile families. When the elder complains that he did not ask to be born, the angel of death admonishes him: "And have I not already told thee, that against thy will thou art created, against thy will thou art born, against thy will thou lives, and against thy will thou must render account for thy actions before the Supreme King of Kings, blessed be He" (translation in Kohut, p. 234).

Although the description of old age sounds like an exception to the universal valuation of life, the context emphasizes that this pathetic figure nevertheless resists his ending. The passage expresses appreciation of the energy and freedom of youth but acknowledges the increasingly heavy cares of supporting a family and the indignities of old age, including loss of function and respect in the extended family. The angel of death's stern speech is reminiscent of the divine response to Job's complaints. Life and the indignities of its ending come without easy explanations, as mystery.

Another version of the stages-of-life motif is found as a comment in the Midrash Rabbah to Qohelet 1:2 on the keystone passage, "Futility! Futility! All is futility!" The presentation of the same stages is unelaborated until the final one: "When he is grown old he is like an ape. What has just been said holds good only of the ignorant; but of those versed in the Torah it is written, 'Now King David was old' (1 Kings 1.1)—although he was 'old,' he was still a 'king.'" Qohelet's despair is midrashically laundered by exempting the learned one, the rabbi, from the ravages of age. The inevitable pathos of the ending is undercut by the revisionist affirmation of the aging- and death-defying powers of Torah study. The 11th-century Midrash Rabbah on Song of Songs 1:10, in contrast, gives a compact, astringent summary of the stages of life of the negative wisdom type—with no promises of amelioration: "When a man is young, he quotes poetry; when he matures, he quotes proverbs; when he grows old he speaks of futilities."

Finally, it is clear that rabbinic law understands the biblical injunction to honor one's parents as the requirement that children care for their aging parents. No matter what virtues an extended life might bring, that the aging require special care is never denied. But that care is almost always seen as a family issue, especially as women's responsibility. Talmud, Midrash and medieval writings deal extensively with the dimensions of the requirements of Torah having to do with aging parents.[17] This source material has been thoroughly treated by Gerald Blidstein (1975) and, in a more concentrated way, by Elliot Dorf (1987). There is relatively little said about the responsibility of the larger Jewish community for the aging who are without means, as Immanuel Jacobovitz (1988) has noted, reflecting that elders were not viewed collectively as a category of people requiring special aid until nearly the modern period (Ben-Sasson)[18]

## THE CAIRO GENIZA DOCUMENTS

Talmud and Midrash give us limited and indirect evidence for reconstructing Jewish attitudes toward aging in Palestine and Babylonia from the Roman period through the 10th or 11th century C.E. A very different kind of literature was recovered early in this century from the Cairo Genizah, which provides extraordinary insight into the social and economic history of lower- and middle-class Jews who lived in Muslim territories, including Palestine, Sicily, and Spain, from the 10th through 13th centuries.

Letters tell stories of parents abandoned as well as parents well cared for or able to care for themselves. S. D. Goitein (1988), who reconstructed this major segment of Jewish civilization in a remarkable five-volume work, theorizes that only 5% of the population reached the age of 70. He cites the 12th-century poets Judah ha-Levi and Abraham Ibn Ezra, who pinpoint 50 as close to the endpoint of life. Judah ha-Levi at one point mocks the elder who tries to ignore his age: "Chasing after youth at fifty/when your days are about to vanish?"[19] Yet those who survived to 70 and beyond were very likely healthy and vital. Many documents indicate that men and women at that age retained control over their own affairs and felt themselves blessed with children and grandchildren. Elderly men were acknowledged for a lifetime of charitable deeds, public service, and learning. Goitein concludes: "In the Bible-oriented society of the Geniza, good old age was the natural reward for (and, therefore, proof of) a virtuous life" (p. 125). Even though the Cairo Geniza documents are far more concerned with business dealings than with pious scholarship, the values represented seem to extend naturally those of Talmudic society, both in positive and negative evaluations.

## *SABA'* IN KABBALAH

Besides the well-known Talmudic injunction against involving oneself with mysticism, Kabbalah, before the age of 40—perhaps implying the last decade of life to many—we can follow the metaphorical use of "elder" into the mystical tradition. The *Zohar*, a 13th-century mystical midrash, is the central text of Kabbalah. Its fragmentary narrative framework has almost a novelistic flavor, with names of mystics constructed as sources of various teachings. One of the most illustrious characters is called *saba'*, the "old man" ("grandfather" in Aramaic). In several passages he mysteriously appears as a donkey driver and surprises the learned rabbis with his marvelous mystical teachings (Matt, *Wisdom of the Zohar*, I: 169–197).

A Kabbalist from the Zoharic period, Moshe de Leon, whom many believe to have authored the Zohar, explicitly disconnects chronological age from the spiritual maturity that comes from mystical wisdom:

> . . . a man who engaged in Mishnah and Talmud all his days . . . began shouting at everyone, "I do not know my own self! . . . All my days I have toiled in Torah until I was eighty years old. But in the final year I attained no more wisdom or essence than I attained in those first years when I began studying. . . . See now how my eyes shine, for I have tasted a bit of this [mystical] honey!" (Matt, p. 7)

The *Saba'* of the Zohar earned the title, not merely by study of Talmud but by his capacity to interpret Torah mystically.

## AGING AND THE ALIENATION OF GENERATIONS IN MODERNITY

The entry of Jews into the modern world in the 19th and 20th centuries brought new forms of literary expression, new contributors, and an ever accelerating rate of publication. As the proportion of elder Jews who survived well into grandparenthood increased, their presence in literature also increased, a theme yet to be thoroughly studied. The older generation came to symbolize something radically different from what it had. The presumption of traditional literature is that the world would remain relatively stable from generation to generation. As far as the rabbis were concerned, Abraham and Moses lived like rabbis and the "world to come" was imagined as an idealization of their world. A long-lived person in such a world might experience personal change but not epochal transitions.

Premodern, traditional literature was concerned with the problem of being a good person—an observer of Torah, a scholar, a moral person in God's creation. Modern Jewish writers have been more focused on boundaries: the problems of remaining a Jew in the face of a secularizing modernity, the conflicted relationships with the past in a world of exciting and frightening change. To be a Jew in traditional society was to be part of an extended family, the usual context for aging. The abrupt entry of Jews into a modernity that had begun without them focused attention on generational differences and the transformation of family structures. The freedom that children sought was experienced by many parents as an abandonment, which often occurred after the most radical dislocation of their lives.

In a perceptive essay, Harry Moody (1986) relates our ability to give meaning to our lives as a whole, to our evaluations of old age. Traditional societies, he notes,

> contain dual, even contradictory images of the movement of aging: a downward movement toward debility and death and an upward movement toward unifying knowledge . . . The sufferings of old age, in the traditional view, are seen against the wider background of the cosmos. (p. 31)

Modernity is characterized by the loss of that "wider background." The positive images are more difficult to construct and less convincing, no longer rooted in the myths, theologies, and philosophies of traditional culture. The recognition of "the downward movement" remains as a continuation of the negative wisdom strand that insists that we should make no attempt to rationalize or justify the sufferings endured by the aged.

The universal modern nuclearization of the family, combined with increased length of life, has resulted in increasing age segregation, especially in the United States. One consequence has been a growing number of "adult living" communities, homes for the aged, nursing homes, and the like. Modern Jewish literature interprets age segregation as a matter of separating out not only bodies but also minds and spirits. A spiritual rift is disclosed that precedes, and certainly accompanies, the crossing of the ocean from Europe. For many that passage was also a crossing of a psychic divide between traditional and posttraditional.

In Jewish fiction and poetry, figures of old men and women or of aging parents often represent the passing of the traditional way of life.[20] Positive or sympathetic presentation of the elderly may signify regret or nostalgia for the loss of the old ways. Presenting youthful impatience with the aging becomes a way to express a desire to be rid of those elements of premodern life that were hindrances to full participation in and enjoyment of the benefits of modern living, benefits that were not only material. In American Jewish and Israeli literature, all of the ambivalence and ambiguities about the Old World, often idealized as the *shtetl* (Yiddish for "town"), became embodied in the figure of the elder.

Modern Jewish literature is immense, so any selection is more or less arbitrary. Stories that feature elderly characters often imaginatively represent and work with the conflicts of old and young. Such themes abound in Yiddish fiction, which bridges Eastern European Jewry to the New World: in Hebrew fiction in which Israelis struggle to relate their political and cultural independence to their Eastern European roots and in American Jewish fiction, which deals with unprecedented identity crises for Jews and Jewish communities. The one nonfiction work that I use to frame this account is anthropolopist Barbara Meyerhoff's (1978) superbly sensitive, empathetic, and intensely personal study of a community of elderly Jews living in Southern California in the early 1970s.

## The "Yiddishe Velt"

For most American Jews, the Judaism of the Eastern European *shtetl* represents their ancestral past. Until recently the same could be said for Israeli Jews, although the rapid influx of Jews from Northern Africa, Arab countries of the Middle East, and now the Soviet Union is changing even the demographics of memory. Meyerhoff (1978) looked to the life of the *shtetl* in order to understand why women as a group dominated the aging immigrant Jewish community she was studying—a dominance co-existing with occasional lip service to male superiority. She found her answers in the prevailing roles and stereotypes of the *shtetl* that could not be transplanted but were remembered. Those answers give us insight into the radical transformation of values about aging expressed in Yiddish literature of transition, as well as In Israeli and Jewish American literature.

The values of the *shtetl* continued the traditional emphasis on male scholarship and piety, removed from affairs of the world and the nitty-gritty of physical survival. The female stereotype included modesty, submission, and service to men and children. The common goals of the society were to maximize study of Torah and piety and to have as many children as possible to walk the same path. In the *shtetl* these women had the responsibility for the basic survival of their families. Men avoided hard labor, yearning for study. The women, Meyerhoff (1978) reasoned, had embodied characteristics that stood them in better stead for aging in the New World than their men had.

Yiddish was the language of the Eastern European *shtetl* and of the first-generation immigrant communities. Its literature included religious voices, but it also provided the first major outlet for secular Jewish voices. European *yiddishkeit* was largely destroyed by the Holocaust. After a brief flowering in America, today it struggles to survive. The ability to understand Yiddish came to designate a generational divide in America and Israel. Yiddish was the language of the old.

Isaac Bashevis Singer, prolific Nobel laureate, and widely translated, writes of the European *shtetl* world and the consequences of the relocation of that consciousness into the New World. "The Little Shoemakers," a seemingly sentimental fable, tells the story of Abba, the "papa." (Howe & Greenberg, 1973, 523–544). In the old country, he was a fine shoemaker, pious, happy, successful, and appreciated in his *shtetl,* and he trained his sons in his craft. After his sons emigrate and open a successful, modern shoe factory, they bring their parents to the New World. Abba feels alien and uprooted until one day he finds his old cobbler tools and sets to work mending the shoes of the household. His sons build him a replica of his old workshop in the backyard and soon find themselves working alongside him, singing along as they had in the old country. But it was on their day off and in the backyard that they worked. Abba's work did not fit in the world of youth and mechanical productivity, but nevertheless it represented to the sons something valuable that was in danger of being lost.

Anzia Yezierska (1975) wrote in English about the Yiddish-speaking worlds of Eastern Europe and of American immigrants. Without sentimentality she tells of the squalor, the crushing poverty, and the struggles between the sexes and generations. Her 1925 novel, *Bread Givers,* presents the struggle for power between father and daughter. The father wants to transport to the New World the oppressive old patterns in which women—wife and daughters—served the patriarchal scholar of Torah, who was incapable of supporting himself, to say nothing of a family. The daughter tries to free herself from her aging father's demands, pulling away to study and acquire a profession:

> I almost hated him again as I felt his tyranny—the tyranny with which he tried to crush me as a child. Then suddenly the pathos of this lonely old man pierced me. In a world where all is changed, he alone remained unchanged—as tragically isolate as the rocks. All that he had left of life was his fanatical adherence to his traditions. (p. 296)

At the end, the issue still undecided, she observes, "It wasn't just my father, but the generations who made my father whose weight was still upon me" (p. 297). She sympathizes with his need to cling desperately and futilely to his traditions, even in her anger at how destructive they had been for her and her family. The old ways that her father represented, the traditional female duties to care for the elder sage, are perceived as oppressive traps.

The story also illuminates how, in the New World, caring for old parents became a question with hard choices to be made, not an automatically assumed duty. Perhaps no other reality of modern life illustrates so clearly the radical transformation of Jewish communal structures and reconfiguring of Jewish identity. Abba in the Singer story and the father in Yezierska's story are both viewed in relation to a non-Jewish scale of social values. The criteria of the negative and positive strands have lost their clarity and can be perceived only through a double vision.

In Cynthia Ozick's (1971) "Envy, or Yiddish in America," we follow an intellectually and emotionally incestuous community of aging Yiddish writers, publishers and translators. Edelshtein, poor, jealous, and envious of the successful Ostrover, chases after a young woman who, he believes, has the power to restore his life and virility by translating his poetry into English. The world of Yiddish writers, says Ozick, is fading away, for there are too few readers. Even the young woman, a phenomenon because she can read but not write Yiddish, is taken only with the famous Ostrover, who can be read in English. Yiddish, for her, is a route to literature—a tool, not a cause. The old, except for the famous Ostrover, are impotent, helpless, and resentful. The question is left undecided—is Edelshtein's poetry good even in Yiddish? Is there automatic virtue in the elder who is ignored? In any case, even the posttraditional secular Yiddish world, with its aging denizens, has no power, no juice, no capacity to reproduce itself. For Edelshtein, it has lost the Darwinian battle for survival.

## Israel

S. Y. Agnon bridged the Old World to the new Israel. One of his legendary-style Hebrew stories, "Tehilah," presents the title character "as comely an old woman as you have seen in your days . . . Righteous she was, and wise she was, and gracious and humble: for kindness and pity were the light of her eyes, and every wrinkle in her face told of blessing and peace" (Blocker, 1965, p. 23). She is the angelic essence of all that was good and sacred about life in the Old City of Jerusalem among the pious. Devout, always performing *mitzvot* of service, Tehilah is filled only with blessings for others—and she is more than a century old. Her counterpoint in the story is the old, cranky *rabbanit*, the rabbi's widow who is sick, bitter, and utterly cynical about the changes approaching. From two different perspectives, the same message comes from the old women. The sacred world, built on the values of scholarship, piety, and *mitzvot,* is ended. Her commitment to the values of the old has filled Tehilah's inner life with pain; she has outlived her life but cannot leave until she finds a way to right a wrong committed long ago by her father against someone already dead. The end of the story is Tehilah's end and is the end of that kind of Judaism, in Agnon's view. The traditional positive images, no longer supported by a traditional community, also age.

Aharon Megged's "The Name," the work of a Polish-born Israeli author, also focuses on new and old in the Holy Land (Blocker, 1965). To the postindependence, native-born Sabra, the ghetto-ish, Yiddish-speaking, religious Jew represents passivity, weakness, cowardice—and being old. Grandfather Zisskind was about to become a great-grandfather. He asks his granddaughter and her husband to name their child Mendele in remembrance of the grandchild who did not survive Hitler. They refuse the memories, the ties, the name. He cracks, and when they bring the great-grandchild to visit, "the aged father did not recognize the great-grandchild whose life would be no memorial" (p. 105). Zisskind's daughter, the new grandmother, seems to represent Megged's viewpoint, "I don't know . . . at times it seems to me that it's not Grandfather who's suffering from loss of memory, but ourselves, all of us."

Hugh Nissenson, an American writer, gives another picture of the old, pious European Jew transplanted to Israel. "The Crazy Old Man" is set in Jerusalem during the 1967 war (Chapman, 1974). The narrator is an intelligence officer who is trying to pry information out of two Arab soldiers. When he aims to kill one to loosen the tongue of the other, his neighbor, an elderly Hasid, tries to convince him that such a murder will defile the holy city. Concerned only with the current battle, the officer takes aim again. The old man grabs the gun, kills the Arab himself, and walks away. The other prisoner talked.

The next time the officer sees the Hasid: "His eyes were blue and slightly glazed with the madness that had made him take my crime upon himself because I had been born in the country into which his God had returned the Jews to give them their last chance" (p. 136). The old man acted with decisiveness and strength, even ruthlessness, but he acted to fulfill the values of the tradition.

## Contemporary American Portraits

Jewish-American fiction presents strong elders and pathetic elders. Their weakness is presented as the result of the normal failings of age—the familiar negative strand—and of the dislocation of the culture—a distinctly modern negative feature. They are admired now for what others perceive as atypical strengths, rather than for their fulfillment of widely accepted roles as traditional Jewish elders.

Bruno Lessing's "The Americanization of Shadrach Cohen" presents a counterpoint to Singer's story about Abba and his sons (Olitzky, 1989). This father too was a pious Russian Jew whose two sons emigrated and, having established a business, sent for him, expecting him to retire and give them his money. They had become "Americanized" and were ashamed of his traditional clothing and ways. In contrast to Abba, the father asserts his economic power over them, takes charge of the store, and teaches them both how to run a business American-style while retaining his patriarchal position and religious practice. He gained their respect because he had proved himself in their world. Lessing gives us an active, aggressive elder who was able to outstrip his sons in the public world of commerce without sacrificing his religion. But in modern style, his Judaism had become his personal way of being.

A number of portraits recall the gloomy picture of old age in Qohelet Rabbah: being mocked, infantilized, and even ignored by one's own family. Such images are mostly of old men and correlate with Meyerhoff's (1978) description of a typical divergence of men and women in the aging process, which must be connected somehow with women normally outliving their partners. She tells of her grandmother Sofie, who, after the death of her husband, lost her home and became a "perpetual visitor in her grown children's households." Toward the end of their life together, Jacob, her husband, "appeared to shrivel while his wife, Sofie, expanded. There was the suggestion of a similar reversal taking place among the old men and women in the Center community" (p. 241).

Eugene Ziller's "Terrible Mistakes" tells the story of a widower who refused to live with his children or spend his time in clubs or sitting on park benches (Olitzky, 1989). He decides to go back to work. There is no job for him in the garment trade where he had worked his whole life. Eventually, he takes a job as a newsstand operator in a subway station, where he is exploited by the manager. Trying to protect his merchandise and job, he is seriously beaten—perhaps killed. An active desire to continue functioning doesn't mean that there will be an appropriate place—or a safe place.

Seymour Epstein's Mr. Isaacs, far more passive externally, sits daily almost immobile on a chair outside the apartment house where he lives with his complaining daughter and her husband (Olitzky, 1989). His inner world is filled with memories of a past full of acts of loyalty and courage but without rewards. Each day as he goes to bed, the same scene repeats itself:

> Now he composes his body for sleep, or death—he knows not which. Often it is for death he decides, but in the moment of choice a figure springs up . . . a shabby figure, pathetic, neither old nor young, but one whose story is so unique, so full of failures close to Mr. Isaacs' heart, so devoid of triumphs, that Mr. Isaacs feels toward it a great compassion—and would linger one more day in a world that contains its presence. (p. 173)

He lives out of pity for an unfulfilled self, as if he were a *dybbuk* occupying his own body.

Yet there are small triumphs when a measure of choice is left. Edna Ferber tells the story of "Old Man Minick," who, after his retirement, his wife's death, and financial disaster, is taken in by his dutiful son and daughter-in-law (Olitzky, 1989). There is not enough room, his daughter-in-law watches carefully what and how much he eats, and he is deprived of the second pillow he loves to fall asleep with. He finds community in political discussions with other old men on park benches; but when winter comes, that too ceases. When he overhears his daughter-in-law telling friends that the reason she doesn't get pregnant is that there is no room for a baby, he takes his life back into his own hands and signs into a "home" where some of his park friends live. In the final scene of the story, he is at the home happily engaged with his park cronies, and he breaks off the discussion to tell an attendant to inform the housekeeper that he wants two pillows on his bed. Meaning and a certain measure of freedom require separation from his family in a world where living arrangements are not designed to include grandparents.

## Women's Voices

As women's voices are heard, the experience of the daughter with aging parents emerges, as we see in Yezierska's (1975) work. In 1983, Kim Chernin published a memoir of four generations of mothers and daughters—her family story. The immigrant great-grandmother of the story suffered and broke under the oppression of an unhappy, frustrated, brutal husband; her story differs little from that told by Yezierska. The grandmother escaped that oppression by her own initiative, working hard for the education that was now available to her. She became radicalized in the process—a Communist organizer who fought for human liberation. Her daughter, a writer, agrees to write her story, and her daughter's daughter's path is still unknown.

Although the loving connection between the generations of women is strong, each ages differently. The patterns of aging for each gender now change from generation to generation with astonishing rapidity. When patterns change, meanings change, and there is less confidence that one can discover some already existing, ageless meaning in any stage of life.

Old age no longer represents an anchor in the past, a reward for fulfillment of ageless values. A stage of life without personal function or social function is a prospect at least as terrifying as physical decomposition.

## POSTMODERN ELDERING

There are no convenient summaries that can embrace traditional, modern, and postmodern worlds. The problems of aging among contemporary Jews are the problems of aging in our society, as more and more people live well beyond their child-rearing and working years. A new periodical, *The Journal for Judaism and Aging*, gathers articles that deal with Jewish issues about aging drawing on traditional sources as well as social-scientific and behavioral studies. The editor, Rabbi Kerry Olitzky, is a member of the faculty of Hebrew Union College.

Not-dying has become a crisis of its own that has created an impetus to ritualize important events in the latter parts of the life cycle. Men and women, who for a variety of reasons did not celebrate their *bar mitzvah* or *bat mitzvah*, their attainment of ritual majority at the age of 13, celebrate at later points in their lives. Many women celebrate their "croning"—their attainment of the wisdom of age, the completion of their childbearing years—in ceremonies created for the occasions (Adelman, 1986; Spiegel (1988/5749).

Rabbi Zalman Schachter-Shalomi (1991/5751), former professor of Jewish mysticism at Temple University and founder of P'nai Or Religious Fellowship, an originator and leader of the Jewish Renewal Movement, is deeply involved in a project he calls "Spiritual Eldering." His hope is to transform the eldering process into an opportunity for self-transformation where elders are enabled to mentor, to share the fruits of their life experience, no longer cut off from other generations by the age segregation that is as much a matter of consciousness as it is of living arrangements.[21]

At those moments when the gap between generations seems the widest, we also find evidence of strong desires to unify the generations, heal the rifts, and see the aging as pioneers in a stage of life that has never before existed in such a massive way in human history. This calls for a radical change of perspective that perceives our elders to be moving ahead of the rest, rather than as relics of the past. Our postmodern world needs a reconfigured positive wisdom image, a recognition that those elders who have learned how to change with integrity in a rapidly changing world are the models we need.

Experience can lend a critical, yet nondogmatic distance to the elder. Saul Bellow's (1970) Artur Sammler, an urbane, cultured European refugee in his 70s, observes and is drawn into the messy realities of an ever-changing world that no one can truly grasp. He is the most intelligent and stable character in *Mr. Sammler's Planet,* consulted—although rarely obeyed—by his unstable daughter, friends, acquaintances, and disciples. There are constant references to the advantages of the perspective of age, the clarity that comes when sexual obsession releases its hold on consciousness. And there are contrasts: the Sammler who can only watch impotently while a virile black thief exposes himself as a warning; the European intellectual Sammler who is abused by the young, ignorant, rude Columbia audience. This generational divide is different, for Sammler is not a traditional Jew but an old-fashioned Enlightenment Jew with liberal politics. His values are still intellectual; and as he ages, Sammler notices that his reading, always omnivorous, now begins to focus on spiritual authors, although more Western than Jewish classics. Yet he holds stubbornly to the apparently outmoded modern ideal of the intellectual tradition as a guarantor of social order. The young are ignorant, callow, chaotic.

Sammler is a wiser Job perhaps, for he has the sense of humor that Job lacks. The ending of Bellow's book is an ironic counterpoint to God's response to Job's complaints about the difficulties of his long life. God assaults Job with his superiority, with the impossibility of knowing the creator's intentions for us. Sammler, viewing the mortal remains of his nephew, muses that he is now "deprived of one more thing, stripped of one more creature. One more reason to live trickled out" (Bellow, p. 285). Gazing at the corpse, he offers a silent eulogy, addressing God:

> Remember, God, the soul of Elya Gruner, who . . . was aware that he must meet, and he did meet—through all the confusion and degraded clowning of this life through which we are speeding—he did meet the terms of his contract. The terms which, in his inmost heart, each man knows. As I know mine. As all know. For that is the truth of it—that we all know, God, that we know, that we know, we know, we know. (pp. 285f.)

## NOTES

[1] The study of aging in Jewish literature and history is rudimentary. There is one modest article in *The Jewish Encyclopedia* (Philipson) and another more recent one in the *Encyclopedia Judaica* (Ben-Sasson, Herr). Both collect the traditional sources; the limited space devoted reflects the relative scarcity of materials for comment. A useful resource is Leopold Loew's (1875) late-19th-century treatment of stages of life in Jewish literature. Sheldon Blank has a very useful article on aging in the Hebrew Bible in the *Interpreter's Dictionary of the Bible.* Recent interest in the topic is a response to an ever-increasing proportion

of elderly in the population. Several years ago, *The Journal for Aging and Judaism* began publication under the editorship of Professor Kerry M. Olitzky of Hebrew Union College. Some articles have examined traditional sources.

[2] Even when Job is in his deepest suffering and spiritual disillusionment, he rejects his wife's suggestion that he "curse God and die," a prescription for a peculiar form of suicide. An early rabbinic tradition tells of a dispute about whether it would have been better for God not to have created humanity, given the resulting aggravation. But the question is asked from the Divine point of view, never questioning the value of life to the human (Urbach, 1987).

[3] See below, p. 160.

[4] *Tanakh* is a common acronym for *T*orah, the *Chumash* (Pentateuch), or the Five Books of Moses; *N*evi'im, "prophets," including historical narratives and the prophetic books; and *K*etuvim, "writings" of various kinds, including Psalms, Proverbs, Job, and Qohelet. Torah in this sense is the most specific use of the term.

[5] Sarah is the only woman in the Bible whose age at death is recorded.

[6] H. H. Ben-Sasson, "Elders" in *Encyclopedia Judaica,* 6:578–581. See also Reviv. Accounts of the powers of elders stretching beyond tribal boundaries probably reflect later attempts to read early Israelite institutional history nationally rather than tribally.

[7] See also Isaiah 47:6 and Lamentations 5:11ff.

[8] This theme appears also in an apocalyptic Talmudic dictum (Sotah 49b) which takes "the lack of respect and courtesy shown by the young toward elders" as a sign of the approaching time of troubles that precedes the coming of the Messiah.

[9] These views continue later, e.g., in the apocryphal *Wisdom of Jesus the Son of Sirach,* later called Ecclesiasticus, which is preserved in Greek, although originally written in Hebrew in Palestine during the early second century C.E.. Its general perspective is very similar to that of Proverbs:

> If you have not gathered wisdom in your youth, how will you find it when you are old? Sound judgment sits well on grey hairs and wise council comes well from older men. . . . Long experience is the old man's crown and his pride is the fear of the lord. (25:3–6)

[10] Quotations from Qohelet are from James L. Crenshaw's (1987) judicious commentary.

[11] Olitzky points to this passage as one of several, beginning with the biblical command to rise before the aged (Lev. 19:32) and continuing with Genesis Rabbah (Toledot 43.6), that directly relate respect for elders with reverence for God.

[12] In a *halakhic* Midrash, Sifra Kedoshim 7:12, we find this parallel, which totally disconnects scholarly attainment from age: "The rabbis held that even a young scholar is called *zaken* and should be honored, while no honor is due the ignorant or sinful, although old."

[13] For the world- and humanity-sustaining powers of Torah study, which sometimes seem theurgic, see Urbach (1987, chap. 12).

[14] Translations of the Babylonian Talmud are from the Soncino edition.

[15] However, in a 15th-century midrash a story is told of a woman whose life had become artificially prolonged by her continuing performance of a *mitzvah* that was not required of her. One can live too long; she was compassionately advised to let go of the *mitzvah* (Patai, 1980).

[16] Olitzky (1989) cites this as another passage that connects deference to elders with respect for God.

[17] Dorf (1987) brings together texts on honoring and caring for parents from traditional sources with a view to illuminating current issues. He finds in tradition both the obligation to care for aging parents and the need to live one's own life, to care for one's own family.

[18] The first Jewish "home for the aged," an institution specifically for caring for the aged, was founded in Amsterdam in the mid-18th century. The need increased with the loss of traditional communal settings (Ben-Sasson).

[19] Goitein (1988) discusses aging as reflected in the Geniza documents in volume 5, pp. 116–128. Judah ha-Levi, translated by Nina Salaman, is cited on p. 119.

[20] As Howe and Greenberg (1973) note, Yiddish fiction tended toward symbolic or "representative" figures. See their introduction, p. 33.

[21] A tape by Schachter-Shalomi entitled "Spiritual Eldering" is available from P'nai Or, 7318 Germantown Avenue, Philadelphia, PA 19119.

## REFERENCES

Adelman, P. V. (1986). *Miriam's well: Rituals for Jewish women around the year.* Fresh Meadows, NY: Biblio Press.

*Babylonian Talmud, Hebrew-English Edition of* (1990). (H. Freedmen, Trans.; I. Epstein, Ed.). London: Soncino Press.

Bellow, S. (1970). *Mr. Sammler's planet.* New York: Fawcett.

Ben-Sasson, H. H. Ageanel the aged. *Encyclopedia Judaica,* 2:343–348. "Elders," *Encyclopedia Judaica,* 6:578–581.

Blank, S. H. (1962). Age, old. In *The interpreter's dictionary of the bible* Vol. 1. (pp. 54–55) New York: Abingdon Press.

Blidstein, G. (1975). *Honor thy father and mother: Filial responsibility in Jewish law and ethics.* New York: KTAV.

Blocker, J. (Ed.). (1965). *Israeli stories.* New York: Schocken.

Chapman, A. (Ed.). (1974). *Jewish-American literature: An anthology.* New York: New American Library.

Chernin, K. (1983). *In my mother's house: A daughter's story.* New York: Harper Colophon Books.

Crenshaw, J. L. (1987). *Ecclesiastes: A commentary (The Old Testament Library).* Philadelphia: Westminster Press.

Dorf, E. N. (1987). Honoring aged fathers and mothers. *The Reconstructionist,* 5314–5320.

Eliade, M. (1963). *Myth and reality* (W. R. Trask, Trans.). New York: Harper Torch Books.

Ginzberg, L. (1961). *The legends of the Jews.* Philadelphia: Jewish Publication Society.

Goitein, S. D. (1988). *A Mediterranean society: The Jewish communities of the Arab world as portrayed in the documents of the Cairo Geniza: Vol. 5. The individual.* Berkeley: University of California Press.

Herr, M. D. Age and the aged. *Encyclopedia Judaica* 2:344–346.

Hillers, D. (1969). *Covenant: The history of an idea*. Baltimore: Johns Hopkins University Press.

Howe, I., & Greenberg, E. (1973). *A treasury of Yiddish stories* New York: Schocken.

Jacobowitz, I. (1988). Ethical guidelines for an aging Jewish world. *Journal for Aging and Judaism, 2*(3), 145–157.

Kohut, G. A. Ages of man, the seven. *The Jewish Encyclopedia* 1:233–235.

Loew, L. (1875). *Die Lebensalter in der Juedischen Literatur* Szegedin, Hungary: Sigmund Berger.

Meyerhoff, B. (1978). *Number our days*. New York: E. P. Dutton.

Matt, D. C. (Transl.) (1983). *Zohar, the book of enlightenment*. New York: Parlist Press.

Moody, H. R. (1986). The meaning of life and the meaning of old age. In T. R. Cole & S. A. Gadow (Eds.), *What does it mean to grow old?* (pp. 9–40). Durham, NC: Duke University Press.

Neusner, J. (1981). *The Tosefta*. New York: Ktav Publishing.

Neusner, J. (1988a). *The Mishnah: A new translation*. New Haven, CT: Yale University Press.

Neusner, J. (1988b). *The way of Torah: An introduction to Judaism* (4th Ed.). Belmont, CA: Wadsworth.

Nickelsburg, G. (1981). *Jewish literature between the Bible and the Mishnah*. Philadelphia: Fortress.

Olitzky, K. M. (Ed.). (1989). *"The safe deposit" and other stories about grandparents, old lovers, and crazy old men*. New York: Markus Wiener.

Ozick, C. (1971). *The pagan rabbi and other stories*. New York: Alfred A. Knopf.

Patai, R. (1980). *Gates to the old city: A book of Jewish legends*. New York: Avon Books.

Philipson, D. Age, old. *The Jewish Encyclopedia*, 1:230–232.

Reuben, S. (1987). Old age: Appearance and reality. *Journal of Aging and Judaism, 2*(2), 117–122.

Reviv, H. (1989). *The elders of ancient Israel: A study of a biblical institution*. Jerusalem: Magnes Press.

Schachter-Shalomi, Z. (1991/5751). The practice of spiritual eldering. *New Menorah: The P'nai Or Journal of Jewish Renewal* (2nd ser.) *22*, 9ff.

Spiegel, M. C. (1988/5749). Becoming a crone: Ceremony at 60. *Lilith, 21*, 18f.

Urbach, E. E. (1987). *The world and wisdom of the rabbis of the Talmud* (I. Abrahams, Trans.). Cambridge, MA: Harvard University Press.

*The Wisdom of the Zohar: An anthology of texts* (F. Lachower & I. Tishby, Trans. [into Hebrew]; D. Goldsmith, Trans. [into English]. (1989). New York: Oxford University Press.

Yezierska, A. (1975). *Bread givers*. New York: Persea Books.

7

# Islamic, Hindu, and Buddhist Conceptions of Aging

*Gene R. Thursby*

---

To complement the discussion in other chapters about conceptions of aging that derive from the majority religious traditions of Judaism and Christianity, this chapter will consider perspectives from three religious traditions whose followers in Europe and North America constituted rather small minorities until quite recently. Over the last quarter-century, however, the number of Muslims, Hindus, and Buddhists emigrating to the United States (Waugh, Abu-Laban, & Qureshi, 1983; Williams, 1988) and elsewhere outside the regions where their religions have held long-established positions of importance has been markedly increasing. Because this pattern of population shift is likely to extend well into the next century and to yield a new kind of multicultural framework in previously Eurocentric societies, a basic knowledge of the values preserved and transmitted by these formerly "foreign" traditions is now gaining a more immediate relevance for citizens of modern Western nations (Smith, 1984).

From a planetary point of view, Islam, Hinduism, and Buddhism are three of the world's major religions. According to a conservative estimate (Barrett, 1982), together the three represent about 2 billion followers or nearly 40% of all human beings now living. Hinduism (about 700 million) is the oldest among them and, like Judaism, is a religion of the ethnic or national type. As the religion of a distinctive people and place, over the centuries most of its participants have entered the religion by birth to Hindu parents or by membership in groups that underwent slow acculturation rather than by individual conversion from other great faiths. However, Hindu religion also spread along with the general cultural influence of India into southeast Asia (Indochina, Indonesia, etc.) and along with the emigration of Hindus from their traditional homeland in the subcontinent of India to other parts of the world. Islam (approaching 1 billion) and Buddhism (about 300 million) are religions of the missionary or universal type, which admit individuals from other faiths, although the latter originated in India and emerged from Hinduism. Especially in earlier centuries, both have engaged in proselytizing and conversion to recruit followers from many of the world's inhabited regions and religions.

The three religions differ from one another in the concepts and prescriptions by which they give shape to their respective visions of life. Islam, in its general attitude toward the world, has discouraged ascetic and monastic styles of life and has celebrated the family. Hinduism has sought ways to balance ascetic with family values. And Buddhism, from the beginning, made its monastic community the model for right living. Moreover, each of the three is a cumulative and complex tradition whose followers have come to include inhabitants of diverse cultures (e.g., Geertz, 1968; Lapidus, 1988), who have represented in various ways their understanding of religious truth. In each tradition, therefore, support can be found for a delimited range of alternative ways to define the stages of human life and to interpret the significance of aging (Geertz, 1973; Ostor, 1984). To treat the three together and to call them "religions" is not to claim that they are simply like one another nor even singular in their own outlook. But despite the considerable differences within and among them, they share the basic assumption that a human lifetime is brief, is nevertheless a great and rare opportunity, and can be rightly understood only in relation to what transcends it (W. C. Smith, 1963).

## ISLAM

Contemporary followers of Islam understand it to be the most recent and complete version of the revealed religions of the Western or Semitic family. Along with Judaism and Christianity, Islam (Peters, 1982) incorporates the biblical heritage that links current Muslim believers with prophets and patriarchs, and back through Abraham and Adam to the one divine Creator. Muslims also trace a line of descent from Ibrahim (Abraham) and Hagar through Ismail (Ishmael) and on down to the first Muslims at Mecca in Arabia in the seventh century of the current era. Most Muslims (Combs-Schilling, 1989) believe that Ismail, not Isaac (as in Gen. 22:2), was the son whom Abraham was called by God to sacrifice. They believe that Hagar and Ismail eventually reached Mecca after Sarah had them cast out of Abraham's household (Gen. 21:9–21) and that when Abraham later visited them, he and Ismail built the Kaba at Mecca to replace a temple to God that Adam himself had first placed there. These beliefs encourage Muslims, the followers of Islam, to see themselves as rightful heirs of the biblical heritage.

The language of scripture and divine revelation in Islam is Arabic, and nearly all of the key terms and concepts of Muslim religious life derive from that language. The world *Islam* is the name given this religion in its own distinctive scripture (Quran 5:5). It means reconciliation or surrender, and it is closely related to the world *salam* meaning peace or salvation. The derivative term *Muslim* refers to the follower of the religion, literally one who has been reconciled or who has surrendered to God. The way of reconciliation and the appropriate attitude to God are the same—submission to the divine will as revealed by the various prophets down through the last great divine messenger, the Prophet Muhammad (570–632 C.E.).

Allah is the Arabic name of God. This revered name refers to the sole divine Creator (Williams, 1963), of incomparable majesty, who is to be supremely praised and respected. As "the center and foundation of Islam" (Esposito, 1988, p. 25), Allah is believed to have revealed perfectly in the Quran, the holy scripture that was transmitted through Muhammad over a period of some 22 years from 610 to 632 C.E., how he intends people to live. The divine message in the Quran was extended and elaborated (Denny, 1985) by exemplary teachings and practices of the Prophet, who, as the final messenger of God, also was considered the most authentic interpreter of the Quran. Muhammad's exemplay words and deeds are known as Sunna and were recorded in collections called Hadith. Together with the Quran, which they complement, they formed the core of traditional Muslim law, the Sharia. Although the Sharia has been enlarged and extended over time by analogical extrapolation from this core, by learned opinion, and by consensus of the community, Muslims still maintain that Allah alone is the ultimate source of Islamic law and of its authority. Therefore, the teachings of the Quran, the precedents preserved in the Sharia, and the practices traditionally prescribed for ritual performance continue to provide the basic framework for Muslim religious life and Islamic values.

The Quran contains only about a dozen passages that make significant reference to elders, old age, and the aging process. Yet few as they are, they clearly and forcefully express the most characteristic features of the Islamic vision (Watt, 1968) of human life that informs the Quran,

Sunna, and Sharia as a whole. The key Arabic terms in the passages that make reference to old age in the Quran (Kassis, 1983) are *shaykh* (an old man, elder, aged), *kabira* (to grow, old age, to be aged, to be an old person), and *qadim* (aged, old, ancient).

Most of the Quran's teachings about elders are set in the context of biblical narratives. Prominent among them is the theme of the great patriarch Abraham and his wife receiving the good news that in old age, when it should be humanly impossible, they are to have a son (11:72, 14:39, 15:54). The tales of other patriarchs and faithful followers of the one God are recounted, too. These include the story of Joseph and his brothers in Egypt (12:78). As related in the Quran, it is assumed that their aged father should be thought to be above them but below God in authority. And Moses (28:23), as he begins his exile from Egypt, performs the good deed of watering the flocks of an elder father in Midian who lacks sons of his own, and he is thereby drawn into that family's life. Finally, the motif of the aged Abraham is repeated in references to Zachariah (3:40, 19:8) who learns in his declining old age that he is to have a son named John.

The attitude toward old age suggested by these and other passages in the Quran takes for granted the relatively weak and limited character of human life in contrast to the absolute power and majesty of Allah. Hence, the Quran tends to regard the loss of capacities that typically are suffered in old age to be only the most obvious evidence of the universal frailty and dependence that is the inevitable condition of all human creatures. The Quran affirms that it is the nature of ordinary human life, as established by divine will, to be limited and to undergo eventual destruction. Old age, according to an extraordinarily intense image in the Quran (2:266), will overtake and destroy a person in the same way that even a flourishing and well-watered orchard will be burned up by a scorching whirlwind. In this vision of life, aging and the human being who suffers it are considered to be neither more nor less than one more sign and reminder (36:68) of the overwhelming mercy, justice, and power of Allah.

Therefore, the true Muslim—the properly responsive and faithful type of human being who is the effective beneficiary of the Quran's clear vision of the nature of life—is called upon to turn away from all individual, private, and personal consolations and to conform to the rules of obedience to the divine will that are revealed in the Quran and subsequent tradition. From the Islamic perspective, only one response to the awareness of human limitation is appropriate when it is beheld in relation to the awesome majesty of Allah, and that is to submit to him and to fulfill the requirements for living as a Muslim. According to Quran 40:67–68 (Ali, 1988):

> It is He who created you from dust,
> then a drop of semen, then the embryo;
> afterwards He brings you forth as a child;
> then you attain the age of manhood,
> and then reach old age.
> But some of you die before you reach the appointed term
> that you may haply understand.
> It is He who gives you life and death.

Ethical standards derived from the Quran assume that those who have been blessed by sufficient resources should take a familial stance toward the less fortunate, less able, and weaker members of society—in particular, the orphaned, the aged, and women. The Quran (4:2–6) requires mature adults to hold in trust the property of orphans until they attain the age at which they can manage for themselves, and it directs (17:23–25) mature adult children to show kindness and respect to aged parents. The Sunna of the Prophet (Suhrawardy, 1941) reinforces the second command by connecting respect shown the elderly with honor offered to Allah. But the unstated premise is that obedience and honor to Allah always take first place in Muslim life; idolators, whatever their age or station, can neither be respected nor tolerated. An incident concerning the great patriarch Abraham in the Quran (26:69–104) reports his response to an encounter with men whose culture was based on the worship of idols. When they tried to justify themselves by saying that they were only continuing a practice that had been passed down to them by their elders, the patriarch nevertheless pronounced a severe judgment on them. In Islam, the unreserved reliance on Allah that is represented by Abraham as a prototype of the true Muslim must take precedence over and thereby qualify all other responsibilities and relationships, including respect for elders.

In traditional Islamic societies the norms applying to women have not been much different from those in most of the traditional cultures that closely interacted with the other major religions. Their proper place was defined as complementary (Nasr, 1975) rather than equal in status to men. Because the primary roles of women were identified with their childbearing function in the family (Ati, 1982), until recent times (Von Grunebaum, 1954) Muslim women tended to be excluded from most public religious, political, and social activities. Although currently (Beck, 1980) there are considerable variations in the status accorded to women and the life-style required of them in the diverse cultures with which Islam interacts (Weekes, 1984), the most characteristic traditional pattern was to subordinate women to men and to value them mainly for bearing sons.

In countries in which Muslims have undertaken experiments in social reform during the colonial era or after national independence was attained, the position of women has been a major point of discussion. In South Asia, for example, where the practice of seclusion of women (*purdah*) in the inner household (*zanana*) has been widespread (Vreede-De Stuers, 1968), Muslim reformers have sought ways to enhance the status of women (Metcalf, 1984) by asserting their moral and religious capacities, their right to receive support in case of divorce, their right to inherit property, their right to education, and in some cases their right to participate in public life so that they no longer would be invisible to society (Minault, 1986). But Muslim sectors of South Asian culture continue to evidence the pattern found in a recent study of rural Bangladesh (Ellickson, 1988), where "the woman, even in old age, remains subdued, withdrawn at least from the public realm and, sometimes, even forgotten" (p. 53). In that kind of cultural setting, there is hardly any convergence of female and male roles in old age. Gender-based status differentiation, in which the wife's standing derives from the husband's, tends to be supported by a patriarchal, patrilocal, and patrilineal family structure throughout the course of life. The eldest male in the household, for example, will retain an age-based seniority in status until death, but his wife will lose her position as female head of the house should she survive him. And as a widow, she is likely to find herself reduced to the position of an inconvenient and apparently anomalous dependent.

Although traditional Islamic law and ethics currently provide some measure of real protection to the less powerful (Esposito, 1982), in the ordinary circumstances of life in third-world Muslim societies, many elderly persons, orphans, and women simply lack the means to secure equitable treatment for themselves (Pathak & Rajan, 1989). A modernist strategy, encouraged by some Muslim jurists who hope for the gradual improvement of this situation (Weeramantry, 1988), has been to frame and propose for general adoption a Universal Islamic Declaration of Human Rights. However, it is an open question whether or not such a strategy ever would reduce the circulation of negative images of older people (Peters, 1986), which are preserved in folk and popular aspects of culture, neither derived from nor supporting Quranic values, that additionally victimize the elderly.

The most certain consolation available to a Muslim in difficult straits during the upward years may be the confidence that Allah knows the plight of every creature and will reward the faithful on the Day of Judgment. In the Quran, the whole of human life is considered to be a trial (Mir, 1987). While a Muslim lives, even a difficult old age is regarded by the devout as an opportunity to strive to perform good action and to remain faithful to God. Then, at precisely the time he determines (O'Shaughnessy, 1969), death will bring the trial to a close. In the hereafter Allah will judge, and punish or reward, each soul. Right through to the end of life and beyond (Smith & Haddad, 1981), the one Creator who alone transcends all earthly joys and woes is trusted to bring about an entirely appropriate deliverance.

## HINDUISM

Among Hindus today, whether they live somewhere in the subcontinent of India or have emigrated elsewhere abroad, there is so great a diversity of religious convictions and practices that inevitably this feature invites special notice (Embree, 1966). There are two general reasons for the extraordinary diversity that characterizes Hindusim. One of them is implicit in the term *Hindu* itself, which was first used by the Persians as a general label to refer to everything that involved India, and so "Hinduism is thus the '-ism' of the Indian people" (Zaehner, 1966). What may be called Hindu, therefore, derives from various human groups, languages, and cultures that have been indigenous to the subcontinent of India over more than 4,000 years. A second reason is that neither a single authority nor a uniform creed, dogma, or statement of doctrine unifies Hinduism (Weightman, 1984). No single founder, savior, or scripture is acknowledged by all who are given or who actively accept the label "Hindu."

Because of the difficulty of establishing a clear and comprehensive definition of Hinduism, colonial administrators in British India (Jones, 1981) treated "Hindu" as a residual category to denote the great majority of the population that remained after Muslims, Christians, Jews, and members of other clearly identifiable religious groups had been counted; and in contemporary independent India, leading intellectuals (Thapar, 1989) continue to puzzle over the theoretical assumptions and practical implications of Hindu identity. But for our purpose here, a sufficiently close approximation to a set of defining features of the Hindu "great tradition" (Singer, 1972) can be derived from the following: the enduring influence of the early incursion into India by the Aryan people, the high respect accorded the Vedic teachings that the Aryans brought with them, the Sanskrit language in which those teachings were preserved and passed on, and the hereditary class of people known as Brahmans, who have functioned as the chief mediators of religious authority (Smith, 1989).

The religious life of the Aryans, at around 1,500 B.C.E., when they entered India through its northwestern mountain passes, was polytheistic. Aryan ritual specialists, acting on behalf of their people, made sacrificial offerings to various divine beings who they believed could control particular features of the operation of the natural world. But, although most of the divine beings to whom the Aryans sacrificed eventually fell from prominence, the ritual specialists who were the mediators between the divine and the human—called Brahmans—became increasingly important. Along with their sacrificial functions, the Brahmans knew and could teach other qualified pupils how to chant the Veda. The Veda was a secret oral tradition transmitted in an early version of the Sanskrit language, and Vedic chants were thought to have a sacred power (also known as *brahman*) that could confer great benefits when properly recited. For that reason, the Veda, the Sanskrit language, and the Brahman specialists who knew how to use them continued to be held in highest esteem.

In the religion of early Indo-Aryan culture, sacrifice served as the principal ritual technique to satisfy divine beings so that in turn they might provide help for human beings. Three of the four oldest sections of the Veda—the Rig, the Sama, and the Yajur—were recited at sacrificial ceremonies. The chants recorded in them contain many general references to goods sought for the patrons of the sacrificial rituals. A similar emphasis is found in the fourth section—the Atharva Veda—which contains charms and spells that were used to bring about more specific remedies. The Brahmans presided at sacrifices in order to obtain for their patrons the divine blessings that would maintain good health, provide protection from natural and human enemies, give healing from afflictions, bring progeny and prosperity, and assure a long life. An expansive affirmation of these aims appears in an invocation in Rig Veda 1.116: "Let me be lord over this world, with good cattle and good sons; let me see and win a long life-span and enter old age as if going home" (O'Flaherty, 1981, p. 184).

The technique-oriented religion of the Aryans in India placed a strong emphasis on life enhancement and life extension. Although it took for granted that there was some kind of survival beyond this life, the notion of the afterlife in early Vedic tradition was a limited one that held little appeal (Basham, 1989). Early Aryans assumed that life is good, that more life would be better, and that the procedures performed by the Brahmans could produce it. An enthusiastic expression of this confidence in sacrificial ritual as a means of securing a ripe old age is found in Atharva Veda 19.67:

> For a hundred autumns may we see,
> for a hundred autumns may we live,
> for a hundred autumns may we know,
> for a hundred autumns may we rise,
> for a hundred autumns may we flourish,

for a hundred autumns may we be,
for a hundred autumns may we become,
—and even more than a hundred autumns!
(Panikkar, 1977, p. 303)*

The practical optimism of the early Aryans who sought to be the beneficiaries of Vedic sacrificial rites may seem familiar, and indeed it is quite similar to that of the old man in a modern American novel (Updike, 1968) who

> felt that he would persist, on this earth, forever; that all the countless others, his daughter and son among them, who had vanished, had done so out of carelessness; that if like him they had taken each day of life as the day impossible to die on, and treated it carefully, they too would have lived without end and have grown to have behind them an endless past, like a full bolt of cloth unravelled in the sun and faded there, under the brilliance of unrelenting faith. (p. 37)

But by about 600 B.C.E., the unrelenting faith in long life as good in itself was failing because of a radical shift away from the idea of the cosmos advocated by early Vedic tradition. The later Vedic view assumed that there is nothing new under the sun, that no event is unique. Every worldly occurrence is instead part of a pattern that recurs in endlessly repeating cycles thoughout vast periods of time. The Upanishads, the last part of the Vedic teachings, exemplify the adaptation of Aryan religion to the revised cosmology. They do not argue the shift in the significance of time and change but take it for granted while continuing to employ the language of sacrificial ritual. In the Upanishads, however, sacrifice becomes a metaphor for the personal striving that is required if one is to engage successfully in ascetic discipline and meditation. Moreover, these practices are considered to be effective means that are crucial to the attainment of an experience of the only dimension of oneself that is unchanging and imperishable (*atman*). Within the context of this world picture, simple life extension lost its appeal.

The later Vedic vision of the cosmos awakened a sorrowful sense that worldly life is part of an oppressive cycle that subjects a person to pain and suffering (*duhkha*) again and again, without cease. Although that ancient evaluation of the plight of the ordinary or unrealized person who is pulled along by time and change might seem far from contemporary attitudes, it has affinities with the modern "theater of the absurd." In the play *Waiting for Godot*, for example, while the other characters sleep, one of them reflects on the human predicament. Part

---

*From Mantramanjari: The Vedic Experience by Raimundo Pannikar. © 1977, University of California Press.

of his soliloquy so closely links together images of coming to life and of departing from it that the two become interchangeably identified with one another (Beckett, 1954): "Astride of a grave and a difficult birth. Down in the hole, lingeringly, the grave-digger puts on the forceps. We have time to grow old. The air is full of our cries. . . . But habit is a great deadener" (pp. 58–59). This convergence of images denies any discernible difference between the birth canal and the burial ground or crematory. The two signify the same thing—a single circle of pain and suffering. The sense of "the absurd" in the later Vedic vision, however, was enlarged by the expectation of a surfeit of lifetimes to be spent in a Hindu version of a "No Exit" (Sartre, 1958) setting in which every soul is subjected to a seemingly endless series of lives in innumerable bodies—including diverse human ones—until all desires and their consequences have been completely extinguished. This idea of *karma* and reincarnation, of a law of action that operates to carry one through countless rebirths, is central to the later Vedic and classical Hindu view of the human dilemma (Keyes & Daniel, 1983; Neufeldt, 1986; O'Flaherty, 1980).

The Hindu vision of the cosmos as a place marked by painful recurrence (*samsara*) had the power to motivate a person to undertake rigorous methods (*yoga*) to attain release (*moksha*). Although the old sacrificial rituals performed by the Brahmans had declined in prestige by 500 B.C.E., partly because their effectiveness was believed to be limited to providing boons within this world of suffering, individual techniques of sense control taught by masters of yoga and meditation were thought to meet the need of the new situation. But they required ascetic withdrawal from the world of sensuous pleasures, material interests, and family responsibilities. Sparsely inhabited forests and hills, therefore, became places for retreat from the world, where people of all ages sought spiritual realization to effect a route of escape from the otherwise endless cycles of rebirth. The joy of the perfected soul, or *atman*, that has succeeded in "shaking off" the body in order to pass into the "uncreated" reality of *brahman* is recorded in a prayer in the Chandogya Upanishad (8.13). Immediately following it, a pupil on the path to perfection is represented by a prayer (Chandogya 8.14; Hume, 1949) that includes this petition: "May I, who am the glory of the glories, not go to hoary and toothless, yea to toothless and driveling [old age]! Yea, may I not go to driveling [old age]!" (p. 273). In sharp contrast to the longing that the aging process attracted in early Aryan culture, here the prospect prompts only disgust.

The search for an ageless, unsullied self within the individual that was so characteristic of the Upanishads remained a minority pursuit within Hindu tradition. Even so, it continued to be an influential one, and representatives of the mainstream of classical Hinduism repeatedly challenged the assumption that withdrawal from the world was the only sure way to attain release from rebirth. The most successful of these mainstream efforts is embodied in the Bhagavad Gita. It is a brief scripture, some 650 Sanskrit verses, that calls itself an Upanishad but is not in fact part of the Veda. Nevertheless, it is widely acknowledged to be "the most important and influential religious text of India" and "also the best-known Hindu text in the West" (Basham, 1989, p. 82). The Gita, dating from about 200 B.C.E., is set within a great epic that concerns a feud between two warrior clans. The Gita's portion of the great epic is a dialogue between a warrior, Arjuna, and his charioteer and spiritual master, Krishna, that takes place just before the decisive battle begins. The dialogue opens with Arjuna's initial shock in anticipation of the bloody battle in which his friends and family members are sure to be killed; it passes through a discussion of the nature of time, change, selfhood, and duty; it considers the value of the old Vedic sacrificial rituals; and then it takes a surprising turn by displaying the hidden identity of Krishna as the presiding personal spirit and continuous creator of the universe, thereby backing the Gita's teachings by the highest authority.

The guidance that is given Arjuna more than once in the Gita is that he should maintain his proper position within the world and learn how to perform all of his rightful duties (*dharma*) without fear, regret, or any attempt to anticipate what might be their outcome. In the Gita, as in the Upanishads, the first step toward mastering this skill derives from the distinction between the apparent individual—the observable psychophysical entity that is subject to time and change—and the unchanging and unborn real self (2:22; Deutsch, 1968): "Just as a man casts off worn-out clothes and takes on others that are new, so the embodied soul casts off worn-out bodies and takes on others that are new." The essential self, not the evident one, establishes the ground for fearless ethical action in the ordinary world. Further support follows from the Gita's reinterpretation of the Vedic concept of *sacrifice* and of the Upanishadic concept of *renunciation* of the world. The two serve as metaphors for diligent performance of right "action . . . done without concern for its fruits" (6:1). The final warrant for the inner-worldly asceticism commended by the Gita is Krishna, when revealed to be the supreme personal spirit. He is at once the tireless source of the cosmos, who must act ceaselessly and disinterestedly in order to maintain it in existence, and the blessing-bestowing heart of reality who cares equally for everyone who is devoted to him. These combined strands of "secret knowledge" mediated by the Bhagavad Gita made it seem possible for a Hindu to experience spiritual freedom without departing from the ordinary responsibilities of human life in the world. And the Gita's influence in tilting the balance toward mastering the responsibilities of worldly life and away from withdrawing from the world in order to seek spiritual fulfillment also lent considerable support to the structure of social values that became the most distinguishing features of classical to modern Hinduism.

The distinctive social norms of Hinduism are based on a theory of classification known as caste (*varna* or *jati*) that establishes a closed hierarchy in which one's position is determined by birth (McGilvray, 1982). The Brahman has the highest status; next is the Kshatriya, or warrior; then the Vaishya, or merchant. All three are termed "twice-born" because their males are eligible to experience the "second birth" of initiation into learning the Veda. Below these three are the Shudra, or laborer, and then anyone else not born into one of the four principal classes. The traditional Hindu social ideal is one in which caste organizes people into separate categories for marriage and other close contacts, justifies a hereditary division of labor, and ranks the various categories of people and their occupations as relatively superior or inferior in relation to one another (Dumont, 1980).

For members of the "twice-born" castes, the standard pattern for the life cycle is defined by a sequence of four stages (*ashrama*) that are supposed to make possible harmonious and complete human development. The first stage is initiation by a Brahman master into Vedic learning. It is open only to the unmarried twice-born male and is marked by his investiture with a sacred cord. He will wear it, until the last stage of life, over his left shoulder. This *brahmacharya ashrama* or student stage may last anywhere from a few hours to several years. The second stage, *grihastha ashrama,* mutually involves both sexes in the sanctification of marriage and in the active responsibility for family life. This householder stage is essential to the ongoing support of the Hindu social order. The third stage, *vanaprastha ashrama,* may be entered following the birth of grandsons who assure the perpetuation of the family line. At this stage the senior couple make a transition from household duties to a more retiring and contemplative mode of life together. If they pass through this stage to the last one, *sannyasa ashrama,* they must undergo a ceremony that will strip them of their familial and social identity. In this fourth stage, the ideal type of human being is a solitary homeless wanderer who is dedicated solely to spiritual realization.

The framework of the caste hierarchy and the four stages generates a structure within which status and age are correlated with specific ethical and behavioral expectations. Hence, the Bhagavad Gita admonishes (18:47; Deutsch, 1968): "Better one's own *dharma,* though imperfect, than the *dharma* of another, well performed." Although everyone is subject to duty (*dharma*), its particular requirements are relative to one's position in the structure. For example, the *dharma* of the student initiate requires temporary withdrawal from worldly responsibilities, obedience to a preceptor, and celibacy. In contrast, the *dharma* of the householder requries dedication to the things of the world (*artha*) and a sexual relationship (*kama*) that is fertile and adds to the family. And these earlier stages are prerequisite to the later and the last. The Hindu tradition assumes that every twice-born male incurs three debts by virtue of being born, and he is required to repay them before the final stage of life. As *The Laws of Manu*, which dates from sometime after 200 B.C.E. and is the most influential text on Hindu *dharma*, allows (6:37; Buhler, 1964): "Having studied the Vedas in accordance with the rule, having begat sons according to the sacred law, and having offered sacrifices according to his ability, he may direct his mind to final liberation."

The traditional ideology of caste and the stages of life remains a significant influence on Hindu cultural values despite the contemporary decrease in exacting penalties for breaking caste rules. Only 30 years ago, in response to an interview by a reporter (Zinkin, 1962) the eldest sister of the great 20th-century Hindu social reformer Mahatma Gandhi

> exploded into toothless anger and tears: Gandhi's insistence on mixing with unclean people, on being his own sweeper, and his trips over the sea, had led to the excommunication of his whole family. For Ralihat Behen this had meant a lifetime of ostracism and humiliation by the people about whom she minded: the orthodox of her own sub-caste and neighbourhood. Far from feeling proud of her brother, she stood there, doubled up by rheumatism, calling him a man so selfish that he had not cared what harm he had done to his family. (pp. 49–50)

Since India became a constitutional republic, most caste rules have lost their legal basis and are rarely enforced (D. E. Smith, 1963); but caste ideals persist because they are suffused with the traditional concern for spiritual liberation and diffused throughout the extended family system. And two recent studies (Hiebert, 1981; Vatuk, 1990) suggest that these traditional ideals continue to serve useful functions among the aging peasantry in South Asian society. Hiebert (1981) observes that the ideal of caste and stages of life in Hinduism "provides its followers with explicit and detailed plans for living, in which age is charted as a series of progressively higher stages of human activity" (p. 211).

Because the most obvious beneficiaries of the traditional values of caste are twice-born Hindu males, there remains the question of the relative status of aging and elderly women. In the polytheistic pattern of traditional Hinduism, goddesses have a prominent place, so the feminine is certainly honored at the level of worship and religious myth (Kinsley, 1988). But unless supported at the social level, this could be an instance of the "apparent paradox between symbolic ascendancy and the social denigration of women" (Sinclair, 1986, p. 112). Evidence on this question is not conclusive (Robinson, 1985), but there are some data suggesting that elderly Hindu women in upper-caste urban settings may be more likely than men to seek new sources of support for their sense of identity in old age. Roland (1988) claims that "the overt hierarchical structure of male dominance which is so evident in any number of ways in the family and other social structures is balanced by the enormous, covert structural powers of the women" (p. 217). But Roy (1975) found that in their later years high-caste women from Bengal tended to shift toward an identity increasingly based on a relationship with a spiritual master, or guru, and away from a family nexus in which support for their status was declining with the onset of old age. As in some Muslim cultures, there is evidence that elderly women in Hindu culture may be more likely than men to be marginalized within the family by the aging process and therefore to be more motivated than elderly men to seek solace in spiritual activities and associations.

## BUDDHISM

Islam promotes family life. Hinduism reveres the renouncer but seeks to protect family values by establishing a balance between the claims of worldly responsibilities and the call of spiritual pursuits that may require their renunciation. The Hindu ethos nonetheless favors the family. "Hindus themselves acknowledge the fascination with renunciation," sociologist T. N. Madan (1989) notes, "and yet postpone it to the very end of a person's life as its fourth stage, after the stages of study, householdership, and retirement. In fact, only a microscopic minority actually renounce the world" (pp. 119–120). But whereas mainstream Islam and Hinduism tip the scale of values toward the home and world, the early and determining orientation of Buddhism was toward the celibate, homeless, wandering world renouncer.

The orientation was not unique to Buddhism. It was shared by the later Vedic tradition, as represented in the Upanishads, and by Jainism—another Indian ascetic movement that eventually came to be regarded as a separate religion. The attitudes and aims of these faiths were deeply influenced by the ancient Shramans (Johnson, 1980), wandering ascetics who were antiworldly counterparts to the Vedic Brahmans. Accordingly, they share a cosmology in which the fate of all beings, as determined by their own *karma* or modes of action over successive lifetimes, is to suffer a ceaseless round of rebirths (*samsara*) into various bodies until they are able to discover and dedicate themselves to an effective method for attaining release.

When Gautama the Buddha (about 560–480 B.C.E.) made a monastic community central to his religious movement, it indicated that status distinctions determined by birth are spiritually irrelevant and that freedom from worldly values is required for release from *samsara*. Although a large lay following later became associated with the Buddhist movement, the monk remained a presiding ideal type. And a characteristic emphasis in Buddhist literature continued to be withdrawal from the world: "One who does not abandon worldly pleasures squanders this life. Therefore, completely sever attachments and ties and remain in secluded mountain dwellings. Yet unlike the birds, deer, and other animals in such secluded places, exert body, speech, and mind in what is virtuous" (Rangdrol, 1989, p. 21).

In Buddhism, and in Jainism and Hinduism as well, the subject of old age serves as a source of object lessons to motivate people to cultivate the attitude of detachment that eventually turns toward a renunciation of worldly values. Therefore, in the spiritual literature of all three traditions there are incisive images of old age in terms of its most painful prospects:

> When old age shatters the body, gradually the limbs become loose; the old person's teeth decay and fall out; he becomes covered with wrinkles and sinews and veins; he can't see far, and the pupils of his eyes are fixed in space; tufts of hair appear in his nostrils, and his body trembles. All his bones become prominent; his back and joints are bent; and since his digestive fire has gone out, he eats little and moves little. It is only with pain and difficulty that he walks, rises, lies down, sits, and moves, and his hearing and sight become sluggish; his mouth is smeared with oozing saliva. As he looks toward death, all of his senses are no longer controlled; and he cannot remember even important things that he had experienced at that very moment. (O'Flaherty, 1988, pp. 100–101)

According to Buddhist tradition (Pye, 1979; Schumann, 1989), Gautama is said to have set out on the search for realization that led him to become the Buddha, the Enlightened One, after seeing four disturbing sights. The first of them was an old man in about the same decrepit condition as just described. That sight, which revealed to the innocent Gautama the consequences of aging, was crucial. The next two, of a sick man and a dead man, further developed the awareness of suffering that had been awakened by the first sight. Then, the fourth sight was of a monk whose appearance represented to the receptive Gautama an alternative way to engage the limited resources and possibilities of a human lifetime.

Traditional versions of the life of the Buddha tell that after his comfortable worldly existence had been interrupted by the preliminary realization conferred by the four sights, he left his home and family in order to find spiritual teachers and to take up the austere life of a Shraman. After some years of study and self-denial, he adopted a more moderate way of living and soon experienced a deep realization of the human predicament. During a long night of quiet sitting, he was able to see the roots of suffering (*duhkha*) in ignorant craving and the means of release from it through the "middle way" of an ordered life that would facilitate meditation and make possible the cultivation of disinterested compassion. From that decisive enlightenment experience (Robinson & Johnson, 1982), the Buddha went out to teach his new Dharma and to enlist disciples into a new monastic community, the Sangha, that was open to all who would follow its rules of discipline (Dutt, 1957).

The Buddha taught a method for attaining release that assumed "the dissolution of suffering depends on the dissolution of the concept of the self" (Little & Twiss, 1978, p. 211). Buddhist meditation (Conze, 1962) became the laboratory for work on the project of dissolving the sense of separate selfhood—which the Buddha had defined as rooted in ignorance and had identified as a link in the chain of desire, craving, and *karma* that distorts reality into repetitive cycles of suffering that give shape to *samsara*. By adopting meditation as his principal technique, the Buddha replaced the procedures of physical mortification required by the Shramans and the Jains with "the mental mortification of the contemplation of universal suffering" (Collins, 1982, p. 235). The Buddhist aim was similar to theirs: release from ceaseless becoming. But the point of departure was different. What set the Buddhists apart was the

> claim that the ontological self is a delusion, and that this delusive sense of self is the fundamental duhkha (frustration) which distorts our experience and disturbs our lives. Contrary to all schools of ego psychology, such a self can never become secure because its very nature is to be insecure. . . . [T]he sense of self is not a thing but a lack, which can conceal its own emptiness only by keeping ahead of itself—that is, by projecting itself into the next thought, action, and so on—which process is craving or desire (Loy, 1988, p. 209)

In the Buddhist analysis of existence, impermanence is the actual condition of life in the world, and the sense of separate selfhood is inevitably a failing, false refuge from it. Any effort to deny the certainty of the aging and death of the embodied self, for instance, merely intensifies "pervasive anxiety that is held at bay only through the strength of forgetting or refusing to look more closely" (Huntington, 1989, p. 87). Rather than denial, the Buddhist method of meditation or mindfulness opens with a preparatory level of practice in which one is required to look closely and repeatedly at all conditions of embodied life until no longer perturbed by them. Then, at a second level of practice, the goal is to settle into calm, clear insight. As support for practice, Buddhism recommends a triple refuge composed of the method and teaching of the Buddha and the life of the monastic order. Together they constitute a path of spiritual development that is directed toward the cessation of a desire-driven separate identity, toward release, toward *nirvana*.

Paradox is prominent in Buddhist teaching at all levels and in all cultures in which Buddhism has been practiced. After the four sights that prompted his searching and Shramanic self-denial, at last sitting quietly the Buddha arrived at decisive clarity and commitment to a middle path. An old Buddhist text presumes to preserve his insight:

> For the attached there is wandering, but for the unattached there is no wandering: without wandering there is serenity; when there is serenity there is no lust; without lust there is neither coming nor going; without coming or going there is neither passing away nor being reborn; without passing away or being reborn there is neither this life nor the next, nor anything between them. It is the end of suffering. (Beyer, 1974, p. 200)

And it is the end of aging as a problem. But most people, even those who find Buddhist truth clear and bracing, find that it is difficult to give up their attachment to the seemingly enduring personal identity that is created by interaction with family, friends, and institutions. Consequently, elite or monastic Buddhism differs greatly from popular or lay Buddhism (e.g., Gombrich & Obeyesekere, 1988; Spiro, 1970; Tambiah, 1970), even though the status of women in Buddhist tradition (Barnes, 1987; Willis 1985) probably differs less from that of men than in Islam or Hinduism. "Canonically," Spiro (1970) observes in reference to monastic religion: "Buddhism is not at all involved in the changes of status that sociologically mark the individual's passage through the life cycle. Although contemporary Buddhism pays greater attention to these points of transition, it too has less involvement in them than is characteristic of other religions" (p. 232). And because it tends not to be involved in these conventional concerns, the practices of its laity tend not to be limited exclusively to Buddhism. Lay Buddhists are likely to consult local charismatic figures, participate in spirit cults, or rely upon other religious traditions for help in crisis situations and for rituals that support transitions through the life cycle.

Buddhist selflessness (*anatman* or *anatta*) and the Hindu unchanging Self (*atman*) that is its polar complement are assumed by their respective traditions to be "autochthonous" (Bharati, 1985, p. 203). Therefore, both of those images of human identity differ radically from the Muslim conception of a personal self whose continuity through old age, death, and beyond is dependent upon a Creator to whom it remains ever responsible. Because of such basic conceptual differences, Shrinivas Tilak (1989) concludes that "what aging is . . . depends upon what is understood by the notion of human beings and their embodiment. It must . . . be determined just what it is that ages" (p. 148). Responses to this question of "what it is that ages," from Buddhist perspectives and addressed to general readers, are represented in recent books by Harding (1988), Kapleau (1989), and Mullin (1986). All three aim to calm anxiety and awaken an "ageless" presence.

## REFERENCES

Ali, A. (1988). *Al-Qur'an: A contemporary translation.* Princeton, NJ: Princeton University Press.

Ati, H. 'Abd al. (1982). *The family structure in Islam.* Lagos, Nigeria: Islamic Publications Bureau.

Barnes, N. S. (1987). Buddhism. In Sharma, A. (Ed.), *Women in world religions* (pp. 105–133). Albany, NY: State University of New York Press.

Barrett, D. B. (Ed.). (1982) *World Christian encyclopedia: A comparative study of churches and religions in the modern world,* A.D. *1900–2000.* Nairobi, Kenya: Oxford University Press.

Basham, A. L.(1989). *The origins and development of classical Hinduism* (K. G. Zysk, Ed.). Boston: Beacon Press.

Beck, L. (1980). The religious lives of Muslim women. In J. I. Smith (Ed.), *Women in contemporary Muslim societies* (pp. 27–60). Lewisburg, PA: Bucknell University Press.

Beckett, S. (1954). *Waiting for Godot.* New York: Grove Press.

Beyer, S. (Ed. & Trans.). (1974). *The Buddhist experience: Sources and interpretations.* Encino, CA: Dickenson.

Bharati, A. (1985). The self in Hindu thought and action. In A. J. Marsella, G. DeVos, & F. L. K. Hsu (Eds.), *Culture and self: Asian and Western perspectives* (pp. 185–230). New York and London: Tavistock.

Buhler, G., tr. (1964). *The laws of Manu.* Delhi: Motilal Banarsidass.

Collins, S. (1982). *Selfless persons: Imagery and thought in Theravada Buddhism.* Cambridge: Cambridge University Press.

Combs-Schilling, M. E. (1989). *Sacred performances: Islam, sexuality, and sacrifice.* New York: Columbia University Press.

Conze, E. (1962). *Buddhist thought in India: Three phases of Buddhist philosophy.* London: George Allen & Unwin.

Denny, F. M. (1985). *An introduction to Islam*. New York: Macmillan.

Deutsch, E. (Trans.). (1968). *The Bhagavad Gita*. New York: Holt, Rinehart and Winston.

Dumont, L. (1980). *Homo hierarchicus: The caste system and its implications* (rev. ed.; M. Sainsbury, L. Dumont, & B. Gulati, Trans.). Chicago: University of Chicago Press.

Dutt, S. (1957). *The Buddha and five after-centuries*. London: Luzac.

Ellickson, J. (1988). Never the twain shall meet: Aging men and women in Bangladesh. *Journal of Cross-Cultural Gerontology, 3*, 53–70.

Embree, A. T. (Ed.). (1966). *The Hindu tradition*. New York: Random House.

Esposito, J. (1982). *Women in Muslim family law*. Syracuse, NY: Syracuse University Press.

Esposito, J. L. (1988). *Islam: The straight path*. New York: Oxford University Press.

Geertz, C. (1968). *Islam observed: Religious development in Morocco and Indonesia*. New Haven, CT: Yale University Press.

Geertz, C. (1973). Religion as a cultural system. In C. Geertz (Ed.), *The interpretation of cultures: Selected essays* (pp. 87–125) New York: Basic Books.

Gombrich, R. & Obeyesekere, G. (1988). *Buddhism transformed: Religious change in Sri Lanka*. Princeton, NJ: Princeton University Press.

Harding, D. E. (1988). *The little book of life and death*. London and New York: Arkana.

Hiebert, P. G. (1981). Old age in a south Indian village. In P. T. Amoss & S. Harrell (Eds.), *Other ways of growing old: Anthropological perspectives* (pp. 211–226). Stanford, CA: Stanford University Press.

Hume, R. E. (Trans.). (1949). *The thirteen principal Upanishads* (2nd ed.). Madras: Oxford University Press.

Huntington, C. W., Jr., with Wangchen, G. N. (1989). *The emptiness of emptiness: An introduction to early Indian Madhyamika*. Honolulu: University of Hawaii Press.

Johnson, W. (1980). *Poetry and speculation of the Rig Veda*. Berkeley: University of California Press.

Jones, K. W. (1981). Religious identity and the Indian census. In N. G. Barrier (Ed.), *The census in British India: New perspectives* (pp. 73–101). New Delhi: Manohar.

Kapleau, P. (1989). *The wheel of life and death: A practical and spiritual guide*. New York: Doubleday.

Kassis, H. E. (1983). *A concordance of the Qur'an*. Berkeley: University of California Press.

Keyes, C. F., & Daniel, E. V. (Eds.). (1983). *Karma: An anthropological inquiry*. Berkeley: University of California Press.

Kinsley, D. (1988). *Hindu goddesses: Visions of the divine feminine in the Hindu tradition*. Berkeley: University of California Press.

Lapidus, (1988). *A history of Islamic societies*. Cambridge: Cambridge University Press.

Little, D., & Twiss, S. B.(1978). *Comparative religious ethics*. San Francisco: Harper & Row.

Loy, D. (1988). *Nonduality: A study in comparative philosophy.* New Haven, CT: Yale University Press.

Madan, T. N. (1989). Religion in India. *Daedalus, 118*(4), 115–146.

McGilvray, D. B. (Ed.). (1982). *Caste ideology and interaction* (Cambridge Studies in Social Anthropology, No. 9). Cambridge: Cambridge University Press.

Metcalf, B. D. (1984). Islamic reform and Islamic women: Maulana Thanawi's *Jewelry of paradise.* In B. D. Mercalf (Ed.), *Moral conduct and authority: The place of Adab in South Asian Islam.* (pp. 184–195). Berkeley: University of California Press.

Minault, G. (1986). Making invisible women visible: Studying the history of Muslim women in South Asia. *South Asia* (ns), *9,* 1–13.

Mir, M. (1987). *Dictionary of Qur'anic terms and concepts.* New York: Garland.

Mullin, G. H. (1986). *Death and dying: The Tibetan tradition.* Boston: Arkana.

Nasr, S. H. (1975). *Ideals and realities of Islam.* Boston: Beacon Press.

Neufeldt, R. W. (Ed.). (1986). *Karma and rebirth: Post classical developments.* Albany: State University of New York Press.

O'Flaherty, W. D. (Ed.). (1980). *Karma and rebirth in classical Indian traditions.* Berkeley: University of California Press.

O'Flaherty, W. D. (Ed. & Trans.). (1981). *The Rig Veda: An anthology.* Harmondsworth, UK: Penguin Books.

O'Flaherty, W. D. (Ed. & Trans.). (1988). *Textual sources for the study of Hinduism.* Totowa, NJ: Barnes & Noble.

O'Shaughnessy, T. (1969). *Muhammad's thoughts on death: A thematic study of the Qur'anic data.* Leiden: E. J. Brill.

Ostor, A. (1984). Chronology, category, and ritual. In D. I. Kertzer & J. Keith (Eds.), *Age and Anthropological Theory* (pp. 281–304). Ithaca, NY: Cornell University Press.

Panikkar, R. (Ed. & Trans.). (1977). *The Vedic experience.* Berkeley: University of California Press.

Pathak, Z., & Rajan, R. S. (1989). Shabano. *Signs, 14,* 558–582.

Peters, F. E. (1982). *Children of Abraham: Judaism/Christianity/Islam.* Princeton, NJ: Princeton University Press. .

Peters, I. (1986). The attitude toward the elderly as reflected in Egyptian and Lebanese proverbs. *The Muslim World, 76,* 80–85.

Pye, M. (1979). *The Buddha.* London: Duckworth.

Rangdrol, T. N. (1989). *The mirror of mindfulness: The cycle of the four Bardos* (E. P. Kunsang, Trans.). Boston: Shambhala.

Robinson, R. H., & Johnson, W. L. (1982). *The Buddhist religion: A historical introduction* (3rd ed.). Belmont, CA: Wadsworth.

Robinson, S. P. (1985). Hindu paradigms of women: Images and values. In Y. Y. Haddad & E. B. Findly (Eds.), *Women, religion, and social change* (pp. 181–215). Albany: State University of New York Press.

Roland, A. (1988). *In search of self in India and Japan: Toward a cross-cultural psychology.* Princeton, NJ: Princeton University Press.

Roy, M. (1975). *Bengali women.* Chicago: University of Chicago Press.

Sartre, J. P. (1958). *No exit: A play in one act* (Adapted from the French by Paul Bowles). New York: French.

Schumann, H. W. (1989). *The historical Buddha: The times, life and teachings of the founder of Buddhism* (M. O'C. Walshe, Trans.). London: Arkana.

Sinclair, K. (1986). Women and religion. In M. I. Duley & M. I. Edwards (Eds.), *The cross-cultural study of women: A comprehensive guide* (pp. 107–124). New York: Feminist Press.

Singer, M. (1972). *When a great tradition modernizes: An anthropological approach to Indian civilization.* New York: Praeger.

Smith, B. K. (1989). *Reflections on resemblance, ritual, and religion.* New York: Oxford University Press.

Smith, D. E. (1963). *India as a secular state.* Princeton, NJ: Princeton University Press.

Smith, J. I., & Haddad, Y. Y. (1981). *The Islamic understanding of death and resurrection.* Albany: State University of New York Press.

Smith, W. C. (1963). *The meaning and end of religion: A new approach to the religious traditions of mankind.* New York: Macmillan.

Smith, W. C. (1984). The modern west in the history of religion. *Journal of the American Academy of Religion, 52,* 3–18.

Spiro, M. E. (1970). *Buddhism and society: A great tradition and its Burmese vicissitudes.* New York: Harper & Row.

Suhrawardy, A. al-M. (Comp.). (1941). *The sayings of Muhammad.* London: John Murray.

Tambiah, S. J. (1970). *Buddhism and the spirit cults in north-east Thailand.* Cambridge: Cambridge University Press.

Thapar, R. (1989). Imagined religious communities? Ancient history and the modern search for a Hindu identity. *Modern Asian Studies, 23,* 209–231.

Tilak, S. (1989). *Religion and aging in the Indian tradition.* Albany: State University of New York Press.

Updike, J. (1968). *The poorhouse fair.* Harmondsworth, UK: Penguin Books.

Vatuk, S. (1990). To be a burden on others: Dependency anxiety among the elderly in India. In O. Lynch (Ed.), *Divine passions: The social construction of emotion in India* (pp. 64–88). Berkeley: University of California Press.

Von Grunebaum, G. E. (1954). *Medieval Islam: A study in cultural orientation* (2nd ed.). Chicago: University of Chicago Press.

Vreede-De Stuers, C. (1968). *Parda: A study of Muslim women's life in northern India.* Assen: Van Gorcum.

Watt, W. M. (1968). *What is Islam?* London: Longmans, Green.

Waugh, E. H., Abu-Laban, B., & Qureshi, R. B. (Eds.). (1983). *The Muslim community in North America.* Edmonton: University of Alberta Press.

Weekes, R. V. (Ed.). (1984). *Muslim peoples: A world ethnographic survey* (2nd ed.). Westport, CT: Greenwood Press.

Weeramantry, C. G. (1988). *Islamic jurisprudence: An international perspective.* London: Macmillan Press.

Weightman, S. (1984). Hinduism. In J. R. Hinnells (Ed.), *A handbook of living religions* (pp. 191–236). New York: Viking.

Williams, J. A. (Ed.). (1963). *Islam.* New York: Washington Square Press.

Williams, R. B. (1988). *Religions of immigrants from India and Pakistan: New threads in the American tapestry.* Cambridge: Cambridge University Press.

Willis, J. D. (1985). Nuns and benefactresses: The role of women in the development of Buddhism. In Y. Y. Haddad & E. B. Findly (Eds.), *Women, religion, and social change* (pp. 59–85). Albany: State University of New York Press.

Zaehner, R. C. (1966). *Hinduism*. New York: Oxford University Press.

Zinkin, T. (1962). *Caste today*. London: Oxford University Press.

8

# Fairy Tales and Spiritual Development in Later Life: The Story of the Shining Fish

*Allan B. Chinen*

Handed down through the ages, fairy tales contain invaluable folk insights about human nature, as psychoanalysts, sociologists, and folklorist have argued (Bettelheim, 1976; Dieckmann, 1986; Dundes, 1986; Grolnick, 1986; Heuscher, 1974; Tatar, 1987; Von Franz, 1977; Zipes, 1979). Because most familiar fairy tales, like "Cinderella" and "Snow White," are about children or adolescents, interpretations of fairy tales have emphasized the psychology of youth—how the stories symbolize important psychological tasks of childhood and help socialize children by inculcating moral and cultural values in them (Degh, 1982; Zipes, 1983). Historically, however, fairy tales were the province of adults, not children. Fairy tales were told by adults, to adults (Heuscher, 1974; Tatar, 1987; Von Franz, 1977) and were about adults. Indeed, in many cultures today, this tradition lives on, and professional storytellers earn their living regaling adults at bazaars and public gatherings. Their stories, understandably, feature adult protagonists with whom mature listeners can identify. These tales constitute a distinct, much-neglected genre of fairy stories, and they are the subject of this chapter. In particular, I will discuss fairy tales that feature "old" people as protagonists, a group that might be called "elder tales" (Chinen, 1989).

As we shall see, elder tales from different cultures share similar plots and themes, distinctly different from those in "youth tales" (fairy stories about children or adolescents). The unique cross-cultural motifs of elder tales, I argue, reveal the psychology of late life, just as youth tales reveal the psychology of youth. Elder tales essentially contain centuries of folk wisdom about aging, and elucidating those insights is the aim of this chapter.

Elder tales, however, offer more than a simple historical record of folk ideas on aging or an archeology of gerontology. The stories remain highly relevant today for two reasons. First, like any other literature that has withstood the test of time, from mythology to Homer and Shakespeare, elder tales reflect deep human aspirations: what can be, rather than what simply is—ideal adult development and the highest measure of humankind. Elder tales thus offer an invaluable corrective to modern psychological research, which focuses on the average, the statistical mean. Second, as we shall see, the focus of elder tales is on spiritual development and the task of transcendence. Elder tales thus provide another welcome antidote to the secular focus of contemporary research in aging, which neglects the transpersonal aspects of later life. Modern psychology, of course, avoids espousing any particular religious outlook for the sake of greater universality. Surprisingly, however, elder tales also exhibit such universality and are quite "nondenominational." The major themes of elder tales are not tied to any particular religion, partly because fairy tales represent an alternative to established religious doctrines and teaching stories: fairy tales typically revel in what church, temple, synagogue, or mosque will not tolerate. Elder tale insights about transpersonal developments in later life are therefore astonishingly relevant to secular society.

## METHOD

A systematic search was made for fairy tales published in English about protagonists called "old," using the libraries of the University of California at Berkeley. For purposes of this study, fairy tales were defined as (1) folktales, (2) not meant to be literally believed, (3) having happy endings, and (4) dealing with ordinary human beings (Bettelheim, 1976; Heuscher, 1974). Hence, the following were excluded: (1) literary fairy tales written by individual authors; (2) legends, which claim to be true; (3) ghost or horror stories, which have unhappy endings; (4) myths, which focus on superhuman protagonists; and (5) fables, which are about animals.

Elder tales were defined as stories that explicitly call their protagonist(s) old; that is, the older person is the central figure, not a secondary character. The latter is the case in most fairy tales: an old man or woman either helps or hinders the young hero and heroine, but the young protagonist retains the dramatic spotlight.

Few elder tales give the actual ages of their protagonists, beyond calling them old, but from clues scattered in various tales, it appears that "old" means anyone over 40 or 50. Although this may be horrifying to modern adults, the historical context of fairy tales must be recalled: the stories presumably originated centuries ago, when the average life expectancy was much less than it is to day. Anyone surviving to 40 or 50 would therefore have been exceptionally old.

Of about 5,000 fairy tales reviewed, approximately 3% qualify as elder tales. There is significant geographic variation, with elder tales most common in Eastern cultures, like those of Japan, Arabia, India, and China, and least common in western Europe. One factor is that Eastern societies traditionally accord older adults more respect than is the case in Western culture and thus more frequently place older people as protagonists in their fairy tales. Historically, however, Western culture has also revered elders (Arnett, 1985), so further explanation is required. A second possible factor is that Western fairy tales, like the Grimms' collection, were published specifically for children because of the growing market among the emerging bourgeoisie in the 1800s. Stories were therefore revised to appeal to children (Rowe, 1986; Tatar, 1987; Zipes, 1979, 1983), and often the role of the older protagonist was reduced or eliminated (Chinen, 1989). Fairy tales from other countries, however, were collected in a much later period, often by anthropologists rather than book publishers, so youth-centered revisions were less common.

When elder tales are identified and compared with each other, recurrent themes are readily identifiable. For the purposes of this study, only themes present in at least two different stories from distinct cultures were analyzed. This comparative method avoids the criticism commonly raised against psychoanalytic interpretations: that they overemphasize idiosyncratic details of a particular story that are absent in other versions of the tale (Dundes, 1986; Grolnick, 1986; Schenda, 1986; Tatar, 1987; Zipes, 1976, 1979).

On the other hand, folkloric studies typically analyze large numbers of fairy tales to elucidate their literary structures—the basic types of plots and characters (Aarne & Thompson, 1961; Propp, 1968; Thompson, 1955). Folkloric studies thus avoid overinterpreting details, but they also tend to neglect the psychological symbolism of stories. Hence, they frequently ignore the rich folk insights in fairy tales. In the present study, therefore, I focused specifically on the psychological themes of the tales, the symbolism of the events and characters, while maintaining a comparative approach. I am hopeful that this method threads a middle way between psychoanalytic and folkloric perspectives.

In this chapter, I will focus on a typical elder tale that exemplifies most of the major themes in elder tales. I will first summarize the story, then discuss its symbolism in comparison with other elder tales, and finally, relate the fairy tale themes to findings from research in the psychology of aging.

## THE SHINING FISH

Once upon a time, an old man and his wife lived in a house overlooking the sea. Through the years, all their sons died, leaving the couple alone and impoverished in old age. The old man barely earned a living by gathering wood in the forest and selling it for firewood. One day in the wilderness, he met a man with a long white beard. "I know all about your troubles," the stranger said, "and I want to help." He gave the old man a small leather bag and when the old man looked in it, he stared in astonishment: the purse was filled with gold! By the time the old man looked up, the stranger was gone. So the old man threw away his wood, and rushed home. But along the way, he began to think. "If I tell my wife about this money, she will waste it all." And so when he arrived at home, he said nothing to his wife. Instead he hid the money under a pile of manure.

The next day, the old man awoke to find that his wife had cooked a wonderful breakfast, with sausages and bread. "Where did you find the money for this?" he asked his wife.

"You did not bring any wood to sell yesterday," she said, "so I sold the manure to the farmer down the road." The old man ran out, shrieking with dismay. Then he glumly went to work in the forest, muttering to himself.

Deep in the woods, he met the stranger again. The stranger laughed, "I know what you did with the money, but I still want to help." So he gave the old man another purse filled with gold. The old man rushed home, but along the way he started thinking again. "If I tell my wife, she will squander this fortune . . ." And so he hid the money under the ashes in the fireplace. The next day he awoke to find his wife had cooked another hearty breakfast. "You did not bring back any firewood," she explained, "so I sold the ashes to the farmer down the road."

The old man ran into the forest, and met the stranger a third time. The man with the long beard smiled sadly. "It seems you are not destined to be rich," the stranger said. "But I still want to help." He offered the old man a large bag. "Take these frogs, and sell them in the village. Then use the money to buy the largest fish you can find—not dried fish, shell fish, sausages, cakes or bread. Just the largest fish!" With that the stranger vanished.

The old man hurried to the village and sold his frogs. Once he had the money in hand, he saw many wonderful things he could buy at the market, and he thought the stranger's advice odd. But the old man decided to follow the instructions, and bought the largest fish he could find. He returned home too late in the evening to clean the fish, so he hung it outside from the rafters. Then he and his wife went to bed.

That night, it stormed, and the old man and woman heard the ocean thundering on the rocks below their house. They prayed for any fishermen who might be caught out in the storm, as their sons had been, years before. In the middle of the night, someone pounded on the door. The old man went to see who it might be, and he found a group of young fishermen dancing and singing outside. "Thank you for saving our lives!" they told the old man.

"What do you mean?" the old man asked. So the fisherman explained that they were caught at sea by the storm, and did not know which way to row until the old man put out a light for them. "A light?" he asked. So they pointed. And the old man saw his fish hanging from the rafters, shining with such a great light it could be seen for miles around.

From that day on, the old man hung out the shining fish each evening to guide the young fishermen home, and they shared their catch with him. And so he and his wife lived in comfort and honor the rest of their days (Calvino, 1978).*

## COMMENTS

The story opens with an old man and his wife living in poverty. The theme is present in virtually every elder tale and can be seen in the Arabian story "The Fisherman and the Djinn" (Burton, 1978), the Japanese tale "The Six Jizo" (Ohta, 1955), and the German story "The Aged Mother"(Grimm, 1944), among many others. A natural interpretation of this motif is that it was literally true when fairy tales arose: unable to manage the hard physical labor required to earn a living long ago, adults presumably suffered great poverty in old age. Historically, however, this was not the case. Even in preindustrial cultures today, elders generally wield significant power through their ownership of property and their mastery of practical skills, guaranteeing them great social respect (e.g., Biesele & Howell, 1981; Hughes, 1961). So the poverty motif is better interpreted symbolically rather than literally. I suggest that the theme symbolizes the multiple losses that older adults fear in later life—the loss of friends or relatives, of youthful beauty and strength, and ultimately, the loss of one's own life. The theme can also be interpreted as a symbol of depression, a common malady of later life (Blazer, 1982; Brink, 1982; Gurland & Cross,1982; Klerman, 1983;

Raymond & Michals, 1980). To make this image of loss even more dramatic, the present story specifically says that the old couple's children had all died, so they have sustained perhaps the deepest grief an adult can suffer. By beginning with such a dismal picture, this story—and it is typical of elder tales in general—warns us that it will not gloss over the problems of growing old. Elder tales are not simply idealistic, romantic fantasies but deal with the very real psychological dilemmas of aging. The present story quickly goes on to elaborate on that theme.

The old couple lives on the seashore at the edge of a forest: they occupy the boundary between land and sea, on the one hand, and between wilderness and civilization, on the other. The same setting can be found in many other elder tales, like the Middle Eastern story of "Fortune and the Woodcutter" and the Arabian tale "The Simple Grasscutter" (Lang, 1914). Forests and oceans are typically symbols of the unconscious in fairy tales and dreams (Jung, 1952/1956; Von Franz, 1980), so the elder's location near them suggests that becoming open to the unconscious is an important development of later life. The present story underscores this motif by saying that the old man gathers wood from the forest for a living. Symbolically, he collects material from the unconscious. This would be an overly elaborate interpretation of a small detail in the story, except for one fact: wood gathering and fishing appear prominently in elder tales from around the world, suggesting that the two occupations are symbolic. (By contrast, fairy stories of middle age emphasize more technical occupations, like weaving or soldiering; and fairy tales of youth, of course, feature protagonists who have no trade at all.)

In fact, psychoanalysts have often noted that older adults in therapy are generally more open to unconscious material than are younger adults (Baker & Wheelwright, 1982; Grotjahn, 1951, 1955; King, 1974), and systematic longitudinal studies have confirmed this phenomenon. For instance, in a long-term study of a select cohort of Harvard college students, Vaillant (1977) observed that during adolescence many individuals did not remember traumatic events from their childhood. (These events were known to the investigators and often were quite dramatic—for example, the suicide of a mother.) From midlife onward, however, these repressed memories returned. As individuals aged, they became more open to the unconscious and had less need to repress unpleasant material. Metaphorically, they moved nearer the boundary between conscious and unconscious, closer to the symbolic forest and sea.

In the present story, the old man meets a stranger who gives him a bag of gold. This is the next major theme of elder tales: magic returns unexpectedly and in the course of ordinary events. The motif appears in virtually every elder tale, including the tales already mentioned: "Fortune and the Woodcutter," "The Fisherman and the Djinn," and "The Six Jizo." The present story then gradually reveals the psychological meaning of this magic.

After receiving the gold, the old man hides the treasure without telling his wife. He acts out of suspicion and greed, and the fact that the old man conceals the gold under *manure* emphasizes the odious nature of his motivations. When the old man's wife inadvertently sells the manure the next day, he is punished for his avarice. Surprisingly, however, the old man receives a second bag of gold from the stranger. The old man hides it again, still acting out of suspicion and greed, but a little less so than previously: the ashes in which he hides the gold are not as foul as manure. But the old man loses his money a second time anyway, much to his regret. Fortunately, the stranger reappears with yet another gift—this time a bag of frogs and a bit of advice about selling the frogs and using the money to buy the largest fish available at the market. The injunction seems odd, as the old man realizes when he sees what else he could buy with his money. Moreover, a single large fish is hardly practical; dried fish, or something less perishable would seem more useful. Though tempted, the old man nevertheless obeys the stranger, and this is a crucial event. We might infer that the old man heeds the stranger's advice because he knows by now how poor his own judgment can be: he lost a fortune twice because of his greed. And here the story introduces two major themes of elder tales: self-reformation and self-transcendence (Chinen, 1989).

The old man was greedy in hiding the gold and trying to keep it for himself, and so he lost it. This is a typical event in fairy tales—greedy or otherwise evil figures are punished. What is distinctive about the present story and about elder tales in general is that the old man is given two more chances and *finally realizes the error of his ways*. This self-reformation theme can be seen even more clearly in the Japanese tale "The Priest's Towel" (Dorson, 1962) and in the Jewish story "The Miser" (Friedlander, 1920). The theme is, moreover, virtually never present in tales of youth. There the good and the bad are clearly demarcated, and the wicked are summarily punished. In the original Grimms' version of "Cinderella," for example, the virtuous young Cinderella marries the Prince and lives happily ever after, while her wicked stepsisters and stepmother have their eyes plucked out by doves. Villains do not reform in youth tales. Indeed, when the young hero and heroine do something evil, their wickedness is typically blamed on an evil spell from another person (Luthi, 1979), leaving the young protagonist blameless. (The villain who cast the spell, of course, is destroyed.)

Elder tales thus suggest, somewhat surprisingly, that older adults are more able to change than are younger ones and are more open to their own faults, less prone toward projecting those shortcomings onto other people. In fact, contemporary research confirms these folk insights. In a longitudinal study based in Berkeley, California (Brooks, 1981; Haan, 1981; Mussen & Haan, 1981), investigators followed a panel of individuals from youth to late middle age and noted the steady decline in projection and "extrapunitiveness"—the practice of blaming others for one's own faults and difficulties. Similar results were obtained by Vaillant (1977) in his longitudinal study of Harvard students. Adolescents and young adults typically protect their tender sense of identity by denying their faults and shortcomings and by blaming other people (usually parents, teachers, and other authority figures). With greater maturity and a more secure sense of identity, older individuals are able to face the unsavory elements within themselves.

Closely associated with the theme of self-confrontation is that of self-transcendence. The old man in our story heeds the stranger's advice, odd though the counsel seems at first. The old man thus breaks free from his greed. This theme of self-transcendence is one of the major motifs of elder tales; it can be seen in "Princess Moonlight" from Japan (Ozaki, 1970), "Stribor's Forest" from Croatia (Berlic-Mazuranic, 1924), "The Cat and the Dog" from Korea (In-Sob, 1979), "The Mortal Lord" from China (Moss, 1979), and "The Aged Mother" from Germany (Grimm, 1944), among others. In each of these stories, an old protagonist is forced to transcend his or her egocentric desires in order to adopt a wider perspective in which the individual is only a small part. The forms of this self-transcendence differ, depending upon whether the story uses a religious, social, or psychological framework, but the process remains the same.

In the German tale "The Aged Mother," for instance, an explicitly Christian tradition holds: an old woman bitterly laments the death of her two young children and her husband years before. In the midst of her sorrow, however, she has a divine vision, revealing why her children and husband died early—to save their immortal souls. With this transcendent understanding, the old woman gives up her egocentric sorrow and finds inner peace.

In the Croatian story "Stribor's Forest," an old woman suffers greatly at the hands of her wicked daughter-in-law, who is really an evil spirit who has enchanted the old woman's son. But a good wizard offers the poor mother a chance to go back in time and live in the happiest period of her life, escaping her suffering. To do so, however, means she must abandon her grown son to the spell of his wife. So the old mother declines her chance at happiness, intent on finding some way of helping her son. But by making her choice she breaks the spell of the wicked daughter-in-law. So the old woman gives up a personal reward for the sake of her son, in the spirit of what Erikson called generativity (Erikson, 1983; Erikson, Erikson, & Kivnick, 1986). Here the context is social and interpersonal rather than religious, but the process of self-transcendence is the same as in "The Aged Mother." In both cases, the individual gives up an egocentric perspective for a larger, more inclusive viewpoint.

Similarly, in "The Mortal Lord" from China, a great king laments the thought of his death and wishes he and all of his friends could live forever. All of the nobles echo the king's sentiments, but one of them laughs and later reveals the reason: if they all lived forever, that would mean that everybody from the beginning of time would still be alive. Hence, the great heroes and sages of history would still live, and, compared to them, the king and all of his friends would be nothing! The king realizes the error of his ways and gives up lamenting the thought of his death. Here the monarch adopts a historical perspective rather than a religious one: just as his predecessors died to make way for him, so must he give way to those after him. Again, however, the *process* of self-transcendence is similar to that in "The Aged Mother" and "Stribor's Forest."

Self-transcendence and spiritual development in later life are important concerns in many religious traditions: Chinese Confucianism stressed the importance of turning to the "Mandate of Heaven" after 50 years of age (Wei-Ming, 1978); the Hindu laws of Manu prescribed giving up material power and responsibility in the second half of life to pursue spiritual enlightenment (Kakar, 1979; Rhadakrishnan & Moore, 1957); Jewish tradition likened old age to the Sabbath and made it a time for contemplating the mysteries of the Torah (Katz, 1975); and medieval Christianity encouraged older individuals to turn away from worldly preoccupations to prepare for death (Curran, 1981). What elder tales offer is a relatively "nondenominational" portrait of spiritual development, not tied to a particular worldview but focused on a general process—that of self-transcendence. This underlying process takes many various forms, suitable for different worldviews, making the theme uniquely relevant to modern pluralistic society.

The present story is unusually complete, however, and goes on to another theme: self-transcendence is not the final end of development in late life. After buying the largest fish he can find, the old man returns home and hangs it outside from the rafters. Doing so seems odd, even in an age without refrigerators, because the fish might be stolen or eaten by animals. The act, however, underscores the fact that the old man has transcended his greed, suspiciousness, and egocentricity. He no longer tries to hoard the stranger's gifts for himself; instead he symbolically offers the fish to the world.

That night a terrible storm breaks out and threatens the lives of several young fishermen. They are saved by the old man's fish, which has been transformed into a magic lantern. The story thus introduces the final theme in elder tales: the old man brings magic into the world, which helps the next generation. He mediates between this realm and the next, benefiting society. The same theme can be seen in the Tibetan story "The Frog" (Hyde-Chambers & Hyde-Chambers, 1981) and in the Arabian tale "The Enchanted Head" (Lang, 1914), as well as in "The Fisherman and the Djinn" and "Princess Moonlight," mentioned above.

Elder tales thus make clear that the task of older person is not simply to transcend themselves and live in a private exalted state of insight but to bring that transcendent wisdom back for the benefit of young men and women. Transcendence must be tempered with generativity. The elder's wisdom, of course, is an important theme in fairy tales of youth: typically, the wise old man or the helpful fairy godmother draws on wisdom and magic to rescue the young protagonist from a dreadful danger. "The Shining Fish" is important in showing how the elder gains the "magic" and wisdom: through a long process of psychological development, involving self-confrontation and self-transcendence.

If elder tales portray the older adult mediating between a supernatural realm and the human order, the stories merely reflect the traditional role of elders in preindustrial societies. Elders act, as David Gutmann (1983) observed, as "bridgeheads to the sacred," linking their people to the gods or the ancestors. This sacred role has been much diminished in modern secular society, depriving older adults of opportunities for transcendent experiences (e.g., Shahrani, 1981). Nevertheless, many older individuals return to spiritual concerns despite social pressures against such a development. Alfred North Whitehead is perhaps the most dramatic example of the process (Chinen, in press; Lawrence, 1968; Lowe, 1985; Whitehead, 1941).

Although religious as an adolescent, Whitehead consciously gave up his spiritual concerns to pursue a career in mathematics. He was elected to the Royal Society at a relatively early age for his *Treatise on Universal Algebra* and then collaborated with Bertrand Russell in writing *Principia Mathematica*, a paragon of logical reasoning. In middle age, Whitehead turned toward more pragmatic pursuits, concerned with the role of mathematics in education (Whitehead, 1917). In his 60s, however, he embarked upon an entirely new area of work—metaphysical philosophy. This was at a time when metaphysics was held in ill-repute, but Whitehead was by this time unconcerned with matters of prestige or academic success. He then went on to elaborate an original theological philosophy (Whitehead, 1925, 1926, 1938) and, through his lectures, seminars, and writing, profoundly influenced a new generation of theologians. Whitehead transcended egocentric concerns about status and success to pursue his spiritual interests and then brought back his insights to the next generation.

Other individuals exemplify the process of transcendence and mediation in more secular ways (McLeish, 1976; Pruyser, 1975). Benjamin Spock, for instance, late in life, risked his reputation as America's premier child care authority to protest the Vietnam War. Unconcerned about losing the respect and honor he had earned from his many years as a physician, Spock committed himself to social reformation as a transcendent value. A similar situation, I should add, occurred with the French philosopher Voltaire (de Beauvoir, 1972). Late in life, Voltaire personally took up several controversial causes and had to flee France on several occasions. He put social reformation, and his sense of justice, above his own safety and reputation.

Transcendence and generativity, however, are not the province only of famous people. In the Berkeley and Harvard longitudinal studies mentioned before, altruism, as measured by time and money donated to charitable causes, increased with age and correlated with better mental health (Haan, 1981; Vaillant, 1977). Other studies with different socioeconomic groups have confirmed the findings (Heath, 1983; Thurnher, 1975; Vaillant & Milofsky, 1980; Viney, 1987). Transcendence put to use in the real world is not merely an ideal of later life; it is a necessity for successful aging.

One final theme in "The Shining Fish" deserves notice, although it is a subtle one. Notice the succession of symbolic objects in the story. The narrative begins with *gold*, moves on to *frogs*, and ends up with a *fish* that is soon transformed into a shinging *light*. Here a mythological framework for interpretation is useful because gold, frogs, and fish appear frequently in myths and legends around the world. Gold, for example, is typically a symbol of human culture and human consciousness (Luthi, 1979; Neumann, 1954). The color of the sun is gold, and the sun—indeed, light in general—symbolizes consciousness. Gold is also used for money in virtually every society. So gold symbolizes secular life and civilization, the highest measure of human consciousness.

The story quickly dispenses with the gold, not once but twice, in case we missed the importance of the event. Material reward and secular achievement are not the goals of the second half of life. Frogs appear next in the story, and their symbolism is complex and profound (Von Franz, 1977). Since frogs are amphibious animals that inhabit the boundary between water and land, they make excellent symbols for the boundary between unconscious and conscious. The old man loses his gold, symbolizing culture and consciousness, and ends up with frogs instead, representing a transitional state. He then exchanges the frogs for a fish. As creatures of water, hidden from sight, fish are frequently construed as symbols of the unconscious by psychoanalysts and mythologists (Neumann, 1954; Von Franz, 1977). Moreover, fish are much less developed than frogs, lacking any limbs at all, so they symbolize a primitive level of existence.

However, in the tale, the fish becomes a shining beacon; that is, a symbol of a primitive state is transfigured. This brings up the traditional iconography of the fish as a symbol of Christ. (The meaning would probably have been known to the Italian, and thus presumably Catholic, narrators of this tale.) The fish therefore symbolizes two things at the same time—an early, basic, or primitive kind of experience, unconscious and undeveloped, on one hand, and spiritual renewal, on the other. The frogs serve as a transition to both the lowest and the highest states man can experience, the beginning and the end.

The theme is reinforced by the frog motif. Frogs are often symbols of renewal and transfiguration (Hyde-Chambers & Hyde-Chambers, 1981). Indeed, Italian folklore associates frogs specifically with Easter and the transfiguration of Christ (Miller, 1976), perhaps because frogs undergo a dramatic physical change around Easter, changing from tadpole to frog. Frogs therefore make a good symbol for the transformation of the material into the spiritual, the natural into the numinous.

This interpretation of the sequence of objects would surely be making a symbolic mountain out of a fairy tale molehill, except for one thing: the same theme can be seen in other elder tales, like "The Old Man Who Lost His Wen" (Ozaki, 1970); "The Six Jizo," from Japan; "The Magic Forest," from Croatia; and the Cossack tale "The Straw Ox" (1895). Together, the stories suggest that older adults return to earlier psychological stages, but those states are transformed into something spiritual and numinous. The theme is somewhat surprising because both folk wisdom and gerontological literature emphasize the regressive changes that occur with age. Older adults in many cultures are said to enter a second childhood, and both cognitive psychologists and psychoanalysts have commented on the apparent emotional and intellectual regression that accompanies old age (Gutmann, 1964, 1987; Labouvie-Vief & Hakim-Larson, 1989; Linden, 1961; Zinberg, 1961). However, the notion that apparently regressive states may actually constitute new and more sophisticated modes of experience has recently become the subject of exploration.

Labouvie-Vief, for instance (Labouvie-Vief & Hakim-Larson, 1989), argues that "mythos" ideally returns in later life, to complement the logos of youth. By "mythos" Labouvie-Vief means subjective, emotional, intuitive, and metaphoric understanding—the language of myth—in contrast to the logic, objectivity, and intellectuality of "logos"—the language of science. Mythos thus resembles the "magical" thinking that reappears in cases of dementia and that represents regression to the child's "primary process" thinking. Labouvie-Vief argues, however, that healthy mature adults do not regress but rather integrate mythos with logos, yielding a deeper, more complex, and inclusive mode of understanding—wisdom rather than wishful thinking. Elsewhere, I have also argued that a mature form of animism reappears in later life and that this does not represent regression to the child's animism but is rather a sophisticated cognitive perspective, closely allied to what spiritual and mystical traditions regard as enlightenment (Chinen, 1985, 1986, 1988, 1989). To be sure, the hypothesis that older adults ideally return to earlier psychological modes, transformed into spiritual states, requires further investigation. The suggestion underscores an important point, however; the folk insights of elder tales not only corroborate modern research in the psychology of aging but also offer stimulating new hypotheses for investigation.

## CONCLUDING REMARKS

"The Shining Fish" exemplifies most of the major themes in elder tales. These motifs appear in stories from around the world and symbolize, I suggest, the drama of late life—the journey beyond the self, toward generativity and the illumination of society. Clearly, this short chapter cannot do justice to the rich insights of elder tales or the complexity of spiritual development in the later years. I also have not addressed how older individuals today use these stories, for example, in psychotherapy. The clinical and personal relevance of elder tales would require a whole separate discussion. My goal in this chapter was simply to put forward three notions. First, traditional fairy tales about old people are rich treasuries of wisdom about aging. Second, these tales address a subject frequently neglected in contemporary gerontology: the development of spirituality and wisdom. And finally, although the fairy tales come from traditional cultures, they offer a surprisingly "nondenominational" perspective, which lends itself readily to modern, secular intepretations. The timeless folk wisdom in these stories is astonishingly relevant to modern life.

## REFERENCES

Aarne A., & Thompson, S. (1961). *The types of the folktale: A classification and bibliography*. Helsinki: Academia Scientarium Finnica.

Arnett, W. S. (1985). Only the bad died young in the ancient Middle East. *International Journal of Aging and Human Development, 21,* 155–160.

Bain, R. N. (1895). *Cossack fairy tales and folk tales.* New York: Stokes.

Baker, B., & Wheelwright, J. (1982). Analysis with the aged. In M. Stein (Ed.), *Jungian analysis* (pp. 256–274). La Salle, IL, and London: Open Court.

Berezin, M. (1961). Some intrapsychic aspects of aging. In N. E. Zinberg & I. Kaufman (Eds.), *Normal psychology of the aging process* (pp. 93–117). New York: International Universities Press.

Berlic-Mazuranic, I. (1924). *Croatian tales of long ago.* London: Allen & Unwin.

Bettelheim, B. (1976). *The uses of enchantment: The meaning and importance of fairy tales.* New York: Knopf.

Biesele, M., & Howell, N. (1981). "The old people give you life": Aging among !Kung hunter-gatherers. In P. Amoss & S. Harrell (Eds.), *Other ways of growing old.* Stanford, CA: Stanford University Press.

Blazer, D. (1982). *Depression in late life.* St. Louis: Mosby.

Brink, T. (1982). Geriatric depression and hypochondriasis: Incidence, interaction, assessment and treatment. *Psychotherapy: Theory, Research and Practice, 19,* 506–511

Brooks, J. B. (1981). Social maturity in middle age and its developmental antecedents. In D. Eichorn, J. Clausen, N. Haan, M. Honzik, & P. Mussen (Eds.), *Present and past in middle life* (pp. 244–269). New York: Academic Press.

Burton, R. F. (Trans.) (1978). *Tales from the Arabian Nights.* New York: Avenel.

Calvino, I. (1978). *Italian folktales* (G. Martin, Trans.). New York: Pantheon.

Chinen, A. B. (1985). Fairy tales and transpersonal development in later life. *Journal of Transpersonal Psychology, 17,* 99–122.

Chinen, A. B. (1986). Elder tales revisited: Forms of transcendence in later life. *Journal of Transpersonal Psychology, 18,* 171–192.

Chinen, A. B. (1988). *Elder tales and the return of wonder in later life.* Paper presented at the Annual Meeting of the Gerontological Society of America, San Francisco.

Chinen, A. (1989). In the ever after: Fairy tales and the second half of life. Wilmette, IL: Chiron.

Chinen, A. (in press). Adult cognitive development: The case of Alfred North Whitehead. In M. L. Commons, C. Armon, L. Kohlberg, F. A. Richards, T. Grotzer, & J. Sinnott (Eds.), *Beyond formal operations: Vol. 3. Models and methods in the study of adolescent and adult thought,* New York: Praeger.

Curran, C. (1981). Aging: A theological perspective. In C. LeFevre & P. LeFevre (Eds.), *Aging and the human spirit: A reader in religion and gerontology* (pp. 68–82). Chicago: Exploration Press.

de Beauvoir, S. (1972). *The coming of age* (P. O'Brian, Trans.). New York: G. P. Putnam's Sons.

Degh, L. (1982). Grimm's *Household tales* and its place in the household: The social relevance of a controversial classic. In M. M. Metzger & K. Mommsen (Eds.), *Fairy tales as ways of knowing: Essays on Marchen in psychology, society and literature* (pp. 21–53). Bern: Lang.

Dieckmann, H. (1986). *Twice-told tales: The psychological use of fairy tales* (B. Matthews, Trans.). Wilmette, IL: Chiron.

Dorson, R. (1962). *Folk legends of Japan*. Tokyo: Tuttle.

Dundes, A. (1986). Fairy tales from a folkloristic perspective. In R. Bottigheimer (Ed.), *Fairy tales and society: Illusion, allusion and paradigm* (pp. 259–270). Philadelphia: University of Pennsylvania Press.

Erikson, E. (1959). *Identity and the life cycle*. New York: International Universities Press.

Erikson, E. (1983). *The life cycle completed*. New York: Norton.

Erikson, E., Erikson, J. M., & Kivnick, H. Q. (1986). *Vital involvement in old age*. New York: Norton.

Franzke, E. (1989). *Fairy tales in psychotherapy: The creative use of old and new tales*. Toronto: Hogrefe & Huber.

Friedlander, G. (1920). *The Jewish fairy book*. New York: Stokes.

Grimm, J. (1944). *The complete Grimms' fairy tales* (Margaret Hunt, Trans.). New York: Pantheon.

Grolnick, S. (1986). Fairy tales and psychotherapy. In R. Bottigheimer (Ed.), *Fairy tales and society: Illusion, allusion and paradigm* (pp. 203–217). Philadelphia: University of Pennsylvania Press.

Grotjahn, M. (1951). Some analytic observations about the process of growing old. *Psychoanalysis and the Social Sciences, 3*, 301–312.

Grotjahn, M. (1955). Analytic psychotherapy with the elderly. *Psychoanalytic Review, 42*, 419–427.

Gurland, B., & Cross, P. (1982). Epidemiology of psychopathology in old age: Some implications for clinical services. *Psychiatric Clinics of North America, 5*, 11–26.

Gutmann, D. (1964). An exploration of ego configurations in middle and later life. In B. L. Neugarten (Ed.), *Personality in middle and late life*. New York: Atherton.

Gutmann, D. (1983). Observations on culture and mental health in later life. In J. E. Birren & R. B. Sloane (Eds.), *Handbook of mental health and aging* (pp. 114–148). Englewood Cliffs, NJ: Prentice-Hall.

Gutmann, D. (1987). *Reclaimed powers: Toward a new psychology of men and women in later life*. New York: Basic Books.

Haan, N. (1981). Common dimensions of personality: Early adolescence to middle life. In D. Eichorn, J. Clausen, N. Haan, M. Honzik, & P. Mussen (Eds.), *Present and past in middle life* (pp. 117–154). New York: Academic Press.

Heath, D. (1983). The maturing person. In R. Walsh & D. Shapiro (Eds.), *Beyond health and normality: Explorations of exceptional well-being* (pp. 152–206). New York: Van Nostrand Reinhold.

Heuscher, J. (1974). *A psychiatric study of myths and fairy tales: Their origin, meaning and usefulness*. Springfield, IL: Charles C. Thomas.

Hughes, C. (1961). The concept and use of time in the middle years: The St. Lawrence Island Eskimos. In R. Kleemeir (Ed.), *Aging and leisure: A research perspective into the meaningful use of time*. New York: Oxford University Press.

Hyde-Chambers, F., & Hyde-Chambers, A. (1981). *Tibetan folk tales*. Boulder, CO: Shambhala.

In-Sob, Z. (Ed.). (1979). *Folk tales from Korea*. New York: Grove Press.

Jung, C. (1956). Symbols of the mother and rebirth. In *Collected Works* (Vol. 5, pp. 207–273). Princeton, NJ: Princeton University Press. (Original work published 1952).

Kakar, S. (1979). Setting the stage: The traditional Hindu view and the psychology of Erik H. Erikson. In S. Kakar (Ed.), *Identity and adulthood* (pp. 2–12). Delhi: Oxford University Press.

Katz, R. L. (1975). Jewish values and socio-psychological perspectives on aging. In S. Hiltner (Ed.), *Toward a theology of aging* (pp. 135–150). New York: Human Sciences Press.

King, P. H. M. (1974). Notes on the psychoanalysis of older patients: Reappraisal of the potentialities for change during the second half of life. *Journal of Analytical Psychology, 19,* 22–37.

Klerman, G. (1983). Problems in the definition and diagnosis of depression in the elderly. In L. D. Breslau & M. R. Haug (Eds.), *Depression and aging: Causes, care and consequences*. New York: Springer Publishing Co.

Labouvie-Vief, G. J., & Hakim-Larson, J. (1989). Developmental shifts in adult thought. In S. Hunter & M. Sundel (Eds.), *Midlife myths: Issues, findings and practice implications*. Newbury Park, CA: Sage.

Lang, A. (1914). *The brown fairy book*. London: Longmans, Green.

Lawrence, N. (1968). *Whitehead's philosophical development: A critical history of the background of process and reality*. New York: Greenwood.

Linden, M. E. (1961). Regression and recession in the psychoses of the aging. In N. E. Zinberg & I. Kaufman (Eds.), *Normal psychology of the aging process* (pp. 125–142). New York: International Universities Press.

Lowe, V. (1985). *Understanding Whitehead: The man and his work*. Baltimore: Johns Hopkins Press.

Luthi, M. (1979). *The fairy tale as art form and portrait of man* (J. Erickson, Trans.). Bloomington: Indiana University Press.

McLeish, J. (1976). *The Ulyssean adult: Creativity in the middle and later years*. New York: McGraw-Hill Ryerson.

Miller, D. (1976). Fairy tale or myth. In *Spring 1976* (pp. 157–164). Dallas: Spring Publications.

Moss, R. (1979). *Chinese fairy tales and fantasies*. New York: Pantheon.

Mussen, P., & Haan, N. (1981). A longitudinal study of patterns of personality and political ideologies. In D. Eichorn, J. Clausen, N. Haan, M. Honzik, & P. Mussen (Eds.), *Present and past in middle life* (pp. 393–414). New York: Academic Press.

Neumann, E. (1954). *The origins and history of consciousness*. Princeton, NJ: Princeton University Press.

Ohta, M. (1955). *Japanese folklore in English*. Tokyo: Miraishi.

Ozaki, T. (1970). *The Japanese fairy book*. New York: Charles Tuttle.

Propp, V. (1968). The morphology of the fairy tale. Austin: University of Texas Press.

Pruyser, P. (1975). Aging: Downward, upward or forward? *Pastoral Psychology, 24,* 102–118.

Raymond, E. F., & Michals, T. J. (1980). Prevalence and correlates of depression in elderly persons. *Psychological Reports, 47,* 1055–1061.

Rhadakrishnan, S., & Moore, C. (1957). *A sourcebook in Indian philosophy.* Princeton, NJ: Princeton University Press.

Rowe, K. (1986). To spin a yarn: The female voice in folklore and fairy tale. In R. Bottigheimer (Ed.), *Fairy tales and society: Illusion, allusion and paradigm* (pp. 53–74). Philadelphia: University of Pennsylvania Press.

Schenda, R. (1986). Telling tales—spreading tales: Change in the communicative forms of a popular genre. In R. Bottigheimer (Ed.), *Fairy tales and society: Illusion, allusion and paradigm* (pp. 75–94). Philadelphia: University of Pennsylvania Press.

Shahrani, M. N. (1981). Growing in respect: Aging among the Kirghiz of Afghanistan. In P. Amoss & S. Harrell (Eds.), *Other ways of growing old* (pp. 175–192). Stanford, CA: Stanford University Press.

Tatar, M. (1987). *The hard facts of the Grimms' fairy tales.* Princeton, NJ: Princeton University Press.

Thompson, S. (1955). Motif-index of folk literature. Bloomington: Indiana University Press.

Thurnher, M. (1975). Continuities and discontinuities in value orientations. In M. F. Lowenthal, M. Thurnher, & D. Chiriboga (Eds.), *Four stages of life* (pp. 176–200). San Francisco: Jossey Bass.

Vaillant, G. (1977). *Adaptation to life: How the best and the brightest came of age.* New York: Little, Brown.

Vaillant, G., & Milofsky, E. (1980). Natural history of male psychological health: 9. Empirical evidence for Erikson's model of the life cycle. *American Journal of Psychiatry, 137,* 1348–1359.

Viney, L. (1987). A sociophenomenological approach to life-span development complementing Erikson's sociodynamic approach. *Human Development, 30,* 125–136.

Von Franz, M. L. (1977). *Individuation in fairy tales.* Dallas: Spring.

Von Franz, M. L. (1980). *The psychological meaning of redemption motifs in fairy tales.* Toronto: Inner City Books.

Wei-ming, T. (1978). The Confucian perception of adulthood. In E. Erickson (Ed.), *Adulthood,* (pp. 113–120). New York: Norton.

Whitehead, A. N. (1917). *The organization of thought, educational and scientific.* London: Williams and Norgate.

Whitehead, A. N. (1919). *An enquiry concerning the principles of natural knowledge.* Cambridge: Cambridge University Press.

Whitehead, A. N. (1920). *The concept of nature.* Cambridge: Cambridge University Press.

Whitehead, A. N. (1925). *Science and the modern world.* New York: Macmillan.

Whitehead, A. N. (1926). *Religion in the making.* New York: Macmillan.

Whitehead, A. N. (1938). *Modes of thought.* New York: Macmillan.

Whitehead, A. N. (1941). Autobiographical notes. In P. A. Schilpp (Ed.), *The philosophy of Alfred North Whitehead* (pp. 3–14). New York: Tudor.

Zinberg, N. E. (1961). The relationship of regressive phenomena to the aging process. In N. E. Zinberg & I. Kaufman (Eds.), *Normal psychology of the aging process* (pp. 143–159). New York: International Universities Press.

Zipes, J. (1976). *Don't bet on the prince: Contemporary feminist fairy tales in North America and England*. New York: Methuen.

Zipes, J. (1979). *Breaking the magic spell: Radical theories of folk and fairy tales*. Austin: University of Texas Press.

Zipes, J. (1983). *Fairy tales and the art of subversion: The classical genre for children and the process of civilization*. New York: Heinemann.

# *PART III*
# *Artistic Expression, Creativity, and Representations of Aging*

9

# Images of Aging in American Poetry, 1925–1985

*Carolyn H. Smith*

In "The Phenomenological Approach to Images of Aging," Michael Philibert (1982 p. 321) concludes that human aging "is a complex process whose biological conditions are embedded in and modified by a social and cultural, which is to say symbolic, context. One cannot study aging independently of the images, naive or sophisticated, in which it is expressed and constituted." The texts that express such images are disparate, as Philibert points out, ranging from myths and movies to stories and poems. The purpose of this essay is to summarize attitudes toward aging embedded in images created by well-reviewed American poets during this century.

For Philibert, the most basic definition of aging is "a process," namely, "the advancing of age" toward "a final period of life." Esposito (1987) similarly defines "aging" as a process, metaphorically a "journey from birth to death." Most studies of images of aging assume this process definition, although they see concern for aging intensifying toward the final stage, variously dated from the late 60s to the 80s. Imagery studies have also indicated, however briefly, whether the images imply a benevolent or cynical attitude. Since the 1970s, studies of images of aging in poetry have been few, but these are perceptive, some analyzing images in the light of general humanistic themes (Clark, 1980; Edel, 1979; Loughman, 1980; Lyell, 1980; Soghnen & Smith, 1978; Watkins, 1988), others following at least one theoretical point of view: Freudian / Lacanian (George, 1986; Muller, 1986; Woodward, 1980), Eriksonian /

Freudian (Salvatori, 1987; Smith, 1989), Jungian (Pruitt, 1982; Zavatsky, 1984), or historical-sociological (Carrington, 1984; Smith, 1976).

These essays also in various ways respond to the argument that images by leading poets are not representative because such poets are too introspective, too involved with academic rather than industrial and governmental systems, and too typically free from such traumas of retirement as role loss (writers remain writers as long as they write), dire poverty, and loneliness (they remain in touch with publishers, interviewers, reading groups, and other writers). Another argument is that the persona a poet adopts for a poem cannot be taken as a source of truth because it may be very distant from, even opposite to, the poet's social self.

One counterargument, most persuasively indicated in Woodward's (1980) *At Last,* is that talented poets are acute in observation and sensory experience; because also skillful in language, they can articulate and even redirect thoughts about common experiences. Furthermore, many poets have experienced poverty and other traumas in their later years, and even those who are relatively comfortable and healthy still have strongly developed imaginations that can evoke images of catastrophes and cosmic emptiness. Finally, like all people, writers experience traumas from the unexpected. As speech-act theorists such as Pratt (1977) have observed, people for centuries have attended to a poet's voice, or persona, not just because of its special language effects (its rhythms, sounds, breathtaking figures of speech) but also because its speech is about the reactions of the self to the unexpected.

For modern poets as for the Romantics, recollection of reactions to crucial events is a form of self-awareness necessary for growth. Robert Penn Warren in his 70s cogently defended the poetry of self-expression by stating in his *Democracy and Poetry* (1975) that an author's works represent "the author's adventures in selfhood" because "the self is a style of being, continually expanding in a vital process of definition, affirmation, revision, and growth, a process that is the image, we may say, of the life process of a health society itself." (p. 89) Warren argued elsewhere that to ignore image-making is to ignore an important part of the human condition: "Man lives by images. They / Lean at us from the world's wall, and Time's" ("Reading Late at Night, Thermometer Falling," *Or Else* 1974).

Like images in painting, those in poetry require close attention if their rich connotations are to be gathered and understood. To heed Achenbaum and Stearns's (1978) warning against superficial and disconnected understandings of texts on aging, I have followed Baltes's (1987) analytical model with its three approaches: historical (biographical, sociological), psychological, and nonnormative (the unexpected). I have also taken a generational approach by focusing on poems by four American poets representing gender and cultural differences within one group, those born early in the 20th century and still writing prize-winning poetry between 1965 and 1985. The four are Robert Penn Warren (1905–1989), Langston Hughes (1902–1967), Gwendolyn Brooks (b. 1917), and Elizabeth Bishop (1911–1979). I will in the end briefly link these writers with representatives of groups little noticed until recently.

The four poets express ambivalence toward aging, an attitude expressed by most Americans (Achenbaum, 1978). Their poems portray some of the aged as emblems of both mortality and wisdom, although wisdom for Warren and Bishop involves self-reliance and self-affirmation, for Hughes and Brooks it involves active service for the common cause of freedom. To all of these poets, wisdom also involves stoic courage in encounters with role loss, physical decline, and death. The poets indicate the emblematic nature of their elderly characters through connotative situations, figures of speech, and allusions. Generally, they ignore details of physical appearance, but they suggest such causes of physical decline as poverty and injustice.

In context, these images of the aged can be seen as projections of the poets' concerns for their own aging and dying. From midlife on, these concerns were sublimated by Warren and Bishop into poems reliving and relieving the past, by Hughes and Brooks into poems urging action for a projected world with justice and freedom. Like Erikson (1982), Jaques (1965) links such signs of late-stage generativity and integrity with childhood nurturing. Although each of the four poets had childhood difficulties (Warren, Hughes, and Brooks because of harsh environments, Hughes and Bishop because of early loss of a parent), all had at least one nurturing grandparent figure. They all read works by classical, Romantic, and those modern writers (Hopkins, Eliot, Frost) who see life as difficult but basically nurturing. The nurturing life course implied by the midlife and late-stage poems of these writers will not mirror every reader's, but taken together, the poems form what Gutmann calls the "collective representations" of aging that the elders of other cultures present as not only true but instructive.

## ROBERT PENN WARREN

I begin with Robert Penn Warren because he was America's first poet laureate, a title he received in 1986 from Daniel J. Boorstin, the Librarian of Congress. Although writing poetry early in life, he wrote his greatest and most numerous work (11 volumes) after turning 50. Warren's style in his major poetic collection of the 1950s, *Promises: Poems 1954–1956* (1957), is the result of external and internal events. He stopped writing poetry during World War II as if the horrors of war undermined his earlier attachments to remote 17th-century English literature, especially Donne and Webster. His first marriage was also collapsing, resulting in a divorce in 1951. He married again in 1952, and he himself saw his second wife, their children, and the two summers with them in Italy as the cause of a rebirth and return to poetry (Farrell, 1982). His poems disclose another cause, his midlife awareness of man's vulnerability in a world of violence and death.

Many of Warren's images in *Promises* are similar to those in his earlier poetry: southern farms, western mountains, birds (especially hawks), and homely people such as tramps, woodsmen, small-town merchants, and country grandparents. More so than in his earlier poems, however, these later images are embedded in more varied, looser, and Whitmanesque structures, and they ponder questions about continuity and mastery (Graziano, Bloom, 1986). One sign that he desired continuity is in his dedication of a group of poems to his daughter and another to his son Gabriel. He also suggests continuity by naming his son after his maternal grandfather. His poems in *Promises* indicate his desire for autonomy.

Midlife fears of loss of autonomy are most dramatically given in "Dark Night of the Soul." These fears are implied in the title and in the main situation, Warren's recollection of the day in his boyhood when a tramp appeared suddenly in the woods bordering his grandfather's farm, a situation also recalled in his short story "Blackberry Winter." The tramp in the story is middle-aged; the tramp in the poem is "old, rough-grizzled, and spent." The middle-aged tramp, like Iago, desires power over others; the old tramp, like Lear, wants to be free from others. The repetition of the tramp image, the shift in age of the tramp, and the echoes of *King Lear* underscore Warren's desire to be autonomous even though aging. In *King Lear*, Edgar sees the flower-wreathed Lear as wise in his "mad" flight from others. Similarly, Warren sees the old tramp's poverty-stricken freedom as more noble than wealth or power, a view both signified and affirmed in the image of the tramp's white hair as "regally wreathed" by the elder blooms screening him from sight. The old tramp also shows a rugged frontiersman's pride in the way he leaves the woods "in joy past contumely of stars or insolent indifference of the dark air."

By bringing the poem to a close with the image of a retreating old man, Warren suggests a separation from the aging like the separation desired by the middle-aged brother, North, in Virginia Woolf's *The Years*.

As Woodward (1986) perceives, North wants to disregard his elderly sister, Eleanor, because she reminds him of mortality. Until his final image, however, Warren devotes some 100 lines to images affirming the tramp. In this affirmation, Warren is more like Woolf's Eleanor, who, as Woodward notes, regards others with a benevolence transcending self-interest. Warren's benevolence can be interpreted as Woodward interprets Eleanor's, as narcissism transformed by pleasure in the signs of human dignity amid loss and death. That Warren sees the old tramp walking proudly away as an emblem of how to meet death is evident from his prayer-like final line: "May we all at last enter into that awfulness of joy he has found there."

Warren also dramatizes his midlife concern for aging and death in his image of a physically strong but humble and stoic old woman in "Foreign Shore, Old Woman, Slaughter of Octopus." Early in the poem she is seen walking on a beach surrounded by signs of loss: she is alone, barefooted, and in black; it is just after sunset, when "the day / Withdraws"; she walks among "volcanic black boulders, at sea-edge," finally coming to rest against a boulder with the remains of a slaughtered octopus, its "pearl slime" glinting "in the last light." At the beginning of the last stanza, Warren separates himself from the old woman and her experience: "This is not my country, or tongue, / And my age not the old woman's age, or sea's age." However, he has already made connections in the lengthy description of her in his previous lines. Furthermore, his description turns into a meditation on what she means. At first, she suggests the inevitability of aging because she is in black, has none of the energy of the young at the day's picnic, and stands without revulsion near the remains of the octopus, "the obscene of the life-wish." But in the next-to-last stanza, she suggests the way to confront death, with a stoic independence and acceptance like that of the sea itself, which knows that in the midst of death there is life, "grain by slow grain." She is "detached in that wisdom" and thus able to endure alone: "Bare flesh of an old foot knows that much, as she stands there."

That Warren transcended a self-regarding view of the old woman is clear when he says at the end that even though he has to leave, her image "may assuage / The mind's pain of logic somewhat, or the heart's rage" whether he is "in the day traffic, or as I stand in night dark." Warren reveals a transcendence over objectification in his benevolent acceptance of the woman. This acceptance is made all the deeper by its echo of "Tintern Abbey," in which Wordsworth calls emblematic figures "beauteous forms" offering the gifts of "tranquil restoration" and "sensations sweet" to one who senses mortality" 'mid the din / Of towns and cities" in "hours of weariness."

Warren's acceptance of the old tramp and old woman was caused in part by their resemblance to his grandfather, whose rugged individualism Warren praises in "Court Martial." Warren spent many summers with his grandfather while growing up, but according to "Court-Martial," he did not see his grandfather as rugged until after he heard him confess that he had hanged ambushers while serving as a cavalry captain during the Civil War. Until that moment, the grandfather had seemed dependent, passive, and unable to be useful because "shrunken, gray," with "Tendons long gone crank and wry," and too ready to forget "mortgage and lien and debt." Immediately after hearing his grandfather's confession, Warren was horrified, but then he imagined his grandfather as a strong horseman riding alone and "large in the sky" with "No speculation in eye."

By displacing the real "spent" grandfather with an imaginary strong horseman, Warren seems to be repressing his awareness of physical decline. By admitting this displacement, however, Warren transcends it. Furthermore, when "shrunken," the grandfather suggested the easy serenity of life circumscribed by the farm: "His pipe smoke lifts, serene / Beneath boughs of the evergreen." After the story, he suggests the harsher but broader and wiser meaning that man sometimes needs to act alone and with cruelty on behalf of justice in an unjust world, a view implied in the last line: "The world is real. The world is there."

The last line of "Court Martial" carries Warren's willingness to accept his grandfather in spite of the destructiveness latent in his individualism. Warren's midlife acceptance of life's destructive aspects is also evident in these writings on his father's death from cancer in 1955 at 86: "Mortmain" (*You, Emperors, and Others: Poems 1957–1960*); "Reading Late at Night, Thermometer Falling" (*Or Else—Poem / Poems 1968–1974*); "Questions You Must Learn and Live Past" (*Rumor Verified: Poems 1979–1980*); and *Portrait of a Father* (1988). According to these works, Warren's father, even when elderly, seemed harsh because he viewed intimacy as less important than the hard work needed to be free from debt and ignorance. Warren first worked on acceptance of his father's jarring autonomy in the five poems forming his elegy "Mortmain." The poem also reveals Warren's attempt to reconcile himself to the irony that man needs autonomy to survive, yet autonomy cannot save him from inevitable aging and death.

In the first poem of the sequence, Warren's father, in his last moments in the hospital, raises his hand as if to make contact with someone, but his hand falls as death comes. By calling the hand "Mortmain," Warren elevates it into an awesome symbol of death's victory over both autonomy and intimacy, a victory especially tragic because his father tried to maintain a facade of mastery by telling no one about his illness until too late (too long you held "your precious secret: / A prostate big as a horse-apple," Warren says poignantly in "Reading Late at Night, Thermometer Falling"). The dead hand also signifies a son's opposite reactions: on the one hand, grief over loss of the helping hand; on the other, relief from the dead hand of the past, that is, the deadening effects a father has on a son's identity formation.

In the fourth poem of the sequence, Warren reveals acceptance of his father's formidable personality and his aging by seeing his father as one who may have discovered the secret of death if only in dying: "In the heart's last kingdom only the old are young."

Concern over aging and dying is conveyed dramatically and symbolically in the last poem of "Mortain" ("A Vision: Circa 1880"). In the first stanza, Warren recalls unexpectedly imagining a boy about to enter a woods in autumn; he realizes the boy is his father. In the second stanza, he calls out to his boy-father down "the tube and darkening corridor of Time." His desire to make contact becomes all the more pressing in the third stanza, when he realizes the boy-father is still standing in a dry and sun-scorched pasture bordering the woods. In the last stanza, the boy-father turns and grins but then disappears into the woods. In the final line, a wind begins to stir the woods, and rain is coming.

On one level, the poem displaces an aging Apollonian, oedipal father with a timeless preoedipal Dionysian boy-god in "patched britches" standing "hieratic" with his brow "bearing a smudge of gold pollen." By this displacement, Warren can release oedipal anxieties and look past the outwardly stern demeanor of his father's aging self to the freer self his father had repressed. As the images of parched earth and encircling woods indicate, the poem also dramatizes the poet's struggle with mortality. The pasture is so parched by the sun's "hot eye" that the cornstalks are shriveled. The phallic imagery connotes oedipal anxiety but also the fear that life leads to a meaningless death. Warren also identifies the whole pasture–woods scene as one from his own childhood. Through this uncanny doubling, Warren himself becomes the boy-father in a dying pasture, although only the boy-father can enter the woods.

By ending with this image of entrance into a shadowy but colorful autumn woods about to receive rain, Warren signifies not only his cutting of libidinal ties but also his view of death as inscrutable yet enticing (a release from phallic anxiety into preoedipal harmony). Warren also implies the belief that if there is no life beyond the shadows of death, there is immortality in the cycle of youth, aging, and death. Also implied is the idea that immortality is in such artifacts as poems, which also signify generativity, integrity, and self-fulfillment in the imagined eyes of another. Although the images of "Mortmain" did not completely relieve mourning, as evident in Warren's subsequent poems about his father, they did provide a means of working through a depressive position over aging and dying that, according to Jaques (1965), is necessary for further creativity.

That Warren experienced creativity later is obvious in the many poems he wrote after "Mortmain," not only about his father but about his boyhood and post-1960s life in New England. Of all of his many late poems, *Chief Joseph of the Nez Perce* (1983) is the most epic in scope. Like the shorter poems, it uses recollection of the past as a means of working through depression over losses caused by aging and death. Less obviously than in "Mortmain," Warren's younger self and his father are portrayed through displacement and doubling. The main narrator is Chief Joseph, who as an old man recalls how in the 1870s he and his tribe were tricked by government troops and politicians into surrender before he could finish leading his tribe to their ancestral home. Besides speaking in his voice as an old and young man, Chief Joseph speaks at times in the voice of his father. In the last section, Warren speaks in his own voice about his trip in 1981 to the western mountains where Chief Joseph had his last battle.

By dating his trip, by quoting from documents of the 1870s, and by doubling, Warren implies that Chief Joseph's losses—the youths of the tribe, his own youthful vigor, community cohesion, heritage, trust in Western culture—represent losses Warren and his country experienced during the 1970s. He is also Chief Joseph when as an old man he questions whether his life's work would have pleased his father: I "think / Of my father and yearn only / That he can think me a man / Worthy the work in dark of his loins." As Chief Joseph, he also asks about cosmic meaning: "But what is a man?" He answers with more cynical questions: "An autumn-tossed aspen, / Pony-fart in the wind, the melting of snow-slush?" Not content with these images of indignity and transiency, he goes on to ponder the wisdom in the more transcendent beliefs of his forefathers: "Unless—unless— / We can learn to live the Great Spirit's meaning / As the old and wise grope for it."

Chief Joseph's late-stage debate about the meaning of life is more clearly Warren's in "Sunset" and "Myth of Mountain Sunrise," with which Warren ended what he must have considered his last volume of poems, *Altitudes and Extensions: 1980–1984* (1985) (he knew he had cancer when publishing this collection). In neither of these poems does Warren refer to his forefathers, but as in his previous poems about himself, his family, and boyhood, he has a pastoral setting. In "Sunset," he is near a mountain. The scene is both oedipal and oceanic—the mountain's phallic peaks are partially covered by clouds touched by the setting sun. The sun arouses both oedipal anxieties and fears of death because it is the "flaming apocalypse of day" when "our errors are consumed / Like fire in a lint-house." Even the stars become "implacable gaggles" indifferent to the identity or status of the person facing the "dire hour" of judgment and death. In Eriksonian terms, Warren is succumbing to the despairing belief that his life has no integrity; in Lacanian terms, he is slipping from a fixed state, the oedipal state, with its names and social placements, to a dissolving state, the fluid pre-mirror, deathlike state, in which identity is fragmented. The pessimistic implications are put into question, however, by the biblical terms ("apocalypse," "errors," "dire hour"), suggesting that late-stage introspection can, like the apocalypse, cleanse and renew. The pessimism is also undermined by the optimism of "Myth of Mountain Sunrise."

A late-stage oneness with life and its cycles is suggested by the setting of "Myth of Mountain Sunrise," a mountain retreat (or room overlooking it) with peaks dimly visible just before dawn. The sounds from brooks and waterfalls create a "wisdom-song against disaster of granite." Soon visible are "the primal flame" of the sun and a spiderweb gleaming "In Pompeian glory." Then a birch tree rising out of a brook turns into a Venus-like young girl with "long, water-roped" hair. However, the connotations of harmony and permanence are undercut by the word "Myth" in the title, by the allusion to Pompeii, by the last words of the poem ("That will be the old tale told"), and by the apocalyptic images of the companion "Sunset." Although seemingly indecisive, Warren gives weight to "Myth of Mountain Sunrise" by placing it last and by hinting through his Venus figure that the words "myth" and "tale" refer not to a lie but to a poetic form of the deeply felt perception that the life cycle has meaning. He also reveals integrity by openly and eloquently expressing his conflicting longings in the main form of his life's work, poetry.

Poetry thus served Warren as both a mediating form of discourse and a means of late-stage identification. His last poems have a continuity with his earliest poems because both show that, like the Romantics, he was open to all experience, whether in a dire hour or on a mountaintop. Warren's late poems do not disclose the serenity that Jaques (1965) finds in the late works of Beethoven or Goethe, but they indicate that during his aging he was willing to contemplate his death and to defy it by admitting the paradox that death has meaning in the life cyle.

## LANGSTON HUGHES

Warren's capacity for seeing the elderly as emblems and aging as meaningful might be attributed to his upbringing in a pastoral, Anglo-

Saxon, middle-class setting. However, Langston Hughes also affirmed the elderly and defied aging. Unlike Warren's poems, Hughes's depict urban settings; he introduces his 92 poems of *Montage of a Dream Deferred* (1951) as one poem "on contemporary Harlem." Because of his many and varied poems on Harlem, he has been called Harlem's "poet laureate" (Davis, 1971). Like other African-American poems, Hughes's have the rhythms and images of jazz, blues, and spirituals. Such rhythms convey a communal as well as a personal voice (Bowen, 1984). Hughes was thus describing his own midlife state as well as the state of his community when he introduced *Montage of a Dream Deferred* as a work "marked by conflicting changes, sudden nuances, sharp and impudent interjections, broken rhythms."

Like Warren's, Hughes's "conflicting changes, sudden nuances" in midlife resulted from conflicts between ideals of freedom and mastery and the reality of aging and death. Warren wanted a self free from any bonds except the nuclear family; Hughes wanted freedom not just for himself but for all blacks, a desire most succinctly evident when he speaks of *Montage of a Dream Deferred* as rooted in "disc-tortions of the music of a community in transition." In his "disc-tortions," Hughes reveals his anguish over lack of freedom in the black community. Like Warren at midlife, Hughes viewed aging as bearable only if there is independence. Unlike Warren, Hughes wrote poems with older persons working in a group for a cause.

Like Warren's views, Hughes's stemmed from a grandparent. When his father left for Mexico because his color prevented his entrance into an American law school, Hughes was left with his grandmother until her death nine years later. In his autobiographical *The Big Sea* (1940), he recalls her "long, beautiful stories about people who wanted to make the Negroes free." He added, "Something about my grandmother's stories (without her ever having said so) taught me the uselessness of crying about anything." This mingling of stern stoicism and cheerful benevolence is reflected in "As I Grew Older" (*The Weary Blues*, 1926), in which the speaker sees growing up as a process of battering down the "thick wall" thwarting dreams; he can smash the wall alone, but he prefers working with others wanting to "break this shadow / Into a thousand lights of sun."

Hughes's older characters embody his grandmother's benevolence and hopefulness. In *The Weary Blues*, the mother in "Mother and Son" tells her son not to "set down on the steps" because "I'se still climbin', / And life for me ain't been no crystal stair." Aunt Sue, in "Aunt Sue's Stories," instills community values in children by telling them stories about "Black slaves / Working in the hot sun." In "The Weary Blues," an aging blues piano player is able, through singing blues songs to others, to overcome suicidal desires. A "black old woman" crooning "In the amen-corner of the / Ebecanezer Baptist Church" arouses hope with her refrain, "De dawn's a-comin!" ("Prayer Meeting," *Fine Clothes to the Jew*, 1927). "Negro Mother," Hughes's most popular poem in his Southern readings in the 1930s, is about an archetypal figure recalling years of climbing "the long dark way" from slavery and surviving because of song, hope, and determination (*A New Song*, 1938). In *Fields of Wonder* (1947), the speaker of "Fulfillment" says that moonlight is "Like an old grandmother" who has "Blessed us with a kiss." In "Sailing Date," old seamen have already "weathered / A thousand storms" and "two wars," but they will return to their work because they have courage and faith in their ship and captain.

Not all of Hughes's poems are hopeful. His midlife collections—*A New Song* (1938), *Shakespeare in Harlem* (1942), and *Fields of Wonder* (1947)—reveal not only midlife depression but awareness of the Depression and World War II. Among the darker poems are those about the elderly, including "Old Sailor," a counterpart poem in *Fields of Wonder* to "Sailing Date." In "Old Sailor," a well-traveled sailor is reduced by age, paralysis, and poverty to little activity except sunning himself alone "In charity's poor chair." "Old Sailor" thus questions the validity of the sailors' vaunted independence in "Sailing Date," just as the grandmother's kiss in "Fulfillment" seems ironic in view of such poems in *Fields of Wonder* as "Night: Four Songs," in which there is only a sorrowful song in the moonlight, or "There," whose speaker says that in the grave, "nothing / Is all" and "I, / Who am nobody" will "become Infinity."

The evocation of anxiety over death through contrasting subjects and seemingly childlike forms links *Fields of Wonder* with William Blake's *Songs of Innocence* (1796) and *Songs of Experience* (1798). Unlike Blake, Hughes has more poems evoking hope and innocence than evil and death. In his post-World War II *One-Way Ticket* (1949), his city-blues images and jazz syncopations suggest the tentative nature of hopefulness. There are also more defiant speakers, starker images of poverty, and bolder suggestions for active resistance to oppression. These changes are noticeable in poems with older characters. The 12 poems forming "Madam to You" are about a middle-aged woman who shows her vitality, dignity, and strength of character by insisting that everyone—rent man, minister, census man—call her madam. In "Sunday Morning Prophecy," an old minister warns his people in a loud voice and with powerful images about the consequences of worldliness; at the end of the sermon he defies his own sermon by boldly asking for money to pay expenses. In "Little Green Tree," the speaker defies those who think that because of old age he (or she) cannot walk to a little tree off in the distance whose "cool green leaves" seem "waitin' to shelter me."

In Hughes's next collection, *Montage of a Dream Deferred* (1951), older people are also depicted according to his hopeful yet realistic and defiant social outlook. The Grandma in "The Dime," like the mother in the early "Mother to Son," is alone except for her grandchildren, she is tired and disillusioned because all she has is "Montage of a Dream Deferred," but she continues to climb stairs with determination. A grandparent in "Freedom Train" has lost Jimmy, a grandson, at Anzio, but even so, he (or she) defies authorities by asking whether Jimmy can ride the Freedom Train. In "Passing," Granny defies those who have become rich but have abandoned the black community and its needs; she remains in Harlem even though she "cannot get her gospel hymns / from the Saints of God in Christ / on account of the Dodgers on the radio."

By the time of his last volume, *The Panther and the Lash: Poems of Our Times* (1967), Hughes was more openly critical of those who failed to work for the black community, including the elderly in "Elderly Leaders." The "leaders" are mocked because "cautious," "opportunistic," and "very well paid" from the egg "Their master's / Goose laid." Hughes draws the poem to a close with five lines of dollar signs, each shorter than the former until the fifth is a single sign; the last line is a period. This series of slash marks climaxing mockery of elders suggests that Hughes, like Warren in "Mortmain," was working through unconscious oedipal as well as death anxieties, possibly a belated release from his own father, from whom he broke in 1922 and whose funeral in 1934 he would not attend. Whether prompted by oedipal anxiety or a desire to be in union with militant younger black leaders, Hughes pays even greater tribute to defiance in *The Panther and the Lash*. In his main title and in such poem titles as "Black Panther" and "Militant," Hughes links himself with the Black Panther movement.

Such militancy, however, is rooted in hope that change is possible. In this sense, in spite of his criticism of the elderly in "Elderly Leaders," Hughes in his 60s maintained continuity with the source of his ideas, his maternal grandmother. Although not referring to grandmother figures in *The Panther and the Lash* (1967), he continues to affirm his grandmother by continuing her method of instilling a belief in freedom by way of stories and songs. Hughes conveys these beliefs and praise for visionary people in such poems as "Color" and "Freedom." Thus, in his last poems, Hughes discloses a combined sense of reality and hopefulness that Jaques (1965) sees as essential for constructive aging. In this respect, Hughes was also consonant with this younger self, ready, as he said earlier, to be in community with those who express "our individual dark-skinned selves without fear or shame. . . . We build our temples for tomorrow, strong as we know them, and we stand on top of the mountain, free within ourselves" (*Hughes*, 1926, p. 694).

## GWENDOLYN BROOKS

Gwendolyn Brooks was one contemporary who saw Hughes in his 60s as an emblem of wisdom. In her words, Hughes at mid-life was "helmsman, hatchet, headlight" in the movement for freedom because of his "Strong speech" and stoic "Muscular tears" ("Langston Hughes," *Selected Poems,* 1963). Like Hughes's poems, Brooks's depict the lives of blacks in the city, mainly Chicago. Because of the power and range of her depictions, she was made poet laureate of Illinois in 1969. Unlike Warren and Hughes, she has been particularly praised for her focus on the domestic and on features in lives of woman that male writers have ignored or misunderstood, including a woman's midlife encounters with death. Like Warren, she is viewed as having a late style because of her obvious shift after 1968 from the domestic scenes and traditional verse forms of earlier poems to more visionary images and rhythms suggesting urgent drumbeats and rally calls. She herself dates her change from the time of the Second Black Writers' Conference at Fisk University in 1967, when she was 50. This was also not long after the death of her father and the beginning of the Black Panther movement. Although her later poems are more politically coded and more rhythmically jagged than earlier poems, they have the same sympathy for the poor and oppressed, including the aging (Mootry & Smith, 1987).

In "Kitchenette Building" (*A Street in Bronzeville,* 1945), a community of gray-haired people (presumably women since they do the cooking) state their communal belief that any "dream" of comfort is undermined by the reality of "onion fumes" and "yesterday's garbage ripening in the hall" of their ghetto living quarters; they have hope, but it is limited to getting lukewarm water from the community bathroom before it runs out. The collapse of their dreams is underscored by their speaking in a truncated form of the sonnet. In *The Bean Eaters* (1960), "Matthew Cole" and "The Bean Eaters" seem to be criticisms of disengaged elderly, but the poems actually criticize the poverty thwarting engagement. Old Matthew Cole is too poor to leave his roach-infested room; he has only memories of poverty to occupy his time. In "The Bean Eaters," the elderly couple eat "beans mostly" on "tin flatware"; in spite of this poverty, they share memories in their "rented back room" with their few but cherished mementoes. In "The Rites of Cousin Vit" (*Annie Allen,* 1949), Cousin Vit's vivacity has helped her transcend poverty and aging. Those attending her funeral see her rise even from her coffin and go back to the barroom where she once danced, laughed, and talked about "guitars and bridgework." Her vitality in aging is conveyed in the narrator's images and form, a well-constructed sonnet with an engaging mixture of one-syllable and singing two-syllable rhymes (door / can't hold her / enfold her / before).

Like the views of Warren and Hughes, Brooks's were rooted in her family experience, as evident in her elegy to her father, "In Honor of David Anderson Brooks, My Father: July 30, 1883–November 21, 1959" (*The Bean Eaters* 1960). As the title makes clear, the poem honors her father for his actions and traits. It also serves as a way of working through grief. Just as Warren's father in "Mortmain" is at first in an unpleasant place a parched pasture, Brooks's father early in his poem is in a chilly and "cramping" chamber. Both fathers enter a place symbolizing an honored death, but whereas Warren's father moves into an autumn woods, Brooks's father "walks the valleys, now—replies / To sun and wind forever." These contrasting settings reinforce David Gutmann's (1980) conclusion that when parenting is over, men think in terms of the feminine (Warren's image of the encircling woods), whereas women move toward the masculine (Brooks's image of the outward-stretching valleys). The two poems also reinforce John Berger's (1973) view that such concepts as the afterlife are rooted in social and economic experiences. Thus, Warren sends his father into a place signifying rest from his drought-prone farming community of the South; Brooks signifies rest for her father by giving him the fresh air he could not have in the ghettoes of early- and mid-20th-century Chicago.

Brooks was willing to praise the elderly who were like her father, able to have a "firm and sculptured door" and to be "innocent of self-interest," ("In Honor of David Anderson"). She was just as ready, even before her militant poems, to criticize the elderly who thwarted freedom, sacrificed freedom for personal comfort, or betrayed community values. Such criticism is evident in *The Bean Eaters* (1960). In "A Sunset of the City," a wife rejected by her husband because of her aging speaks about herself indirectly through images of her cold house, dying summer flowers, and sunset. The wife also contemplates suicide as better than a long and lonely aging. In "The Old-Marrieds," an old couple have "time for loving," but they do not take it because they have lost touch with each other. The title "On the Occasion of the Open-Air Formation of the Olde Tymers' Walking and Nature Club" reinforces the poem's mockery of elderly club members avoiding both their aging and their ghetto lives by acting out unrealistic fantasies.

In *The Bean Eaters*, Brooks in "The Sundays of Satin-Legs Smith" uses T. S. Eliot's images and rhythmic patterns of "Prufrock" to mock an aging self-centered man; the mockery is all the more telling because Smith is an exact inversion of Prufrock, seeing too little of the poverty near his apartment and believing too much that he is attractive to women. Form also emphasizes content in "Old Relative" (in "Notes from the Childhood and the Girlhood," *Annie Allen* 1949). In the first three stanzas, the speaker describes old age negatively as a time of "baths and bowel work" leading to the coffin. The view seems true because emphasized by the matching rhymes of the opening three-line stanzas. The concluding two-line stanza, however, forms a whiplash because the two rhymes underscore the speaker's point that the negative view of the elderly is held by a self-centered, shallow young girl annoyed by the prohibition against popular songs during the funeral.

In the last section of "The Womanhood" (*Annie Allen* 1949), Brooks criticizes fathers who, instead of living up to the saying "What's old is wise," give daughters unwise advice about how to behave in marriage. Even worse, daughters in the modern world can no longer look to "timely godmothers" for guidance. "We" (younger women but also women like Brooks at midlife) must either "combine" or "Wizard a track through our own screaming weed." By personifying the weed as screaming and by turning *wizard* into a verb, Brooks indicates her anger over this repression; she also shows that one way of overcoming anger is by way of sublimation in a poetic figuration. This foreshadows her later release of anger through political activism and through elliptical poetry in *Riot* (1969), *Family Pictures* (1970), and *In the Mecca* (1968). In *Riot*, she personifies herself, now in her early 50s, as a Black Philosopher who calls for "*black*blues," sees "Crazy flowers" hissing "This is it," and recalls how "the hurt mute" have risen like the Phoenix. In *Family Pictures*, she speaks directly to the young, urging them to act not just for victory but for the fullness of life "in the along."

Brooks ends the collection of her late 50s, *Beckonings* (1975), by describing herself as "Beckoning" to "Black Boys" so that they will "battle for breath and bread." Because of the aggressive nature of her imperatives ("Hurry / Force through the sludge. / Wild thick scenery subdue"), she might be defined as a woman disclosing unrestrained aggressiveness at midlife according to Gutmann's (1980) midlife masculine / feminine model, but she also asks for compassion ("It is too easy to cry 'Attica' / and shock thy street") and humility ("beware the imitation coronations"). Her "Black Love" (1981) seems to lack compassion because it rebukes "the Elders" for inaction, but she is pointing to the healthy and wealthy who choose the "luxury of languish and of rust" rather than help the oppressed.

Like Hughes, she has been seen in her later years as wise, courageous, and creative, a continuation of the figure eulogized by Hughes in his "Negro Mother." Representative are these poets in *To Gwen With Love* (1971): Carole Gregory Clemmons compares Brooks to the preacher who "sings the second sermon" ("Black Children"); Alicia I. Johnson connects her with "grandmothers / rocking / and humming" on porches "that under & overstand [*sic*]" ("Some Smooth Lyrics for a Natural People"); Etheridge Knight asks her to "hum your lullabies / and soothe our souls" ("To Gwendolyn Brooks"). In "Black Love" (1981) Brooks herself speaks at 66 much as the woman in her earlier "Weaponed Woman" (*Selected Poems*, 1963) spoke, as one who "fights with semi-folded arms" and "does Rather Well."

## ELIZABETH BISHOP

Although six years younger than Brooks, Bishop seems very remote, partly because she was not an activist nor group-minded. Her poems, like Warren's, are about country and seaside settings and about the self rather than a community. Like Brooks, she has concrete details about interiors and about the appearance of the elderly, but the implications are more cosmic and more pessimistic, although derision is forestalled by overall politeness and attention to the specific details of another person's dress and setting. As she aged, she became more tolerant of the elderly and of aging.

Like Hughes, she experienced family breakup early in life, but unlike Hughes, she was an infant when she lost her father because of his untimely death. Her mother had several breakdowns because of unresolved grief. When Bishop was five, her mother was permanently institutionalized, and Bishop never saw her again. Until going to Vassar, Bishop lived with various relatives in Massachusetts and Nova Scotia. She recalled that she was "very isolated as a child"; she was given books to read, and perhaps "poetry was my way of making familiar what I saw around me" (Travisano, 1988).

As Erikson (1982) might have predicted, Bishop's poems do not portray older people as representing any trustworthy beliefs other than inscrutability and mortality. Less predictable are her politeness and her interest in specific details, undoubtedly stemming from her desire to imitate her favorite writers. Good manners and attention to detail are features of writers Bishop admired, particularly Frost, Dickinson, and Marianne Moore, who was her mentor from 1934 until her death in 1972. The benevolence can also be seen as coming from Bishop's maternal grandparents, who were kind even if not very intimate, although Bishop's desire to be kind and to look carefully may have been caused by the fear that before she could do or see enough, others might collapse and disappear as her mother had done. Then too, she was as aware, as were other writers during the Depression and war periods, that benevolence and carefulness are necessary yet ironic in the face of irrevocable losses and uncontrollable violence.

This mingling of tolerant irony and love of detail is evident in one of her earliest portraits of an aging person, the frail, bedridden, and deranged old lady with "fine white hair" in "Faustina, or Rock Roses" (*Poems* 1955). The title, the rose imagery, the interior setting (the old lady's bedroom), and highlighted details (bed, nightstand with salves and pills, roses from a visitor) suggest that the woman became deranged by despair over the perception that because of aging she will no longer receive a "Gather ye rosebuds" invitation. Like the woman in Gwendolyn Brooks's "A Sunset of the City," (*The Bean Eaters,* 1960) she has lived a domestic life and thus has no outlet for despair except to go mad or die. To show sympathy, a visitor has brought roses. However, the visitor, like the servant Faustina, perceives the foolishness in the *carpe diem* lure, yet she fears rejecting it since it offers, even if briefly, intimacy desirable in a lonely universe. This irony of death in life is symbolized in the ironic image of rock petals in the title and in the visitor's concluding act of "awkwardly" leaving "her bunch / of rust-perforated roses" and wondering "oh, whence come / all the petals." No words of wisdom come from the old lady.

Though the lady is old and apparently Italian, she seems to be a displacement of Bishop's mother after the death of Bishop's father. Another midlife poem, "At the Fishhouses" (*Poems,* 1955), is a more obvious dramatization of fear that as one ages, intimacy will lead to confining security, maddening domesticity, and dislocation. The setting is both dreamlike (it is a moonlight night and details are clear yet obscure) and also like the village in Nova Scotia where Bishop and her mother lived with her maternal grandparents until her mother's breakdown. The old fisherman in the poem is called "a friend of my grandfather," a phrase that helps establish the reality of the setting and also the fisherman's link with family intimacy. Besides the grandfather, the old fisherman has friends on a herring boat whose return he awaits. Like the boy-god in Warren's "Mortmain," he is Dionysian: he is almost invisible in the gloaming, yet his clothes are clearly "a dark purple-brown"; the fishscales on his vest look like sequins; the objects near him are iridescent with moonlit fishscales. Even the signs that he is Father Time—his black knife, the dead fish, the flies, his conversation about the decline in herring—are alluring because touched by moonlight. As if fearing that a desire for intimacy is a death wish, Bishop leaves him for the sea's edge. Here she links herself with the sea, icy cold, but "clear, moving, utterly free." At the sea's edge the self relies on itself, free from bonds with the elderly Fisher-King and Fisherman Saviour, and free also from a stasis that can cause early aging.

Bishop's ambivalence toward domestic elderly is more evident in the first two poems of the "Elsewhere" section in *Questions of Travel* (1965). In the time period of Bishop's childhood, the grandfather in "Manners" gives advice to his grandchild on how to behave when driving a horse-drawn buggy; the child is polite but notes that when automobiles rush by in whirling dust, his advice seems foolish, a foolishness reinforced by the poem's slant and doggerel rhymes. The complex and fixed rhyme scheme of "Sestina" similarly reinforces the complexity in a grandmother's seemingly simple act of making tea. The grandmother makes tea to hide her tears from her granddaughter; the granddaughter sees the tears anyway. Also, by unthinkingly hanging an almanac and letting the teakettle boil, the grandmother arouses the child's perception of two causes of tears, the passing of time and entrapping domesticity. Although she likes her grandchild, the grandmother offers no advice nor comfort and, as in Bishop's childhood, no mother is about to appear. As a consequence, the child draws "another inscrutable house" in a coloring book. Similarly in "In the Waiting Room" (*Geography III,* 1976), older figures fail to help a child distressed by pictures of aging, struggle, and death in a *National Geographic* she is reading while alone in a dentist's waiting room.

Later in life, however, as other late poems in *Geography III* (1976) reveal, Bishop accepted intimacy, although she restricted this to only a few friends, in particular a Brazilian friend with whom she lived in Brazil from about 1950 to 1970 (Travisano, 1988). Her villanelle "One Art" is supposedly her lament on this friend's death, as is the aged Crusoe's lament for his deceased Friday in "Crusoe in England." In "A Moose," a lonely bus ride is interrupted by a female moose coming out of "the impenetrable woods" as if to signify nurturing in a lonely universe. The moose is seen only briefly because the bus goes on its journey, yet for Bishop, in her 60s, it remains a dreamlike vision, towering "high as a church" but "safe as houses." In "Poem," Bishop affirmed her grandparents; whereas she turned her back on their village in "At the Fishhouses," in "Poem" she sees the village as "still loved," its details offering "the little of our earthly trust," not much, but "touching."

When Bishop's *The Complete Poems* appeared in 1983, the poet Mark Strand called Bishop a "survivor" (Travisano, 1988). As her late poems indicate, one reason for her survivorship was her willingness to defy death's lure of escape from struggle while at the same time developing a capacity to integrate intimacy with autonomy. Thus, her works taken together create an image connoting the defiance and integration Jaques (1965) sees as necessary for constructive aging.

## CONCLUSION

Although a poet of specificity, Bishop did not describe an elderly person's face with any detail, nor did Hughes nor Brooks, who were more concerned with the living conditions and rights of the elderly than with their loss of physical beauty. In "Old Flame" (*Now and Then: Poems 1976–1978*), Warren (1978) confesses that he can recall the girlhood braids of a schoolday's friend but "Never, never" her aging face, "grisly," with "false teeth, gray hair." In "Re-internment: Recollection of a Grandfather" (*Altitudes and Extensions, 1985*) he recalls, as he did in "Court Martial," the details of his grandfather's appearance; this time he also recalls the "croak," the "choked weeping," and thinning hair. However, he laments the fading of these details from memory.

Reactions to bodily signs of aging are infrequent but eloquent and benevolent in the modern Native Indian poetry recently collected by Duane Niatum (1988) for Harper's. For example, Mary TallMountain (b. 1918) sees her grandmother as a "Gnarled mother-vine / ancient / As vanished ages" whose spirit remains "Nourished / Nourishing me ("Matmiya: For My Grandmother"). Elizabeth Cook-Lynn (b. 1930) admires her Crow Creek Sioux grandfather when he "bares his chest / but keeps a scarf tied on his steel-gray braids ("Grandfather at the Indian Health Clinic"). In his earlier collection, *Carriers of the Dream World*, Niatum (1975) remembers an old woman whose face "wrinkles / Into a smiling heap of eggshells," whose "eyes do figure eights on thin ice" as she tells stories of her grandchildren, and who, after dropping her false teeth into her pocketbook, looks blissful, as if her mind "breathes with the apple peasants of the world / And chews time like a white rabbit" ("Old Woman Awaiting the Greyhound Bus"). Similarly, Janice Mirikitani, a third-generation Japanese born in the 1940s, notes that her mother's skin is "soft like tallow" when as an older woman she testifies on treatment of the Japanese during the war ("Breaking Silence," *Survey of American Poetry*, 1984), and Mei-Mei Berssenbrugge, now an American but born in Peking in 1947, describes an old man fishing, his "eyes lost in thick spectacles listening to birds" ("Old Man Let's Go Fishing in the Yellow Reeds of the Bay," Fisher, 1980).

In his memoir *The Names* (1976), N. Scott Momaday indicates the importance of grandparents in a child's growing up among the Kiowas. Niatum (1975) points out in his introduction to *Carriers of the Dream World* that all Native Indian groups revere the elderly for their words of wisdom, stories, and songs; as Brian Scott says in his introduction to Niatum's collection for Harper's (1988), grandparents are seen as "keepers of the faith" and "symbols of rooted continuity," a view Lance Henson summarizes in the Harper's collection in his image of his grandfather as "red sage of sunset" whose name "the night hawk sings" ("Grandfather"). Even in poems noting physical details, reverence for the elderly is evinced, as it is in the poems by Mirikitani and Berssenbrugge. The Chicana poet Lorna Dee Cervantes (b. 1954) admiringly signifies her grandmother's courage in the way she wears her hair "in loose braids" tucked close to her head "with a yellow scarf" even though her life is hard and drab in a run-down apartment ("Beneath the Shadow of the Freeway," Fisher, 1980).

A greater readiness to note details of physical changes as well as personality is exhibited by another recently identified group, elderly women writers. In one collection, *Women and Aging* (1986): Sue Saniel Elkind (b. 1913) recalls her sister at 82, her face "a map / Of many roads travelled," her "body bent withered / a dying tree," yet ready to laugh and "rest old antagonisms" ("Sisters"); Arlene S. Jones (b. 1928) describes herself among the hospitalized, some with "bones bracketed in steel / breath fractured," some with hearts "crazy, dancing like madmen," some with straggly hair like "the stubble / left in the spring field," all emblems "of hope standing / like ninepins" ("Country Hospital"); Meridel Le Sueur (b. 1900) sees "spiders creep at my eyes' edge" and her body "a canoe turning to stone," but she still feels "luminous with age" ("Rites of Ancient Ripening").

In their individual poems, even these elderly women poets imply greater admiration for cheerful stoicism than for disgruntlement or despair. In their respective works, Achenbaum (1978), Gadow (1983), and Cole (1984) have warned against an overglorification of traits associated with frontier rugged individualism at the expense of frailty, silence, and withdrawal in the face of family breakdown, violence, and loss of spiritual meanings. If poems are read not as single, separate artifacts but together as collective representations, readers can see that at times, aging poets will feel physically frail but spiritually in touch with the deepest perceptions about life and death; at other times, they will feel despair, but out of that sunset experience may come a moving poem about that sunset despair or about a sunrise aftermath. By observing varied images of aging in a variety of poems in context, readers may form a better understanding of aging, their own aging as well as that of another. As Warren (1985) said in one of his last essays, poetry is not the primary concern of mankind, "but it is an activity, for writer or reader, valuable and unique, and a fundamental measure of the quality of any civilization." Reading poems on aging may add to the quality of this civilization.

## REFERENCES

Achenbaum, W. A. (1978). *Old age in the new land: The American experience since 1970*. Baltimore: Johns Hopkins Press.

Achenbaum, W. A. & Stearns, P. N. (1978). Old age and modernization. *Gerontologist, 18*, 307–312.

Alexander, J., Barrow, D., Domitrovich, L., Donnelly, M., & Mclean, C. (Eds.). (1986). *Women and aging*. Corvallis, OR: Calyx Books.

Baltes, P. B. (1987). Theoretical propositions of life-span on the dynamic between growth and decline. *Developmental Psychology, 23*, 611–626.

Berger, J. (1973). *A way of seeing*. New York: Viking Press.

Bishop, E. (1955). *Poems: North & south-A cold spring*. Boston: Houghton Mifflin.

Bishop, E. (1965). *Questions of travel*. New York: Farrar, Straus & Giroux.

Bishop, E. (1976). *Geography III*. New York: Farrar, Straus & Giroux.

Bishop, E. (1983). *The complete poems: 1927–1979*. New York: Farrar, Straus, Giroux.

Bloom, H. (Ed.). (1986). *Robert Penn Warren*. New York: Chelsea House.

Bowen, B. E. (1984). Untroubled voice: Call and response in *Cane*. In H. L. Gates, Jr. (Ed.), *Black literature and literary theory* (pp. 187–203). New York and London: Methuen.

Brooks, G. (1945). *A street in Bronzeville*. New York: Harper & Brothers.

Brooks, G. (1949). *Annie Allen: Poems*. New York: Harper.

Brooks, G. (1960). *The bean eaters*. New York: Harper & Brothers.

Brooks, G. (1963). *Selected poems*. New York: Harper & Row.

Brooks, G. (1968). *In the Mecca: Poems*. New York: Harper & Row.

Brooks, G. (1969). *Riot*. Detroit: Broadside Press.

Brooks, G. (1970). *Family pictures*. Detroit: Broadside Press.

Brooks, G. (1975). *Beckonings*. Detroit: Broadside Press.

Brooks, G. (1981). Black love. *Ebony, 36*, 50.

Carrington, R. G. (1984). *"What are years?" The late poems of Marianne Moore, 1958 to 1970*. Ph.D. diss., University of Maryland.

Clark, M. (1980). The poetry of aging: Views of old age in contemporary American poetry. *Gerontologist, 20*, 188–191.

Clemmons, C. G. (Ed.). (1971). *To Gwen with Love: An anthology dedicated to Gwendolyn Brooks*. Chicago: Johnson Publishing.

Cole, T. R. (1984). Aging, meaning, and well-being: Musings of a cultural historian. *International Journal of Aging and Human Development, 19*, 329–336.

Davis, A. P. (1971). Langston Hughes: Cool poet. In T. B. O'Daniel (Ed.), *Langston Hughes, black genius: A critical evaluation* (pp. 18–38). New York: William Morrow.

Edel, L. (1979). Portrait of the artist as an old man. In D. D. Van Tassell (Ed.), *Aging, death, and the completion of being* (pp. 193–214). Philadelphia: University of Pennsylvania Press.

Erikson, E. H. (1982). *The life cycle completed: A review*. New York: W. W. Norton.

Esposito, J. L. (1987). *The obsolete self: Philosophical dimensions of aging*. Berkeley: University of California Press.

Farrell, D. (1982). Poetry as a way of life: An interview with Robert Penn Warren. *Georgia Review, 36*, 314–331.

Fisher, D. (Ed.). (1980). *The third woman: Minority women writers of the United States*. New York: Houghton Mifflin.

Gadow, S. (1983). Frailty and strength: The dialectic of aging. *Gerontologist, 23*, 144–147.

George, D. H. (1986). "Who is the double ghost whose head is smoke?" Women poets on aging. In K. Woodward & M. M. Schwartz (Eds.), *Memory and desire: Aging—literature—psychoanalysis* (pp. 134–153). Bloomington: Indiana University Press.

Gutmann, D. (1980). Psychoanalysis and aging: A developmental view. In S. I. Greenspan & G. H. Pollock (Eds.), *Adulthood and the aging process* (pp. 489–517). Washington, DC: National Institute of Mental Health.

Hughes, L. (1926). The Negro artist and the racial mountain. *Nation, 122,* 692–694.

Hughes, L. (1926). *The weary blues.* New York: Alfred A. Knopf.

Hughes, L. (1927). *Fine clothes to the Jew.* New York: Alfred A. Knopf.

Hughes, L. (1938). *A new song.* New York: International Workers Order.

Hughes, L. (1942). *Shakespeare in Harlem.* New York: Alfred A. Knopf.

Hughes, L. (1947). *Fields of wonder.* New York: Alfred A. Knopf.

Hughes, L. (1948). *The big sea: An autobiography.* New York: Alfred A. Knopf. 1940

Hughes, L. (1949). *One-way ticket.* New York: Alfred A. Knopf.

Hughes, L. (1951). *Montage of a dream deferred.* New York: Holt.

Hughes, L. (1965). *Selected poems.* New York: Alfred A. Knopf.

Hughes, L. (1967). *The panther and the lash: Poems of our times.* New York: Alfred A. Knopf.

Jaques, E. (1965). Death and the mid-life crisis. *International Journal of Psychoanalysis, 46,* 502–514.

Loughman, C. (1980). Literary views of the isolated elderly. *Educational Gerontology, 5,* 249–257.

Luke, D. (1978). How is it that you live, and what is it that you do? The question of old age in English romantic poetry. In S. F. Spicker, K. Woodward, & D. D. Van Tassel (Eds.), *Aging and the elderly* (pp. 221–240). Atlantic Highlands, NJ: Humanities Press.

Lyell, R. G. (Ed.). (1980). *Middle age, old age: Short stories, poems, plays and essays on aging.* New York: Harcourt, Brace, Jovanovich.

Momaday, N. S. (1976). *The names: A memoir.* New York: Harper & Row.

Mootry, M. K., & Smith, G. (Eds.). (1987). *A life distilled: Gwendolyn Brooks her poetry and her fiction.* Urbana and Chicago: University of Illinois Press.

Muller, J. (1986). Light and the wisdom of the dark: Aging and the language of desire in the texts of Louise Bogan. In K. Woodward & M. M. Schwartz (Eds.), *Memory and desire: Aging—literature—psychoanalysis* (pp. 76–96). Bloomington: Indiana University Press.

Niatum, D. (Ed.). (1975). *Carriers of the dream wheel; Contemporary Native American poetry.* New York: Harper & Row.

Niatum, D. (Ed.). (1988). *Harper's anthology of 20th century Native American poetry.* New York: Harper & Row.

Philibert, M. (1982). The phenomenological approach to images of aging. In P. L. McKee (Ed.), *Philosophical foundations of gerontology* (pp. 303–322). New York: Human Sciences Press.

Pratt, M. L. (1977). *Toward a speech act theory of discourse.* Bloomington: Indiana University press.

Pruitt, V. D. (1982). Yeats, the mask, and the poetry of old age. *Journal of Geriatric Psychiatry, 15*, 99–112.

Salvatori, M. (1987). Thomas Hardy and Eugene Montage: In mourning and in celebration. *Journal of Aging Studies, 1*, 161–185.

Schaie, K. W. (1982). Toward a stage theory of adult cognitive development. In P. L. McKee (Ed.), *Philosophical foundations of gerontology* (pp. 261–270). New York: Human Sciences Press.

Soghnen, M. & Smith, R. J. (1978). Images of old age in poetry. *Gerontologist, 28*, 181–186.

Smith, C. H. (1989). Richard Eberhart's poems on aging. *Journal of Aging Studies, 3*, 75–80.

Smith, H. (1976). Bare ruined choirs: Shakespearean variation on the theme of old age. *Huntington Library Quarterly, 39*, 233–249.

*Survey of American poetry, midcentury to 1984.* (1986). Great Neck, NY: Poetry Anthology press.

Swann, B. (1988). Introduction: Only the beginning. In D. Niatum (Ed.), *Hanper's anthology of 20th century Native American Poetry.* New York: Harper & Row.

Travisano, T. J. (1988). *Elizabeth Bishop, her artistic development.* Charlottesville, VA: University Press of Virginia.

Warren, R. P. (1957). *Promises: Poems, 1954–1956.* New York: Random House.

Warren, R. P. (1960). *You, emperors, and others: Poems 1957–1960.* New York: Random House.

Warren, R. P. (1974). *Or Else—: Poem / Poems, 1968–1974.* New York: Random House.

Warren, R. P. (1975). *Democracy and poetry.* Cambridge, MA: Harvard University Press.

Warren, R. P. (1976). *Selected poems, 1923–1975.* New York: Random House.

Warren, R. P. (1978). *Now and then: Poems, 1976–1978.* New York: Random House.

Warren, R. P. (1981). *Rumor verified: Poems, 1979–1980.* New York: Random House.

Warren, R. P. (1983). *Chief Joseph of the Nez Perce, who called themselves the Nimipu, "the real people."* New York: Random House.

Warren, R. P. (1985). *Altitudes and extensions: 1980–1984.* New York: Random House.

Warren, R. P. (1985). Introduction. In Academy of American Poets (Eds.), *Fifty years of American poetry.* New York: Harry N. Abrams.

Warren, R. P. (1988). *Portrait of a father.* Lexington. KY: University Press of Kentucky.

Watkins, F. C. (1988). "The body of this death" in Robert Penn Warren's later poems. *Kenyon Review, 10*, 31–42.

Westbrook, F. (1980). Death, separation, and autumn imagery in early Chinese poetry. *Advanced Thanatology, 5*, 38–61.

Woodward, K. M. (1980). *At last, the real distinguished thing: The late poems of Eliot, Pound, Stevens and Williams.* Columbus: Ohio State University Press.

Woodward, K. (1986). *The look and the gaze: Narcissism, aggression, and aging* (Critical Reappraisals of Continental Thought Seminar Series, Working Paper No. 7). Milwaukee, WI: University of Wisconisn–Milwaukee, Center for Twentieth-Century Studies, 1986.

Zavatsky, B. (1984). Journey through the feminine: The life review poems of William Carlos Williams. In M. Kaminsky (Ed.), *The uses of reminiscence* (pp. 167–191). New York: Haworth Press.

10

# Old Age in Contemporary Fiction: A New Paradigm of Hope

*Constance Rooke*

This essay is not intended as a survey of contemporary fiction concerned with old age, or as a review of what other literary critics have seen in such fiction, or as a summary of gerontological debates as these may apply to literary practice. Instead, it abstracts from a great array of primary texts a set of characteristics and theoretical concerns that are at work in the production and reception of these texts. Eccentrically, perhaps, it offers an introduction to my own conclusions about what is currently afoot in the fiction of old age.

Contemporary novels and stories are surprisingly well stocked with old people. Indeed, their numerical presence in today's fiction is increasing at a rate at least equal to that of their burgeoning share in the world's population. But far more important than this quantitative measure is another: the fact that when they appear in fiction old people are now much less likely to be afforded only the passing glance or minor role that was customary in the past, and considerably more likely to be granted their fair share of the author's gaze and the available print. Often marginalized and stereotypically reduced in life, old people are now regarded by the writers of fiction as interesting; increasingly, they are now assigned major roles.

The reasons for this change seem clear enough. As life is prolonged and the population ages, we must face the realities both of an increasing presence of the elderly in our lives and of becoming old ourselves. We therefore have a vested interest in regarding old people as unique individuals; we want to destroy the stereotypes that would reduce the old people we love or are or will become. We also have an increasing curiosity about old age. We have an interest in reading about it, almost, perhaps, as we might devour travel books prior to a departure for Italy—or Siberia. This is not to say that we choose the destination of old age; admittedly, our tickets have been prearranged and our passage is very nearly obligatory. Still, we are curious, because for many of us today the habit of denial is wearing thin. We have begun, in a combination of hope and dread, to imagine ourselves in the country of the old.

Curiosity about our fate as aged human beings has grown in both readers and writers. Certainly the reader's increased interest in old age has made it easier for novels and stories concerned with this subject to find an audience. (This interest is especially pronounced among readers who are inclined to favor what we call serious or literary fiction, as opposed to bodice rippers and the like.) But the extent to which the reader's increased willingness to engage with elderly characters in fiction has summoned those characters into being is an open question. Obviously, writers respond in varying ways to the exigencies of the marketplace. Many would argue that they ignore it altogether, that they write what they must, that the reader's (and therefore the publisher's) presumed tastes are irrelevant to any genuine product of the author's imagination. However true or false that may be in any individual case, the situation is undeniably complicated by the fact that writers are also readers, with tastes that can be developed. Words that are "alive" spawn other words; each new novel that reveals the power of old age as a subject for fiction increases not only the possible audience for such fiction, but also the appeal of that subject for the writer's imagination.

Fiction concerned with old age is on the rise, then, for both literary and sociological reasons. These are not opposed categories; they interpenetrate because literature is responsive to and constructive of social realities. More such literature is being written and read because old age is an increasingly insistent fact of life; writers and readers of serious fiction both feel this particular claim of reality on their imaginations. But novels and stories about old age are also proliferating in response to the existence of powerful predecessors. (The apposite titles will, of course, vary from one writer to the next.) Other people's books inevitably help to shape and augment the writer's interest in old age itself *and* to reveal the literary potential of this material.

Simone de Beauvoir (1970/1972) argued two decades ago, in *The Coming of Age*, that "if an old man is dealt with in his subjective aspect he is not a good hero for a novel; he is finished, set, with no hope, no development to be looked for . . . nothing that can happen to him is of any importance" (p. 210). This statement involves some blurring of the possibly divergent perspectives of reader and writer, and implicitly it raises the question of whether the experience of the old person lacks "importance" from his own point of view. Since de Beauvoir's tone seems embittered and to some degree ironic, it is not entirely clear whether she herself believes that "nothing . . . of any importance" can happen to an old man. Is this a view she projects on others because (as her book makes clear) she regards society as plagued by the denial of old age? Is she then, at least to some degree, parroting or parodying the views of less thoughtful people? Or is this her own toughness speaking, her own refusal to engage in a denial of the misery of old age, her own existential despair?

Simone de Beauvoir's fierce assault in this passage is clearly problematic. Is it the reader or the writer who denies "importance" to the experience of the aged? Does de Beauvoir suppose that writers had given up on old people because they were not marketable in fiction, because audiences caught up in the denial of old age would not "buy" them? Or does she think that writers themselves reject such depiction for the same purposes of denial? Another possibility is that, at least in the context described by de Beauvoir, the lives of old people really are lacking in "importance." In that case, we must ask whether de Beauvoir holds out any hope for an amelioration of that climate in the country of the old; we must ask to what extent that climate is our fault. And we must ask—as Simone de Beauvoir herself does not—what role fiction might have to play in determining it.

It is clear from *The Coming of Age* that de Beauvoir is asking us to see ourselves in old people. She suggests that if we can overcome our denial sufficiently to accomplish that task, we will cease to acquiesce in the misery of old age. What is much less clear is the extent to which de Beauvoir believes our refusal to acquiesce in that misery will be effective in removing it. Thus, while she is passionate about the need to improve the economic climate of old age, she is less hopeful of the emotional climate. Her gaze is fixed on the external rather than the internal—although of course one affects the other—because when she looks at the inner or "subjective" experience of old age, she despairs. She seems to hope only for a small amelioration, through externals. She wants us to change those, because those—she thinks—are all that can be changed.

We may conclude, then, that at least to some degree Simone de Beauvoir's own despair is at work in her claim that "if an old man is dealt with in his subjective aspect he is not a good hero for a novel." If it is true that there is "no hope" in old age, fiction that takes us into the "subjective" presence of that final despair cannot succeed. In arguing this, de Beauvoir is assuming what few people would deny, that the force of literature is affirmative. Her point, however, is not simply that such fiction would be depressing, but that the plot (the engine of the story) would be as nearly dead as the characters themselves. She is approaching the matter from what seems the pragmatic point of view of a technician: just as a car with too many miles on it is an unwise investment and unlikely to take us very far, so an elderly protagonist is incapable of projecting us into the future. But here de Beauvoir's argument itself breaks down, because the engines of the imagination are more subtle, more multidirectional, and more powerful than this. They can also take us into the past and seek both narrative tension and affirmation there, for time is not linear in fiction; and they can extend our sense of the "importance" of the present moment, for time in fiction is not measured strictly by the clock. And none of this is a sterile trick; all of it is transportable from fiction to life. The understanding we gain through literature can actually change the emotional climate of old age.

In any case, Simone de Beauvoir's remarks seem dated—for contemporary fiction proves her wrong, resoundingly. We know from several hundred good books and several dozen superb ones, in the last few decades especially, that an old man or woman can in fact be "a good hero for a novel." But what is particularly striking in de Beauvoir's statement is the notion that elderly protagonists cannot engage our interest if "dealt with in [their] subjective aspect." For this is exactly the aspect of old age that contemporary fiction chooses to reveal. When the closed subject becomes an open book, when the mask of stereotypical old age is torn away and the icon stirs, when the elderly character in fiction is allowed to reveal himself or herself as *subject,* we may discover that indeed there is "development to be looked for." In the fiction of old age, that development is looked for—by author, character, and reader—all the more urgently because of the constraints that operate against it.

## THE VOLLENDUNGSROMAN

The recent proliferation of novels about old age should cause us to ask whether a new genre has come into being and, if so, what we might call it. A literary genre is constituted by a significant number of texts that share a significant number of characteristics; as a discernible kind or type of literary production, it has a tendency to call other examples into existence. We appear to have reached that point in the production of novels that are centrally concerned with old age. The *Vollendungsroman* (from the German for "winding up") is a term proposed and coined by the present author, on the model of the bildungsroman; the latter is commonly used in literary criticism to refer to novels of growing up, of youth and development (such as Charles Dickens's *David Copperfield* or James Joyce's *A Portrait of the Artist as a Young Man*). The *Vollendungsroman* is proposed as a complementary term, to refer to the novel of completion or winding up.

These genres have come into being because they treat critical phases in the life cycle; they offer to the novelist (whose vast, perennial subject is human life) a reasonably distinct time frame, a limited but imaginatively expandable segment of the individual life story. The two genres can profitably be studied together; indeed, there is nearly always some recapitulation and reassessment of the matter of the bildungsroman in the *Vollendungsroman*. Both are concerned with basic identity themes, with the relationship of the individual to society, with an assessment of what living well means, and with the question of what comes next. Poised on either side of that extended period in which the individual is most fully engaged in the business of life, and often too preoccupied for reflection, novels concerned with youth and age offer the writer a natural "platform" from which to address large questions.

In Figure 10.1 life is represented as a circle. We arise from the unknown quadrant marked "Universal" and are born into the "Particular" life story we will gradually construct, in response to an array of forces. Commonly, we regard the first phase of the life cycle (childhood and youth) as a preparation for life in society. The matter of the bildungsroman is accumulated in this phase; such novels typically end with the protagonist poised on the brink of the next quadrant, having made at least preliminary moves on such vital issues as love and work. The middle phase (the prime of life) allows participation in society and the exercise of our developed powers. The last phase (old age) involves leaving the social stage, or disengagement; here the *Vollendungsroman* begins.

This simplistic model, which would seem to deny to children and the elderly the right of participation in society, cannot be excused in practice. Nor can it be reconciled conceptually with a continuous circle of "narration," the pattern of self-actualization enacted over a lifetime, except by a radical shift. The task of our first life phase is sometimes given as the construction of ego; this notion is congruent with the progression from an inchoate infancy to a carefully designed and self-assured maturity. The task of old age may be given as the deconstruction of ego, which may in some instances be translated as a willingness to let go of social power. It is easy enough to detect a vested interest in the allocation of these tasks. The process may be recommended as spiritually

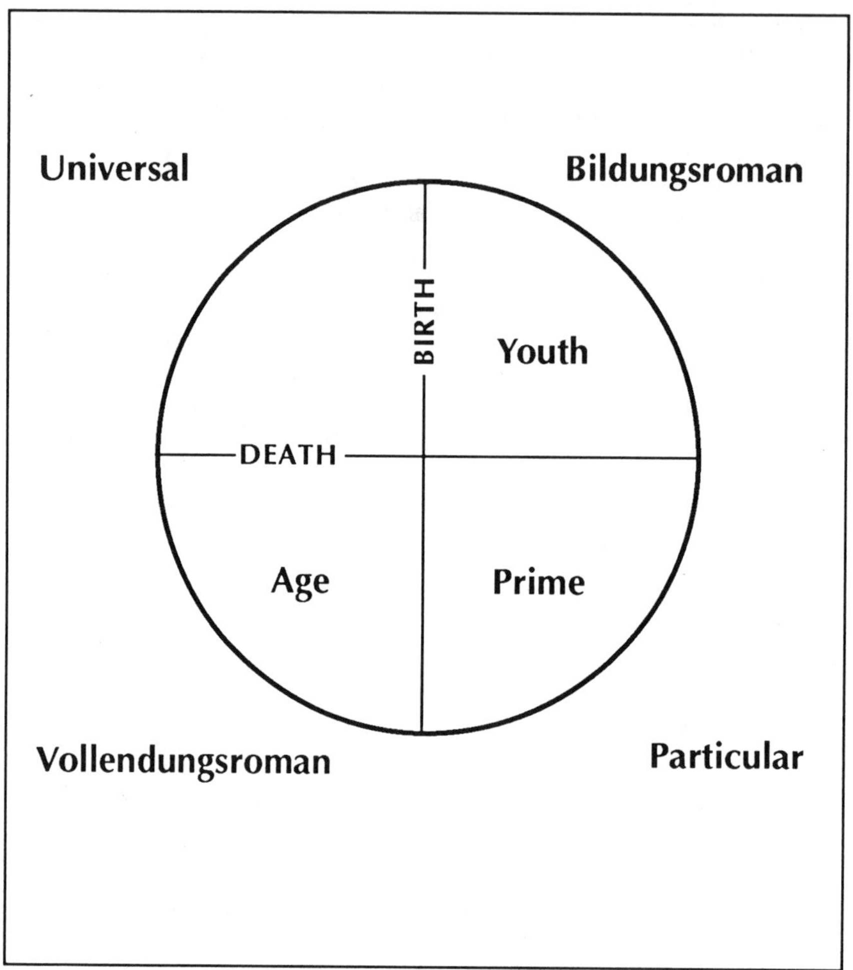


**FIGURE 10.1 Critical phases in the life cycle.**

advantageous for the old, when its egotistical motive (on the part of those in their prime) is simply to reduce clutter or competition in the circle.

Disengagement may be resisted. Old people in life and fiction often resist it to good effect; television and popular films resist it with sometimes cloying or suspect images of aged gusto. And gerontologists, of course, have for some time now abjured their own or their predecessors' valorization of this concept. In both glib and subtle considerations of this issue, there has been a considerable shift in our attitudes to disengagement. We have been sensitized to its hidden agenda and to the need for activity and a sense of involvement in the life stream. Sometimes, however, this new liberality—this cheering on and cheering up of the old—has a trivializing and perniciously totalizing effect. To persist (as far as possible) in the behaviors and values that were central in youth and middle age may be a source of great strength for the elderly, but such persistence is not necessarily a good thing. Human beings, as the subtleties of good literature help us to understand, *vary* from one to another; they also change, for good or ill.

Thus, it remains a possibility that disengagement will benefit the old. If we shift our gaze, to regard that singular achieved ego as (necessarily, at least in part) a failure, as only a fractional representation of what the human being ought to be, then disengagement or the deconstruction of ego will seem a vital task. Wholeness, indeed, if that is regarded as an ideal, may require a multiplicity of selves; and ego may be an impediment to growth. Less radically, we may say that some departure from accustomed behaviors will assist the completion of the human figure.

The literature of old age, from Shakespeare's *King Lear* through to such recent examples of the *Vollendungsroman* as David Malouf's (1978) *An Imaginary Life*, has wrestled long and hard with the issue of disengagement. On the one hand, we see plainly the need (and often the right) of elderly characters to hold onto the social identity that has been constructed over time; frequently, such texts will insist upon the desirability of this and the villany or self-interest of characters who would deprive the elderly protagonist of his ego's trappings. On the other hand, such texts nearly always discover some benefit that accrues to the elderly character through disengagement. One characteristic form of that benefit is illustrated by Lear and by Ovid, Malouf's protagonist. As Lear loses his kingdom and rages on the heath, so the sophisticated Latin poet of *The Metamorphoses* is forcibly exiled from Rome and sent to live on the barren steppes among the barbarians. And both men learn something of the reality underlying the specious aspects of what they had constructed in the social realm. Both discover, through loss of station and a kind of metamorphosis, their place in the natural world; through a deconstruction of ego, each becomes more truly humane. In Ovid's case, the story ends with an ecstatic return to the universal at the point of death; but in Lear's case, the spectacle of error and waste threatens to outweigh the value we may place on the aged monarch's spiritual growth.

One of the most characteristic thematic features of the *Vollendungsroman* is this vital concern with the advantages and penalties of disengagement. In *King Lear* and *An Imaginary Life*, a specific dramatic act projects the aged man into a new space; but symbolically, in these texts and in the *Vollendungsroman* generally, it is old age itself that effects the change. Although events such as retirement or the loss of a mate or removal to an institution provide sudden jolts and propel the plot of the *Vollendungsroman*, disengagement is typically regarded as a continuous process—and not always or only as a progressive deterioration. Frequently, these events unleash recognitions so that new meanings are constructed even as the ego or life of the individual is deconstructed. In many texts, the elderly protagonist rebels against disengagement and (armed with a determination born of values asserted in the face of loss) reinserts herself or himself in the social realm. This reengagement may involve a return to past skills and past behaviors, or it may illustrate the capacity to actualize previously dormant aspects of the self. But there is almost always a qualitative difference, an intensification or an ironic tone that comes from the knowledge that this renewal within the quotidian is temporary. Disengagement may be continuing on another level, and typically the protagonist acknowledges more fully than he or she has done before that death—the last stage of disengagement—is unavoidable.

The task of the *Vollendungsroman* is to discover for its protagonist and for the reader some kind of affirmation in the face of loss. We might also say, however, that this is the task of literature generally. Literature teaches empathy and performs a salvage operation. It helps us to see and to value in our own lives and the lives of other people things that we may have overlooked. It works in the face of loss and of abundant and varied opposition, on the side of life. All lives are temporary; all are circumscribed by the reality of death. But this is felt more strongly in fiction concerned with old age, so that a special intensity, resulting from the proximity to darkness, characterizes the *Vollendungsroman*. The writer's imagination is challenged by the prospect of the character's demise and by the need to "capture" a life before it vanishes. Behind this, and quite apart from the question of how old the writer is, lurks the specter of the writer's own prospective death. Writing is always an act directed against death, but it may become that more specifically and more urgently when the writer's subject is old age.

Old age is also an occasion for humor. The proximity of death makes the absurdity of individuals who are stuck in certain patterns of behavior or response all the more striking. Their stubbornness (which, of course, can also be shown as heroic) may seem comic—futile and therefore absurd—when it is enacted in close proximity to the end of life. Theorists of humor have recognized for a long time that one of the great sources of comedy is the spectacle of a human being who is "stuck," who responds automatically rather than with the flexibility (the capacity to adapt and change) that we expect of ourselves and our fellow citizens. Into the gap between this social ideal and the reality, laughter rushes. But not all humor is so dependent as this description may imply upon the separation of the one who laughs and the one who is laughed at. One of the great lessons of the *Vollendungsroman* is that we are *all* terminal cases; the fiction of old age (whether it employs black comedy or humor of a gentler sort) reminds us that the "joke" is on us too.

A major part of humor is critique; its thrust is that something ought to be otherwise. But there is another important thing that happens when we laugh: often, we forgive and celebrate ourselves and other people through laughter. We express through laughter not only contempt—a dismissal to the category of distant "other"—but kinship, a recognition of shared human foibles. And sometimes we laugh out of sheer joy, out of exhilaration: that yes, this thing we toss up into the light *is* marvellous, and all the more so for the darkness out of which it comes.

The subject of old age is a powerful one for other reasons too. The invisibility or marginalization of old people, their reduction to stereotype, their occupation of a zone behind the mask—all of this may provide special impetus to one of the writer's most crucial drives, which is to *see* other human beings clearly. The indignities suffered by the elderly—as their bodies betray them, as memory fails, as social power is stripped away and condescension mounts—may also stimulate the writer's need to proffer dignity through art.

Questions such as these relate to the elderly person's claim upon a writer's empathy or compassion. But the elderly character is also attractive for a number of more technical literary reasons. To begin with, she (or he) makes available to the writer nearly the whole span of a life history, as opposed to just that truncated, glibly predictive bit before the heroine decides whom to marry. She picks up the human story at a pivotal and richly dramatic point, when the evaluation of life seems most urgent and when the old dramatic question of what comes next is most especially poignant. She may also function for the writer as a touchstone (and victim or champion) of social attitudes that have shaped our past and that operate still even in a climate of radical revision.

## AFFIRMATION IN OLD AGE

Margaret Laurence's (1964) *The Stone Angel* is a classic example of the *Vollendungsroman*. It illustrates the need for affirmation and the consequences of an author's decision to give us the elderly character from the inside. A cantankerous old woman, Hagar Shipley is an obstacle and a problem for her family; but we take her side to a remarkable degree because we are given access to it. We see what Hagar says and does, and much of that we would judge harshly; but because Hagar is allowed to tell her own story, because we enter her consciousness and live there, we can respond to her more fairly. We learn to value her rich sensuality and the free play of her wit; we see the other side of the coin, the capacity for joy, all of the positive qualities that have been so tragically denied in Hagar's presentation of self to the world. We come to understand as well the social forces—familial, patriarchal, and puritanical—that have led her to this distortion.

All of this raises a set of interesting questions about the "credit" we as readers are prepared to grant to characters in fiction. In general, we honor characters for their admirable behavior (especially against heavy odds) or, if they have misbehaved, for proof that they have changed or reformed. In Hagar's case, which is typical of many elderly characters in contemporary fiction, time has nearly run out; although she comes to a partial recognition of her mistakes, she cannot rectify them. Instead, she makes the gestures of atonement that are symbolic of a will to be and do otherwise, and that are often so persuasive in the fiction of old age. From a strictly existential point of view, such as Simone de Beauvoir might espouse, human beings are neither more nor less than the sum of their actions; and gestures such as Hagar's would not weigh heavily in the balance.

But this view is too harsh. Pessimism in old age is partly a function of two questionable assumptions: that only time matters and that only actions count. These two limitations enforce one another in old age, as time is running out and as the arena and capacity for action are diminished. Contemporary fiction acknowledges this, but it does not stop there. It seeks—as literature must, as human beings must—to affirm the value of human life. To affirm is always to affirm *despite* something, despite all that would seem to contradict or "liquefy" or "drown" that which we attempt to make "firm" in affirmation. If in old age this affirmation is especially difficult, it is also therefore especially heroic. Affirmation is achieved not by denying the forces of negation but by confronting them and by maintaining that *still* there is value in human life and cause for celebration.

Affirmation is not always so hard won, and it comes in many forms. Sometimes the elderly protagonist will find a great deal to value in his or her life. But only rarely does a text conclude with a ringing endorsement of what the developmental psychologist Erik Erikson refers to as the old person's "one and only life." An exception of this kind is Willa Cather's (1932) "Neighbor Rosicky" which ends with the statement that

"Rosicky's life seemed to [the doctor] complete and beautiful" (p. 71); in Cather's novella, the life itself is regarded as a finished work of art, and closure comes without a pang. But *The Stone Angel*, in which Hagar is struggling desperately to change and grow, in which categorically she refuses to gloss over her mistakes and deprivation, is a far more typical case. Affirmation here—as in the case of Tillie Olsen's (1956) *Tell Me a Riddle*—comes with great difficulty. While it involves something more than the assessment of a single human life, it does nevertheless ring out and console and incite joy in an old woman at the point of death.

For characters like Laurence's Hagar and Olsen's Eva, affirmation is wrested out of a life that has been filled with disappointment. Similarly, Lucy Smalley, the elderly heroine of Paul Scott's (1977) *Staying On*, can look back on her life and think, "Yes, from the beginning I had a sad life. . . . A life like a flower that has never really bloomed, but how many do?" (p. 67). Affirmation, in texts like these, is dependent upon the will to "flower" and upon the hope that for future generations the ground (the structures and values of society) will prove more nurturing, more amenable to the fulfillment of human potential. A kind of evolutionary ideal is apparent in many of these texts, an ideal that survives (even if the individual does not) because Hagar and Eva and Lucy are capable of embracing it. Affirmation is achieved for the reader partly through a recognition of the potential for "flowering" that each of these women has retained; we can recognize that potential and feel its partial actualization because we are allowed to enter the consciousness—the interior, "subjective" space—of the elderly character. If it is sometimes too late for these characters to act or change their lives in ongoing and externally verifiable ways, we can nevertheless affirm that it might have been otherwise and can be for future generations; we can affirm that it partly *was* otherwise, because they have found things to celebrate and because consciousness is also real. We can understand that dreams, even when they have not been actualized, are a part of life and not to be despised.

The term *Vollendungsroman* (for the novel of completion or winding up) has been proposed with a certain measure of irony because a characteristic of these texts is the recognition that human projects are rarely—perhaps we may say that they are never—completed. Closure is always arbitrary; and the tension between affirmation and regret, or between the desire to wrap things up and the recognition that in any life there will inevitably be loose threads, is surely one of the most powerful features of the fiction of old age. But affirmation and regret are not mutually exclusive, and affirmation is not dependent upon a sense of completion.

## SPEECH IN THE *VOLLENDUNGSROMAN*

The act of speech operates in the *Vollendungsroman* in several ways. Broadly or metaphorically speaking, it is all of the *writing* performed on the protagonist's behalf by the writer; it may include the inner or silent discourse of the protagonist; and finally, of course, it is all speech performed out loud by the protagonist. Speech of this most literal kind may be divided further. Often, there is something to be said to other characters, usually in order to free them for their own lives. It is typical of the *Vollendungsroman* that the "truth" of a crucial act of speech should be in question; what seems to matter is that the thing be said, the gist of it, before the power of speech is gone. Although the theme of the message is enormously important in the *Vollendungsroman*, the writer often and very interestingly underplays the message itself at the point of delivery. Often, too, the elderly protagonist is tormented by the memory of characters who have died (or vanished) before some vital message can be delivered or received, and then eased when a surrogate figure is supplied to participate in the desired exchange. (Margaret Laurence's (1964) *The Stone Angel* is a powerful example.) A third kind of significant speech for the elderly protagonist is one that strikes a new tone or reveals him or her in a new light.

Words that are delivered to surviving characters, messages that are routed to the dead through intermediaries (so that the elderly character may be delivered from the burden of silence or mistaken speech), talk in which the aged protagonist may exercise a freer version of the self—these are the most typical acts of speech that point toward affirmation in the *Vollendungsroman*. Always, they are imperfect or imprecise. But that is necessarily the case because the *Vollendungsroman* negotiates between speech and silence, between the lived and the unlived life. Desire is never fully satisfied; what seems to matter is that it be expressed.

Speech is also important in a broader sense: as the *story* of a life. Contemporary fiction generally has been interested in the need human beings feel to turn their lives into story, and in the insistent analogy that obtains between fiction and life. As fiction mirrors life, so life reflects (or enacts) the shaping behaviors of fiction. This theme is especially pronounced in the *Vollendungsroman*, in which elderly characters are running out of time and therefore determined to let the story be told. Previous versions of a life story may need to be revised in an attempt to construct some final "authorized" version. All stories, however, are stories; all are partial or incomplete. But if contemporary fiction emphasizes the necessary imperfection or unreliability of any such construction, the value of the life story (for teller or listener) is not diminished by this recognition. Storytelling is understood as one of the great devices by which we assert both our individuality and our place in the community.

## STRUCTURE, THEME, AND IMAGERY

The life review, one of the most common themes of the *Vollendungsroman*, is also a common structural device. The protagonist is located within a present time frame, a few days or months perhaps of that character's old age; and then through memory the character is transported into past time, often through a narrative voice that assesses past experience in a new light. Thus, memory is important because it gives the reader (and the character) access to the past, and because it is being shaped by the character in the present. Memory *is* present experience; it is not simply a dodge that allows the writer to escape from the country of the old. Sometimes memories are so fragmentary that they do not disrupt the narrative line; sometimes they do disrupt it, but are clearly secondary to the present time of the fictional world. The issue here is not only the duration of the memory, but also the mode of representation, the extent to which we remain aware of the filter that memory supplies. Sustained flashbacks, however, can create an additional—sometimes equally important—dimension of the plot. At the other end of the continuum, the protagonist's old age may become inconsequential if it functions simply and briefly as a narrative frame. (In this case, of course, the term *Vollendungsroman* would cease to be applicable.)

So far, this discussion has emphasized the considerable attention paid by contemporary fiction to an elderly protagonist engaged in an assessment of his or her life. Especially in texts of this kind, the circumstances of old age—however important these may be—are less insistent than the humanity of the character. But there are also many fictional works that seem to be centrally concerned with the task of *depiction*, texts that are concerned with revealing the tribulations and perhaps the consolations of being old. There is no clear distinction between these types; rather, they form another kind of continuum. Often works at the sociological (rather than what might be termed the psychological or spiritual) end of this continuum will deploy a large cast of elderly characters in order to ring the changes on old age. But sophisticated novels, even those that are most notably concerned with old age—including "group" novels such as Kingsley Amis's (1974) *Ending Up*, Muriel Spark's (1959) *Memento Mori*, Elizabeth Jolley's (1983) *Mr. Scobie's Riddle*, and John Updike's (1959) *The Poorhouse Fair*—are always concerned with much more than the depiction of old age. Indeed, this anti-ghettoizing of theme in the best of our contemporary writers is a measure of how far we have come.

Themes that are important in the *Vollendungsroman,* and in contemporary short stories that treat old age, naturally overlap with themes that have interested gerontologists. Intergenerational conflicts, societal change, disengagement, the life review, poverty, loneliness, sexuality, body image, frailty, memory loss, illness, loss of independence, loss of friends and family, stereotypical reduction and marginalization, the motivation and behavior of caregivers, the terrors and possible benefits of institutionalization, attitudes toward religion and death—all of this is powerful fictional material. The conditions of old age are moving to us as human beings and therefore *useful* to fiction. But it is equally clear that contemporary fiction is useful to our understanding of these matters in life. It is useful primarily because fiction contextualizes and particularizes the problems of gerontology; it does so by reminding us forcibly that "old" is only one of many adjectives that may be applied to the old person, and by giving us access to the infinitely complex "subjective" experience of aging. Fiction is less abstract or theoretical than gerontology; it is also (in a seeming paradox) less narrowly pragmatic or concrete.

The imagery that characterizes the *Vollendungsroman* is particularly interesting. The frequency with which certain images recur may suggest the operation of archetypes or at least that there are strong determinants affecting the way the imagination approaches the subject of aging. The extent to which these determinants are specifically literary is hard to assess, but in any case it is clear that they also arise "naturally" out of the experience of old age. Such images include, for example, the mirror and the fall and the circle. Literal concerns, like the old person's entirely sensible fear of falling (since old bones refuse to knit), are developed in elaborately symbolic ways.

The figure of the child and images associated with birth—recalling the old rhyme of womb and tomb—are especially important. Often, as in David Malouf's (1978) *An Imaginary Life,* the plot will feature an encounter between the elderly character and a child, and will suggest that in this way the old person is symbolically establishing vital contact with an earlier version of the self. And highly charged tableaux involving the aged child's vision of his parents are often placed at the emotional center of the text. Also remarkably prominent in the fiction of old age are animals and animal images. Sometimes—as in Elizabeth Taylor's story "Mice and Birds and Boy" or Doris Lessing's "An Old Woman and Her Cat"—animals feature as the companions of old people who have been cast aside by society. Often, and in complex ways, they signify a fear of death; the animal (shark or rat or hyena, for example) figures as potential killer, but the animal is also the self that will die like other animals. Insult and deterioration and the loss of beauty typically unleash animal images, as if in old age the human being becomes inevitably a lesser breed.

One of the most compelling images in the fiction of old age is the house. Again, this arises "naturally" out of experience. Old people in life (as in fiction) are often desperate to hold onto their homes, because the house represents the self in society and contains (through memory and memorabilia) the "furniture" of identity—or simply because they fear removal to an institution, which is regarded as the antechamber to the grave. The house is a marker of belonging or social status and may prop up the elderly in that way, but it can also be a "time capsule" that protects the elderly inhabitant from the judgmental, frighteningly changed outside world. And it is a shelter against the "outside" forces of nature, so in this way too it becomes symbolically a barrier or a stay against death. In part because we regard ourselves as "living in" the body, the house is essentially an image of the body; and the dilapidation or disorder of the house is often used to signal the body's decline. A struggle generally ensues—either between the old person and those who would remove her from her home (and thus, symbolically, from her social identity and her body) or between the house itself and nature which would invade it. Sometimes, though, the elderly character flees the house (usually to avoid institutionalization) and escapes into the natural world; there, unhoused and gypsy-like, she embraces the "deconstruction" of the ego.

One last image that is especially striking in the fiction of old age is water, which in its formlessness and mobility is often opposed to the firmness of the house. A surprising number of old people in fiction are frightened of water or drawn to it; almost always, it represents the universal unknown from which life came and toward which life flows once more as the end approaches. Water, if it expresses dissolution, also may expresses "solution"—an inclusive and transformative embrace. It can seem (in the case of *The Stone Angel* or *An Imaginary Life*, or in several texts by John Cheever) almost an adventure or a holiday after the stolid sameness of the house. Over water, finally, we venture out into death or parts unknown.

## CONCLUSION: AN HONOR ROLL

This discussion of old age and contemporary fiction has attempted to address in a preliminary way a number of theoretical issues and to argue for the importance of its subject. In order to achieve these goals in a limited space, it has not negotiated the terrain of critical discourse on this topic; neither has it engaged in any extensive description or analysis of particular literary texts. Thus, its claims go forward without the usual intellectual "proofs." In lieu of these, it seems appropriate to end with a brief, representative list of contemporary *Vollendungsromans* so that the reader of this essay can begin to test its claims independently.

## REFERENCES


Alford, E. (1981). *A sleep full of dreams*. Lantzville, BC: Oolichan.
Amis, K. (1974). *Ending up*. London: Jonathan Cape.
Amis, K. (1986). *The old devils*. London: Hutchinson.
Anderson, J. (1978). *Tirra lirra by the river*. London: Macmillan.
Bailey, P. (1967). *At the jerusalem*. London: Jonathan Cape.
Barnes, J. (1987). *Staring at the sun*. Toronto: Random House.
Bellow, S. (1970). *Mr. Sammler's planet*. New York: Viking.
Beresford-Howe, C. (1973). *The book of Eve*. Boston: Little, Brown.
Blackwood, C. (1986). *Corrigan*. Harmondsworth: Penguin.
Blackwood, C. (1977). *Great Granny Webster*. London: Duckworth.
Calisher, H. (1987). *Age*. New York: Weidenfeld and Nicolson.
Cheever, J. (1982). *Oh, what a paradise it seems*. New York: Knopf.
Figes, E. (1981). *Waking*. New York: Pantheon.
Fischer, M. F. K. (1964). "Sister age." New York: Vintage.
Gardner, J. (1976). *October light*. New York: Knopf.
Gloag, J. (1988). *Only yesterday*. London: Grafton.
Hall, R. (1983). *Just relations*. New York: Viking.
Ishiguro, K. (1986). *An artist of the floating world*. New York: Putnam's.
Ishiguro, K. (1989). *The remains of the day*. New York: Knopf.
Johnson, B. S. (1971). *House mother normal: A geriatric comedy*. New York: New Directions.
Jolley, E. (1983). *Mr. Scobie's riddle*. Melbourne: Penguin.
Laurence, M. (1964). *The stone angel*. London: Macmillan.
Lessing, D. (1972). An old woman and her cat. In *The story of a nonmarrying man*. London: Jonathon Cape.
Lessing, D. (1985). *The diaries of Jane Somers*. Harmondsworth: Penguin.
Lively, P. (1987). *Moon tiger*. London: Deutsch.
Malouf, D. (1978). *An imaginary life*. London: Chatto and Windus.
Morris, W. (1971). *Fire sermon*. New York: Harper & Row.
Morris, W. (1973). *A life*. New York: Harper & Row.
Olsen, T. (1961). Tell me a riddle. In *Tell me a riddle*. New York: Dell.
Pym, B. (1977). *Quartet in autumn*. London: Macmillan.
Rule, J. (1987). *Memory board*. Toronto: Macmillan.
Sarton, M. (1973). *As we are now*. New York: Norton.
Scott, P. (1977). *Staying on*. London: Heineman.
Spark, M. (1959). *Memento Mori*. London: Macmillan.
Taylor, E. (1965). Mice and birds and boy. In *A dedicated man and other stories*. New York: Viking.

Updike, J. (1958). *The poorhouse fair*. New York: Knopf.
Wharton, W. (1981). *Dad*. New York: Knopf.
White, P. (1973). *The eye of the storm*. London: Jonathan Cape.
White, P. (1961). *Riders in the chariot*. London: Eyre and Spottiswoode.

# Walking to the Stars

*Mary G. Winkler*

> The human body is an instrument for the production of art in the life of the soul.
> —Alfred North Whitehead

> The principal task of the artist is to introduce appropriate meaning.
> —Rudolph Arnheim

Toward the end of his life, Vincent Van Gogh (1959) reflected on the distant stars. About the time he painted *Starry Night* (Figure 11.1) he confided to his brother Theo:

> For my own part I declare I know nothing whatever about it [dying], but looking at the stars always makes me dream, as simply as I dream over the black dots representing towns and villages on a map. Why, I ask myself, shouldn't the shining dots of the sky be as accessible as the black dots on the map of France?
>
> Just as we take the train to get to Tarasçon or Rouen, we take death to reach a star. One thing undoubtedly true in this reasoning is that we cannot get to a star while we are alive, anymore than we can take a train when we are dead.
>
> So it seems to me possible that cholera, gravel, tuberculosis and cancer are the celestial means of locomotion, just as steamboats, buses and railways are terrestrial means. To die quietly of old age would be to go on foot. (Letter 506, p. 605)

The idea of walking to the stars suggests a pilgrimage perceptible in the work of some artists. Van Gogh's fleeting meditations open us to further reflections on the relationship between a long life and the artist's task and on analogies between the life journey and the meaning and purpose of art. If we all seek meaning in life, and if it is the artist's principle task to introduce appropriate meaning (Arnheim, 1966), then

**FIGURE 11.1 The Starry Night. Vincent Van Gogh. 1889. Oil on canvas. 29 × 361/14". Collection, The Museum of Modern Art, New York. Acquired through the Lillie P. Bliss Bequest.**

a study of how various artists have introduced meaning to aging offers guidance for reflecting on the end of the life course.

In art we find innumerable depictions of the aged. Some depictions are naturalistic, some romantic, some didactic—and a few transcend their theme to offer previously unimagined insights and comfort. Images of aging draw from the whole range of subjects found in images of humanity in general. Thus, we find virtue and vice, sensuality and spirituality, striving and repose.

Amid the wealth of depictions of aging in Western art I see three themes emerge: grotesque or despicable old age, wise old age, and old age transcended in the face of death. From the abundance of examples of each theme, I have chosen only a few for discussion. Some, like the works of Michelangelo, are well known; others, less so. All are accessible to contemplation and understanding. And all may be used as charts for the journey.

## OLD AGE DELUDED, EMBITTERED

The first examples do not address the viewer gently. Sometimes art is cruel. The artist does not always soothe us with images of beauty and harmony, and if we dare remove veils of flattery and sentimentality, we face the potential ugliness of lives lacking in wisdom and self-knowledge.

In *The Historie of Life and Death* (published in 1638), Francis Bacon (1977) harshly pronounced that people's spiritual state may be inferred from the wizened, crippled state of their bodies: "old men's minds being visible would appear as deformed as their bodies" (p. 279).

Although we reject this statement as unkind and unjust, we still appreciate the artist's unique opportunity not only to "make minds visible" but to demonstrate through the aged body the results of misdirected life journeys derailed by vanity, self-absorption, or greed. To those choosing such detours, poets and artists show no mercy. The following three examples of aged minds made visible are no dainty fare for the sentimentalist of old age.

The first is Francisco Goya's *Hasta la Muerte* (Figure 11.2), one of a series of 90 aquatints published in 1799 under the title *Caprichos*. Until 1792, Goya enjoyed a reputation as a court painter, but, as Robert Hughes (1990) observed, if he had died then we would not remember him as a great painter. That year, however, he suffered a severe illness that shattered his self-confidence and left him permanently deaf. Bitter and disillusioned, he retreated into solitude and into an artistic vision very different from the "polite discourse of court art" (p. 30). At the age of 53, he issued his manifesto, the *Caprichos* (published in 1799), a series of satirical works flirting with the demonic and psychosexual.

*Hasta la Muerte* (Until Death) is one of Goya's merciless depictions of the follies of the aged. Essentially a variation on the vanity theme (vanity of vanities, all is vanity), this work shows an old crone trying on an extravagantly beribboned bonnet before a mirror that reveals to the viewer her self-satisfaction and lack of true insight. Completely absorbed in her image, she plays the coquette while the two gentlemen in attendance sneer. One stifles his laughter behind his hand while the other rolls his eyes to heaven. The much younger servant girl leans her elbows on the toilette table and joins the mockery.

The work is savage. The old woman's face is reduced to a mask with pig eyes, sunken cheeks, a bulbous nose. Goya invites the viewer to scorn her—not because she is old but because she fails to really *see*

**FIGURE 11.2 Hasta La Muerte. Aquatint from *Los Caprichos*. Francisco Goya. (5th edition, Madrid, Calcografía Nacional, c. 1881–1886.) The Huntington Library, San Marino, California.**

herself. The mirror is the artist's visual play on both narcissism and the opportunity for self-knowledge. The aged coquette has chosen to use it as a narcissistic tool, and Goya, therefore, allows us to despise her. He allows this not because she wishes to be an object of sexual desire but because her desire is warped by egotism and vanity. She neither truly sees herself nor those around her, and in her blindness of spirit she clings to youth with a tenacity that Goya shows to be delusional. Rather than the beauty that reflects a wise and loving heart, she has chosen the glittering and lying mirror's image.

Vanity and egotism are not female prerogatives, and seldom have these human failings been more minutely dissected than in the work of George Grosz. Grosz is best known for his angry, penetrating satires on German society between the two world wars. Born in 1893, he enlisted in the infantry at the beginning of World War I, but he spent a portion of his military service in a mental institution, his own art used against him as evidence that he was a lunatic and unfit for military service

**FIGURE 11.3 Drawing. George Grosz. 1919. From *Ecce Homo*, Grove Press, New York, 1966. © Estate of George Grosz / VAGA, New York, 1991.**

**FIGURE 11.4 Spring Awakening. Drawing. George Grosz. 1922. From *Ecce Homo,* Grove Press, New York, 1966. © Estate of George Grosz / VAGA, New York, 1991.**

(Bruckner, Chwast, & Heller, 1984). In the postwar years he concentrated on revealing the hypocrisy, venality, incompetence, and depravity that he saw in his defeated homeland. For this, his work was vilified as subversive and blasphemous, and under Hitler he was forced to emigrate.

His vision is not for the faint-hearted nor for those who deny ugliness. Like the later work of Goya, it is a harsh reminder of the depths to which human beings can go. No one is spared, least of all the aged. Often, in fact, Grosz uses the aged as examples of the evils he saw around him. Two works (Figures 11.3, 11.4) from his series *Ecce Homo* (first published in 1923) demonstrate the savage penetration of his gaze. The first is a drawing of an old man, his body tense with rage. Where Goya's old woman had her eyes fixed on a mirror, Grosz's old man sees nothing—his eyes are *clenched* shut in impotent anger. His gnarled hands are tightened into clawlike fists. This raised fist does not epitomize virile force of strength and self-control. Rather, this gesture symbolizes a grasping, illegitimate lust for control. The old man tries to impose his will on the world but is ineffectual and powerless. If we could hear his voice, it would be the peevish wail of a spoiled infant.

The second work depicts a perverted "love scene." A variation on a very ancient theme, this is Grosz's version of a May–December romance. But there is no love here, only lust and sly greed. Here, a corpulent older man looks knowingly at his companion, a naked young girl. Everything about the man is carnal and gross, from his bloodshot eyes to the thick fingers dangling a phallic cigar. The whole figure suggests greedy sexuality. The young girl with her schoolbook and pigtail is, however, no mere innocent victim. She returns his hot gaze with a look both sly and calculating. Their eye contact reveals that they are accomplices in the perversion of love.

If there is a "misspent youth," say Goya and Grosz, there is also a misspent old age, one we must look at with pity and fear. This view is harsh. The viewer is not allowed to escape into the sentimentality of greeting cards or the false heartiness of television commercials, where old people sell hospital products as if their lives could be reduced to commercial panacea. These are works about the consequences of lives lived without generosity and grace, and they are truly disturbing—not because they reveal our common fear of decay and death but because they embody minds devoted entirely to the material and the sensual.

## OLD AGE, BLESSED AND WISE

There is, however, a gentler perception of aging, one that serves as an antidote to the harrowing view we have just seen. The vision of old age as a time of wisdom and reflection has a long history in Western art. One of the earliest genres in the depiction of age is that of the philosopher in Hellenistic sculpture. In this genre, the aged philosopher becomes the prototype for "good" aging. This tendency to personify the concept of "good" old age continues through the Middle Ages in depictions of prophets and saints. For centuries, the concept of the individual proceeding through life on the solitary journey toward death had been an important *topos* in Western spirituality.

Beginning in the Renaissance, however, there was an increasing interest in exploring the relationship of aging to the individual. Two themes emerge here as paramount. One is a peaceful transcendence of the aging flesh; the other, acceptance of mortality by embracing the continuity of generations. One of the most beloved portraits of aging is Domenico del Ghirlandaio's portrait of an old man with his grandchild

**FIGURE 11.5 An Old Man and His Grandson. Panel c. 1480. Domenico Ghirlandaio. Musée du Louvre, Paris.**

(c. 1480) (Figure 11.5). It is a simple composition, grandfather and child before a window; from the window a winding road, a lone tree, a church, a distant mountain. The portrait is famous for the old man's extremely deformed nose. The viewer's eye is continually drawn to it;

even the child seems to wonder, "Grandpa, what happened to your nose?" But that is not what finally holds us. It is the

> honesty of studied detail that lessens the effect of the portrait's ugliness; the inner gentleness of expression; the graceful light on the smooth and consistent surfaces; the brilliance of the color; the beauty of the distant landscape; and the strange rigidity and inflexibility of the elements of composition, which combine a distinct archaism with all the studied naturalism of the artist's drawing. (Hartt, 1975, p. 308)

The picture speaks of the relationship between the old man and the child. The focus is the interaction of their eyes. The artist simplified everything to suggest the unity and strength of the relationship. The red pyramid of the old man's gown protects the child and creates a powerful and stable force in the composition. But the whole scene is opened and illuminated by the window, which serves as an analogy for the spiritual life.

The old man is firmly grounded in this world. This is clear by his weighty presence in the composition and by the child who represents the succession of generations. But there is also a transcendent future. The window speaks of a "life beyond" the daily pleasures and struggles of the material world. The old man's vista is open to a distant mountain traversed by way of the church. When viewed not just as a record of Italian bourgeois life but as a parable of the good life, the picture becomes poignant. Perhaps soon the man will leave the child to begin the journey to the mountain. Someday the child will leave the same house to make the same journey. Thus, Ghirlandaio has turned a simple family portrait into a vision of harmony between a good life (here in the late medieval Christian sense) and the transcendence of matter through spirituality.

Another powerful evocation of old age and the succession of generations is Rembrandt's *The Return of the Prodigal Son* (Figure 11.6), executed in 1663. Rembrandt chose his text from one of the parables of Jesus (Luke 15:11–32), the story of the reconciliation between a loving father and a wayward son. Although the parable—and the painting—deal with divine rather than human love, the humanity of the artistic concept is so great that even nonbelievers are moved by the exquisite sweetness of the relationship between old man and youth. Kenneth Clark (cited in Halewood, 1982) characterized the spirit that conceived this vision of love and mercy as "a feeling of compassion so intense that it has the power of healing" (p. 61).

The Ghirlandaio painting shows the graceful transition from one generation to another and offers an ideal of continuity and acceptance

**FIGURE 11.6 The Return of the Prodigal Son. Rembrandt. Oil painting. c. 1665. Hermitage Museum, Leningrad.**

of life's seasons. The Rembrandt work is more complex and suggests ambiguities and struggles not present in the sunny world of Ghirlandaio's family life. The story it tells is both painful and compelling. Rembrandt, working in a Protestant environment, was clearly aware of the implications for reformed, evangelical theology. The parable of the Prodigal Son was a staple of Protestant iconography because it supported the teaching of the reformers on the proper relationship of grace to faith and works: the son is forgiven *not* through his own merits but through the father's boundless mercy. The parable contains one of the central themes of intergenerational conflict. The younger of a man's two sons chafes at waiting for his inheritance. The father gave the son his inheritance, and the son "departed to a far country." There he squandered his wealth and in his poverty and despair thinks of his childhood home. He determines to return and beg his father's forgiveness: "Father, I have sinned against heaven and in thy sight, and am no more worthy to be called thy son." Instead of greeting the son with coldness or reprimands, the father embraces him with joy, calling for feasting and merriment. "For this my son was dead, and is alive again; he was lost, and is found." Rembrandt used a moment of ineffable *human* joy to portray the mystery of transcendent, divine love. A family story reveals the mystery of God's love.

But there is another level of meaning. Rembrandt's depictions of the aged contain a penetrating but tender insight. Discussing the artist's *Portrait of an Old man* (1632), John C. Gilmour (1986) pinpoints the qualities that draw us to these depictions.

> His wordless message presents us with an understanding of old age, loneliness, vulnerability, and loss. We receive this message directly, without apparent mediation by thought. Both the mood and the features of the old man's face seem to be there on the surface. . . . This painting reveals an emotional context, while simultaneously linking it to its physical setting. We find ourselves moved by the portrait and we also gain understanding from it. Although the old man seems to be uniquely himself, we also see general traits of humanity in his face. Therefore, we encounter more than a portrait of a single human being, we encounter something universal. Rembrandt has brought alive a portion of the world, and has opened it up for us to inspect. The face of the old man becomes a mirror to our own humanity. (p. 61)

## OLD AGE AND MEANING

"In life," writes John Berger, "meaning is not instantaneous. Meaning is discovered in what connects, and cannot exist, without development. Without a story, without an unfolding there is no meaning. . . . Certainty may be instantaneous; doubt requires duration; meaning is born of the two" (Berger & Mohr, 1982, p. 89). When Van Gogh wrote about walking to the stars, he did not suggest a meaning for the journey. Yet we all know that we have a quite different experience when we walk than when we ride. We achieve our destination more quickly in a car or a plane, but we lose the detail. In a sense, the artists whose work we have examined have walked, no matter what their individual life spans. Their journeys help us see details that would ordinarily rush by in a blur. Through revelation of detail the artist has unique means for teaching us. As Berger observes, "Revelation was a visual category before it was a religious one. . . . By its nature revelation does not easily lend itself to verbalization. The words used remain aesthetic exclamations" (Berger & Mohr, 1982, p. 89).

In the detail of the bonnet ribbons, the convulsed finger, the tender glance, the artist reveals depths of meaning that speak through the eyes to the heart. In the works of Goya and Grosz we read the stories of lives devoted to barren self-absorption—a concentration on self that does not bear the fruit of insight. The meaning of these works becomes a criticism and a warning. They warn against self-delusion, vanity, and a grasping hold on youth. They offer meaning by demonstrating lives of the perverted certainty that ends in self-delusion.

The two works of Ghirlandaio and Rembrandt offer another kind of meaning. In both, a gracious harmony results from loving lives directed toward others. Here are ideals of plenitude, of continuity, and love. Here, the old ones hold by letting go.

## AGE TRANSCENDED

We have looked at two of the themes of aging in art, the theme of grotesque and perverted old age and the theme of blessed old age. The third, the theme of transcendence of mortality has two faces. One is the theme *in* art. The other is how art itself may serve as a means of transcendence.

The focus of discussion of the third theme is the works of two artists, Michelangelo, one of the most famous artists of all time, and Käthe Kollwitz, a woman of our own century. There lives were separated by centuries. They came from different cultures, had completely different life stories, but finally—by different roads—arrived at the same destination.

Each artist returned again and again to one theme to offer an understanding of aging, yet without having aging, or the old, as the express subject. I want to focus on the evolution of Michelangelo's understanding of death through his exploration of the Pietà, the dead Christ in the arms of his grieving mother. I also want to look at Käthe Kollwitz's succession of self-portraits, beginning in her youth and ending in 1945, the last year of her life. With these themes each artist speaks of the stages of a private journey and reveals a lifetime's understanding of the human condition.

Michelangelo and Kollwitz had long careers that spanned two of the most turbulent periods in the history of Western culture. Michelangelo's career began in the heady optimism of the Italian Renaissance and ended after Western Christendom had been rent by the Protestant Reformation and territorial and religious wars. Kollwitz's life and career were racked by the devastation of two world wars. The art of each reveals the evolution of both artistic sophistication and spiritual depth. Each suffered from the cataclysmic events of their time, and each explicitly attempted to understand these events in the context of a personal artistic journey.

Michelangelo practiced his art against the backdrop of the intense religious longings of his time. That these longings coexisted with hardness of heart, brutality, and skepticism did not escape him, for although he devoted the last decades of his life to the Roman Catholic church and the papacy, he was engaged in a tortured spiritual struggle. He came to fear that his love of his art overshadowed his love of God (Steinberg, 1975). In his mature years, however, he began to understand that his art could speak for the faith. Thus, he chose as his motto Psalm 50:15, "I will teach the unjust thy ways: and the wicked shall be converted unto thee" (Steinberg, 1975). It is significant that he created his most poignant religious art and poetry in his 70s and 80s. Nearly a decade before his death in 1564, he wrote to his friend and biographer that "the image of death" was engraved on his every thought (Vasari, 1965). He had come to doubt the worth of his artistic career, believing that it caused him to neglect the true meaning of life—contemplation of God (Steinberg, 1975).

Charles de Tolnay (1968) wrote of Michelangelo's spiritual state in his last years as an oscillation between "burning faith and inner emptiness," between awareness of an intimate communion with God and a desperate feeling of being separated from Him. But de Tolnay perceives in Michelangelo's late work, and particularly in his Pietàs, a "consoling certainty" that "at the end of the struggle there awaits ultimate peace" (p. 47).

One of his most renowned sculptures is the Pietà in St. Peter's, executed between 1498 and 1500, when Michelangelo was in his early 20s (Figure 11.7). So greatly beloved in reproduction that its popularity teeters on the brink of kitsch, this Pietà is accessible because it avoids too deep an engagement of the viewer on the real subject of the work. Rather than contemplating the horrible physical torture inflicted on the son and the nearly unbearable psychological suffering borne by the mother, the viewer is drawn to meditate on a tableau of exquisite and

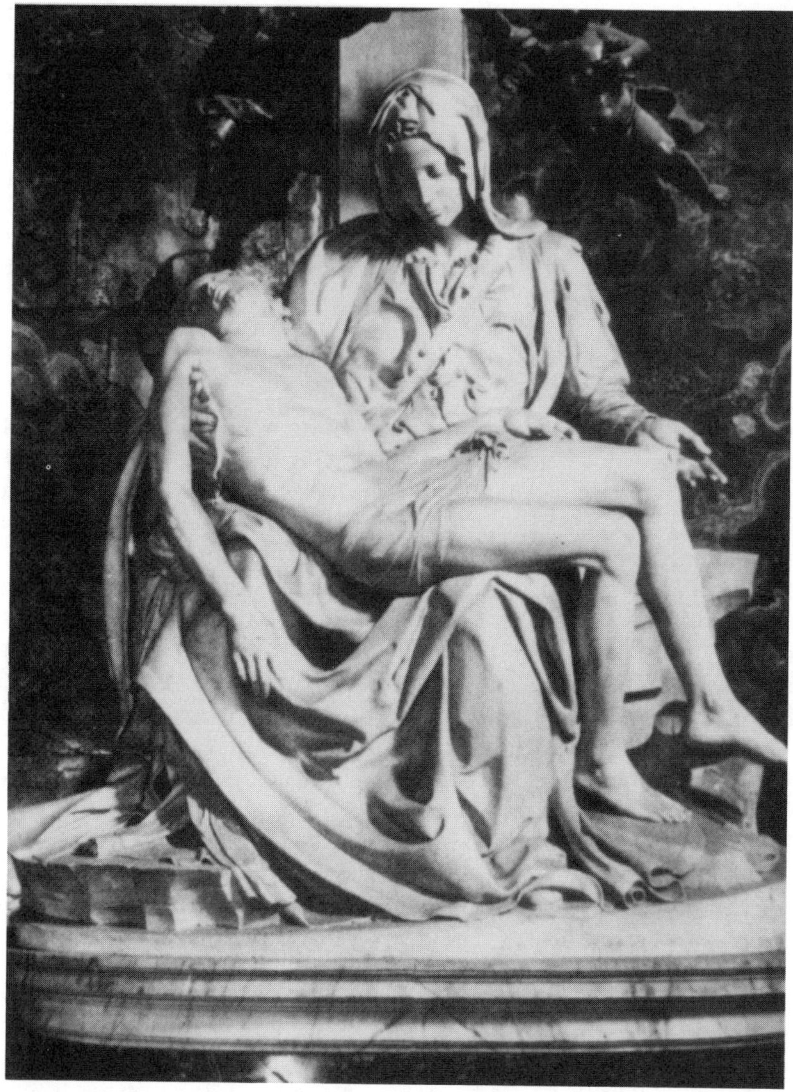

**FIGURE 11.7 Pietà. Michelangelo. c. 1499. St. Peter's, Rome.**

delicate beauty. "Never," as Frederick Hartt (1975) observed, "did [Michelangelo] carry refinement and delicacy to a higher pitch than in the complex and spasmodic linear rhythms of the drapery or the exquisitely finished, long torso and wiry limbs of the Christ" (p. 416).

The Christ seems to sleep on the knees of a woman so young that an untutored viewer might imagine that she was his sister or his bride. Contemporaries of Michelangelo noticed this discrepancy in ages, and we have his response.

> Do you know that chaste women remain much more fresh than those who are not chaste. How much more, therefore, must this be true of the Virgin who never entertained the least immodest thought which might have troubled her body. . . . Do not be surprised, therefore, if for these reasons I have represented the Very Holy Virgin, the Mother of God, much younger than her years would require and I have given the Son his real age. (Clements, 1968, p. 47).

This, then, is the young artist's dream of how the body may reflect the soul. It is a work in which suffering and aging do not alter or distort. It is a work in which the beauty and purity of the spirit are expressed directly in the beauty of the human form. Hence, the artistic "refinement and delicacy" become metaphors for inviolability.

In his last years Michelangelo returned to work with the subject again. In the two final Pietàs, an aging man sums up the whole of his artistic vision and offers himself—and us—a visible form of his loneliness and his faith. The first Pietà (Figure 11.8), a work the artist fashioned for his own tomb, is dated 1555. In this group, a pyramidal composition with Christ supported and surrounded by Mary Magdalene, Mary the Mother, and Joseph of Arimathea, Michelangelo has given Joseph his own grieving features.

At roughly the same period that he worked on his tomb sculpture, he began another Pietà. After abandoning the work for a decade, he returned to it in February 1564, only a few days before his death. As perhaps the great artist's last work, this so-called Rondanini Pietà (Figure 11.9) deserves our attention. Until now we have looked at depictions of the aged as artists' vehicles for expressing their understanding of the last stage of life. Now we have an artist, himself at the last stage of life, returning to a theme that had gained him fame in youth. What did this theme suggest to Michelangelo, and what has it to do with the theme of aging in art?

De Tolnay (1968) writes that despite Michelangelo's lifelong oscillation between faith and despair, at the end of life there came about a kind of resolution, a "consoling certainty" that emanated from these last Pietàs, a certainty that "at the end of the struggle there awaits ultimate peace" (p. 79). The result suggests a mystical experience, a vision of meaning in which matter simply doesn't matter. In the Rondanini Pietà, de Tolnay says, Michelangelo gives up his exploration

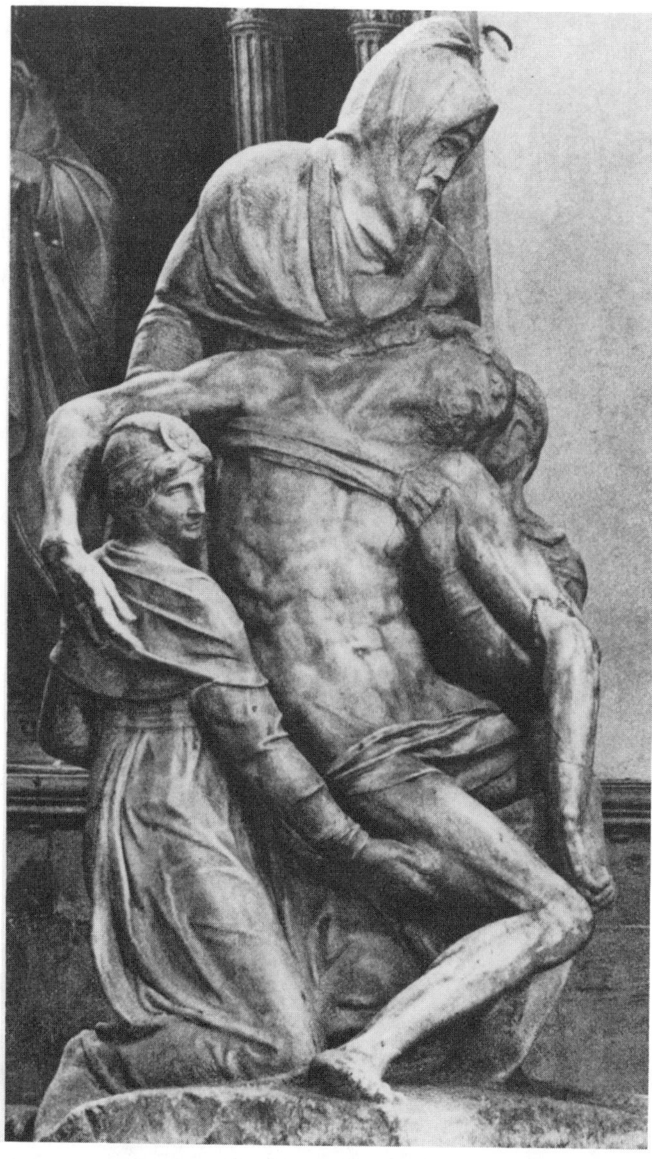

**FIGURE 11.8 Pietà (Disposition of Christ). Michelangelo. c. 1550–1555. Museo dell' Opera del Duomo, Florence.**

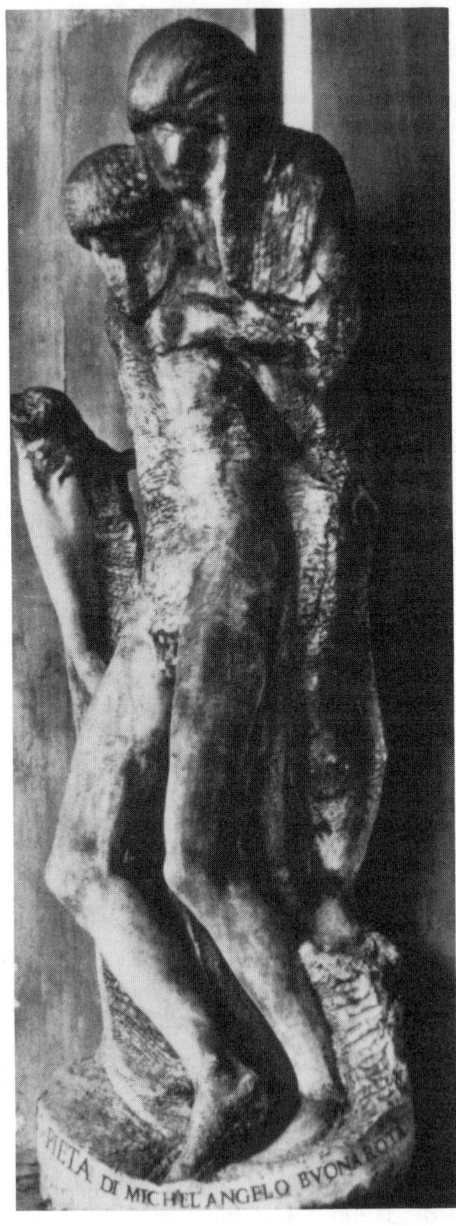


**FIGURE 11.9 Pietà called the Rondanini Pietà. Michelangelo. c. 1555–1564. Castello Sforzesco, Milan.**

of "Renaissance principles of causality and the representation of the rationally possible. What he achieved is an image contradicting the law of gravity and, yet, speaking with utmost immediacy to the heart of the beholder" (p. 92).

In his youth, Michelangelo had balanced grace and delicacy with the exploration of powerful forms. In maturity he concentrated on the heroic struggle of powerful, masculine bodies. At the end of life he let the spirit slip its envelope. The final message is of peace—not the harmonious quiet that characterizes the Pietà of his youth but the peace achieved at the end of a life marked by suffering, illness, intellectual activity, fear, doubt, love, and hope. In the end the work speaks of redemption and "is addressed to no human audience, but to God" (Janson, 1986, p. 458).

Käthe Kollwitz's self-portraits remind us of Bacon's cynical comment that if the minds of the old were visible, they would appear as deformed as their bodies. Kollwitz's work belies these words, by offering an ideal of beauty that makes conventional models seem insipid and trivial. Kollwitz probably never was conventionally beautiful. In her memoir, written in 1922 when she was 55, she writes of her father's decision to give her an artist's training, noting that although she was female she was not pretty, so affairs of the heart were not likely to interfere with her career (Kollwitz, 1981). In a youthful self-portrait (Figure 11.10) the viewer first meets the budding character that flowers fully in her old age. Both shy and forthright, the young woman gazes from the page. It is not a pretty face. It *is* a strong face and a sensitive one; and because it is the young artist's own face, we know that it is the face of an individual determined to soften nothing, yet to view all with compassion.

The daughter of a religious mother and a radical Social Democratic father, from childhood Kollwitz developed an attitude toward her work that merged Christian charity with socialism. As her life evolved, she consciously created an artistic oeuvre that expressed her sense of calling. Her diary entry of March 17, 1917, paraphrases scripture: "I want to live and work, so long as daylight remains" (Kollwitz, 1981, p. 76). And at the end of her life she wrote:

> Now that my life is drawing to its end, I can see it more clearly than I could before. I felt myself "called" to an undertaking that only I could carry out. Now, if it becomes necessary for me to lay down the burin, I know that I have accomplished what it was in my power to do. (p. 144)

Five years later she wrote again after returning from an exhibit: "True, my art is not pure in the sense of, for example, Schmid-Rottluff. But—nevertheless, art. I understand that my art has a purpose. I want

**FIGURE 11.10 Self portrait. Drawing. Käthe Kollwitz. © Estate of Käthe Kollwitz. Reprinted by permission of Arne Kollwitz, Berlin.**

to work in this time, when people are so confused and in need" (Kollwitz, 1981, p. 108).

Because she did have a sense of calling, she devoted her artistic endeavor to revealing the humanity of the downtrodden, the ill, and despairing. But her art is not an art of despair. Rather, it calls us viewers to really *see* beneath the surface, to love what we see, and therefore to hope.

The love Kollwitz's work teaches is not the false love of the sentimentalist. In the introduction to a collection of her drawings, Herbert Bittner (1959) makes this clear. "The substance of Käthe Kollwitz's art is dominated by compassion, strength and self-control. This compassion has nothing to do with *Schwermut* or *Wehmut* or with the weakness of a sentimental heart" (p. 1). And from her self-portraits we see that her art and her life developed into one. In her youthful self-portrait she looks out at us, determined to speak the truth *of* herself and *to* herself, private, but trusting. The portraits of midlife have the same rigor and the same psychological penetration, but now experience and suffering have intervened.

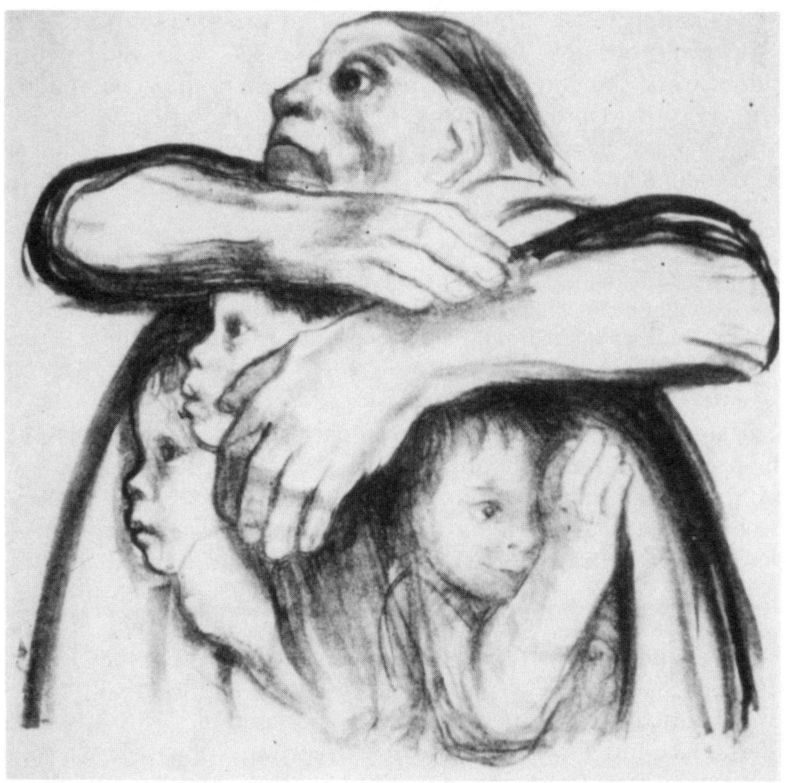

**FIGURE 11.11 Thou Shalt Not Grind the Seed Corn. Drawing. Käthe Kollwitz. © Estate of Käthe Kollwitz. Reprinted by permission of Arne Kollwitz, Berlin.**

It was a suffering familiar to multitudes of her generation. In November 1914, she lost her son Peter on the battlefield; and in 1942, her grandson, also named Peter. Her diary and correspondence are full of the pain of these losses and a deep understanding that her own pain was the pain of millions. Work could be the anodyne: first, a memorial to her son that would, in the end, become a monument to all of those fallen in war, to all of those who bore their loss. Finally, her art stands as a reminder that behind the hysteria and kitsch of war propaganda lies the truth of war—irreplaceable loss, deprivation, and waste. This is all offered without bitterness or self-pity but rather as an attempt to turn her pain into a gift for others—into art. This struggle to speak her stern but loving message continued to the end of her life. In 1942, the year of her grandson's death, she made a lithograph of a mother with children that stands both as a protest against war—any war—and as direct defiance to the Nazi mythologizing of motherhood in the service of the totalitarian state. "Thou shalt not grind the seed corn" is a work of anger and of hope (Figure 11.11). At the age of 75, after two horrendous wars, she dares to imagine a world where the good and loving have strength to protect the weak, and she offers that vision to us. During her last days in 1945 she held the following conversation with her granddaughter, who observes that if there were no war, people would have to invent it. Kollwitz replies:

> It would be invented, yes, and people would wage war as they have done for so long. But some day a new ideal will arise and there will be an end to all wars . . . I am dying in this faith. People will have to work hard for that new state of things, but they will achieve it.

The granddaughter asks, "You mean pacifism?" Kollwitz replies, "Yes, if by pacifism you mean more than merely anti-war feeling. It is a new idea, the idea of human brotherhood" (Kollwitz, 1988, pp. 198–199).

Kollwitz's repeated turning to herself as a subject in her last years gives us, her viewers, an entree into the private spirit that inspired the political persona. At midlife her portrait-self begins to turn away, looking back at us, her eyes reflecting what she knows of human weakness and cruelty (Figure 11.12). The eyes reveal that in facing these things she has determined to face herself and to speak to herself without flinching in response to what she continues to learn. At the end, the face turns away. In the last self-portrait Kollwitz has become a form as monumental as one of her sculptures and hardly an individual at all (Figure 11.13). In perhaps her last letter to her son Hans, written on April 16, 1945, she writes, "The war accompanies me to the end" (Kollwitz, 1988, p. 198–199). This has the force of symbolic truth. She

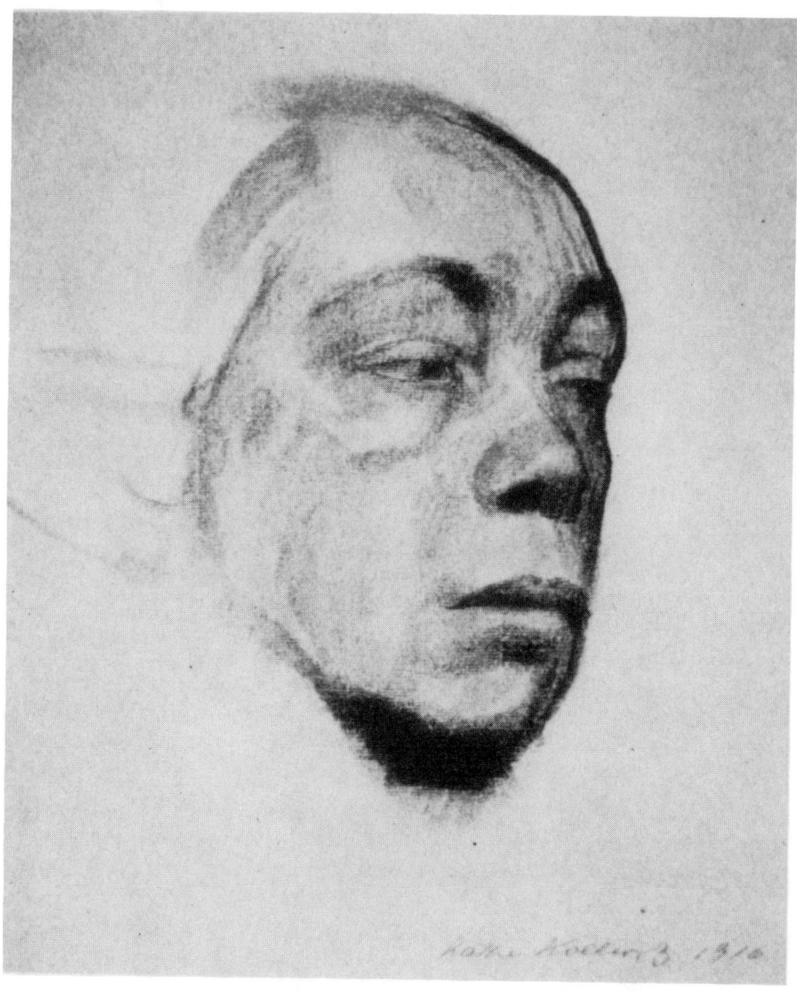

**FIGURE 11.12 Self portrait. Drawing. Käthe Kollwitz. © Estate of Käthe Kollwitz. Reprinted by permission of Arne Kollwitz, Berlin.**

writes here of World War II, but one is led to a deeper meaning of her words: she devoted art—her calling and her gift—to a loving war against the meanness of spirit and hardness of heart that blinds our eyes to our common humanity. The war in Europe would end just weeks after her death. Her private war continues. Contemplating her last self-portrait (Figure 11.13) and her "Thou shalt not grind the seed corn" (Figure 11.11) side by side, is one way of making Van Gogh's long journey to the stars.

**FIGURE 11.13 Self portrait in profile looking right. Lithograph. Käthe Kollwitz. 1938. National Gallery of Art, Washington, Rosenwald Collection. © Estate of Käthe Kollwitz. Reprinted by permission of Arne Kollwitz, Berlin.**

## BEYOND SENSUAL TRUTH

Kollwitz's last diary entry, dated May 1943, ends with these words of Goethe: "But let us stop worrying our particular religions like a dog its bone. *I have gone beyond purely sensual truth*" (Kollwitz, 1981, p. 154).

This is the culmination of any artist's work on aging. The works I have described seek in their various ways to go beyond purely sensual truth. But they employ sensual means to achieve this. In the works of Goya and Grosz, the poverty of a truth that is *only* sensual is revealed. In painting the grandfather and the child, Ghirlandaio finds in the goodness of mundane relationships a suggestion of supramundane beatitude. Rembrandt, Michelangelo, and Kollwitz, on the other hand, use the theme of parent and child to symbolize and express an all-encompassing and transcendent love. Finally, Kollwitz employs her self-portraits to record her own journey to self-knowledge and death.

Earlier I suggested that there was an analogy between the metaphor of aging as a pilgrimage to the stars and the function of art. I selected art works about aging or by aged artists to seek possible connections. This has resulted in an attempted synthesis of two themes: one, the *altersstil*, the almost universal style of old age; the other, the mythic function of the artist.

Rudolf Arnheim, an authority on the psychology of art and aging, is especially helpful with the first theme. In a ground-breaking article published in 1978, Arnheim describes a pattern of artistic development, defining three stages related to life stages. First is childhood, a period of little differentiation between self and others, when one perceives in broad generalities. Maturity, the time of interest in the facts of outer reality and growing capacity for discrimination, follows. Finally comes a stage characterized by the detachment of contemplation from practical application and a shift from hierarchial patterning to coordination of elements: similarities become more important than differences. Arnheim stresses that longevity does not ensure arrival at this final stage (as it does not ensure wisdom or peace). But when an artist achieves it, the result is an art reminiscent of the art of childhood. It is as if the artist's imagination comes full circle. Perhaps a spiral is a more appropriate symbol, for the intervening life experience separates "a state of mind that cannot yet discriminate from one that no longer cares to" (Arnheim, 1978, p. 153). Knowledge of that difference resonates through Goethe's statement that he has gone beyond purely sensual truth. And that knowledge defines Michelangelo's final *Pietà* and Käthe Kollwitz's last self-portrait. Using the spiral to symbolize a life's endeavor allows us to combine the rich imagery of the circle with the idea of ascent.

For centuries, poets and scholars have alternately used the symbolism of the cycle and of decline and ascent to describe the life course. For example, de Tolnay (1968) calls Michelangelo's inner development a work of art "in which we find the chief stages of human ascension" (p. 94), and Arnheim (1978) contrasts the idea of physical and mental decline with an ideal of wisdom achieved through the ascent of spirit over matter. But the circle symbolism is equally evocative. In *The Power of the Center*, Arnheim (1988) equates artistic composition with balance in life. In both he finds the interaction of "centric" and "eccentric" tendencies. The centric he takes to stand for the self-centered attitude that characterizes the individual at the beginning of life. The eccentric represents actions directed outward to tasks or goals—or to others. He concludes:

> ... the interaction of the two tendencies represents a fundamental task of life.... The tension between the two antagonistic tendencies trying to achieve equilibrium is the very spice of human experience ... neither total self-centeredness nor total surrender to outer powers can make for an acceptable image of human motivation. (p. 2)

It is "the tension between" that makes both life and art. The greatest of our artists understood this and employed it to fulfill one of the artist's principal tasks—the introduction of appropriate meaning. When artists willingly accept this tension, they become mythic figures. Within the mystique that surrounds the artist hides a truth recognized in ancient religion *and* in modern theories of culture and personality. As Erich Neumann (1973) pointed out, artists are uniquely and uncannily sensitive to the needs of their times even though they may not wish the burden of such sensitivity" (p. 13). In "following the drive or the psychic substratum" (p. 13), artists speak not only for themselves but for their time.

This almost priestly function in which the artist offers ourselves *to* ourselves is one we must take very seriously, for the gift of the great artist is knowledge of the meaning of our humanity. This has always been important, but it may have special significance for modern people. In the history of Western culture there has been an accelerating evolution toward individualism, often leaving modern men and women with a painful sense of loneliness or isolation. Norbert Elias (1985) has astutely connected this unease with the civilizing process that has characterized our culture since the Renaissance. We have gained much from this process in comfort and freedom but may have paid for those gains with deep confusion about the meaning of our lives. Elias argues that we can find meaning only in our recognition of our dependence and interdependence on and with others. Modern individuals seek meaning in isolation, each hoping to find a meaning "for oneself alone, a meaning independent of all other people" (p. 34). Yet meaning *requires* others, because our meaning lies precisely in what we mean to others, both in the past and the future. It is one function of the artist to show us our dependence on and our relationship to others—to reveal that meaning to which we would otherwise remain blind.

But in wonderful instances the artist may transcend art. This transcendence rests, according to Neumann (1973), on the individual development of the artist who loosens ties with collective humanity and "attains a level of timelessness." And, he continues, "reluctant as we are to use such terms, this stage of artistic creation cannot be characterized without such words as 'eternity, intuition of essence, and metaphysical experience'". It is precisely these concepts that we wish to recall when we reflect on a "good" culmination of the long journey of aging. We dream that, like the great artist, we might somehow break our bonds of self-centeredness, ignorance, fear, and greed, and rise, buoyant, to the stars. But the life journey, like the artist's struggle, is sometimes treacherous and dark. The works I have discussed here may serve as signposts. In them—and in others if we choose to look—we may see not only our own reflection but choices and paths. Because we are human with nothing human foreign to us, we may recognize incipient selves in the works of Goya or Grosz. In blessed moments we may also see ourselves in Rembrandt. We may be guided by works that teach us self-knowledge, commitment to others, and love. We may thus see that there is little difference between the artist's pencil and the pilgrim's staff, and we may choose to make our own journey to the stars a work of art.

## REFERENCES


Arnheim, R. (1966). *Toward a psychology of art.* Berkeley and Los Angeles: University of California Press.

Arnheim, R. (1978, Spring). On the late style of life and art. *Michigan Quarterly Review*, pp. 149–156.

Arnheim, R. (1988). *The power of the center.* Berkeley, Los Angeles, London: University of California Press.

Bacon, F. (1977, originally published 1638). *A short historie of life and death.* NY: Arno Press.

Berger, J., & Mohr, J. (1982). *Another way of telling.* New York: Pantheon Books.

Bittner, H. (1959). *The drawings of Käthe Kollwitz.* New York: Thomas Yoseloff.

Bruckner, D. J. R., Chwast, S., & Heller, S. (1984) *Art against war.* New York: Abbeville Press.

Clements, R. J. (1968). *Michelangelo—a self-portrait.* New York: New York University Press.

De Tolnay, C. (1968). *Michelangelo: the Final Period.* Princeton, NJ: Princeton University Press.

Elias, N. (1985). *The loneliness of the dying.* Oxford: Blackwell.

Gilmour, J. C. (1986). *Picturing the world.* Albany: State University of New York Press.

Halewood, W. H. (1982). *Six subjects of Reformation art: A preface to Rembrandt.* Toronto: University of Toronto Press.

Hartt, F. (1975). *History of Italian Renaissance art.* Englewood Cliffs, NJ, and New York: Prentice-Hall and Harry N. Abrams.

Hughes, R. (1990). The liberal Goya. *New York Review of Books, 36,* 90 28.

Janson, H. W. (1986). *History of art.* Englewood Cliffs, NJ: Prentice-Hall and Harry N. Abrams.

Kollwitz, H. (Ed.). (1988). *The diary and letters of Käthe Kollwitz.* (R. Winston & C. Winston, Trans.). Evanston, IL: Northwestern University Press.

Kollwitz, K. (1981). *"Ich will wirken in dieser Zeit."* (H. Kollwitz, Ed.). Frankfurt am Main and Berlin: Ullstein.

Neumann, E. (1973). Art and time. In J. Campbell (Ed.), *Man and time* (p. 13). Princeton, NJ: Princeton University Press. Bollingen Series XXX. 3.

Steinberg, L. (1975). *Michelangelo's last paintings.* New York: Oxford University Press.

Van Gogh, V. (1959). *The complete letters of Vincent Van Gogh* (Vol. 2). Greenwich, CT and London: New York Graphic Society.

Vasari, G. (1965). *Lives of the artists.* Harmondsworth, UK: Penguin Books.

# 12

# The Creative Process: A Life-span Approach

*Robert Kastenbaum*

## WHAT IS THE QUESTION?

"What is the answer? What is the answer?" According to those present, the dying woman had roused herself from a comatose state to speak these urgent words. Her aged head dropped again to the pillow, her eyes again closed. But a moment later, the mischievous eyes of Gertrude Stein opened for one last time. Inspecting her bedside collection of friends, Stein now imposed another demand upon them: "What was the question?" *Finis!*

This vignette suggests that even the final scene in a long life can be transfigured by a creative mind. But it also reminds us that questions may rival answers as a source of understanding. We begin, then, by surveying the types of question that have guided inquiry into the creative process across the life span. We will then examine representative findings and contentions related to each type of question and conclude with a few suggestions toward an integrated theory of creativity in later life.

The following questions govern most of the (limited) attention that has been given to creativity in the life-span developmental / gerontological literature:

1. What is the pattern of growth and decline for creative *ability* through the life span?
2. How does creativity function as a *strategy* for reducing intrapsychic conflict and anxiety?

3. How can creativity be induced and channeled as a *tool* for problem solving?
4. How can elderly adults be encouraged to engage in creative *activity*?
5. What is creative *thinking*?

Significantly less attention has been given to the following questions:

1. What is the *meaning* of creativity from youth through old age?
2. Does creativity across the life span serve any fundamental psychobiological *purpose*?
3. Why does creativity appear to be a *life-or-death issue* to some people?

Despite this proliferation of questions, creativity has seldom been invited into the realm of core topics as indexed, for example, by textbook and course coverage. A newcomer to gerontology is most likely to encounter creativity in its guise as an ability or set of abilities. The "average expectable" article or textbook discussion is a gloss on the Lehman / Dennis controversy (see below) that concerns the production of creative works in youth, middle age, and old age. The psychoanalytic literature includes treatises on creativity as an attempt to cope with intrapsychic and interpersonal conflict, but these are seldom consulted and cited by gerontologists. The management literature—also of limited appeal to gerontology—offers an abundance of material on "brainstorming" and other techniques for utilizing creativity as a corporate tool. The cognitive-processes literature, familiar to psychologically oriented gerontologists, offers research into the components of creative thinking. Much more common within the gerontological literature itself are articles, books, and videos that advocate "creative activities" to overcome passivity and social withdrawal. This approach is closely related to what might be called the *eugeros* mission: the attempt to counter ageism by selecting and emphasizing information that supports a favorable image of the older person.

Those who read only mainstream gerontology are likely to become acquainted with the *ability* and possibily with the *activity* viewpoints. The improbable person who also delves into psychoanalysis, management, and factor-analytic study of intelligence will have a broader range of vision yet may never come across contributions that focus on the *meaning* or *purpose* of creativity and the urgent *life-or-death* context in which the issue of creativity may arise.

This chapter attempts to provide a convenient starting point for those who are interested in the entire spectrum of approaches to life-span creativity. Special emphasis will be given to those facets of creativity that are most likely to be important to gerontology in the long run, even if they have not been well represented up to this time. We begin, however, with the approach that has received by far the most attention: creativity as an ability.

## CREATIVITY AS AN ABILITY

Social and behavioral scientists have found it most appropriate to think of creativity as an ability when they choose to think of creativity at all. The story begins with Francis B. Galton, the person who is most frequently honored (or blamed) for introducing the measurement of human abilities. Galton hoped to improve society by improving the genetic quality of its citizens. Both the eugenics and the abilities-testing movements eventually spun far out of his control. However, his own contributions (Galton, 1869) provided the foundation for the cradle-to-grave assessment of abilities that shadows our lives today. Galton identified "persons of genius" (mostly from the upper classes) and traced their hereditary lines. He also devised procedures to assess human abilities in the laboratory and then subjected the results to statistical analyses. From Galton's work it became apparent that (a) abilities could be identified, assessed, and expressed in statistical terms and that (b) major individual differences existed in the extent of these abilities. His results favored the proposition that genetic endowment is the major source for creative potential.

Although Galton had chosen *Hereditary Genius* for the title of his major work on this topic, he later criticized "genius" as a vestigial and obsolescent concept (Albert, 1983). It is misleading and not very useful to say that a gifted person *is* a genius. Instead, Galton would describe that person as showing certain outstanding qualities of intellect and disposition. This more functional approach has not fully established itself even today. Some writers continue to speak of genius (or creativity) as though quoting directly from 18th-century texts on "faculty psychology," if not from medieval treatises on the powers of the soul. Nevertheless, Galton had offered a fresh alternative that challenged the implicit dichotomy between the "genius" and the ordinary person. We all might have a potential for creativity, although this talent, along with most other talents, is not distributed equally. Nevertheless, many subsequent writers and researchers have continued to focus on the distinguished few, rather than on the creativity that might be found in people unknown to fame.

The approach taken by Galton and most who followed in his footsteps accorded little attention to developmental processes. The way to become a gifted old person was to enter this world with an elite set of genes and then to display the diligence to make the most of this potential. One should also be a male because early studies were sexist, concentrating on "men of distinction." In this early period of investigation, two competing answers might have proposed themselves: (a) creativity is based upon genetic endowment; therefore, it should continue throughout the life span if the individual is free from debilitating illnesses; (b) creativity is a set of abilities, and aging erodes all abilities.

The one exception was provided by George Beard (1874), a neurologist who had already made distinguished contributions, although still in his 30s. He attempted to determine the age at which more than a thousand famous people had made their major contributions or achievements. He recognized that the then-infant science of brain physiology was too primitive to yield results based upon microscopic or chemical studies. He was also far from naive about the criterion problem; reputation would have to be his basis for selecting cases, but this amounted to little more than "the settled opinion of mankind." A sample of illustrious contributors to civilization would no doubt include some whose credentials had been exaggerated while other worthy persons had been entirely overlooked. Acknowledging these difficulties, Beard nevertheless made a detailed examination of available biographies on "great men of history."

Beard (1874) concluded that "seventy per cent of the work of the world is done before 45, and eighty per cent before 50. . . . The best period is between 30 and 45" (p. 7). With classical resonations and a bit of flair, Beard offered the following characterization of the adult life course in terms of distinguished achievements and contributions. Note that the decades are not arranged age-sequentially but in order of merity, with the brightest leading the way.

| | |
|---|---|
| The *golden* decade | Between 30 and 40 |
| The *silver* decade | Between 40 and 50 |
| The *brazen* decade | Between 20 and 30 |
| The *iron* decade | Between 50 and 60 |
| The *tin* decade | Between 60 and 70 |
| The *wooden* decade | Between 70 and 80 |

According to Beard (1874), there is a "very striking" differential between the frequency of achievements in the brazen and the iron decades; a sharp decline was found as "great men" entered their fifth decades of life. These men tended to be long-lived, but, generally, "the last *twenty* years in the lives of original geniuses are unproductive" (p. 8). Beard called attention to notable exceptions: men such as Titian, Dryden, Defoe, and Christopher Wren did some of their best work at an advanced age. All in all, though, creative elderly men tended to do whatever had made them famous while they were young.

Beard (1874) offered conclusions that were both vivid and sweeping:

> The same law applied to animals. Horses live to be about twenty-five, and are at their best from eight to fourteen; this corresponds to the golden decade of man. . . . Fruit bearing trees . . . are most prolific at a time of their average life corresponding pretty nearly to the golden and silver decade of man. Children born of parents one or both of whom are between twenty-five and forty, are, on the average, stronger and smarter than those born of parents one or both of which are much younger or older than this. . . . It should be noted also, that in women, the procreative function ceases between forty and fifty, just the time when the physical and mental powers begin to decline, as though nature had foreseen this law and provided that the world should not be peopled by those whose powers had fallen from their maximum.

Why hasten, then, to study creativity in the later years of life when all of nature seemed to be set against it? It would take some time before researchers would again arouse themselves to investigate this topic. And so—without pausing to learn Beard's equally melancholy conclusion about the egg-laying capacity of the aging hen—we "fast forward" now to the post–World War II era and its rapidly growing interest in gerontology. Just beneath the surface of much gerontological activity at this time was the question "What are we going to do with all these old people?" The pioneering gerontologists were often concerned either with the need to develop new social attitudes, policies, and practices for an aging society or with documenting age-related decrements. Creativity did enter the spotlight, however, with the publication of a slender book entitled *Age and Achievement* (Lehman, 1953). The author had compiled lists of outstanding creative contributions in the arts, literature, music, philosophy, and science. He then determined the age at which these contributions had been made, using a method that did not differ greatly from Beard's. Harvey Lehman's data showed that the peak of creative achievement generally occurred when people were in their 20s and 30s. From the age of 50 onward, there was a decline in creative output. He also reported an interesting secondary finding: the peak of creative output differs somewhat from field to field (e.g., earlier in music, later in philosophy). The major conclusion, however, was that creative ability tends to express itself fairly early in life and to decline thereafter. Essentially, it was a confirmation of Beard's study.

Lehman's methodology and conclusions were soon challenged by Wayne Dennis (1956). Lehman promptly responded (Lehman, 1956), and the ensuing controversy temporarily aroused interest in creativity among some gerontologists. Part of the debate concerned technical issues such as the identification and selection of creative accomplishments, choice of age intervals, and how best to take differential longevity into account. However, the nastier—and therefore more entertaining—exchange centered around the threat that Lehman's findings seemed to present to any positive view of old age.

Dennis (1956) presented his critique as though defending a worthy if fragile cause against a brutal aggressor. Lehman hinted that Dennis simply refused to face such facts as the decline of athletic performance with age. In retrospect, it is clear that both Lehman and Dennis agreed on two major points: (a) that some creative work of high quality has been accomplished in old age and (b) that decline, if it exists, is not to be explained by a vague reference to "the aging process." At this point, however, an open-minded reader could hardly avoid drawing the tentative conclusion that the rate and probability of creative production declines with age. And one of Dennis's own studies a few years later also found an age-related decline in productivity. Although the drop-off in productivity was not as great as had been suggested by Lehman's study, there was a marked deterioration in the *quality* of artistic creativity with advancing age (Dennis, 1966).

A renewal of research interest in recent years has brought additional methodologies to bear on the thesis that creativity is an ability that may or may not decline with age. Several cross-sectional studies involving University of Southern California faculty and students have explored creativity among people selected from the general population, rather than the eminent individuals favored by earlier investigators (e.g., Alpaugh, 1976; Alpaugh & Birren, 1977; Alpaugh, Parham, Cole, & Birren, 1982; Ruth & Birren, 1985). Taken together, these studies found that older adults showed less fluency, flexibility, and originality on tasks intended to assess verbal creativity. The younger adults performed on a level superior to that of the older adults on both quantitative and qualitative measures of creativity. Additionally, men earned higher scores on ability measures that tapped technical and practical knowledge as well as "pure" creativity. Creativity as an ability (or set of abilities) had again been found to express itself less vigorously among older adults.

Among active researchers, Dean Keith Simonton has set new standards for the quantitative investigation of creativity-related abilities. Simonton's work includes sophisticated computer modeling of age and achievement and is further distinguished by its attention to historical period and to instructive details of the creative product itself (e.g., Simonton, 1975a, 1975b, 1977, 1984, 1988, 1989). In one study, for example, he examined "interdisciplinary relationships among 15 kinds of creative achievement... over 130 generations of European history" (Simonton, 1975b). In another study, he found that composers tended to write their most popular melodies in their youth (Simonton, 1980).

Simonton's refined and industrious research supports the most basic conclusions reached by earlier investigators: (a) creative achievement occurs more frequently and at a higher level in the earlier adult years, and (b) the peak age for creative achievements varies somewhat according to the modality (e.g., teenagers have written memorable poems and contributed important innovations to mathematics, but scientists tend to make their major discoveries in their late 30s and novelists produce their best works in their early 40s). Allowing for individual differences and exceptions, the general rule seems to be that creative ability expressed itself most robustly in youth and early adulthood.

It should be observed that these conclusions are drawn almost exclusively from studies of creative achievements within the Euro-American tradition. An innovative study of "The Old Man as Creative Artist in India" (Maduro, 1981) offers an alternative view that will be considered later. But even within the mainstream Western tradition, there are questions that are not fully resolved by the quantitative study of creative achievements by age.

## LIMITATIONS OF THE CREATIVITY-IS-AN-ABILITY APPROACH

The general conclusion that creative achievements become more infrequent with advancing adult age cannot be ignored. However, many significant questions remain. Two will receive attention here: *Why* does creative achievement decline with age? What are the *meanings* and *functions* of creative activity in the later years of life?

The "why" of decline has not been investigated directly by most of the available studies, although the authors sometimes offer interesting speculations. In my view, a fundamental limitation and source of potential misinterpretation has been the assumption that the product is a dependable guide to the process. In science, for example, a major contribution might be the fortunate outcome of unusual persistence, superior equipment, and a bit of luck. A competent but not particularly bold and original researcher might earn deserved recognition for the contribution. Meanwhile, numerous other colleagues may have far exceeded the winner in the quality of their creative thinking but failed to grasp the prize for any number of other reasons. Much creative activity will go unrecognized, then, because it does not result in a recognized and certifiable achievement-outcome, although mere competency rings the bell for others. In the arts, public and even critical response may penalize creativity and reward derivative works that meet the needs and expectations of the moment. Beethoven's late string quartets, for example, were rejected by many as unmusical and unlistenable, if not completely mad. As the same time, written-by-formula pieces in a familiar style received favorable hearings.

It is possible that both the very young and the very old creative person will be judged, at least for a time, by standards that do not address their distinctive creative spirit and style. Young Tennyson's first published poetry, for example, was criticized as both too conservative and too modern (Martin, 1980). Albert Berne's last paintings—at the age of 96—eluded many viewers because they were almost too rich in their terraced symbolism (as explicated by O'Connor [1979] and by his own letters). To put this another way: both standard empirical research techniques and public expectations may be better suited to evaluate the work of creative persons who have crossed the threshold to acceptance but have not yet discovered what might be called their own "personal universals." The finding that achievements tend to cluster within the moderately young adult years might represent society's zone of comfort more than the actual creative spirit that informs the achievements.

Other limitations of the creativity-as-ability approach have been noted by Romaniuk and Romaniuk (1981). These limitations include (in Beard, Lehman, Dennis, and some Simonton) reliance upon information whose reliability is difficult to establish. In some other studies, the age-related declines were based upon cross-sectional data. Alpaugh and Birren (1977) themselves note that their findings might represent the influence of cohort differences rather than factors associated with age as such. Today's older people, for example, were taught when young to rely more heavily on principles of memorization than on techniques of problem-solving, and this emphasis could be deleterious to creativity (Baltes & Schaie, 1974). Other problems include the insufficiently studied role of physical impairments on creative production in later life and the possible bias in tests intended to assess abilities relevant to creativity. For example, "a creative problem-solving task which is considered to be fun and challenging may be . . . boring and unchallenging to a different age or cohort group" (Romaniuk & Romaniuk, 1981, p. 373). The "same" test also might call upon different abilities among younger and older adults, for example, "the Product Improvement Test may be tapping remote memory processes for a relatively unfamiliar object for older examinees while younger ones may be utilizing recent memory with a relatively familiar object" (p. 373).

Added to these difficulties are differences in test-taking attitudes between young and older adults and a variety of inconsistencies in the measurement process itself (e.g., subjective criteria developed by relatively young adults that are then applied to the creative productions of older adults).

There are also substantive issues whose impact on creativity is difficult to evaluate. How much of the decline in creativity is a function of social expectations for the aging person? It has been widely noted that Western industrial nations tend to expect people to become less rather than more "useful" with advancing age, and expectations for creativity may be even more negative. How much is a function of reduced opportunity? In music, for example, there are many awards available specifically for young composers. I know of none that are set aside for composers who are at least 60 or 80 years of age. And how much of the apparent decline actually represents a transfer of creativity to realms of activity in which there are fewer obvious "products" to certify and count? Connie Goldman's "Late Bloomer" interviews, for example, include many men and women who entered into the most creative phase of their lives after "retirement" (Goldman, 1989). Conventional ways of identifying creative products would miss such people as "Mildred," who has now taught a new generation of Native American children to relish their heritage, or "Magda," who developed group therapy techniques to help other elderly woman overcome a low self-image.

In summary, creativity *can* be regarded as an ability, but there are reasons to hesitate before accepting this view as either flawless or comprehensive. The observed decline in documented creative achievements with advancing age may be in part factual and in part artifactual. Furthermore, what remains to be explained adequately is not only the general pattern of decline but also the numerous exceptions. If even one aged man or woman has demonstrated exceptional creative activity, then we cannot end our inquiry with aggregate statistics—and exceptional creative activity has been demonstrated repeatedly by aged men and women.

This brings us to the second set of questions in which the functions and meanings of creativity come to the fore. This shift in questions also occasions a shift in method. It becomes essential to enter the lives of individuals in some detail and depth and also to place these individuals within their sociohistorical contexts. How many compositions of what type that J. S. Bach composed at various points in his life would be less relevant than analyzing the circumstances under which he wrote *Art of*

*Fugue* even as death seized his hand. Furthermore, one would also attend closely to the specific style and quality of this composition both as music and as a statement of the human spirit. It is within this realm that the study of creativity seems to hold the most promise for answering Old Man Hoppergrass's question. Stephen Vincent Benet's (1942) character laments:

> . . . Wake at night and ease me
> But it does not please me,
> Stick I am, sick I am,
> Apple pared to quick I am.
> . . . A stone's a stone
> And a tree's a tree,
> But what was the sense
> of aging me? (pp. 414–415)*

## ON THE FUNCTIONS AND MEANINGS OF CREATIVITY IN LATER LIFE

There would be little value in proposing a static list of the functions and meanings that are associated with creative activity in later life. Instead, we will visit a few lives to illustrate the terrain that remains to be explored more thoroughly by those willing to invest in the time-consuming process of person-by-person inquiry.

### Tennyson, Picasso, and the Creative Transcendence of Time

Creativity in old age can be approached through life-span developmental models. In my study of Tennyson and Picasso (Kastenbaum, 1989), an attempt was made to discover the idiosyncratic model developed by each creative person himself, as well as the functions served and meanings engendered.

The poet Tennyson (1809–1892) and the artist Picasso (1881–1973) differed not only in their primary creative modality but in nationality, generation, family structure, and personality. Inward, self-doubting, devoted to wife and family, and often convinced that creativity and energy had abandoned him, Tennyson contrasted sharply with the confident, outgoing, and fiercely energetic Picasso, who attracted, conquered, and exploited woman after woman. Nevertheless, there were also striking parallels in their progression through life. These include the following:

---

*Nine (9) lines from: "Old Man Hoppergrass." From: The Selected Works of Stephen Vincent Benet. Holt, Rinehart, & Winston, Inc. Copyright 1937 by Stephen Vincent Benet. Copyright renewed, © 1965, by Thomas C. Benet, Stephanie B. Mahin. Reprinted by permission of Brandt & Brandt Literary Agents, Inc.

1. A childhood shadowed by conflict, loss, and a sense of apartness from most other people.
2. The early emergence of death as a major personal theme: for Tennyson, a feeling of death-in-life and impulse toward suicide; for Picasso, an intense preoccupation with death as an enemy that must be defeated.
3. In youth, the sudden death of a close personal friend: Tennyson's talented but melancholy confidant, Arthur Hallam, and Picasso's erratic "trainee," Carles Casegamas (who took his own life).
4. In the wake of their friends' deaths, both Tennyson and Picasso experienced intensifications of their personal death-centered anxieties (including, for Tennyson, the thought of suicide).
5. Each responded to the death by creating masterpieces in a new style. Furthermore, each selected old men as subjects. Young Tennyson wrote *Ulysses*, depicting the legendary wanderer as a land-locked old man; Picasso lavished the craft and compassion of his new-found Blue Period on *The Old Guitarist*. (Other kindred creations by both Tennyson and Picasso were also analyzed.)
6. The creation of ardent and compelling old men by the troubled young men seemed to help them transcend the personal crises they were experiencing at the moment.
7. Both young men not only survived into old age but also remained creative. Furthermore, death continued as a persistent theme that each, in his own way, continued to mine for artistic creation.
8. Both wove personal and historical pasts together with the present in their very late creations, for example, Tennyson's "Crossing the Bar" (age 80) became epilogue for the *Ulysses* he had envisioned as a youth, while Picasso's *Musketeer with Guitar* (age 91) served a similar function for his youthful masterpiece, *The Old Guitarist*.

In a sense, Tennyson and Picasso produced versions of possible future selves and brought to these creations a deeper and more complete mastery than had distinguished their previous creations. They could engage in emotional and symbolic interaction with these future selves who, by their very existence, represented survival. In advanced age, both "stayed in character" by innovating further variations on the themes that had beset and inspired them for so many years.

There is no reason to suppose that all creative people engage in such time-transcendent dialogues between their young and older selves, nor that all wrestle with the same dragons as the English poet and the Spanish artist. However, there is also no reason to suppose that Tennyson and Picasso are the only people who have been intensely motivated in youth to create potential futures and then, in age, to weave past and future together into a wholeness.

## The Observed Self: Creativity Through Intimate Journals

Harry J. Berman has called attention to intimate journals as a potential source of information for gerontologists. His own analyses suggest that diaries and autobiographies can also provide the opportunity for creative thinking by men and women confronting the challenges of old age. Indeed, these sources may be indispensable for those who are more interested in the process than in palpable products. Berman (1986) takes as one of his examples the political columnist Alan Olmstead, who retired at age 65. Olmstead's diary, writes Berman, is

> a disciplined and sharply crafted work. There is an entry every day. . . . The entries are consistently three- to four-hundred words long. Each entry has a title and is a reflection on a clearly focused idea. The entries are laced with wry humor and often build to a concluding sentence which flashes out at the reader like the punch line of a good story. The fact that the entries are so carefully crafted does not mean that they are any less personal or revealing. To the contrary, the journal is like a guided tour of an *interior* terrain. It is as if Olmstead is saying: "OK folks, here's what you'll encounter on the first part of your trip. . . . Don't forget to watch out for those dangerous feelings on the left. . . . After a while you'll begin to have this other thought." (p. 4).

Olmstead's diary exemplifies those people who achieve a continuity between pre- and postretirement life by calling upon the same skills and modality that had previously served them well. In Olmstead's case, he applied his creative process to identifying the inner and outer dangers he perceived in his own new world of age and then offering a kind of "tour book" for others. It is also instructive to note that Olmstead moves easily between objective prose and poetic metaphor, a characteristic that Chinen (1989) has observed in folktales that feature old people. For example, while ostensibly speaking about a blighted elm tree outside his window, Olmstead writes that "one day the elm will come down, porous and crumbled. Meanwhile, it feels good still to be gripped, firmly, by something, even late flowering dreams."

Other themes and functions emerge in the study of other intimate journals, as Berman (1986) demonstrates. For example, Elizabeth Vining's *Being Seventy: The Measure of a Year* (1978) expresses a keen sensitivity to the dynamics of impending change and culmination, for example,

> A door shuts. It is shut not in one's face, but behind one. In front is a new landscape, bleak perhaps at times, lit no doubt at others by mysterious

> beauty, but cut off in the distance by a wall, which for the first time is close enough to be visible. (pp. 4–5)

Another dominating theme for Vining is the absurd fact that she herself is now one of "them," the old people. How *could* she be old? "Inside I feel often as gauche, as shy, as incapable of wise or effective action as I did at sixteen, or as surprised and delighted by unexpected beauty" (p. 4). It is probable that this is one of the more common themes that, for some people, induces gloom and resignation and, for others, a stimulus to creative thought. One cannot help but think of Yeats's blast at "decrepit age that has been tied to me / As to a dog's tail" (Yeats, 1989, p. 194).

Another theme evident in Vining's writings was also expressed by many of Goldman's (1989) late bloomers and creative artists (Goldman, 1988) interviewees and appears again in Florida Scott-Maxwell's (1979) autobiography, *The Measure of My Days*. "Another secret we carry is that that though drab outside—wreckage to the eye, mirrors a mortification—inside we flame with a wild life that is almost incommunicable" (pp. 32–33).

Even from these brief glimpses into intimate journals it can be seen that old people have a wealth of themes that "come natural" to their situation and can provide the impulse for creative activity.

## Maya Rupa: The Old Man as Creative Artist

> I am a very old man and people say I am very creative. I agree with them. I try to look at things in a different way—a new way all the time. I have lost interest in everything external to my artistic efforts. . . . Even though I stand before darkness and death—ready—still I try to incorporate everything that is natural in my paintings. I therefore try to get closer to God. . . . The mind of the really creative painter is different from others. And I tell you clearly: after the householder stage he who is the creative painter is equal to God—he performs the highest acts of creation (Maduro, 1981, p. 79).

These comments from an aged artist of Northern India exemplify only the qualitative side of Renaldo Maduro's unique study. The Indian-born psychiatrist also carried out an objective inquiry into perceived artistic merit of younger and older artists (utilizing the Barron-Welsh Revised Art Scale) and then combined both components into an interculturally informed, neopsychoanalytic framework. The qualitative and quantitative reports add up to a coherent picture. According to the Hindu concept of aging, childhood is followed by four overlapping "resting places" or stages (*ashramas*). For the Brahmins of Nathdrwara in Northern

India, the quality of artistic creation is seen as attaining higher levels as individuals move from one *ashrama* to the next. The descriptions would seem to be at home in disengagement theory (although the Hindu conception was formed long before the advent of modern gerontology).

Relatively few Indian men live into old age, and those who bring with them both health and artistic talent are rarer still. This means that the cultural ideal of continued spiritual and artistic growth can be realized only in the exceptional person. However, there is no contradiction here. The Hindu conception of life-span development does not emphasize numbers, nor does it deny that many people fail to progress. The relatively small number of creative old men[1] are valued the more for having persevered in their long and arduous personal journeys. What is perhaps of most interest in Maduro's study for the present purposes are the following conclusions and implications:

1. The old creative artist in India is fulfilling a cherished cultural value by emphasizing inner development. "Disengagement" from external and utilitarian concerns does not lead to a reduced status as a useless and expendable person.
2. Continued inner development is also seen as an ever-increasing affinity with God.
3. Aged artists believe that they can draw upon an "inner reservoir of creative power" known as *Maya rupa*. This traditional Hindu concept resonates with Jungian ideas about "ideal energized affect images."
4. Creativity itself is viewed not simply as the act of producing a painting or other artistic object but rather as "an overall act of becoming or manifesting interior contents of the psyche, a process which may take weeks, days, or hours" (Maduro, 1981, p. 88).
5. Just as there is no guarantee that a person will progress from one *ashrama* to the next, so there is also no guarantee that an artist will solve the problems that are confronted in contemplating every work.
6. The aged artists studied by Maduro actually did show more creativity, whether as judged by other artists or by their own test responses.

Overall, the view from Northern India contrasts sharply with prevailing assumptions and attitudes in Western industrialized nations.

[1] In limiting his focus to men, Maduro was staying within the established cultural tradition. However, the female principle (*shakti*) is considered essential to the creative process, which must integrate female and male principles.

Creativity is seen as a significant, an essential human activity and one that can reach its highest expression in old age. There is, nevertheless, a point of contact with the research literature on creativity as an ability. Creative old people are none too plentiful, whether one is correlating achievements with age in the manner of Beard (1874) and his successors or cherishing the admirable few artists who draw deeply upon the power of *Maya rupa* in their old age. However, the fact that works of the highest quality can be produced by aged artists is more clearly evidenced in Maduro's (1981) study than in the usual aggregate statistical approach favored by mainstream gerontologists.

## THE "LATE STYLE" CONTROVERSY AND THE SWAN SONG

Is it possible to identify a particular set of characteristics in the creations of old artists? And if so, would this perhaps tell us something significant about both the meaning of aging and of creativity? The concept of "late style" is often encountered in biographical, historical, and aesthetic studies of people who have been creative in the arts. It is most often asserted that the artist's oeuvre can be divided into "early," "middle," and "late" periods, each of which possesses distinctive characteristics. Furthermore, there has also been special interest shown in a creative artist's very last work—the Opus Ultimum, as trenchantly discussed by Alfred Einstein (1937), or the "swan song" in more common usage. On this view, several successive styles are followed by an epilogue in which the composer / artist / writer takes leave of this world through an offering that somehow represents a completion or culmination of a lifetime of creative activity.

Both concepts are appealing and can provide a stimulating introduction to creative achievements throughout the entire life span. For example, the allure of late style invites us to explore the continued unfolding of Giuseppe Verdi's creative development over 60-plus years of life and achievement, and the 71-year-old Franz Josef Haydn himself referred to his fragmentary 83rd string quartet as a swan song. If late style and the swan song can be taken as secure foundations, then it should be possible to construct a more comprehensive theoretical structure regarding the meaning and purpose of creativity within the total life-span context.

But it's just not that easy! Some of the flaws, limitations, and hazards in this approach can be illustrated within the realm of musical creativity:

1. The basic facts may be more in doubt than one would assume and subject to significant revision. For example, the first publication of J. S.

Bach's final composition, *Art of Fugue*, concluded with a chorale-prelude that was taken to represent his last musical thoughts. It was subsequently discovered that the publisher has simply tacked this piece to the end of *Art of Fugue* to prevent the purchasers from feeling cheated because Bach's actual swan song had been left incomplete: a triple fugue that ended at the 239th measure as the composer fell dead. That there are consequential differences between these two different accounts of Bach's final composition can be readily appreciated when we note that the composer had introduced his own name (in German notation of the time: B-flat, A, C, B) as one of the fugal themes, literally writing himself into his music and out of this world. This is by no means an isolated example. Subsequent discoveries have required biographers and musicologists to revise their views of the lives and stylistic development of many other composers.

2. How compositions are analyzed and judged has proved to be even more subject to variation over time. Both the musical establishment and the public often have particular difficulty in responding to the later achievements of composers who had become popular through earlier works. For example, composers as different as Franz Liszt and Igor Stravinsky puzzled and alienated many admirers by the "strangeness" of the works written in old age, and even the adored Verdi, at 84, left many opera lovers disconcerted by his final stage work, *Falstaff*. Did Liszt, Verdi, and Stravinsky suffer a decline in creativity as they aged, or did they explore newer realms of musical thoughts? The sobering fact is that one cannot simply impose an answer—the disagreement continues, and reminds us that conclusions about life-span creativity often rest upon the changing sands of critical and public opinion. It is worth noting, however, that over the span of approximately a century there has been growing appreciation for the uniqueness and adventuresomeness of the music composed by Liszt and Verdi in their old age. Stravinsky may have to be patient; he has not been dead long enough, and his final works are often still thought to be esoteric and unrewarding.

3. Both late style and the swan song must be considered within their situational contexts. There is a temptation to treat the individual creative person as though a specimen one can study in isolation. How far this temptation might take a "researcher" can be illustrated all too well by Haydn's postmortem adventures. One of his "friends" at court arranged to have Haydn's head severed from his body so that the brain could be dissected and the secrets of creativity discovered (Landon, 1976). This covert operation was, in fact, carried out, but it failed to explain the composer's genius, as has many another reductionistic study since that time. Many other—though fortunately less grisly—examples abound. For example,

- Haydn's astounding development as a composer of symphonies was intimately related to the simultaneous emergence of a prosperous middle class for whom the public concert hall was devised.
- Richard Strauss, renowned for exuberant orchestral show pieces such as *Don Juan* and *Ein Heldenleben*, created a radically different kind of music in his eighth decade. Now appreciated as a masterpiece, his *Metamorphosen* is written for strings alone and displays a purity, inwardness, and restraint one would hardly have associated with its composer's oeuvre. But this music tells us as much about the times as it does about its aged creator. Strauss was mourning the destruction that had befallen his beloved city of Munich during World War II and, more universally, the assault upon the human spirit everywhere that violence had engendered.
- Jimmy Yancey, a pianist whose innovations helped to create a new blues-and-jazz style, spent his later adult years as a groundskeeper for a baseball team. Like many other jazz-oriented musicians, his opportunity to develop and share a late style was blocked by racial discrimination and economic pressures. Both late style and swan song may become casualities of circumstance; therefore, conclusions about the inherent or intrinsic creative potential of aging composers (artists, writers, etc.) must contend with this bias of large but uncharted proportions.

4. Mahler was a relatively young man when he composed death-haunted symphonies, yet he realized that he probably did not have long to live. A sense of time urgency rather than anything associated with chronological age seemed to engender what might be called his "early late style." Although their circumstances differed in many ways, Tchaikovsky was still an active and prolific middle-aged man when reflections on mortality inspired the unique final movement of his final symphony (No. 6). Age per se may have relatively little to do with the emergence of a late style.

Other types of difficulty with the concepts of late style and swan song could be mentioned, along with examples drawn from various spheres of creative activity. Enough has been said, however, to sound a caution against hasty conclusions and undisciplined generalizations. These imperfect concepts do not lack merit; they simply require a more systematic and encompassing type of scholarship for thorough evaluation. Here are a few illustrative aspects of late style / swan song that invite further inquiry:

1. Late style may be a means of achieving an integrated balance between two strong and competing impulses: (a) the desire to encompass a wide variety of artistic expressions and yet (b) control and

perfect these varied expressions within a powerful aesthetic structure. *The Art of Fugue*, already mentioned, applies the "learned fugue" as a stringent organizing technique for musical materials that are themselves of diverse and wide-ranging character. In fact the fugue, with its formidable intellectual demands, has been embraced not only by Bach, the supreme master of this genre, but also by elderly composers for whom the fugue previously had held only incidental or academic interest (listen, for example, to some of the last works of long-lived 20th-century composers, Stravinsky and Arnold Schoenberg). An aged composer may express a broad range of musical thought and feeling within the same opus (e.g., Haydn's last complete set of string quartets, op. 76) or within one individual work (e.g., Verdi's last composition, the *Te Deum*). Moment by moment, there is nothing in the final works of Haydn or Verdi to suggest "old age," but listened to in their entirety, there is an impression of unlimited mastery, especially in the ability of integrating disparate expressive impulses.

Do such artistic accomplishments indicate that the aged composers are carrying out a similar transformation within their own selves? Is this an aspect of the "generativity versus despair" (Erikson, 1979) and "life review" (Butler, 1963) that has not yet been well elucidated? Perhaps the creative product, for all of its distinctive qualities, is but a token of inner growth.

2. The late style often is characterized by an economy of means, a conciseness of expression in which the essence is communicated without a superfluous brush stroke, word, or note. Maduro (1981) observed this trait in the work produced by the aged artists of Northern India. One discovers it repeatedly in the compositions of aged composers: prime examples can be found in the symphonies composed by Havergal Brian (1876–1972 [1988]). Of these, the most accessible for study is Symphony No. 31, composed at 92 years of age. In the span of about 13 minutes Brian develops a complete symphonic drama of a type one would ordinarily expect to require a much longer performance time (his Symphony No. 7, composed at age 52, is on the same compact disc and runs for more than 40 minutes). Concentrated artistic thought and "no nonsense," then, is a frequent although by no means a universal characteristic of late style. (For example, Brian's British countryman, Ralph Vaughan-Williams, imbued his Symphony No. 8, composed at age 83, with a spirit of expansive merriment).

3. Late style may also be an outcome—or casualty—of the aging individual's confrontations with the prospect of cessation and the hope of renewal. For people who have lived many years within the whirlwinds of creative activity, "cessation" often has the equivocal meanings of "death" and "silence" (stagnation or nonproductivity). The challenge

may be triggered by the current situational context (e.g., "Should I accept this commission to write a new opera or symphony—do I still have it in me?"). However, the challenge is also likely to represent a continuing lifelong effort to cope with personal anxieties, losses, and sorrows. Leos Janacek (1854–1928), for example, was preoccupied with the theme of decay and regeneration in a philosophical as well as a personal sense. Almost all of the music that has fostered Janacek's current high reputation was composed in the last few years of his life after he renewed himself through a late-life love relationship. By contrast, Jean Sibelius (1865–1957) quickly established himself as his nation's preeminent cultural hero but, after producing a series of symphonies and various other works, offered no new compositions during the last three decades of his life. There have been both reports and denials that he did complete another symphony (No. 8), although only to reject and destroy it. The sustained burst of creativity that marked Janacek's later years and the silence from Sibelius appear to represent two vastly different responses to the universal challenges of aging and mortality. And yet even a small piece of additional information can suggest a different perspective; it has recently come to light that in his 92nd year Sibelius did take up his pen once again to orchestrate, with his own distinctive mastery, a song from Shakespeare's *Twelfth Night*: "Come Away, Death." One cannot help but think that Sibelius's inner relationship with life, death, and creativity was far more complex than we are ever likely to understand. Late style and swan song concepts may prove useful, then, in directing attention into fruitful areas for inquiry, including nonreductionistic psychoanalytic approaches such as those of George Pollock (1989) and William Neiderland (1989), who see the creative process as a distinctly human way of coping with sorrow, loss, and limits.

## SOME CONCLUDING THOUGHTS

Creativity is a term that is encountered with increasing frequency among life-span developmentalists and gerontologists. A quantitatively oriented research literature has been accumulating alongside (although seldom interfaced with) critical, historical, and biographical studies. Both types of approach have been described in this chapter. The sociobehavioral data, heavily weighted toward quantitative methods, suggest that creative productivity does occur throughout the total life span but with decreasing frequency in the advanced years. There is still room for differing opinions on the "why" of declining creativity and certainly for more definitive scholarly contributions.

Contextual and qualitative approaches also offer a variety of starting points for further inquiry: creativity in later life seems to be influenced by cultural expectations, by economic opportunity, and, very likely, by many other contextual variables. Creative thinking lends itself to a variety of functions. These include helping a person to get from "here" (e.g., frustrated and alarmed youth) to "there" (a desired grown-up self), balancing the surge of expressive impulses with the demands of coherent structure and discipline, confronting the challenges of aging and mortality, and, of course, experiencing pleasure through the creative process itself.

In neither the quantitative nor the contextual / qualitative approach is there any compelling evidence for the proposition that age "causes" stagnation or cessation of creative activity, just as there is no compelling evidence that youth "causes" the first stirrings of creative activity.

Perhaps when wiser minds write more informative chapters on this topic, we will have learned the following:

- Creativity is an attitude and a philosophy of life as much as it is a set of cognitive / aesthetic skills.
- Creativity belongs not at the periphery but at the center of all studies of human experience, as a psychobiological resource for survival of both individual and species and as an intimate link between the individual and what gods, spirits, forces, or whims have given rise to mindedness in an entropy-addicted universe.
- The dynamics of personal growth versus stagnation throughout the total life span (Kastenbaum, 1981; Norris-Baker & Scheidt, 1989) are closely related to the processes that result in creative achievement; in the act of creation, we may also create and re-create ourselves.
- Aging tests the creative spirit in a way that might be compared with the ordeal of the saint (Kastenbaum, 1990), though few of us be saints. The triumph of the creative spirit in old age—no matter how personal and unobserved a triumph—would be cherished by a more perceptive society as perceptive people now cherish a glowing sunset at the end of a long and eventful day.

## REFERENCES

Albert, R. S. (1983). The concept of genius and its implications for the study of creativity and giftedness. In R. S. Albert (Ed.), *Genius and eminence* (pp. 6–18). New York: Pergamon Press.

Alpaugh, P., & Birren, J. (1975). Are there sex differences in creativity across the adult life span? *Adult Development, 19,* 461–465.

Alpaugh, P., & Birren, J. (1977). Variables affecting creative contributions across the adult life span. *Human Development 2*, 240–248.

Alpaugh, P., Parham, I., Cole, K., & Birren, J. (1982). Creativity in adulthood and old age: An exploratory study. *Educational Gerontology, 8*, 101–116.

Baltes, P. B., Schaie, W. K. (1976). On the plasticity of intelligence in adulthood and old age—where Horn and Donaldson fail. *American Psychologist, 31*, 720–725.

Beard, G. (1874). *Legal responsibility in old age*. New York: Russell's American Steam Printing House.

Benet, S. V. (1942). Old Man Hoppergrass. In B. Davenport (Ed.), *Stephen Vincent Benet: Poetry* (pp. 414–415). New York: Farrar & Rinehart.

Berman, H. J. (1986). The use of intimate journals in geropsychology: Olmstead's journal of retirement. Presented at the annual meeting of Gerontological Society of American in San Francisco, Nov. 1986.

Berman, H. J. (1988). Admissable evidence: Geropsychology and the personal journal. In S. Reinharz & G. D. Rowles (Eds.), *Qualitative Gerontology* (pp. 47–63). New York: Springer Publishing Co.

Brian, H. (Composer). (1988). Symphony #31. Hayes Middlesex, England: EMI Angel Compact Disc CDC 495582.

Butler, R. N. (1963). The life review: An interpretation of reminiscence in the aged. *Psychiatry, 26*, 65–76.

Chinen, A. B. (1989). *In the ever after*. Wilmette, III: Chiron.

Dennis, W. (1956). *Age and Achievement*: A Critique. *Journal of Gerontology 11*, 331–333.

Dennis, W. (1966). Creative productivity between the ages of 20 and 80 years. *Journal of Gerontology, 21*, 1–8.

Einstein, A. (1937). Opus ultimum. *The Musical Quarterly, 22*, 269–286.

Erikson, E. H. (1979). Reflections on Dr. Borg's life cycle. In D. D. Van Tassel (Ed.), *Aging, Death, and the Completion of Being* (pp. 29–68). Philadelphia: University of Pennsylvania Press.

Galton, F. B. (1869). *Hereditary genius*. London: Macmillan.

Goldman, C. (Producer). (1988). Elders of the tribe. Audio cassette. Fairfax, VA: Connie Goldman Productions.

Goldman, C. (Producer). (1988). Late bloomer: Stories of successful aging. Audio cassette and booklet. Fairfax, VA: Connie Goldman Productions.

Kastenbaum, R. (1981). Habituation as a model of human aging. *International Journal of Aging & Human Development, 12*, 159–170.

Kastenbaum, R. (1989). Old men created by young artists: Time-transcendence in Tennyson and Picasso. *International Journal of Aging & Human Development, 28*, 81–104.

Kastenbaum, R. (1990). The age of saints and the saintliness of age, *International Journal of Aging & Human Development, 30*, 95–118.

Landon, H. C. R. (1976). *Haydn: Life and chronicle* Vol. 4. London.

Lehman, H. C. (1953). *Age and achievement*. Princeton, NJ: Princeton University Press.

Lehman, H. C. (1956). Reply to Dennis' critique of *Age and Achievement*. *Journal of Gerontology, 11*, 331–337.

Maduro, R. (1981). The old man as creative artist in India. In R. Kastenbaum (Ed.), *Old age on the new scene* (pp. 71–101). New York: Springer Publishing Co.

Martin, R. B. (1980). *Tennyson and the unquiet heart.* Oxford: Clarendon Press.

Neiderland, W. G. (1989). Trauma, loss, restoration, and creativity. In D. R. Dietrich & P. C. Shadad (Eds.), *The problem of loss and mourning* (pp. 61–82). Madison, WI: International Universities Press.

Norris-Baker, C., & Scheidt, R. J. (1989). Habituation theory and environment-aging research: Ennui to joie de vivre? *International Journal of Aging & Human Development, 29,* 241–258.

O'Connor, F. V. (1979). Albert Berne and the completion of being: Images of vitality and extinction in the last paintings of a nienty six year-old man. In David D. Van Tassel (Ed.). *Aging, death, and the completion of being* (pp. 255–289). Philadelphia: University of Pennsylvania Press.

Pollock, G. H. (1989). The mourning process, the creative process, and the creation. In D. R. Dietrich & P. C. Shabad (Eds.), *The problem of loss and mourning* (pp. 27–60). Madison, WI: International Universities Press.

Romaniuk, J. G., & Romaniuk, M. (1981). Creativity across the life span: A measurement perspective. *Human Development, 24,* 366–381.

Ruth, J. E., & Birren, J. (1985). Creativity in adulthood and old age: Relations to intelligence, sex, and mode of testing. *International Journal of Behavioral Development, 8,* 99–110.

Scott-Maxwell, F. (1979). *The measure of my days.* New York: Penguin. (Original work published in 1968.)

Simonton, D. K. (1975a). Age and literary creativity: A cross-cultural and transhistorical survey. *Journal of Cross-Cultural Psychology, 6,* 259–277.

Simonton, D. K. (1975b). Sociocultural context of individual creativity: A transhistorical time-series analysis. *Journal of Personality & Social Psychology, 32,* 1119–1113.

Simonton, D. K. (1977). Eminence, creativity, and geographic marginality: A recursive structural equation model. *Journal of Personality & Social Psychology, 35,* 805–816.

Simonton, D. K. (1980). Thematic fame, melodic originality, and musical Zeitgeist: A biographical and transhistorical content analysis. *Journal of Personality & Social Psychology, 38,* 972–983.

Simonton, D. K. (1984). *Genius, creativity, & leadership.* Cambridge: Cambridge University Press.

Simonton, D. K. (1988). *Scientific genius: A psychology of science.* Cambridge: Cambridge University Press.

Simonton, D. K. (1989). The swan-song phenomenon: Last-works effects for 172 classical composers. *Psychology and Aging, 4,* 42–47.

Vining, E. (1978). *Being seventy: The measure of a year.* New York: Viking Press.

Yeats, W. B. (1989). The tower. In R. J. Finneran (Ed.), *The collected works of W. B. Yeats Vol. I. The Poems* (p. 194). New York: Macmillan.

# 13

# Story of the Shoe Box: On the Meaning and Practice of Transmitting Stories

*Marc Kaminsky*

Storytelling has traditionally been, and in radically altered ways remains, a common social practice in old age. No longer the sacred and technological archives of the tribe, tales are still used to offer counsel on being and doing well. A specifying history of the changing forms of older adult storytelling, and the changing uses to which stories are commonly put, remains to be written.

Scholars and gerontological practitioners alike "work with" the stories that old people tell and hence have been interested in interdisciplinary writing that links individual reminiscence and life review with collective history and the transmission of culture. As actual processes, the need to resolve archaic personal conflicts, the wish for immortality, the will to bear witness and the desire to create a lasting image of one's life and world are complexly intertwined: they evidently cannot be parceled out among psychology, religion, anthropology, and literary or art criticism. The object of study—cultural creativity that takes life history as its materials and its project—traverses all these disciplines. Interdisciplinary studies tend to demonstrate the connections among some, but not all, of the categorically separated realms of activity. The occluded areas of activity tend to be politics and economics. Cultural studies, using the cultural theory of such marxist thinkers as Mikhail Bakhtin (1981) and Raymond Williams (1986), investigate the interrelation of all the connected spheres of human activity that constitute the object of study. Social discourse of all kinds (artifacts, texts, symbolic behavior, cultural productions and performances) is interpreted by a specifying rhetorical analysis that seeks to demonstrate the ways in which the discourse reflects and refracts a whole way of life that is grounded in history.

Cultural studies on *late-life* storytelling have yet to be written. (Walter Benjamin's [1969] classic essay, "The Storyteller," and John Berger's [1967] work, notably *A Fortunate Man*, are among the few texts that demonstrate the contribution that cultural theory has to make to studies on aging). We have, however, many strong interdisciplinary studies on storytelling in old age. Myerhoff's contribution and her broad appeal to scholars and practitioners have to do precisely with the interdisciplinary character of her project: she offered narrative and theoretical descriptions of "the culture of aging" that connected personal narrative and cultural transmission.

Myerhoff's ethnographic work takes the breakdown of tradition as its historical given and describes the cultural creativity of old people under historical conditions of permanent crisis: they have been "robbed of their natural heirs." This creates the social break for a radically altered process of cultural transmission. Scholars and practitioners stand in for the missing children and "kinfolk." They—*we*—assume the role of cultural next-of-kin, of the preservers and custodians of endangered traditions. The occupational hazards here are evident: professional self-aggrandizement takes the specific form of appropriating the other's spirituality so that secular studies subtly lay claim to value as a form of substitute religion. The storms of privatization that do violence to *communitas* and the competitive individualism that in practice tears apart "moral" social relations are placed outside interdisciplinary discussions that promote and interpret their object of cultural study in terms of spiritual and moral community. Then, too, as the critiques of the "textualist movement" have shown, middle-class professionals, as the preservers and transmitters of other folks' traditions, are quite unreliable and tend to efface and subordinate difference. (See, for instance, the essays by Renato Rosaldo and James Clifford in *Writing Culture* [Clifford & Marcus, 1986]). Myerhoff's essays are among the first to focus reflexively on the collaboration between professional interviewer and elder and to view the professional as a "natural" role-bearer in the process of cultural transmission. Her texts concurrently assume this social relationship—that is, treat it as a normal if lamentable fact of life—and problematize it. But they soften—spiritualize—their implicit critique of the culture of capitalism by evading the necessary analysis of the interrelation between the culture and the historical forces that have "distanced" children from their (working-class, immigrant, socialist) parents. Hareven (1982) has shown that cultural discontinuity was imposed by the historic transfer of many of the family's functions to state institutions and by a segmentation of the life cycle that was tied to the stratification and division of labor. These factors are crucial in the lives of Myerhoff's subjects, but (given the distaste of liberal discourse in the human sciences for anything that smacks of class analysis) are not cited in the background history of her "elders." Her major ethnographic papers on the immigrant generation, like her work on a later generation of Jews who survived the Holocaust, celebrates the culture of professionalism as a means of coping with larger historical crises.

Myerhoff's pioneering reflexive work remains invaluable both for interdisciplinary studies as well as more fully developed cultural studies on aging. It offers specifying descriptions of how members of a minority group resist the dominant culture by creating face-work rituals and other cultural performances that repair their wounded dignity, oppose their invisibility, and assert their worth; thus, it movingly portrays the creativity of a stigmatized group as inseparable from its project of cultural resistance in one of the enclaves of socioeconomic difference that the globalization of the market and the universalization of capitalism has been erasing in all corners of the earth.

This text, written five years ago for presentation at a conference,[1] participates in the transmissive practices it describes. It remains, as I now see it, too much inside the culture of professionalism that it reflexively analyses. One always starts out from somewhere, and critical understanding comes slowly and with difficulty. This Bakhtinian investigation of Myerhoff's work on storytelling initiated a critique that is worked through elsewhere.[2]

## STORY OF THE SHOE BOX

I was told by a colleague who was close to Barbara Myerhoff and myself that she told the story of the shoe box at least 15 times in his presence: at conferences, in classes and workshops, in conversation. Here is the version of it that I heard:[3]

"I was working with a man who was a survivor, and he was a Hungarian. When he was 11, they knew in his family that the time was limited, everyone knew that, and he was told to pack some things because they would be leaving in a hurry, and he pondered as to what he should take. This pondering of what to take from his little room has always fascinated me.

"I watch old people look around their houses and wonder what to take [to the nursing home], and watch how every object becomes a container and synthesizes an entire lifetime, becomes a reservoir of memories. 'And *that* should be left behind?' I mean, we all get shaped when you clean a drawer [*sic*]. Or you find you can't turn out letters. These are not just things, these are parts of one's life.

"So picture an 11-year-old child looking around his room, knowing his life is about to be destroyed: what should he take? And he was frozen in the dilemma of the choice. And so he made himself two shoe boxes. In one shoe box he put pictures of his family, he put some poetry he had written, he put a postcard from a girl—his treasures, his autobiography of things. And in the other he put an extra pair of shoes and some underwear and a hanky and a knife and a watch. And I think he probably put in a toothbrush. And he came home from school one day and he was told, 'Now! Run!' And he ran in and grabbed the shoe box. And they left.

"When they stopped again, he looked into the box, and he had taken the wrong one. He had the hanky and the shoes and the toothbursh and so on.

"And he thought, 'What did I want this box for? What did I want the other box for? What did the other box mean—to anybody?' And he said, 'It was as though I was standing at the edge of the sea, and I knew I would be pushed into the sea with my box, and the only thing that mattered was that I not sink with the box. It was as if I would try to throw the box back onto shore, and maybe somebody would catch it.'"

## THE SURVIVOR'S STORY: THE QUESTION OF PLOT

When we first hear this story, our attention is gripped by our concern for the survivor. Stories claim us through our desire to know: what will happen next? And then? And then? The "and then" is the mortar out of which stories are constructed. Our curiosity or narrative desire is met by the plot, which presents us with an image of fate. In stories, the fate of a character is decided. It is often said that there are only a limited number of basic stories. In the story of the shoe box, we encounter, for the millionth time, the story whose central conflict concerns redemption or perdition.

"Plot," writes Paul Ricoeur (1980),

> is the intelligible whole that governs a succession of events in any story. This provisory definition immediately shows the plot's connecting function

> between an event or events and the story. A story is *made out* of events to the extent that plot *makes* events *into* a story. (p. 167)

Plot, then, is that totality of which each event is a unique, contributing part.

The story of the survivor is constituted of a sequence of four abbreviated events. At the onset of the time of crisis, the boy is told to pack some things in preparation for an abrupt departure. The now-time of preoccupation begins: the future he faces is close at hand and offers no hope. He knows "his life is about to be destroyed." And: "Everyone knew that." A significant ambiguity binds his personal death to the destruction of a way of life that is his: this is a tale, then, of collective destiny and personal fate.

The content of the initial event is constituted by the boy's action, his response to the crisis: "he made himself two shoe boxes."

This sets up the second event: the moment of choice and the moment of crisis are joined in a single event. The arrival of the Nazis is never directly shown. It is condensed into two words that mark the end of normal routines: "Now! Run!" As in biblical narrative, all description of place is suppressed. What matters is what human beings do, and what often matters more than that is what they say.

The third event is a recognition or judgment scene. The refugees stop. The boy has a chance to examine the contents of the shoe box. He, and we, discover *his* mistake, and perhaps ours. It is possible that we have *preferred* the wrong box.

The final event is also a recognition scene, occurring more than 40 years later, in and through the storytelling situation itself. The survivor discovers and articulates the meaning of the act of creation—the shoe boxes as significant objects are "made"—by which he faced death.

Of these few events the story is made. The ending that the story seeks is illumination. At the end, the grown man discovers or creates the meaning of the boy's preoccupation, act of creation, and moral choice.

As a statement of the plot, this is too general, since it omits the shoe box, which is carried through all four events and unifies them. The object of the plot is the shoe box, which makes the events into a story of *re-membered life*. This key term in Barbara Myerhoff's vocabulary is the "intelligible whole" that makes what happens in the story significant to her:

> To signify this special type of recollection, the term "Re-membering" may be used, calling attention to the reaggregation of members, the figures who belong to one's life story, one's own prior selves, as well as the significant others who are part of the story. Re-membering, then, is a

> purposive, significant unification, quite different from the passive, continuous fragmentary flickerings of images and feelings that accompany other activities in the normal flow of consciousness. The focused unification provided by Re-membering is requisite to sense and ordering. A life is given a shape that extends back into the past and forward into the future. It is a tidy edited tale. Completeness is sacrificed for moral and aesthetic purposes. The same impulse for order informs them all. Perhaps this is why Mnemosne, the goddess of Memory among the Greeks, is the mother of the muses. Without Re-membering we lose our histories and our selves. Time is erosion, then, rather than accumulation. (Myerhoff, 1980a, p. 111)

The contents of the shoe box, like the interiors of those small boxes assembled by the American sculptor Joseph Cornell, represent an attempt to hold an accumulation of life by spatializing time: to compose a narrative frame of cardboard or wood in which moments lived will be emblemized by appearances, as they are in photographs. The shoe box, with its highly selected, symbolic autobiography, is a desperate version of the photograph album: an improvisation in extremis that seeks, like photographs, to be the material form of memory.

In "The Uses of Photography," John Berger (1980) writes:

> Memory implies a certain act of redemption. What is remembered has been saved from nothingness. What is forgotten has been abandoned. If all events are seen, instantaneously, outside time, by a supernatural eye, the distinction between remembering and forgetting is transformed into an act of judgment, into the rendering of justice, whereby recognition is close to *being remembered* and condemnation is close to *being forgotten*. Such a presentiment, extracted from man's long, painful experience of time, is to be found in varying forms in almost every culture and religion. (p. 54)

Nothing comes closer to accounting for the connection that Myerhoff made among memory, storytelling, and visibility. The concept of cultural performance is the idea under which she studied this connection. Through dramatized storytelling, the old people of the Israel Levin Senior Center (in Venice, California) made their memories visible, so that they might attain a secular mode of redemption.

## THE LISTENER'S STORY: THE QUESTION OF VOICE

When we listen to this story a second time, released from its plot interest, we can hear the shifting play of its voices. The first voice is that of the anthropologist-storyteller, who is the narrating "I" of the story.

The second is that of the subject, the narrated "he" of the story. The third cannot be simply equated with a biographical person or character: it is an actual part of the process of communication without corresponding to an actual speaker and hence is readily overlooked in many accounts of social discourse. This transpersonal "linguistic zone" is created by the combination of the first narrator's voice, that of the survivor, and the second narrator's voice, that of the anthropologist. Bakhtin's (1981) discourse theory provides us with the first systematic method of analysing this hitherto vast and unchartered area in communication (both oral and written). The shifting and often hidden interplay and combination of different voices, with their different intonations and evaluations of things, constitutes what Bakhtin called "double-voiced discourse" and what Myerhoff called "the third voice." Double-voiced discourse takes over somebody else's word and gives it another accent, another evaluation, another interpretation. Bakhtin describes with exhilirating particularity the social process in which the other's word is "dialogized," that is, saturated with altered intentions and tones. In the listener's tale, the survivor's word "shoe box" is dialogized when it is informed by Myerhoff's reception (interpretation, symbolization) of it. Or, in Myerhoff's phrase, this co-authored word, generated in and through the act of communication, is uttered "in the third voice, which is neither the voice of the interviewer nor the voice of the informant, but the voice of their collaboration."[4]

As we listen to the interplay of voices, we become aware that this is the second telling of the story: we are hearing the events at one remove, as told to us by the listener. In the version of the story that Myerhoff heard, the first-person narrator and the subject of the story were the same person: the survivor told his story in his own way. Now, a second formulation has been added; another consciousness has interposed itself between the events and an audience. The voice of the story's second narrator—Myerhoff, the expert on aging—appropriates the events to constitute a story in which it is a subject. The story, as we hear it, begins: "I worked with a man who was a survivor." The original narrator is displaced; he is now the object of the professional interviewer's verb: "I worked with . . ." This speaking "I," in its orientation toward its listeners—an audience of gerontological social workers—blurs the difference between anthropological researcher and gerontological social worker. This is the voice, then, of a generic professional listener who works with the elderly.

Although its professional category is generalized, this voice has its particular intonation and function; it is clearly marked off. "This pondering of what to take has always fascinated me." This distinct voice presents its responses to the unfolding events as a way of evaluating and interpreting them: of intensifying them, of giving them another emphasis and value. Myerhoff's reception of the story is deployed in an exemplary way: we are to model our own attentiveness on hers. Her rhetorical intervention is an advocate's plea that we give her client a fair hearing.

Then Myerhoff suspends the plot entirely and gives us a discourse on old people and on the way in which they—and we—commonly ritualize the life-review process: "I mean, we all get shaped when you clean a drawer."[5] This is an important part of the story she has to tell, and she gives one-fifth of this very brief narrative over to it, although it formed no part of the story that she heard from the survivor. In this discourse, the second narrator universalizes the survivor's story, and turns the first event of the boy's preoccupation into a metaphor: the correspondence between what happens in the boy's room and in the rooms of old people on the brink of institutionalization is proposed. This is then elaborated when the narrator's voice does a bit of role playing for us: it assumes the voice of an unnamed old person. Like an actor stepping into one part and out of another before our eyes, the narrator says, "And *that* should be left behind?" This fleeting ventriloqization suffices to evoke the image of a bereft old person, gazing at a precious memento during the crisis of leave-taking. Thus, this second narrative voice, through its dramatized storytelling, openly demonstrates that narration is a performative activity.

Obviously, then, the story of the shoe box is not intended to be a faithful copy or exact replica of an original, nor is a greater degree of reality to be accorded to the survivor's narration than to the later construction of those events in the anthropologist's narrative. It is evident that the second narrator's voice belongs to what Clifford Geertz (1983) has called a "blurred genre." In seeking to present a documentary report for pedagogical and inspirational purposes, it employs imaginative modes, forms of fiction, and does not shrink from elaborations that are possibly invented. Here we have left the linguistic zone of the empiricist social scientist and entered an area of indeterminacy.

This indeterminate linguistic zone becomes more apparent in a playfully ambiguous addition to the list of objects in the boy's survival kit: "And I think he probably put in a toothbrush." Is this an ethnographer or a fiction writer speaking? Does this estimate of probabilities signify the documentarian reaching deeper into her memory for a half-forgotten detail or the imaginative ethnographer elaborating the material a bit, making an educated guess, and winking at us as she does so? This utterance plays with what Myerhoff considered a naive sense of reality and of narrative as existing in a one-to-one correspondence with each other. Again, her interventions are intended to make us more educated listeners to the story she is telling and, in the telling, constructing. In this playful utterance, she is hinting that storytelling and reality are both social and cultural constructions and that the line between the documentary mode and the imaginative mode is so fine as to be permeable.[6]

In tracing the voice of the listener, we have seen that, while many statements clearly belong in the linguistic zone of the voice of this professional, the boundaries of this zone become blurred as it moves into an area of indeterminacy.

When we follow the traces of the first narrator in the story, the same thing happens. Certain utterances clearly belong to the voice of the survivor: "And he came home from school one day and he was told, 'Now! Run!'" This is the linguistic zone or reported speech, plain and simple. The survivor reported his parents' utterance to the anthropologist who, it seems, reported his total report, including the quoted words. Most of the plot statements have the same quality of reported speech: here the story has been transmitted to us, we think, in the form in which it was received.

The survivor doesn't speak to us directly, through the listener's tale, until we arrive at the very end. Then we hear: "And he thought, 'What did I want this box for? What did I want the other box for? What did the other box mean—to anybody?'"

This question and the answer to it, taken together, end the story. And here, we have unmistakably arrived at the linguistic zone of the third voice. Even if Barbara Myerhoff did not lend words of her own to the survivor, which I consider to be unlikely, this passage would still belong to the third voice. Inscribed in this utterance is the dialogic collaboration of the storytelling situation itself, with its question-and-answer structure, and the participation of a mirroring listener. The survivor's words, even if he actually spoke them as Myerhoff has given them to us, belong to the listener's tale because the listener, by offering recognition, collaborated in the discovery and utterance of that final image of the man at the edge of the sea. And in that collaboration lies the meaning of the Bakhtinian claim that the listener coauthors the story.

The listener's tale generalizes the survivor's story. When we return to the discourse on old people, we see specifically how it uses amplification to raise the particular contents of the shoe box to the level of generalization. In the room of the old people, "every object becomes a container and synthesizes an entire lifetime, becomes a reservoir of memories." The word *container* fuses all the objects in the story into an abstract category, which is then given further meanings when the containers and the things they contain—shoe boxes and drawers and postcards and poems—are liquefied as "reservoirs of memoirs." Later, further amplification heightens the value of such containers: each one is and holds a treasure, an autobiography-in-things. These symbolic elaborations are enlisted in the service of plot work, which binds the events into a unified story about re-membered life: these symbols run the unifying meaning and texture through the various episodes, thereby communicating an unfinished experience that has been made whole.

In formulating the concept of the third voice, Myerhoff sought to explain and legitimate her text-making interventions. She had moved beyond editing and fitting together shards of table talk, to compose rare amphoras of meaning, and was now providing some of the missing pieces herself. Her work had moved from the "imaginative identification" that is the accepted practice of the participant-observer, to imaginative interventions that we consider to belong more to the humanities and arts than to the social sciences. This, for her, was standing at the edge of an abyss. We all "believe" in interdisciplinary work, but to cross the no-man's- / no-woman's-land that separates the disciplines can be frightening. In the story of the shoe box, Myerhoff took the leap into the third voice.

The final passage of this story is the place where, probably for the first time, she fully and legitimately attained the third voice. (Shmuel's speeches in *Number Our Days* [Myerhoff, 1978] are her hidden, earlier masterpieces in this genre.) And the secret of the power of this passage is that it conflates the boy's abyss with Barbara Myerhoff's. All her conviction about the value of storytelling and her immense powers of persuasion are concentrated in its final images. Even if these lines were given to her verbatim by the survivor, she seized them and made them her own.

For Myerhoff and her listeners the final passage is, explicitly, an image of the desire for symbolic immortality. It is saturated with a conflict that animates all her strong work. The wish for enchantment—for spiritual community, belief, transcendence—must contend with the sober gaze that disenchants everything it sees. Myerhoff's work is grounded in the impassable distance that separates the skepticism of the professional social scientst from the dance of the Hasidim, whose ecstasy she values more than the middle-class life she leads. This betwixt-and-between position gives her a hard-won insight into "the made-upness of culture." From this lived-through knowledge, a series of brilliant ethnographic papers on "the work of ritual" proceeds. Once, talking to a group of colleagues in the humanities, social sciences, and arts, Myerhoff said that the danger underlying all "our" rituals—she was specifically including the symbolic activity of storytelling here—

> is that they always present us, through their artifice and their performative quality, with the possibility that we have made those up, and extrapolating

> from that, there is the possibility that we have made everything else up. And where do you go from there? If we see our formulations as constructions against nothingness or chaos, then we become endangered, not only as witnesses to our own dramas, but as anthropologists studying the culture of another people. Then we don't know anymore; we are at the edge of the abyss. (Myerhoff, 1980b, pp. 33–34)

This is not the place to deconstruct Myerhoff's attempt to ward off the deconstructionism that had already entered into her analysis of rituals. This much can be said: Myerhoff was standing, here, at the brink of the debate concerning "the breakup of master narratives."[7] This issue has been at the center of the polemic and the extraordinary studies of culture that are being conducted in terms of postmodernism. Through Myerhoff's appropriation of it, the survivor's abyss is shifted onto new terrain, to become hers—and ours.

In the hands of the second narrator, then, the story is universalized (in terms of the professional discourse concerning the life review of old people), and its contents are transferred, in part, from the storyteller to the listener. In the survivor's gesture of transcendence, the listener locates the meaning of her role and her work, which she offers to listeners who come to her in hope of overcoming the danger that they face: burnout.

If the story begins "I worked with" a survivor, it ends with the hope of the appearance of the listener, the "someone who would be there to catch it." That redemptive figure is, of course, Barbara Myerhoff, who received the survivor's story. This is the listener's tale not only in the sense of being her version of the story; it makes her partnership the transformative agent that alters the survivor's fate: the lost past is recovered in and through the listener's intervention.

In all her work on storytelling, Myerhoff stressed the significance of the listener. In working with the elderly, she keenly felt "the pathos of the absent listener." (Bakhtin [1981] speaks of the suffering brought on due to "nonrecognition" in the absence of a "watchful listener.") In the story of the shoe box, Myerhoff finds an emblem for the pathos of the absent listener, as well as the pathos of the absent story, the story that doesn't get told, which is our modern story. Many writers (since World War I) have been obsessed with silence, with the danger of silence. So, too, are survivors of Auschwitz and Hiroshima. And in another sense, silence is the theme of Holocaust narrative and the literature on survivorhood: again and again, witnesses say that only silence can render the story's horror and that this speaking silence was itself nearly buried in silence.

The story of the shoe box presents us with an isolated speaker, a figure by Giacometti or Beckett: this is the figure of the modern storyteller, the witness who has looked into the bleak Medusa face of reality and not been turned to stone. And this is the figure of the modern stroyteller—a witness who reports on a vanished world—because she lacks not only an auditor but also the very materials with which to make her report. Language, whose conventions formerly held good, fail the victims of horror. And the survivor has brought the wrong box: no symbols are available to him with which to communicate what he has lived through, only a few useful things—"a hanky, a toothbrush"—that cannot convey his meanings. He knows his position is hopeless: even if he had that tool kit of culture, a box of symbols, his message ("reservoirs of memories") face dissolution in the "sea" (of historical crisis).

If Barbara Myerhoff had done nothing more than turn the lighthouse of her attention on this Hungarian survivor, her searching, intensely mirroring gaze created a space for the story, by surrounding the teller with the sense that at last being beloved and being believed and being heard were one and the same. If she had done nothing but lend the teller the profound light of her listening, she would have silently coauthored the story. This dialogical listening enacts a secular form of faith: that hope (for recognition, illumination, and continuity) is still possible.

## THE LISTENER'S STORY RETOLD: THE QUESTION OF IDEOLOGY

The ideological dimension of Barbara Myerhoff's stories and talks on storytelling account for the tone that is an indispensable part of their power: their vehemence, the authority of their conviction. This is, specifically, the impassioned tone of the lay sermon, which runs through much of American critical, poetic, scholarly, and didactic talk and writing since Thoreau and Emerson made it native to our speech.

People left Myerhoff's lay sermons converted. But to what? To storytelling itself. Myerhoff's commitment was to her work as a professional listener of the stories people tell. For this reason, people engaged in what may be called the storytelling and story-listening professions—gerontologists and writers, anthropologists and filmmakers, actors and therapists, folklorists and social historians—felt uplifted by her talks and returned to work not only with a greater knowledge of what they were doing but with an enhanced sense of its value.[8]

The story of the shoe box as a lay sermon is addressed to us in our professional capacity and in "our common humanity." In speaking to us as people professionally concerned with narrative—and if we are not already, her discourse anticipates that we soon will be—the story tells us how to live and offers the listener as a model for identification. In speaking to us in "our common humanity," the story tells us how to die and offers the survivor as a model for identification.

The story as lay sermon is concerned with the making of a moral choice. The listener's moral choice is enacted implicitly: she is the "someone" who appears in the final metaphor to hear the story that would otherwise be unheard. Think of the qualities that we normally ascribe to someone who is willing to listen: concern, compassion, disinterestedness, patience, and so on. These are moral qualities, and listening is, whatever else it may be, a moral act.

The plot is manifestly concerned with the issue of the moral choice that the boy—and we—must make because we must all face death. This moral issue is concentrated in the most extreme moments of a story composed entirely of extreme situations. These are the moments of actual choice, when life is endangered and the boy must flee, and the moment of illumination, nearly 40 years later, when the man, in the imagination, returns to the abyss.

As we review these events a third time, we can hear the storyteller at work, constituting the moral order that the narrative itself appears to propose.

The story dramatizes the debate between two attitudes, two systems of value. The first shoe box represents a "this-worldly" position; the second, an "otherworldly" position. Many formulations of this value dilemma, which the boy lives as an immediate crisis, can be offered: the "outer life" versus "the inner life," "the practical" versus "the symbolic." The narrative evidently repudiates "things" for the sake of "meanings." As a sermonic text, it expounds its values dialogicially, that is, through argumentation: by its opting away from what one ideological language (the humanist tradition) calls "materialism" and another (marxism) calls "commodity fetishism."

The survivor's story about his boyhood experience is, on the face of it, plainly a tale of loss, utter loss. The record is lost; the treasured things that could have evoked the past, a whole way of life, are lost. But is that the story we get? As it comes to us, transformed through Myerhoff's way of listening and retelling it, the story is redemptive. It redeems loss with meaning, with the discovery and articulation of meaning. This story crosses and closes the space that separates the survivor's discovery that he has taken the wrong box and the knowledge, discovered decades later, of what the right choice meant. The story transcends the chronicle of loss with the arrival of meaning, which is co-created in the storytelling situation.

Notice, in Myerhoff's version of the tale, this statement: "He ran in and grabbed the shoe box." The central conflict is glossed over, suspended, held in abeyance. This sleight-of-hand reproduces the boy's state of mind at the time of taking flight: all question as to which is the right box is out of the question now. And we, listening to this, are led to assume that the dilemma has been worked out and that he is taking the box that interwines "testimonials of self" and cultural testimony. The story has set up this expectation, so we are doubly shocked: with the news that we too got it wrong and with the finality and terribleness of his loss. It seems irrevocable. This is the point at which the narrator makes explicit the evaluation that she had led us to assume the boy had made.

Because of the device of concealing the actual choice, we are made to suffer what the boy does. The storyteller's art, both Myerhoff's and possibly the survivor's, creates channels for empathy to flow so that we can live through the experience as a form of knowledge. And that is the function of art as well as social science: to raise experience to the level of knowledge.

The narrative organizes its moral as much by what it leaves out as by what it puts in and the way it interrelates the included materials. And so, by its constellation of meaning, the story does not invite us to think about the events that were historically necessary for the loss to be transcended: the boy survived to tell the tale. For the purposes of this story, the narrative of the boy's physical survival is out of place, and images of such events are unwarranted, because the most salient aspect of the protagonist is that he is always standing in immediate danger of death. Why is it significant to point to this nonarticulation of his survival as narrator—a fact that is implicit?

We must distinguish between the loss of objects and the loss of narrative possibility: this distinction, made to me in conversation by Eric Santner after we had seen *Shoah,* has significant implications with respect to the story of the shoe box and survivors' stories generally. The loss of objects, including loved ones, was not necessarily fatal; the loss of narrative possibility was. As countless survivors have testified, it was the will to bear witness that not only made it possible for them to endure a hell constituted by the loss of all significant objects; the will to bear witness was lived through as a moral obligation and a form of faith. It was, for countless victims of terror, the only way of fighting back. We know the unimaginable measures that the Nazis took to exterminate all traces of their extermination of the Jews and other populations. The crematoria in the back woods sought not only the death of its objects but the second death of narrative possibility. The physical survival of the victims was, in part, contingent upon the conviction that the machinery of mass destruction would not succeed against the countermeasure of "story."

The story of the shoe box, like all survivors' stories, pries apart narrative possibility from the death of objects for the sake of survival. And it does so by its transformation of a stock image in the shipwreck tales that are the survivors' stories of an earlier age. The Hungarian survivor or Barbara Myerhoff, or both of them through their collaboration, could not have come upon the image of the *thrown* shoe box had it not been for the deeply familiar story of the message-in-the-bottle thrown into the sea by the marooned survivor seeking to be rescued. The story of the shoe box has its way with us—we "believe" it—because it (probably unconsciously) reaccentuates one of the great storytelling conventions: the seaman's tale of the shipwreck. Both the motif of the bottle and the motif of "sunken treasure" evoke the age-old narrative structure that stands behind this tale and makes it possible.

The storyteller, having arrived at the second ending of the story, reaches for the metaphor of the sea as a way of imaging what Lifton (1967) has called grotesque death, for death by drowning was the form by which an earlier age represented anonymous mass death. In this we see the pathos of our transmitted symbols, which were not adequate to communicate our experience. Benjamin (1969), in "The Storyteller," speaks of the "incommunicability of experience" as a modern crisis that befell the soldiers who left the trenches of World War I—these men who had grown mysteriously silent were seen again and again, as vast populations were sundered from traditional bearings.

The story of the shoe box, emblematic of the precariousness of the transmission of culture and of legacies in our brutal century, embodies as one of its meanings, for Myerhoff, our nearness to meaninglessness, our difficult knowledge of how close we now always are to the darkness, which she symbolized as "the death without throwing the box . . . and our lives without catching the box." Adrift in our moment, without a past that provides orientation on earth, without certainty of a livable future, we make sense of our way of being in time through narrative. And so Myerhoff transferred onto storytelling itself the moral passion that, in traditional society, was reserved for the sacred beings and events that stories pointed to, beyond themselves.

## THE SECOND GENERATION OF THE STORY: THE QUESTION OF METAPHOR

Imaginative works are changed by the deaths of their creators, none more so than works that appear to gaze at death. Giacometti's statues, those emaciated witnesses that once visibly returned their creator's speculative gaze, now look through us to the absence of the sculptor.[9] Barbara Myerhoff's death changed the story of the shoe box in a similar way.

When Barbara Myerhoff found out she had lung cancer, she faced a crisis comparable to that of the boy in the story. In her study, she was surrounded by cartons filled with unfinished manuscripts, file cabinets filled with field research, correspondence, grant proposals, lecture notes, tapes, slides, and photographs: 19 voluminous, meticulously indexed three-ring binders filled with 20 years of papers, her own and others'; and notes toward projects she would now never live to complete.

"Can I join my work to yours?" she asked me. In despair, she asked me, "How can I let those survival stories just die?" She was speaking of the tales she had collected from Hasidim, refuseniks, survivors, and others in the Fairfax community of Los Angeles. These questions were being posed, in various ways, to each of the colleagues and friends whose legacy-bearing help she sought. As the weeks passed and she steadily lost weight, she threw cans of film, brown envelopes filled with typed pages between whose lines spidery corrections crawled, as well as numerous other tasks, across the widening gap that separated her from the completion of her projects.

During one of our discussions about what tasks I might take on, I mentioned that I had taped a talk she had recently given on life-history work, aging, and survivorhood. "That's it," she said. "That's where to begin. Turn that talk into a text. For publication."

The story of the shoe box is taken from that talk. Titled "Stories as Equipment for Living"—a phrase she took "from the master, Kenneth Burke"—this was, in her view, her culminating statement on storytelling. As scriptor / editor of her talk, my work was to preserve her words or, as she put it in her absence-haunted double negative, "erase their oblivion."

Now the dilemma I faced in preparing *this* text corresponds to the boy's dilemma, and to Barbara's. Of the treasures contained in those cardboard boxes, of all of the talks and texts that she threw to me, what to choose? What to leave out? How to represent her legacy? I wished, in addition to comprehending everything, to summon her presence—her living voice—along with her knowledge. Perhaps I should simply read one of the transcripts that I had edited? Finally, as we often do with the dead whose voices we internalize, I consulted her, just as she had often turned to Shmuel the tailor.

"So, Barbara, what do you want me to do?"

"I already told you. Do 'Stories as Equipment for Living.'"

"Yes, I thought I'd read the section that begins 'Killroy was here' and concludes with your minimum definition of story as the desire to leave a trace, and also the section where you evoke the shamanic ancestry of the storyteller, and then the passage on the storyteller as a latter-day Jacob who wrestles a blessing from the Angel of Death." I proceeded to enumerate other passages that, taken together, miniaturize two decades of scholarship and turn it into an aria of sorts.

"No, no, there's no time for all this. You'll have to triage. Try telling a story. It's the most condensed and unified way of containing in a little space one or two themes I've developed."

"You are speaking of the story of the shoe box?"

"Well, I'm glad you thought of it."

"Barbara, how many stories about containing 'infinite riches in a little room' do you tell in that talk?"

"That's true. Still, you read my intention correctly."

"You know, Barbara, the thought of having to 'present your legacy' is . . . it's overwhelming. I'd love just to read your words. Or, as you put it, to sound your text."

"Impossible. For one thing, my words are now inseparable from the words of those who have passed into mine. For another, it will make a better symposium if you add your own voice. Isn't that what storytelling and transmission is all about? Besides, there's nothing I'd like better than to hear you retell the story of the shoe box. Go ahead. I'm listening."

To override any possible waning of conviction, Barbara donned the mantle of anthropological authority and cited a dozen or so cultures in which the dead sit around listening to progeny and friends retell their stories. So you have it on good authority that Barbara is present as I retell the story of the shoe box.

As you hear it again, the story is changed. This transformation is accomplished through metaphor. The Greek word *metapherein* literally means to bear over, to transfer. Metaphor carries meanings across the boundaries that separate objects. In rhetoric, metaphor is the construction of an implied analogy that imaginatively identifies one thing with another. Imaginative identification, rhetorically and culturally, is the way in which meanings are transmitted.

For a story to remain alive as it enters its second generation, for it to present an experience that we take to be usable and true, it has to change. It is metamorphosed through the (not always conscious) metaphor making of subsequent tellers and listeners, who co-create it, both to adapt a valued narrative to changed conditions and to adapt themselves to new conditions through the use of narrative. The myth that sacred and traditional stories remain the same gives them their stabilizing power. The continuity of their manifest content maintains this illusion. Meanwhile, the generations go on infiltrating the story and reorientating the meanings and latent contents that stories bear in their metaphors. Stories survive their immediate occasions only by having change—personal, cultural, social, and historical change—inscribed in their metaphors.

As I tell the story again, the shoe box, which grew symbolic to contain Barbara's voice, is returned, anew, to the ground of experience: it becomes actual in the realm of practice that we share. What is happening, here in this room, and what happened more than four decades ago in that boy's room in Hungary are brought into relation: the imaginative identification of these dissimilar places is demonstrated by a metaphorical identity equation whose middle term is Barbara's study. Through her story, his story gives me metaphors for mine. And as my story, it becomes, literally, the legacy that Barbara transmitted to me—as a task, a privilege, and a problem—to pass on.

Telling this story, then, becomes a living enactment of the process of cultural transmission, through which the death of the teller or culture-bearer is transcended. And this is what stories are for: arms with which to fight death, arms for mortal oarsmen to go back over the wide water of forgetfulness, so that we may continue to make the round trips toward meaning that stories make possible.

## NOTES

[1] This is a revised version of a paper that was presented at the 1985 annual conference of the Gerontological Society of America, at the President's Symposium on the Humanities and Arts, titled "Life-History Work and the Experience of Aging: The Legacy of Barbara Myerhoff." This text was prepared for publication under the auspices of the Myerhoff Center at the YIVO Institute for Jewish Research. Grateful acknowledgment is made to Dr. Maury P. Leibovitz, President of the Center; Polly Howells and Diane Demeter, co-chairs of the Committee on Research and Publication Projects; Dr. Deena Metzger, Founding Co-director; and to Dr. Steven Demeter, Naomi Newman and Micah Taubman.

[2] See my Introduction to Myerhoff's *Remembered Lives: The Work of Ritual, Storytelling and Growing Older* (1992).

[3] The colleague, Arthur Strimling, co-taught a seminar on life history and performance with Myerhoff at New York University and at the Hunter / Brookdale Center on Aging. Myerhoff presented this version of the story at a 1983 conference on "survival stories" that I organized at Hunter / Brookdale.

[4] Myerhoff presented the notion of the third voice at a panel discussion, "Storytelling: Cultural Transmission and Symbolic Immortality," that I organized in collaboration with her and Harry Moody and that was offered at the 1983 annual meeting of the Gerontological Society of America.

[5] The complexity and contradiction of the participant-observer's "subject position" is inscribed in this utterance: the shift in pronoun, which violates

the consistency of subject required by the conventions of syntax, precisely communicates Myerhoff's movement back and forth between a position of "scientific" detachment and "imaginative identification." Here, the break in grammar foregrounds what elsewhere is either hidden or described in terms of conflict-free transitions: "they" becomes "we" becomes "you," in writing that stands at the boundary between active solidary relations with the "elders" and disidentification. In the present instance, the utterance moves from the identification of the speaker with the old people to an identification of the middle-class listener (the "you") with them. At stake is "managing" the actual cultural and historical conflicts between politically radical and ethnically unassimilated "ancestors" and their American "progeny." Also at stake is glossing over the hidden conflict in Myherhoff's ethnographic papers: solidarity with the old people's cultural resistance versus alignment with the hegemonic view of them. The narrative of Americanization that, in part, governs Myerhoff's interpretation of the old people's cultural production is the liberal myth of "the one-generation proletariat," which Irving Howe discredits in *World of Our Fathers.*

[6] This issue is at the center of scholarly research and debate today and is engaged in major work by such diverse social thinkers as Foucault, Geertz, Raymond Williams, Jameson, and Aronowitz; and it is *the* problem addressed by the "textualist movement" in contemporary American anthropology. This is a profoundly difficult investigation that seeks nothing less than to analyze and describe the relation between discourse and "reality." In my Introduction to *Remembered Lives* (Myerhoff, 1992), I have discussed at length Myerhoff's position as a forerunner and initiator of the "textualist movement," as well as the development of her own critique against empiricist social science. To epitomize my evaluation of her problematic position, I would say that the use of "literary devices" in the representation of social life is legitimate when these devices and their ideological orientation are made as explicit as the author's reflexive knowledge can make them. Myerhoff's "novelization" of her informants' lives and utterances is at once a source of the power of her work and, in places, an extreme, cunning, and problematic writing practice, which is, significantly, representative of the "crisis in representation" in the human sciences. Toward the end of her life, she was moving toward openly avowing her "artistic" interventions and toward openly contesting the norms of empiricism. The notion of the third voice was a crucial move in this direction. But she was far from having worked through her thinking and conflicts with respect to principles of text construction in ethnography. One of the most problem-laden discoveries that I made, after her death, involved the story of the shoe box. After completing this paper, I found the field notes in which she had written up the survivor's story from memory, soon after the interview. The first half of the story differs from Myerhoff's version in one significant fact: the age of the boy is given as 9, not 11. Here is the second half:

> Then one day I came home from school. The whole block next door was gone, simply gone, smoking ruin. My family was waiting. "Quick, come at once." I ran inside and grabbed the box with the useful things, I was crying and I knew all along that at that moment I left my childhood behind. We arrived at our [hiding] place and I opened the box. Mistakenly I had taken the box with the poems and things. Such a shock. What would I do with it? I spent the rest of my life wondering what to do with that box. What good was it to me? No chance of taking it with me into the camps. What could it mean to any other living soul? I have thought it was as though I sank into a

> lake, drowning, and all I wanted to do was heave the shoe box to the shore where someone else could catch it. Anyone. Just so it still goes on existing.

In the "heat" of delivering her talk, did Myerhoff forget this earlier version—also her rendition of the survivor's story—and switch shoe boxes? If so, how do we evaluate such "forgetting"? It is also crucial to stress that, although a key moment in the plot is reversed, the meanings of the narrative—hers and the survivor's in old age—are left intact. The ratio between "unconscious" and deliberate transformation of the story finally matters less than this: the tale she tells is consistent with the vision and method she espouses. In retelling this story, she has practiced what she preaches: she has made this into a "tidy edited tale." What she has suppressed is discontinuity. In the survivor's story, the boy's choice—his whole evaluative orientation—is different from that of the survivor in old age. This accounts for the shift in age: at 11 a Jewish boy would be near enough to ritual adulthood at age 13 to think like the man who he will soon be. Myerhoff's version not only "invents" the survivor's lifelong selfsameness, it also removes any discontinuity between the survivor's now-unified moral vision and Myerhoff's authorial intention. This is an instance, then, of the suppression of difference that is the basis of the profound critique that non-marxists and marxists alike have been making of conventionalist ethnographic narrative. A simple moralism is out of place here, on many grounds. Suffice it to say that this "transgression" is inseparable from Myerhoff's contribution. She is widely and rightly recognized for her pioneering use and espousal of "reflexivity" and "narrative" in formal ethngraphic case studies. Too, her investigation of the whole area of life-history work begins with the insight that cultural creativity in this domain is driven by the desire to transcend discontinuity, and what is in fact created are imaginative forms of continuity that meet commonly felt human needs, including needs that are irreducibly spiritual. That they proceed from the imagination does not make them any the less social facts, once they are objectified as ritual, tradition, and other types of social discourse.

[7] This is a key concept in Jean-Francois Lyotard's (1984) *The Postmodern Condition*. See also Frederic Jameson (1984).

[8] Myerhoff was—and for this she was admired and loved by her students and colleagues—a great courage-teacher. Her inspiration sustained the morale of people whose work has been increasingly marginalized. There is, nonetheless, a problematic aspect to the profoundly needed repair work she did. Her "moral teachings" and, vitally, her "moral example" were separated from a critique of the institutional practices that were wounding—marginalizing and demoralizing—her professional audiences in the first place. The increase of managerialism in university life, the use of efficiency measures to cost-account the "productivity" of helping professionals, the monopolization and corporate control of communications systems and of production and distribution systems in the arts (i.e., the demise of independent publishing houses and booksellers)—these institutional implementations of the culture of capitalism have come to dominate and, in certain spheres of activity (notably the arts), to dismantle the social space in which an independent scrutiny of society can be offered and a more caring response provided. Macro-forces such as monopolization and managerialist rationalization cut across disciplinary and professional boundaries and have a direct, and often devastating, effect upon the worklife of people in the "liberal" professions, who were Myerhoff's constituency. Cultural hegemony is the affliction for which discourse such as hers seeks to administer

an antidote. However, social knowledge that can, in the long run, prove sustaining must link the legitimation—and even celebration if need be—of marginalized practices with a rigorous critique that inspires sustained opposition to the homogenizing dominant institutional practices and values.

[9] This idea is taken from John Berger's (1980) essay "Giacometti" in *About Looking*.

## REFERENCES


Bakhtin, M. M. (1981). *The dialogic imagination: Four essays* (M. Holquist, Ed.; C. Emerson & M. Holquist, Trans.). Austin: University of Texas Press.

Benjamin, W. (1969). The storyteller. In H. Arendt (Ed.), *Illuminations* (H. Zohn, Trans.). New York: Schocken Press.

Berger, J. (1967). *A fortunate man*. New York: Pantheon.

Berger, J. (1980). *About looking*. New York: Pantheon.

Clifford, J., & Marcus, G. E. (1986). *Writing culture: The poetics and politics of ethnography*. Berkeley: University of California Press.

Geertz, C. (1983). *Local knowledge: Further essays in interpretive anthropology*. New York: Basic Books.

Hareven, T. K. (1982). The life course and aging in historical perspective. In T. K. Hareven & K. J. Adams. (Eds.), *Aging and life course transitions: An interdisciplinary perspective* (pp. 1–26). New York: Guilford Press.

Lyotard, J.-F. (1984). *The postmodern condition*. Minneapolis University of Minnesota Press.

Lifton, R. J. (1967). *Death in life: Survivors of Hiroshima*. New York: Random House.

Jameson, F. (1984). Postmodernism, or the cultural logic of late capitalism. *New Left Review, 146*, 53–92.

Myerhoff, B. (1978). *Number our days*. New York: E. P. Dutton.

Myerhoff, B. (1980a). Life history among the elderly: Performance, visibility, and re-membering. In K. W. Back (Ed.), *Life course: Integrative theories and exemplary populations*. American Association for the Advancement of Science.

Myerhoff, B. (1980b). Telling one's story. *Center Magazine, 13*(2), 22–40.

Myerhoff, B. (1992). In M. Kaminsky (Ed.), *Remembered lives: The work of ritual, storytelling, and growing older*. Ann Arbor: University of Michigan Press.

Ricoeur, P. (1980). Narrative times. In W. J. T. Mitchell (Ed.), *On narrative*. Chicago: University of Chicago Press.

Santner, E. (1990). *Stranded objects: Mourning, memory and film in postwar Germany*. Ithaca, NY: Cornell University Press.

Williams, R. (1961). *The long revolution*. New York: Columbia University Press.

Williams, R. (1986). The uses of cultural theory. *New Left Review, 158*, 19–31.

# *PART IV*
# *Humanistic Gerontology: The State of the Art*

14

# Literary Gerontology Comes of Age

*Anne M. Wyatt-Brown*

Literary critics have been slow to recognize the role that aging plays in the creative process. Of course, some gerontological scholars had already discussed the contributions that literature makes to our understanding of aging, but Kathleen Woodward (1978, 1980a) and Janice Sokoloff (1986, 1987) were the first to argue convincingly that aging is an essential but missing variable in literary criticism itself. Until their studies, the impact of aging on the artist's life and work had been largely ignored by scholars of literature—and still is, according to Woodward (1988). As a result, the relationship between aging and literature has been largely relegated to educators, librarians, and social and behavioral scientists with literary interests.

The few pioneers who, along with Woodward and Sokoloff, were determined to enlighten literary critics and gerontologists alike discovered that they had a daunting task. They had to study gerontological issues and theories, master an unfamiliar social science vocabulary, and attract an interdisciplinary audience capable of responding intelligently and critically to their insights. Needless to say, such an enterprise took time, but a review of current material suggests that sophisticated literary approaches are beginning to appear, a sign that academic legitimacy may be in the offing.

Literary scholars first began to address the subject of aging in a systematic way in 1975, when the Conference on Human Values and Aging took place at Case Western Reserve University in Cleveland. The

This is an adaptation of materials presented in different form in "The Coming of Age of Literary Gerontology," *Journal of Aging Studies*, 4 (1990): 299–315.

papers from the conference include two psychoanalytically informed literary analyses by Leon Edel and Leslie Fiedler. Edel's (1979) study of Goethe, Tolstoy, and Henry James addresses the question of creativity in old age, and Fiedler (1979) analyzes the unconscious strivings of "dirty old men." A third major participant at the conference was Erik Erikson (1979), whose reflections on Bergman's film *Wild Strawberries* provide a successful interdisciplinary model, one that transcends narrow categories. Unfortunately, despite the success of the conference, relatively few scholars followed their example. Indeed the annotated bibliography of Polisar, Wygant, Cole, and Perdomo (1988) identified only 46 essays that are literary in nature, with about 100 more that are peripheral to the field. Of the literary ones, 33 have been written since 1980, with 15 in 1986 alone.

Such a meager scholarly record must mean that until recently few incentives existed to encourage literature specialists to address gerontological issues. For one thing, with the exception of *The Gerontologist,* which published the first qualitative studies in literature (Haynes, 1962; Ricciardelli, 1973), gerontologists have preferred the kinds of quantitative studies unfamiliar to humanists. Thus, it is not surprising that relatively few literary scholars have written on aging except when energetic editors have put together edited volumes (Porter & Porter, 1984; Spicker, Woodward, & Van Tassel, 1978; Van Tassel, 1979; Woodward & Schwartz, 1986). But now that there is a greater interest in qualitative research, more literature scholars have mastered gerontological theory, thereby bridging the gap between the two fields and creating a legitimate subspecialty in literary studies.

The material published so far in literary gerontology can be divided into the following categories. Briefly, they consist of (1) analyses of literary attitudes toward aging; (2) humanistic approaches to literature and aging; (3) psychoanalytic explorations of literary works and their authors; (4) applications of gerontological theories about autobiography, life review, and midlife transitions; and (5) psychoanalytically informed studies of the creative process.

## ATTITUDES TOWARD AGING

The first group of humanists to enter the field addressed the problem of literary attitudes toward old age with particular emphasis on negative stereotyping of the elderly. Studies of fiction for children and adolescents tend to be less interpretive and more statistical in nature (Ansello, 1977; Blue, 1978; Clark, 1980; Peterson & Karnes, 1976). Their chief goal is to determine whether an individual work provides a balanced or distorted view of aging. Although the researchers fear that readers, especially young ones, might develop negative attitudes toward the elderly from what they read, their findings do not support such anxieties. On the whole they report that fiction provides a fairly balanced view of old age.[1] These essays, many of which focus on children's literature, are of particular interest to teacher trainers, classroom teachers, and librarians.

Another group of scholars (Berdes, 1981; Freedman, 1978; Loughman, 1977, 1980; Sohngen, 1975, 1977, 1981; Sohngen & Smith, 1978; Tamke, 1978) had a university audience in mind. The essays by Berdes, Sohngen, and Sohngen and Smith furnish abstracts of many contemporary novels and poems for those who are planning courses (Sohngen, 1978), but their commentaries are extremely short. Inevitably, that constraint has affected the literary value of their work. They have produced "efferent" (instrumental) rather than "aesthetic" readings (those in which the experience of reading itself is primary), to borrow a useful distinction from the literary critic Louise Rosenblatt (1978), and as a result have ignored questions of language, genre, style, and imagery altogether. Sohngen (1975) allows herself an occasional literary insight, particularly in the least statistical essay, but never extends her insights into a close reading of selected texts. A cross-cultural study, *Perceptions of Aging in Literature* (Bagnell & Soper, 1989), is disappointing in that regard as well. The brief essays offer an overview of the literature of nine cultures. Fortunately, the contributors included excerpts from the works they discuss. As a result, the readers can challenge the sometimes superficial analyses.

Loughman's (1977) study of contemporary novels by Kingsley Amis, Muriel Spark, Saul Bellow, and Junichiro Tanizaki also evaluates attitudes toward the aged in fiction. Her goal is to discover common trends in the thinking of contemporary novelists, but she overstates her case. Unquestionably, the four novels provide chilling views of aging. Yet it seems unlikely that "invariably contemporary novels of senescence focus on the inevitable process of degeneration and decay." By the time she wrote her later essay, "Eros and the Elderly" (1980), she had modified her views somewhat, suggesting that literature's "humane and sensitive portrayal" of the later years challenges stereotypes of aging. I would hope that someone as widely read in the field as Sohngen would challenge or validate Loughman's two arguments. Barbara and Allan Lefcowitz's (1984) essay, "Old Age and the Modern Literary Imagination," begins such an effort. Examining selected works from European, Russian, English and American literature, they discover four models of aging: stoical elders with impressive powers of endurance, admirable elders who are contrasted favorably to greedy youths, elders whose plight demonstrates the inadequacy of society's response to aging, and elders whose behavior mirrors social values. At the same time, they ignore certain pertinent issues. They fail to ask how old the authors were when they wrote these novels, what kinds of attitudes about youth and middle age they expressed, and what their social and political attitudes are. Such questions would guard against the temptation of overgeneralizing from limited data.

In contrast, Freedman (1978) starts from a different premise when he argues that literature's "true greatness . . . lies precisely in its ability to face unflinchingly the lowest, least 'humane' instincts of human beings" (p. 50). His approach should interest gerontologists because he has carefully provided the autobiographical context for the gerontophobic material that he collected. For example, he suggests that Swift's hostile portrait of the immortal but aging Struldbruggs in *Gulliver's Travels* reflects the author's personal anxiety about losing his mind in old age, not a reasoned analysis of what extending life would really be like. As a result, Freedman's essay provides a useful model for analyzing negative attitudes toward aging rather than deploring them. There are other examples of equal worth: Tamke's (1978) study of Victorian children's literature, for instance. The essay provides a carefully delineated context for the works in question, thus extending statistics into the realm of literary analysis. Another recent essay, which uses some literary sources to depict attitudes about elderly sexuality in the Middle Ages (Covey, 1989), has aroused a spirited rebuttal (Donow, 1989). Such controversy cannot by itself cause a shift in community attitudes toward the sexual rights of the aged, but debates of this nature may well encourage more medievalists to take an interest in the subject.

## HUMANISTIC GERONTOLOGY

The second category, humanistic gerontology, is best exemplified by the essays in Porter & Porter (1984), Spicker, Woodward, and Van Tassel (1978), and Van Tassel (1979). According to Butler (1984), this approach combines literature with history, religion, philosophy, and the arts. At their best, studies of this type provide a very complex reading of literary texts. Some insightful essays include Bronsen (1978) on the plays of Ibsen and Beckett, Festa-McCormick (1984) on Proust, and Moss (1978) on Turgenev. The risks, however, are that too intense a focus on gerontological issues sometimes overshadows literary questions (Porter, 1984) or results in a distorted reading of the text (Ricciardelli, 1973). Ideally humanistic gerontology should bring new insights into *both* literary and aging studies.

## PSYCHOANALYTIC INTERPRETATIONS OF LITERATURE

The third group, psychoanalytic interpretations of literature, is one that is growing in numbers and refinement. These critics have used a wide variety of analytic approaches, drawing upon Freud, Jung, Erikson, Winnicott, Kohut, and Lacan. The essays in this category, however, can be divided according to the research questions that are asked.

### Evidence of Creativity and Transcendence

The first subdivision consists of essays in which the author provides evidence of enhanced creativity and transcendence in old age. Journals, memoirs, and novels are the primary source materials, and the life-stage theories of Jung, Erikson, and Levinson et al. (Levinson, Darrow, Klein, Levinson, & McKee, 1979) provide most of the interpretations. To cite one instance, Berman (1986) uses ideas from Jung and Levinson et al. (1979) to inform his reading of the journals of Florida Scott-Maxwell, who was herself a Jungian. Analyses of novels by May Sarton and Doris Lessing belong in this category because of the influence of Jung's thoughts on the writers. Two examples include Woodward's (1980b) thoughtful essay on May Sarton's early journals and *As We Are Now*, Sarton's revolutionary novel about life in a nursing home; another is Waxman's (1985) study of two novels by Doris Lessing. Woodward's reading stands up extremely well despite the fact that Sarton has published several works since the essay was written. Furthermore, she legitimately questions Sarton's attitudes when she asks if the writer has espoused the Jungian model "because it refuses a rootedness in a sociohistorical context that she would deny?" (Woodward, 1980b, p. 114). Waxman's (1985) essay on Lessing is less critical; she accepts all of Lessing's attitudes about aging without question. But Lessing's presentation of aging in *The Summer Before the Dark* should not go unchallenged. Instead, Waxman admiringly reports Lessing's conviction that when one of the heroines stops dyeing her hair, she no longer fears death. Of course such a decision can be symbolic of acceptance, but in the absence of psychological evidence of change, Lessing's technique tends to trivialize death anxiety.

Although these studies have value, this particular approach has potential problems. Indeed, there are hazards in applying psychoanalytic theories to literature too programmatically. The important contributions that Erikson and Jung have made to an understanding of human nature evolved from a synthesis of their life experiences, their clinical and theoretical research, and their reading. Furthermore, Erikson has not hesitated to refine his theories of old age in the light of his own experience of aging. Steven Weiland (1989) pointed out that, in *The Life Cycle Completed* (Erikson, 1985), for the first time Erikson has placed old age at the beginning rather than at the end of his famous chart of the life cycle, thereby achieving new insights into the pattern of human life. Six years later Erikson suggested that the psychic lessons of early life are reinterpreted and reintegrated in old age (Goleman, 1988). But each subsequent application of Erikson and Jung, such as in Levinson et al. (1979), reduces these organic theories to a systems analysis. The literary critic, however, must be especially careful not to impose any psychoanalytic theory on literary texts without regard for their particularity.

Second, theories about the male life cycle, be it Erikson's or Levinson's, have only limited value in discussion of the journals of a woman writer. Berman (1986) is generally cautious about which aspects of the life cycle theory he emphasizes, but unfortunately he ignores relevant research into the psychology of women. At no point does he make any reference to Carol Gilligan's (1982) *In a Different Voice*, a study that provides an important new interpretation of women's development. In the future, I would hope that those who write about the lives of women will take account of Gilligan's research as well as that of such psychoanalytic feminist theorists as Nancy Chodorow (1978, 1989) and Jean Baker Miller (1986).

Third, caution is most advisable when the search for signs of creativity in old age is underway. Although Kastenbaum (1973) has wisely predicted that "the better we become as students of creativity, the more creativity we will see" (p. 704), the question is whether truly creative work and creative efforts are distinguishable. In the present enthusiasm for a process method of studying creativity over the older product approach (Kogan, 1973), it is possible that an excessively enthusiastic endorsement of creative efforts might end by cheapening our notion of what constitutes genuine creativity.

Fourth, literary scholars should be aware that humanistic values must embrace more than simple notions of individualism. Unrestrained "self-actualization" can result in blatantly selfish behavior. In a recent interview, Erik Erikson used words like agape, *caritas*, humility, and empathy to describe the culminating values of old age (Goleman, 1988). Although his emphasis was ethical rather than overtly religious, clearly he was discussing a reality that transcends middle-class, individualistic aspirations to find oneself. Like it or not, such wise elders as Erikson (Goleman, 1988) and Kohut (Woodward, 1986a), as well as the middle-aged Kohlberg (1973), have appealed to this higher reality. I would counsel, therefore, even the skeptics among us to take their concerns seriously.

A thorough grounding in historical, cultural, and social matters should inform these Jungian readings as well. Examples of illuminating research include the highly textured, cross-cultural work done on the life cycle by members of the Chicago school, in particular Gutmann (1977, 1980a, 1980b, 1985, 1987), Neugarten (1973, 1977), and Neugarten and Datan (1973). Yet another cross-cultural approach is exemplified by Chinen's (1985, 1986, 1987) perceptive (and charming) essays analyzing the moral and social world of the elder tale. Chinen (1989) has also recently published a book-length version of his work, *In the Ever After: Fairy Tales and the Second Half of Life*. According to him, the elder tales demonstrate the values described by adult psychologists, particularly in the social realm. The elders in the tales are able to emancipate others because they learn to confront and reform their own weaknesses (Chinen, 1985, 1989). All of these approaches provide an important corrective to the modern tendency to value the search for self over responsibility for others.

Another productive way of avoiding cultural relativism is suggested by Hendricks and Leedham (1987). They advise applying the concepts of dependency theory, an economic model describing the interdependency of countries, to an analysis of literature. Using this method one could determine, for instance, who is supporting the individual's search for creativity and ask what price others pay for that person's privacy and withdrawal. Indeed, the writer May Sarton (1984), whose journals record her sometimes relentless search for privacy, admits at moments of insight and humility that her efforts to free herself from the demands of others are not always admirable. But on the whole the Jungian celebration of quest, growth, and change has been so ingrained in the American consciousness that only Moody (1985) has directly challenged its pervasiveness in aging studies.

## Explorations of the Writer's Psyche

Another active group within the psychoanalytic circle consists of those literary critics who use these approaches to explore a writer's psyche over the life span in relation to the problems of aging that appear in the literary work itself. Fortunately, these psychoanalytic theorists are no longer as reductionist as their Freudian predecessors (Eissler, 1978). In recent years a more eclectic approach has emerged. Scholars apply a variety of ideas from Freud, Winnicott, Kohut, and Lacan to literary texts. Unlike the optimistic Jungians, they tend to produce fairly grim pictures of old age. The essays collected in Woodward and Schwartz's (1986) *Memory and Desire*, however, are of such a high caliber that they demand special attention.

For example, Norman Holland (1986) displays a troubling picture of old age in some incidental remarks about the adult life of Little Hans, one of Freud's most famous cases. Holland disputes the assumption of the Jungian school that change implies growth and improvement. He bluntly insists that "We age . . . into parodies of ourselves." He sees old age as decrement because "we spend the last quarter losing the abilities we spent the first three-quarters learning, *but*—and this is the hard part—growing more identity." He concludes somewhat pessimistically that although "identity-growth *uses* the abilities arrived at by the other kind of growth," it is our "ability-growth" that allows us to be ourselves (p. 72). Holland finds the threat of physical decline sufficiently unpleasant that he concludes that Graf (Little Hans) "seems to have been spared the undignified deteriorations of being 'old elderly.'" In consequence, even Holland's declaration that "there is a kind of joy, a final triumph of the self against decay" (p. 73) sounds like a hollow hope. As a partial answer to the despairing undertones of his remarks, one can turn to evidence of late-style development in writers, such as Woodward's (1978, 1980a) sensitive study of four American modernist poets.[2] Nonetheless, one must not overpraise the artistic productions of the elderly. Holland's (1986) belief that we parody ourselves in old age is sometimes reinforced by the later works of once productive writers and artists. At the same time his blunt pessimism can and should be challenged, an exercise that might well enrich our understanding of aging and the creative process.

## The Phenomenology of Aging

Woodward's (1986b) essay on Proust raises another set of troubling questions. In her analysis, she proposes a suggestive hypothesis about the "mirror stage" of old age, one that parodies, to use Holland's (1986) term, Lacan's "mirror stage" of infancy. She points to a crucial scene in Proust's *The Past Recaptured* in which Marcel discovers that he too is old. From this series of incidents she deduces that because the elderly generally avoid their mirror image to evade signs of the ravages of time, they often learn of their change in status from the reactions of others. Freud's account in "The Uncanny," in which he reports the shock of an unexpected glimpse of his mirror image, is offered as further testimony. Woodward suggests that Marcel handles his anxiety by repressing his observation; each of us must decide, she argues, if we will accept this social view of ourselves as accurate or gain our sense of self some other way.

Although Woodward's analysis is impressive, a few mitigating points can be suggested. In the first place, Festa-McCormick (1984) points out that Proust draws a distinction between the artificial and unpleasant aging of the aristocrats and that of Marcel's grandmother, whose inner beauty remains because of her "deep integrity" (p. 113). Second, mirror shock is not merely a problem for old age. In a newspaper comic strip (May 19, 1988), a contemporary heroine, Cathy, is unable to open her eyes to look in the mirror when trying on bathing suits in a store. Of course, her problem is being too fat not too old, but her behavior illustrates that narcissistic injury is not confined to the aged. Third, Susan Sontag (1979) has made a persuasive argument that attitudes toward physical aging are related to the intertwined issues of gender and power. She urges women to improve their sense of competence and self-worth rather than attempting to hold onto a youthful appearance. Perhaps now that more women are achieving positions of power, society will allow them to age without reproach as men have customarily been permitted to do.

Finally, Woodward (1986b) herself speculates whether the limitations of aging might, at least in the case of Proust, heighten his creativity. After all, as she herself points out, he was convinced that creativity and illness are linked. Thomas Mann, for another, also believed that illness can bring about heightened sensitivity and artistic productivity (Kleinschmidt, 1978). There are other examples as well: illness and the shock of aging apparently heightened creativity in old age for at least two other writers, Barbara Pym and Penelope Mortimer (Wyatt-Brown, 1988). Certainly, the question ought to be studied in the lives of other writers in future.

Besides the Woodward and Holland pieces, several other articles represent innovative and important psychoanalytic literary work with implications for gerontologists. One view is fairly negative but impressive. In Ragland-Sullivan's (1986) brilliant Lacanian analysis of *The Portrait of Dorian Gray*, she suggests that Oscar Wilde's homosexuality was translated into the metaphor of aging, a psychic burden equally isolating and unmasterable. In contrast, George (1986) demonstrates that some contemporary women poets have used their creativity to refashion their later lives. According to her readings, these poets have turned to their mothers as a potential source of power and authority, and in order to invoke this power, they use language that is confrontational, angry, tender, unashamed, and naked. Not only do George's findings confirm Gutmann's discovery that women tend to become more assertive and "agentic" in late middleage (Cooper & Gutmann, 1987; Gutmann 1980b, 1985, 1987), but she extends his interpretation. She writes convincingly that women writers use their poetry to forge a relationship with their dead or dying mothers that "partakes of the sacred" (George, 1986, p. 139), even though in traditional cultures only men can be "bridgeheads to the sacred" (Gutmann, 1980a, p. 433; 1987).

Important as these articles are, gerontologists may well find themselves overwhelmed by the amount of unfamiliar psychoanalytic and specialized literary critical concepts and language, a problem that Cohler (1986) mentions in his review of *Memory and Desire* (Woodward & Schwartz, 1986). At the moment, unfortunately, there are two different audiences for literary scholarship on aging and precious little communication between them. The particular psychoanalytic critics mentioned above write for their colleagues in English departments. Woodward is an exception. She has written successfully for both groups, but most of the essayists in *Memory and Desire* are unfamiliar with the work of gerontologists. Still, if literary gerontology has any hope of legitimizing its endeavors, it must build upon their important insights. The essays represent an approach to a theory of the literature about aging. In future it would be desirable if all writers on literature could learn to combine gerontological and literary theories in language that is accessible to all.

Woodward is the author of two other psychoanalytic essays that were not included in Woodward and Schwartz (1986). The first is a suggestive study of Eiseley's *All the Strange Hours*. In it she connects his obsession with evolution to his feelings about aging. The connection contains a paradox. On the one hand, his fascination with the past and the history of evolution was one way of avoiding his fear of aging, disintegration, and death, but at the same time he regarded "his aging and death as the descent down that [evolutionary] ladder" (Woodward, 1982, p. 58). Woodward's second essay (1986a), an analysis of Virginia Woolf's *The Years*, is even more interesting, as well as more difficult. Woodward clarifies the complex and ambivalent interaction of middle-aged and older family members at the end of the novel. She begins by analyzing the confused feelings that one of the middle-aged nephews has about his Aunt Eleanor, the aged protagonist. But when she points out that Eleanor herself ignores her middle-aged nieces and nephews because of her preoccupation with the aesthetic pleasure of observing the young, then the nephew's reactions become more comprehensible. In view of the fact that *The Years* has been long underrated in literary circles, Woodward's sensitive and urbane reading is most welcome. The only point that could possibly be added to her analysis is a biographical detail about Woolf that lends a note of poignancy to that final scene. Woodward (1986a) describes the closing pages, in which the middle-aged cousins are entranced by the tableau temporarily created by the family's omega generation. She says "this portrait, this still life of the elderly has something of the eerie about it: brilliant, it is also tinged with death, with the cadaverous. But for us in the late twentieth century, this image of the elderly must inevitably possess a utopian quality as well" (p. 21). The scene was utopian for the writer as well. Woolf herself grew up in a large family in which sudden death carried off many of her relatives, both elders and her age mates (Wyatt-Brown, 1989b). This final scene represents an act of the imagination triumphing for a moment over the horror of death.

## APPLICATIONS OF GERONTOLOGICAL THEORY LIFE REVIEW AND AUTOBIOGRAPHY

The fourth category focuses on life review, reminiscence, and autobiography. Life review is a term attributed to Butler (1963), who argues in a seminal paper that reminiscence serves an important function in the lives of aging people, even though the recollections might well seem tedious or repetitive. The tendency of older persons to review the past, Butler claims, helps them to face death with equanimity and "participates in the evolution of such characteristics as candor, serenity, and wisdom among certain of the aged" (p. 65). Clearly, his work has aroused an almost inspirational fervor in those who, like Kaminsky (1984), have discovered how naturally elders turn to life review when they are asked to keep journals. Yet Woodward (1986c) has disputed some of Butler's conclusions. In a different spirit she analyzes some of the literary works to which Butler refers and concludes that one cannot create meaning for a life by reliving it imaginatively. Butler's theory, she contends, is based on an outworn Aristotelian idea that lives form a coherent whole. Instead, the modernist and postmodernist nature of the very works to which he refers belie that assumption. No doubt Woodward provides a fresher reading of the Joyce Cary novel, the Henry James story, and the Beckett play than does the psychiatrist Butler. But his point is more valid than Woodward concedes. After all, real lives, unlike postmodern novels, have their psychic coherence. They can display the Aristotelian characteristics of a beginning, middle, and end. Postmodernists may justly question our ability to find genuine meaning or provide a sense of psychological closure at all times, but even they cannot dispute all of Butler's clinical findings.

In fact, there are recent literary corroborations of the life-review theory. Zavatsky (1984), for instance, indirectly validates Butler's position. His findings also challenge Woodward's criticism of Butler's ideas as too subjective and romantic. In his study of William Carlos Williams, the American physician and poet, Zavatsky suggests that life review is almost always triggered by someone else because it fulfills the needs of both the asker of the questions and the elder answering them. In his moving account of the way in which Williams encouraged his mother's stories, Zavatsky shows how both parties were helped by the process. Not only did Williams create a memorial for his mother by writing his account of her life review, but his later poetry was enriched by the enterprise (Zavatsky, 1984).

Three other essays lend support to Butler's theory of the life review. In the first, Nicholl (1984–85) analyzes five short stories about dying characters, the plots of which, she claims, demonstrate the validity of both Elisabeth Kübler-Ross's stages of dying and Butler's theory of life review. In a moving reconstruction of these plots, Nicholl suggests that the final reveries of each character confirm Butler's finding that the outcome of the review can be either "psychologically positive or self-destructive" (p. 95).

In the second essay, Salvatori (1987) has made a thoughtful study of the way in which life review transforms mourning in two cycles of poems by Thomas Hardy and Eugenio Montale. Salvatori is one of the few scholars who, like Woodward, manages to combine a thorough knowledge of literary and gerontological theory, a feat that is rarer than it ought to be. Salvatori argues convincingly that both poets in different ways use their recollections of the fragments of experience to reestablish a sense of the continuity of their relationship with their dead wives. Her sensitive exploration describes a process of creation that is not unlike the one Kaminsky (1984) undertook when he turned fragments from individuals' journals into a more coherent story of their past.

Finally, Constance Rooke (1988) addresses Woodward's criticisms of Butler's theory of life review in her impressive essay on Margaret Laurence's *Stone Angel*. Rooke coins the term *Vollendungsroman*, which stands for a "novel of . . . 'completion' or 'winding up'" (p. 34). She declares that life review is "perhaps the most common form" of that genre (p. 37), because it offers characters an opportunity for psychic growth even as they face death. However, she argues that Laurence's novel avoids creating an overly determined sense of closure—the kind of ending that Woodward felt Butler was endorsing. Instead, "it seizes upon the open ending and upon filaments launched into the future; it discovers hope paradoxically, through recognition of failure" (p. 40). All of these studies make clear that reclaiming and redeeming the past does not necessarily force the novelist or scholar into oversimplifying life experiences. The work begun in this area ought to be encouraged.

## Autobiography and the Creative Process Over the Life Span

The overarching question of finding meaning in one's life is approached in yet another group of essays, which explore the autobiographical elements of fiction, particularly in relationship to the creative process over the life span. Taken as a group, these studies have provided some of the most interesting theoretical explorations to date. For example, Carolyn H. Smith (1989) shows how Richard Eberhart's poetry reveals his "'cognitive plasticity'" (p. 76) in old age. She argues that from an early age Eberhart developed a precocious interest in this aging relatives and acquaintances. From their brave integrity he garnered a positive view of the possibilities of old age, an attitude that has stood him in good stead in his later years.

Several literary scholars have begun to demonstrate the truth of Neugarten's (1973) contention that one can predict the nature of one's aging from behavior at midlife. They are beginning to focus attention on transitions in midlife creativity in order to look at the creative life span as a whole. Bertram Wyatt-Brown (1989) shows how depression increased Walker Percy's fictional creativity in his midlife. Wyatt-Brown suggests that because so many members of the Percy clan committed suicide, Percy turned to fiction as a safe arena for writing about the family tragedies that helped trigger his own depression. According to Wyatt-Brown, Percy's strategy was so successful that his later work lacks the tension and richness of the novels of his middle age (for example, Percy avoided the problems of aging altogether by writing about protagonists far younger than himself). Wyatt-Brown comes perilously close to wishing that Percy's old age had been less serene so that his novels would provide a more interesting example of late style.

The whole question of late style in art, literature, and music was first elaborated by the psychoanalyst Elliott Jaques (1965), whose seminal essay on midlife crisis and creativity concentrated exclusively on the lives of male artists. He argues that men face the reality of death for the first time in their late 30s, and for some that discovery marks the end of their work. Those who can recover from the shock, however, experience dramatic changes in their style and write or paint in a more careful, sculpted fashion. No one would wish to quarrel with the importance of Jaques's contribution to our understanding of creativity, but the work of more recent scholars suggests essential modifications of his insights. For example, Gutmann (1980b) argues that even though Jaques's description was "the most sophisticated psychoanalytic statement on the aging process," it contributed to a generally "catastrophic view of aging" (pp. 489–490).

Further, one can complain that Jaques's (1965) focus on male artists is one-sided. If Carol Gilligan (1982) is correct about the different psychological development of men and women, then it is possible that creative women, as Carolyn Heilbrun (1988) suggests, may experience this midlife transition in different ways. For example, it seems likely that the career of Anita Brookner demonstrates that women's lives modify the patterns described by Jaques (Wyatt-Brown, 1989a). For one thing, Brookner's reaction to the crisis of mortality came later in her life than 37, the age Jaques had identified as crucial to male development. Second, her reaction was not to alter her existing style but to branch out into a new realm of creativity in a most exciting way. By producing a series of novels in her 50s, Brookner has illustrated Gutmann's (1985) description of agentic women at midlife. Moreover, a recent novel, *Latecomers* (1988), provides a breakthrough of a slightly different sort. For the first time the novelist writes movingly about the sustaining friendship of two middle-aged males, rather than bemoaning the fate of female victims, the subjects of her first seven novels. Eleven novels in eleven years seems an admirable outcome for a midlife crisis.

Margaret Gullette's (1988) study of the midlife progress novel, *Safe at Last*, implicitly challenges the pessimistic overtones of Jaques's (1965) study. Her analysis of the "life-course fiction" of Saul Bellow, Margaret Drabble, Anne Tyler, and John Updike suggests that middle age can be a period of renewal of hope and an affirmation of life's possibilities, rather than a last creative gasp or a portrait of the artist's declining years. Her point is that "aging is a cultural construction" and that there have been at least "two ideologies of aging," one a story of decline and the other of progress (M. M. Gullette, personal communication, June 9, 1989). The final chapter of her book argues eloquently for the importance of a fiction of amelioration. She insists that pessimism does not necessarily provide a more accurate view of the human condition than does the informed optimism of her chosen subjects.

Of course, eloquent though Gullette may be, she will not have the final word in this debate. Kathleen Woodward's forthcoming book, *Aging and Its Discontents: Freud and Other Fictions* (in press), will provide an equally eloquent account of the losses of aging that are not remedial. Woodward focuses on the narcissistic injury that aging people often experience and relates this sense of loss to a rich body of literature (Wyatt-Brown, in press). Her focus and conclusions are quite different from Gullette's, indicating that at last literary gerontologists are beginning to contribute to the debate about the phenomenological nature of aging in the modern world. Scholars, like writers, have their own perceptions and views of reality. It is hardly surprising that these two talented scholars do not agree.

## CONCLUSION

Despite the many categories that exist, some topics have not been adequately covered. Only one short study of aging blacks in fiction exists

(Deck, 1985), and few scholars employ a feminist perspective (George, 1986). Further, the choice of topics suggests that many critics assume that Americans and Britons are the sole writers of English. This ethnocentrism should be challenged by analyses of the novels of Margaret Atwood, Elizabeth Jolley, V. S. Naipaul, Shiva Naipaul, R. K. Narayan, and Chinua Achebe, among others. Of course, we look forward to further contributions to the questions Gullette and Woodward have raised, as well as to studies that shed light on the creative process. In this regard the work of the British psychoanalyst Anthony Storr (1972, 1988a, 1988b) will be especially helpful. His eclectic Jungian approach makes him especially responsive to the plight of gifted depressives, who, like Walker Percy, have used their creative talents as a way of mastering their sense of isolation and unhappiness. Further work that combines psychoanalytic insights with an exploration of the creative process over the life span would be especially useful.

Even though one could wish for an even greater development of new areas of interest, as well as the extension of established approaches, it is apparent that literary gerontology is soon to become an important academic subject. Not only can we expect more studies of writers and their work, but our standards of judgment will surely become more demanding. As Steven Weiland (1989) has suggested in his intelligent analysis of the way in which aging has been treated in some recent biographies, we need to encourage "methodological pluralism" (p. 194). With an influx of well-trained literary scholars, in time the field of literary gerontology will grow. To gain recognition, we must present our findings to literary as well as gerontological audiences so that mainstream literary scholars will find it impossible to continue to ignore the dimension of age in their analysis of texts, a phenomenon Woodward (1988) so eloquently deplored. After all, Carolyn Smith and Constance Rooke's chapters in this volume suggest that in recent years novelists and poets have made aging a major theme. It is time that the literary establishment recognizes its cogency. We need also to increase the number of courses that combine literature with gerontological theory. Although superficially a crude measurement, an increased visibility would be a sign that literary gerontology has finally come of age.

## NOTES

[1] In contrast to children's literature, poetry and American sheet music reveal more negative pictures of aging (Cohen & Kruschwitz, 1990, Sohngen & Smith, 1978).

[2] Woodward's description of T. S. Eliot's later years, however, seems unnecessarily gloomy. Although she accurately suggests that in the poetry of

his middle age he "imposes a dark vision of old age on his middle years" (Woodward, 1980a, p. 56), his friends all agreed that his old age was notable for its unexpected serenity. His last play, although flawed, contains "tender love scenes" unique in his writing (Ackroyd, 1984, p. 323).

## REFERENCES


Ackroyd, P. (1984). *T. S. Eliot: A life*. New York: Simon & Schuster.

Ansello, E. F. (1977). Old-age and literature: An overview. *Educational Gerontology, 2,* 211–218.

Bagnell, P. V. D., & Soper, P. (1989). *Perceptions of aging in literature: A cross-cultural study*. New York: Greenwood Press.

Berdes, C. (1981). Winter tales: Fiction about aging. *Gerontologist, 21,* 121–125.

Berman, H. J. (1986). To flame with a wild life: Florida Scott-Maxwell's experience of old age. *Gerontologist, 26,* 321–324.

Blue G. F. (1978). The aging as portrayed in realistic fiction for children 1945–1975. *Gerontologist, 18,* 187–192.

Bronsen, D. (1978). Consuming struggle vs. killing time: Preludes to dying in the dramas of Ibsen and Beckett. In S. F. Spicker, K. M. Woodward, & D. D. Van Tassel (Eds.), *Aging and the elderly: Humanistic perspectives in gerontology* (pp. 261–281). Atlantic Highlands, NJ: Humanities Press.

Brookner, A. (1988). *Latecomers*. New York: Pantheon Books.

Butler, R. N. (1963). The life review: An interpretation of reminiscence in the aged. *Psychiatry: Journal for the Study of Interpersonal Processes, 26,* 65–76.

Butler, R. N. (1984). Foreword. In L. Porter & L. M. Porter (Eds.), *Aging in Literature* (pp. ix–xii). Troy, MI: International Book Publishers.

Chinen, A. B. (1985). Fairy tales and transpersonal development in later life. *The Journal of Transpersonal Psychology, 17,* 99–122.

Chinen, A. B. (1986). Elder tales revisited: Forms of transcendence in later life. *The Journal of Transpersonal Psychology, 18,* 171–192.

Chinen, A. B. (1987). Fairy tales and psychological development in late life: A cross-cultural hermeneutic study. *Gerontologist, 27,* 340–346.

Chinen, A. B. (1989). *In the ever after: Fairy tales and the second half of life.* Wilmette, IL: Chiron.

Chodorow, N. (1978). *The reproduction of mothering: Psychoanalysis and the sociology of gender*. Berkeley: University of California Press.

Chodorow, N. J. (1989). *Feminism and psychoanalytic theory*. New Haven, CT: Yale University Press.

Clark, M. (1980). The poetry of aging: Views of old age in contemporary American poetry. *Gerontologist, 20,* 188–191.

Cohen, E. S., & Kruschwitz, A. L. (1990). Old age in America represented in nineteenth and twentieth century popular sheet music. *Gerontologist, 30,* 345–354.

Cohler, B. J. (1986). Reconciling aging and desire. [Review of *Memory and desire: Aging—literature—psychoanalysis*]. *Readings: A Journal of Review, 1,* 28–33.

Cooper, K. L., & Gutmann, D. L. (1987). Gender identity and ego mastery style in middle-aged, pre- and post-empty nest women. *Gerontologist, 27,* 347–352.

Covey, H. C. (1989). Perceptions and attitudes toward sexuality of the elderly during the Middle Ages. *Gerontologist, 29,* 93–100.

Deck, A. A. (1985). Depictions of elderly blacks in American literature. *Explorations in Ethnic Studies, 8,* 15–33.

Donow, H. S. (1989). Sexuality in Chaucer. *Gerontologist, 29,* 416–417.

Edel, L. (1979). Portrait of the artist as an old man. In D. D. Van Tassel (Ed.), *Aging, death and the completion of being* (pp. 193–214). Philadelphia: University of Pennsylvania Press.

Eissler K. R. (1978). Remarks on an aspect of creativity. *American Imago, 35,* 59–76.

Erikson, E. H. (1979). Reflections on Dr. Borg's life cycle. In D. D. Van Tassel (Ed.), *Aging, death and the completion of being* (pp. 29–67). Philadelphia: University of Pennsylvania Press.

Erikson, E. H. (1985). *The life cycle completed: A review.* New York: Norton.

Festa-McCormick, D. (1984). Proustian old age, or the key to time recaptured. In L. Porter & L. M. Porter (Eds), *Aging in literature* (pp. 105–113). Troy, MI: International Book Publishers.

Fiedler, L. A. (1979). Eros and Thanatos: Old age in love. In D. D. Van Tassel (Ed.), *Aging, death and the completion of being* (pp. 235–254). Philadelphia: University of Pennsylvania Press.

Freedman, R. (1978). Sufficiently decayed: Gerontophobia in English literature. In S. F. Spicker, K. M. Woodward, & D. D. Van Tassel (Eds.), *Aging and the elderly: Humanistic perspectives in gerontology* (pp. 49–61). Atlantic Highlands, NJ: Humanities Press.

George, D. H. (1986). "Who is the double ghost whose head is smoke?" Women poets on aging. In K. Woodward & M. M. Schwartz (Eds.), *Memory and desire: Aging—literature—psychoanalysis* (pp. 134–153). Bloomington: Indiana University Press.

Gilligan, C. (1982). *In a different voice: Psychological theory and women's development.* Cambridge, MA: Harvard University Press.

Goleman, D. (1988, June 14). Erikson, in his own old age, expands his view of life. *New York Times,* National edition, pp. 13, 16.

Gullette, M. M. (1988). *Safe at last in the middle years: The invention of the midlife progress novel.* Berkeley, CA: University of California Press.

Gutmann, D. (1977). The cross-cultural perspective: Notes toward a comparative psychology of aging. In J. Birren & K. W. Schaie (Eds.), *Handbook of the psychology of aging* (pp. 302–326). New York: Van Nostrand Reinhold.

Gutmann, D. (1980a). Observations on culture and mental health in later life. In J. E. Birren & R. B. Sloane (Eds.), *Handbook of mental health and aging* (pp. 429–447). Englewood Cliffs, NJ: Prentice-Hall.

Gutmann, D. L. (1980b). Psychoanalysis and aging: A developmental view. In S. I. Greenspan & G. H. Pollock (Eds.), *The course of life: Psychoanalytic contributions toward understanding personality development: Vol. 3. Adulthood and the aging process* (pp. 489–517). Adelphi, MD: National Institute of Mental Health, Department of Health and Human Services.

Gutmann, D. L. (1985). The parental imperative revisited: Towards a developmental psychology of adulthood and later life. In J. A. Meacham (Ed.), *Contributions to human development: Vol. 14. Family and individual development* (pp. 31–60). Basel: Karger.

Gutmann, D. (1987). *Reclaimed powers: Toward a new psychology of men and women in later life.* New York: Basic Books.

Haynes, M. S. (1962). The supposedly golden age for the aged in ancient Rome (a study of literary concepts of old age). *Gerontologist, 2,* 93–98.

Heilbrun, C. (1988). *Writing a woman's life.* New York: Norton.

Hendricks, J., & Leedham, C. A. (1987). Making sense of literary aging: Relevance of recent gerontological theory. *Journal of Aging Studies, 1,* 187–208.

Holland, N. N. (1986). Not so little Hans: Identity and aging. In K. Woodward & M. M. Schwartz (Eds.), *Memory and desire: Aging—literature—psychoanalysis* (pp. 51–75). Bloomington: Indiana University Press.

Jaques, E. (1965). Death and the mid-life crisis. *International Journal of Psychoanalysis, 46,* 502–514.

Kaminsky, M. (1984). Transfiguring life: Images of continuity hidden among the fragments. In M. Kaminsky (Ed.), *The uses of reminiscence: New ways of working with older adults* (pp. 3–18). New York: Haworth Press.

Kastenbaum, R. J. (1973). Loving, dying, and other gerontologic addenda. In C. Eisdorfer & M. P. Lawton (Eds.), *The psychology of adult development and aging* (pp. 699–708). Washington, DC: American Psychological Association.

Kleinschmidt, H. (1978). *American Imago* on psychoanalysis, art, and creativity: 1964–1976. *American Imago, 35,* 45–58.

Kogan, N. (1973). Creativity and cognitive style: A life-span perspective. In P. B. Baltes & K. W. Schaie (Eds.), *Life-span developmental psychology: Personality and socialization* (pp. 145–178). New York: Academic Press.

Kohlberg, L. (1973). Continuities in childhood and adult moral development revisited. In P. B. Baltes & K. W. Schaie (Eds.), *Life-span developmental psychology: Personality and socialization* (pp. 179–204). New York: Academic Press.

Lefcowitz, B., & Lefcowitz, A. (1984). Old age and the modern literary imagination. In L. Porter & L. M. Porter (Eds.), *Aging in literature* (pp. 129–148). Troy, MI: International Book Publishers.

Levinson, D. J., Darrow, C. N., Klein, E. B., Levinson, M. H., & McKee, B. (1979). *The seasons of a man's life..* New York: Knopf.

Loughman, C. (1977). Novels of senescence: A new naturalism. *Gerontologist, 17,* 79–84.

Loughman, C. (1980). Eros and the elderly: A literary view. *Gerontologist, 20,* 182–187.

Miller, J. B. (1986). *Toward a new psychology of women* (2nd ed.). Boston: Beacon Press.

Moody, H. R. (1985). Review essay: Late life creativity & wisdom. *Gerontologist, 25,* 95–98.

Moss, W. G. (1978). Why the anxious fear? Aging and death in the works of Turgenev. In S. F. Spicker, K. M. Woodward, & D. D. Van Tassel (Eds.), *Aging and the elderly: Humanistic perspectives in gerontology* (pp. 241–260). Atlantic Highlands, NJ: Humanities Press.

Neugarten, B. L. (1973). Personality change in late life: A developmental perspective. In C. Eisdorfer & M. P. Lawton (Eds.), *The psychology of adult behavior and aging* (pp. 311–335). Washington, DC: American Psychological Association.

Neugarten, B. L. (1977). Personality and aging. In J. E. Birren & K. W. Schaie (Eds.), *Handbook of the psychology of aging* (pp. 626–649). New York: Van Nostrand Reinhold.

Neugarten, B. L., & Datan, N. (1973). Sociological perspectives on the life cycle. In P. B. Baltes & K. W. Schaie (Eds.), *Life-span developmental psychology: Personality and socialization* (pp. 53–69). New York: Academic Press.

Nicholl, G. (1984–1985). The life review in five short stories about characters facing death. *Omega, 15,* 85–96.

Peterson, D. A., & Karnes, E. L. (1976). Older people in adolescent literature. *Gerontologist, 16,* 225–231.

Polisar, D. Wygant, L., Cole, T., & Perdomo, C. (Eds.). (1988). *Where do we come from? What are we? Where are we going? An annotated bibliography of aging and the humanities.* Washington, DC: Gerontological Society of America.

Porter, L. (1984). *King Lear* and the crisis of retirement. In L. Porter & L. M. Porter (Eds.), *Aging in literature* (pp. 59–71). Troy, MI: International Book Publishers.

Porter, L., & Porter, L. M. (Eds.). (1984). *Aging in literature.* Troy, MI: International Book Publishers.

Ragland-Sullivan, E. (1986). The phenomenon of aging in Oscar Wilde's *Picture of Dorian Gray*: A Lacanian view. In K. Woodward & M. M. Schwartz (Eds.), *Memory and desire: Aging—literature—psychoanalysis* (pp. 114–133). Bloomington: Indiana University Press.

Ricciardelli, R. M. (1973). King Lear and the theory of disengagement. *Gerontologist, 13,* 148–152.

Rooke, C. (1988). Hagar's old age: *The stone angel as* Vollendungsroman. In K. Gunnars (Ed.), *Crossing the river: Essays in honour of Margaret Laurence* (pp. 25–42). Winnipeg, Manitoba: Turnstone Press.

Rosenblatt, L. M. (1978). *The reader the text the poem: The transactional theory of the literary work.* Carbondale, IL: Southern Illinois University Press.

Salvatori, M. (1987). Thomas Hardy and Eugenio Montale: In mourning and in celebration. *Journal of Aging Studies, 1,* 161–185.

Sarton, M. (1984). *At seventy: A journal.* New York: Norton.

Smith, C. H. (1989). Richard Eberhart's poems on aging. *Journal of Aging Studies, 3,* 75–80.

Sohngen, M. (1975). The writer as an old woman. *Gerontologist, 15,* 493–498.

Sohngen, M. (1977). The experience of old age as depicted in contemporary novels. *Gerontologist, 17,* 70–78.

Sohngen, M. (1978). Humanistic approaches to gerontological education in the colleges. *Gerontologist, 18,* 577–578.

Sohngen, M. (1981). The experience of old age as depicted in contemporary novels: A supplementary bibliography. *Gerontologist, 21,* 303.

Sohngen, M., & Smith, R. J. (1978). Images of old age in poetry. *Gerontologist, 18,* 181–186.

Sokoloff, J. M. (1986). Character and aging in *Moll Flanders. Gerontologist, 26,* 681–685.

Sokoloff, J. (1987). *The margin that remains: A study of aging in literature* (American University Studies, Series 4, English Language and Literature, Vol. 37). New York: Peter Lang.

Sontag, S. (1979). The double standard of aging. In J. H. Williams (Ed.), *Psychology of women: Selected readings* (pp. 462–478). New York: Norton.

Spicker, S. F., Woodward, K. M., & Van Tassel, D. D. (Eds.). (1978). *Aging and the elderly: Humanistic perspectives in gerontology.* Atlantic Highlands, NJ: Humanities Press.

Storr, A. (1972). *The dynamics of creation.* New York: Atheneum.

Storr, A. (1988a). *Churchill's black dog, Kafka's mice, and other phenomena of the human mind.* New York: Grove Press.

Storr, A. (1988b). *Solitude: A return to the self.* New York: Ballantine Books.

Tamke, S. S. (1978). Human values and aging: The perspective of the Victorian nursery. In S. F. Spicker, K. M. Woodward, & D. D. Van Tassel (Eds.), *Aging and the elderly: Humanistic perspectives in gerontology* (pp. 63–81). Atlantic Highlands, NJ: Humanities Press.

Van Tassel, D. D. (Ed.). (1979). *Aging, death, and the completion of being.* Philadelphia: University of Pennsylvania Press.

Waxman, B. F. (1985). From *Bildungsroman* to *Reifungsroman*: Aging in Doris Lessing's fiction. *Soundings, 68,* 318–334.

Weiland, S. (1989). Aging according to biography. *Gerontologist, 29,* 191–194.

Woodward, K. M. (1978). Master songs of meditation: The late poems of Eliot, Pound, Stevens, and Williams. In S. F. Spicker, K. M. Woodward, & D. D. Van Tassel (Eds.), *Aging and the elderly: Humanistic perspectives in gerontology* (pp. 181–202). Atlantic Highlands, NJ: Humanities Press.

Woodward, K. (1980a). *At last, the real distinguished thing: The late poems of Eliot, Pound, Stevens, and Williams.* Columbus: Ohio State University Press.

Woodward, K. (1980b). May Sarton and fictions of old age. In J. Todd (Ed.), *Gender and literary voice* (pp. 108–127) (Women and Literature, NS 1). New York: Holmes and Meier.

Woodward, K. (1982). The uncanny and the running man: Aging and Loren Eiseley's *All the strange hours. Southern Humanities Review, 16,* 47–60.

Woodward, K. (1986a). *The look and the gaze: Narcissism, aggression, and aging* (Working paper No. 7). The University of Wisconsin–Milwaukee Center for Twentieth Century Studies.

Woodward, K. (1986b). The mirror stage of old age. In K. Woodward & M. M. Schwartz (Eds.), *Memory and desire: Aging—literature—psychoanalysis* (pp. 97–113). Bloomington: Indiana University Press.

Woodward, K. (1986c). Reminiscence and the life review: Prospects and retrospects. In T. R. Cole & S. A. Gadow (Eds.), *What does it mean to grow old?*

*Reflections from the humanities* (pp. 137–161). Durham, NC: Duke University Press.

Woodward, K. (1988). Simone de Beauvoir: Aging and its discontents. In S. Benstock (Ed.), *The private self: Theory and practice of women's autobiographical writings* (pp. 90–113). Chapel Hill: University of North Carolina Press.

Woodward, K. (1991). *Aging and its discontents: Freud and other fictions.* Bloomington: Indiana University Press.

Woodward, K., & Schwartz, M. M. (Eds.). (1986). *Memory and desire: Aging—literature—psychoanalysis.* Bloomington: Indiana University Press.

Wyatt-Brown, A. M. (1988). Late style in the novels of Barbara Pym and Penelope Mortimer. *Gerontologist, 6,* 835–839.

Wyatt-Brown, A. M. (1989a). Creativity in midlife: The novels of Anita Brookner. *Journal of Aging Studies, 3,* 177–183.

Wyatt-Brown, A. M. (1989b). The narrative imperative: Fiction and the aging writer. *Journal of Aging Studies, 3,* 55–65.

Wyatt-Brown, B. (1989). Walker Percy: Autobiographical fiction and the aging process. *Journal of Aging Studies, 3,* 81–89.

Wyatt-Brown, A. M. (1992). Review of K. Woodward, *Aging and its discontents: Freud and other fictions. Medical Humanities Review, 6*(1).

Zavatsky, B. (1984). Journey through the feminine: The life review poems of William Carlos Williams. In M. Kaminsky (Ed.), *The uses of reminiscence: New ways of working with older adults* (pp. 167–191). New York: Haworth Press.

15

# Aging in America: The Perspective of History

*Carole Haber and Brian Gratton*

---

Until the mid-1970s, historians expressed little interest in the study of old age. Historical studies, even those produced by the "new" social historians, focused almost entirely upon the activities of the young and the middle-aged. The experiences of older people, in contrast, seemed to contribute little to our understanding of history. Despite (or perhaps because of) the dearth of scholarship, few gerontologists questioned whether we possessed a clear understanding about the roles and behavior of the old in past societies. Lacking a historical perspective, scholars interested in aging relied upon a broad sociological model for an explanation of the treatment of the elderly before the present century. In many textbooks on aging, this history was summed up in a cursory section early in the first chapter. Relying on an ill-defined past, the texts explained that the old had once reigned as the most valuable members of the community. They held complete power in their families, ruled unchallenged over councils of government, and prescribed social values through their religious and cultural authority. Then, the texts continued, a radical transformation occurred. The status of the old fell sharply; they became outcasts in societies that celebrated youth and vitality (Burgess, 1960; Crandall, 1980; Holmes, 1976; Roscow, 1974).

To explain the assumed shift, gerontologists and sociologists depended largely upon modernization theory (Clark & Anderson, 1967; Cowgill & Holmes, 1972; Simmons, 1945). According to this thesis, the once high status of elderly males was based on four basic and seemingly obvious factors. First, modernization advocates posited that aged members of society had once retained great authority through their unquestioned and irrefutable role as patriarchs of extended families. Second, such aged individuals were assumed to have controlled land and resources that assured the continued respect and dependence of their kin. Third, in preindustrial societies, elderly workers were believed to have been subject to few laws dictating their retirement from employment or withdrawal from society. And, fourth, as repositories of needed knowledge and skills, the elderly were presumed to have played essential and irreplaceable roles in their communities.

All of this changed, according to modernization theorists, with the advent of industrialization and urbanization. In the factory and the office, the old neither controlled the young nor retained economic independence. Furthermore, the demographic changes that led to the modern family meant the end of their patriarchal power. Now members of limited nuclear families, they spent their final years in the "empty nest," apart from their grown children. Finally, professionalization and the growth of literacy made the skills of the old seem useless and outdated. With urban and industrial growth, modernization theorists concluded, the status of the old had sharply declined; they became useless and irrelevant in modern society (Achenbaum & Stearns, 1978).

In many gerontological textbooks, a related historical assumption often accompanied this "great transformation" model. Several scholars argued that the present-day old have no relevant past. According to that thesis, the current conditions of the elderly, based on events of the post-Depression era, bear little resemblance to the lives of the old in other centuries. In part, this assumption was drawn from the historical narrative sketched by modernization theorists. If the agrarian elderly of a century or two ago were uniformly respected, their past experience bore little relationship to the problems of today's aged population.

The assertion of the unique nature of the experiences of the present-day elderly was based on an additional belief. Gerontologists seemed to assume that, prior to recent times, the old were not only too secure but too rare to attract much concern. As the author of one recent college-level text stated, "In the past, the aged received little attention from writers, poets, philosophers, or scientists because they were so few in number" (Crandall, 1980, p. 25). As a result, contemporary old-age policies have been said to possess few meaningful antecedents. In much of the current gerontological literature, issues such as nursing homes, pension plans, and geriatric medicine are discussed as if they were born full grown, the sole result of extremely recent demographic and economic realities.

In the past 10 years, a small group of scholars has begun to examine historical theories in gerontology and to challenge assumptions basic to the field. Their research, as we shall see, has evolved in terms of both subject and approach. At first, historians generally focused upon the culture of growing old. Major questions revolved around attitudes toward old age, the growth of negative beliefs about senescence and the factors that led to such fatalistic sentiments. Central to the research was the existence of a colonial gerontocracy. Had the elderly ever ruled as the most powerful members of society? And, if so, when and why had they fallen from such exalted heights?

In formulating these questions, historians generally assumed that by the early 20th century, old age had become an economically and socially disadvantaged stage of existence. According to turn-of-the-century experts on aging, the future of the once powerful and respected old had become increasingly dim. In the modern world, the elderly no longer had a vital role to play in their families or in the productive world. In the second phase of historical inquiry, then, scholars began to focus upon this pessimistic evaluation of the social and economic status of old age. Turning from broad questions of culture, historians explored the actual work, family, and residence patterns of the elderly. The conclusions, as we shall see, often differed sharply from the assertions of contemporary experts. Not only were a majority of the old not doomed by the forces of modernization, but their lives were hardly uniform; their advanced ages alone did not determine the nature of their existences. Rather, their relationships with the children, as well as the structure of their work and even the meaning of their last years, varied greatly depending on their race, religion, ethnicity, region, class, and gender.

This critical reassessment of the lives of the old led historians into a third phase of research. If the depiction of the old as completely diseased and dependent was not entirely valid, then the establishment of programs to assist the old were not easily explained. Welfare programs could not be seen simply as a reaction to growing poverty; institutions did not serve only to shelter large numbers of isolated elders. Rather, historians came to debate the motivations, expectations, and outcomes of policies and programs that affected the lives of the old and social expectations about senescence.

In this essay, we shall trace the evolution of the historical inquiry into old age and focus upon key issues in the literature that have led to considerable debate. Such controversy is, in a sense, ironic. Before in-depth historical research was published, growing old in the past could be presented in broad and clear strokes: the once venerated position of the old had eroded with the advent of the modern era. The old had little hope of retaining power or respect in the urban-industrial world. Current work has clearly complicated the narrative; the outlines of the new history are no longer so indisputable or precise.

## THE FIRST PHASE OF INQUIRY

Scholars have long had reason to question at least part of the modernization thesis. Work in the family history of both 17th-century England and colonial America demonstrated the fallacy of the belief that the old had once gained respect through dominance over large kinship groups. As John Demos (1970), Peter Laslett, (1972, 1977), and Lawrence Stone (1977a) have shown, the family of the 17th century was largely nuclear in structure. For the most part, only two generations—parents and unmarried children—resided together. In England and Wales, from the late 16th century until the first decade of the 20th century, English and Welsh households contained, on average, only about 4.75 persons (Laslett, 1972). In Western Europe, at least, there existed few aging patriarchs whose power rested on co-residence with numerous generations of kin.

Beginning in the late 1970s, new historical research, directed specifically to aging, then added additional challenges to modernization theory. Advocates of modernization had tied respect of the old firmly to the agrarian economies and linked decline in status to the advent of urban and industrial change. In the first major study of the history of aging, David Hackett Fischer (1977) directly attacked this assumption. In *Growing Old in America,* Fischer argued that modernization had little direct effect upon the old. Rather, the key to understanding status lay in changing cultural beliefs—ones that well preceded the processes of urban and industrial change. According to Fischer, religion, political theory, and philosophy, far more that economics, determined the nature and timing of the elderly's loss of position.

Despite Fischer's (1977) sharp disagreement with the modernization thesis, his study did not completely depart from the traditional model. According to the author, a time did indeed occur when the elderly comprised the most powerful group in society. During the colonial period, Fischer contended, a gerontocracy had clearly existed; the old, rather than the young or middle-aged, established social roles and behaviors. All of this changed, however, in the decades between 1770 and 1820. With the revolutionary generation, the elderly were removed from positions of authority. In place of deference toward the old, a new cultural paradigm was born. America presented itself to the world as a young republic founded on revolutionary ideas of liberty and equality. With all people free and equal, little reason could be found to conform to the hierarchy of age.

The first question posed by subsequent historians of aging rested on the very existence of the hierarchy of age. Fischer (1977) had argued that a firmly established gerontocracy existed in early America; the old, without challenge, controlled the young of the community. Was there ever, in fact, a number of historians asked, a time when old age was celebrated as the most glorious and powerful stage of existence?

The answer they developed was ambiguous; even in the colonial period, great variation appeared in society's treatment of elderly persons. In his article, "Old Age in Early New England," John Demos (1978) argued that many of the elderly, in fact, did command great respect. Yet Demos asserted that such high status generally arose not out of cultural prescriptions for deference but as a result of specific economic and demographic factors. As Philip Greven (1970) and John J. Waters (1976) demonstrated, in early America fathers generally held onto their estates—and the respect of their offspring—until their deaths. In their refusal to deed their land to their kin, they guaranteed their exalted position.

Demos (1978) concluded, however, that in early New England, old age was not always a time of honor and privilege. Even in the 17th century, senescence was often portrayed in harsh and unrelenting terms. The elderly were depicted as "touchy, peevish, angry, and forward"; they were found to be "hard to please, and . . . full of complaints of the present times" (Bridge, 1679). Although no laws dictated the elderly's retirement, those who remained too long in positions of power were apt to feel the resentment of would-be successors. Children coveted the land of their fathers; aspiring middle-aged leaders jealously eyed the power of aging magistrates, jurists, and ministers. "To summarize," Demos (1978) wrote, "the position of the elderly in early New England was sociologically advantageous, but psychologically disadvantageous. Their control of important resources seemed to command honor and respect, but not affection or sympathetic understanding" (p. 155). According to Demos, the hierarchy of age described by Fischer appeared to be based more on power and property than on ideological consensus.

Daniel Scott Smith (1978), in his article "Old Age and the 'Great Transformation': A New England Case Study," largely confirmed Demos's conclusions. Smith found that honor for the old was based on their ability to perform needed services and their control of valued assets. In contrast to Fischer, Smith suggested that in the 18th century, middle-aged men, rather than the elderly, exerted the greatest power in society. In was they who possessed the wealth of the community, ruled over the councils of government, and controlled the unmarried children in their households. Moreover, the economic and demographic factors that helped to bolster the position of the old were fragile indeed. By the late 18th century, an increasing scarcity in land served to deprive the old of their economic power over the young. As a result, Smith concluded, "the older matrix of values sustaining respect for the aged withered" (p. 296).

The work of Demos, Smith, and others raised serious questions about Fischer's simple gerontocracy (Boyett, 1980; Faragher, 1976; Haber, 1983; Laslett, 1977; Stearns, 1982; Stone, 1977b; Thomas, 1976). Even in the early 17th century, they argued, the actual position of the old seemed insecure. If the elderly continued to control family, assets, or occupations, they might provoke hostility from the young; if they retired, they were likely to be judged to have outlived their usefulness. And for those who faced old age alone and poor, their last years often brought scorn rather than the admiration of the culture. Elderly persons who failed to possess valued assets quickly learned that age alone brought few rewards. Such poverty-stricken individuals were placed at the rear of the meetinghouse and greeted with disrespect; their physical ailments and weaknesses were treated with contempt.

Nonetheless, aging in colonial America did appear different from the experience of growing old in later periods. Despite disagreements among historians, a general consensus existed that, in the 17th and early 18th centuries, the elderly often exerted power, and the young were admonished to show them respect. Both cultural prescriptions and economic factors combined to support the prestige and the active participation of a sizable proportion of the elderly.

Despite disagreement over the existence of an influential gerontocracy, Fischer's (1977) study clearly set an early agenda for historians and generated an important new construct for the study of the aged. In his attack on modernization, Fischer argued that, at least for the history of the old, the nation's political and intellectual philosophy was far more influential than economics or demographics. Throughout the course of American history, cultural beliefs, rather than urbanization or industrialization, shaped the social worth of all aged individuals.

The second major history of aging, W. Andrew Achenbaum's (1978) *Old Age in a New Land*, clearly endorsed the new axiom. "Ideas about the worth and function of the elderly," Achenbaum wrote, "have a life of their own: the unprecedented denigration of older Americans arose independently of the most observable changes in their actual status" (p. 86). Again, the forces of modernization were found to have little effect upon perceptions of old age. Instead, negative attitudes toward the old were portrayed as the driving force in shaping the elderly's history.

Fischer and Achenbaum, however, did disagree on one key issue; their studies presented radically different interpretations as to when the "great transformation" in beliefs and attitudes occurred. Fischer saw veneration for the old dissipating with American Revolution; Achenbaum continued to find signs of respect in the early Republic. During the first half of the 19th century, he argued, the old continued to be held in veneration as symbols of longevity and guardians of virtue. New ideas of liberty and equality made little impact on their status. Only after the Civil War, Achenbaum stressed, did the elderly begin to lose the power and honor they once had possessed.

This conclusion lead inevitably to a second major problem in the historiography of aging. Several historians attempted to discover the source of the elderly's dramatic fall from grace. Although Fischer and Achenbaum disagreed over the timing of this important change in attitudes, they both concluded that by the early 20th century respect for old age had turned into unrelenting ageism. As a group, the elderly were demeaned for their numerous years and debased for the physical decline that often accompanied old age. How then could the development and widespread acceptance of such ageism be explained?

One answer was provided by Thomas Cole. According to Cole (1980, 1986), a distinctive antagonism to old age arose with the development of 19th-century middle-class culture. The central beliefs in activity, vitality, and self-control devalued the worth of the old. The elderly's once-honored experiences were now judged to be of little use. Their habits were old-fashioned; their ideas were simply obstacles to progress. Moreover, the physical signs of age had clearly become distasteful. Gray hair and wrinkles—once signs of honor and respect—had evolved into unwanted reminders of inevitable decay and death.

For Cole (1980), the Second Great Awakening played an especially crucial role in the transformation of these cultural beliefs. In the second quarter of the 19th century, religion, once the foundation on which a hierarchy of age had been built, now exalted those who advocated reform and change. From their pulpits, ministers stressed the importance of youth. In adolescence, possibilities were limitless, and salvation lay close at hand. For the old, however, little solace could be extended; the time for redemption had long passed.

In delineating the new belief system, Cole emphasized that it was more than simply a revolt of children against their fathers or a rejection of hierarchy during a revolutionary age. "If old age in America had only suffered the usual misfortune of being identified with an old order," Cole wrote, "the impact might have been short-lived. But old age not only symbolized the 18th-century world of patriarchy and hierarchical authority, it also represented an embarrassment to the new morality of self control." In the bourgeois world of civilized morality, he explained, the old came to signify "dependence, disease, failure and sin" (Cole, 1986, p. 61).

In *Beyond Sixty-Five,* Carole Haber (1983) found a similar characterization of old age evolving in 19th-century America. For Haber, however, the source for these stereotypes lay more specifically in the ideas of doctors, social workers, statisticians, and businessmen who came to categorize and thus to treat all elderly individuals as members of a uniquely needy group. Basing their work on an increasingly popular medical model of aging, these professional groups depicted advanced age itself as a progressive and inevitable disease. Newly described changes in physiology and anatomy of the old meant that the elderly could no longer compete with the young. Their advanced chronological age could be taken as a reliable sign that they required professional care, retirement, and segregation.

In the late 19th century, according to Haber, this model of aging was then institutionalized in the programs and policies that were established to assist the elderly. The founders of nursing homes, mandatory retirement programs, and geriatric medicine all shared the belief that old age was a time of particular disease and dependence. In their view, all old men and women would eventually become both physically and mentally senile. There was little reason to hope that they could remain active in the industrialized world.

In contrast to Achenbaum, Haber did not agree that such ideas "about the worth and functions of the elderly have a life of their own" (Achenbaum, 1978, p. 86.) In her study, as in the work of Michel Dahlin (1983), this characterization of the old grew directly out of the daily experience of the professional workers who dealt with the elderly. Largely urban in their orientation, these individuals and their organizations perceived radical change in the condition of the old. In almshouse rosters, outdoor relief rolls, and hospital wards, they discovered an aged population that was separated from its kinship network and deprived of profitable wage labor. Social analysts were convinced that increasing structural poverty among the old accounted for their deteriorating status. Experts on the elderly, such as Edward T. Devine (1909), Abraham Epstein (1922), I. M. Rubinow (1913), and Lee Welling Squier (1912), had little doubt that the old had been relegated to "the industrial scrap heap."

This negative perception of the status of the elderly led social advocates to argue that specific bureaucratic responses were required in the face of the elderly's deteriorating physical, economic, and social conditions. In stressing the need for state pensions, old age homes, and "family-like" almshouses, they characterized old age as a time of complete dependence (Anderson, 1983; Butners, 1980; Gratton, 1985; Katz, 1984). Yet even in this characterization, it appeared clear that not all old people were treated similarly. Old age homes were provided for the native-born and almshouses for immigrants, and in the large cities of the South, segregated institutions served as houses of death for the most unfortunate of elderly blacks (Gratton, 1985; Haber & Gratton, 1987).

In the initial wave of historical work, attitudes and ageism—themes gerontologists know well—served to shape the research and the debates among scholars. In their investigation of the existence of a gerontocracy or in the search to explain the loss of status of the old, Fischer (1977), Achenbaum (1978), Cole (1980, 1986), Haber (1983), and others generally emphasized the importance of cultural beliefs. Yet their lack of agreement as to when the "great transformation" in attitudes occurred also raised questions as to the precise economic and social condition of the old through the course of American history. Although historians have generally agreed with Fischer's (1977) account of the higher status of many of the old in the 17th century and their subsequent decline in position by the late 19th century, they came to question the validity of contemporary experts' perceptions. Was the early 20th-century belief that industrialization had diminished the worth of the old an adequate assessment of their condition? Had old age truly evolved into a social serious problem?

## THE SECOND PHASE OF INQUIRY

In an attempt to answer these questions, historians turned from general questions of cultural perceptions to an investigation of economic and social realities. According to their findings, it appeared that the early social analysts and the later modernization theorists had been categorically wrong. By examining the actual employment, residential, and familial status of the old, historians concluded that, in the late 19th and early 20th centuries, the old did not in reality undergo a dramatic and revolutionary displacement in either the home and the work place. Despite the harsh warnings by reformers such as Epstein (1922) and Rubinow (1913), the elderly were neither uniformly deserted by their children nor relegated to obsolescence.

Historical research on the economic and social conditions of the old in the late 19th century, in fact, revealed family and employment patterns far different from those depicted by contemporary social analysts. With urbanization and industrialization, the lives of the old did not change abruptly. The aged did not suddenly find themselves outcasts in the modernizing world. According to Howard P. Chudacoff and Tamara K. Hareven, in the second half of the 19th century, few dramatic transitions actually disrupted the final stage of life (Chudacoff & Hareven, 1978, 1979; Hareven, 1976, 1978, 1986). The central demarcations of old age—loss of control over children, household, and employment—never occurred for a majority of old persons. Even in the industrial city, most old men remained employed and heads of their households (Dahlin, 1980).

Moreover, Chudacoff and Hareven (1978, 1979) argued that, in the late 19th century, the families of a majority of elderly persons changed little with advancing age. In contrast to today, the old rarely experienced the "empty nest syndrome"; most spent the majority of their lives with at least one child in the home. Such co-residence may, in fact, have actually grown with urban and industrial growth. In sharp conflict with assumed theory, Chudacoff and Hareven, along with Michael Anderson (1971) and Steven Ruggles (1987), argued that the economic transformation of the late 19th century increased the likelihood that the old would live in an extended family. Especially in cities where economic hardship and a shortage of housing existed, Anderson (1971) concluded, the old maintained a desired commodity: a relatively inexpensive place to reside. The young, in search of affordable living space, turned to homes either owned or rented by their elders. As a result, intergenerational exchange of valuable resources created strong familial ties.

While challenging the notion that all aged individuals were abandoned to urban poverty, the discovery of complex family structures in the late 19th century also revealed that the elderly made up an extremely diverse segment of the population; they followed no single residential, familial, or employment pattern. Although the majority of men continued to labor, a minority searched futilely for work. Although most continued to live with their spouse and children, others resided alone, and a small group sought institutional refuge. Through a study of the 1900 census, Daniel Scott Smith (1986) found that the elderly adopted a wide variety of living arrangements. For some, and especially for widows, aging did bring sharp changes in family structure; not all retained the patterns of their middle age. Most old, married, and employed men continued to head their households, but the death of a spouse or long-term unemployment often meant that new strategies for the survival of the family had to be devised.

Moreover, as Thomas A. Arcury (1986), Hal Barron (1984), and N. Sue Weiler (1986) showed, differences in the ethnic background of the old, their place of residence, their gender, or their class also shaped the nature of their family structure. The race of aged individuals, as well, affected their existence. From family relationships, through patterns of work, to the nature of their relief, the lives of blacks often departed significantly from those of their white counterparts. To be old hardly guaranteed a single life-style or a uniform family relationship (Gratton, 1987a; Smith, Dahlin, & Friedberger, 1979).

Clearly, the family that historians have recovered from the past is not one in which every old person struggled to survive alone; the work has shown the stark pronouncements of the Progressive-era social analysts about the isolation of the old from their families to be sharply exaggerated. Similarly, historians have come to question the reformers' generalizations about the impact of industrialization upon the working lives of the old. Was economic change, as Epstein (1922) and Rubinow (1913) stated, the major force that led to the elimination of the old from the labor market and caused them to require extensive state and federal assistance?

Again, historians have offered a wide variety of responses to these questions. In *Growing Old in America,* David Hackett Fischer (1977) categorically answered no. Economic change had little effect: the trend toward the displacement of the old began between 1790 and 1820, well *before* industrialization could take its effect. W. Andrew Achenbaum (1978) also rejected industrialization as a key determinant, stating that the displacement of the old from the labor market did not begin until *after* 1890. Citing figures that showed a steady decline in employment rates from 1890 to the present, he declared that only at the turn of the century did age-based retirement begin on a significant scale. Had economic change been the primary factor in displacing the old, Achenbaum reasoned, a larger proportion of the old would have become unemployed in the mid-19th century. Achenbaum declared that ageism, rather than urban or industrial growth, was the key factor that ultimately displaced and demeaned the old.

In contrast to Fischer and Achenbaum, more recent historical work has suggested that industrialization did have an impact upon the old, although one far different from that suggested by contemporary social analysts. Research by Brian Gratton (1985, 1987b) and R. Ransom and R. Sutch (1986) has challenged both the validity of the 19th-century employment figures and their interpretation. In "The Labor of Older Americans," Ransom and Sutch (1986) argued that late-19th-century census takers grossly exaggerated the number of aged workers by including men who were permanently unemployed or living on income earned through property or investments. Providing their own estimates, the authors suggested that very high levels of retirement or withdrawal from the labor force could be observed by 1870. Moreover, this level of labor force participation was essentially unchanged between 1870 and 1930. The authors contended, in fact, that industrial workers of the

1930s may actually have been less likely to retire than were their counterparts of the 1870s.

In *Urban Elders* and "The Labor Force Participation Rates of Older Men, 1890–1950," Brian Gratton (1985, 1987b) also challenged the accepted employment figures for the old. Little real change, he contended, existed in labor force participation rates of the old from 1890 to 1930, although such rates varied according to the race, ethnicity, and location of the workers. For Gratton, the catalyst causing mass retirement of the old was not a sweeping attitudinal change or persuasive ageism. Instead, he argued, large numbers of aged individuals did not depart from the work force until the adoption of Social Security. The establishment and growth of the welfare state, rather than widely shared antagonism against the aged worker or sweeping economic transformation, caused a majority of elderly laborers to retire.

In addition, Gratton suggested that, in sharp contrast to the assertion of experts like Epstein or Rubinow, the impact of industrialization upon the old was not uniformly negative. According to his findings, industrialization neither led to a steady decline in employment for the old nor impoverished aged employees. Rather than displacing the old from the labor market, the economic transformation actually increased the per capita income of workers and offered many elderly laborers far better existences.

The revised labor force participation rates provided by Gratton (1985, 1987b), as well as by Ransom and Sutch (1986), challenged both the early modernization thesis of displaced aging and the more recent explanations based on cultural ageism. Even in the 1870s, it appeared, large numbers of old people either accumulated sufficient savings, permitting them to leave the work force voluntarily, or continued to work or seek employment. Certainly, they were affected by the economic transformation of the country, although not necessarily displaced and discredited. Moreover, if, as Gratton and Ransom and Sutch have contended, the labor force participation rates of the early 20th century did not steadily decline, the effect of ageism remains unclear. Did industrial employers actually fire large numbers of elderly workers or discriminate against them because of their advancing age? What role did cultural expectations play in the actual experience of old age?

## THE THIRD PHASE OF INQUIRY

The reassessment of the labor force participation rates, then, posed a final problem for historians of aging investigation. Previously, both the timing and widespread acceptance of national old age welfare policies had been easily explained. According to this thesis, beginning in 1890, the old faced steadily growing ageism and resulting unemployment. By the Great Depression, the elderly's poverty-stricken state could no longer be ignored; the public acceptance of Social Security was an understandable and, in fact, seemingly inevitable step. By examining the actual social and economic condition of the old, however, historians challenged this simple explanation. If, as recent research has implied, the unemployment rate did not steadily grow from 1890 to 1930, what then accounted for the creation and national establishment of the welfare state?

No issue in the history of aging has raised greater controversy among historians. The American welfare model clearly stood apart from its European counterparts. In terms of both its late acceptance and its reliance upon the contributions of workers, it spoke of a particular history. Scholars have attempted to explain the adoption of the welfare policy and its ultimate effect upon the aged. The government's actions—its timing, purpose, and impact—were all subject to considerable debate. According to W. Andrew Achenbaum (1983, 1986a, 1986b), Social Security was primarily a benevolent response on the part of policymakers to increasing unemployment and poverty among the old. Over time, as entitlements grew, the program combined both welfare and insurance. It provided relief for the poverty-stricken old while guaranteeing the independence of the middle class.

For William Graebner (1980), however, the establishment of Social Security rested on the state's need to control the size and composition of its labor force. Relying on management practices dating back to the late 19th century, Graebner argued, New Deal policymakers hoped to provide work for the young; with the enactment of Social Security, the old would no longer compete for limited employment. In contrast to Achenbaum, Graebner argued that the needs of the elderly were never the primary concern of policymarkers. First and foremost, New Dealers sought to correct unemployment and bring recovery and reform to a severely troubled economy. (See Myles, J. for debate.)

In *The Transformation of Old Age Security*, Jill Quadagno (1988) extended Graebner's approach, arguing that the welfare state was established to shape and control the labor market through the evolving nature of the relief it allocated to the needy. Failure to provide nationally for the old at an earlier date, she argued, could not be explained by the relative prosperity of the old or their steady decline in employment. Rather, the delayed establishment of Social Security, especially in comparison to other industrialized Western countries, resulted from three factors: the failure of American unions to organize mass production workers, the strength of the private sector, and the power of sectional interests in

American politics. Moreover, even during the Great Depression, these forces continued to shape the conservative nature of American welfare. Southern planters and business leaders combined to determine the provisions of Social Security, rewarding specific groups with government-supported retirement while assuring the continued employment of others. Even today, she concluded, such policies continue to influence the welfare state and the nature of support for the elderly. Other scholars, however, strongly disagreed, arguing that elites hardly played the positive role in formulating policy that Quadagno had assigned to them (Skocpol & Amenta, 1985).

## FUTURE RESEARCH

The historiography of aging illustrates that the field has challenged longstanding beliefs and raised new problems for future research. The experiences of the old in the past have differed sharply from the assumptions drawn from modernization theory. In 17th- and 18th-century America, the elderly did not rule over extended families; their power and prestige came from control over their own land, wealth, and offspring, rather than from purely cultural prescription. Nor did industrialization and urbanization cause the old to be suddenly displaced and abandoned. In the burgeoning cities of the 19th century, as well as in the countryside and small towns, the elderly and their families developed a variety of strategies that enabled them to exist and, at times, even prosper. Furthermore, the history of Social Security can no longer be seen as the simple and direct charitable response to the steadily increasing unemployment of old workers. Above all, current research has revealed that the history of aging in America is extremely complex; no simple theory can sufficiently explain the diverse nature of growing old in America's past. As historians have shown, the elderly have never comprised a unified group whose age alone dictated their experience. Their history has varied with race, gender, region, class, and ethnicity; theirs is an extremely diverse past.

For gerontologists, these conclusions are extremely significant. Without question, research has demonstrated that the attitudes and experiences of the present day have historical precedents. The limited number of old persons in other centuries did not prohibit them from influencing those around them; similarly, their assumed high status did not protect them from the vagaries of aging. Clearly, past generations of elderly people were neither invisible nor invulnerable. Even before the advent of the urban and industrial world, some elderly individuals were displaced from positions of authority, and others altered their lives and family arrangements in order to survive. Furthermore, historical research has shown that modern-day policies do have important links to the past. Old age homes, geriatric medicine, and welfare policies were not the creation of the mid-20th century but must be understood in terms of their 19th-century antecedents.

For historians, as well, these findings have importance. Most certainly, they demonstrate that the elderly did not simply play a secondary role in other centuries; to assume so is to be shaped by present-day biases that equate old age with powerlessness. In the past, despite their small numbers, the old represented a significant part of the adult population and an even more important proportion of those holding wealth, resources, and power. As they shaped their lives, they played a crucial role in the transformation of work, family, and welfare in America.

Yet, although this research has revealed that many assumptions about the history of aging are false, it also has left significant questions unanswered. Among historians of aging, five central issues continue to shape the debates. First, the history of old age must be fully addressed in terms of its diversity. As historians have just begun to show, the character of an individual's old age was dependent on a great number of variables; not everyone who aged was a middle-class, urban, Protestant male. Race, religion, ethnicity, class, region, and gender, as well as the person's own cohort experience, all need to be studied and understood as having an impact upon growing old in the past.

Second, although scholars have traced the evolution of cultural biases against the elderly in the course of the 19th century, the meaning of such ageism has yet to be explored. Cultural sentiments against the old certainly began to be visibly apparent by the mid-19th century, but the effect of such beliefs on the employment and residential patterns remains unclear. Did feelings against the elderly actually limit their opportunities, or were such beliefs simply a convenient and consistently invoked rationale for otherwise-determined behavior?

Third, although we have a better understanding of what industrialization did not do in terms of displacing the old or removing them from their families, we are still unclear as to the effect of broad economic change. We cannot simply dismiss industrialization and urbanization, concluding that the most dramatic changes in old age history occurred before and/or after. We are still faced with understanding how industrialization and urbanization effected the work, family, and wealth of a variety of cohorts of elderly individuals.

Fourth, we need to understand the impetus behind social measures "for" the elderly. Ranging from outdoor relief and almshouse residency through Social Security, these measures dictated roles for the old and developed a language through which the aging process could be interpreted. Historians have shown that need alone cannot explain the rise of the policies; as we have seen, the pronouncements by welfare authorities were clearly exaggerated. What, then, led to programs that defined old age as a time of dependence and disability? And as it now appears conceivable that the old, as a whole, did not experience a steady decline in employment and wealth in the early 20th century, how can we explain the creation of a welfare state that removed elderly workers from the labor force and made old-age poverty a national concern?

Finally, we need to understand the historical experience of aging from the perspective of those who have grown old. Traditionally, historians have focused on how the elderly were perceived and treated. Attitudes toward old age, rather than the attitudes of the old, have shaped their research. As a result, the elderly of the past often appear to be little more than pawns controlled by economic forces or passive patients waiting to be assisted and, ultimately, dissected by ever-growing numbers of professionals. Yet, as historians are beginning to show, old age had diverse meaning to those who experienced it. From the elderly women of the early republic to the Gray Panthers of the late 20th century, the meaning of old age is clearly shaped by those who live it (Cole, 1985; Cole & Premo, 1986–87; Premo, 1990).

Historians are now addressing these issues. Their findings, of course, will not end all debate. Certainly, we can expect scholars to present a variety of hypotheses. Nevertheless, the work should be of great importance to both gerontologists and historians. In the future, gerontologists may no longer relegate the history of old age to a cursory section at the start of the text, treating present-day policies, attitudes, and experiences as if they were totally devoid of any usable past. Similarly, historians may have to revise their narratives of family, work, and welfare; the old can no longer be portrayed as the passive victims of modernization. Current research clearly demonstrates that both the experience of the old and attitudes toward old age have had great significance. To ignore the new historiography of aging is to limit both our vision of the past and our understanding of the meaning of growing old in present-day America.

## REFERENCES

Achenbaum, W. A. (1978). *Old age in the new land.* Baltimore: Johns Hopkins University.

Achenbaum, W. A. (1983). *Shades of gray.* Boston: Little, Brown.

Achenbaum, W. A. (1986a). The elderly's social security entitlements as a measure of modern American life. In D. Van Tassel & P. Stearns (Eds.), *Old age in a bureaucratic society* (pp. 156–192). Westport, CT: Greenwood Press.

Achenbaum, W. A. (1986b). *Social security.* Cambridge: Cambridge University Press.

Achenbaum, W. A., & Stearns, P. (1978). Old age and modernization. *Gerontologist, 18,* 307–312.

Anderson, A. (1983). *The institutional path of old age.* Unpublished doctoral dissertation, University of Virginia.

Anderson, M. (1971). *Family structure in nineteenth-century Lancashire.* Cambridge: Cambridge University Press.

Arcury, T. (1986). Rural elderly household life-course transitions, 1900 and 1980 compared. *Journal of Family History, 11,* 55–76.

Barron, H. S. (1984). *Those who stayed behind.* New York: Cambridge University Press.

Boyett, G. W. (1980). Aging in seventeenth-century New England. *New England Historical and Genealogical Register, 134,* 181–193.

Bridge, W. (1679). *A word to the aged.* Boston: John Foster.

Burgess, E. W. (1960). *Aging in Western society.* Chicago: University of Chicago.

Butners, A. I. (1980). Institutionalized altruism for the aged. Unpublished doctoral dissertation, Columbia University.

Chudacoff, H., & Hareven, T. (1978). Family transitions into old age. In T. Hareven (Ed.), *Transitions.* New York: Academic Press.

Chudacoff, H., & Hareven, T. (1979). From the nest egg to family dissolution. *Journal of Family History, 4,* 69–83.

Clark, M., & Anderson, B. G. (1967). *Culture and aging.* Springfield, MA: Clark Thomas.

Cole, T. (1980). *Past meridian: Aging and the northern middle class.* Unpublished doctoral dissertation, Stanford University.

Cole, T. (1985). Aging and meaning: Our culture provides no compelling answers. *Generations, 10,* 49–52.

Cole, T. (1986). Putting off the old. In D. Van Tassel & P. Stearns (Eds.), *Old age in a bureaucratic society* (pp. 49–65). New York: Greenwood.

Cole, T., & Premo, T. (1986–87). The pilgimage of Joel Andrews. *International Journal of Aging and Human Development, 24,* 79–85.

Cowgill, D., & Holmes, L. D. (1972). *Aging and modernization.* New York: Appleton-Century-Crofts.

Crandall, R. (1980). *Gerontology: A behavioral science approach.* Reading, MA: Addison-Wesley.

Dahlin, M. (1980). Perspectives on the family life of the elderly in 1900. *Gerontologist, 20,* 99–107.

Dahlin, M. (1983). *From poorhouse to pension.* Unpublished doctoral dissertation, Stanford University.

Demos, J. (1970). *Family life in Plymouth Colony.* New York: Oxford University Press.

Demos, J. (1978). Old age in early New England. In M. Gordon (Ed.), *The American family in social-historical perspective* (2nd ed.; pp. 220–256). New York: St. Martin's Press.

Devine, E. T. (1909). *Misery and its causes.* New York: Macmillan.

Epstein, A. (1922). *Facing old age.* New York: Alfred A. Knopf.

Faragher, J. (1976). Old women and old men in seventeenth-century Wethersfield, Connecticut. *Women's Studies, 4,* 11–31.

Fischer, D. (1977). *Growing old in America.* New York: Oxford University Press.

Graebner, W. (1980). *A history of retirement.* New Haven, CT: Yale University.

Gratton, B. (1985). *Urban elders.* Philadelphia: Temple University.

Gratton, B. (1987a). Familism among the black and Mexican-American elderly: Myth or reality: *Journal of Aging Studies, 1,* 19–32.

Gratton, B. (1987b). The labor force participation of old men, 1890–1950. *Journal of Soical History, 20,* 689–710.

Greven, P. (1970). *Four generations.* Ithaca, NY: Cornell University.

Haber, C. (1983). *Beyond sixty-five.* New York: Cambridge University Press.

Haber, C., & Gratton, B. (1987). Old age, public welfare and race: The case of Charleston, South Carolina, 1800–1949. *Journal of Social History, 21,* 263–279.

Hareven, T. (1976). The last stage. *Daedalus, 105,* 13–23.

Hareven, T. (1978). Family time and historical time. In A. Rossi, J. Kagan, & T. Hareven (Eds.), *The family* (pp. 58–70). New York: W. W. Noton.

Hareven, T. (1986). Life course transitions and kin assistance. In D. Van Tassel & P. Stearns (Eds.), *Old age in a bureaucratic society* (pp. 110–125). Westport, CT: Greenwood Press.

Holmes, L. D. (1976). Trends in anthropological gerontology. *International Journal of Aging and Development, 7,* 211–218.

Katz, M. (1984). Poorhouses and the origins of the public old age home. *Milbank Memorial Fund Quarterly / Health and Society, 62,* 110–140.

Laslett, P. (1972). *Household and family in past time.* Cambridge: Cambridge University Press.

Laslett, P. (1977). *Family life and illicit love in earlier generations.* Cambridge: Cambridge University Press.

Myles, J. (1986). Citizenship at the crossroads: The future of old age security. In D. Van Tassel & P. N. Stearns (Eds.), *Old age in a bureacratic society* (pp. 193–216). New York: Greenwood.

Premo, T. (1990). *Winter friends.* Urbana: University of Illinois.

Quadagno, J. (1988). *The transformation of old age security.* Chicago: University of Chicago Press.

Ransom, R., & Sutch, R. (1986). The labor of older Americans. *Journal of Economic History, 46,* 1–30.

Roscow, I. (1974). *Socialization to old age.* Berkeley, CA: University of California.

Rubinow, I. M. (1913). *Social insurance.* New York: Henry Holt.

Ruggles, S. (1987). *Prolonged connections.* Madison: University of Wisconsin.

Simmons, L. (1945). *The role of the aged in primitive society.* New Haven, CT: New Haven Press.

Skocpol, T., & Amenta, E. (1985). Did capitalists shape social security? *American Sociological Review, 50,* 572–575.

Smith, D. S. (1978). Old age and the "Great Transformation." in S. F. Spicker, K. M. Woodward, & D. D. Van Tassel (Eds.), *Aging, death and the completion of being* (pp. 97–113). Atlantic Highlands, NJ: Humanities Press.

Smith, D. S. (1979). Life course, norms, and the family system of older Americans in 1900. *Journal of Family History, 4,* 285–298.

Smith, D. S. (1986). Accounting for change in the families of the elderly in the United States 1900–present. In D. Van Tassel & P. Stearns (Eds.), *Old age in a bureaucratic society* (pp. 87–109). Westport, CT: Greenwood Press.

Smith, D. S., Dahlin, M., & Friedberger, M. (1979). The family structure of the older black population in the American South in 1880 and 1900. *Sociology and Social Research, 63,* 544–549.

Squier, L. W. (1912). *Old age dependency in the United States.* New York: Macmillan.

Stearns, P. (1982). *Old age in preindustrial society.* New York: Holmes and Meier.

Stone, L. (1977a). *The family, sex and marriage in England 1500–1800.* New York: Harper & Row.

Stone, L. (1977b). Walking over Grandma. *New York Review of Books, 24,* 10–16, 48.

Thomas, K. (1976). *Age and authority in early modern England.* London: British Academy.

Waters, J. (1976). Patrimony, succession, and social stability. *Perspectives in American History, 10,* 131–160.

Weiler, N. S. (1986). Family security or social security? *Journal of Family History, 11,* 77–95.

16

# Elders in World History

*Peter N. Stearns*

---

The juxtaposition of themes explicit in viewing old age and older people through world history is far from commonplace. Few historians who have dealt with old age have thought in global terms; relatively few indeed have looked beyond a single society or culture. For their part, few of the growing breed of world historians, concerned with large international patterns and comparisons, have seriously taken up the topic of old age. The stuff of world history involves commercial exchanges, missionary religions, and the formation of empires, and old age has not been isolated as a significant facet of these topics. Even cultural diffusion, potentially the most salient standard interest, has not been probed in terms of the place of the elderly.

Not surprisingly, as a result, the texts devoted to world history either avoid old age as an explicit subject or confine coverage to comments about 20th-century issues in advanced industrial societies, where new demographic patterns (falling birthrates and rising longevity) push the elderly to new statistical and policy prominence. The indexes of the textbooks tell the story: either no listings for old age or a reference near the end, in dealing with the rise of social security in late 20th-century Japan or the West (as an example of the latter, see McDay, Hilliard, & Buckler, 1984). For a scholar versed in some of the exciting debates about old age history, particularly as they have applied to premodern periods, this result can be severely disappointing.

Nevertheless, without pretending that old age is yet emerging as a significant item in global treatments, the relationship between world history approaches and an understanding of old age is not entirely inchoate. Important themes in world history can be applied to placing old age in cultural context and to viewing it as part of basic processes of historical change. Several facets of old age history, in turn, lend themselves to global perspectives.

After dealing briefly with the current limitations of world history as a venue for humanistic study of old age, we can turn to the several channels where connections have been made that are illuminating in themselves and permit extension through further research. It must be emphasized that even an approximation of a world history of old age awaits its scholars. This essay captures some of the important fragments available, from anthropology as well as history, and some of the further connections that may prove fruitful.

## A DIALOGUE DELAYED

Attention to world history has surfaced in fits and starts at various points in the 20th century, but it clearly predates serious historical attention to the phenomenon of old age. World historians like H. G. Wells and Arnold Toynbee focused particularly on patterns of rise and fall in various major civilizations, an essentially political story, though with moral and cultural overtones. Neither hypotheses nor data about the role of old age in this process were included, and it would be the bold theorist even today who could spin out a plausible connection. A second round of world history writing crested in the 1960s, signaled particularly by William McNeill's (1970) *Rise of the West.* Attention to civilizational patterns remained, and McNeill was particuarly fascinated by creative periods in the great societies of the Old World. There was a new interest, however, in features of world history besides rise and fall, especially in connections among otherwise discrete civilizations through invasions, trade, and above all, cultural imitation. Here was a more sophisticated version of world history, with hints of a more genuinely global framework, but it was still silent on issues of age structure of elders' experience. Finally, during the 1980s another surge of world history occurred, closely connected to perceived teaching needs but complete this time with professional organization and fledgling journal outlets such as the *Journal of World History* (Allardyce, 1990). This latest generation of world history scholarship has emphasized (in addition to the earlier themes) serious attention to previously neglected parts of the globe, such as Africa and Latin America; still-greater interest in the phenomonon of global connections, which allow division of world history into significant time periods, not on the basis of coincidential pauses in individual civilizations but through analyzable changes in international context; and finally, utilization of social-historical as well as political and high-culture themes in assessing both civilizational patterns and global periodization. Still, however, attention to age structure is largely ignored, as one of the many details that must be omitted (at least until the demographic innovations of the 20th century are encountered, with the resultant increase of the old age sector) if the gargantuan task of capturing the essential world past is to remain manageable.

Obviously, the most recent styles of world history open a potential connection to the study of old age through the social history window, which emphasizes the experiences and outlook of ordinary people. The fact is, however, that the study of old age has not yet reached sufficient prominence in the social history of individual societies to command ready attention at the world history level. World historians have been extremely interested in integrating hotter, and more politically charged, new items, such as the history of women, though not always with great success beyond identification of large categorizations such as patriarchy plus discrete details for individual societies. Though not directly relevant, this work offers something of a model for extending attention to other facets of the human experience, such as aging, plus an indication that conceptions of world history can prove expansive.

On the other hand, the two other emphases in recent world history scholarship may at least temporarily discourage incorporation of old age and the elderly. Growing interest in international context, as shaped by exchanges of goods, diseases, and ideas, has not to date pointed toward the later phases of life, if only because the most active exchangers—as explorers, merchants, missionaries—are normally of a younger age. Some exchanges may well affect the phenomenon of old age, so mutual exclusion is far from complete, but these ramifications have yet to be traced. The most sophisticated current theorizing about world history, involving the development and evolution of world systems beyond single civilizations, leaves out old age.

New concern for international scope raises another set of issues, as world historians incorporate more than the great classical civilizations of Asia and the Mediterranean. The simple fact is that we lack even rudimentary historical data concerning the elderly in a number of key societies, such as pre-Columbian America and early Latin America, Africa, and Russia. Again, the contrast to women's history is striking, for some mention of women's roles and status is possible in all of the areas, as well as time periods, world historians try to embrace, even though detail and analytical subtlety continue to vary widely.

The most obvious gaps involve the interests of historians themselves. Family history has lagged in dealing with societies such as Latin America and Russia, and though the gaps are beginning to be repaired, the spillover into a focus on the elderly has yet to occur. In certain instances other factors may contribute. It has been speculated that in some parts of South America, such as the Andean lowlands, distinctive mortality patterns reduced the normal numbers of people surviving to old age. In some areas, again including Latin America, the experience of colonization cut into cultural autonomy; forced conversions to Christianity attacked Amerindian ancestor worship, meaning that for some centuries older people were less visible and less significant in transmitting knowledge through stories than had been the case. Old age history may prove to be particularly arduous, and its significance may be unusually limited in some settings. The main point, however, is that existing historical inquiry is spotty, with some societies, vital for world history in other respects, largely omitted to date. There is no reason to assume that fuller knowledge will not develop along with the maturing of sociohistorical inquiry. In the meantime, gaps, when juxtaposed with the legitimate desire for more extensive geographical coverage, complicate the inclusion of the elderly in world history.

The point need not be labored: a juncture between world history and elder history is conceivable, and it fits the growing interest in using a wide range of social facets as part of characterizing civilization development. The juncture has not yet arrived, and both practical and theoretical impediments complicate its prospect.

This said, a series of more positive approaches can be emphasized that use the substantial data available on elder history in certain areas toward a picture relevant to world history, even if not yet fully global. Equally important, world history frameworks can already be applied to the history of the elderly, with suggestive results, including a challenging context for the interpretation of main lines of historiography on the subject.

For world history, despite its immense potential detail, has a certain elementary simplicity in its most basic rendering, readily applicable to major findings about old age in the past and indeed blending surprisingly readily with these findings. World history scholarship is normally structured as follows: after some bows to early societal development through the Neolithic revolution, attention concentrates on the formation of major civilization traditions, from 3500 B.C. until (usually) the 15th century A.D. This huge period, defined in terms of the elaboration of the potentials of agriculturally based civilizations and the growing capacity to organize substantial regions in single market, cultural, and (sometimes) political networks, is obviously not changeless. The advent of new religions and their growing spread between the 5th and 10th centuries A.D constitutes just one of several innovation themes. Nevertheless, emphasis remains on the formation of great and in many ways durable traditions—such as Hinduism and the caste system in India—duly adapted to periodic challenges. Analytically, in building out from the discrete civilizations, the chief integration device involves comparison, allowing scholars to identify common patterns as well as the differences among social, political, and cultural systems.

Modern world history, in contrast, focuses on the interaction between the great traditions and novel forces that to some extent range over the entire globe. In the most sophisticated formulations, the period from about A.D. 1000 to about 1500 sees a first version of this pattern, though around the Indian Ocean and the Mediterranean Sea rather than literally internationally, through the cultural contacts and commercial exchange sponsored particularly by Arab Islam. More familiar are the still more pressing innovations and more genuinely international scope of the forces of change ushered in by Western expansion and increased world trade. This basic pattern underwent successive iterations as, for example, the industrial revolution and more full-blown global imperialism were introduced into the equation in the 19th century; in the 20th century a varied but steady international diet of political upheaval and secularization of culture occurred.

Elder history, though not usually decked with such explicit organizational markers, has already acquired a somewhat parallel dynamic, involving for the long centuries of civilizational or cultural establishment an emphasis on basic traditions and social forms, followed by a period (in some cases, a quite recent period) of more substantial change, the transition involving a host of questions about the impact and directions of the modernization process. Parallel dynamic, in turn, permits further exploration along world-historical lines, despite the absence of any commanding literature beyond single-civilization bounds. Here is the basis for a vigorous sense of the interactions between old age and world history, some of them well established, others a challenge for additional inquiry.

## THE NEOLITHIC REVOLUTION: AGRICULTURAL CIVILIZATIONS AND HUNTING / GATHERING PRECEDENTS

A world history of the elderly logically begins where world history scholarship normally begins: with the formation of agricultural societies and the emergence of civilizations as a type of social and cultural organization, beginning in the Middle East between 7000 and 3500 B.C. These huge changes in human history undoubtly had an impact on the role of the elderly, both male and female, though interestingly (again in contrast to kindred topics such as status of women) the transition has rarely been evoked. The initial framework of analysis in world history, which uses the contrast between agricultural societies and resultant civilizations and their hunting and gathering predecessors to launch inquiry into change and continuity in our global past, has not been systematically applied to old age and the elderly.

Several key points are clear, nevertheless. In the first place, old people existed in significant numbers in hunting and gathering societies. They did not form a substantial percentage of the population because, given high infant mortality and birthrates, over half of the total consisted of young children. Average life expectancies at birth were low, which has sometimes led historians to assume that almost no one reached old age—a mistake implied, for example, in Simone de Beauvoir's (1972) famous survey of the subject. If a person survived childhood diseases, he or she had a quite decent chance of living to 50 or even beyond, though men, free from the dangers of childbirth, usually did better than women. All societies had experience with old age well before the advent of civilization or more sophisticated economies, and they developed roles and cultural expectations accordingly. The advent of agriculture may have improved slightly the chances for living to later age; certainly, the likelihood of an adult living to later age remained reasonably good despite, still, the low life expectancies due to massive child morality. Old age continued to be a relevant interest.

This said, further generalization is complicated by the second fact about the elderly in preagricultural settings, derived from contemporary anthropological evidence. Their conditions varied greatly, and this constrains any generalizations about the results of change. The contrast with women's history is revealing. It is generally agreed that the key economic roles of women in preagricultural economies assured them functions and status that can be contrasted with the characteristic, and subordinating, institutions of patriarchal agricultural societies despite interesting diversities on both sides of the chronological divide (Ahmed, 1986; Lerner, 1986). The elderly, on the other hand, might have enjoyed an important position in preagricultural settings, or they might have been treated with scornful brutality.

Cultural anthropologists such as Philip Silverman and Robert Maxwell have attempted to construct typologies predicting and explaining such huge variations (Maxwell & Maxwell, 1980; Maxwell & Silverman, 1970, 1983). Harshness toward the elderly, including killing older people who had passed their economic prime and in some cases brutalizing, even cannibalizing them as well, follows in part from the rigors of the environment and related problems of food supply. Tribes in cold or arid settings thus often (though not invariably) turn against their decrepit old. Information exchange is another interesting variable, potentially relevant to economically more advanced societies as well. Isolation of many hunting and gathering groups can help firm up the importance of older people in passing on vital knowledge and values, whereas hunting and herding societies in contact with other areas—the societies most likely to generate civilizations—may prefer to take their information from exchange, downgrading their evaluation of the elderly in the process. No set of predictors thus far uncovered works perfectly to explain variation, however. Some hunting and gathering societies establish an abrasive pattern of social relationships, starting with parental treatment of children, that readily spills over into behavior toward the vulnerable old age sector; others are consistently more benign. Some hunting societies reserve marriage rights for men who have passed their physical prime, whereas others downgrade the status of older men. The combinations are fascinating, in determining widely divergent cultures of veneration or belligerence, widely different role assignments ranging from vital educational and political roles to virtual worthlessness. This same extensive variety makes a simple judgment of the impact of the rise of agriculture and then civilization on improving or worsening the lot of the elderly literally impossible. (For older studies, see Koty, 1934; Simmons, 1945; a fine introduction to recent work is the *Journal of Cross-Cultural Gerontology*, 1986ff.)

What the advent of agriculture and the subsequent emergence of civilization did accomplish, in all probability, was a certain standardization in the conditions of most older people, previously scattered in more isolated local cultures. As social class distinctions increased in what had become a hierarchical society, the likelihood of living to old age almost certainly varied, with people in the upper classes benefiting from a higher living standard, winning the greater opportunities. This, along with the importance of older people inherited from a hunting and gathering past, helps explain why old age emerged fairly early on as a theme in art, literature, and philosophy in many agricultural civilizations.

The establishment of property concepts, essential to almost all agricultural economies except slash-and-burn varieties, gave older people an economic tool lacking in hunting and gathering societies. Most major agricultural settings, from the age of the river-valley civilizations until a scant century ago, find older people using control of property and the right to determine aspects of inheritance as a means of assuring their economic livelihood. Disproportionate control of property gave many elders an ability to maintain function and purpose and to claim no small amount of deference (respect for elderly being an obvious theme in most of the major cultures established under the aegis of agricultural civilizations). Most families, from peasants on up, developed patterns designed to assure support in old age, by instilling respect in children and by manipulating property transmission so as to assure some care. The patriarchal tendencies of agricultural civilizations that resulted in some consistent tendencies concerning the treatment of women had similarly consistent implications for the status of older people, save in the lowest social classes. While older men were the principal beneficiaries of property control, many older women also gained status, either through their sons or, in some but not all civilizations, through property rights as widows. (The widowhood theme is one facet that is now explored for Latin American history [Metcalf, 1990].)

Specialization of functions possible in agricultural economies allowed certain other activities to fall disproportionately to a favored minority of older people (though in many instances these functions had been anticipated by activities of older leaders in the more benignly organized hunting or herding societies). More specialized organization of religion often conduced toward the top priestly and scholarly functions being assigned, at least de facto, to older men, as was ultimately the case in the hierarchy of the Christian church. Hereditary kingships and aristocracies often allowed older men to maintain political power, though this might be disputed by younger rivals. A recurrent drama in the political histories of many agricultural civilizations, such as the Arab caliphate or medieval Europe, pitted aging rulers against younger claimants.

The roles and assurances possible for older people in agricultural civilizations were not, of course, uniform. In this aspect of life as in most others, wealth counted strongly. Propertyless elderly, including slaves, though usually a minority, were often scorned or neglected (Pollard, 1981). Older women had far fewer functions and rights than older men had, again because they were typically limited in property control or excluded outright. Here, however, a tendency did emerge in a variety of agriculturally based civilizations for older women to win significant social power as leaders of other women in an extended family structure, as sons' wives as well as unmarried daughters were urged to defer to the family matriarch. Widows' property control, however, was frequently more limited in fact than in law.

Property control, a surrounding culture that urged devotion toward older parents, plus some specialized functions for older men in politics and religion—these are virtual commonplaces of cultures and civilizations formed on the basis of agriculture in Asia, Europe, and Africa. Their consistent emergence testifies to an important, if as yet not fully charted, series of changes as agricultural civilizations emerged in the first place, replacing the less predictable variety of conditions characteristic of hunting and gathering operations.

## CULTURAL TRADITIONS: THE COMPARATIVE APPROACH

This general framework established, the next obvious point about old age in world historical context—a point that links centrally to most of the historical work done on the elderly before modern times—is that the various agricultural civilizations developed distinctive modulations in cultural tone and to an extent in the treatment older people might expect, the self-image they might form. Old age displayed some of the comparative differences among civilizations visible in other aspects of culture and society (Sokolovsky, 1983). This claim must be launched carefully, for it does not, in fact, contradict the conclusions about some general consistencies across civilizational lines. All agricultural civilizations, at least from the classical period (roughly 800 B.C.–A.D. 450) onward, display important common features, revolving around the emphasis on veneration linked to the authority older property owners maintained and older mothers could claim in an extended family. Much of the history of old age consists, however, in the various embellishments possible within this general framework, and this in turn invites a grasp of the significance of diverse cultural traditions and their evaluation through comparative analysis.

The essential case is simple enough: within a common patriarchal framework, the different value systems of key civilizations led to varied opinions about older people and about the state of old age itself. Old age, in turn, fits into the comparative approach fundamental in standard world history coverage as major civilizations take center stage.

The best-developed contrast, implicitly comparative, involves Chinese civilization from pre-Confucian centuries onward and Western civilization from Greek and biblical references onward. Chinese emphasis on veneration of elders is familiar enough; incorporated into Confucianism, it became one of the staple features of culture, apparently shared by various social classes, though most pronounced among ruling elites (De Bary, 1970). Respect for the authority of elders, gaining a religious quality through ceremonies honoring family ancestors, anchored familial stability and linked it to the wider political order. Not surprisingly, a wide variety of Chinese writings celebrated the idyllic potential of later age, and the Confucian classics (notably the late work entitled the *Book of Filial Piety*) moved the principle of veneration for later age into the basic texts of elite political training (Ebrey, 1981). Considerable interest in promoting longevity followed from this culture of later age, though this emanated more from Taoist than Confucian sources (Needham, 1982).

Early patterns in the Mediterranean societies that ultimately produced Western civilization are characterized not by a negative view of old age and older people but by considerably more ambivalence than was characteristic of China. Some early histories, including Simone de Beauvoir's pioneering study that relied so heavily on Western cultural imagery, to be sure, accented the negative in noting the many laments about senescent decline and the many criticisms of the childishness or avarice of older people that dot classical Greek and Roman literature and persist into later renditions such as those of Montaigne (Hendricks & Hendricks, 1977–78). More recent work, although agreeing on the importance of basic cultural traditions as an entry to old age history, stresses rather the mixture of emphases in the Western orbit (Minois, 1987). Biblical treatments, to be sure, building on earlier Middle Eastern values (Arnett, 1985), held a long life to be a reward for piety and a source of religious inspiration for others, with exemplary patriarchs easily living 70 years or more (Stahmer, 1978). Greco-Roman thought, however, clearly introduced the theme of ambivalence. Medical authorities, though not deeply interested in the problems of the elderly (Finley, 1984), produced considerable testimony to what proved to be a durable idea that old age was itself a disease (Quandt, 1986). Individual writers such as Pliny, eager to assert the wisdom older people might gain from their experience and freedom from distracting appetite, nevertheless bemoaned decrepitude and the loss of youthful vigor (Bertram, 1976; Finley, 1984). Even Hebrew culture produced mixed reviews for old age; whereas elders testified to piety and transmitted traditional values, they might abuse their power as part of a futile effort to keep time at bay. Overall, respect for wisdom and a recognition of old age as a life stage equal in value to those that preceded it, was balanced by a tendency to scorn physical and mental decay and a persistent identification of selfishness and abuse of authority associated with the later years.

The ambivalence of Western culture produced not only diversity in evaluations but also a tendency toward oscillation over time, with some centuries producing distinctly more favorable cultures than others (Foltz, 1980; Thomas, 1976; Tobriner, 1985). Recent French historiography has been particularly useful in tracing cultural shifts from ancient times through the Renaissance, around the theme of change within a framework of ambivalence (Bois, 1989). Medieval art and literature thus stressed themes of veneration with less reserve than Roman culture had done, but the late Middle Ages returned to a less favorable view. Sixteenth-century literature, both secular and religious, became still more negative, holding the vaunted wisdom of old age to be largely a sham, promoted by people who were in fact losing their grip. Important also was a growing tendency to attack the avarice of older people, which essentially applied earlier concern about abuse of power to a more commercial economy in which money played a growing role. Cultural shifts of this sort again contrast with trends in China, where consistency was much stronger literally until the 20th century (De Bary, 1970; Spence, 1975).

The comparative distinctions show finally in characteristic discussions of older women, a subordinate theme in both Chinese and Western cultures, given women's inferiority and their lesser likelihood of attaining old age in the first place because of high adult mortality rates (Laslett, 1977). Chinese writers extended their assumptions of wisdom and authority attached to age in the respect due to family matriarchs, whereas Western discussions tended to play up the uselessness of older women who had outlived their primary reproductive role (Stearns, 1980).

Distinctions in cultural approach, established early in the civilization tradition, thus tended to endure and to amplify, predicting the amount of change and fluctuation over time and extending to valuations of older women. Old age clearly mirrored more general differences between Western and Chinese culture: the importance of physical (including military) prowess as opposed to contemplation and scholarship, emphasis on a certain individualism versus a more distinctly hierarchial strain, and the sheer frequency of cultural change as against a stronger attachment to continuity.

Culture, to be sure, is not the whole story of old age history in the great civilizations. Historians' interest in literary or artistic renderings of old age may skew our understanding, as against actual health conditions, material standards, and the outlook of older people themselves. Still, cultural traditions clearly had impact beyond the musings of essayists. Older people themselves could hardly fail to be touched by ideas around them that promoted a sense of esteem or, more Western-style, that tempered pleas for veneration with lament and criticism.

Furthermore, culture could impact on material conditions. Generational tensions that can be noted in the Greco-Roman tradition surely helped produce a premodern Western reality that, as we increasingly realize, frequently lined adult children in a battle for resources against older property owners—their parents—and forced the elderly, even when relinquishing power, to make detailed contractual arrangements to assure their support (Stearns, 1983). Note that contracts to assure provision for older parents also developed in parts of China, including contemporary Taiwan, which means that the most facile contrasts with the West, based on general culture, can be overdrawn. Nevertheless, Chinese contracts are based on assumptions of the obligation of support and, if they reflect tension, normally focus on disputes among sons; the anguished bargaining of Western elders in the 17th and 18th centuries, over simply making sure that some potatoes would be available, is not characteristic (Cohen, 1976). Certain societies, in sum, were more likely to provide carefully for older people even in essential retirement than was the West, based on different family arrangements (the Chinese traditionally married younger than did most Westerners during the early modern centuries and therefore provided more years of generational overlap) and on different cultural emphases. Ideas about the elderly seem, at least in the present stage of our historical knowledge, both to have caused and to have reflected wider differences in the way older people were treated.

The causal-plus-mirroring role of culture applies also to important institutional developments in the situation of the elderly that again contrast Western history and its East Asian counterpart. The establishment of the "European style" family pattern in the later Middle Ages, with its stress on the individual acquisition of property as the basis for family formation (as against a more purely extended family tradition) and attendant emphasis on the nuclear family, with a tendency to relegate surviving older parents to a subordinate (often residentially separate and inferior) position, was in no simple sense caused by larger ideas about old age (Burguière et al., 1986; Hajnal, 1964). It was consistent with the cultural strand that denigrated old age and chafed against elderly power wielders, however, and it could not have emerged in a more respectful cultural context than that of China.

Ideas about old age thus form a significant feature of larger cultural traditions and can be explored as part of a more general comparative approach that recognizes common patterns in agricultural societies but also sees durable cultural variations as a fundamental ingredient of world history. Comparative analysis remains in its infancy, on this subject as on many others. A fuller understanding of the actual conditions of older people might modify the cultural impressions. Cultural differences themselves, although clearly linked to larger tendencies in philosophy and ethics, need fuller explanation. Some recent Western scholarship has begun to include political factors, for example, in the assessment of the status of the elderly (Bois, 1989), and this raises interesting possibilities in any comparison with China. On the other hand, the transmission of respect for old age to Japan, as part of cultural diffusion from China, seems largely to have overridden huge distinctions in political systems within the East Asian orbit (Palmore, 1975).

There is also the obvious need for comparable cultural inquiry into the history of old age in other major civilizations, to amplify the comparative possibilities. Indian traditions, while having nothing to do with Confucianism, seem to have produced a respect for old age not dissimilar to that in China, but they have not been as extensively probed through historical research (Vatuk, 1980, 1983). Some interesting work has stressed the veneration of old age in sub-Saharan Africa cultural tradition, seeing a transmission of these values to Afro-American families in the New World (Pollard, 1981). Despite important indications of this sort, a full comparative mapping is not yet available. Further, some previous intrepretations, such as Palmore's (1975) characterizations of Japanese deference, have more recently been challenged or qualified. Even societies that have been studied historically, in other words, have often been presented in oversimple fashion, a fact that reflects the exciting flux of current research but severely complicates incorporation of old age into world history generalizations.

Nevertheless, although further analysis is vital, an important claim has been sketched, and it meshes with the civilizational approach that undergirds world history before the modern centuries: Major civilizations generate a durable, identifying set of impulses early on, which continue to work through subsequent change and mark off political institutions, social structure, and even familial relationships relevant to gender and life stages over long stretches of time. Culture is the most important variable in dealing with the comparative analysis of old age in the great civilizations, producing values that might be transported even amid huge disruptions such as the transatlantic slave trade. Cultural distinctions not only contrast major civilizations; they also set the basis for dealing with the second facet of world history—the advent of forces that cut across civilizational lines during the past five centuries.

## TRANSITIONS

The great civilization traditions were clearly established in most inhabited parts of the world by the end of the first millennium A.D. In many cases they had evolved considerably from their origins under the impact, for example, of major new religions, but they generally maintained recognizable continuities as well. The centuries that have filled the most recent millennium, particularly the period from about 1500 onward, have been marked in world history by an overlapping series of changes that, though differential in impact, have been literally global in scope. Commericial ties increased, involving the Americas in the world system for the first time, and a pattern of dominance or dependency was established within the world economy. World population began to increase, spurred by adoption of New World foodstuffs, though there was new disease exchange as well. Western economic and political influence spread until quite recently, and the impact of Western cultural forms continues to this day (Von Laue, 1987). New cultural, political, and social patterns spread, first in the West itself, in a process that can loosely be labeled "modernization," and centered on new government functions and rapid technological and industrial change (Cowgill & Holmes, 1972). Most of these shifts had clear implications for the roles of the elderly, though these implications varied depending on an area's position amid the international currents and its own prior traditions. Again, old age history has not been explicitly inserted into this sweeping panorama of change, but some well-established findings fit readily within the framework and set some guidelines for further scholarship.

The West itself changed first, which is one reason that considerable attention has focused on the early modern centuries (1500–1800) as a time of confused, in many ways painful transition in the status of the elderly. Western developments built on the mixed cultural legacy concerning old age, but they added important new ingredients, some of which have been confounded with "tradition" in a society that was rapidly becoming untraditional even five centuries ago.

Shifts in the economy and in culture hold center stage, though a rising birth rate in the 16th century may have altered the symbolic importance of the elderly by reducing their relative share in the population; increasing adult longevity in the 18th century produced pressure on resources of a more direct sort. Economically, the big development was commercialization. More and more farming regions as well as urban centers began producing for the market and for profit (a development that occurred in New England late in the 18th century, setting in motion a reevaluation of deference to old age in American culture). Commercial relationships challenged earlier community hierarchies and exacerbated tensions between aspiring adults and older property-holders. New divisions between propertied respectability and an identifiable proletariat created anxieties about the poor and a revulsion against traditional charity and community responsibility (Hufton, 1974; Quadagno, 1982). The elderly, if unpropertied, clearly suffered from this division. One of the many reasons for witchcraft hysteria's focus on older people, particularly women, in the 16th and 17th centuries followed from these tensions and may have worked to force a new docility among older women (Bever, 1983). Religious divisions, the spread of literacy and the rise of science and more egalitarian political beliefs worked gradually, through the 18th century, to challenge the elderly as voices of authority or recipients of special deference.

Western historians have quite properly warned against facile modernization theses that would point to simple contrasts between a benign past and modernized deterioration where the elderly are concerned (Hendricks & Hendricks, 1977–78). Jean–Pierre Bois (1989) and David Troyansky (1989), for example, have recently emphasized new cultural factors opening greater interest in old age, from Enlightenment fascination with longevity to Romantic sentimentalizing about older family members. (But see also Peterson & Rose, 1982). New commerical patterns could provide functions for elders, as Michael Anderson (1971) has shown, particularly when work moved out of the home and caretakers for children became essential. The declining importance of land could reduce tensions over inheritance and ease antagonisms with older relatives. The picture is complex, but the sense of a vital transition in the roles and perceptions of the elderly, extending in Western society from the 15th century through the early phases of industrialization, sets some basis for evaluating new pressures and opportunities for the elderly in an international context in recent centuries (Shanas et al., 1968).

## WORLD REVOLUTIONS

International currents of change outside the West during the early modern centuries have not been intensely scrutinized from the standpoint of old age history. New patterns of disease plus outside political and cultural control may explain the absence of old age as a discernible theme in Latin American history from the Spanish Conquest until quite recent decades. Peter the Great's westernization effort in Russia placed a premium on youth and new learning among the Russian elite in the 18th century. The clearest themes of change, however, await the 19th and 20th centuries, and they raise vital issues for the status of the elderly in a host of traditional civilization centers.

The most salient general forces of change are threefold, with a fourth related factor applicable in many instances. They might be loosely summarized as part of a pattern of modernization (Cowgill & Holmes, 1972) but are most effectively treated separately.

The first factor involves changes in the economy and related work patterns. Certainly, where outright industrialization develops (as in Japan) but also where new commercial ventures disrupt traditional, familial production patterns (as in Africa or Latin America), family cohesion and the power elders wield through property control are jointly challenged. When labor becomes a market commodity pure and simple and when work moves outside the home to factories, mines, or commercial agricultural estates, questions inevitably develop about the effectiveness of elders' contributions and about the influence they can wield through ownership or through political leadership in family and village (Stearns, 1976).

The second factor involves pervasive belief change, fed by Western influence and the spread of mass education and scientific and technical training. When traditions are challenged and when knowledge is conveyed by missionaries or teachers rather than by customary local authority, an international phenomenon over the past century amid quite different stages of economic development, questions again arise about the role of the elderly and about past cultural patterns that hold the elderly in respect. Novelists like Chinua Achebe (1981, 1985) in Africa have traced a process of religious conversion and also cultural secularization that, though not specifically directed against the elderly, challenge village and family cohesion and lead many Africans, however painfully, to rethink family obligations in favor of new religious allegiances or an individualistic achievement and consumer ethic.

The third factor, though more variable, involves demographic change. Societies that in the 20th century pull into the pattern of low birthrate and increased life expectancy that the West began to develop somewhat earlier inevitably face new issues of old-age support. Even societies that have yet to undergo full demographic transition, in which the elderly do not rapidly increase as a percentage of total population, nevertheless encounter increased adult life expectancy that gradually augments the elderly population.

It must be remembered that many adults did live into old age, defined as 60 or beyond, in agricultural civilizations or in hunting and gathering societies, producing an "old age sector" of up to 4% of the population total even amid characteristic high birth and infant mortality. By the late 19th century and the 20th century, however, chances of surviving to 60 improved further—for women, by way of example, with reduced infection during childbirth. In cases when the birthrate also dropped significantly, the percentage increase of the elderly in the overall population was noticeable, and the convenience of assuming, as most agricultural societies had done, that old age problems were family matters alone opened to new challenges.

The final factor involves a pattern of political change that, through colonial controls followed by decolonization or through political revolution, displaces hereditary leadership at the top of society. These changes do not necessarily supplant the political power of older leaders, which may be reasserted through democratic elections, Communist bureaucracies, or authoritarianism, but they again raise questions about customary legitimacies that had often assumed a natural governmental function for selected elders.

The general impact of these factors in contemporary world history is complicated by prior culture and by differential combinations that depend on extent of industrialization, presence or absence of political revolution, and the nature of belief change. The factors, in other words, raise a common set of questions for recent world history, but they do not assure uniform answers.

Several societies have been extensively studied within this overall framework and compared to modern Western patterns. Erdman Palmore (1975), in a provocative and now controversial brief study, argued that a culture of veneration in Japan produced distinctive benefits for Japan's older population amid extensive modernization. Japan's demographic transition was still, in the mid-1970s, a bit different from the West's; the elderly comprised a slightly lower precentage of the population. Widespread retirement at age 55 did not, in fact, end work careers, as most older Japanese continued part-time work and greatly aided the economy through the flexibility as well as the experience they added to the labor force. Family cohesion remained substantial, with many older Japanese living in extended family arrangements. Above all, a culture of respect persisted, visible in ceremonial deference to the elderly in private and public settings alike, continued authority in familial decisions, and careful government promotion of elders' status. (Witness a 1963 law that urged: "The elders shall be loved and respected as those who have for many years contributed toward the development of society, and a wholesome and peaceful life shall be guaranteed to them.") Palmore concluded, before the plea became fashionable in other respects, that the West should imitate Japan. His argument forcefully urged that the modernization process need not lead to a single end result.

The dramatic focus for 20th-century China involves the force of political revolution, first under Sun Yat-sen and his successors and then under Mao, in challenging an old regime culture in which veneration for the elderly was a central ingredient (Solormon, 1971). The authority of older people had to be attacked as part of democratic political and familial reforms and as part of a push toward rural land reform and economic modernization. Yet the hold of culture remained strong, and the establishment of a new bureaucracy built in a protection for seniority. The result has been considerable change, admixed with what to Western eyes remains of surprising amount of countinuity, in a story whose end has not yet been written.

Contemporary Indian history, not surprisingly, displays continuity even more strongly. Although life expectancy has increased, high birthrates keep the elder percentage modest in the total population (though its overall size more than tripled in recent decades). Changes in beliefs vary greatly with social class position, with the majority still able to enforce family traditions, including the obligation to support older parents, even in new economic circumstances associated with urbanization. Arranged marriages promote parental control and minimize generational conflict. Rituals defining the position (and circumscribing the behavior) of widows continue with little alteration; co-residence of elderly with married sons remains the norm. Continuity should not, however, be overplayed: A growing number of rural elderly do live alone, as urbanization moves the young disproportionately; anxiety about support by children has increased, particularly on the part of widows and / or where sons are lacking; status within the family may have dropped even amid apparently traditional arrangements. India represents another case of mixed continuity and change, where a Western-derived modernization model does not fit but where important evolution must be acknowledged (Vatuk, 1980, 1983).

Comparative old age history, viewed as an interactions between tradition and new (though differentially applicable) international factors resulting from economic, political and cultural contacts, fits obviously into a wider interpretive scheme that sees change conditioned by civilizational traditions. Urbanization and other "modernizing" factors have some general effects but do not produce uniform results. Old-age history rests thus in a wide world historical context and neatly illustrates some fundamental patterns in which civilization traditions and widespread currents of change must be combined to grasp 20th-century history.

Although the interaction between tradition and challenge links old age to key interpretive questions in recent world history, its results must not be interpreted too facilely. "Traditional" elements are neither uniform nor simple. Agricultural civilizations offered varied traditions, of varying adequacy for elders; and rarely are conditions within a given civilization uniform or likely to respond to innovation in uniform fashion. Recent comparative work, particularly in anthropology, reminds us that apparently customary arrangements may work to the disadvantage of many older people; thus, residence with younger kin may provide solace and support, but it also may encourage brutality and neglect. This may be particularly true as families cease to be units of production, in third world economies that are changing even without full-fledged industrialization, but it may have affected more literally traditional arrangements as well (Goldstein, Schuler, & Ross, 1983). Historians dealing with Western history over the past four centuries have worked hard and successfully to show that an equation of tradition and modern with good and bad is simply inaccurate (Hendricks & Hendricks, 1977–78; Smith, 1984). The same message almost surely applies to 20th-century world history.

## POLICY HISTORY

In the more advanced industrial societies, the forces of change in modern old-age history have produced important policy responses over the past century. These responses have attracted a final and particularly focused comparative historical scholarship. A global framework, to be sure, is missing because the developing nations continue to rely primarily on familial support for the elderly. In both Eastern and Western Europe, the United States, and Canada, and Japan, however, a general trend toward governmental assurance of minimal old age support (and, usually, medical care) is shaped, once again, by distinctive specific contexts.

Purely national case studies of the emergence of social security systems raise their own complexities, to be sure. The systems do not break as free from traditional, alms-centered thinking about the dependent elderly as their authors imagine (Quadagno, 1982). They may serve to regiment the elderly and promote marginalization rather than being statesmanlike responses to a preexisiting economic crisis for elders. Issues of this sort have been vigorously debated in the U.S. history of social security policy (Van Tassel & Stearns, 1986). A comparative approach, more suitable from a world history standpoint, produces additional analytical perspectives by treating this aspect of old age in a large context.

Thus, overall political climate, including the stance and role of trade unions, must be factored into the timing and extent of old-age support systems even in rather similar nations like Britain and Sweden (Heclo, 1974). Larger political culture plays a vital role. Arnold Heidenheimer (1975) persuasively points to a durable tendency in American history to look to the provision of education (and thus of opportunity) as legitimizing the government's social role, a stance that reduces sanction for government intervention against symptoms of inequality in adult life, which are seen as individual flaws and not a social responsibility. Western Europe, traditionally less enamored of social mobility and more open to the idea of government involvement in mitigating the worst consequences of an inevitable social hierarchy, evinces greater willingness to use welfare systems to underwrite the worst risks of poverty and misfortune, including, of course, old age and attendant health care issues (Marmor, 1973). Even basic work values come into play. The United States ended up pushing for more systematic retirement than was common in much of Western Europe, Juanita Kreps (1979) argues, because it was less innovative in augmenting leisure opportunites during adult working years.

The most specific comparative efforts have centered on a Western context, but they can be applied more widely. Japanese traditions promote elaborate government interest in the status of the elderly but not, ironically, in a Western-style social security system. Precisely because the Japanese look to the elderly to serve as a flexible ingredient of the labor force and because they assume ongoing family support, they redistribute fewer social funds to the elderly than is common in the West. A starkly materialistic comparative assessment of old age differs, by the later 20th century, from the more general assessment of cultural prestige; and as the numbers and longevity of Japan's elderly increase, the disparities become more marked. Here, obviously, distinctive recent political histories combine with an ironic twist on cultural traditions to produce distinctive policy results.

The comparative approach can be applied not only to the formation and inital impact of modern social security systems but to ongoing evolution seen in terms of contemporary history. In the past two decades, the United States has responded differently to new pressures on old age social security than has Western Europe. It has been able to introduce fewer modifications in benefits and has tended to try to push retirement age up rather than trying to meet more general employment problems by facilitating early retirement. (Stearns 1985; "Social Security Problems" 1989) Once again, a more rigorous symbolic insistence on work ethic may be in play here. Certainly, the United States's concentration on social security rather than a more general welfare system reduces political flexibility, creating greater political tensions—and greater sacrosanctity—around this particular policy facet. There may be irony in the fact that by the 1980s the greatest agonies about preserving social security virtually intact arose in the United States, given a modern historical tradition not particularly friendly to old age. The result suggests the importance of an ongoing historical assessment, open to new factors, including the impact of recent policy itself, and not wedded to assumptions about unchanging cultural contexts alone.

## CONCLUSION

Consideration of old age in world history points obviously to many important gaps in historical knowledge. We know too little about old-age history in many societies. What early history there is may lean too heavily on cultural factors (known in more modern times to be relevant but hardly all-encompassing). Too few explicit comparative analyses are available, and a number of known transitions in world history have not yet been tested in terms of impact on and involvement of elders.

The same broad framework, however, highlights a number of important findings, including several comparative vantage points. Cultural continuities loom large. A number of civilizations seem to form basic approaches to the evaluation of old age early on, and traces remain (sometimes with unexpected results) to our own day. Cultural orientation can also be used as a skein into which what we know about work roles and about familial roles of elders can be woven. Emphasis on culture and the invitation to explain different cultural approaches also invites attention to a broad context for interpreting old age history. Basic political as well as religious values, attitudes toward work and individualism, and evaluation of sources of knowledge all enter into a explanation of why old age is viewed as it is in any single civilization and how it responds to innovation.

Research in a world-historical frame also insists on certain key points of change, in addition to shifts within particular societies. The advent of agriculture and the emergence of new kinds of cultural and commercial contacts are important moments in international old-age history as in world history more generally. The world history approach also confirms some notion of modernization, though as a set of issues rather than a set of predetermined outcomes, as in the simpler versions of this approach. International contacts and imitations do raise a common range of questions about old age during the past century or more, but the answers depend on the precise mix of change and on prior traditions. Although innovations are widespread, from family settings to state policy, variety among different civilizations does not necessarily diminish. A tolerance for complexity is vital when viewing old-age history seriously and certainly on a world stage, but by the same token old-age history, properly understood, can illumine important facets of world historical processes in its own right.

## REFERENCES


Achebe, C. (1981). *No longer at ease.* New York: Heinemann.

Achebe, C. (1985). *Things fall apart.* New York: Heinemann.

Ahmed, L. (1986). Women and the advent of Islam. *Signs, 2,* 665–691.

Allardyce, G. (1986). Toward world history: American historians and the coming of the world history course. *Journal of World History, 1,* 23–76.

Anderson, M. (1971). *Family structure in 19th century Lancashire.* Cambridge: Cambridge University Press.

Arnett, W. S. (1985). Only the bad die young in the ancient Middle East. *International Journal of Aging and Human Development, 21,* 155–160.

Beauvoir, S. de. (1972). *Coming of age.* New York: Putnam.

Bertram S. (1976). *The conflict of generations in ancient Greece and Rome.* Amsterdam: Gruener.

Bever, E. (1983). Old age and witchcraft in early modem Europe. In P. N. Stearns, (Ed.), *Old age in preindustrial society.* New York: Holmes and Meier.

Bois, J.-P. (1989). *Les Vieux, de Montaigne aux premieres retraites.* Paris: Fayard.

Burguière, A. , et al. (1986). *Histoire de la famille.* 2v. Paris: Armand Colin.

Cohen, M. (1976). *Houses united, Houses divided: A Chinese family in Taiwan*. New York: Columbia University Press.

Cole, T. R., & Winkler, M. G. (1985). Aging in Western medicine and iconography: History and the ages of man. *Medical Heritages, 5*, 335–347.

Commission of the European Community. (1982). Social security problems: Points for consideration. Brussels: European Economic Community.

Cowgill, D. O., & Holmes, L. D. (Eds.). (1972). *Aging and modernization*. New York: Appleton-Century-Crofts.

Davis-Friedmann, D. (1983). *Long lives: Chinese elderly and the Communist Revolution*. Cambridge, MA: Harvard University Press.

De Bary, W. T. (1970). *Self and society in Ming thought*. New York: Columbia University Press.

Delhi School of Social Work. (1977). *A study of the aged in Delhi*. Delhi: University of Delhi.

Ebrey, P. B. (1981). *Chinese civilization and society: A sourcebook*. New York: Free Press.

European attitudes toward retirement. (1980). *Social Security Bulletin, 43*, 26–28.

Falk, G., et al. (1981). *Aging in America and other cultures*. Saratoga, CA: Century Twenty-One Publishing.

Finley, M. I. (1984). The elderly in classical antiquity. *Ageing and Society, 4*, 391–408.

Foltz, J. D., Jr. (1980). Senescence and renascence: Petrarch's thoughts on growing old. *The Journal of Medieval and Renaissance Studies, 10*, 207–237.

Goldstein, M. Schuler, S., & Ross, J. C. (1983). Social and economic forces affecting intergenerational relations in extended families in a third world: A cautionary tale from South Asia. *Journal of Gerontology, 38*, 716–724.

Guest, D. (1980). *The emergence of social security in Canada*. Vancouver: University of British Columbia Press.

Guillemard, A.-M. (1986). State, society and old age policy in france: From 1945 to the current crisis. *Social Science and Medicine, 23*, 1319–1326.

Hajnal, J. (1964). European marriage patterns in perspective. In D. U. Glass, & D. F. C. Eversly (Eds.), *Population in history* (pp. 101–143). Chicago: Aldine Press.

Heclo, H. (1974). *Modern social politics in Britain and Sweden: From relief to income maintenance*. New Haven, CT: Yale University Press.

Heidenheimer, A. J. (1975). *Comparative public polity: Policies of social choice in Europe and America*. New York: St. Martin's Press.

Hendricks, J., & Hendricks, C. D. (1977–78). The age old question of old age: Was it really so much better back when? *International Journal of Aging and Human Development, 8*, 139–154.

How many votes in a French dole queue? (1981, April 4). *The Economist*, p. 279.

Hufton, O. (1974). *The poor of eighteenth century France 1750–1789*. Oxford: Clarendon Press.

Kebric, R. B. (1983). Aging in Pliny's letters: A view from the second century A.D. *Gerontologist, 23*, 538–545.

Koty, J. (1934). *Die Behandlung der Alten und Kranken bei den Naturvölkern*. Stuttgart: Hirschfeld.

Kreps, J. (1979). Human values, economic values and the elderly. In D. Van Tassel (Ed.), *Aging, death and the completion of being* (pp. 11–28). Philadelphia: American Philisophical Society.

Laslett, P. (1977). The history of the aging and the aged. In P. Laslett (Ed.), *Family life and illicit love in earlier generations* pp. 174–213. Cambridge: Cambridge University Press.

Lerner, G. (1986). *The creation of patriarchy.* New York: Oxford University Press.

Marmor, T. (1973). *The politics of Medicare.* Chicago: Aldine.

Maxwell, E. K., & Maxwell, R. J. (1980). Contempt for the elderly: A cross-cultural analysis. *Current Anthropology, 24,* 509–580.

Maxwell, R. J., & Silverman, P. (1970). Information and esteem: Cultural consideration in the treatment of the aged. *Aging and Human Development, 1,* 361–392.

Maxwell, R. J., & Silverman, P. (1983). Cross cultural variation in the status of old people. In P. N. Stearns (Ed.), *Old age in preindustrial society* (pp. 46–49). New York: Holmes and Meier.

McKay, J. P., Hillard, B. O., & Buckler, J. (1984). *A history of world societies.* Boston: Houghton, Mifflin.

McNeill, W. H. (1970). *Rise of West: A history of the human community.* Chicago: University of Chicago Press.

Metcalf, H. C. (1990). Women and means: Women and family property in colonial Brazil. *Journal of Social History, 24,* 277–298.

Minois, G. (1987). *Histoire de la vielillesse en Occident, de l'Antique à la Renaissance.* Paris: Fayard.

Needham, J. (1982). *Science in traditional China.* Cambridge, MA: Harvard University Press.

Palmore, E. (1975). *The honorable elders: A cross-cultural analysis of aging in Japan.* Durham, NC: Duke University.

Peterson, M., & Rose, C. L. (1982). Historical antecedents of normative vs. pathological perspectives in aging. *Journal of the American Geriatric Society, 30,* 289–294.

Pollard, L. J. (1981). Aging and slavery: A gerontological perspective. *The Journal of Negro History, 66,* 228–234.

Quadagno, J. S. (1982). *Aging in early industrial society: Work, family, and social policy in 19th century England.* New York: Academic Press.

Quandt, P. J. (1986). Growing old, growing aged. *Pharos, 49,* 26–31.

Shanas, E., Townsend, P., Wedderburn, D., Fris, H., Milh, P. & Stehouwer, J. (1968). *Old people in three industrial societies.* New York: Atherton Press.

Simmons, L. (1945). *The role of the aged in primitive society.* New Haven, CT: Yale University Press.

Smith, D. S. (1983). Historical change in the household structure of the elderly in economically developed societies. In P. N. Stearns, (Ed.), *Old age in preindustrial society* (pp. 248–273). New York: Holmes and Meier.

Smith, R. M. (1984). The structure of dependence of the elderly as a recent development: Some skeptical historical thought. *Ageing and Society, 4,* 409–428.

Social security problems in Western European countries. (1984). *Social Security Bulletin, 47,* 17.

Sokolovsky, J. (Ed.). (1983). *Growing old in different societies: Cross cultural perspectives.* Belmont, CA: Wadsworth.

Solomon, R. H. (1971). *Mao's revolution and the Chinese political culture.* Berkeley: University of California Press.

Spence, J. (1975). *Emperor of China: Self portrait of K'ang-hsi.* Cambridge, MA: Random Books.

Stahmer, H. M. (1978). The aged in two ancient oral cultures: The ancient Hebrew and Homeric Greece. In S. F. Spicker, K. M. Woodward, & D. D. Van Tassel (Eds.), *Aging and the elderly* (pp. 25–36). Atlantic Highlands, NJ: Humanities Press.

Stearns, P. N. (1976). *Old age in European society: The case of France.* New York: Holmes and Meier.

Stearns, P. N. (1980). Old women: Some historical observations. *Journal of Family History, 5,* 44–57.

Stearns. P. N. (Ed.). (1983). *Old age in preindustrial society.* New York: Holmes and Meier.

Stearns. P. N. (1985). Contemporary social security in comparative perspective: What kind of crisis? In Special Committee & Aging, V. S. Senate, *Fifty years of social security: Past achievements and future challenges* (pp. 73–87). Washington, DC: U.S. Government Printing Office.

Thomas, K. (1976). Age and authority in early modern England. *Proceedings of the British Academy, 62,* 205–248.

Tobriner, A. (1985). Honor of old age: Sixteenth century pious ideal or grim delusion. *Journal of Religion and Aging, 1,* 1–21.

Troyansky, D. G. (1989). *Old age in the Old Regime: Image and experience in eighteenth-century France.* Ithaca, NY: Cornell University Press.

Van Tassel, D. D., & Stearns, P. N. (Eds.). (1986). *Old age in a bureaucratic society.* Westport, CT: Greenwood Press.

Vatuk, S. (1980). Withdrawal and disengagement as a cultural response to aging in India. In C. Fry (Ed.), *Aging in culture and society: Comparative viewpoints and strategies.* New York: Praeger. 126–148.

Vatuk, S. P. (1983). Old age in India. In P. N. Stearns (Ed.), *Old age in preindustrial society* (pp. 70–103). New York: Holmes and Meier.

Von Laue, T. H. (1987). *The world revolution of westernization: The twentieth century in global perspective.* New York: Oxford University Press.

Younger people and employment. (1983, June). *European Industrial Relations Review,* pp. 25–27.

# 17

# Bioethics and Aging

*Harry R. Moody*

Bioethics, or the disciplined examination of value dilemmas in health care, is a field with enormous relevance for policy and practice in gerontology. The same advances in medical technology that now enable increasing numbers to reach old age also confront us with inescapable and difficult choices. These questions of bioethics and aging are treated in this chapter, which offers an overview of major developments in the past 20 years.

The most dramatic questions of bioethics are the ethical dilemmas of death and dying—for example, to prolong life or to hasten dying, perhaps by terminating treatment or withdrawing nutritional support. Who is to make such decisions and under what principles or authority? These problems are not unique to care of the aged. Yet because more than two-thirds of deaths now occur among those over age 65, the dilemmas arise disproportionately with elderly patients.

There are distinctive problems of diminished mental capacity that are very common among those of advanced age. We may point to Alzheimer's disease and other forms of dementia or mental impairment that occur commonly among older people, raising questions about informed consent under conditions of diminished capacity. Beyond mental capacity, there are related questions posed by physical frailty. The frail elderly living at home or in the community are vulnerable to what has come to be known as elder abuse. But it is not always easy to know when protective intervention is justified.

Then, too, there are collective health policy issues, particularly those tied to the escalating cost of health care. Efforts at cost-containment have already highlighted serious problems about justice and the allocation of resources. As we devote more and more resources to prolonging the lives of the very aged, we confront dilemmas that have no easy answers. What is the purpose for which we are so frantically seeking to prolong life? When have people lived "long enough"? How do we define what quality of life consists of? How do we understand the meaning of life and the meaning of old age (Cole & Gadow, 1986)?

All of these issues—death and dying, autonomy and consent, the allocation of resources—are familiar in the literature of bioethics. Can the conventional methods of bioethics simply be extended to the class of patients who are elderly? What is distinctive about the very old, and how appropriate are the methods and principles of bioethics to the task of illuminating their problems? To understand how bioethics has approached the problem of aging, we need to look at the historical origins of bioethics in recent philosophical thought and then consider the position of bioethics in contemporary society.

## EMERGENCE OF CONTEMPORARY BIOETHICS

Until well after the first half of this century philosophical ethics was not an exciting field of work. The literate public paid little attention to philosophical ethics, and academic philosophers were just as happy to keep it that way. In the Anglo-American world, from the time of G. E. Moore (*Principia Ethica,* 1911), modern ethics took on an increasingly detached, professional and academic tone. Analytic philosophy deliberately, even proudly, removed itself from politics or culture and in fact from all of the pressing social issues of the day. As practiced by analytic philosophers, ethics, the most practical of fields, turned away from practice.

In the past generation all of this has changed. The result has been something of an academic revolution in philosophy. Since the late 1960s there has been a revival of work in normative ethics as a subdiscipline within philosophy. This development signaled a dramatic departure from the style of analytic philosophy that was so influential by the middle of this century. With the revival of normative ethics and applied ethics, philosophers no longer confined themselves to examining the logical basis of moral discourse or metaethics. Instead, they became interested again in substantive ethical problems in the world around them. A landmark in this movement was John Rawls' (1971) theoretical treatise, *A Theory of Justice.* But major stimulus also came from controversies about war and peace, racial discrimination, and advances in biomedical technology. For the first time in this century, philosophers in large numbers ventured outside the academy and promoted "applied ethics"—symbolized, for example, by the influential journal *Philosophy and Public Affairs.*

During the late 1960s and early 1970s the new discipline of bioethics burst upon the scene and quickly captured public attention. The late 1960s were the years of the first heart transplant and other new technologies of medical care that posed perplexing questions. A benchmark for the arrival of a new discipline of bioethics was the founding of the Hastings Center and its interdisciplinary journal, *The Hastings Center Report,* in 1969. During the early 1970s bioethics was preoccupied with the definition of death and debates about the criteria for brain death, an issue made pressing by advances in organ transplantation and technology for life prolongation. Throughout the 1970s bioethics as a discipline acquired stronger intellectual underpinnings and attracted the attention of academic thinkers as well as practitioners, policymakers, and the wider public. Coinciding with this growth of bioethics was the expansion of gerontology in higher education and increasing attention to issues of aging.

By the early 1980s, the two fields of bioethics and gerontology were beginning to exhibit mutual influence, and by the late 1980s a solid body of literature in bioethics and aging was discernible. The first edited collections devoted exclusively to the subject of ethics and aging did not appear until the mid-1980s (Fahey, 1985; *Law, Medicine, and Health Care,* 1985; Lesnoff-Caravaglia, 1985; Moody, 1985; Thornton, 1987). At about the same time a series of important full-length books devoted to specialized topics also appeared (Callahan, 1987; Daniels, 1987; Melnick & Dubler, 1985; Spicker, 1987).

When we look at the two decades of the 1970s and 1980s, certain broad trends are now clear. First, there was the rise of bioethics from a marginal or fledgling enterprise in the late 1960s to a broadly influential framework for analysis. A milestone here was the President's Commission on Biomedical Ethics and its landmark volumes (1981–1983) on defining death, informed consent, forgoing medical treatment, and access to health care. A prominent role in this whole development was played by the simultaneous flowering of medical technology, applied ethics, public interest law, and the consumer movement on behalf of patients' rights. Bioethics was at the intersection of all these trends.

In the second place, over the last two decades there was the growing role of the courts in extending the principle of autonomy and self-determination even to the point of permitting termination of treatment and deliberate death under circumscribed conditions. Whatever the origins of these legal decisions, the implications for the elderly were unavoidable. Under the stimulus of both technology and law, the timing of death has increasingly become subject to intentional determination. Issues of bioethics, aging, and legal rights have became ever more closely intertwined.

Third, in the 1980s we saw the emergence of resource allocation and distributive justice as major themes in health policy. In the 1960s and 1970s the dominant theme was access to health care. Today, increasingly, it is cost. The force of cost-containment has come to equal medical technology as a factor driving the behavior of the health care system in America. Here again, the elderly are at the center of the story. Comprising 11% of the population, people over 65 now account for more than 30% of health care expenditures. New questions about cost, access, and age have barely begun to be matters of public debate. Yet the answers will be crucial in shaping what kind of society America will be in the future.

## DEATH AND DYING

The earliest and most persistent stimulus to thinking about ethics and aging has come from decisions about death and dying. Two trends here are noteworthy: first, gains in longevity that have displaced death more and more into late life; and second, with advancing medical technology, the increased scope for explicit human decisions on the timing of death.

The ethical dilemmas of death and dying encompass a range of acts and omissions that extend from forgoing treatment to intentionally withdrawing life-sustaining therapy and, for some, even to the extreme point of direct killing (Cassem, 1981; Rachels, 1986) or adopting a positive view of "rational suicide" on grounds of age (Battin, 1987; Prado, 1990). Perhaps the classic example of allowing to die, or "passive euthanasia," is the nontreatment of fever (Brown & Thompson, 1979). Traditionally, pneumonia was called "the old man's friend" because it promised a quick, painless exit from life. During the past decade a clear consensus of opinion, in both law and ethics, has been willing to defend an explicit choice—as a rule, on grounds of patient autonomy—that would shorten life by either withholding or withdrawing treatment. There is still some debate on the matter (Cody, 1986), and there are strong minority views at the extremes of the debate: for example, to preserve life regardless of circumstance, on the one hand, or to engage in active euthanasia, on the other. But the public, along with most clinicians, now seems to occupy a middle ground here, as illustrated by the recent *Guidelines on Termination of Treatment* issued by the Hastings Center (1988).

The historical movement toward this consensus is marked in a series of court cases, many originating in New Jersey, announced in the late 1970s and early 1980s, that extended the judicial basis for approving termination of treatment decisions (Ball, 1984). The decisive cases were those of Quinlan, Brother Fox, and Earle Spring (Annas, 1981); later, Saikewicz, Brophy, Peter, Jobes, Conroy. The case of Earle Spring (age 77) was notable because Massachusetts courts declared "senility" to be sufficient reason to terminate medical treatment (Glantz, 1982; Kart, 1981). The cases of Peter and Conroy also have special significance for geriatric ethics because they exhibit recurrent problems of quality of life and diminished decision-making capacity in a nursing home environment. The Conroy case, a landmark decision in geriatric ethics, established a legal basis for withdrawing treatment from a patient in a persistent vegetative state (Connery, 1985; Marzen, 1985). But many were unhappy with the procedural hurdles introduced by Conroy (McIntyre, 1986), and the legal decision still leaves much room for debate on the ethics of such withdrawal of treatment in specific cases.

Amid the complexity of case law and legal debate, certain principles stand out. To begin with, competent patients, under law, clearly have the right to refuse treatment. But if a patient is incompetent, a legal guardian or proxy must decide. As a practical matter, the ethical dilemmas of caring for the dying incompetent remain especially troubling (Dyck, 1984) because the patient cannot make an informed choice. Early on, the problem of proxy consent (Baron, 1981) was raised because many impaired elderly exhibit doubtful capacity to make decisions. Debate continues to arise around specific forms of intervention: for example, resuscitation and do-not-resuscitate (DNR) orders in the nursing home (Beck, 1985). Still another question that may be raised is whether the nursing home environment in itself introduces some special ethical problems (Besdine, 1983).

It is important to understand how law and biomedical ethics are increasingly intertwined in America. Claims to a "right to die" may be based on either a constitutional right to privacy or a common law right to refuse treatment. Again, as a practical matter, health care providers are often preoccupied with whether withholding or withdrawing life supports will expose them to lawsuits (Kapp, 1985). Beyond the matter of withdrawal or withholding of treatment, there are cases in which the patient seeks to directly end life, which raises questions about the ethics of active euthanasia and suicide (Bromberg & Cassel, 1983).

One of the most controversial and disturbing issues that has been raised is the matter of withdrawal of nutrition and hydration (Bexell et al., 1980; Callahan, 1985; Lynn, 1987). Many ethicists, supported by rulings from the American Medical Association, insist that artificial nutrition and hydration (e.g., a nasogastric tube) are properly regarded as forms of "treatment." Yet many health care providers and ordinary citizens continue to feel that food and water cannot be construed as medical treatment, and their withdrawal might be justified (Meilaender, 1984).

This whole historical line of development raises some unanswered questions for the future. A major uncertainty today is just how far one may go in "pulling the plug" or otherwise intentionally "allowing to die" in the case of a patient who might otherwise survive. When we look back over the last decade or more, we cannot help but recognize a movement along points of a so-called slippery slope. First, there was the definition of brain death, followed by acquiescence in termination of treatment for those terminally ill, followed in turn by termination of treatment for those in a permanent coma or "persistent vegetative state." This is the issue at stake in the Nancy Cruzan case, decided by the Supreme Court in 1990. In this whole historical trend there are major implications for ethics and aging. For example, is the next step withdrawal of life support, including food and water, from Alzheimer's disease patients? What about those demented or otherwise debilitated who have a poor quality of life, however this is judged? Right-to-life proponents, as well as advocates for the disabled, have been persistent in raising these concerns.

A diminished quality of life has sometimes been cited as a sufficient reason for withdrawing a feeding tube (Lo & Dornbrand, 1984). But a global quality-of-life standard could easily become a covert form of age discrimination where quality of life surreptitiously becomes tantamount to "worth of life" (Annas, 1984). Clearly, ethical judgments about quality of life for the impaired elderly will be a major point of contention in years to come (Thomasma, 1984b). As long as medical technology puts in human hands the decisions about prolongation of life and the timing of death, the ethical debates about death and dying will persist. Decisions about death and dying in old age will be a central part of the ethics of aging in the future.

## THE ETHICS OF DECISION-MAKING

Over the past two decades growing public and professional acceptance that it is legitimate to terminate treatment has been based on broad agreement about a fundamental idea of medical ethics: the idea that the patient has the ultimate right to decide. In American law and ethics, this idea has been tied to the principle of informed consent (Applebaum, Meisel, & Lidz, 1985).

Most discussions of the ethics of decision making in geriatric ethics start from a premise favoring autonomy over beneficence and rejecting the practice of paternalism (Childress, 1984; Cohen, 1985; Halper,

1980). Paternalism is often defined as coercive interference for another person's own good. But some ethicists have argued that ideals of autonomy and informed consent require special interpretation when applied to the dependent aged (Thomasma, 1984). Attempts to protect the vulnerable elderly sometimes lead to new forms of paternalism (Regan, 1981). Others have questioned whether the key idea of "mental competency," which is a fundamental requirement for informed consent, should play the prominent role it tends to play in debates on the subject (Caplan, 1985).

As a practical matter, both clinicians and ethicists have tried to get around the conflict between autonomy and beneficence by urging some variety of advance directives or proxy consent (Steinbrook & Lo, 1984). Even in the absence of such explicit legal instruments, the principle of "substituted judgment" may be favored when making decisions for incompetent patients. The difficulty is that, in practice, these methods often fail to work. Few people bother to sign Living Wills or other legal instruments.

One of the most difficult areas for decision making arises with patients suffering from dementia (Pratt, Schmall, & Wright, 1987; Winslade et al., 1984), particularly in the nursing home environment (Rango, 1985). Many clinical settings, such as the nursing home, are dominated by an atmosphere of paternalism that remains troubling to most ethicists (Hofland, 1988). Familiar controversies about withdrawal of nutrition arise with the demented elderly (Mehr et al., 1984). Still another area of great ethical controversy concerns the role of protective services for mentally impaired elderly living in the community, for example, those who may be subject to elder abuse (Quinn, 1985). Finally, there is the vexing question about the place of paternalistic intervention within the family (Mallary & Gert, 1986). This matter assumes special importance for long-term care decisions, for example, "coercive" nursing home placement.

## AGE AND THE ALLOCATION OF HEALTH CARE RESOURCES

The late 1960s, continuing through the 1970s, was a time of massive expansion of geriatric health care, fueled by increased Medicare and Medicaid funding. In those years there was a lively discussion of allocation problems, but discussion tended to be limited to issues such as organ transplants or other exotic technology. The early debate about distributive justice in health care did not extend to the elderly. In those years, a liberal consensus viewed the elderly as part of the "deserving poor." There was no question that the health care needs of the old could and should be met.

Yet during those same years the unconstrained growth in public spending for geriatric health care was sowing the seeds for future problems. The mood changed abruptly with the decade of the 1980s, when new policies of cost-containment came into effect. The new mood coincided with Reagan-era cutbacks in all social spending after 1981. And the change from expansion to cost-containment was not limited to the executive branch nor inspired exclusively by conservative ideology. Limits to spending were approved by policymakers across the board. In a single year, 1983, Congress passed legislation to resolve a major Social Security financing crisis and also approved serious cost-containment reform, the prospective payment system (DRGs) for the financially troubled Medicare system. Both moves reflected Congressional and public feeling that earlier free spending for social and health benefits to the elderly could not continue unchecked.

The response by ethicists was, at first, to uphold the status of the elderly as a group deserving special care and concern (Childress, 1984). But by the middle of the 1980s it had become possible to look again, now in more critical terms, at issues of distributive justice in geriatric health care (Gill & Ingman, 1985; Kayser-Jones, 1986). The new prospective payment reforms had changed the rules of the game in hospital admissions and discharge planning. Now it promised to change the physician's role as well (Cassel, 1985a). The new mood of cost-containment posed a distinct risk to the traditional role of the physician, threatening to turn doctors into medical gatekeepers (Pellegrino, 1986). Throughout the decade health professionals remained deeply troubled by these new cost-containment initiatives.

At the same time, theoretical work began to lay the basis for a new understanding of cost-containment and aging. Prominent ethicists came out in favor of rationing based on age. In a single year, 1987, four full-length books on age and the allocation of health care resources appeared in print, including an edited collection (Smeeding, 1987). One of these, Daniel Callahan's (1987) *Setting Limits,* was widely reviewed and set off a storm of controversy. Callahan boldly proposed to use chronological age as a factor in cutting off health care resources for some patients. Callahan's conclusion was frequently rejected, but the framework he proposed—distributive justice in life-span perspective—was becoming widely shared among ethicists.

Daniels (1987) derived a life-span perspective from liberal premises of John Rawls (1971). His recommendations were more circumspect and couched in abstract philosophical terms. Like Callahan, he favored more financial support for palliative, "low tech" care. But he too opened the door to age-based denial of treatment. Robert Veatch (1981) compared the very old with the terminally ill; both groups, he suggested, might have already consumed more than their "fair share" of health care resources. Still another voice was that of Margaret Battin (1987), who argued that, instead of rationing health care, voluntary, rational suicide was the most fair and economical solution to the problem of allocating health resources in an aging society.

Clearly, something had changed in the conventional wisdom about ethics, aging, and the allocation of resources. Yet all of these harsh proposals about age and the allocation of health resources should not be seen as "ageism" or lack of sympathy for the needs of the elderly. The new mood was rather part of an unfolding debate of the late 1980s about justice, priorities, and the rationing of health care (Blank, 1988; Churchill, 1987). Throughout the 1980s most liberals remained skeptical of any proposals that urged "limits" to health care spending. But many were becoming aware of the British experience of withholding kidney dialysis on the basis of age, a practice documented in an influential volume, *The Painful Prescription* (1983) (Halper, 1985).

As DRGs and other cost-containment steps took effect, critics charged that already in America something similar to rationing was taking place. But it was implemented indirectly, without any open admission that it was taking place. The liberal view held that collective decision making through national health care could reduce this distressing prospect of denial of treatment (Evans, 1985). Physicians in particular tended to reject the idea of "bedside rationing," and the public at large continued to reject use of chronological age as any kind of criterion for withholding treatment (Siegler, 1984). Other analysts warned against cost-benefit analysis, maintaining that such utilitarian standards involved a kind of covert age discrimination (Avorn, 1984). But political elites continued to wrestle with the problem of limits to health care spending.

A continuing focus of concern was Medicare, the single largest public health care entitlement in America (Fahey, 1985). During the 1980s the Medicare program itself became an item of interest, not only to budget cutters but to ethicists (Bayer & Callahan, 1985; Collopy, 1985). By promising to underwrite the health care needs of the aging population, Medicare had been at the center of liberal hopes for the Great Society. But during the 1980s, these hopes receded. With the Social Security crisis and prospective payment reforms of 1983, fears of cost-cutting increased. At least one analyst could seriously ask if the first Medicare generation might not be the last (Bayer, 1984). An effort to expand Medicare on an incremental basis—the Catastrophic Health Coverage Act of 1988—was actually an abandonment of the intergenerational model of social insurance. By the end of the decade, the earlier liberal consensus on behalf of expanding health care access for the aged had lost its confidence.

Public debate in the 1980s finally faced up to questions of distributive justice between generations: the specter of interage group competition (Clark, 1985). What became known as "generational equity" for a time captured attention from the media, as well as academic and policy elites. In the years after 1983 public confidence in the future of Social Security plummeted drastically. The year 1985 saw the formation of Americans for Generational Equity, a small but highly vocal Washington-based group. The response of organized aging interest groups was one of great discomfort with any attempt to look at distributive justice along age lines. Instead of competition between generations, aging advocates naturally favored "interdependence" of generations, as urged in *Ties That Bind* (Kingson, Hirschorn, & Cornman, 1986), a counterattack against the proponents of generational equity.

By the middle of the 1980s public opinion surveys on both income and health care provision for the aged revealed contradictory sentiments. On the one hand, the public supported more liberal provision for the elderly under social insurance programs. The aged remained a favored constituency in the eyes of most Americans. Yet on the other hand, people were pessimistic about the future solvency of Social Security and Medicare. Contradicatory public sentiment was echoed in elite opinion circles (academics, journalists, and legislators) by the spread of generational equity as a policy framework for thinking about entitlement programs. The appeal of generational equity corresponded to a fundamental political dilemma: how to finance expanded health care benefits? Democrats in Congress, along with most bioethicists, favored some form of national health insurance. Yet the Reagan and, later, the Bush administrations, echoing public sentiment, were resolutely against new taxes to pay for expanded care. It was not clear how this "policy paralysis" could ever be overcome.

There were attempts to break out of the gridlock. A landmark event was the Catastrophic Health Coverage Act of 1988, hailed as the first major expansion of Medicare in 20 years. This liberalization of the Medicare program was explicitly designed to be both revenue-neutral (no increase in the federal deficit) and generationally neutral (no new burdens on younger taxpayers). The result was a departure from the principle of social insurance and a challenge to what had so recently been the liberal consensus on health care and aging. Congressional and elite opinion had resolved to finance expanded benefits from the elderly themselves rather than from younger generations. Instead of seeing older people as the "deserving poor," the new policy reflected a growing awareness of the heterogeneity of rich and poor among the elderly themselves.

But the progressive surtax used to finance the Catastrophic Act's benefits proved to be the law's undoing. A tax revolt, sparked by more affluent elderly, resulted in repeal of the Catastrophic Act less than a year later. Catastrophic coverage became a political catastrophe. Repeal brought widespread disillusionment, shared by both the public and Congressional leaders, with this failed effort to expand Medicare on a pay-as-you go basis. Subsequently, Congress appointed the blue-ribbon Pepper Commission to look into alternatives. The commission recommended coverage for the 37 million Americans without health insurance and also proposed a new program of long-term care insurance covering all age groups. But the commission could not agree on how to finance these new benefits. When aging advocates urged greater public financing of long-term care, Congressional leaders proved cautious, partly because of the dismal experience of the Catastrophic Act.

As the 1980s drew to a close, issues of financing and cost-containment remained at the center of debates. Just as the concept of autonomy and informed consent decisively reshaped health care ethics in earlier decades, so now the issue of justice between generations had begun to influence health care policy in an aging society. In years to come, we can expect to see a growing "old-old" population and continuing public support for health care expenditures for the old. But we are also likely to see more open, explicit recognition of the limits on financing new health care benefits. The result is that justice and the ethics of allocation in an aging society will be controversial for many years to come.

## LONG-TERM CARE

When many people think of old age, the first image they think of is a nursing home. But the image is largely inaccurate. At any given time, only 5% of the nation's older people live in nursing homes. Yet concern about long-term care is appropriate because between 20% and 25% of people over 65 will spend time in a nursing home before they die. Thus, the ethical issues of quality of life in long-term care have great importance for the elderly. More to the point, long-term care presents some distinctive ethical dilemmas worthy of special attention. Wetle (1985), for example, could speak of a "taxonomy" of ethical issues in long-term care, issues that in many instances overlapped with well-established problems of bioethics, such as paternalism and autonomy, termination of treatment, and distribution of scarce resources.

The history of the modern nursing home goes back to 16th-century England and the Elizabethan Poor Law. In America, nursing homes were quickly distinguished from hospitals. Long-term care facilities took the form of the poorhouse or almshouse. After the passage of the Social Security Act in 1935, public funding gave a subsidy to private, proprietary homes for the aged, which have continued to be the overwhelming pattern in America. The passage of Medicaid in 1965 created another major stream of public funding and stimulated a new spurt of growth (Achenbaum, 1978).

Attention to ethical issues in long-term care has coincided with the growing numbers of elderly people living in nursing homes. With deinstitutionalization of the mentally ill in the early 1960s and then with the availability of Medicaid funding, there came a dramatic expansion of nursing home beds, a trend continuing into the 1970s. Before long there followed a series of nursing home scandals in the mid-1970s, greeted in turn by new laws and regulations. A widespread failure to ensure rights and autonomy of institutionalized elderly was matched by close attention to the issue by public interest lawyers and advocates for the elderly. Questions were raised about forced transfer of patients into nursing homes (Hessman, 1979). During the 1980s, DRGs and demographic trends began changing the character of nursing homes and residential facilities for the elderly. There was "aging in" of retirement communities and housing projects, and there was the rising level of age and frailty of nursing home residents.

Enthusiasm for promoting rights of nursing home residents—for example, through the nursing home resident's "Bill of Rights"—eventually had to confront more troubling questions: for example, are such rights actually enforceable (Wilson, 1978)? Do these rights include a so-called right to treatment for the mentally ill (Barnett, 1978) comparable to persons placed in state-run institutions? What about the use of physical or chemical restraints on patients who may be confused—"wanderers," for example, or those who are a danger to themselves or others? Another major issue in ethics and long-term care is the matter of nursing home placement (Bayer et al., 1987). Difficult questions here involve conflicting interests of different family members and the issue of how to safeguard the rights of elderly persons who may be placed in nursing homes against their will. Once again, the questions are complicated, the answers uncertain.

The 1980s witnessed some efforts to seek answers to these troubling questions. For example, in 1985, the Retirement Research Foundation announced a $1.5 million, 4-year grant program focused on ethical issues in autonomy and decision making for frail and impaired elderly (Hofland, 1988). Projects sponsored by the foundation covered a wide range: conceptual inquiries to define the many meanings of "autonomy," empirical studies of decision making in long-term care, the problem of diminished capacity to give informed consent, and specific programmatic steps to increase the scope of self-determination for nursing home residents. What is notable about this Retirement Research Foundation project is the way it successfully brought together multiple perspectives of empirical research, philosophical inquiry, legal remedies, and pragmatic forms of clinical intervention. The national impact of the effort will be felt for years to come.

In the future, it seems likely to that nursing home ethics, like other subdivisions of geriatric ethics, will focus in a more differentiated way on very specific questions that have been largely neglected by the mainstream literature on bioethics. Bioethics as a discipline has tended to focus on dramatic, life-and-death issues. Yet the ethical dilemmas in long-term care may have more to do with small details of daily life than with dramatic choices.

The study of these small details of life—"everyday ethics," or the "morality of the mundane"—has already illuminated some of the neglected questions of long term care (Diamond, 1988; Kane & Caplan, 1990). It has also drawn attention to issues of enormous controversy, such as the use of physical and chemical restraints (Schafer, 1985). Along parallel lines, ethicists have also turned their attention to issues arising in home health care, which are not entirely the same as those in a nursing home setting (Collopy, Dubler, & Zuckerman, 1990). In home care a continuing topic of concern remains the role of public financing versus family responsibility (Buchanan, 1984; Freedman et al., 1983).

Related to these broader policy questions are ethical issues that arise not within the public system of formal service provision but in the informal system, among family members, who, in fact, provide over 80% of the care for the frail elderly in America today (Sherlock & Dingus, 1985). The burden on these caregivers—mainly middle-aged women—has increasingly become recognized as a major issue of social policy, but it is an ethical matter as well (Pratt et al., 1987). A serious question concerns the limits of caregivers' responsibilities for the demented elderly (Howell, 1984). Other questions arise from the special bond between children and parents (Schorr, 1980), that is, the ethics of filial responsibility. It is only recently that philosophers have have given serious attention to these questions of family ethics (Callahan, 1985b; Sommers, 1986). But any assessment of the ethics of long-term care will necessarily have to take better account of the private as well as the public domain of ethical decision making.

## ETHICS OF RESEARCH WITH THE AGED

The field of research involving the elderly became identified as an area of important concern during the 1970s. In the early part of the decade that concern was limited (Bernstein & Nelson, 1975). But with the establishment of the National Institute on Aging (1976) there was an upsurge of federal funding for research on aging. It became clear that ethical dilemmas in geriatric research would have to be faced. Reich (1978), for example, cited five areas where special ethical concern was appropriate: anti-aging research, the vulnerability of the elderly to coercive participation in research, assessing mental competency, the use of surrogate consent, and special problems of consent for residents of nursing homes. There was an initial fear that elderly subjects would bear all of the risks while the benefits would accrue to society at large (Berkowitz, 1978). When abuses of earlier medical experimentation came to light, it was natural to urge a policy protecting "high risk" subjects such as prisoners, children, and institutionalized populations. The aged might well fall into this high-risk category, at least in the eyes of institutional review boards (Makurushka & McDonald, 1979).

But before long it became clear that neither clinicians nor researchers were altogether happy with putting the aged as a group into a "suspect" category for recruitment as research subjects. Ratzan (1981), for example, challenged the conventional approach to securing informed consent for participation in research. If simply "being old means you're different," then doesn't exclusion from research paticipation imply a lack of uniform competence on the part of the elderly as a group? The initial view of the elderly as research subjects stressed their vulnerability and the need to protect them from exploitation, but this view was obviously one-sided. By the mid-1980s this view had become more balanced.

An especially problematic case was research on Alzheimer's disease, where the exclusion of elderly subjects of diminished mental capacity might mean drastically curtailing the pace of biomedical research in dementia (Melnick & Dubler, 1985). Clearly, if one were concerned with the well-being of the elderly, there were two sides to the issue of research. On one side there was the promise of a relieving the scourge of Alzheimer's disease. On the other side, there was the fear of exploiting demented and vulnerable elderly. Researchers wondered if, along with protecting the vulnerable, was there not perhaps even a duty to actively promote research on the elderly (Miller et al., 1985)? If geriatric research was not undertaken, wouldn't the result be tantamount to excluding older people from possible benefits of new medical advances—in effect, an unintentional type of "ageism"?

Once again, bioethicists found themselves facing dilemmas on both sides of an issue. Clearly, more creative solutions to the problem needed to be found. A practical problem was the deficiency of short-term memory often found in aged subjects (Stanley et al., 1984; Taub, 1980), which made informed consent difficult to obtain. An experimental subject might give consent, then later on completely forget the transaction. Was the consent still valid? One possible approach urged was the use of a two-step, verbal and written consent procedure, accompanied by follow-up tests of comprehension, with oversight by an ethics committee (Denham, 1984). In years to come further refinements of research instruments and protocols may build on this model.

Reviewing the debate of the past decade, then, one can discern a broad shift in research ethics away from a view of the elderly as simply a vulnerable population in need of protection to a more balanced view that recognizes both an obligation to do research and also a duty to secure valid consent. The task for the future will be to maintain that balance among competing principles and ideals (Cassel, 1985b).

## METHODOLOGICAL ISSUES IN BIOETHICS AND AGING

In this overview of bioethics and aging, I have so far avoided discussion of methodological issues, prefering to focus instead on substantive questions and on the broad history of those questions over the last two decades. The assumption here has been that applying the methods of bioethics to problems of aging is a straightforward exercise and that success can be found by extending established principles to new questions raised by aging. But in fact the history of bioethics over the past two decades shows that the characteristic methods of bioethics arose in contexts quite different from geriatric health care. We may wonder: Are the questions of geriatric health care in some way distinctive? Will methods arising in a different context serve us well for issues of ethics and aging?

Contemporary bioethics has developed a powerful style of conceptual analysis that will continue to prove fruitful in the years ahead. Yet the limits of contemporary bioethics should also be noted. Most work in bioethics grew up almost entirely in the field of acute care medicine and medical technology. But for just that reason bioethics may be ill-equipped to offer illumination about the most characteristic dilemmas of geriatric health care. In fact, if the results and methods of bioethics as developed to date are simply extrapolated to the geriatric context, the result will not be satisfactory.

I want to elaborate this point by first outlining what I will call the "Dominant Model" of bioethics. The Dominant Model bioethics is illustrated in popular textbooks, academic articles, and policy debates. It is defined less by consensus about answers than by a shared style of analysis and problem solving, as shown. The Dominant Model stresses the role of rules and principles, above all centered on three leading principles of Beneficence (roughly, promoting individual well-being), Autonomy, and Distributive Justice. It then becomes the task of bioethics to clarify conflict among these principles and ultimately to develop rules and strategies for professional action or public choice. The shared style of the Dominant Model can be characterized as follows:

1. *Analytic philosophy.* Bioethics can be seen, in large part, as a species of applied philosophy. The prevailing style among American philosophers has been analytic philosophy, which, earlier in this century, was allied first with logical positivism and later with linguistic analysis, particularly as derived from the later work of Wittgenstein and others. This same style, characterized by application of logic, principles, rules, and conceptual analysis, has been carried over into applied ethics. In applied ethics, however, there have been modifications. Instead of the "thought experiment" or "counter-example" methods used in analytic philosophy, bioethics has been preoccupied with the case study approach. In this approach principles and rules are invoked that allow us to clarify choices open to agents facing a problematic clinical decision, an approach Caplan (1983) has described as the "engineering model." Ethical dilemmas—sometimes called "quandary ethics"—arise when principles come into conflict, as they often do (Pincoffs, 1986). Ethical analysis then consists of clarifying or resolving the conflict while at the same time uncovering presuppositions and implications brought out by the case at hand.

2. *Legal concepts.* A second point about the Dominant Model worth noting is the prevalence of legal principles and modes of argument (due process, precedent, burden of proof, analogy, etc.). Certain legal principles are almost sacrosanct in contemporary bioethics, for example, the doctrine of informed consent related to the ethical ideal of autonomy. Thus, the conflict between autonomy and beneficence gives rise to specific legal instruments—guardianship, conservatorship, power-of-attorney, and so on—that all take for granted the priority of individual autonomy. In general, the prevalence of legal concepts in the Dominant Model reflects the power of law, both liability law and constitutional law, in shaping American health care practice today. The language of rights is deeply embedded in American culture and serves to reinforce the power of law in the Dominant Model of bioethics.

3. *Time-limited action focus.* A third feature of the Dominant Model is its time-limited or action-focused quality. The Dominant Model of autonomy focuses on dramatic events of acute care. A specific problem or issue demands our immediate attention, and the case study method accentuates this mood of dramatic crisis or conflict in which a decision is

required. The critical question is always "What is to be done?" That is, what act (or decision) is to be taken, under what intentions and with what foreseeable consequences? An emphasis on intention points to Kant's deontological (duty-based) ethic, whereas an emphasis on consequences points to Mill's utilitarianism. But in either case, it is always a specific, delimited act or choice that is the focus, not, for example, an ongoing human relationship or social institution nor a still deeper question about character and virtue. The analysis of the Dominant Model is focused on actions, not on what kind of human beings we are or what our choices might mean in some larger scheme of things.

Yet a little reflection reveals how much has been left out by the Dominant Model of bioethics (Toulmin, 1981), and what has been left out becomes a serious problem for ethics and aging. The Dominant Model is based on a concept of rights and duties. It is, in Toulmin's phrase, "an ethics of strangers," and the Dominant Model often seems abstract and remote from practice. It is no secret that among clinicians and practitioners the conclusions of bioethics for practice are sometimes regarded with skepticism or even hostility (Clements & Sider, 1983). For example, the overwhelming consensus among bioethicists against paternalism in all but exceptional situations is a good instance where the conclusions of analytic bioethics seems sharply at odds with the practice of clinicians (Whitbeck, 1985). What is missing in the Dominant Model is an appreciation for the more intuitive and interpersonal ingredients of ethical deliberation: the role of narrative in individual character, the texture of lived experience, and the interpersonal dynamics of communication. The problems of "everyday ethics" so prominent in chronic care situations tend to be neglected by the Dominant Model (Christie & Hoffmaster, 1986).

In the remainder of this chapter, I want to consider three alternative methodological approaches that can correct some of the deficiencies in the Dominant Model of bioethics. These three approaches are virtue ethics, phenomenology, and the communicative ethics of Critical Theory.

## Virtue Ethics

In recent years, stimulated by the work of Alsadair MacIntyre (1982), there has been revival of interest in the tradition of virtue ethics. What virtue ethics urges is that we return to questions about character and human relationships, which historically have been at the center of thinking about ethics. Instead of an ethics of acts or principles, virtue ethics is more interested in the ethics of agents embedded in historical communities or traditions of discourse. MacIntyre's approach to virtue ethics is accompanied by an appeal to what he calls the "narrative unity of human life," a concept with rich but ambiguous implications for clinical decision making (Long, 1986).

Virtue ethics can contribute in important ways to remedying the deficiencies of the Dominant Model of bioethics. In the problems of geriatric care, crucial ethical issues revolve around attitudes and day-to-day caregiving rather than discrete or time-limited decisions and treatments. For that reason, it seems more appropriate to think in terms of virtue or character rather than rules or principles. Yet the ethics of virtue and the ethics of rules need not be understood as mutually exclusive. Without virtuous practitioners, we could have no confidence that rules and principles would be honored in practice. Even the ideal of informed consent proves unworkable if the virtue of empathy is not present among professionals (Rosenberg & Towers, 1986).

Furthermore, unless we appreciate the power of virtues, we simply cannot make sense of supererogatory acts undertaken by family caregivers who are caught between "imperative duties and impossible demands." An ethics of filial responsibility based on simple ideas of justice will not explain the obligations felt by caregivers. The caregiver's sense of moral obligation arises precisely from a lifelong relationship, in which the duty is experienced as part of one's historical identity as a spouse, son or daughter, and so on. The moral imperative is understood as an ineluctable feature of my history and personal identity, not simply as an obligation justified under contractual reciprocity.

Virtue ethics also proves crucial when we confront the catastrophic loss of hope or commitment to go on working, living, striving. The loss of hope can occur among patients, caregiving families, or professionals. We see it in the familiar phenomenon called burnout. Ethical dilemmas involving termination of treatment decisions or motivation for rehabilitation therapy often turn on just how we are to think about the prospect of hope for the future. Yet the psychology of hope is probably better understood by the categories of virtue or character than in terms of rules or principles. To speak of hope against a horizon of inevitable aging and death ultimately raises questions about the meaning of suffering and the meaning of the last stage of life itself.

## Phenomenology

Most analysts who write on ethical issues of aging have not themselves experienced old age. Nor, as a rule, have they had firsthand experience providing care for the very old. This lack of shared experience with the subject under study is a formidable barrier and one that has not been sufficiently acknowledged in the literature of gerontology or ethics. Yet appreciation for the experience of illness, of the aging body, seems crucial if we are to illuminate the dilemmas faced by practitioners, patients, and their families. It is precisely on this point that the perspective of phenomenology can prove most helpful in geriatric ethics (Agich, 1990; Kestenbaum, 1983; Zaner, 1988).

A phenomenological approach may result in different conclusions from the Dominant Model of bioethics. Specifically, ethicists writing from a phenomenological standpoint have challenged the conventional emphasis on autonomy as a central principle in geriatric ethics. It is argued that this emphasis misplaced because an excessively rationalistic view of autonomy ignores embodiment, temporality, and finitude (Spielman, 1986). The traditional view of autonomy, we know, thinks in terms of a competent, rational, and free decision maker. On this view, anything departing from that ideal tends to be viewed as a suspect form of paternalism. According to a common version of the matter, respect for autonomy as independence simply means noninterference, or leaving people alone. As the cliché has it, "Whose life is it anyway?" Yet, as Agich (1990) observes, this conventional language of autonomy and rights seem ill-suited for the tragic choices and moral ambiguities of long-term care.

Agich, writing from a phenomenological perspective, argues that the mainstream liberal view of autonomy is inadequate. On a theoretical level he argues that the liberal theory of autonomy provides too weak and too thin an account of what it means to be a person. Concrete lived experience seems remote from the abstractions of the liberal theory of autonomy. The standard account cannot help people in long-term care settings because its concept of the autonomous individual is abstract and idealized. We need an alternative framework based less on autonomy as independence than on respect for persons in their full concrete reality. This phenomenological perspective challenges the tendency to extend the discourse of autonomy from mainstream medical ethics to the environment of long-term care without understanding the lived reality of the situation.

This critique of the liberal theory of autonomy is not confined to phenomenologists but has been echoed by others inspired by Marxist and feminist theory. Writing along similar lines, Whitbeck (1985), for example, points to the primacy of relationships and contrasts the ethics of caring with the ethics of principles, in much the same way that Carol Gilligan does in her argument against Lawrence Kohlberg. O'Nora O'Neil, like Whitbeck, has also stressed the need for an ideal of autonomy based on a concrete picture of persons. This line of argument parallels the perspective of virtue ethics but underscores the importance of gender roles, a topic with immense implications for care of the aged because the overwhelming proportion of residents in long-term care facilities are women, as are caregivers as well.

Still another case where the phenomenological perspective can prove helpful is chronic illness. A recent report from the Hastings Center charges that chronic illness has been seriously neglected in the field of bioethics (Jennings, Callahan, & Caplan, 1988). The implications of this neglect for ethics and aging are very serious because the prevalence of chronic disease is a prominent feature of old age. Without a deeper phenomenological appreciation for the experience of chronic illness, it is doubtful if bioethics can offer insights helpful to practitioners concerned with questions such as nursing home placement, compliance with rehabilitation therapy, or the quality of life in daily living with handicaps.

Still another example of the same problem is to be found in ethical dilemmas of dementia and Alzheimer's disease. In looking at dementia we need to understand in concrete terms what it means for memory and selfhood to disintegrate over time. We also need to recognize how structures of consciousness remain intact, for example, to appreciate the complex relationship between long-term memories and personal identity. Failure to adopt a phenomenological perspective can lead to serious ethical misunderstanding. For example, one prominent philosopher, using a strict analytical framework, has urged us to look upon deteriorating Alzheimer's disease patients in the same way we look upon animals and to think of our duties to them in terms of animal rights (Brock, 1988).

But this conclusion misunderstands the lived experience of Alzheimer's disease for the victim as well as for the caregivers. From a phenomenological perspective, we cannot isolate the properties, or rights, of individual "personhood" outside the web of social relationships in which personal identity is embedded. Among families of Alzheimer's disease patients, their own identities are affected by the gradual disappearance of memory and identity of a central figure in their lives. The ethical dilemmas of caregivers must be understood in terms of social transactions in which life stories or narratives are constructed and validated through human relationships. It is just here that the analytic philosophical approach can oversimplify and therefore be misleading. Without a phenomenological grasp of the experience of Alzheimer's disease, we are in danger of ignoring the existential issues in the management of the demented elderly patient (Levine et al., 1984).

## Rights or Virtues?

Cassel, both geriatrician and ethicist, has suggested that contemporary biomedical ethics is excessively dominated by the "three C's:"

Competency, Consent, and Confidentiality. The real interests of older patients, she has argued, are not necessarily captured by those three C's. Instead, she has proposed that attention be shifted to another three C's: Care, Commitment, and Courage. Cassell's critique, once again, amounts to a call for virtues, such as patience, compassion, and prudence. This familiar contrast between two forms of ethical thinking, rights against virtues, has a long history in ethics. It seems clear that the virtues have special relevance for aging because geriatric care, whether in the family or in a long-term care facility, is more suited to the ethics of intimacy than to the ethics of strangers.

But is the appeal to virtue ethics really enough to solve the dilemmas of death and dying or Alzheimer's disease or justice between generations? Even if virtue ethics is updated, it's hard to see how the virtues alone will resolve the complex ethical dilemmas of an aging society. Moreover, virtue ethics and the traditional language of medical codes of ethics down through the centuries can all too easily be used to support open-ended professional discretion (Katz, 1984). That road leads to the temptations of extreme paternalism, particularly in an environment in which vulnerable old people lack defenders and where, too often, the most elemental rights are disregarded.

The problem with the virtue model and the rights model is that both tend to place exclusive attention on traits or claims by individuals. The ethics of rights and the ethics of virtue both ignore the social or institutional context of ethics, which is of a different order than that for isolated individuals. What is called for is not an ethics of individual decisions, whether patients' rights or professional virtues, but a genuinely social ethics, a communicative ethics based on deliberation and negotiation. Instead of the three C's of the rights model (Competency, Consent, and Confidentiality) or the three C's of the virtue model (Care, Commitment, and Courage), a different set of three C's is called for: Communication, Clarification, and Consensus-building.

## CRITICAL THEORY AND COMMUNICATIVE ETHICS

A third, quite different perspective comes from looking at the problems of ethics and aging not as questions of individual rights or virtues but as problems dependent on social structure and the history of institutions. Instead of looking for abstract principles or rules, on the one hand, or hoping to promote virtue or character, on the other, we need to take a critical view of the social institutions and patterns of communication in which ethical dilemmas arise. This third perspective is derived from the tradition of Critical Theory, as elaborated first by Adorno and Horkheimer and then by the later work of Jurgen Habermas. Critical Theory can make a contribution to elucidating the social and historical context of bioethical debates (Benhabib, 1986). The perspective of Critical Theory can be especially illuminating for gerontology (Moody, 1989).

Instead of accepting ethical claims at face value, Critical Theory would ask us to look at the way in which ethical thinking embodies or reflects political and economic structures. By considering more deeply the historical and institutional fabric in which ethical conflict unfolds, we come to see that ethics is never separate from politics and history. Critical Theory constitutes a critique of instrumental reason in favor of the normative ideal of communicative reason. Because this normative ideal is always bound to concrete conditions of history, there is a need for collaboration between philosophy and the social sciences, if only to understand the ideologies of professionalism, bureaucracy, and the dominance of interest groups over the common good. Most important, the normative ideal of communicative reason is distinct from the ethics of "procedural liberalism" of Kant or Rawls and thus from the fetish of autonomy deriving from social contract theory. As against hypothetical freedom—embodied in courts, mass media, the marketplace—Critical Theory would look at those forces that distort free communication, such as advertising, professional hegemony, and elite control of technologies.

Critical Theory, basing itself on Marx's critique of political economy, is concerned to disclose those human interests that are otherwise concealed under traditional theoretical frameworks (Roderick, 1986). On the positive side the values and interests at stake are those of emancipation of the human subject from domination, for example, from the dominating modes of prediction and control characteristic of social technologies in advanced industrial society.

This dialectic between human interest and emancipatory knowledge is of central concern in the writings of the contemporary exponent of Critical Theory, Jurgen Habermas (1974, 1979). Habermas favors what he describes as a "communicative ethics" based on shared discourse among persons who respect each other's position in the communication process itself. In this perspective, finding the "correct answer" to an ethical dilemma may be less a matter of agreeing on abstract principles than it is a matter of sharing a commitment ot free and open communication and working on behalf of institutional structures that support that communication. This normative goal—the "ideal speech condition"—constitutes the ultimate aim of ethical action. The problem is to define and to promote the concrete conditions that favor such communication in all stages of life, including old age.

This ideal standard of communication is admittedly very far from what we find in most arenas of contemporary life. Habermas has argued that it is characteristic of advanced industrialized societies that we encounter "systematically distorted communications," which serve to frustrate open communication. In mass media, in the educational system, in the workplace, in political communication—everywhere we find an evasion or falsification of discourse. Instead of open deliberation we see domination by power or manipulation.

The development of human services for the aging has followed precisely this pattern. For example, the rise of the nursing home industry does not empower older people to make decisions about their lives. Instead, the elderly become a new class of consumers subject to the expanding domination by professionals in the "Aging Enterprise" (Estes, 1979). Instead of freedom, we have the "colonization of the life-world" in old age, and the last stage of life is emptied of any meaning beyond sheer biological survival.

This whole development is part of a social and historical process, not at all a matter of individual choice. Therefore, it is not surprising that the traditional ethic of individual autonomy has been helpless to halt this erosion of freedom. The ethics of patient autonomy may insist on informed consent or encourage advance directives. But those very instruments are compromised by the institutional structures and systematically distorted communications in which the elderly receive care.

The control of health care decisions by third-party payers increasingly has the effect of distorting and disguising the nature of real choices made, for example, a bias toward elaborate medical technology or life prolongation rather than social support for patient decision making. One result of this pattern of domination is that free communication or deliberation about choices and values in geriatric health care becomes difficult if not impossible. The natural weaknesses of age are compounded by the structured dependency of old age (Townsend, 1981).

Collective decisions about the allocation of resources follow the same pattern. Technocratic medicine becomes ever more expensive and is at the same time accompanied by unremitting pressures for cost-containment. In the face of spiraling costs, the elderly are portrayed as both victims and villains. The health care system prolongs their lives while geriatric care consumes more and more social spending. Younger generations plunge deeper into poverty, and "rationing" becomes the new form of rationality. Yet the political system, in the grip of policy paralysis, increasingly loses any rationality it may have had. Both the public and the elderly are more than ever mystified by a "system" that seems beyond the reach of individual choice or the judgment of ethics.

It is precisely against this historical background, which is the history of our own time, that we can grasp the importance of open communication about ethical dilemmas of health care and aging. The novelist Bernanos remarked that "the worst and most corrupting of lies are problems wrongly stated." If free and open communication about ethics can do anything, it can help us to state, and thus to confront, the real problems that are before us.

In our time the experience of advanced age has more and more become a normal, predictable part of the human life course. In public discourse our conventional ethical concepts about truth-telling, respect for persons, and allocation of resources take little account of the distinctive ethical problems of the last stage of life. Yet, intuitively, most of us understand that age makes a difference in how people see their lives. The view from 20 is not the same as the view from 80. Despite that awareness, we keep the dilemmas of old age, like the fact of death, in the shadows of consciousness. Just as we separate the elderly from the rest of society, so we separate old age from the rest of life.

The recent demand for more self-determination and autonomy in geriatric health care is a welcome protest against all forms of domination. But, given our history, it is not, it cannot be the whole answer. Indeed, the ideal of autonomy itself, so incompatible with many existential facts about old age, may inadvertently become a new myth promising us a fulfillment that is bound to leave us disappointed. Perhaps we should call to mind the Greek figure Tithonus, who was granted by the gods his wish for immortality but, alas, without also receiving youth.

Along with Tithonus, we should call to mind the story of Oedipus, not the Freudian version but the original Greek myth, which includes the last chapter of that fateful life of King Oedipus at Colonnus. Sophocles' last play is the story of Oedipus in old age, wandering in blindness but finally achieving wisdom, submission, and reconciliation with the order of the universe. This vision was achieved only by Sophocles in his own old age, his 89th year of life, and it is a far-reaching vision indeed. Confronting the ethical dilemmas of old age may demand a vision no less far-reaching from all of us.

## REFERENCES

Aaron, H., & Schwartz, W. (1984). *The painful prescription.* Washington, DC: Brookings Institution.

Achenbaum, W. A. (1978). *Old age in the new land.* Baltimore: Johns Hopkins University Press.

Agich, George, "Reassessing Autonomy in Long Term Care," *Hastings Center Report* (November / December, 1990), 20:6, 12–17.

Annas, G. J. (1981). Termination of life support systems in the elderly: Legal issues. *Journal of Geriatric Psychiatry, 14*(1), 31–43.

Annas, G. (1984). The case of Mary Hier: When substituted judgement becomes sleight of hand. *Hastings Center Report, 14*(4), 23–25.

Annas, G. (1985). When procedures limit rights: From Quinlan to Conroy. *Hastings Center Report*, 24–26.

Appelbaum, P. S., Meisel, A., & Lidz, C. (1985). *Informed consent: Legal theory and clinical practice.* New York: Oxford University Press.

Avorn, J. (1984). Benefit and cost analysis in geriatric care: Turning age discrimination into health policy. *New England Journal of Medicine, 310*(20), 1294–1301.

Ball, J. R. (1984). Withholding treatment: A legal perspective. *Journal of the American Geriatrics Society, 32*, 528–530.

Barnett, C. F. (1978). Treatment rights of mentally ill nursing home residents. *University of Pennsylvania Law Review, 126*(3), 578–629.

Baron, C. H. (1981). Termination of life support systems in the elderly. *Journal of Geriatric Psychiatry, 14*(1), 45–70.

Battin, M. P. (1987). Choosing the time to die: The ethics and economics of suicide in old age. In S. Spicker et al. (Ed.), *Ethical dimensions of geriatric care*, (pp. 161–189).

Bayer, R. (1984). Will the first Medicare generation be the last? *Hastings Center Report, 14*(3), 17–22.

Bayer, R., & Callahan, D. (1985). Medicare reform: Social and ethical perspectives. *Journal of Health, Politics, Policy and Law, 10*(3), 533–547.

Bayer, R., Caplan, A., Dubler, N., & Zuckerman, C. (Eds.). (1987). Coercive placement of elders: Protection or choice? [Special issue]. *Generations, 11*(4).

Beck, P. (1985). Do not resuscitate orders in nursing homes: The need for physicians to communicate and to document. *North Carolina Medical Journal, 46*(12), 633–638.

Benhabib, S. (1986). *Critique, norm and utopia: A study of the foundations of critical theory.* New York: Columbia University Press.

Bergsma, J., & Thomasma, D. (1982). *Health care: Its psychosocial dimensions.* Pittsburgh: Duquesne University Press.

Berkowitz, S. (1978). Informed consent, research and the elderly. *The Gerontologist, 18*(3), 237–243.

Bernstein, J. E., & Nelson, F. K. (1975). Medical experimentation and the elderly. *Journal of the American Geriatric Society, 23*, 327–329.

Besdine, R. W. (1983). Decisions to withhold treatment from nursing home residents. *Journal of the American Geriatric Society, 10*, 602–606.

Bexell, G., et al. (1980). Ethical conflicts in long-term care of aged patients: The tube-feeding decision. *Ethics in Science and Medicine, 7*(5), 141–145.

Blank, R. H. (1988). *Rationing medicine.* New York: Columbia University Press.

Brock, D. W. (1988). Justice and the severely demented elderly. *Journal of Medicine and Philosophy, 13*, 73–99.

Brody, E. (1985). Parent care as a normative family stress. *The Gerontologist, 25,* 19–29.

Bromberg, S., & Cassel, C. (1983). Suicide in the elderly: The limits of paternalism. *Journal of American Geriatric Society, 31*(11), 698–703.

Brown, N. K., & Thompson, D. J. (1979). Nontreatment of fever in extended-care facilities. *New England Journal of Medicine, 300,* 1246–1250.

Buchanan, R. J. (1984). Medicaid: Family responsibility and long term care. *Journal of Long Term Care Administration, 12*(3), 19–25.

Callahan, D. (1985a, Winter). Feeding the dying elderly. *Generations,* pp. 15–17.

Callahan, D. (1985b). What do children owe elderly parents? *Hastings Center Report, 15*(2), 32–33.

Callahan, D. (1987). *Setting limits: Medical goals in an aging society.* New York: Simon & Schuster.

Caplan, A. (1983). Is aging a disease? In S. Spicker & S. Ingman (Eds.), *Vitalizing long term care.* New York: Springer Publishing Co.

Caplan, A. (1985, Winter). Let wisdom find a way: The concept of competency in the care of the elderly. *Generations,* pp. 10–14.

Caplan, A. (1983). Can applied ethics be effective in health care and should it strive to be? *Ethics, 93,* 311–319.

Cassel, C. (1985a). Allocation decisions: A new role in the new Medicare. *Journal of Health Politics, Policy and Law, 10*(3), 549–564.

Cassel, C. (1985b, Winter). Ethical issues in research in geriatrics. *Generations,* 45–48.

Cassel, C. K., & Meier, D. E. (1986). Selected bibliography of recent articles in ethics and geriatrics. *Journal of the American Geriatric Society, 34,* 399–409.

Cassem, N. H. (1981). Termination of life support systems in the elderly: Clinical issues. *Journal for Geriatric Psychiatry, 14*(1), 13–21.

Childress, J. F. (1984). Ensuring care, respect, and fairness for the elderly. *Hastings Center Report, 14*(5), 27–31.

Christiansen, D. (1978). Ethical implications in aging. *Encyclopedia of Bioethics.* New York: Macmillan.

Christie, R., & Hoffmaster, C. B. (1986). *Everyday ethics for family physicians.* New York: Oxford University Press.

Churchill, L. R. (1987). *Rationing health care in America: Perceptions and principles of justice.* Notre Dame, IN: University of Notre Dame Press.

Clements, C. D., & Sider, R. C. (1983). Medical ethics' assault upon medical values. *Journal of the American Medical Association, 250,* 2011–2015.

Cody, M. (1986). Withholding treatment: Is it ethical? *Journal of Gerontological Nursing, 12*(3), 24–26.

Cohen, E. (1985). Autonomy and paternalism: Two goals in conflict. *Law, Medicine and Health Care,* 145–153.

Cole, T., & Gadow, S. (Eds.). (1986). *What does it mean to grow old? Views from the humanities.* Durham, NC: Duke University Press.

Collopy, B. J. (1985). Medicare: Ethical issues in public policy for the elderly. *Social Thought, 11*(2), 5–14.

Collopy, B. (1988). Autonomy in long term care: Some crucial distinctions. *The Gerontologist, 28* (Suppl.), 10–17.

Collopy, B., Dubler, N., & Zuckerman, C. (Eds.). (1990). The ethics of home care: Autonomy and accommodation [Special supplement]. *Hastings Center Report, 20*(2).

Connery, J. R. (1985). In the matter of Claire Conroy. *Linacre Quarterly, 52*(4), 321–328.

Daniels, N. (1987). *Am I my parents' keeper?* New York: Oxford University Press.

Daniels, N. (Ed.). (1988). Justice between generations and health care for the elderly [Special issue]. *Journal of Medicine and Philosophy, 13.*

Denham, M. J. (1984). The ethics of research in the elderly. *Age and Ageing, 13,* 321–327.

Diamond, T. (1988). Social policy and everyday life in nursing homes: A critical ethnography. *Social Science and Medicine, 23,* 1287–1295.

Dyck, A. J. (1984). Ethical aspects of caring for the dying incompetent. *Journal of the American Geriatrics Society, 32,* 661–664.

Engelhardt, T. (1986). *The foundations of bioethics.* Oxford: Oxford University Press.

Estes, C. (1979). *The aging enterprise.* San Francisco: Jossey-Bass.

Evans, R. (1985). Illusions of necessity: Evading responsibility for choices in health care. *Journal of Health, Politics, Policy and Law, 10*(3), 439–467.

Fahey, C. (Ed.). (1985). Ethics and aging [Special issue]. *Social Thought, 11*(2).

Freedman, R. M., et al. (1983). Why won't Medicaid let me keep my nest egg? *Hastings Center Report, 13*(2), 23–25.

Gilfix, M., & Raffin, J. A. (1984). Withholding or withdrawing extraordinary life support: Optimizing rights and limiting liabilities. *Western Journal of Medicine, 141,* 387–394.

Gill, D. G., & Ingman, S. (1985). Geriatric care and distributive justice: Problems and prospects. *Social Science and Medicine, 23*(12), 1205–1215.

Gilligan, C. (1982). In a different voice: Psychological theory and women's development. Cambridge, MA: Harvard University Press.

Glantz, L. H. (1982). The case of Earle Spring: Terminating treatment on the senile. In A. E. Doudera & J. D. Peters (Eds.), *Legal and Ethical Aspects of Treating Critically and Terminally Ill Patients.* Ann Arbor, MI: AUPAA Press.

Habermas, J. (1974). *Theory and practice* John Viertel, (Trans.) London: Heinemann. (Original work published 1963).

Habermas, J. (1979). *Communication and the evolution of society* (T. McCarthy, Trans.). Boston: Beacon Press.

Halper, T. (1978). Paternalism and the Elderly. In S. Spicker et al., (Eds.), *Aging and the Elderly* (pp. 321–339). Atlantic Highlands, NJ: Humanities Press.

Halper, T. (1985). Life and death in the welfare state: End-stage renal disease in the United Kingdom. *Milbank Memorial Fund Quarterly, 63*(1), 52–92.

Hastings Center. (1988). *Guidelines on termination of treatment.*

Hessman, L. (1979). Case studies in bioethics: Forced transfer to custodial care. *Hastings Center Report, 9*(3), 19–20, 26.

Hofland, B. (1988). Autonomy in long term care: Background issus and a programmatic response. *The Gerontologist,* 28: pp. 3–9.

Howell, M. (1984). Caretakers' views on responsibilities for the care of the demented elderly. *Journal of the American Geriatrics Society, 32,* 657–660.

Jennings, B., Callahan, D., & Caplan, A. (1988). Ethical challenges of chronic illness. Special Supplement, *Hastings Center Report.*

Kane, R. A., & Caplan, A. L. (1990). *Everyday ethics: Resolving dilemmas in nursing home life.* New York: Springer Publishing Co.

Kapp, M. (1985). *Geriatrics and the law: Patient rights and professional responsibilities.* New York: Springer Publishing Co.

Kapp, M., Pies, H. E., & Doudera, A. E. (Eds.). (1985). *Legal and ethical aspects of health care for the elderly.* Ann Arbor, MI: Health Administration Press.

Kart, C. S. (1981). In the matter of Earle Spring: Some thoughts on one court's approach to senility. *The Gerontologist, 21*(4), 417–423.

Katz, J. (1984). *The silent world of doctor and patient.* Glencoe, IL: Free Press.

Kayser-Jones, J. S. (1986). Distributive justice and the treatment of acute illness in nursing homes. *Social Science and Medicine, 23*(12), 1279–1286.

Kestenbaum, V. (1983). *The humanity of the ill: Phenomenological perspectives.* Knoxville, TN: University of Tennessee Press.

Kingson, E., Hirschorn, B. A., & Cornman, J. (1986). *Ties that bind.* Washington, DC: Seven Locks Press.

*Law, Medicine and Health Care.* (1985). [Special issue on aging].

Lesnoff-Caravaglia, G. (Ed.). (1985). *Values, ethics and aging.* New York: Human Sciences Press.

Levenson, S. A. (1986). Ethical dilemmas of the 80s. In R. J. Ham (Ed.), *Geriatric medicine annual.* Oradell, NJ: Medical Economics Books.

Levine, N. B., et al. (1984). Existential issues in the management of the demented elderly patient. *American Journal of Psychotherapy, 38,* 215–223.

Lo, B., & Dornbrand, L. (1984). Guiding the hand that feeds: Caring for the demented elderly. *New England Journal of Medicine, 311*(6), 402–404.

Long, T. D. (1986). Narrative unity and clinical judgment. *Theoretical Medicine, 7*(1), 75–92.

Lubitz, J., & Prihoda, R. (1984). The use and costs of Medicare services in the last two years of life. *Health Care Financing Review, 5*(3), 117–131.

Lynn, J. (1986). Ethical issues for caring for elderly residents of nursing homes. *Primary Care, 13,* 295–306.

Lynn, J. (1987). *By no extraordinary means.* Bloomington: Indiana University Press.

MacIntyre, A. (1982). *After virtue.* Notre Dame, In: University of Notre Dame Press.

Macklin, R. (1986). The geriatric patient: Ethical issues in care and treatment. In Mappes and Zembaty (Eds.), *Biomedical ethics.* New York: McGraw-Hill.

Makarushka, J. L., & McDonald, R. D. (1979). Informed consent, research, and geriatric patients. *The Gerontologist, 19,* 61–66.

Mallary, S. D., & Gert, B. (1986). Family coercion and valid consent. *Theoretical Medicine, 7*(2), 123–126.

Marzen, T. J. (1985). In the matter of Claire C. Conroy. [Note] *Issues in Law and Medicine, 1*(1), 77–84.

McCullough, L. B. (1984). Medical care for elderly patients with diminished competence: An ethical analysis. *Journal of the American Geriatrics Society, 32*(2), 150–153.

McIntyre, R. L. (1986). The Conroy decision: A "not-so-good" death. In J. Lynn (Ed.), *By no extraordinary means* (pp. 260–266). Bloomington, IN: Indiona University Press.

Mehr, D., et al. (1984). Feeding the demented elderly. *New England Journal of Medicine, 22*(311), 1383–1384.

Meilaender, G. (1984). On removing food and water: Against the stream. *Hastings Center Report, 14*(6), 11–13.

Melnick, V. L., & Dubler, N. (Eds.). (1985). *Alzheimer's dementia: Dilemmas in clinical research.* Clifton, NJ: Humana Press.

Miller, S. T., et al. (1985). Clinical trials in elderly persons. *Journal of the American Geriatrics Society, 33*(2), 91–92.

Moody, H. R. (Ed.). (1985). Ethics and aging [Special issue]. *Generations 10*(2).

Moody, H. R. (1988). From informed consent to negotiated consent. [Special supplement on autonomy and long-term care]. *Gerontologist, 28.*

Moody, H. R. (1989). Toward a critical gerontology: The contributions of the humanities to theories of aging. In J. Birren & V. Bengtson (Eds.), *Theories of aging.* New York: Springer Publishing Co.

Moody, H. R. (1992). *Ethics and aging.* Baltimore: Johns Hopkins University Press.

Neugarten, B. (1982). *Age, society and the law: An annotated bibliography.* Evanston, IL: Northwestern University.

Neugarten, B. (1983). *Age or need?* Beverly Hills, CA: Sage.

Neugarten, B., & Havighurst, R. J. (Eds.). (1976). *Social policy, social ethics and the aging society.* Washington, DC: U.S. Government Printing Office.

O'Neill, O. (1984) Paternalism and partial autonomy. *Journal of Medical Ethics, 10,* 173–178.

Pellegrino, E. D. (1986). Rationing health care: The ethics of medical gatekeeping. *Journal of Contemporary Health Law and Policy, 2*(2), 23–45.

Pincoffs, E. (1986). *Quandaries and virtues: Against reductivism in ethics.* Lowrence: Kansas University Press.

Prado, C. G. (1990). *The last choice: Preemptive suicide in advanced age.* Westport, CT: Greenwood Press.

Pratt, C., Schmall, V., & Wright, S. (1987). Ethical concerns of family caregivers to dementia patients. *The Gerontologist, 27*(5), 632–638.

President's Commission for the Study of Ethical Problems in Medicine. (1981–1983). *Defining death* (1981); *Making health care decisions: The ethical and legal implications of informed consent* (1982); *Deciding to forego life-sustaining treatment* (1983); *Securing access to health care* (1983). Washington, DC: US Government Printing Office.

Quinn, M. J. (1985, Winter). Elder abuse and neglect raise new dilemmas. *Generations,* pp. 22–25.

Rachels, J. (1986). *The end of life: Euthanasia and morality.* New York: Oxford University Press.

Rango, N. (1985). The nursing home resident with dementia: Clinical care, ethics and policy implications. *Annals of Internal Medicine, 102,* 835–841.

Ratzan, R. M. (1981). The experiment that wasn't: A case report in clinical geriatric research. *The Gerontologist, 21*(3), 297–302.

Rawls, J. (1971). *A theory of justice*. Cambridge, MA: Harvard University Press.
Regan, J. J. (1981). Protecting the elderly: The new paternalism. *Hastings Law Journal, 32*, 1111–1132.
Reich, W. J. (1978). Ethical issues related to research involving elderly subjects. *The Gerontologist, 18*(4), 326–337.
Rosenberg, J., & Towers, B. (1986). The practice of empathy as a prerequisite for informed consent. *Theoretical Medicine, 7*(2), 181–190.
Schafter, A. (1985). Restraints and the elderly: When safety and autonomy conflict. *Canadian Medical Association Journal, 132*, 157–160.
Schorr, A. (1980). *"... Thy father and thy mother": A second look at filial responsibility and policy*. Washington, DC: Social Security Administration.
Scitovsky, A. A., & Capron, A. (1986). Medical care at the end of life: The interaction of economics and ethics. *Annual Review of Public Health, 7*, 59–75.
Shelp, E. (Ed.). (1985). *Virtue and medicine: Explorations in the character of medicine*. Dordrecht, The Netherlands: Reidel.
Sherlock, R., & Dingus, C. M. (1985). Families and the gravely ill: Roles, rules and rights. *Journal of the American Geriatrics Society, 33*(2), 121–124.
Siegler, M. (1984). Should age be a criterion in health care? *Hastings Center Report, 14*(5), 24–27.
Smeeding, T. M. (Ed.). (1987). *Should medical care be rationed by age*? Totowa, NJ: Rowman and Littlefield.
Sommers, C. H. (1986). Filial morality. *Journal of Philosophy, 83*(8).
Spicker, S., Ingman, S., & Lawson, L. (Eds.) (1987). *Ethical Dimensions of Geriatric Care*, Dordrecht: Reidel.
Spielman, B. J. (1986). Rethinking paradigms in geriatric ethics. *Journal of Religion and Health 25*(2), 142–148.
Stanley, R., et al. (1984). The elderly patient and informed consent. *Journal of the American Medical Association, 14*, 1135–1137.
Steinbrook, R., & Lo, B. (1984). Decision making for incompetent patients by designated proxy. *New England Journal of Medicine, 310*, 1598–1601.
Taub, H. (1980). Informed consent, memory, and age. *The Gerontologist, 20*(6), 686–690.
Thomasma, D. (1984a). Ethical judgments of quality of life in the care of the aged. *Journal of the American Geriatrics Society, 32*, 525–527.
Thomasma, D. (1984b). Freedom, dependency, and the care of the very old. *Journal of the American Geriatrics Society, 32*, 906–914.
Thornton, J. (Ed.). (1987). *Ethics and aging*. Vancouver, BC: University of British Columbia Press.
Toulmin, S. (1981). The tyranny of principles. *Hastings Center Report, 11*(6), 31–39.
Townsend P. (1981). The structured dependency of the elderly: A creation of social policy in the 20th century. *Ageing and Society, 1*(1), 5–28.
U.S. Office of Technology Assessment. (1987). *Life sustaining technologies and the elderly*. Washington, DC: US Government Printing Office.
Veatch, R. M. (1979). *Life span: Values and life-extending technologies*. New York: Harper and Row.

Veatch, R. M. (1981). *A theory of medical ethics.* New York: Basic Books.

Veatch, R. M. (1988). Justice and the economics of terminal illness. *Hastings Center Report, 18*(4), 34–40.

Wetle, T. (1985, Winter). Long term care: A taxonomy of issues. *Generations* pp. 30–34.

Whitbeck, C. (1985). Why the attention to paternalism in medical ethics? *Journal of Health Politics, Policy and Law, 10*(1), 181–187.

Wilson, S. H. (1978). Nursing home patients rights: Are they enforceable? *The Gerontologist, 18*(3), 255–261.

Winslade, W. J., Lyon, M. A., Levine, M. L., & Mills, M. J. (1984). Making medical decisions for the Alzheimer's patient: Paternalism and advocacy. *Psychiatric Annals, 14*(3), 206–208.

Zaner, R. (1988). *Ethics and the clinical encounter,* Englewood Cliffs, NJ: Prentice-Hall.

18

# Wisdom and Method: Philosophical Contributions to Gerontology

*Ronald J. Manheimer*

Outside the field of biomedical ethics, few contemporary scholars trained in philosophy or housed in its departments have ventured to comment professionally on the process of aging or the phenomenon of growing old. Simone de Beauvoir (1972) in her systematic study of aging as reflected in European literature, *The Coming of Age*, is an important exception. But philosopher Patrick McKee's (1982) recent compendium, *Philosophical Foundations of Gerontology*, leaves a vast lacuna between the reflections of thinkers ancient and modern—only two, Montaigne and Schopenhauer, fill the gap; whereas for contemporaries, just two or three formally trained philosophers are included.

In fact, the vast majority of philosophical contributors to the study of aging are from the social sciences and from fields of the humanities other than philosophy. Members of these disciplines have crossed traditional departmental boundaries to expound on aging and a variety of topics: wisdom (Clayton & Birren, 1980), social philosophy and theory construction (Rosenmayr, 1980, 1981), ethics (Callahan, 1987), philosophy of education (Lowy & O'Conner, 1986), logic and teleology (Labouvie-Vief, 1980), the status and construction of meaning (Cole, 1985; Kaufman, 1986), philosophical reasoning (Chinen, 1989), to name some of the topics and interlopers in the field. They are joined by a smaller circle of formally trained philosophers such as Moody (1976, 1986, 1988), Norton (1976), and Prado (1986), but not all of these scholars are affiliated with academic philosophy. Although it is interesting to ask why so few professional philosophers have entered this arena, it is equally interesting to ask why nonphilosophers have been drawn to issues of aging and epistemology, ontology, ethics, hermeneutics, and philosophy of science. Several answers are possible.

The study of aging and later life is a relatively new science and an enticing one at that. Its scope is both personal and universal; it is relevant to generations past, present, and future, and it raises or provokes many of life's big questions—its purpose, value, meaning, potential, and mystery. By its very nature, gerontology is interdisciplinary.

But besides personal and interdisciplinary factors, there is a third motive that has led students of aging into philosophical discourse. The early, formative years of gerontology were dominated by positivist and behaviorist approaches of the medical, biological, and social sciences. Although significant advances were made, a corresponding flatness settled into gerontology, stemming from a reductivist orientation that established one-dimensional cause-and-effect relationships (Kenyon, 1988; Philibert, 1979), leading to a focus upon what has been termed the "failure model" of aging. This contributed, for example, to the biological view that old age was a pathological condition, immutable and universal in its effects, or to the sociological view, that withdrawal from community life was a normal (i.e., necessary) correlate of growing old. Aging tended to be viewed as a disease, problem, weakness, or deficiency. An ideology of dependency and obsolescence pervaded and shaped the perceptions of scientists and scholars, though they were unaware of holding any normative viewpoint (Esposito, 1987).

In response, a thoughtful body of literature arose that attempted to restore complexity and dimensionality to the study of aging by reasserting a wide array of variables such as the importance of historical periods and events, cultural values and ethnic traditions, multivariate explanations, phenomenological descriptions, and the qualitative gains of later life. Philosophically, many of these studies revealed issues of values and ideology as key influences operating where value-free claims had been made. Moreover, methodologies used in the study of aging and their fundamental presuppositions were called into question, especially since, it was argued, certain research techniques tended actually to produce, rather than just permit, discovery of their results (Gubrium & Lynott, 1983). The tools of critical analysis and interpretation used by these investigators showed the influence of such 20th-century philosophers as Heidegger, Husserl, Schutz, and Merleau-Ponty (phenomenology); Ricoeur and Gadamer (hermeneutics); Horkheimer, Adorno, and

Habermas (critical theory). The contributions of European rather than Anglo-American thinkers seem to have exercised the greatest influence.

How then have these philosophical contributions added to our understanding of aging? The following is an attempt to examine the issues and topics in which gerontology and philosophy have crossed paths. This is not a historical survey because only the last 10 years or so are considered, and only major or representative contributions are included. Rather, it is an effort to articulate the critical issues and evaluate the progress that has been made. The field of aging and biomedical ethics, which has been fertile ground for philosophers, will be only touched on because it is dealt with elsewhere in this volume (see Moody, chap. 18). In some cases, it will be necessary to show that a particular piece of research and descriptive exposition does, in fact, contain philosophical content or make philosophical assertions. In other cases, this will be obvious.

Two interrelated philosophical themes are reviewed here. The first includes studies that critique reductivist and narrow ideological presuppositions in order to advance humanistic views aimed at restoring personal and social meanings of aging and later life. The second considers studies that identify positive developmental features of later life while acknowledging simultaneous areas of decline and that offer critical analysis of the single-end or linear life-course models. Both sets of studies deal with issues concerning research, methodology, interpretive modes, qualitative versus quantitative approaches to research, and the communication of research findings, especially the uses of narrative methods.

## SAVING THE MEANING OF AGING

The problem of meaning in later life has been discussed from several related points of view. It is argued that old age has lost its societal meaning because we no longer share commonly held expectations, values, or understanding of its place in the life course (Cole, 1985). Though liberated from social and cultural stereotypes of the predestined and immutable character of old age as a time of inevitable decline, the new old age is besieged by theorists, marketeers, and the media, who advocate an ethic of activity, whether in the form of social participation, education, volunteerism, or recreation. This, in turn, has contributed to new normative stereotypes also conveying impoverished social meanings of aging and old age. These can be traced historically to post-Victorian theological and hygienic moralisms (Cole, 1983), the ideology of consumer capitalism (Moody, 1986), and the denial of frailty and death (Gadow, 1983).

Added to the loss of an adequate social role, it is argued that the elderly suffer from personal meaninglessness because their past experiences are considered obsolete or, at most, quaint and sentimental snapshots of a time gone by. From certain developmental points of view, the old have run out of growth potential. The most they can hope for is successfully to perform a series of life adjustments that gerontologists, perhaps reflecting the work ethic, insist on calling "tasks" (Havighurst, 1952). Even in the innermost self of the aged, meaninglessness takes the form of despair over the sense of one's having led an arbitrary, fragmented, and incomplete life (Erikson, 1975) that, in the face of impending death, produces anguishing loss of self-esteem (Butler, 1963), leaving the psyche prey to dominating unconscious forces, such as narcissism (Downing, 1981; Jung, 1933; Woodward, 1986).

Rallying to meet the multiple challenge of saving the personal and social meaning of old age, those who have articulated the problem also have posed new directions and solutions for the restoration and, indeed, interpretive expansion of a multiplicity of meanings.

Cole and Moody, for example, are inspired by the work of philosopher Alasdair MacIntyre (1981) who has called for "the unity of a narrative quest," which, in the study of aging, means formulation of the view that old age is an intrinsic part of life while providing a coherent account depicting the significant moral and intellectual roles the old can play in the larger schema of the generations. Cole's (1983) historical narrative critiques the current "enlightened" view of aging. In contrast, he believes that by overcoming the fragmentary treatment of later life and studying the unity and interdependence of life stages, a meaningful, because holistic, understanding will be possible. For Cole, the proponents of the "use it or lose it" activity paradigm of old age exceed a healthy attitude toward the elderly. The obsession with activity can be a denial of frailty and mortality. His study of sermons during the Victorian era convinces Cole that a new type of moralism has emerged that regards as "sinful" states of being such as the vulnerability of old age, in which the person is less in control of his or her life. Such a covert attitude has led to imposition of a new stereotype: the healthy, vigorous, self-controlled, successfully aging older person.

Moody's narrative quest began some 12 years ago, when he studied attitudes toward education for older adults (Moody, 1976). Presuppositions about education in later life included "rejection," that there was no point in educating the old; a social service mentality that saw education as an ameliorating, socializing activity for the dependent elderly; a participation approach emphasizing the "normalizing" benefits of lifelong learning; and Moody's own preference for education in later life as a means to "self-actualization" through release of personal potential leading to ego integrity. But Moody's concerns over the years have led him to a more elaborate social-political philosophy. Drawing on the Frankfort School of "critical theory," he has sought to make gerontology a more self-reflective science, critically aware of its own value-laden assumptions and ideological leanings. "Emancipation" has replaced "self-actualization" in Moody's recent work (1988) as he analyzes the need for intergenerational cooperation, group initiative (such as self-help groups), mentoring roles the old can play for the young (especially the disenfranchised poor and minority), and release from the dominating ideologies found in public policies that preempt the initiative of the elderly or that pit the old as a special interest group against the needs of other age groups.

Both Cole and Moody regard later life as a time when unique metamorphoses of self and society are possible. But they regard self-change and greater social freedom as neither imminent nor purely voluntary—willed reconstructions of reality or remaking of "metaphors of self." Their approaches imply an a priori moral order, old age as a time for "participation in cultural forms" passed down through the great traditions. In this, they affirm MacIntyre's historico-philosophical quest for the recovery of traditional "virtues."

If Cole and Moody advocate that later life holds the promise of personal transformation and social renewal of roles and contributions when guided by traditional values, others hold a more modest, if not conservative position. They regard later life as primarily a time for adjustments to changing life circumstances. An accommodation process, coming to terms with personal and social limitations, need not exclude the possibility of qualitative change. But a strict interpretation of adaptation implies certain notions of fixed limits to growth—whether of self or society. The distinction between transformational and adaptational perspectives can be further subdivided. Those, like Moody and Cole, who argue for age-appropriate roles guided by cultural traditions and classical virtues are "traditionalists," especially when compared to student of aging who reject notions of age-appropriate roles and behavior as social stereotyping. For these "modernists," later life is an unwritten history that is yet to be evolved by each person, limited only by personal imagination and pressures of society to conform (Manheimer, 1987).

A transformational position is suggested in the work of developmental psychologist Lawrence Kohlberg (1973), who has speculated on what, in his hierarchy of moral stages, constitutes a "seventh," or postconventional, stage. Triggered by the realization of the finitude of one's life, stage seven begins with despair stemming from the experienced contradiction of a finite self in a world of infinite possibilities. This clearly Kierkegaardian formulation leads Kohlberg to the observation that somewhere in middle age to later life, individuals who are highly morally developed may experience a "field and ground" type of ontological reversal of self and world. "We sense the unity of the whole and ourselves as part of that unity," explains Kohlberg, though he is clearly uncomfortable moving into a realm that lacks the formal rigor and unilinear structure of stages one through six of his theory.

Other theorists have addressed this postconventional stage as a mode of individual consciousness rooted in culture and society but revealing personal values transcending self-interest (Reker & Wong, 1988) or as acceptance of the need for detachment from the futile impulse to complete oneself (Muller, 1986), and so on. The modernist attitude places greater emphasis on the act of choice itself than on the thing chosen. Self and social construction—à la the "multiple realities" social phenomenology of Alfred Schutz (1962)—are the results of deliberate acts, not acceptance of or surrender to a superordinate reality. The ultimate transformational modernist view is that of unconstrained choice indifferent to age restraints and contributing to an "age-irrelevant" society (Neugarten & Neugarten, 1986) in which the older person is simply that, a person, free to actualize his or her own individual potential (Gruman, 1978).

What is especially interesting about these transformational narratives of later life, traditionalist and modernist, is their emphasis on the strengths and contributive assets of old age while not denying aspects of loss and decline in late life—the so-called trade-off point of view. Restoring the meanings of old age requires attention to subtle changes in a person's life: growing interiority, the complex interplay of personal and public history, cultural and religious values, the influence of ethnicity and gender. To approach these qualitative dimensions, theorists we have cited make use of literary sources such a autobiographies, biographies, journals and diaries, novels, poems and plays, oral histories, folklore, as well as sources from the visual arts. These "texts" allow theorists of aging to explore the concrete, emotional, paradoxical, changeable, multifaceted cultural and historical dimensions of aging and old age. In fact, scholarly investment in the narrative approach can yield accounts that seek to capture and even evoke the transformation of later life, turning academic writing into an art form. These studies give dramatic form to retelling the story of late-life transformation in which disability, frailty, limitation, dependency, and despair undergo an inversion, becoming qualities such as capability, strength, possibility, autonomy, and wisdom. Elsewhere we have referred to these as narratives of "secular redemption" (Manheimer, 1989) because they bear striking resemblances to traditional accounts of spiritual development.

The quest for a coherent life-course narrative has its own pitfall. The overly unified life-course narrative has been critiqued by Cohler (1989), who values the narrative approach but cautions against a Western, post-Reformation tendency to assume a single-track, linear life-course model. The coherent life story may be too coherent, suppressing the diversity of life events and simultaneous levels of experience because of a pre-occupation with continuity. This can lead to the problematic view that the end of one's life is the ultimate test of its meaning—a form of retrospective attribution that is as flawed as prospective determinism.

The question of the meaning of old age for the individual and for society is directly related to the questions of the purpose of old age. This is seen very clearly in Daniel Callahan's (1987) assertion that the purposive role of the older person is to serve as a model of unselfish care for the young of society, to display "grace under adversity" as one accepts the travails of decline and the inevitability of death, and to act one's age with dignity so as to "redeem its meaning as a stage of life." Such a purposeful old age will, presumes Callahan, be a meaningful one.

The philosophical difficulty we encounter in these arguments about what constitutes a meaningful and purposeful later life is in finding adequate criteria for determining their validity and evaluating their explanatory power. It is not always clear when these descriptions of later life are to be understood as empirical statements, normative declarations, advocative utterances, or hypothetical ideals. A large body of literature, drawing from empirical, quantifiable studies as well as from oral histories and personal documents has convincingly shown that, for a variety of reasons such as identity loss from retirement or absence of a sense of productivity, old age can bring about a crisis of meaning in one's life that is, at the same time, a social malaise amplified by certain values and social arrangements. But the cure for the crisis of meaning is harder to observe, measure, or logically deduce. Is the role of philosophy in gerontology to produce ideals, to advocate for change, to posit values—in short, to liberate older adults?

The strengths of philosophy in gerontology would seem to lie in contributions adding critical analysis along historical, political, ethical, and epistemological lines, with a penchant for synthesis of ideas making up an evaluative-normative construction of later life's purpose and meaning. But the discomfort of humanistic endeavors in a field dominated by clinical and behavioral science reveals itself even more clearly in the corresponding critique of investigative methodologies and their reporting narratives, especially when these deal with asserted strengths of aging. The problem of the method of studying the purpose of old age surfaces in the study of wisdom and other positive qualities.

## WISDOM AND METHOD

Erikson's (1964) notion that wisdom may emerge in the last stage of life has brought about a vast and enthusiastic popular and scholarly literature. However, his general life-cycle framework has been criticized on the grounds that it is more normative than empirical, difficult or impossible to substantiate, and lacks sufficient explanatory power to account for how change comes about. Moreover, according to Clayton and Birren (1980), Erikson's concept of wisdom is difficult to operationalize and validate because it is unclear how "the intellectual or reflective components of wisdom are utilized in the psychosocial evolution of the individual." Hence, the argument for an adaptational rather than transformational framework.

What is the advantage of wisdom, both for the individual and society? Apart from providing inner solace through reconciliation to one's life struggles—as in Erikson's (1979) sensitive treatment of Dr. Borg in Ingmar Bergman's *Wild Strawberries*—is it possible that wisdom has an adaptational value? Clayton and Birren (1980) sense that, in this respect, Erikson was on the right track. Their study of wisdom proceeds along parallel epistemological avenues: investigating the nature of human understanding that transcends intelligence, adopting a research methodology that reflects accepted standards of scientific objectivity. Where Erikson could be classified a transformational pietist (he has been especially concerned with transformations in the lives of major spiritual figures such as Luther and Gandhi), Clayton and Birren's study of wisdom and aging is adaptational and modernist. They forgo use of an in-depth narrative method in favor of more readily quantifiable questionnaires. The ultimate value of wisdom for them is biological—perhaps to justify to their colleagues in the behavioral sciences the validity of attempting to bring an elusive and normative topic under empirical investigation.

Clayton and Birren (1980) set about to review the history of wisdom in ancient Western and Eastern traditions, focusing on the behavioral manifestations in overt actions of wisdom rather than its inwardness. They pursue aspects of wisdom in old age in order to find out whether wisdom could be viewed as a unique quality of later life, a key element of successful adaptation, and possibly an evolution-favoring (species-survival) characteristic which Birren, elsewhere, has termed "strategic adaptability" (Birren, 1988).

Plato or Lao Tse might have smiled to hear that the "underlying structure of wisdom," as perceived by individuals at different points in life, could be distinguished by the use of such research tools as the multidimensional scaling (MDS) algorithm (TORSCA8), a word association–value preference test the researchers applied to a pool of subjects, young and old.

Smile as they may, the ancients, especially of the Eastern tradition, would have approved of Clayton and Birren's conclusion that wisdom represents "the integration of general cognitive, affective, and reflective qualities." The triad of thought, feeling, and intuition runs throughout the Western philosophical and religious tradition, though, from the time of Plato and Aristotle, there has always been a distinction between practical, moral wisdom (ethics) and theoretical, contemplative wisdom (metaphysics). Clayton and Birren (1980) also found that although older persons did not regard themselves or later life as in greater possession of wisdom, they did judge affective qualities of understanding and empathy as more similar to wisdom than chronological age or experience. Younger age groups, on the other hand, did link wisdom with aging.

If, as the researchers contend, empirical investigation shows that wisdom is manifested in actions, judgments, values, and personality characteristics, which may be factors of education and environment, it may be possible to advocate for those social circumstances most conducive to the advancement of wisdom.

We have concentrated on Clayton and Birren's (1980) study because it exemplifies the attempt to deal with a teleological issue—the ineffable quality and lofty ideal of wisdom as potentially the essence of the last stage—and a crucial methodologically issue, how one could go about ascertaining the nature and presence of wisdom by using procedures holding to the standards of objectivity and empirical quantifiability. Unfortunately, their functional definition of wisdom, given philosophy's long and complex history of trying to come to terms with its own mission (its pursuit), seems unoriginal, but their discovery that younger generations project a link between growing older and growing wiser, though older people do not, is a profoundly suggestive result of their study. It echoes the famous Socratic denial of the attribute. Their pragmatic interpretation of wisdom is reminiscent of Dewey's notion of intelligence in humans as a form of evolutionary adaptability—a perhaps useful but extremely narrow and reductive view of the human mind.

The epistemological quandary in Clayton and Birren's (1980) work reveals a parallel problem found in other studies that try to show that whereas later life involves a series of biological declines, simultaneously it may show a series of social and psychological advances. The paradigmatic problem is to determine, empirically, how a longer life and more experience can lead to enhancement of personal judgment (drawing on long-term memory) and a greater contributive capability based on the "self-generating" capacity of the human nervous system to "override" the somatic system and thus transcend biological, psychological, and social barriers (Birren, 1988). In other words, how do people grow wiser when the rest of them may be falling apart? How does one correlate the determinist criteria of evolutionary biology with self-generative acts deriving from wisdom? "Self-generative" suggests acts of superordinate self-regulation that are difficult to foresee, predict, anticipate, and explain.

Self-generated self-regulation is an operational definition for freedom understood as autonomy. But, as Kant has shown, freedom can neither be proved nor disproved; it is a logical antinomy. It defies determinism. Yet, obligated to demonstrate that wisdom—as an example of a positive development in old age—can be profitably studied within a behavioristic-empirical framework, Birren (1988) is drawn into applying biological metaphors (self-generative, adaptive, etc.), and, hence, to a determinist (and materialist) view of what, in the great tradition, has been considered transcendent of determinism (and, often, of materialism). This is not to deny the value of Birren's approach because it is important to ask whether wisdom can be defined and its acts observed, whether it can be taught or fostered, whether it is one thing or many, and whether, if one had it, one would know one had it.

Despite these problems, Clayton and Birren (1980) have identified the need for future research on the nonlinear, simultaneous loss–gain phenomenon of aging.

The related work of psychologist Labouvie-Vief (1980, 1982) provides an additional critique of unilinear theories of development that posit single and end-states or stages and hence can only project advancement and then decline. For Labourvie-Vief (1980), "growth and regression are interwoven at all points of the life span." She regards the extrapolation of child development theories to midlife and old age as the imposition of false norms deriving from a linear logic. Contradicting the unilinear model, studies showing both decrement and stability in older adults led to the theory of fluid and crystallized forms of intelligence—where fluid intelligence is exemplified by abstract reasoning and crystallized intelligence to gains in judgment and understanding based on learning and experience. A revision of this theory led to the distinction between competence and performance and evidence that decline in competence can be influenced by educational and environmental factors.

What is interesting about Labouvie-Vief's work, given our emphasis on narrative structures and the use of first-person accounts, is that a third revision of the nonlinear theory emerged because she was "forced by research participants themselves into an altogether different approach" (1980). She includes their comments and her dawning realization that the aging subjects felt that research tests were trying to push them into demonstrating declining cognitive ability, whereas they felt that the tests were belittling and were testing only the things they did less well (and found boring), not any of the things they did better with age.

She then found that contrary to the elementary building-block theory of cognitive development—that development goes in a straight line from simpler to more complex cognitions—there is in fact a trade-off, that "to gain a new integration, one must give up an earlier one." Her studies dovetail with Birren's (1988) at this point because she posits the notion that adaptive, pragmatic necessities in adulthood and old age exercise a force on the individual that triggers a reintegration of the cognitive system. From her reformulation, logic—the end-state of cognitive development in Piaget's theory of the development of operational thinking—is not the goal of development but the tool that, in turn, is subordinated to social-system needs of adulthood. But whereas Birren is inclined to regard the self-generative capacity of the individual as potentially socially transcendent, Labouvie-Vief sees it is limited by dependence on cognitive constructs available in the society. Labouvie-Vief holds to the notion that, ultimately, it is social adaptability that qualifies adult development. She is aware of the ideological implications of this view as a form of conservatism (i.e., preservation of the status quo) but argues that characteristics of flexibility and toleration for complexity contribute to stability instead.

Though she does not label it as such, Labouvie-Vief's (1980) story of how her subjects made her aware of some of the prejudicial components of her research model and methodology is an example of the "hermeneutical circle" that some theorists (Philibert, 1979, Rosenmayr, 1980) have insisted is required in the study of aging. Researchers must practice a self-critical role in making their presuppositions and evaluative commitments self-conscious in order to recognize their influences and to make these a part of their investigations. Gerontology, in this sense, becomes a dialectical science, studying itself as it studies its subjects. Moreover, it should practice this same dialectic from the side of the aging subject by considering as valid the self-interpretations and self-constructions, "biographical work" (Starr, 1983) that introduce the subjective, historically embedded reality of later life.

What will be found, according to social theorist Rosenmayr (1981), once research on the older adult takes history, biography, and generationally influenced social values into account as part of a subjective–objective dialectic, is that the individual does not move toward "compact oneness" but is a "multitude of life-threads." The concept of the singular self, integrated in later life (Erikson's "wisdom"), can function as a denial of further innovations in old age, just as Labouvie-Vief's "stability" can function as a justification for conservativism on the part of the elderly.

Methods in gerontology need to be as complex as the subject of aging, according to Rosenmayr (1980). And he advances the same concern found in other philosophically minded students of aging: that theory not be allowed to function as a form of suppression through promoting singular norms and then testing for them. Like others, he searches for the element of freedom in the narrowing world of the elderly, transforming the causal logic of human development (with its interplay of deterministic forces) into a narrative of "fulfillment" through "chances of renewal" in later life. For Rosenmayr, fulfillment is not a product but a process: continual self-chosen activity, experience of progress through one's efforts. Rosenmayr is a transformational modernist in his emphasis on late-life qualitative change and on the action of doing rather than on the structure and content of what is done or discovered.

## THE AGING OF PHILOSOPHERS

It is appropriate that, bringing this essay full-circle, we conclude by turning to a philosophical contribution to gerontology that looks at the aging of philosophers themselves as an influence on their reasoning. Allan Chinen (1989), a psychiatrist and frequent contributor to aging studies, uses biographies, a novel, and their own philosophical texts to theorize about transformations from quantitative to qualitative reasoning in the work of two 20th-century philosophers, Wittgenstein and Whitehead. He finds in their early thinking a preoccupation with and delight in precision, abstraction, conceptual reduction, and mathematical description. He points out, in the case of Wittgenstein's *Tractatus*, a self-confident "declarative tone." But at some point in midlife, the philosophical reasoning of the two philosophers changes toward growing emphasis on concrete situations, broader contexts, pragmatic problem solving, and a greater tolerance for ambiguities. In the case of Whitehead, Chinen identified a third developmental stage: "After years of pragmatic problem-solving, the obligations and compromises of midlife give way to an intuitive, transcendent and holistic mode of reasoning, exemplified by Whitehead's metaphysical work."

The life course itself, Chinen implies, produces a philosophical movement away from logical positivism to forms of reasoning more attuned to the qualitative, ineffable, intuitive, and indeterminate. One is reminded of Kierkegaard's three stages of life interpretation: the aesthetic, ethical, and religious. The aesthetic might be akin to Chinen's attribution of "youthful cleverness"; the ethical, to pragmatic problem solving; and the religious, to the metaphysical.

Chinen's (1989) essay again has this theme of inversion as a critical transformation in midlife and old age. Only now, instead of trying to understand aging from a philosophical point of view, we are regarding philosophical thought from an aging, developmental point of view.

Does the shift from quantitative to qualitative reasoning imply the superiority of one to the other? Is narrative interpretation, with its tendency toward secular redemption of aging, the solution to reductionist analyses of growing old? These questions are yet to be resolved.

Philosophical contributions to aging and human development help to map the richness and complexity of a fledgling field that belongs to both the natural and human sciences. Although the philosophical approaches tend to be self-critical and reflective, they are not automatically free of presuppositions or normative inclinations. But these contributions do serve to inquire about the difference between normal (sometimes static) and ideal (perhaps liberative) views of aging. Philosophical inquiry can introduce new possibilities into our understanding of aging and later life. Where, before, we had seen only impasse and one-dimensionality, we now recognize opportunity and complexity.

## REFERENCES

Beauvoir, S. de (1972). *The coming of age* (P. O'Brien, Trans.) New York: G. P. Putnam's Sons.

Birren, J. E. (1988). A contribution to the theory of the psychology of aging: As a counterpart of development. In J. E. Birren & V. L. Bengston (Eds.), *Emergent theories of aging* (pp. 152–176). New York: Springer Publishing Co.

Butler, R. W. (1963). The life review: An interpretation of reminiscence in the aged. *Psychiatry, 26,* 65–76.

Callahan, D. (1987). *Setting limits, medical goals in an aging society.* New York: Simon and Schuster.

Chinen, A. B. (1989). From quantitative to qualitative reasoning: A developmental perspective. In L. E. Thomas (Ed.), *Research on adulthood and aging: The human science approach.* Albany: State University of New York Press.

Clayton, V. P., & Birren, J. E. (1980). The development of wisdon across the life span: A reexamination of an ancient topic. In P. B. Baltes & O. G. Brim, Jr., (Eds.), *Life-span development and behavior* (Vol. 3, pp. 103–135). New York: Academic Press.

Cohler, B. (1982). Personal narrative and life-course. In P. Baltes & O. G. Brim, Jr. (Eds.), *Life-span development and behavior* (Vol. 4, pp. 205–241). New York: Academic Press.

Cohler, B. J. (1989). Personal narrative and maintenance of morale in later life. Paper presented at Institute of the Medical Humanities, The University of Texas Medical Branch at Galveston.

Cole, T. R. (1983). The enlightened view of aging: Victorian morality in a new key. *Hastings center report, 13,* 34–40.

Cole, T. R. (1985). Aging and meaning: Our culture provides no compelling answers. *Generations, 10,* 49–52.

Downing, C. (1981). Your old men should dream dreams. In J. R. Staude (Ed.), *Wisdom and age.* Berkeley, CA: Ross Books.

Erikson, E. H. (1964). *Insight and responsibility.* New York: W. W. Norton.

Erikson, E. H. (1975). *Life history and the historical moment.* New York: W. W. Norton.

Erikson, E. H. (1979). Reflections on Dr. Borg's life cycle. In D. D. Van Tassel (Ed.), *Aging, Death, and the Completion of Being* (pp. 29–68). Philadelphia: University of Peansyluania Press.

Esposito, J. L. (1987).*The obsolete self.* Berkeley, CA: University of California Press.

Gadow, S. A. (1983). Frailty and strength: The dialectic in aging. *Gerontologist, 23,* 144–147.

Gruman, G. J. (1978). Cultural origins of present day "ageism": The modernization of life cycle. In S. F. Specker, K. M. Woodward, & D. Van Tassell (Eds.), *Aging and the elderly.* Atlantic Highlands, NJ: Humanities Press.

Gubrium, J. F., & Lynott, R. J. (1983). Rethinking life satisfaction. *Human organization, 42.*

Havighurst, R. J. (1952). *Developmental tasks and education.* New York: McKay.

Jung, C. G. (1933). *Modern man in search of a soul.* New York: Harcourt, Brace and World.

Kaufman, S. (1986). *The ageless self: Sources in meaning in later life.* Madison: University of Wisconsin Press.

Kenyon, G. M. (1988). Basic assumptions in theories of human aging. In: J. E. Birren & V. L. Bergtson (Eds.), *Emergent theories of aging* (pp. 3–18). New York: Springer Publishing Co.

Kohlberg, L. (1973). Stages and aging in moral development: Some speculations. *Gerontologist, 13.*

Labouvie-Vief, G. (1980). Adaptive dimensions of adult cognition. In N. Datan & N. Lohmman (Eds.), *Transitions of aging* (pp. 3–26). New York: Academic Press.

Labouvie-Vief, G. (1982). Dynamic development and mature autonomy. *Human development, 25,* 161–191.

*Life-sustaining technologies and the elderly.* (1987). Washington, DC: U.S. Office of Technology Assessment.

Lowy, L. & O'Connor, D. (1986). *Why education in the later years.* Lexington,iMA: D. C. Heath.

MacIntyre, A. (1989). *After virtue: A study in moral theory.* Notre Dame, IN: University of Notre Dame Press.

Manheimer, R. J. (1987). *Adjustment versus transformation in late life narratives.* Paper presented at the 40th Annual Scientific Meeting of the Gerontological Society of America, Chicago, November 1987.

Manheimer, R. J. (1989). The narrative quest in qualitative gerontology. *Journal of Aging Studies, 3*(5), 231–252.

McKee, P. L. (Ed.). (1982). *Philosophical foundations of gerontology.* New York: Human Science Press.

Moody, H. R. (1976). Philosophical presuppositions of education for our age. *Educational Gerontology, 1,* 1–16.

Moody, H. R. (1986). The meaning of life and the meaning of old age. In T. R. Cole R & S. A. Gadow (Eds.). *What does it mean to grow old?* (pp. 11–40). Durham, NC: Duke University Press.

Moody, H. R. (1988). *Abundance of life, human development policies for an aging society.* New York: Columbia University Press.

Muller, J. (1986). Light and the wisdom of the dark: Aging and the language of desire in the texts of Louise Bogan. In K. Woodward & M. M. Schwartz (Eds.), *Memory and desire.* Bloomington: Indiana University Press.

Neugarten, B. L., & Neugarten, D. A. (1986). Age in the aging society. *Daedalus, 115*(1),

Norton, D. L. (1976). *Personal destinies.* Princeton, NJ: Princeton University Press.

Philibert, M. (1979). Philosophical approach to gerontology. In J. Hendricks & C. D. Hendricks (Ed.), *Dimensions of aging* (pp. 379–394). Cambridge, MA: Winthrop.

Prado, C. G. (1986). *Rethinking how we age.* Westport, CT: Greenwood Press.

Reker, G. T., & Wong, P. T. P. (1988). Aging as an individual process: Toward a theory of personal meaning. In J. E. Birren & V. L. Bergston (Eds.), *Emergent theories of aging* (pp. 153–176). New York: Springer Publishing Co.

Rosenmayr, L. (1980). Achievements, doubts, and prospects of the sociology of aging. *Human Development, 23.* 46–62.

Rosenmayr, L. (1981). Objective and subjective perspectives of life span research. *Aging and society, 1,* 29–49.

Schutz, A. (1962). *Collected papers: Vol. 1. The problem of social reality.* The Hague: Martinus Nijhoff.

Starr, J. M. (1983). Toward a social phenomenology of aging: Studying the self process in biological work. *International journal of aging and human development, 16*(4), 257–270.

Woodward, K. (1986). The mirror stage of old age. In K. Woodward & M. M. Schwartz (Eds.), *Memory and desire.* Bloomington: Indiana University Press.

19

# The Older Student of Humanities: The Seeker and the Source

*David Shuldiner*

In recent years, options for late-life humanities study have continued to grow, not only in terms of subject but of venue as well. Community and senior centers, libraries, nursing homes, churches, synagogues, and colleges throughout the country have offered educational programs and courses for older adults on subjects ranging from creative writing to local history. An increasing number of educational institutions, particularly community colleges, have older-student organizations, whose members not only attend regularly scheduled classes but organize courses, lectures, and other programs of their own. Apart from institutional settings, many elders are engaged in some form of self-directed learning, whether alone or among groups of like-minded explorers in the world of ideas.

To provide a more complete picture of this world of late-life humanities study, I will look at the following areas:

1. Age and lifelong learning.
2. Social/historical contexts and late-life humanities study.
3. Humanities, literacy, and oral tradition.
4. Forms of late-life humanities study.

I wish to acknowledge the sage council of Prof. Mary Alice Wolf, Director of the Gerontology Program at Saint Joseph College; our discussions helped me clarify the overview and direction of this article.

## MATTERS OF AGE

> Now, I can appreciate more, I can read slower, and really get the meaning. Before, when I was younger, I used to read faster, I used go through books much faster, and not too much in depth like now. Now I try to get more in depth when I read, I try to get myself involved more in what the author has to say. . . . I am interested in the plot in the sense of what's going on, instead of how it is said . . . also the human emotions involved. . . . I think it comes with age . . . and with experience. (Octavio Toro, retired medical technician)

Recent thinking on the subjects of aging, learning attitudes, and learning capacity has provided new perspectives that bear on the discussion of late-life humanities learning. "Life course" studies tend to stress the conditional relevance of age to personal outlook, worldview, and so on, revealing age to be but one of severable variables in late-life identity formation (see, e.g., Hareven & Adams, 1982). Such factors as historical experience and class and ethnic background may be just as influential as chronological age in providing a context for identity and its forms of expression among older adults. Any of these factors, including age, may provide direction for the study of humanities in later life.

A corollary to this view is the notion that the identity and interests of older adults represent a continuity with the past, that we bring into old age a set of characteristics shaped by earlier life experiences. Chronological age often brings wisdom tempered by experience, but just as often that wisdom may represent but the maturation of a worldview set at a much earlier formative stage. Yet it is equally true that the potential for enlightenment is ageless, that the desire for knowledge may emerge at any time (prompted by many circumstances, including the offering of a humanities class at a local senior center) and that interests and pursuits may radically change with differing circumstances of age (e.g., the potential "liberation" of retirement). In fact, the range of interests—and therefore subjects older persons choose for study—are just as varied as for any other arbitrarily designated age group. Further, levels of development in the capacity for critical thinking vary as much among older adults as among younger persons. I will discuss forms and formats for humanities study among older adults that address this diversity of backgrounds and interests.

## LIFELONG LEARNING

There is very little in the way of literature specifically on older students of humanities. However, general approaches to older adult education and lifelong learning (i.e., continuing education) offer useful insights. It is generally agreed among educational gerontologists that the ability to learn is undiminished by age. Although motor functions may slow down and short-term memory may lag, the capacity for associative thinking—a vehicle of critical thought—is not necessarily diminished. Differences in the readiness of older adults to learn may be more often a function of previous learning experiences than of age-related cognitive (dis) abilities (Darkenwald & Merriam, 1982).

One factor that may be considered age-relevant is what James Birren (1964) calls "social intelligence" (70, 182), that is, a verbal comprehension that has been developed over a lifetime of social interaction and discourse. What Birren is describing is an experiential knowledge that comes with the "praxis" of social relationships, of living in the world. Measured by technical standards, the average older adult may be slower in the performance of certain intellectual tasks (e.g., demonstrating perceptual skills, making quick judgments, etc.) but more than compensate with those cognitive skills that accrue with the accumulated experience of human interaction (Darkenwald & Merriam 1982).

It is precisely in this area that elders bring a special set of cognitive skills and sensibilities to the study of humanities. At the core of all humanities disciplines is the attempt to understand the human experience—the relationship of people to each other and to the world—be it through history, philosophy, literature, or the arts. The "social intelligence" of age enables older persons to apply a special measure of personal and social expertise to the study of that human experience, bringing to bear accumulated knowledge—in particular, the memory of past events and activities—that may be compared to or contrasted with those encountered in the course of humanities learning. Whatever the specific subject of study may be, personal experience becomes the touchstone for humanities learning among older adults.

For the older student, in fact, that accumulated social knowledge becomes the functional equivalent of formal training in a humanities field when drawn upon in forming opinions and discussing issues. What an older person may lack (and what does not necessarily accompany the wisdom of years) is a method of critical thinking and inquiry that enables her or him to identify and interrelate concepts in disparate works under consideration. It may well be argued (given the frequent complaints by professors in institutions of higher education) that teaching modes of critical inquiry has not historically been a high priority in our public educational system. So an older adult is not necessarily any more at a disadvantage than the average college undergraduate in her or his capacity to grapple with humanities subjects. It is breadth of perspective that counts, and it is in this respect that elders—specifically, those who have achieved the potential for a broadened perspective that often comes with age—have the distinct advantage.

Although these age-related factors in humanities learning are significant, they are not necessarily manifest in all older persons. The range of intellectual background, capabilities, and modes of learning among older persons is just as great as for other age groups. Many older students of humanities—often, but not exclusively, those with extensive formal education—are versed in methods of critical inquiry integral to humanities learning; others have seldom engaged in critical thinking, let alone humanities study. The issue here is not intelligence but rather degrees of familiarity with tools of analysis, reflected in differences in the level of discourse. It is just as important to accept variations in the capacity for humanities learning as it is to recognize the broad spectrum of interests that older persons may (or may not) have in humanities subjects.

Still, "life-stage" models continue to impose universal age-dependent conditions upon the intellectual activities of older persons. A prevalent model posits old age as a period during which the search for self-realization (a cornerstone of humanities learning) becomes an urgent task, especially so if the process has never before been initiated. Perhaps it is more a desire for closure—tying loose ends together, completing "unfinished business"—that is being identified. For the road to self-discovery may be entered at any age and is (at least potentially) lifelong, a path of continuous development and maturation, interrupted only by death (Wolf, 1988). Although it is important to acknowledge the urgency with which many older persons seek "final" enlightenment, it is just as important to recognize that many elders, while seeking ultimate wisdom, may also pursue humanities learning with an ageless enthusiasm—a savoring of the moment—that reflects their own lifetime interests.

Although contemporary life course studies have replaced the pathological model of deterioration in old age with one of lifelong growth and development, the fact remains that development is an uneven process. Just as older people vary in their interests and outlook, so do they also differ developmentally in their perspective or orientation to the humanities. Many older persons have a well-defined worldview through which they "work through" the subjects and issues with which they are confronted. Others are just discovering their own inner world. Late-life humanities programs have often been catalysts in this process.

In a dialectics of aging there is both continuity and change, degeneration and growth. Although there are losses (physical and otherwise) associated with age, there is also the possibility of living a new life (in retirement), of gaining a "richness in the quality of experience"

(Moody, 1985). Psychologists identify this "quality" variously as self-actualization (Maslow), integration (Erikson), individuation (Jung), and countless other terms (cited in Moody, 1985). One may view it as a stage of personal development often reached only in old age. In educational gerontology it has become commonplace to identify as an important goal in late-life learning the pursuit of self-enlightenment, mediated through the process of self-reflection, one of the key modalities of humanities learning. (The National Council on the Aging's series of reading anthologies for older adults [discussed below] is, at least from this perspective, most appropriately titled "Self-Discovery Through the Humanities.")

## Humanities and Liberation

> I think [my wife and I] were both fortunate having, early in life, adult role models who encouraged us to question, encouraged us to look behind things, and not take things for granted—that that's the way it's supposed to be. (Joseph Dimow, retired machinist)

The decision to explore the world of the humanities in late life is just as bound by historical circumstance (personal, social, economic, political) as it is by individual personality or chronological age. Recognition of, let alone seeking, the rewards of humanities study, spiritual and intellectual, is contingent. For some, the motivation to learn, to explore the human experience, to discover oneself, may be sublimated at any age by other priorities, not the least of which is the need to work for personal and family survival. Humanities study, deferred throughout the life course, is for many elders not the first item on the agenda for late-life activities. For others, like Joe Dimow, critical inquiry, encouraged from childhood, has continued throughout their working lives; the time of age simply provides an opportunity for more formal exploration.

> I did, after retiring, take a course in the history of western civilization. . . . And that was the first formal course I had in anything that you might call humanities. And I took it mostly because I had heard a lot about some different figures or events in history or periods in history that I knew the names [of] but I wasn't really sure that I knew what they signified. I didn't read a lot of books. But I did follow the text, listened to the lecturer, and discussed questions with him, and tried to gather something from the way that the students responded, too. That was more of what I was interested in. . . . When I walked through the corridor with the professor, we talked as equals. Sometimes we were stopped by a student who was concerned with what date will the exam be.

For Joe Dimow, the "luxury" of formal humanities study was, of necessity, deferred until after his career as a full-time machinist had been completed. Humanities study in general has been an activity historically reserved for the privileged few. For those older persons who for social, economic, or cultural reasons have lived out their working lives with little or no exposure to the humanities or modes of critical thinking, the "luxury" of late-life study can be a liberating experience.

## HUMANITIES AND THE POLITICS OF CRITICAL THOUGHT

That critical thinking is inseparable from humanities study may explain why so may people in this conforming, nonreflective society reach old age without adequate exposure to a field whose mode of inquiry has not been encouraged in school, factory, or office. Yet, for some elders, like Joe and his life partner, Lillian—members of a cultural minority of working-class intellectual and political rebels—humanities as critical inquiry (formal or nonformal) has been an integral part of political and social movements in which they have been lifelong participants. Continuing a European "tradition" here, many immigrants who arrived in the United States at the turn of the century brought with them the legacy of "workers' schools." Radical precursors of the adult education system, they were designed to provide a political education for those in the trade union movement but also to provide a cultural education denied to the working class (see, e.g., Harrison, 1961, pp. 90–151). Many immigrant workers joined a "Labor Lyceum," where not only political lectures were offered but also discussions of literature and the arts, including forums for working-class authors. Many older "veterans" of this milieu continue to carry on this political connection with the humanities through a variety of vehicles, ranging from literary club meetings to gatherings of old poets on park benches.

By whatever route an older adult has taken, whether newly discovered or lifelong, the exploration and interpretation of human experience (humanities in its broadest sense) can be a vehicle not only for understanding acquired knowledge and experience but for acting on it in ways that bring about personal and social change.

## HUMANITIES AND LITERACY

Cutting even deeper into the issue of access to the liberating aspects of humanities discourse is the problem of literacy—the ability to read the writing on the wall, let alone act upon the message. Attention has been given in recent years to the role of humanities in literacy programs. This is partly in response to the need for more "mature" material to use in teaching reading skills to older adults. Also, in educational programs in developing countries, literacy campaigns are political tools used to bring not only needed reading skills but also exposure to and appreciation of national culture (see, e.g., Arnove & Graff, 1987). In the literature on literacy programs may be found accounts of the experience of elders who have been touched by these campaigns. Often elders are encouraged to use poetry as a first vehicle for their newly acquired literacy skills (see, e.g., Eisen, 1984; Hirshon & Butler, 1983).

In North America, there is a significant minority of older adults who have never learned to read (Jacobs, 1986). A far greater number are functionally illiterate. Many more older persons did not make reading a regular activity during their working lives; they shy away from humanities learning because they find themselves intimidated by the printed word. Those who would provide opportunities for such people to engage in humanities study will have to confront its traditional grounding in the written text (see "Modes and Models" below).

## Oral Tradition and Literary Tradition

An issue that comes up in the discussion of approaches both to literacy and to humanities in general is that of the role of oral tradition. Among scholars and practitioners alike, there is a growing recognition that social and cultural memory is of comparable worth to that of written documents in deepening our understanding of personal, social, and historical place. The value of oral tradition is taken for granted in nonliterate societies, where it is the sole means of transmitting cultural knowledge. In some literacy campaigns, for example, the importance of oral tradition is recognized in programs in which young students are encouraged to record and transcribe the oral wisdom of elders as one means of gaining language competence.

Among practitioners in aging, the value of oral tradition is viewed from the perspective of the therapeutic value of reminiscence (see, e.g., Butler, 1963); oral historians have taken this positive feedback to heart (Baum, 1980–81). In *The Uses of Reminiscence*, Marc Kaminsky (1984) discusses and presents a variety of perspectives demonstrating the importance of reminiscence and the valuing of elders as repositories of memories. All of this underscores the recognition that reminiscence/life review is a primary modality informing the experience of late-life humanities learning.

What the oral historian gains from a structured elicited life story is a unique personal perspective on historical events, a view of history as a lived-in experience. This story—a narrative of memories and a repository of cultural wisdom—is the primary "text" that serves as the foundation upon which late-life humanities learning is based. (Examples of humanities study based directly on reminiscence are described in "Modes and Models" below).

### The Seeker and the Source: Elders as Humanities Texts

I have deliberately identified oral history not only as memory but also as "text" to draw attention to its functional equivalence with the written word as a modality for humanities discourse. The essence of humanities learning lies not in the particular medium of communication but in the nature of the discourse. It would follow from this that the "texts" that serve as the basis for humanities study can be any that facilitate inquiry into the nature of human experience, without regard to the particular form of their expression.

Within such a perspective it would be most appropriate to consider the cultural wisdom and memories of elders as "living texts" that, like the written (book) or visual (film) text, are set within a specific framework—cultural, historical, stylistic—and may therefore constitute as apt a subject or medium for humanities discourse as other "conventional" forms. One well-known example of a humanities class for older adults structured around the "living text" model in that of the "living history" classes conducted by anthropologist Barbara Myerhoff (1978) as one means of recording the cultural knowledge and personal / historical memory of members of a community of Jewish elders in Venice, California. I will describe below several other types of humanities programs for older adults that have engaged participants in the process of drawing from their own "living texts" of experience, "translating" given subjects into the language of their own memories, and integrating what they have learned into the (dis)course of their own lives.

## MODES AND MODELS OF HUMANITIES LEARNING

Educational gerontologists and other proponents of lifelong education have come to recognize the virtues of the interactive mode of learning with older adults (Courtney & Long, 1987; Moody, 1986). There are three major reasons for favoring such an approach in late-life humanities learning, each of which draws from observations that I have made earlier. First, the centrality of reflection and reminiscence in the discourse of elders demands a framework in which, as I have argued, personal experience (as nonformal knowledge) can be valued and exchanged as readily as the formal subject being studied and discussed. Second, interactive learning favors "social intelligence," the strong suit of elders (as outlined above): the working out of humanities issues, of the interpretation of human experience, drawing on knowledge of human relationships while engaging in a close relationship with other older humanities learners. Last, the egalitarian nature of interactive learning carries with it the potential for empowerment by validating both the personal identity and memory of participants while instilling confidence in their capacity to act upon what they learn in the world around them. The Brazilian adult educator Paulo Freire (1972) recognized this when he stressed the necessity of "co-intentional" education, where teachers and students, "co-intent on reality, are both Subjects, not only in the task of unveiling that reality, and thereby coming to know it critically, but in the task of recreating that knowledge" (p. 56).

Whether or not they are guided by Freire's larger visionary goal of creating an egalitarian society through egalitarian education, many organizers of programs and their elder participants have recognized that participatory learning acts as a leveling device, providing a structure within which people, regardless of their background or formal education, may freely exchange views. In discussing learning strategies for lifelong education, R. H. Dave (1975), echoing Freire's model, describes one such approach as "inter-learning," a process in which participants in educational programs frequently exchange the roles of teacher and learner but without the stifling teacher-student hierarchy.

One route to the democratization of late-life humanities study has been self-directed learning (see, e.g., Knowles, 1975). Elders in many parts of the country have set up their own peer-led study groups, often under the aegis of local educational institutions. Partly this has been a response to the special educational needs and interests of retired persons. Another factor lies in the political economy of education.

I have observed that, until recently, humanities study was to a large extent a luxury pursued by the privileged. In reviewing organized (group) forms of humanities study for older people, it is instructive to consider that older-adult education in general has followed the trend of worker education; in other words, it has emerged from activism. Henry Lipman, former director of the Institute for Retired Professionals (IRP, housed at the New School for Social Research in New York City), recently (summer 1989) reviewed this background for a group of older adults in New Haven interested in forming a similar educational group. He pointed out that 70 years ago there was only one such institute. In the intervening years assumptions have changed about the ability of older persons to learn and about the variety of modes of learning. Another impetus for the rapid growth of educational opportunities for elders in the last few decades has come from the efforts of unions (especially retiree groups) and aging-advocacy groups such as the Gray Panthers who, like members of the earlier workers' schools, organized educational programs for social action.

This has had a profound impact on the ways in which many educational programs for elders have been organized. For one thing, a number of groups are self-generated. The IRP, for example, is composed of paying members who select their own subjects for study and draw from their own ranks for facilitators. Another characteristic of such groups is their egalitarian nature. Freed from the constraints of formal education (including both its competitive and hierarchical nature, aspects that have often mirrored their working lives), they have tended to dissolve traditional teacher-student dichotomies, organizing study groups in which people share responsibility for researching and sharing views (Hirsch, 1980; Midwinter, 1984).

More "traditional" educational models have taken root but with significant differences. The most striking model is that of Elderhostel. Established in the 1970s as a modest series of weeklong intensive educational programs, mostly held on college campuses, it has experienced a phenomenal growth, with courses offered throughout the year at hundreds of host sites both in North America and abroad. Although the Elderhostel catalog presents a conventional list of course offerings (the majority of which are humanities subjects), the actual experience varies considerably. "Students" live at the host site for a week or more, where they may attend lectures, engage in seminar-like discussions, take field trips, and socialize with fellow "hostelers" (see Brady, 1987; Knowlton, 1980.)

Although Elderhostel has, with good cause, a large and devoted following, there has been a growing recognition among its founders that it has tended to attract an elite clientele composed largely of well-educated, moderate- to high-income elders (Manheimer, 1987–88). To their credit, Elderhostel staff have a "hostelship" program waiving the "tuition" for lower-income elders, and they have made efforts to encourage elder ethnic minority group members to apply. In addition, they have recently established the Elderhostel Institute for Learning in Retirement, which is helping to seed community-based educational programs organized and run by elders with the cooperation of local educational institutions, which provide space and faculty support.

However, the problem of reaching out beyond its present base of largely well-educated retired professionals remains.

Ironically, the distinct class division (and the ethnic division that often accompanies it) separating the participants in self-generated educational programs for older adults from the rest of the elder population underscores the de facto exclusion of "blue-collar," lower-income, and minority elderly from alternative (let alone adequate) educational opportunities, something that they have experienced throughout their lives.

In the wake of the civil rights, women's, peace, and other progressive movements, there have been efforts to reach out to the disenfranchised through educational programs that validate personal and cultural identity and provide participants with the tools for analyzing and changing their conditions. Many practitioners among the aging have come to recognize the value of humanities programs as vehicles for acknowledging cultural identity and self-worth and therefore their importance in any program for promoting personal and social health and integrity. Their "target population" has largely been those elders with little or no exposure to concepts and methods in humanities (for examples of some of these programs, see Administration on Aging, 1984 Balkema, 1986).

One of the most successful of these efforts has been the National Council on the Aging's (NCOA) "Discovery Through the Humanities." Since 1976, the NCOA has developed a series of reading anthologies with short readings designed for a discussion group format. An introductory handbook outlines the philosophy behind the series:

> [The anthologies] are based on the assumption that the humanities offer mature Americans unlimited opportunities for self-discovery and personal growth. Older persons find their rich fund of experiences illuminated and clarified in literature, philosophy and history. And in turn, their recollections and critical, creative vision can contribute to understanding in these fields. Exploring the humanities can make the later years a time of expansion of interest as well as one for reflection and synthesis. (Senior Center Humanities Program, 1984)

The *Discovery* series is based on an interactive learning model. A *Manual for Leading Humanities Discussion Groups* stresses the social as well as intellectual value of group interaction: "Participants have creative resources that the [program] can stimulate and help develop . . . in an atmosphere that also enhances [their] appreciation of and relationship with their peers through a collective exploration of themes of universal human concern" (Senior Center Humanities Program, 1985). In this way, the *Discovery* series is especially designed to reach older persons with little or no formal humanities education. An *Evaluation Report* issued in 1981 noted that slightly more than one-third of program participants to date had ever engaged in college-level humanities study (Moody, 1981).

The role of the discussion leader has been viewed as crucial to the success of the program. Although great stress is placed upon their skills in facilitating group interaction, it is apparent that discussion leaders are called upon to introduce methods of humanities inquiry to participants who are, more often than not, being exposed to those methods for the first time. The *Evaluation Report* revealed that, although fewer than 20% of discussion leaders in *Discovery* programs to date were professionally employed teachers or scholars, over 90% were college-educated, and most had taken college level humanities courses (Moody, 1981). Thus, skilled intervention has been as integral a component of NCOA's approach to late-life humanities study as has the interactive learning model.

The most difficult thing to evaluate is the degree to which qualitative changes take place in terms of outlook, method, and level of discourse in the course of any of these humanities programs designed for (and occasionally by) older students. The most telling evidence—and perhaps the most appropriate—is anecdotal. Participants in the NCOA *Discovery* have linked critical evaluation of issues discussed in programs with the process of evaluating their own lives and their relationships with others. Their comments, while terse, are revealing: "It enlightens my understanding of how much alike all people are"; "It was a time of reminiscing [about] our own past history and comparing similarities"; "The Humanities Program is awakening in me a knowledge of myself [and] of how the whole universe is ever in the process of change"; "[The] material stimulated others to share their background, experiences and philosophies"; "I find it so interesting to see how communicating on a deeper level overcomes surface irritants that cause discord"; "I feel that I am now more aware of more things than I have ever been in my entire life"; "I believe that one's reaction to this course is exactly how much one puts into it. . . . One's past interest in humanities—whether it is nonfiction or fiction—does help"; "[It] inspires me to think quietly and deeply about the present and the past and makes me more efficient in making decisions about the present and the future which is very gratifying to one's self-esteem" (Moody, 1981).

As "Humanist in Residence" at the Connecticut State Department on Aging, I have encountered a wide range of responses to programs I have organized and led. As a scholar-in-residence working under a grant from the Connecticut Humanities Council, now as a Humanities Program

Coordinator, I have designed programs with the specific aim of stimulating humanities learning, especially among those with little or no exposure to humanities subjects. The results have been generally successful if measured by the positive response to programs but mixed in terms of depth of discussion or development of critical responses to issues. Over the past few years, I have collaborated with the Humanities Council, as well as many local public libraries, in offering scholar-led discussion programs using both the NCOA *Discovery* series, as well as film series on local history, literature, the arts, and folklore. In each case, discussion leaders were "instructed" to encourage free exchange of ideas, intervening mainly to share pertinent information or keep the discussion focused on the subject at hand.

The film series were offered not only to add variety in format but also to overcome a problem evident in many of the sites—senior centers, nursing homes, and public housing facilities for the elderly—namely, that many elders were intimidated by the written word. Some were functionally illiterate; others had simply not been granted either the good fortune of favorable (or any) exposure to serious literature or the luxury of reading for their own pleasure. In film discussion programs, the films were treated as "texts" and subjected to analysis as for any written passage.

I vividly remember the words of one participant in a film series held in the community room of a public housing project for the elderly. The program, which consisted of five titles from the PBS "American Short Story" series, was led by an English professor from a local college, who encouraged participants to discuss the authors' motivations for portraying and developing characters in the ways that they did. One woman exclaimed at the end of a program: "I never thought that I would be a critic!" This remark not only vindicated the aim of going beyond conventional notions of humanities "texts" but also demonstrated that the depth of humanities inquiry need not be sacrificed to reach those without formal training in its methods.

Nevertheless, the issues of scope and method in late-life humanities learning are still open questions. One could argue that many "humanities" programs for elders are little more than structured reminiscence sessions. There is nothing inherently wrong with that; regardless of the specific subject matter of programs that are offered, reminiscence often becomes a common denominator for discussion, for participants invariably draw upon their own memories and experiences in relation to the particular subjects under consideration.

Reminiscence is itself, in fact, often a central source of critical inquiry in many of the most popular forms of humanities programs for older adults, for participants may become author, critic, *and* text. Among the many forms such programs may take are the aforementioned "living history" programs (Myerhoff, 1978); reminiscence-based poetry workshops, in particular, those pioneered by Marc Kaminsky (1974) and Kenneth Koch (1974); and life-writing projects (Coberly, McCormick, & Updike, 1984). The interpretation of personal experience among older persons has taken dramatic form as well, in the largely improvisational "living history" theater, as pioneered by Susan Perlstein through the New York–based Elders Share the Arts (ESTA) and "oral history theater," based on transcriptions of recorded interviews with elders (a notable example of the latter is the work of Christine Howard Bailey [1986], who studied with Perlstein). Through such creative explorations, older persons collaborate in the interpretation and presentation of their lived-in experiences in dramatic form.

One issue that is raised by reminiscence-based humanities study is a pedagogical dilemma: that the distinction between critical inquiry and nostalgia may become murky. The "fine line" fades even more when considering materials designed to minimize barriers to interaction. A case in point is an imaginatively conceived series of products called Bi-Folkal Kits. Aptly titled "multisensory experiences," each kit includes slides, audiocassettes, song sheets, artifacts, and other materials that may engage elders with various levels of (dis)ability, enabling them to participate in discussions focused on such themes as "Remembering 1924," "Remembering the Depression," "Remembering the Automobile," and "Remembering Work." Bi-Folkal Kits have been especially popular in nursing homes, where even patients with cognitive deficits can be drawn into interaction through one or more of the various sensory modalities exploited among the materials stuffed into the brightly colored gym bags of each kit. Although carefully assembled and historically accurate, they are designed primarily to stimulate reminiscence and only secondarily to generate critical inquiry. They are most likely to be used by practitioners with little or no formal humanities background. Their principal virtue is their accessibility to the most neglected potential late-life humanities learners: those who have had minimal formal education or who are trapped in ailing bodies and minds. To their credit, Bi-Folkal Kits are thoughtfully researched and have the potential to act as effective—and highly adaptable—vehicles for critical discussion at varying levels of discourse, based upon the capacities of program participants and leaders.

## SUMMING THINGS UP

A number of observations have been made about the character of older students of the humanities, the forms of their inquiry, and the subjects they explore. A central theme is that although there are indeed age-relevant factors in humanities study, the critical mode of thought to which it is wedded may emerge at any time, informed and enriched by age. What may make a real difference in approach to humanities study among older adults are such factors as prior education, socioeconomic status, cultural background, and personal experience.

Given their varied backgrounds, experiences, and capacities for learning, older persons have explored the humanities through a wide range of learning modalities and at varying levels of discourse. Among the lessons we may draw from the diverse paths that they taken are the following:

1. Self-validation, personal growth, and empowerment for changing self and society are all aspects of a process of learning through the humanities, one that is lifelong and can begin at any time.
2. The expression of critical thought in late life will be as divergent in character and kind as the personal, class, ethnic, gender, occupational, political, and intellectual backgrounds and interests of elder humanities students. And the implications of critical thought among elders is potentially just as politically charged as for any other age group (just witness Gray Panther leader Maggie Kuhn's rallying call: "Learning and sex until rigor mortis!").
3. The most challenging and empowering forms of humanities study in late life are cooperative ventures—interactive and "intertextual" learning experiences in which participants exchange ideas as social and intellectual equals and in which the texts of their lives are as valued as those of the thinkers and writers who throughout history have tried their hand at interpreting the human experience.

## REFERENCES

Adminstration on Aging. (1984). *Education for older persons: Illustrative local project profiles.* Washington, DC: U.S. Department of Health and Human Services.

*Adult education and the elderly.* (1985). (Adult Education and Development, No. 24). Bonn: German Adult Education Association.

*Another perspective: Humanistic approaches to aging.* (1982). *Convergence on Aging, 1* [Special issue].

Arnove, R. F., & Graff, H. J. (1987). *National literacy campaigns: Historical and comparative perspectives.* New York: Plenum Press.

Bailey, C. H. (1986). Oral history theatre: Its practice and roots. *New England Association of Oral History Newsletter, 9,* 9–30.

Balkema, J. B. (1986). *The creative spirit: An annotated bibliography on the arts, humanities and aging.* Washington, DC: National Council on the Aging.

Baum, W. (1980–81). Therapeutic value of oral history. *Aging and Human Development, 12,* 49–53.

Birren, J. E. (1964). *The psychology of aging.* Englewood Cliffs, NJ: Prentice-Hall.

Brady, E. M. (1987). Patterns of learning among the active elderly: The case for Elderhostel. *Activities, Adaptation and Aging, 9*(4), 69–77.

Brady, E. M. & Fowler, M. L. (1988). Participation motives and learning outcomes among older learners. *Educational Gerontology, 14*(1), 45–56.

Butler, R. (1963). The life review: An interpretation of reminiscence in the aging. *Psychiatry, 26,* 65–76.

Coberly, L. M., McCormick, J., & Updike, K. (1984). *Writers have no age: Creative writing with older adults.* New York: Haworth Press.

Courtenay, B. C., & Long, H. B. (1987). New perspectives on the education of the elderly in the United States. In H. Long (Ed.), *New perspectives on the education of adults in the United States* (pp. 83–105). London: Croom Helm.

Darkenwald, G. G., & Merriam, S. B. (1982). *Adult education: Foundations of practice.* New York: Harper and Row.

Dave, R. H. (1975). On learning strategies for lifelong education. In R. H. Dave (Ed.), *Reflections on lifelong education and the school.* Hamburg: UNESCO Institute for Education.

*Education and older adults: Implications of the age of aging.* (1985). *Convergence, 18* [Special issue].

Eisen, A. (1984). Education for emancipation. In A. Eisen (Ed.), *Women and revolution in Viet Nam* (pp. 216–228). London: Zed Books.

Freire, P. (1972). *Pedagogy of the oppressed.* New York: Herder and Herder.

Glendenning, F. (1985). *Educational gerontology, international perspectives.* New York: St. Martin's Press.

Hareven, T. K., & Adams, K. J. (Eds.). (1982). *Aging and life course transitions: An interdisciplinary perspective.* New York: Guilford Press.

Harrison, J. F. C. (1961). *Learning and living 1790–1960: A study in the history of the English adult education movement.* Toronto: University of Toronto.

Hill, A. D. (1977). *In praise of age.* Providence, RI: St. Martin de Porres Multiservice Center.

Hirsch, H. (1980). The educated senior citizen: Continuing education after retirement. In P. H. Apt (Ed.), *Higher education and the older learner* (pp. 57–64). New York: Human Sciences Press.

Hirshon, S., with Butler, J. (1983). *And also teach them to read.* Westport, CT: Lawrence Hill.

Houle, C. O., & Houle, B. E. (1970). The continuity of life. In (no author) *Lifelong education.* New Delhi: Asian Institute of Educational Planning and Administration. 127–152.

Jacobs, B. (1986). *Tutoring older adults in literacy programs* (Literacy Education for the Elderly Project). Washington, DC: National Council on the Aging.

Kaminsky, M. (1974). *What's inside of you it shines out of you.* New York: Horizon Press.

Kaminsky, M. (1984). *The uses of reminiscence.* New York: Haworth Press.

Knowles, M. S. (1975). *Self-directed learning.* New York: Association Press.

Knowlton, M. P. (1980). The Elderhostel philosophy. In P. H. Apt (Ed.), *Higher education and the older learner* (pp. 65–70). New York: Human Sciences Press.

Koch, K. (1977). *I never told anybody: Teaching writing in a nursing home.* New York: Random House.

*Late life learning.* (1987–88). *Generations,* Winter [Special issue].

Manheimer, R. J. (1984). *Developing arts and humanities programming with the elderly.* Chicago: American Library Association, Reference and Adult Services Division.

Manheimer, R. J. (1987–88). The politics and promise of cultural enrichment programs. *Generations, 12,* 26–30.

McClusky, H. Y. (1982). Education for older adults. In C. Eisdorfer (Ed.), *Annual review of gerontology and geriatrics* (pp. 403–428). New York: Springer Publishing Co.

Myerhoff, B. (1978). *Number our days.* New York: E. P. Dutton.

Midwinter, E. (1984). *Mutual aid universities.* London: Croom Helm.

Moody, H. R. (1981). *Evaluation report.* Washington, DC: National Council on the Aging, Senior Center Humanities Program.

Moody, H. R. (1985). Philosophy of education for older adults. In D. B. Lumsden (Ed.), *The older adult as learner* (pp. 25–49). Washington, DC: Hemisphere.

Moody, H. R. (1986). Late life learning in the informational society. In D. A. Peterson (Ed.), *Education and aging* (pp. 122–148). Englewood Cliffs, NJ: Prentice-Hall.

Peterson, D. A. (Ed.). (1986). *Education and aging.* Englewood Cliffs, NJ: Prentice-Hall.

Ray, D., et al. (1983). *Values, life-long education and an aging Canadian population.* London, Ontario: Third Eye Publications.

Senior Center Humanities Program. (1984). *Discovery through the humanities: Introductory Handbook* (rev. ed.). Washington, DC: National Council on the Aging.

Senior Center Humanities Program. (1985). *Manual for leading humanities discussion groups* (rev. ed.). Washington, DC: National Council on the Aging.

Sherron, R. H., & D. B. Lumsden (Eds.). (1985) *Introduction to educational gerontology* (2nd ed.). Washington, DC: Hemisphere.

Wolf, M. A. (1985). The meaning of education in late life. *Geriatrics and Education, 5*(3), 51–59.

Wolf, M. A. (1988). *Self-development: What older adults bring to education.* Paper presented to the American Association for Adult and Continuing Education, Tulsa, OK.

20

# Afterword: Integrating the Humanities into Gerontologic Research, Training, and Practice

*W. Andrew Achenbaum*

---

Roughly 50 years ago, John Dewey (1939) suggested an appropriate way to integrate the humanities into gerontologic research, training, and practice. "Science and philosophy meet on common ground in their joint interest in discovering the processes of normal growth and in the institution of conditions which will favor and support ever continued growth," Dewey wrote in his introduction to E. V. Cowdry's *Problems of Ageing*.

> When we shall envisage social relations and institutions in the light of the contribution they are capable of making to continued growth, when we are capable of criticizing those which exist on the ground of the ways in which they arrest and deflect processes of growth, we shall be on our way to a solution of the moral and psychological problems of human aging. (p. xxvii)

John Dewey, of course, was not the first philosopher to grapple with the problems and potentials of human aging. Some metaphors, aphorisms, and images of old age, which date back to ancient Hebraic literature and Graeco-Roman civilizations, still pervade our culture (for a survey, Achenbaum, 1985; Fischer, 1977). Nor on the eve of his 80th birthday was Dewey necessarily the member of his cohort who best illuminated the dimensions of late life through materials and methods associated with humanistic disciplines. Two others merit notice. G. Stanley Hall (1922) in retirement compiled *Senescence*, a companion piece to his two-volume *Adolescence* (1904). Hall "tried to present the subjects of Old Age and Death from as many viewpoints as possible" to document "what ripe and normal age really is, means, can, should, and now must do, if our race is ever to achieve its true goal" (pp. v, ix). Bessie Richardson, on the other hand, eschewed composing a broad overview, contrasting instead past and present conditions in *Old Age among the Greeks* (1933); her monograph remains a valuable commentary.

Even if not wholly original, Dewey's (1939) paradigm for integrating the humanities into gerontologic research, training, and practice provided a useful way of promoting cross-disciplinary work. Long before C. P. Snow offered his critique, *The Two Cultures*, Dewey pointed out that science and philosophy typically operate in independent spheres. "Biological processes are at the roots of the problems" of aging, he asserted, but these biological processes "take place in economic, political, and cultural contexts" (p. xxvi). Dewey doubted that scientific theory and measurement alone could capture, much less comprehend, all of the relevant factors and dynamics associated with aging, the scope of which had "no precedent in human history." Hence, experts in the humanities, according to Dewey, might ably serve two roles in nurturing gerontology as a field of scientific inquiry. First, they should embellish insights made by bench scientists: the humanities have powers of description and synthesis essential for understanding growth and aging. Second, philosophers had to communicate scientific advances broadly. Sometimes humanists had to criticize conceptual and social barriers within and without the academy. Often they had to recommend ways society could alleviate the aged's problems.

Few initially carried out Dewey's strategy. Biomedical investigations of senescence and inquiries into the psychology of aging increased; social workers, private agencies, and public officials devised ways to improve housing, employment opportunities, and social services for the elderly. There was little interest, however, in using the humanities to link aging research and practice. One exception was a concern about late-life spirituality. In *Older People and the Church* (1949), Paul Maves and J. Lennart Cedarleaf summarized points of convergence they saw between theology and gerontology. They also offered clergy practical guidelines on how to meet the aged's spiritual needs and enable older people to serve the young more effectively. Their ideas were discussed in a session on Religious Programs and Services held at the 1950 National Conference on Aging (Thurston, 1951; Tibbitts, 1951).

Before the 1970s, social scientists and clinicians committed to the advancement of gerontology actually did more than historians, philosophers, and other critics in promoting humanistic perspectives on aging. *The Role of the Aged in Primitive Societies* (1945) by anthropologist Leo Simmons (1945) documented how diversely norms manifest themselves and showed the influence of cultural context in late life. Following in the tradition of I. L. Nascher and M. W. Thewlis, who recounted key moments in the establishment of geriatrics, several pioneers in gerontology staked out the field's historical perimeters. The late Nathan W. Shock included historical references in his *Classified Bibliography of Gerontology and Geriatrics.* Frederic D. Zeman (1945–1947) wrote historical essays and gathered graphics of pioneers in aging. The late Joseph Freeman (1979), a prominent Philadelphia clinician active in the Gerontological Society from its founding, collected original copies of classic texts on aging and prepared bibliographic guides. Gerald Gruman, MD (1966), who also earned a PhD in the history of science, produced a monograph on prolongevity published by the American Philosophical Society. James Birren (1961) and Klaus Riegel (1977) wrote on the history of the psychology of aging.

Simone de Beauvoir (1972/1970) was probably the first contemporary author steeped in the humanities whose work fulfilled Dewey's hope that humanistic gerontology ultimately would highlight the normative foundations of old age and ameliorate its cultural milieu. Having published *The Prime of Life* (1960) and *A Very Easy Death* (1966) in her 50s, de Beauvoir was predisposed to think about *The Coming of Age.* "The meaning or the lack of meaning that old age takes on in any society puts that whole society to the test, since it is that that reveals the meaning or the lack of meaning of the entirety of the life leading to that old age" (p. 16). And as one might expect from the provocative author of *The Second Sex,* de Beauvoir intended to "break the conspiracy of silence . . . [to] compel my readers to hear" (p. 2) the voices of the aged.

Though *The Coming of Age* begins with a chapter on "old age and biology," de Beauvoir does not view interactions between gerontology and the humanities as Dewey did. Hers is an historicist approach: universal themes concerning body imagery or fear about decrepitude (and thus ambivalence about old age) matter less than changes in how different cultures deal with these phenomena. Nor does de Beauvoir take her cues from scientific research; scientists' opinions are invoked mainly when they bolster her narrative point. Instead, de Beauvoir's analysis relies heavily on ethnographic data, examples from literature, and historical evidence informed by a Marxist critique of society. In tone as well as execution, *The Coming of Age* is shaped by the author's "philosophy." Such an idiosyncratic approach, its seeming comprehensiveness notwithstanding, has led some critics to complain that *The Coming of Age* is uninviting, even ageist due to the author's personal anxieties (see, for instance, Walzer, 1988; Woodward, 1988). Still, her emphasis on political economy and the hypocrisy of middle-class values anticipated motifs that shortly would be elaborated by other critics.

I suggest that Dewey and de Beauvoir offer two possible "ideal" models for linking the humanities and aging. Dewey points the way toward *humanistic gerontology*. Because aging is a phenomenon experienced on biological, psychological, and cultural levels, gerontology perforce is a multidisciplinary endeavor. Students of the humanities must develop expertise in biomedical and behavioral aspects of senescence if they want to bridge "science" and "philosophy." Yet mastering the basics of aging is not enough. To advance humanistic perspectives on aging requires experts to distance themselves from the gerontologic community of discourse so that they can assess strengths and weaknesses in current practices. Furthermore, research in Dewey's model ideally leads to social action: fresh ideas should foster interventions and reforms that benefit older men and women.

Those who follow de Beauvoir's lead, in contrast, will produce works in the *gerontological humanities*. Unlike Dewey's, the goal of their inquiry is not a comprehensive understanding of the dynamics of aging. Instead, emphasis is placed on demonstrating the value of certain humanistic theories and methods in understanding what it means and how it feels to grow older. Grasping what scientists think that they "know" about mechanisms of aging in this mode of discourse is as important as conveying the "reality" of phenomena measured by biomarkers of aging. And although de Beauvoir thought that experts in the humanities should serve as critics, her conception of the role resembles Michael Walzer's (1987) prophetic mode: "Social criticism is less the practical offspring of scientific knowledge than the educated cousin of common complaint. We become critics naturally, as it were, by elaborating on existing moralities and telling stories about a society more just than, though never entirely different from, our own" (p. 65); de Beauvoir's ideal social critic does not necessarily include command of the instrumental techniques essential in Dewey's model.

Pioneers on both sides of the Atlantic evinced interest in bridging the humanities and aging. French philosopher Michel Philibert (1968) advanced humanistic gerontology by establishing Le Centre Pluridisciplinaire de Gerontologie with Dr. Robert Hugonot at the University of Grenoble Medical Center (Spicker, 1978). Historian Walter Moss facilitated work in the gerontological humanities by compiling *Humanistic Perspectives on Aging: An Annotated Bibliography and Essay* (1976). But money—more than fresh ideas—seems to have been the catalyst that enticed experts in the humanities in the 1970s to break new ground in gerontologic research, training, and practice. Between 1974 and 1978, the Public Program Division of the National Endowment for the Humanities (NEH) funded at least 14 projects that utilized various media to communicate ideas (Moss, 1978).

Perhaps the most ambitious research venture was directed by David Van Tassel. With NEH support, "Human Values and Aging: New Challenges to Research in the Humanities" enabled distinguished senior scholars (including Leon Edel, Erik Erikson, Leslie Fiedler, Joseph Fletcher, Juanita Kreps, and Peter Laslett) to share their insights on aging with rising stars (including Sally Gadow, Daniel Scott Smith, Stuart Spicker, David Stannard, Maris Vinovskis, Evelyn Eaton Whitehead, Kathleen M. Woodward) as well as graduate students and other observers.[1] Van Tassel hoped to mobilize a cadre of researchers who in turn would provoke interest in gerontology within their disciplinary ranks and attract graduate students to build on work already underway. As we shall see, Van Tassel's pioneering effort resulted in follow-up conferences and more scholarly interest.

Training grants facilitated educational initiatives undertaken with similar enthuasiasm. Once again the NEH support, Van Tassel conducted a 2-year summer institute for college-based historians, philosophers, musicians, social scientists, and English teachers who wanted to introduce aging issues into the curricula. The Institute of Gerontology (IoG) at the University of Michigan offered summer workshops on the history of old age in America. In 1978, in conjunction with a conference on Aging and the Art of Living, IoG unveiled "Images of Old Age in America, 1790 to the Present," a visual representation of my dissertation, with graphics selected by Peggy A. Kusnerz. Over the next decade, the Smithsonian Institution Traveling Exhibition Services took the exhibit to nearly every state in the continental United States (Achenbaum & Kusnerz, 1978).

A significant number of experts in the humanities moved beyond academic bases to share their interest in old age and older people with the public. Historians gathered oral histories to preserve folk culture and to gain insights into the experiences of blacks, immigrants, and women. Inspired by the goals of the 1960s, and goaded by employment woes of the 1970s, some became "public" scholars who helped communities recapture their past. Such activities put historians in close contact with senior citizens (Benson, Brier, & Rosenzweig, 1984; Howe & Kemp, 1986).[2] Similarly, poets and literary critics often went into nursing homes, where they enabled residents to write about their dreams, wishes, and fears. Philosophers moved into key positions at the Hastings Center, the Brookdale Center on Aging, hospitals, and nursing homes, where they helped health care professionals to wrestle with ethical issues affecting the dignity and treatment of their patients.[3] Between 1978 and 1988, the National Council on the Aging produced 16 workbooks and anthologies for its Discovery Through the Humanities program, as well as bibliography and other resources that made scholarship accessible. This NCOA commitment inspired other experiments in grassroots adult education.

Over time more scholars became intrigued by the intellectual possibilities and career opportunities associated with linking aging and the humanities. Those who had been graduate student observers at Van Tassel's "Human Values and Aging" symposia published their first articles and monographs. Changing intellectual fashions focused attention on old-age issues: consider the recent flurry of interest in the "elderly's welfare state" at the interstices of social (welfare) history and historical sociology.[4] Recognizing the growing interest in the gerontological humanities, an area that he has probed in his own intellectual career, Robert Kastenbaum in 1982 added a historical section to his *International Journal of Aging and Human Development.*[5] Social scientists also acknowledged the importance of humanistic perspectives in analyzing the dynamics of aging:

> One of the dramatic changes that took place in the field in the 1980s—beginning quietly, but now in full swell—has been the tremendous increase in attention paid to adult life-course (and sometimes the full life-course) context in which persons age. . . . An understanding of the life course has become integral to social scientific studies of aging, whether that understanding is incorporated prospectively through longitudinal design or is obtained retrospectively through analyses of successive cohorts and the historical periods and social conditions through which they have lived. (Streib & Binstock, 1990, p. 1)

As gerontologists (re)discover the centrality of *time,* both as marked by history and experienced through aging, more will rely on humanistic research.

Furthermore, as higher education responded to the graying of America, geriatric and gerontologic education took on the shape and scope of other academic specialities. This created niches for historians like Thomas Cole to gain invaluable clinical experiences that enrich scholarship as he broadens physicians' training. (The Institute of Medical Humanities at the University of Texas Medical Branch, Galveston, offers the country's only PhD in this field.) And just as most teachers in the humanities nowadays try to convey to their students the importance of gender, race, and class, so too some attention is gradually being paid to the elderly. At the University of Michigan, Maris Vinovskis and I feature unit(s) on the elderly in our respective U.S. history surveys, which regularly draw 400 undergraduates a term.

Indicative of the humanities' new visibility is the recognition accorded them in the Gerontological Society of America (GSA). Dr. Joseph Freeman proposed in 1976 the creation of an Ad Hoc Committee on Humanism and the Humanities. In due course, largely under the guidance of Freeman and Van Tassel, this body became a standing committee. By the early 1980s, the Arts and Humanities luncheon session was one of the most popular at the annual meeting, largely because a well-known personality was invited to speak. Since 1985, experts in the humanities have convened an annual Presidential Symposium, which draws together experts from several disciplines to discuss a timely ethical issue. The last three editors of *The Gerontologist* have included at least one historian, philosopher, or literary critic on the editorial board; the first historian joined the board of the newly reorganized *Journal of Gerontology: Social Sciences* in 1990.[6]

Although I have focused on developments in the United States, I hasten to mention similar trends in Europe, apparent in efforts by two British scholars. Peter Laslett (1977, 1989), renowned for his scholarship into John Locke's philosophy and his direction of the Cambridge Group for the History of Population and Social Structure, has edited a collection of essays on old age and recently published *A Fresh Map of Life*, which deals with the consequences of societal aging. Laslett's has hardly been a donnish purview: he also has tirelessly written editorials, given radio broadcasts, and sponsored several adult education initiatives aimed at people over 60. Meanwhile, Alan Walker (1981, 1983) several decades Laslett's junior, has been a chief architect of British models of "the political economy of aging," willing to test some of his theories about dependency by designing alternatives to existing social services.[7] On the continent Anne-Marie Guillemard, Martin Kohli, and Hans Schroots (among others) have infused an historical temperament into gerontology. The International Association of Gerontology and the British *Ageing and Society* provide other scholarly vehicles for this interest.

Without discounting accomplishments to date, the extent to which the humanities have been integrated into gerontologic practice, teaching, and research must not be exaggerated. Few professionally trained historians, philosophers, literary critics, or theologians in fact apply their expertise in interactions with senior citizens. Most teach younger people, work with their peers in bureaucracies, or look forward to the greater independence retirement will bring. Surely this is not surprising. Unlike psychology or sociology graduate programs, "applied" fields of humanistic inquiry are fairly new. Their placement records are modest.

The number of aging courses offered in humanities divisions of colleges and universities grows, but not fast. Seminars in "historical gerontology," "images of old age," or "portraits of aging artists" tend to be (s)elective, given at the pleasure of a professor who happens to be interested in the topic. "Aging" does not fit neatly into the subfields of history, literature, philosophy, or religion; there is not yet a critical mass of knowledge to justify its designation as a subfield sui generis. Designers of gerontologic curricula do not put much emphasis on the humanities—unless a colleague tenaciously lobbies for their inclusion. In part, this reflects the novelty of *any* educational programs in aging. Only the University of Southern California and the University of Massachusetts at Boston currently offer PhDs in gerontology. Nor is there great interest in the humanities among roughly 300 schools that offer degrees or certificates in aging. In a 1980 survey on "Foundations for Gerontological Education" prepared by the GSA and the Association for Gerontology in Higher Education (AGHE), only 9% of the biomedical scientists, 21% from the psychosocial sciences, and 28% of the experts in socioeconomic/environmental subjects felt that the humanities, arts, and media were essential content clusters. AGHE's 1989 report on standards and guidelines for gerontology programs never mentions a need to include a humanities component (Connelly & Rich, 1989; Johnson et al., 1980).[8]

Even in the research arena, the record is uneven. The scope of the humanities, as the articles in this *Handbook* attest, is wide-ranging, but some topics attract greater attention than others. Historians have made progress in reconstructing key meanings and experiences of growing old(er) in the United States. Initial surveys challenged the mistaken impression that shifts in attitudes toward aging and the treatment of the elderly occurred in a linear, predictable manner. Recent monographs have underscored with greater specificity elderly people's diverse lifestyles and have shown the importance of the local economy, demographic patterns, and power structure in influencing the aged's choices and constraining their activities. Yet there is far more to learn about variations by gender, race, class, region, occupation, and disability, especially in advanced ages. Interpretations of 19th-century trends lately have generated more disputations than new data. It is unfortunate that so few historians have analyzed 20th-century developments: if gerontologists could see the relevance of such research to their own endeavors, they might get more interested in broader historical sweeps.

In a word, professional humanists still play a *marginal* role in gerontologic circles. Though several hundred members of GSA have expressed a secondary interest in the arts and humanities, it is doubtful that there soon will be sufficient numbers of philosophers, critics, artists, or historians to warrant independent section status. Nor is it evident that experts in the humanities would be more inclined to talk to one another than they are to make contact with colleagues in the biomedical, behaviorial, or social sciences. Those competent at "deconstructing" texts, after all, quickly become frustrated trying to communicate with peers who have never read Foucault, Derrida, or Rorty; it may be more fruitful to talk with psychologists who have.

Many humanists keep abreast of the social science literature, but the converse does not necessarily follow. One historian contributed an article in the first (1977) edition of the *Handbook of Aging and the Social Sciences;* two wrote something for the 1985 edition. None appeared in the third edition because, the editors wrote, the "classic analysis of 'societal perceptions of the aging and the aged' in the last edition cannot easily become dated by research developments in the humanities" (Binstock & George, 1990).[9] Such a statement suggests that breakthroughs in the humanities are not as rapid as they are in "social supports and social relationships" or the economics of aging (which required three chapters to summarize). But scant reference was made in the 1985 essays to the political economy of historical aging: the debate over when and to what extent older men began to withdraw from the labor force had not yet erupted. Similarly, no expert in the humanities contributed to *Qualitative Gerontology* (1988); the only professionals cited in the Introduction were Carole Haber and Mary Sohngen, though reference was made to Ronald Blythe, May Sarton, and Florida Scott-Maxwell (Reinharz & Rowles, 1988).

For the gerontological humanities to have realized its initial potential would have required a steady flow of new people. Yet during the very period in which aging should have become a "hot" topic, three countervailing trends inhibited growth. First, funding for graduate education dried up, and job prospects for newly minted PhDs in history, English, philosophy, religious studies, and the arts became bleak. Thus, those willing and able to serve as dissertation mentors found few promising candidates. Second, the comparative advantages of investing time and energy in "aging" seemed debatable at all academic ranks. Junior faculty feared that gerontology was a "fad" that would taint their candidacy for tenure. The concurrent Balkanization of history, philosophy, religion, and literary criticism made other topics at least as appealing. Third, ageism doubtless infects academics no less than ordinary citizens. Thus, it is not by accident that those who contributed articles to David Van Tassel's 1983 symposium tended to be those already published in the field or the mentors of those who did (Van Tassel & Stearns, 1986). Without the synergy associated with new activity, growth was bound to be gradual, not geometric.

Prospects for advancing humanistic gerontology were worse. Becoming an expert in one field takes time; mastering a second, unrelated speciality appears daunting. Few in *any* field of inquiry are likely to match James Birren, Bernice Neugarten, Matilda White Riley, or Nathan Shock for their capacity for interdisciplinarity. In any case, the best hopes from the humanities tended to follow the example of John Dewey and Simone de Beauvoir: they produced a masterpiece, and then never wrote on the topic of aging again. Shifts in NEH funding, moreover, created disincentives. Whereas the Carter years encouraged the spread of humanistic inquiry into new areas, NEH under subsequent Republican administrations has viewed humanistic gerontology as an oxymoron. That the National Institute on Aging and the Administration on Aging are also unreceptive—few adept at competing for NEH support are viewed as "scientists" by the former or deemed qualified to "serve" by the latter—adds to the frustration among experts in the humanities.

What can those committed to integrating the humanities into gerontologic research, training, and practice do to bolster their cause? There are three options. The first is just to continue doing their very best. Optimists will appreciate this scenario. It presumes that colleagues sooner or later come to recognize quality. Experts in the humanities can deliver what gerontologists in the biomedical, behavioral-social science ranks and practitioners want: a cogent sense of how our future selves and social structures may differ from past times, of how well current policies mesh with prevailing ethics and mores, and of how people's late-life potential can be stimulated through thinking and reading. A laissez-faire variant of this approach will appeal to cynics. Nearly every discipline recently has undergone a crisis of confidence. Subfields proliferate around shrinking "cores." In such a milieu, the marginality of the humanities in gerontologic circles is relative: where, after all, is the center when there is no "there" there anymore?

The second option urges experts in the humanities to be more open to collaborating in research, teaching, and service. This tack takes for granted that disciplinary-specific research will remain the sine qua non for academic advancement as long as departments are the main units of higher education. It recognize's that research in the humanities typically is a solitary enterprise, but it also acknowledges that joint ventures in these disciplines have been successful. Because few gerontology institutes can afford to hire people who cannot reasonably be expected to recapture their salary through grants, those interested in advancing humanistic gerontology may have to adjust their modus operandi. Precedents exist. In this country, historians, ethicists, and literary critics serve on research projects headed by physicians, social workers, public health experts, and social scientists. In Europe, philosophers and historians have been joining sociologists, political scientists, and economists in rethinking the dynamics of age in welfarism.

The moment is right for imaginative grantsmanship. Private foundations such as the Carnegie Corporation, Rockefeller Foundation, and the Twentieth Century Fund have supported historians interested in old age whose work promised to stimulate cross-disciplinary thinking. The Department of Veterans Affairs is expressing an interest in providing research and training grants to ethicists and historians whose work complements their mission. Professors should insist upon getting an increase in departmental FTEs when they help to train students from other disciplines in how to integrate the humanities into gerontology. They might also seek funding, such as that provided by NIA for Special Emphasis Research Career awards, so that they can assist midcareer nurses, gerontologists, policymakers, and physicians to acquire intensive graduate-level training in the humanities.

A third option is to mobilize resources within our own ranks and by collaborating with colleagues in other disciplines to advance a *critical gerontology*. "The perspective of the humanities can offer an alternative ground for theories of aging to embrace both the contradictions and emancipatory possibilities of late life," contends Harry R. Moody (1988, p. 9). Instead of settling for multidisciplinary coexistence, architects of critical gerontology would call into question the instrumentalism that prevails in much gerontologic theory, method, and practice. They should invite frank debate over the scholarly reification of human development, challenge positions that pretend to be "value-free," and criticize instruments of control that dominate for bureaucratic convenience.

> Critical gerontology would seek to thematize the subjective and interpretive dimensions of human aging.... Gerontology would be based no longer on technology but on the primacy of praxis.... It] would entail new relationships... between the academic world and the world of practitioners. Finally, a Critical Gerontology is an emancipatory enterprise. It would aspire toward liberation from the meaning of old age inculcated by the spirit of modern culture. (Moody, 1988, p. 36)

U.S. philosophers, historians, and literary critics have begun to formulate a critical gerontology.[10] Some work appears in editorials in gerontologic journals (Weiland, 1990). Far more must be done.

Note how the pursuit of a critical gerontology transforms previous options in radical ways. Rather than view their marginality with regret or detachment, as the laissez-faire tack supposes, experts in the humanities are empowered to capitalize on their (belated) commitment to gerontology. Critics, Michael Walzer (1988) observes, "must look for a way of talking in tune with but also against their new accompaniment.

They need a place to stand, close to but not engulfed by their company" (p. 26). This suggests, in turn, that historians, philosophers, theologians, and critics need not emphasize their distinctiveness vis-à-vis "scientists" and the "public," as the second model implies. Becoming a critical gerontologist means one is willing to subject *all* gerontologic assumptions to critical judgment while acknowledging a common stake in humanity. Critical gerontology challenges every researcher, teacher, and practitioner to act as a true intellectual, who functions "not as the inhabitant of a separate world, the knower of esoteric truths, but as a fellow member of this world who devotes himself, but with a passion, to the truths we all know" (Walzer, 1988, p. 44).

Ideally, a critical gerontology can synergize both gerontologic humanities and humanistic gerontology. Its appeal to some will lie in its radical orientation toward both the object and subject of our endeavors and its postmodermist mode of discourse. Others will discern that its prophetic, integrative stance has ancient roots. Risks abound in urging historians, theologians, philosophers and critics to demand that gerontologists become more systematic in theory building and in applying ideas in the classroom and their policy analyses. But the price of rethinking basic issues will prove less costly to this emerging field than continuing to proliferate disparate studies and projects that fail to clarify where we are heading and why.

## NOTES

[1] The essays of the "senior" writers appeared in Van Tassel (1979); those of the "rising stars," in Spicker, Woodward, and Van Tassel (1978).

[2] Even mainstream historians were influenced by this movement; see Hareven (1983) and Hareven and Langenbach (1978).

[3] For poets in nursing homes, see Marc Kaminsky (1974) and Kenneth Koch (1978). Successive issues of the *Hastings Center Report* attest to the prominence of philosophers discussing euthanasia and the ethics of acute care for the frail elderly.

[4] See Carole Haber (chap. 16, this volume). See also the essays by Ellis Hawley, Brian Balogh, Edward Berkowitz, and me in Critchlow and Hawley (1988), as well as the three volumes—*Democracy and the Welfare State* (A. Gutmann, Ed.), *The Politics of Social Policy in the United States* (M. Weir, A. S. Orloff, & T. Skocpol, Eds.), and *Social Security* (T. R. Marmor & J. L. Mashaw, Eds.)—by Princeton University Press (1988) for the Project on the Federal Social Role.

[5] Among other things, Kastenbaum presented his own commissioned play, *Ump*, "a searching character study of an ebullient, hesitantly introspective, aging enforcer of rules and arbiter of baseball disputes" (Carson, 1986) at a 1984 conference on Aging and Meaning organized by Thomas Cole and Sally Gadow at the Institute for Medical Humanities in Galveston.

[6] Some of the credit for these initiatives must be accorded to Jack Cornman, GSA's former executive director, who considers such efforts a bridge-building indispensable for the Society's future.

[7] Walker presented his plans for the Sheffield experiment at the second conference on "The Future of Adult Life," Leeuwenhorst, The Netherlands, July 1990.

[8] The picture is even more dismal if we expand the relevant pool to include the nearly 1,200 colleges and universities that presently offer at least one credit course in gerontology.

[9] Peter Laslett had an essay, "Societal Development and Aging," in the first two editions; my piece is in the second edition (1985).

[10] Besides co-editing *Emergent Theories of Aging,* James Birren also is co-editor with Gary M. Kenyon and J. J. F. Schroots of a volume on metaphors of aging to be published by Springer Publishing Co. in 1991. The editors of this volume and I also hosted a conference on "critical gerontology" in 1991 to serve as a companion piece to this volume. Readers might also profitably consult articles emanating from a largely European symposium (Johnson, Thomson, & Conrad, 1989), which tackled the generational equity issue from a broader perspective than is typical in the United States. See also Phillipson and Walker (1987).

## REFERENCES

Achenbaum, W. A. (1985). Societal perceptions of aging and the aged. In R. H. Binstock & E. Shanas (Eds.), *Handbook of aging and the social sciences* (2nd ed.; pp. 129–148). New York: Van Nostrand Reinhold.

Achenbaum, W. A., & Kusnerz, P. A. (1978). *Images of old age in America.* Ann Arbor, MI: Institute of Gerontology.

Benson, S. P., Brier, S., & Rosenzweig (Eds.). (1986). *Presenting the past.* Philadelphia: Temple University Press.

Binstock, R. H., & George, L. K. (1990). Preface. In R. H. Binstock & L. K. George (Eds.), *Handbook of aging and the social sciences* (3rd ed., p. xvi). New York: Academic Press.

Birren, J. E. (1961). A brief history of the psychology of aging. *Gerontologist, 1,* 69–77, 127–134.

Carson, R. A. (1986). Introduction. In T. R. Cole & S. Gadow (Eds.), *What does it mean to grow old?* Durham, NC: Duke University Press.

Connelly, J. R., & Rich, T. A. (1989). *Standards and guidelines for gerontology programs.* Washington, DC: Association for Gerontology in Higher Education.

Critchlow, D. T., & Hawley, E. W. (Eds.). (1988). *Federal social policy.* University Park, PA: Penn State University Press.

de Beauvoir, S. (1972). *The coming of age.* New York: G. P. Putnam's Sons. (Original work published 1970).

Dewey, J. (1939). Introduction. In E. V. Cowdry (Ed.), *Problems of ageing.* Baltimore: Williams & Wilkins.

Fischer, D. H. (1977). *Growing old in America.* New York: Oxford Univeristy Press.

Freeman, J. T. (1979). *Aging: Its history and literature.* New York: Human Sciences Press.

Gruman, G. J. (1966). *A history of ideas about the prolongation of life.* Philadelphia: American Philosophical Society.

Hall, G. S. (1922) *Senescence: The last half of life.* New York: D. Appleton.

Hareven, T. K. (1983). *Family time and industrial time.* New York: Columbia University Press.

Hareven, T. K., & Langenbach, R. (1978). *Amoskeag.* New York: Pantheon.

Howe, B. J., & Kemp, E. L. (Eds.). (1986). *Public history.* Malabar, FL: Robert E. Krieger.

Johnson, H. R., et al. (1980). Foundations for gerontological education: Part 2. *Gerontology, 20,* 52.

Johnson, P., Thomson, D., & Conrad, C. (1989). *Workers and pensions.* Manchester: Manchester University Press.

Kaminsky, M. (1974). *What's inside you it shines out of you.* New York: Horizon Press.

Koch, K. (1978). *I never told anybody.* New York: Vintage Books.

Laslett, P. (1977), *Family life and illicit love in earlier generations.* New York: Cambridge University Press.

Laslett, P. (1989). *A fresh map of life.* London: Weidenfield and Nicolson.

Maves, P. B., & Cedarleaf, J. L. (1949). *Older people and the church.* Nashville, TN: Abingdon-Cokesbury Press.

Moody, H. R. (1988). Toward a critical gerontology. In J. E. Birren & V. L. Bengtson (Eds.), *Emergent theories of aging* (pp. 19–40). New York: Springer Publishing Co.

Moss, W. G. (1978). Humanities, aging and the public. *Gerontology, 18,* 581.

Philibert, M. (1968). *L'echelle des age.* Paris: LeSeuil.

Phillipson, C., & Walker, A. (1987). The case for critical gerontology. In S. diGregorio (Ed.), *Social gerontology: New directions* (pp. 1–13). London: Croom, Helm.

Reinharz, S., & Rowles, G. D. (Eds.). (1988). *Qualitative gerontology.* New York: Springer Publishing Co.

Riegel, K. F. (1977). History of psychological gerontology. In J. E. Birren & K. W. Schaie (Eds.), *Handbook of the psychology of aging* (pp. 70–102). New York: Van Nostrand Reinhold.

Richardson, B. E. (1933). *Old age among the Greeks.* Baltimore; The Johns Hopkins Press.

Simmons, L. W. (1945). *The role of the aged in primitive societies.* New Haven, CT: Yale University Press.

Spicker, S. F. (1978). The role of humanities in geriatric education. *Gerontologist, 18,* 579.

Spicker, S. F., Woodward, K. M., & Van Tassel, D. D. (Eds.). (1978). *Aging and the elderly.* Atlantic Highlands, NJ: Humanities Press.

Streib, G. F., & Binstock, R. H. (1990). Aging and the social services: Changes in the field. In R. H. Binstock & L. K. George (Eds.), *Handbook of aging and the social sciences* (pp. 1–16). New York: Academic Press.

Thurston, J. L. (1951). First National Conference on Aging. *Industrial and Labor Relations Review, 4,* 163–172.

Tibbitts, C. (1951). Conservation of our aging population. *North Carolina Medical Journal, 12,* 481–485.

Van Tassel, D. D. (1979). *Aging, death and the completion of being.* Philadelphia: University of Pennsylvania Press.

Van Tassel, D. D., & Stearns, P. N. (Eds.). (1986). *Old age in a bureaucratic society.* Westport, CT: Greenwood Press.

Walker, A. (1981). Towards a political economy of old age. *Ageing and Society, 1,* 73–94.

Walker, A. (1983). Social construction of dependent social and economic status in old age. In A.-M. Guillemard (Ed.), *Old age and the welfare state* (pp. 143–168). Beverly Hills, CA: Sage.

Walzer, M. (1987). *Interpretation and social criticism.* Cambridge, MA: Harvard University Press.

Walzer, M. (1988). *The company of critics.* New York: Basic Books.

Weiland, S. (1990). Gerontology and literary studies. *Gerontologist, 30,* 435–436.

Woodward, K. (1988). Simone de Beauvoir: Aging and its discontents. In S. Benstock (Ed.), *The private self* (pp. 90–113). Chapel Hill: University of North Carolina Press.

Zeman, F. D. (1945–47). Life's later years: Studies in the medical history of old age [10 parts]. *Journal of Mount Sinai Hospital, 11–13.*

# Index